Transformation of Agricultural Research Systems in Africa

Transformation of Agricultural Research Systems in Africa

LESSONS FROM KENYA

Cyrus G. Ndiritu, John K. Lynam, and Adiel N. Mbabu, editors

Michigan State University Press • *East Lansing*

Michigan State University Press
East Lansing, Michigan 48823-5202

Printed and bound in the United States of America.

07   06   05   04   1   2   3   4   5   6   7   8   9   10

LIBRARY OF CONGRESS CATALOGING-IN-PUBLICATION DATA
Transformation of agricultural research systems in Africa : lessons from
Kenya / Cyrus G. Ndiritu, John K. Lynam, and Adiel N. Mbabu, editors.
p. cm.
ISBN: 0870137395 (pbk.: alk. paper)
Includes bibliographical references and index.
1. Agriculture—Research—Kenya. 2. National agricultural research
systems—Kenya. 3. Kenya Agricultural Research Institute. I. Ndiritu,
Cyrus G. II. Lynam, John K. III. Mbabu, Adiel N.
S542.K4T73 2005
630'.72'06762—dc22
2004015266

g **green**
press
INITIATIVE Michigan State University Press is a member of the Green
Press Initiative and is committed to developing and encouraging ecologically responsible publishing practices. For more information
about the Green Press Initiative and the use of recycled paper in book
publishing, please visit *www.greenpressinitiative.org*.

Cover and book design by Sharp Des!gns, Inc., Lansing, MI

Cover photograph provided by International Maize and Wheat Improvement Center (CIMMYT)

Publication of *Transformation of Agricultural Research Systems in Africa*
was made possible by support from the Rockefeller Foundation.

Visit Michigan State University Press on the World Wide Web at
www.msupress.msu.edu

Contents

Part 1: Setting the Scene

Part 2: The Transformation (Reorganization of Research Systems)

Part 3: Strategic Alliances

Part 4: Resource Mobilization

Part 5: Synthesis and Conclusions

Illustrations

Figures

Tables

Boxes

Acknowledgments

First and foremost, the editors thank the authors of the various chapters, who shepherded the book into being through a series of formal and informal consultations from which initial drafts germinated and developed. That the book contains up-to-date information bespeaks the patience, resolve, and professional awareness of the authors.

Special mention is made of the Kenya Agricultural Research Institute (KARI). Thanks to many years of focused, uninterrupted, and problem-oriented research, the institute provided vital information on which the book hinges. Many other national as well as regional organizations, both public and private, fed into the book in one way or another. Our sincere appreciation goes to them, much as we find it difficult to list all of them here. At the final stages of the work, it was decided to enlist the services of a professional freelance editor, Mrs. Annie Jones, and concomitantly bring on board a coordinator/editor, Dr. J. O. Mugah of KARI.

Throughout the planning and preparation of this book, we relied heavily on Mrs. Wanjiku Kiragu of the Rockfeller Foundation, who gave unstintingly of her vast administrative expertise, hospitality, and quiet inner strength to provide much-needed facilitation and guidance from the foundation. Special thanks go to the Rockfeller Foundation for financial and general support, and to the Bellegio Centre for hosting the entire team of authors in their lovely facilities for one week. In particular, we thank John Lynam, the foundation's associate director in charge of food security, for actively participating in the preparation of the book throughout all the stages, and, notably, for writing the introduction to the book.

About the Editors

Cʏʀᴜs Gᴀᴛʜɪʀᴜᴀ Nᴅɪʀɪᴛᴜ was director of the Kenya Agricultural Research Institute (KARI) from 1989 to 2000. He is currently a private consultant in agricultural systems and rural development. He graduated from the University of Nairobi in 1974, gained his M.Sc. at the University of California, Davis in 1976, and his Ph.D. at the University of Nairobi in 1982. He worked with the Wellcome Foundation's Foot and Mouth Disease Laboratory in Kenya and Pirbright, UK, until the mid-1980s.

In 1990, he was appointed board chairperson of the KEVEPAPI, a board member of the KETRI, a member of the Administrative Council for the SR-CRSP. From 1991 to 1993 he was chairperson of the Crop Management Research and Training Committee, the tripartite responsibility of KARI, Egerton University, and CIMMYT, in an attempt to decentralize training efforts from Mexico to the Africa region. In 1992 he was appointed a member of the board of KEPHIS, a service body responsible for the quarantine and quality control of the plant materials entering or leaving Kenya. That same year he became a member of a core team of the East and Central Africa Research organization coordinated by SPAAR that planned the formation of ASARECA. He was later appointed to oversee the organization through the initial stages until a secretariat was established in Kampala. In 1993, he was appointed advisor to GTL, a corporate body in the Republic of Kenya that deals in the application of innovative science in supporting agricultural development in Kenya and East Africa. He was also appointed a member of the CGIAR's specialist committee on the livestock that culminated in the formation of ILRI. In 1994, he was appointed chairperson of the NARS-CGIAR Committee to find ways of enhancing collaboration between the NARS and IARCs. In 1995 he was appointed chairperson of the CGIAR task force to review the "Ecoregional Approach to Agricultural Research." In 1996, he was appointed a member of the Board of Trustees of CIMMYT and a member of the Technical Advisory Committee of the CGIAR. He was appointed a member of the Executive Council of the University of Nairobi in 1998.

More recently, he has been involved in the review of the CGIAR relationship with the African NARS generally and Kenya in particular; and has served as a consultant for the World Bank-sponsored project of setting up the FARA. He is also involved in the WHO-sponsored Biotechnology Study on Modern Food Biotechnology.

In recognition of his outstanding national contribution to agricultural research and development, Cyrus Ndiritu has been awarded the OGW and EBS by His Excellency the president of Kenya. He was admitted into the 2001 edition of the International Biographical Centre, Cambridge, UK, publication of the outstanding scientists of the twentieth century.

Jᴏʜɴ K. Lʏɴᴀᴍ is associate director of the Food Security Division, Rockefeller Foundation, Nairobi, Kenya. He obtained his B.Sc. from Ohio State University in 1970, his M.Sc. from Stanford University in 1974, and his Ph.D., also from Stanford, in 1978. He was a commodity analyst for the Foreign Agricultural Service of the U.S. Department of Agriculture (USDA) from 1970 to 1972, and a visiting research fellow at the Institute for Development Studies, University of Nairobi, from 1974 to 1975. From 1977 to 1988, he was head of the Economics Section, Cassava Program of CIAT, where he designed and directed economic research on cassava.

In his present position with the Rockefeller Foundation, his duties include developing a funding program for agricultural research in eastern Africa, developing a banana research program in Uganda, social science research at ICIPE and KARI, developing an integrated soils research agenda in East Africa, and integrating GIS and modeling in agricultural research planning and priority setting. He was responsible for the management of the collaborative study of cassava in Africa (COSCA), directed by IITA, and the development of a research program for crop and resource husbandry in agricultural faculties in East Africa.

Aᴅɪᴇʟ Nᴋᴏɴɢᴇ Mʙᴀʙᴜ is technical officer for planning at ASARECA with the basic responsibility of assisting agricultural research networks, projects, and programs in the ten ECA countries in planning their respective agricultural research and development activities. He received his B.A. in sociology in 1979 and his M.A. in 1984 from the University of Nairobi. He earned his Ph.D. in rural sociology from the University of Missouri-Columbia in 1988. From 1989 to 1990, he was resident scientist for the SR-CRSP sociology project, on behalf of the University of Missouri-Columbia, in collaboration with KARI. This was followed by a research fellowship with ISNAR that included on-the-job training in agricultural research management. From 1993 to 2000, he was the planning, management, and evaluation advisor/interim assistant director of the socioeconomics and biometrics division at KARI. As technical advisor, he was responsible for strengthening planning, management, and evaluation in all research programs in KARI. As interim assistant director, he was charged with the responsibility of strengthening and managing the socioeconomics research program of the institute.

Adiel Mbabu served as a member of the advisory committee of the African Career Awards of the Rockefeller Foundation. He facilitated the Workshop on Gender Disaggregated Data in Mukono, Uganda, in 2000, and the strategic planning process of the Agricultural Research System in Rwanda. He has also served on various advisory panels and committees, including the Scientific Advisory Panel to the Directorate of Personnel Management, Office of the President, Republic of Kenya, and has served as chairperson of KARI's Gender Task Force, and KARI's PM&E Task Force, among others.

Foreword

Agricultural researchers in sub-Saharan Africa have for decades faced a plethora of challenges in the pursuit of improved agricultural technology in their respective countries. Relative to the rest of the world, the African countries in which they live and work are poor. Many of them have gone through cycles of economic growth, followed by downturns and stagnation. Immediately after independence the gross domestic product in many countries grew at impressive rates. However, unfavorable developments in the world economy, environmental calamities, civil strife, poor governance, and changing donor priorities have dampened and in some cases reversed economic growth.

The diversity of problems facing the agricultural sector has led to the establishment of national agricultural research institutes with broad mandates. Understandably, but paradoxically, the human, financial, and physical resources required to run such institutes have outstripped the national capacity to finance them. Thus, invariably, the budgets allocated to the agricultural sector and to research in particular remain parsimonious and do not, in most cases, reflect the enormity, diversity, and dynamism as well as the special economic significance of the sector.

The overall objective of this book is to analyze the process of institution building and institutional transformation in Africa in a long-term perspective. The book makes the case that institution building is a continuous process of significant complexity, and that this process should not be sacrificed to shorter-term perspectives and goals. After more than three decades of stops and starts, there is now a knowledge base for transforming basis for transformation of national agricultural research systems (NARS) into effective institutions producing a continuous flow of public goods.

The book is divided into four parts, with a final section devoted to a synthesis and conclusions. The first section demonstrates the interaction between the structure, dynamics, and resource base of the agricultural sector and the organization and priorities of the agricultural research system. The second moves from the external environment to an analysis of the internal issues such as setting research priorities. The objective is to analyze both the process of and the various components critical to positive institutional change and transformation. This section reviews the history of agricultural research in Kenya, the process of building a National Agricultural Research Organization (NARO), and the various elements involved in the internal transformation of the Kenya Agricultural Research Institute (KARI) into an effective research organization. Among these elements are internal organizational structures, the balance between centralization and decentralization, and the development of a range of research management structures. This section reviews the tension between spatial dispersal of research activities and infrastructure and the search for economies of scale and scope.

The third section evaluates the institutional context in which KARI operates. The objective is to analyze the NARS and how these independent institutions interact. The section reviews agricultural extension and the universities. Biotechnology is an example of successful links to advanced research laboratories.

The fourth section reviews options and constraints on financing of agricultural research, because adequate financing is essential to the effectiveness and productivity of the national agricultural research system. The development of a more diversified and sustainable funding base is reviewed, including devolution to an expanding private sector.

The premise of this book is that agricultural research and technological development are central to the growth in food and livestock production, to alleviation of rural poverty, and to maintenance of the natural resource base. This book is timely because African policymakers want to see how research is contributing to improving the economy and the welfare of rural and urban people. Farmers are looking to agricultural research institutes for solutions to the myriad problems impacting on their farming activities.

The choice of KARI as a case study for this book is appropriate because Kenya has the largest NARO model of research in sub-Saharan Africa, and it has enjoyed a long period of stability and uninterrupted research. It is my hope that those involved in the planning and management of agricultural research in Africa and other parts of the developing world will find this book indispensable.

J. O. Mugah, *Kenya Agricultural Research Institute*

Acronyms and Abbreviations

Currency Equivalents *(exchange rate effective July 2004)*

CURRENCY UNIT = KENYA SCHILLINGS
79.1 = US$1

Acronyms

A-AARNET	ASARECA Animal Agriculture Research Network
AARINENA	Association of Agricultural Research Institutes in the Near East and North Africa
ABSF	African Biotechnology Stakeholders Forum
ABSP	Agricultural Biotechnology for Sustainable Productivity, KARI, Kenya
ABU	Ahmadu Bello University, Nigeria
ACIAR	Australian Centre for International Agricultural Research
ACMV	African common mosaic virus
AD	assistant director
ADC	Agricultural Development Corporation, Kenya
AERC	African Economic Research Consortium
AEZ	agro-ecological zone
AFC	Agricultural Finance Corporation
AfDB	African Development Bank
AFRENA	Agroforestry Research Network for Africa (ICRAF)
AFRENA–ECA	Agroforestry Research Networks for Africa-Eastern and Central Africa
AFRENA–SA	Agroforestry Research Networks for Africa-Southern Africa
AgGDP	agricultural gross domestic product
AGNPP	average aboveground net primary productivity
AHI	African Highlands Initiative
AHP	analytic hierarchy process (a multiple-criteria method)

AHRSC	Animal Husbandry Research Sub-Centre, KARI, Kenya
AI	artificial insemination
AIA	appropriations in aid
AID	Agency for International Development, Washington
AIDS	Acquired Immunodeficiency Syndrome
AIE	authority to incur expenditures
AIK	agricultural indigenous knowledge
AKIS	agricultural knowledge information system
AO-R	assistant agricultural officer
AOs	agricultural officers
APAARI	Asia-Pacific Association of Agricultural Research Institutions
ARC	Agricultural Resource Center, Egerton University
ARD	Agricultural Research Division of MoA, Kenya
?ARD	agricultural research and development
ARF	Agricultural Research Fund, Kenya
ARI	Advanced Research Institution
ARO	agricultural research officer
ARP	Adaptive Research Program, Kenya
ARSC	Agricultural Research Sub-Centre, KARI, Kenya
ARTP	Agricultural Research and Training Project, Uganda
ASAL	arid and semi-arid lands
ASARC	Agricultural Sciences Advisory Research Committee, Kenya
ASARECA	Association for the Strengthening of Agricultural Research in Eastern and Central Africa
ATD	Africa Technical Department of the World Bank, Washington
ATIRI	Agricultural Technology and Information Response Initiative project of the KARI, Kenya
AU	African Union
AVHRR	advanced very high resolution radiometer (image)
AW	all-weather roads
BARNESA	Banana Research Network for Eastern and Southern Africa
BBK	Brooke Bond Kenya
BRC	Beef Research Centre, KARI, Kenya
BRU	Biotechnology Research Unit
Bt	*Bacillus thuringiensis*
CARE	Cooperative for American Relief Everywhere
CBD	Convention on Biodiversity
CBK	Coffee Board of Kenya
CBS	Central Bureau of Statistics, Kenya
CBPP	contagious bovine pleuropneumonia
CCPP	contagious caprine pleuropneumonia

CCTA	Commission de coopération technique en Afrique au sud du Sahara
CCUS	Committees for the Conservation and Utilization of Soils
CERAAS	Centre d'étude regionale pour l'amelioration de l'adaptation a la secheresse
CFs	contact farmers
CGIAR	Consultative Group on International Agricultural Research
CH	central highlands zone, Kenya
CIAT	Centro International de Tropical Agriculture (Colombia)
CIDA	Canadian International Development Agency
CILSS	Comité inter-états de lutte contre la sécheresse au Sahel
CIMMYT	Centro Internacional de Mejoramiento de Maíz y Trigo (*International Maize and Wheat Improvement Center*), Mexico
CIP	Centro Internacional de la Papa (*International Potato Center*), Peru
CIRAD	Centre de coopération internationale en recherche agronomique pour le développement, France
CIRAD-MICAP	Plant Breeding Division of CIRAD
CL	coastal lowlands zone, Kenya
CORAF	Conférence des responsables de recherche agronomique en Afrique de l'Oueste et du Centre
CORNET	Coffee Research Network of ASARECA
COSCA	Collaborative Study of Cassava in Africa
COTEPA	Coffee and Tea Parliamentary Association, Kenya
CRAC	Center Research Appraisal Committee, Kenya
CRACCUS	Central Region of Africa Committee for the Conservation and Utilization of Soils
CRF	Coffee Research Foundation, Kenya
CRO	Chief Research Officer
CROACCUS	Western Africa Region Committee for the Conservation and Utilization of Soils
CSA	Conseil scientifique pour l'Afrique sud du Sahara
DAO	district agricultural officer
DARES	Department of Agricultural Research, Eritrea
DEO	district experiment officer
DFID	Department for International Development, UK
DGIS	Directorate General for Development Cooperation of Dutch Ministry
DGIS-BIOTECH	Special Program Biotechnology of the DGIS
DM	disease management
DOA	Department of Agriculture, Kenya
D-P-I	diagnostic review, planning, and implementation framework
DRT	Department of Research and Training, Tanzania

DSE	German Foundation for International Development
DSK	Dansk Chrysanthemum Kultur, Denmark
DVS	Department of Veterinary Services, Ministry of Agriculture, Kenya
EAA&FC	East African Agriculture and Fisheries Council
EAAFRO	East African Agriculture and Forestry Research Organization
EAARI	East African Agricultural Research Institute
EAC	East African Community
EACSO	East African Common Services Organization
EAGNPP	expected average aboveground net primary productivity
EAHC	East African High Commission
EAPGREN	Eastern Africa Plant Genetic Resources Network
EARCCUS	East Africa Regional Committee for the Conservation and Utilization of Soils
EARO	Ethiopian Agricultural Research Organization
EARRNET	Eastern Africa Rootcrops Research Network
EASB	European Agricultural Settlement Board
EAVRO	East African Veterinary Research Organization
EBS	Elder of the Burning Spear award, Kenya
EC	European Community
ECA	eastern and central Africa
ECABREN	Eastern and Central Africa Bean Research Network
ECAMAW	Eastern and Central Africa Maize and Wheat Research Network
ECAPAPA	Eastern and Central Africa Program for Agricultural Policy Analysis
ECARSAM	Eastern and Central Africa Regional Sorghum and Millet network
ECSARRN	Eastern, Central and Southern Africa Rice Research Network
EEC	European Economic Community
EL	eastern lowlands zone, Kenya
EMBRAPA	Empresa Brasileira de Pesquisa Agropecuária, Brazil
EPMR	External Programme and Management Review
EPTD	Environment and Production Technology Division, IFPRI
ERR	economic rate of return
ESA	European Space Agency
EU	European Union
FAO	Food and Agriculture Organization of the United Nations, Rome
FARA	Forum for Agricultural Research in Africa (formerly SPAAR)
FEW	front-line extension worker
FFA	frameworks for action, of SPAAR
FOFIFA	Centre national de recherche appliquée au développement rural, Madagascar

FOODNET	Postharvest Processing Network, under ASARECA
FPEAK	Fresh Producers Exporters Association, Kenya
FPPE	Finnish Post-Graduate Program in Economics
FPR	farmer participatory research
FRC	Farmer Research Committee of KARI, Kenya
FSA	farming systems approach
FSA-RET	farming systems' approach to research, extension, and training
FSR	farming systems research
FSRE	farming systems research and extension
FTC	farmer training center
Fte	full-time equivalent
FURP	Fertilizer Use Recommendation Project
GA	Gender Advisors of GTF, KARI, Kenya
GAM	gender analysis matrix
GCTE	Global Change and Terrestrial Ecology
GDP	gross domestic product
GFAR	Global Forum on Agricultural Research
GF-SC	Global Forum Steering Committee
GICs	General Investigation Centers
GIS	geographic information systems
GLIP	Grain Legume Improvement Project, under SACCAR
GMO	genetically modified organism
GMR	Guaranteed Minimum Return scheme
GO	government organization
GoK	Government of Kenya
GTF	Gender Task Force of KARI, Kenya
GTL	Genetic Technology Limited, Kenya
GTZ	Deutsche Gesellschaft für Technische Zusammenarbeit (*German Agency for Technical Cooperation*)
HAI	household agricultural income
HCDA	Horticultural Crops Development Authority, Kenya
HHU	household unit
HIV	Human Immunodeficiency Virus
HPM	high potential maize zone, Kenya
HR	human resource
IAC	International Agricultural Center, the Netherlands
IADP	Integrated Agricultural Development Project, Kenya
IAEA	International Atomic Energy Agency
IAR	Institute for Agricultural Research of ABU, Nigeria

IARC	International Agricultural Research Center
IBRD	International Bank for Reconstruction and Development (now World Bank)
IBS	Intermediary Biotechnology Service
ICIPE	International Centre of Insect Physiology and Ecology, Kenya
ICR	Implementation/Completion Review of NARP by the World Bank
ICRA	International Center for Development-Oriented Research in Agriculture, the Netherlands
ICRAF	International Centre for Research in Agroforestry, Kenya
ICRISAT	International Crops Research Institute for the Semi-Arid Tropics, India
IDA	International Development Association
IDRC	International Development Research Centre, Canada
IDS	Institute for Development Studies
IFAD	International Fund for Agricultural Development
IFPRI	International Food Policy Research Institute, USA
IGAD	Intergovernmental Authority on Development
IGO	intergovernmental organization
IITA	International Institute of Tropical Agriculture, Nigeria
ILAMB	International Laboratory of Molecular Biology for Tropical Disease Agents
ILCA	International Livestock Centre for Africa (now ILRI)
ILO	International Labor Office
ILRAD	International Laboratory for Research on Animal Diseases (now ILRI)
ILRI	International Livestock Research Institute, Kenya
IMF	International Monetary Fund
INEAC	Institut national pour l'étude agronomique du Congo
INERA	Institut national pour l'étude at la recherche agronomiques, Democratic Republic of Congo
INFORM	Information for Research Management tool of ISNAR
INIA	Instituto Nacional de Investigacíon Agraria, Uruguay
INIAP	Instituto Nacional Autónomo de Investigaciones Agropecuarias, Ecuador
INM	integrated nutrient management
INSAH	Institut du Sahel
INTA	Instituto Nacional de Tecnología Agropecuária, Argentina
IPGRI	International Plant Genetic Resources Institute, Rome, Italy
IPM	integrated pest management
IPM-DM	integrated pest management and disease management
IPRs	intellectual property rights
ISAAA	International Service for the Acquisition of Agribiotech Applications

ISABU	Institut des sciences agronomiques du Burundi
ISAR	Institut des sciences agronomiques du Rwanda
ISNAR	International Service for National Agricultural Research (now a division within IFPRI)
IT	Intermediate Technology
IV	instrumental variables (technique)
JICA	Japan International Cooperation Agency
JICU	Junta de Investigações Científica do Ultramar
JKUA	Jomo Kenyatta University of Agriculture, Kenya
KABP	Kenya Agricultural Biotechnology Platform
KAMPAP	Kenya Agricultural Monitoring and Policy Analysis Project
KARI	Kenya Agricultural Research Institute
KBL	Kenya Breweries Ltd.
KCC	Kenya Cooperative Creameries
KDB	Kenya Dairy Board
KENGO	Kenya Energy and Environmental Organization
KEPHIS	Kenya Plant Health Inspection Service
KESREF	Kenya Sugar Research Foundation
KETRI	Kenya Trypanosomiasis Research Institute
KFA	Kenya Farmers Association
KMC	Kenya Meat Commission
KNA	Kenya National Archives
KNFU	Kenyan National Farmers Union
KPCU	Kenya Planters Cooperative Union
KSA	Kenya Sugar Authority
KSC	Kenya Seed Company
KTDA	Kenya Tea Development Authority
LAC	Latin America and the Caribbean
LDSB	Land Development and Settlement Board, Kenya
LH	lower highland zone, Kenya
LM	lower midland zone, Kenya
LPAP	length of photosynthetically active period
LUS	land use system
MADIA	Managing Agricultural Development in Africa (discussion papers)
MIAC	Mid-American International Consortium
MIRCEN	Microbiological Resource Center Project, Kenya
MoA	Ministry of Agriculture, Kenya
MoALD	Ministry of Agriculture and Livestock Development, Kenya

MoALDM	Ministry of Agriculture, Livestock Development, and Marketing, Kenya
MOH	Ministry of Health, Nairobi, Kenya
MOU	Memorandum of Understanding between MoALD and MRTTT, Kenya
MRS	marginal rain shadow zone, Kenya
MRTTT	Ministry of Research, Technical Training, and Technology, Kenya
MSV	maize streak virus
MTC	Ministry of Transport and Communication, Kenya
NA	northern arid zone, Kenya
NACBAA	National Advisory Committee on Biotechnology Advances and their Applications, Kenya
NAEP	National Agricultural Extension Project of the World Bank
NAHRC	National Animal Husbandry Research Centre, KARI, Kenya
NAI	New Africa Initiative
NALEP	National Agricultural and Livestock Extension Program, Kenya
NALRC	National Arid Lands Research Centre, KARI, Kenya
NAMA	Network for Agricultural Mechanization in Africa
NARC	National Agricultural Research Centre, KARI, Kenya
NARC	National Agricultural Research Council
NARI	National Agricultural Research Institute
NARL	National Agricultural Research Laboratory
NARM	National Agricultural Research Master Plan, Tanzania
NARO	National Agricultural Research Organization
NARP	National Agricultural Research Programme of the KARI, Kenya
NARP-I	NARP, Phase I
NARP-II	NARP, Phase II
NARS	national agricultural research systems
NASCOP	National Acquired Immunodeficiency Syndrome (AIDS)/Sexually Transmitted Diseases (STDs) Control Programme, Kenya
NCF	noncontact farmer
NCPB	National Cereals and Produce Board, Kenya
NCST	National Council for Science and Technology, Kenya
NDDP	National Dairy Development Project, Kenya
NDFRC	National Dryland Farming Research Centre, KARI, Kenya
NDVI	normalized difference vegetation index
NEP	National Agricultural Extension Project, Kenya
NEPAD	New Partnership For Africa's Development
NFRC	National Fibre Research Centre, KARI, Kenya
NGOs	nongovernmental organizations
NHRC	National Horticultural Research Centre, KARI, Kenya
NIB	National Irrigation Board, Kenya

NLO	Netherlands Liaison Office
NPBRC	National Plant Breeding Research Centre, KARI, Kenya
NPRC	National Potato Research Centre, KARI, Kenya
NPV	net present value
NRC	National Research Center
NRELC	National Research Extension Liaison Committee, Kenya
NRM	natural resource management
NRP	National Research Program, Kenya
NRRC	National Range Research Centre, KARI, Kenya
NUTMON	nutrient monitoring
NVRC	National Veterinary Research Centre, KARI, Kenya
OAU	Organization of African Unity
OCD	Oil Crops Development Ltd., Kenya
ODA	Overseas Development Administration, UK (now DFID)
ODI	Overseas Development Institute, UK
OECD	Organization for Economic Cooperation and Development, Paris
OED	Operations Evaluation Department of the World Bank, Washington
OFCOR	on-farm client-oriented research
OGW	Order of the Golden Warrior Award, Kenya
ORSTOM	Office de la recherche scientifique et technique d'outre-mer, France
OPV	open pollinated varieties
PAD	photosynthetically active decades
PADA	provincial assistant directors of agriculture of MoA, Kenya
PAM	Participatory Agro-Ecosystem Management Approach
PARTS	Policy Analysis, Research and Technical Support of USAID
PAV	photosynthetically active vegetation
PBK	Pyrethrum Board of Kenya
PCR	polymerase chain reaction
PCSA	Production to Consumption Systems Approach
PD	population density
PDA	provincial director of agriculture, Kenya
PFMS	Project Financial Management System
PIB	Pig Industry Board, Kenya
PLAR	Participatory Learning Action Research Approach
PLC	public limited company
PM&E	planning, monitoring, and evaluation
PMEU	Program Monitoring and Evaluation Unit of KARI, Kenya
PPF	Project Preparation Facility, for NARP, Kenya
PPP	purchasing power parity
PPU	primary production unit

PRA	participatory rural appraisal
PRAPACE	Programme régional d'amelioration de la culture de la pomme de terre et la patate douce en Afrique Centrale et de l'Est
PRASAC	Pôle régional de recherche appliquée au développement des savanes d'Afrique Centrale (*regional pole of applied research for the development of the central savanna*), CORAF
PRASAO	Pôle régional de recherche appliquée au développement des savanes d'Afrique de l'Oest (*regional pole of applied research for the development of the west African savanna*), CORAF
PREP	Phosphorus Resource Exploratory Project, western Kenya
PS	production systems
PSI	Pôle régional de recherche sur les systèmes irrigués (*regional research pole for irrigated systems in the Sudano-Sahelian zone*), CORAF
PTD	participatory technology development
RAC	Research Advisory Committee of TRFK, Kenya
RAIN	Regional Agricultural Information Network, under ASARECA
R&D	research and development
R&E	research and extension
RCC	Research Coordinating Committee, KARI
REDSO	Regional Economic Development Services Office for Eastern and Southern Africa of USAID
RELD	Research Extension Liaison Division of MoALDM
RELO	Research-Extension Liaison Officer of RRCs, Kenya
RENACO	ICRISAT cowpeas network
RET	research, extension, and training
RF	Rockefeller Foundation
RFMC	Research Fund Management Committee, KARI, Kenya
RHBS	Rural Household Budget Survey, Kenya
ROR	rates of return
RPP	regional productivity potential
RRA	rapid rural appraisal
RRC	Regional Research Center, KARI, Kenya
RREAC	Regional Research-Extension Advisory Committee, Kenya
RRP	Regional Research Program, Kenya
RRSC	Range Research Sub-Centre, KARI, Kenya
RSC	Regional Steering Committee
SACCAR	Southern Africa Center for Coordination of Agricultural Research
SADC	Southern Africa Development Community
SADCC	Southern African Development Coordination Conference
SAL	semi-arid lands

S&T	science and technology
SAP	Structural Adjustment Program, Kenya
SAR	Staff Appraisal Report
SARCCUS	Southern Africa Regional Committee for the Conservation and Utilization of Soils
SAREC	Swedish Agency for Research Cooperation with Developing Countries
SARRNET	Southern African Roots and Tubers Research Network
SB	Sisal Board, Kenya
SCU	Sector Coordination Unit of SADC
SFC	Staff and Finance Committee of TRFK, Kenya
SFPNRP	Soil Fertility and Plant Nutrition Research Program of the KARI, Kenya
SIDA	Swedish International Development Authority
SLEMSA	Soil Loss Estimation Method for Southern Africa
SMIP	Sorghum and Millet Improvement Program of ICRISAT
SMP	Soil Management Project of KARI, Kenya
SMS	subject matter specialist
SOM	soil organic matter
SPAAR	Special Program for African Agricultural Research (now FARA)
SPFMV	sweet potato feathery mottle virus
SPGRC	SADC Plant Genetic Resources Center
SPU	secondary production unit
SR-CRSP	Small Ruminant Collaborative Research Support Project
SRD	Scientific Research Division, MoA, Kenya
SRO	subregional organization
SSA	sub-Saharan Africa
STABEX	Stabilising Export Earnings, the European Community's compensatory finance scheme
STD	sexually transmitted disease
SWMNet	Soil and Water Management Network, under ASARECA
TA	tropical alpine zone, Kenya
TAC	technical advisory committee
TALIRO	Tanzania Livestock Research Organization
TARO	Tanzania Agricultural Research Organization
T&V model	Training and Visit (extension) model
TOFNET	Trees on Farm Network of ASARECA
TRF	Tea Research Foundation, Malawi
TRFK	Tea Research Foundation of Kenya
TRIEA	Tea Research Institute of East Africa
TSP	triple super phosphate

UH	upper highland zone, Kenya
UM	upper midland zone, Kenya
UNAIDS	United Nations Program on AIDS
UN/BIOCHEM	University of Nairobi Biochemistry Department
UNCS	University of Nairobi Crop Science Department
UNDP	United Nations Development Programme
UNESCO	United Nations Educational, Scientific, and Cultural Organization, France
USAID	United States Agency for International Development, Washington
USLE	universal soil loss equation
VILs	Veterinary Investigation Laboratories of MoA, Kenya
VRD	Veterinary Research Division of MoA, Kenya
VRSC	Veterinary Research Sub-Centre, KARI, Kenya
WAA	weighted average age (index)
WARDA	West Africa Rice Development Association
WB	World Bank, Washington
WCAMRN	West and Central African Maize Research Network, ICRISAT
WCASRN	West and Central African Sorghum Research Network, ICRISAT
WH	western highlands zone, Kenya
WHO	World Health Organization
WL	western lowlands zone, Kenya
WT	western transitional zone, Kenya
WTO	World Trade Organization

PART 1

Setting the Scene

Introduction

JOHN LYNAM

On no other continent is the need for agricultural research greater than it is in Africa; similarly, nowhere are the complexities of producing well-adapted agricultural technologies more binding than in Africa, and yet the basic institutions supporting agriculture are some of the weakest in the developing world. In Africa, the challenge of increasing food supply to keep pace with population growth and rising urban demand, of producing the agricultural technologies that will fuel that process, and of designing the basic institutions that will create and deliver these technologies, remains largely unfulfilled. Nevertheless, this does not imply that there are not some positive experiments that provide insight into how to close this complicated circle. In analyzing these experiments, a better understanding can be reached on how to harness the science and transform the institutions that will lead to equitable and sustainable models of agricultural development on the African continent. This volume is a case study of Kenya, focusing on the least understood piece of the circle, namely the agricultural research institution, and in the process underlining the complex process by which science can be molded and managed to serve more effectively the agricultural development process in Africa.

Linking Science and Agricultural Development

Professor Thomas Odhiambo (1967) first gave expression to the idea of molding and orienting science and scientific institutions to resolve the problems of agricultural development in Africa. Science would be used to explain and then resolve the problems of African agriculture. In so doing, scientific institutions would be organized around solving problems. Technology development, in turn, would be an interactive process between farm-level diagnostics, development of a scientific understanding of relevant systems and problems, pursuit of knowledge and development of techniques to resolve those problems, and an analysis of the application of those techniques at the farm level. How to structure and organize institutions around this agenda, fund those institutions, and link them to both the innovators in science around the world and to rural development practitioners in the field were the issues that defined how effective this link between science and development would be (Chema, Gilbert, and Roseboom 2003; Byerlee and Echeverria 2002).

Science and Agricultural Intensification in Africa

Agricultural development in Africa must take place within the context of constraints that differentiate it from the development process in Asia and Latin America. First, rural population growth rates in Africa are at historically high levels, and this growth is occurring at a stage when the economies of these rural areas remain agrarian in structure. The high mortality rate because of Acquired Immunodeficiency Syndrome (AIDS), in East and Southern Africa especially, presents its own challenge as increasing mortality rates shift from economically inactive to economically active cohorts (Yamano and Jayne 2004). Second, agricultural intensification and productivity increases in Africa must take place almost exclusively within tropical environments, where the agricultural research base remains extraordinarily underdeveloped, as compared to that in more temperate regions. Moreover, the inherent productivity of the agricultural resource base in Africa is in general poorer than that of the principal agricultural areas of Asia and Latin America, being limited either by poor soils or by insufficient rainfall. Third, transport and market infrastructures are highly underdeveloped in Africa. They are underdeveloped in relation both to the concentration of most agricultural areas away from the coast and to the level of investment in such infrastructure in Asia and Latin America at the period of their yield "take-off" (Spencer 1996). Fourth, African countries must compete in tropical agricultural export markets (e.g., oil palm in Malaysia or bananas in Central America) where comparative advantage is now primarily defined by technological progress rather than by traditional determinants such as factor endowments and agricultural potential. That is, technological progress is the principal basis for competitieveness in a world market economy where there are rapidly declining terms of trade. In the face of this challenge, Africa's percentage of global exports declined from 6 percent in 1990 to 2 percent in 2002 (UNCTAD 2003).

These constraints are then juxtaposed against a structural food deficit in Africa. Some argue that the problem resides in state-controlled economic policies that have retarded the development of the private sector and therefore growth. A neo-industrial argument has emerged more recently (Ellis 1999), asserting that the agricultural sector is so highly constrained that development must proceed by bypassing the agricultural sector and jump-starting the informal and industrial sectors. As Eicher (1999) notes, this means potentially repeating the failed policies followed by most African countries at independence and disregarding the most critical lesson emerging from any understanding of the modern agricultural development process—namely, the critical role of increasing agricultural productivity as necessary to economic growth in the industrial and service sectors. Nevertheless, the target condition for economic transformation remains a sustained growth rate of at least 4 percent in agricultural gross domestic product (GDP), where some combination of increases in land and capital

4

productivity will allow for necessary increases in rural labor productivity and income. As structural adjustment programs have taken hold across the continent, the experience has demonstrated that economic policy change was necessary, but by no means sufficient, to meet these targets. Revitalizing the scientific and institutional basis for agricultural productivity gains is equally critical in the attempt to meet these growth rate targets (Jayne, Minde, and Agrwings-Kodhek 2002).

Technical change in most of Africa will be based on increasing yields in small-holder farming systems, but within the constraints noted previously. Yield increases will not rely, as in Asia and Latin America, on either purchased inputs or irrigation. Rather, yield gains will be based on the production of crop varieties better adapted to their environment, exploitation of ecosystem services for plant nutrient supply, and pest and disease control. Where practical, yield gains may be based upon the integration of livestock and trees in the farming system, and highly efficient use of limited supplies of mineral fertilizer within a context of improved nutrient cycling. Yield gains in such circumstances will be more management and labor intensive. The research and extension systems that produce and disseminate such technologies must adapt more traditional areas of agricultural science (e.g., crop breeding and soil science) to a low-resource context, develop new disciplines (e.g., agroforestry), and adapt other sciences to agriculture (e.g., ecology and molecular biology). Thus, much of the science that will drive African agriculture will need to be developed around the particular needs of African farming systems, especially within the context of tropical, rain-fed agro-ecosystems (Buddenhagen 1996) that are insufficiently supported by access to input, output, and credit markets.

Linking Agricultural Research and Rural Development

Policy changes in the last decade have resulted in a depreciation of the role of agricultural research in rural development. Two related, but independent, forces are contributing to this. The first is uncertainty surrounding public policy in agriculture after structural adjustment and market liberalization. With the liquidation of grain marketing boards; the liberalization of fertilizer, seed, pesticide, and veterinary services; and a restructuring of regulatory bodies, ministries of agriculture have both lost their voice within budgetary negotiations and been lax in redefining their public-sector role and function within a liberalized economy. Policy levers such as price supports, input subsidies, grain storage, and agricultural taxes have largely disappeared under structural adjustment programs. Policy, in turn, has primarily collapsed to the public-sector investment role, with agricultural research being a principal public good investment as well as a dominant institutional presence. However, agricultural research institutes are caught in a conundrum—they have been marginalized in national budgetary priorities, and yet with the contraction of extension services and the insufficient private sector response under liberalization their perceived role has been substantially broadened. The lack of clarity in agricultural policy has led to agricultural research institutes being pulled in many directions at once, with a resultant loss of strategic focus (Eicher 2003).

5

The other, and even more recent, trend has been a shift in donor and national government policy toward poverty alleviation as central to rural development policy (Mansuri and Rao 2004). In Africa, the locus of poverty is principally in the rural areas, and improvement in the welfare of the poor will depend on access to and provision of basic social services, as well as increases in rural incomes and access to markets. Public-sector reform has taken place within the framework of decentralization of government functions—to what is termed a district focus. Health sector reform and universal primary education have made significant demands on national and district budgets, and priorities and budgets for rural development are now set within a broader framework than just an agricultural policy. Investments in social services are now viewed as having more immediate impact on the welfare of the poor and as being more politically acceptable than in the past in newly democratizing countries.

Decentralization is occurring at the same time that new forms of agricultural extension are being designed, as Training and Visit extension has been abandoned as a model. Poverty alleviation programs have produced a more immediate demand for readily available agricultural technologies and demand-driven extension services. Because agricultural research institutes remain the pivotal actors in the sector, they are being pulled into defining their role in transferring and disseminating technology and designing research to better target technology to the needs of the poor. Thus, although the demands on appropriately structuring research to achieve the necessary yield gains are large and complex, to this must be added other societal demands on research to contribute to more immediate impacts on poor rural households.

However, putting boundaries on the research agenda is difficult within an African context. The portfolio of crops and livestock is large, the biotic problems are complex, and technology design is difficult where inputs are often not available to farmers. Given that these are low-input, rain-fed systems, stability and sustainability are often added as research objectives to the more singular quest for productivity gains. These issues have given rise to the role of biodiversity, soil biology, and organic matter dynamics in regulating agricultural system performance through time. To the scope and complexity of this research agenda is often added an environmental and natural resource agenda. Agricultural land use and its productivity are the key determinants of water, forest, wetland, and wildlife management across most of the continent. Thus, the National Agricultural Research Organization (NARO) mandate in Uganda includes forestry, fisheries, and wetlands. Because of its research capacity, the Kenya Agricultural Research Institute (KARI) has developed a program in association with the Kenya Wildlife Service on wildlife diseases, of key importance to the Kenyan economy.

Thus, the current demands on agricultural research in Africa are almost limitless, and yet the resources available to undertake them are by comparison extraordinarily limited, creating pulls on research effectiveness and efficiency. Although agricultural research is the pivotal public-sector institution in the agricultural sector, resource and efficiency concerns are forcing strict limits on that role, with a large question being how best to achieve an appropriate balance.

The Co-Evolution of Institutions and Development

Until recently the role of institutions, especially public institutions, in the development process has not been a large topic within the development literature. These institutions have been either subsumed under processes such as technical change, resource mobilization, financial intermediation, and human capital investment, or analyzed as functional aggregates, such as the public sector, the banking and financial sector, the education and health sector, or agricultural research and extension. The focus has been on investment, resource flows, and productivity, rather than on organizational structure, level of centralization, internal incentive structures, institutional change, and organizational efficiency. The key role of organizations, especially public organizations, in the development process often has ben lost or seen only in a historical context. Yet institutions are fundamental to the shape and direction of the development process, and economic growth and structural change, in turn, influence the role, function, and structure of these institutions, in a process known in the biological sciences as co-evolution. This is clearly the case with agricultural research, agricultural extension, and universities.

It is not often stressed, but Africa is an extraordinarily late arrival in terms of the development of public institutions. Institutional development depends on written language, and in sub-Saharan Africa this developed only in Ethiopia, as opposed to its much broader development in Arab culture, Western culture, and most Asian cultures. Basic institutions in Africa had to wait for the arrival of the colonial system in the mid-1800s. This was late compared to the experience of Latin America, which by that time had three hundred years of colonial experience and was going through its independence. The institutions that were imported into Africa were those of emerging industrial societies and oriented to the economic and political objectives of colonial regimes. In the post–World War II period, when the rest of the world was going through a time of rapid structural, technological, and economic change, Africa had to focus on developing basic political, governmental, and educational institutions and on training the manpower that would staff those institutions. The necessary preconditions to initiating an indigenous development process, as well as participating in the larger world order, were not in place in Africa as they were in Asia and Latin America. Institutional development was built on imported structures and responded to external models and influences, and in the process often failed to develop an adaptive response to local realities or demands.

African countries are primarily agrarian economies. In Africa, health and demographic transitions will have to be accomplished within a rural context. Investments in education will compete with agricultural investments (at a public policy level) and agricultural labor use (at the farm level). The funding for basic agricultural public institutions, such as research, extension, and universities, will depend primarily on an agricultural tax base, but will compete for those funds with urban infrastructure and social services. Such institutions also tend to be located in urban settings at the expense of needed linkages to rural constituencies. Serving large, diverse, and resource-constrained rural populations is a challenge for public institutions in Africa.

Decentralization is the most recent response to that challenge, but faces the constraints imposed by limited public-sector funds and increased stringency in government budget deficits and deficit financing. How to build institutions with large, complex mandates, broad geographical territories, and yet severe budgetary constraints is a puzzle that African countries are currently trying to solve.

Organizational Change and Institutional Crisis

Agricultural research institutes are an excellent example in Africa of the difficulties in transforming organizational structures that mostly served colonial economic interests (particularly tropical export crops) to institutions that better serve local, especially food crop, interests, under conditions of scarce manpower and tight resource constraints. (Roseboom, Pardey, and Beintema [1998] give a good historical overview of this process across the continent). Directly after World War II, regional agricultural research structures expanded greatly, especially in the British colonies. Unlike during the prewar period, the metropolitan government largely financed these regional systems, especially in British East Africa. Independence brought with it the need to build up national systems from very small and focused research institutes. This restructuring process reoriented agricultural research to domestic requirements, particularly those of the many smallholders outside the commercial crop sector; collapsed regional structures into national systems; and staffed those systems with indigenous scientists. Funding shifted to local sources, aided in the 1960s and 1970s by reasonable growth in the agricultural sectors of many African countries and the initially small institutional base.

The first twenty years after independence saw a huge growth in agricultural research systems. This growth, although necessary, was by no means systematically planned, and came at some cost to research effectiveness. The process was fragmentary, as different departments within different ministries built up their own research capacity. Responsibility for research institutes often shifted between ministries and research councils (Eicher 1989). No organizational model drove and directed this growth process, nor was there any notion of an interlocking research system of agricultural research institutes, agricultural faculties, and agricultural extension, with investments in research and extension often proceeding in out-of-phase cycles. Universities had an even later start than research institutes and an even more rapid growth process, increasing from fewer than 20 in 1960 to 160 by 1996 (Beintema, Pardey, and Roseboom 1998). The arrival in the 1960s of scores of fledgling and barely formed nation-states, with huge institutional voids in their capacity to function as modern nation-states, was unprecedented. The big bang of institutional growth that filled this void was simultaneously creative and destructive, producing only an emergent organizational form.

The economic downturn of the 1980s produced the conditions that led to a process of consolidation. When expansionary institutional growth met inflation, economic stagnation, and strained government budgets, the result was institutional crisis. Operational budgets declined in relation to salaries, and salaries declined as staff levels were maintained while budgets declined in real terms under inflation. The best managerial and research talent was lost, and there were virtually no maintenance or capital budgets. All these factors led to a loss of internal incentive structures, loss of morale, and, in the end, ineffective institutions. This was true of research institutions, universities, and extension systems (Eicher 1999). The public sector played a dominant role in agriculture during this period, not only in the production of public goods, but also in terms of service provision, input and output marketing, and investments. Yet the economic downturn produced a negative, reinforcing interaction between the declining health of public institutions and the performance of the agricultural sector.

The way out of this crisis came in the form of structural adjustment programs. Although heavily criticized at the time, nevertheless some components of these programs were accepted across the continent. In many ways this adjustment process would not have been possible without the interplay among the multilateral agencies, the International Monetary Fund (IMF), and the World Bank. The programs undertaken at this time encompassed macroeconomic stabilization, fiscal stringency, liberalization of foreign exchange and agricultural markets, and in essence the withdrawal of the public sector from management of the agricultural economy. This structural adjustment was supposed to produce the fiscal flexibility to both reorder government spending priorities and rationalize public-sector staffing and salaries. As Pardey, Roseboom, and Craig (1999) note, "The World Bank was party to a total of 57 lending operations with civil-service reform components in 27 African countries between 1981 and 1992." It is probably fair to say that because of its political ramifications, civil service reform was the most difficult piece of the structural adjustment agenda, and progress has been slower here than in most other components.

The civil service reform process provided the political space for the needed consolidation and restructuring of agricultural research across much of the continent, as it also coincided with renewed donor interest in funding national agricultural research in Africa. The most common organizational model chosen was what Roseboom, Pardey, and Beintema (1998) call NARO (National Agricultural Research Organization). According to this model, research units, staff, and infrastructure were pulled out of the different ministries, especially ministries of agriculture and livestock, and were consolidated under a single, semi-autonomous structure. As Roseboom, Pardey, and Beintema (1998) note, "The motivation behind this development was to lower the transactions costs of agricultural research and development (R&D) across otherwise disparate agencies, and to streamline the allocation of limited resources, thereby improving the focus of research—spatially and otherwise. In 1991, 28 of the 48 countries (in the study) in Africa had adopted a NARO structure." Donor funding facilitated this process of pulling research components out of line ministries into the NARO and creating the administrative superstructure to manage the institution. However, the process of internal consolidation and creating a scientific institution that creatively and efficiently produced agricultural technologies required time and nurturing.

Moreover, the process resulted in a shift to reliance on donor financing (Pardey, Roseboom, and Craig 1999). Agricultural research lost its traditional budgetary support within the line ministries at a time of budget stringency and reordering of government budgets. This donor "crowding out" of national budgetary support—that is, apart from salaries—reflected at the time a quid pro quo inherent in the restructuring process. However, such decisions were forgotten when in the late 1990s donor concerns shifted to the issue of sustainable financing as they sought to shift priorities.

As African agricultural research systems move into the new century, they find themselves centrally placed within the agricultural sector. The thirty-year structural food deficit remains and increasing agricultural productivity is necessary to overcome it. A revitalized private sector increases the demand for and potential application of new technology, with the potential for even further division of labor and complementarity between public- and private-sector roles. Nevertheless, the process of internal consolidation and organization remains a stumbling block for agricultural research institutes in Africa. The internal productivity and efficiency of these institutes has to be increased, and yet there are no good road maps for how this is to be achieved. At the same time, the effectiveness of the downstream, extension linkage needs to be improved, the necessary role of universities needs to be strengthened, and the upstream linkages to scientific and research expertise need to be established in ways that form interactive partnerships. This process is the subject of this book.

Global Science and African Agriculture

The scientific method has always presumed a community of peers that would maintain the quality and "verifiability" of the scientific research that was done. With the advent of the Internet and information and communication technologies, that process has become global—the so-called globalization of science. Africa has lagged behind the rest of the developing world in participating in this process. Telecommunication capacity remains underdeveloped over the African continent and Internet connectivity, although increasing rapidly in the last few years, still remains limited over much of the continent. This, however, will change over the course of the next decade. The question is whether Africa will be able to participate in the world scientific community as it comes out of this "virtual" isolation. A reflection of the continuing gulf between the African and world scientific communities is African participation in the more traditional, published scientific literature. One estimate suggests that research from Africa forms less than 2 percent of that world literature. As agricultural research institutions better organize themselves to create research support systems for their scientists, reinforcement of that research culture and the process of making it more productive will rely on fuller participation in the world scientific community.

How African agricultural research institutes position themselves in relation to the rapid changes in the international scientific community will be a key challenge over the coming decade. What capacity in strategic research should be built, especially when it competes for resources devoted to applied and adaptive research? How can this research be made relevant to African conditions and effectively linked to applied capacity; and what mechanisms are available to harness global science to work on African problems? These issues play out most forcibly in the rapidly expanding areas of molecular biology and genetic engineering. These techniques have been primarily applied to high-input, temperate agriculture (James 1998), but they can equally be applied to improve the productivity of low-input, tropical systems if the research can be directed toward those targets (Wambugu and Wafula 1999). That redirection, however, is critical. No sub-Saharan African country, apart from South Africa, has the resources to invest in the basic strategic research for most of the crops important to Africa. Development of the transformation and regeneration systems, the molecular maps and markers, and the promoters for tropical crops such as cassava, highland banana, and millet is an international public good in which no single African country would have the incentive or the capacity to invest. Rather, African research institutes would be interested in developing capacity in the applied aspects of biotechnology, such as tissue culture, the use of molecular markers in crop variety development, the introgression of genes from transformed plants, and disease diagnostics. African participation in much of world science, therefore, will not be direct, but rather will be mediated through intermediate institutions, in the form of either research partnerships or international consortia.

This is not to imply that Africa should not or will not be an active participant in the world scientific community. By devoting itself to its own research agenda, Africa has a contribution to make to world science. Management of tropical soils through soil biology, organic matter dynamics, and nutrient cycling—that is, without reliance on large applications of mineral fertilizer—is a complex research agenda that has spin-offs into the broader area of sustainable agriculture in temperate systems. The same applies to integrated management of pests and diseases within tropical environments where chemical control is not a viable option. Crop breeding for multiple stresses and marginal environments with the assistance of molecular markers also has scope for applying new science to very different problems. Increasing the scientific capacity for tropical agriculture will not only work toward meeting the needs of African countries, but also ensure an appropriate place for Africa in a world scientific community where terrestrial ecology and climate change are seen as global issues, with severe under-representation from tropical areas, especially in Africa. The challenge is to create the institutional structures that will cultivate and launch such science, with linkages that ensure participation of African researchers as peers in the global scientific community.

Transforming the Agricultural Research System

The restructuring of national agricultural research that has taken place over the last decade leaves in its wake two key challenges in the transformation of these systems into productive scientific institutes. First is the challenge to develop effective internal organizational and management structures that lead to cost-effective production of research outputs. The second challenge is to develop the linkages to other key institutions that will produce an efficient national agricultural research and extension system. The internal organization of these NAROs is designed to achieve the necessary economies of size, scale, and scope (see chapter 7 for a discussion of these concepts)

11

and at the same time to align the institutions and their programs to effectively inter-act with both their stakeholders and complementary institutions. This internal orga-nizational structure determines the overall productivity and cost-effectiveness of the research process. Yet the literature gives little guidance on how these economies are to be achieved within an African setting. If anything, the direction is toward trading such economies for the potential of more demand-driven approaches through decen-tralization of activities.

This book focuses on the NARO, a semi-autonomous agricultural research insti-tute that manages more than 70 percent of the agricultural research undertaken in Kenya. There is a strong presumption that this organizational structure is more efficient for agricultural research in Africa than the decentralized, multi-agency model found in such large countries as Nigeria and South Africa or relatively small countries such as the Central African Republic. As Roseboom, Pardey, and Beintema (1998) note, "Most African (research) agencies are still very small and fragmented by international standards, making it difficult to realize the scale and scope of economies that seem increasingly evident in agricultural R&D conducted elsewhere." Thus, the trend over the last decade has been toward consolidation within single agencies, and the remain-ing agenda is to determine how to effectively organize these institutes.

Internal transformation of NAROs

The consolidation of a multiplicity of research entities into a single agency required an initial, internal organizational structure as a template. By necessity these structures drew on experience elsewhere, providing the initial framework around which more adaptive changes in both organizational structure and management systems could be made, as existing research entities adapted to, and integrated themselves into, the new organization. Nevertheless, the process often did not start with a clean slate, but rather required negotiation between often-competing governmental entities with very dif-ferent self-interests. As a result, even the initial structures often reflected compro-mises rather than the search for optimal organizational forms. Moreover, it is an obvious fact (although often forgotten, especially by financing agencies) that such institutional development is an organic process and as such takes time. The results of this consolidation process have therefore been uneven around the continent.

The search for an optimum internal organizational structure involves three prin-cipal issues. The first, certainly most central and probably most contentious, is opti-mum size. The size issue embodies the appropriate balance between the complexity of the research enterprise in Africa and the limits on the financial resources for its execution. Certain size thresholds allow the attainment of economies of scale and scope, and yet these are difficult to achieve given the pulls toward overextension. Even in small countries the diversity in agro-ecologies, commodities, and livestock species is extraordinarily large (Eyzaguirre 1996), especially given that much of the applied research, and all of the adaptive research, has a large element of location specificity. To this is added the complexity of the research enterprise, when the focus is on smallholders under rain-fed conditions with very limited access to purchased inputs. Moreover, the political pressures are for a national system to address at some level the spatial extent of this diversity.

Yet the financial and human resources available to carry out the research enterprise rarely match its scope. As Eicher (1999) has noted, the technological successes on the continent usually come out of relatively small, highly focused, and long-term research efforts. Obviously, building such units within a larger NARO is not impossible, but the question is how many of these units should there be, and how should they be organized? The limited size and sustainability of the financial base is often used as an argument that research systems in Africa are too large. Yet Roseboom, Pardey, and Beintema's (1998) analysis of twenty-two NAROs (in thirty-seven countries) shows that a third have less than fifty researchers. One-third have between one hundred and two hundred researchers (similar to the size of an average International Agricultural Research Center [IARC], but with an extraordinarily more diverse research mandate). Only five have more than two hundred researchers. The overall size of these institutes thus remains small by international standards, which forces the argument back to strategies to increase the size of the financial base and to achieve better internal organization in order to achieve greater resource efficiency.

The second organizational issue is how to structure the research programs themselves. This is a complex undertaking, because it relates to various factors such as the number of research programs and their mandates, and the size of individual research teams and their spatial distribution. It also relates to the thematic structure (i.e., whether commodity, factor, discipline, agro-ecology, or production system is used as the organizational basis for the research program), and functional type of research (i.e., whether strategic, applied, or adaptive research). There are no easy models for how such internal organization of the research program can be achieved. Initially, existing research units and their location in existing research stations determined this. However, as research institutes consolidated, real divides appeared. These concerned whether to organize along commodity lines or on the basis of agro-ecologies—the same issue has applied to the Consultative Group on International Agricultural Research (CGIAR)—or whether to combine strategic, applied, and adaptive research in individual research programs or to functionally separate them into different research teams. Central to these decisions is the ability to achieve focus and economies of scale and scope within the research teams and the need to minimize internal transaction costs. Again, little empirical work exists on this issue, and yet such structural decisions have real implications for resource allocation and research efficiency within the institution.

The third organizational issue, which is related to size constraint and research structure, is the internal level of centralization or decentralization. This issue influences decision making, accountability, resource flows, transaction costs, and institutional linkages. Part of the rationale of a NARO is that certain management functions and services can be centralized, reducing overhead for research programs. In fact, Roseboom, Pardey, and Beintema's (1998) analysis of fourteen NAROs shows that just over 40 percent of researcher staff reside at headquarters, while the rest are distributed

13

across an average of eleven stations, with an average staffing of about seven researchers per station. This suggests a real tension between the development of centralized management, support, and laboratory services, the need for stations to serve diverse ecologies, and real size limits on staffing of individual stations and programs. Such limits on decentralized staffing raise additional questions about the ability of the NAROs to better position themselves in relation to the decentralization process and absorb more downstream functions, including even extension. Although there are small, pilot experiments on how to achieve more bottom-up, demand-driven approaches to technology development (Sutherland, Martin, and Salmon 1998), the staffing and resource constraints on configuring the NAROs to achieve this have yet to be adequately taken into account. Moreover, such repositioning comes at a time when the research programs themselves are not very mature and there is danger of overextending these institutions.

The internal organizational structure evolves as an iterative process with the development of the management systems within the institution and the demand for these systems obviously influencing the size and staffing at headquarters. Allocation of limited financial and personnel resources is at the heart of most of these management systems. The three principal pillars to the development of these resource allocation systems are a priority-setting framework, a budgeting and research planning system, and a financial management and control system. Each is a highly differentiated system, requiring specific skills to design and implement, and each is usually housed in a different unit of the institute. They are usually developed out of synchrony with each other; yet, to effectively plan and manage the organization and structuring of the research process, the three systems have to interface in concert. The challenge in developing these systems is enormous, but nothing compared to the task of making them operational within the institution. That is, priority setting and budgeting have to be integrated into the research planning process at different hierarchical levels and the flow of funds integrated accordingly. In many instances, research or corporate plans are driven by the requirements for external financing, often through the aid of consultants, and end up being used only for that purpose. Appropriate institutionalization of these management systems cannot be short-circuited.

Developing effective priority-setting and budgeting and financial control systems, in turn, forms the basis for developing a training and manpower development plan. It also allows the decentralization of budgeting, research planning, and financial management. The system also facilitates the development of appropriate internal incentive structures, ensuring sufficient operating funds for professional advancement and adequate salary emoluments to secure retention of productive staff. Finally, when linked to a planning, monitoring, and evaluation system, the capacity then exists for adaptive management of the research process, as well as continued internal experimentation with organizational models. This process of internal transformation of African NAROs is one that will rely on close monitoring and assessment of each of these areas individually, and evaluation of the collective impact on research productivity and technology adoption.

Linkages and the Development of the Research and Extension System

The restructuring and consolidation process of the last decade and a half now finds itself faced by two countervailing forces. The first is a reassessment and possible rationalization of the research portfolio based on a clearer notion of NARO comparative advantage. The search for more sustainable funding mechanisms and continued improvement in research efficiency are principally driving this reassessment. Positioning public-sector research in better relation to an expanding private sector is one element of this rationalization, while the other is developing a better division of labor with universities, which underwent faster expansion than even agricultural research over the last three decades.

With market liberalization, the role of the private sector has significantly expanded, although nowhere near the high expectations of policy planners. With better development of input and output markets, a better economic environment is certainly created for the uptake of technology, which in turn could provide potential incentives for private-sector investment in agricultural research. This has occurred in large parts of Latin America and Asia where there are large commercial sectors and input-based agriculture. In Africa, the potential for devolution of research areas to the private sector is only at the margin. Research on export crops such as coffee, tea, and cacao is already primarily carried out in producer-supported research institutes, building on the capacity in these crops that was developed during the colonial period. Private research investment has also helped in developing new export crops, such as horticulture and floriculture (Kangasniemi 2002). However, for the bulk of the agricultural economy (i.e., basic food crops and livestock) the public sector will be the source of technological advance. Areas such as hybrid maize seed may have some potential, but even here the private sector will depend on the public sector for research, as it has in India (Morris 1998) on such problems as striga, grey leaf spot, or stem borer. An effective NARO will be attuned to the potential for private-sector involvement in agricultural research, either as a collaborative exercise or in devolution of activities, but the potential for this will continue to be limited until the agricultural sector is more radically transformed.

Universities and faculties of agriculture suffered similarly from the institutional crisis of the 1980s, but probably more so because of the very large increase in undergraduate enrollments during a period of declining resources. The important result of these two trends was the loss of the ability of most faculties to do research. This had a host of very important ripple effects. Disciplinary knowledge stagnated, quality of teaching declined, quality of graduate science programs suffered, and as a result many of the new staff coming into the NAROs were not adequately trained. Certainly the faculties lost their ability to provide new disciplinary directions for the highly complex problems of smallholder agriculture, and to be a focal point for importing new knowledge and methods from the global scientific community. Rebuilding research capacity in agricultural faculties thus becomes a necessary part of the transformation of the agricultural research systems in Africa. Deepening faculty and graduate science research through joint programs with the NARO becomes a vehicle by which to better

15

meld disciplinary expertise with problem solving. Mechanisms such as competitive research funds have developed in a few countries to facilitate this process. Joint supervision of postgraduate work, collaborative research programs, NARO scientists teaching at the universities, and joint peer review of research are other mechanisms to begin to forge improved linkages between NAROs and universities. As chapter 10 notes, revitalization of the agricultural research and extension system will depend critically on improving the quality of faculty teaching and research capacity.

The other countervailing force is the pressure on the NARO to deepen its capacity in adaptive research and even extension. Competition and distrust, rather than a truly functional division of labor, have characterized the history of the development of effective linkages between research and extension. Competition for resources, separation of research and extension into different ministries, and lack of synchronization in cycles of funding are principal reasons for the lack of effective linkages. The situation was made more difficult in the 1990s by the virtual collapse of Training and Visit extension systems in Africa. Various factors have combined to create uncertainty about how to organize the extension function. One factor is the movement to increase farmer participation in research and extension (the Food and Agriculture Organization's [FAO] recent promotion of farmer field schools in Africa is an example). Other contributing factors are the increasing emphasis on information- and management-intensive, rather than input-based, technologies, and the need to better position research and extension in the decentralization process. With the strengthening of adaptive research in the NAROs, agricultural research institutes have developed better internal linkage points to extension, although at a time when extension systems have been severely weakened. The combination has pulled the NAROs into some aspects of the extension function. Shifts in donor funding to more downstream activities have heavily influenced all of these trends.

Research institutes are still experimenting with internal organizational models, still wrestling with the size and resource allocation problem, and only just addressing the internal decentralization process (Besley and Ghatak 1999). Adding the extension function to research institutes adds completely new organizational, staffing, and resource issues to an organizational change process that in many cases is only just reaching some sense of internal cohesion. How to rethink and redesign the extension function within the national agricultural research and extension system is a difficult issue, given the lack of well-tested models, current political and donor pressures, and the lack of certainty on the organizational structure of the NARO itself. The two countervailing forces are thus pulling the NARO in two different directions at the same time, and that could overtax the internal transformation process.

Scale Economies through Regionalization

Africa is divided into far more countries than is any other continent. Given the significant diversity existing within often small national boundaries, and given the limited financial resource base, achieving economies of size and scale is difficult and is possible, if at all, in only very limited areas. The British government's increased investment in African agriculture in the immediate postwar period focused on building regional structures and, given the current reliance of African agricultural research on international public funds, the last decade has seen a move in the development and funding of regional frameworks for agricultural research.

During the colonial period, development of regional programs varied by region. In West Africa, regional programs were built around a limited number of export crops, especially tropical tree crops. In East Africa, regional capacity was developed in disciplines that backstopped national capacity as well as some regional division of labor in areas such as sugarcane or coffee breeding. Regional capacity in this period was structured around a limited number of strategic areas, in which long-term, well-trained scientific capacity was built. Independence led to the collapse of these regional frameworks and their incorporation into national systems.

The formation of the Southern Africa Development Community (SADC) provided the impetus for the first regional agricultural research association, the Southern Africa Center for Coordination of Agricultural Research (SACCAR), in Southern Africa. The structure was originally based on building regional centers of excellence in particular research areas and in so doing defining a regional division of labor. The Association for the Strengthening of Agricultural Research in Eastern and Central Africa (ASARECA) in East and Southern Africa organized regional programs around networks, and over time SACCAR has also come to rely more on networks. The Conférence des responsables de recherche agronomique en Afrique de l'Oueste et du Centre (CORAF) in West Africa was a former organization of networks supported by the French government in Francophone Africa. It is providing the initial organizing structure for the West African regional framework. The donors under the Special Program for African Agricultural Research (SPAAR) led this process, at least initially, and particularly the formation of ASARECA and CORAF. Significant donor funding supported these structures, which has created two interacting processes, namely the restructuring of CGIAR activities in Africa in relation to the regional bodies and the development of regional networks to assist the NAROs.

More than 40 percent of the CGIAR's research resources are spent in sub-Saharan Africa. Four centers are located on the continent, and all of the other eleven centers have programs or activities of varying size on the continent. To a large extent the regional frameworks were built on existing IARC networks, especially the formation of ASARECA in East and Central Africa. These networks were principally commodity-based, with research and training activities tending to be organized around germplasm and breeding activities. Commodity IARCs with headquarters outside Africa have established over time African-based breeding programs in crops such as beans, sorghum, maize, groundnuts, and sweet potatoes. Although these programs draw on centralized germplasm improvement capacity, African-based breeding has been essential to meet the particular challenges of African environments. Networks have provided the potential for an effective division of labor with national crop improvement programs.

The CGIAR's development of ecoregional programs coincided with the development of regional frameworks in Africa (Eicher and Rukuni 2003). The search for economies of scope in CGIAR regional activities coincided with the search for an organizational framework for research on natural resource management (NRM). However, the CGIAR's ecoregional programs have not been able to achieve an effective and functional integration with the three African regional frameworks. Several factors have worked against such integration. First, the ecoregional framework within the CGIAR has been slow in becoming an effective organizational structure. This is partly because of the difficulties in individual IARCs devolving responsibility and decision making to a more independent, regional program. Partly, this has been caused by the lack of an effective framework for organizing NRM research. Second, melding two highly different management structures has not been easy. The International Institute of Tropical Agriculture's (IITA's) ecoregional structure, the Forum for Agricultural Research in Africa (FARA), in West Africa has been seen as competing to some extent with the development of the CORAF regional framework. The African Highlands Initiative (AHI) in East Africa has been scaled back to an NRM Andean Region subproject network, which is one among other prospective networks. Southern Africa has no CGIAR ecoregional program.

The integration of the NAROs into regional frameworks represents a very different challenge. Whereas the organizational task for the CGIAR is to better integrate autonomous and relatively highly specialized research programs into a more interactive whole, the task for the NAROs is to attempt, within a geographically and programmatically diversified institution, to foster and tap regional economies of scale. This depends on defining a basis for a regional division of labor. For the commodity networks, this is frequently possible where expertise can be developed in different biotic and abiotic areas, often linked to breeding subprojects. For NRM-based programs a division of labor is less clear. Thus, the challenge for NAROs within a regional framework is how to adapt their own priorities, research planning, and resource allocation in order to achieve regional-scale economies. Achievement of this objective is anything but straightforward, except in the simple—and to date relatively rare—case of direct technology borrowing from the IARCs. It requires some subversion of national interests, a reliance on effective programs throughout the region, a sophisticated and integrated national and regional research-planning framework, and a mechanism for funding regional transaction costs.

Thus, regional frameworks represent an opportunity and at the same time a significant risk for both national systems and the CGIAR. Several big issues remain to be resolved. First, how sustainable will they be? If both national and international research programs are to be restructured around these frameworks, continuity will be critical. Yet these regional programs depend wholly on international public funds. Donors should not see these regional programs as a mechanism for reducing the overall costs of agricultural research on the African continent; rather, they may increase research productivity and effectiveness. Yet adding another organizational layer will, if anything, only increase overall research costs, certainly if the recent growth of ASARECA to nineteen networks is indicative. Nevertheless, funding for these programs is almost certain to come at the expense of either national system funding or

CGIAR funding. Second, the regional frameworks' major task is to facilitate a restructuring of both CGIAR and national research programs, but by minimizing the growth of intermediate management structures. Given the organizational constraints on both sides of this equation, the ability to act as middleman has been possible only where donor funding has been significant and has built on existing structures. However, real organizational change on either side has remained limited, with no real blueprint for how to effect such change, other than to rely and build on the network modality. One necessary change will be for the CGIAR to move forward more effectively with its ecoregional structure. Thus, the second-generation development of regional research structures will be very different from the first.

Why Kenya and Why This Book?

The development of strong and effective institutions is a long-term, organic process; history, internal structures, and the external environment always condition institutional reform. This book analyzes this transformation process for national agricultural research systems (NARS) in Africa at a point in time where crisis has loosened old structures and there is a receptiveness to reform and a growth process that will produce effective institutions. Agricultural research systems are a useful focus for understanding institutional transformation in Africa, in that, compared to universities or medical or education systems, they have a longer history than these other institutions. They have also undergone more radical restructuring, and are linked to both internal and external processes that reinforce the reform process.

This book analyses institutional transformation by focusing on one country, Kenya, and its agricultural research system, and then uses this case study to draw implications for sub-Saharan Africa as a whole. The decision to focus on Kenya makes it possible to achieve a greater understanding of institutional change through time, the interaction with the agricultural economy, the intricacies of the internal restructuring and transformation process, and the linkages between different components of the overall research system. As such, this book complements and deepens the recent cross-sectional analysis of NARS in Africa made by the International Food Policy Research Institute (IFPRI) and the International Service for National Agricultural Research (ISNAR) (Chema, Gilbert, and Roseboom 2003). The book is built around the analysis of the transformation process in KARI and is complemented by an analysis of the agricultural sector, of the other institutions in the overall system (especially extension and faculties of agriculture), and of the financial base that supports public agricultural research.

Kenya has been chosen for this study even though no single country or system can be said to be representative of sub-Saharan Africa, given the great diversity that exists. Kenya's economy has performed well below its potential in recent years. In fact, average GDP growth has declined from about 7 percent in the 1970s to just over 2 percent in the 1990s. Moreover, Kenya's agricultural sector is performing poorly; the average agricultural GDP fell from 3.5 percent during the 1980s to 1.0 percent in the 1990s.

However, Kenya and KARI bring together the range of issues that most countries in Africa have to face in mobilizing science and technology to transform traditional agriculture. Another reason that Kenya has been chosen is that it has the third-largest agricultural research system in sub-Saharan Africa after Nigeria and South Africa. However, of these three countries, Kenya is the only one that has adopted an organizational model based on a NARO, making KARI the largest NARO in sub-Saharan Africa. The large size of KARI arises from both Kenya's history, particularly the absorption of much of the East African Agricultural and Forestry Research Organization (EAAFRO), and from the significant range of both agroclimatic potential and rural population density, creating a large diversity in crop and animal systems. Moreover, Kenya has been an early adopter of new organizational modalities, including restructuring into a NARO and the implementation of the Training and Visit extension model. The depth in scientific manpower and research programs, and the experience gained by KARI and the overall research system, provides more potential for evaluating the transformation process than would be the case in many other African countries. Eyzaguirre (1996) analyzed the small country case, which covers many African countries.

The overall objective of this book is to analyze the process of institution building and institutional transformation in Africa in a perspective that covers a long time frame and considers the complexity in some depth. Perspectives on institution building in Africa, especially donor and policy perspectives, often have a project time frame and a project focus, and impact is expected, if rarely achieved, in jumps rather than increments. The recent shift in donor funding to poverty alleviation has precipitated a focus on downstream service provision, social safety nets, and integrated livelihood approaches. This has come at some expense to a long-term perspective on the institution building process in Africa, especially for agricultural research. Withdrawing from that process at this point in time could set it back for decades, undercutting the achievement of longer-term poverty goals. This book makes the case that institution building is a continuous process of significant complexity, and that this process should not be sacrificed to shorter-term perspectives and goals (Eicher 1999). After more than three decades of stops and starts, a basis now exists for systematic transformation of NARS into effective institutions producing a continuous flow of public goods. This book provides the evidence for this case, arguing that the costs would be significant should the process be retarded at a point when effectiveness is close to being realized.

The specific objectives of this book track its organization into four sections. The first objective is to demonstrate the interaction between the structure, dynamics, and resource base of the agricultural sector and the organization and priorities of the agricultural research system. This may seem intuitively obvious, but this interface is mediated by such factors as political and power relationships, internal scientific culture, and the strength of the connection between farmers and scientists. The tightness of this interaction influences the technology design process and the appropriateness of the research, the ability to reinforce growth of production in the agricultural sector, and the ability to incorporate policy and social weights in the research process. The agricultural sector largely defines the external environment in which the agricultural research system must operate and respond. For NAROs this environment is both spatially complex and temporally dynamic and requires organizational forms that are flexible and responsive, while at the same time able to maintain the continuity necessary given the long-term nature of the technology development process.

The second section moves from the external environment to an analysis of the internal environment of the agricultural research system in Africa. The objective here is to explain in some depth both the process and the various components critical to institutional change and transformation. This section reviews the history of agricultural research in Kenya, the process of restructuring into a NARO organizational form, and the various elements involved in the internal transformation of KARI as an effective research institute. Among these elements are internal organizational structures, the balance between centralization and decentralization, and the development of a range of research management structures. This section examines the tension between spatial dispersal of research activities and infrastructure and the search for economies of scale and scope, especially where the supply of Ph.D. scientists is limited. Financial, research planning, and personnel systems must then be adapted to a spatially distributed system with an appropriate division of labor between headquarters and individual research stations. To a significant extent these issues determine the productivity and efficiency of the research process (World Bank 2004).

The third section evaluates the larger institutional context in which KARI operates. Achievement of increases in agricultural productivity depends on these institutions interacting as a whole. The objective here is to analyze the NARS and how these independent institutions interact (Chema, Gilbert, and Roseboom 2003). The section reviews agricultural extension and the universities. Biotechnology provides the framework for analyzing links to advanced research laboratories, and a chapter on the emergent regional structures reviews the links to CGIAR centers and to research networks. The focus is on KARI's adaptation of its research programs to link effectively to, and take maximum advantage of, these institutional flows of personnel, information, and research products. A strong argument is made for simultaneous and interlinked transformation of all of these institutions. One weak institution produces ineffectiveness in the whole system, as each serves a necessary function and all are needed to produce and deliver improved agricultural technologies.

The final section reviews options for and constraints on the financing of agricultural research. Development of adequate financing for the NARS is essential to achieving effectiveness and productivity for the overall system. Yet in Africa, government budgets are highly constrained, reflecting both the limited economic base of African countries and the constraints on developing an efficient and adequate tax base (Brinkerhoff, Gage, and Gavian 2002). Moreover, a range of competing demands is made on government budgets. Even as a clear public good, government budgetary support for agricultural research is often highly limited. The options in developing a more diversified and sustainable funding base are reviewed, including devolvement to an expanding private sector.

21

The premise of this book is that agricultural research and technological development will be key to the growth in food production, to rural poverty alleviation, and to maintenance of the natural resource base in Africa. This book examines that issue through the lens of the agricultural research institution, its capacities, and its constraints. How to organize agricultural research effectively on the continent is an under-researched area, and this volume hopes to contribute to an appreciation of the complexity of that process.

REFERENCES

Beintema, Nienke M., Philip G. Pardey, and Johannes Roseboom. 1998. Educating agricultural researchers: A review of the role of African universities. Environment and Production Technology Division (EPTD) Discussion Paper No. 36. The Hague: International Food Policy Research Institute (IFPRI) and International Service for National Agricultural Research (ISNAR).

Besley, Timothy, and Maitreesh Ghatak. 1999. Public-private partnerships for the provision of public goods: Theory and an application to NGOs. Development Economics Discussion Paper Series, No. 17. London: London School of Economics.

Brinkerhoff, D. W., J. D. Gage, and S. Gavian. 2002. *Sustainable agricultural research systems: Findings and lessons from reforms in Côte d'Ivoire, Ghana, Senegal, Tanzania, and Uganda.* Bethesda, Md.: Abt Associates.

Buddenhagen, W. Ivan. 1996. Modern plant breeding: An overview. In *Biotechnology and integrated pest management,* ed. Gabrielle J. Persley, 205–13. Wallingford, UK: CAB International.

Byerlee, Derek, and Ruben Echeverria, eds. 2002. *Agricultural research policy in an era of privatization.* New York: CABI Publishing.

Chema, Sam, Elon Gilbert, and Johannes Roseboom. 2003. *A review of key issues and recent experiences in reforming agricultural research in Africa.* The Hague: ISNAR.

Eicher, Carl K. 1989. *Sustainable institutions for African agricultural development.* Working Paper No. 19. The Hague: International Service for National Agricultural Research (ISNAR).

———. 1999. *Institutions and the African farmer.* Third distinguished economist lecture. Mexico: International Maize and Wheat Improvement Center (CIMMYT).

———. 2003. Flashback: Fifty years of donor AID to African agriculture. Paper presented at an International Policy Conference "Successes in African Agriculture: Building for the Future." Sponsored by In Went, IFPRI, NEPAD, and CTA, Pretoria South Africa, 1–3 December. Available at *www.ifpri .org/events/conferences/2003/120103/papers/paper16.pdf.*

Eicher, Carl K., and Mandwamba Rukuni 2003. *The CGIAR in Africa: Past, present, and future.* Washington, D.C.: World Bank Operations Evaluation Department.

Ellis, Frank. 1999. Rural livelihoods and diversity in developing countries: Evidence and policy implications. Natural Resource Perspectives No. 40. London: Overseas Development Institute (ODI).

Eyzaguirre, Pablo. 1996. *Agricultural and environmental research in small countries: Innovative approaches to strategic planning.* Chichester, UK: John Wiley.

James, Clive. 1998. *Global review of commercialized transgenic crops.* International Service for the Acquisition of Agri-biotech Applications (ISAAA) Briefs No. 8. Ithaca, N.Y.: ISAAA.

Jayne, T. S., Isaac J. Minde, and Gem Agrwings-Kodhek, eds. 2002. *Perspectives on agricultural transformation: A view from Africa.* New York: Nova Science.

Kangasniemi, Jaakko. 2002. Financing agricultural research by producers oganizations. In *Agricultural research policy in an era of privatization,* ed. Derek Byerlee and Ruben G. Echeverria, 81–104. New York: CABI Publishing.

Mansuri, Ghazala, and Vljayendra Rao. 2004. Community-based (and driven) development: A critical review. Working Paper No. 3209. Development Research Group. Washington, D.C.: World Bank, February.

Morris, Michael L., ed. 1998. *Maize seed industries in developing countries.* Boulder, Colo.: Lynne Reiner.

Odhiambo, Thomas. 1967. East Africa: Science for development. *Science* 158:876–81.

Pardey, Phillip G., Johannes Roseboom, and Barbara J. Craig. 1999. Agricultural R&D investments and impacts. In *Paying for agricultural productivity,* ed. Julian M. Alston, Phillip G. Pardey, and Vincent H. Smith, 31–68. Baltimore, Md.: Johns Hopkins University Press.

Roseboom, Johannes, Phillip G. Pardey, and Nienke M. Beintema. 1998. The challenging organizational basis of African agricultural research. EPTD Discussion Paper No. 37. Washington, D.C.: International Food Policy Research Institute (IFPRI) and International Service for National Agricultural Research (ISNAR).

Spencer, Dunstan S. C. 1996. Infrastructure and technology constraints to agricultural development in the humid and subhumid tropics of Africa. *African Development Review* 8:68–93.

Sutherland, Alistair J., Adrienne Martin, and Jon Salmon. 1998. *Recent experiences with participatory development in Africa: Practicioner's review.* Natural Resource Perspectives No. 25. London: Overseas Development Institute (ODI).

UN Conference on Trade and Development (UNCTAD). 2003. *Economic development in Africa: Trade performance and commodity dependence.* Geneva: UNCTAD.

Wambugu, Florence, and John Wafula, eds. 1999. *Advances in maize streak virus disease research in eastern and southern Africa.* Workshop Report. Nairobi: Kenya Agricultural Research Institute (KARI) and International Service for the Acquisition of Agri-biotech Applications (ISAAA), AfriCentre.

World Bank. 2004. *Agricultural investment sourcebook.* Washington, D.C.: World Bank.

Yamano, Takashi, and T. S. Jayne. 2004. Measuring the impacts of working-age adult mortality on small-scale farm households in Kenya. *World Development* 32(1): 91–119.

2

Kenya's Agricultural Sector: The Research Management Context

GEM ARGWINGS-KODHEK

The Historical Context

The history of Kenya's agricultural sector is well told in many sources and has its roots in the colonial experience (Heyer 1981; Bates 1989; Lele and Meyers 1987; Lele 1989; and Winter-Nelson 1995). The need to cover the costs of the Mombassa-Uganda railway led to two major settlement programs in 1920 and 1946 for European producers of export commodities, primarily wheat, maize, coffee, and tea. These immigrant producers were supported on the one hand by a system of preferential tax policies, and on the other hand by restrictions on African competition that freed up African labor. First the colony and then the larger metropolitan government invested in infrastructure, training, research, and extension. A system of centralized marketing boards helped reduce marketing costs. Trade and tariff restrictions also were used to raise the incomes of European food crop producers. Credit was made available through a Guaranteed Minimum Return (GMR) scheme under which the government would purchase a guaranteed quantity of produce at a pre-announced price. An insurance element in the program guaranteed protection against weather-induced crop failures, and best production practices were extended, and demanded, by a well-qualified and funded extension service. This system of guarantees was the basis of input credits secured by a lien on the marketed crop and repaid through the monopoly marketing agents.

Land policies, especially the creation of native reserves, and taxation measures (per hut or per head) were used to force Africans to seek employment on the settler farms, where they were offered land for subsistence production and the keeping of livestock. The introduction of mixed farming in the highlands required the elimination of the disease-carrying cattle of the African squatters, forcing their return to the crowded reserves, or into wage labor. Pressure for land was a key stimulus to the struggle for independence, and a key element of the post-independence transition arrangements. The Swynnerton Plan of 1954 marked the transition to integration of the African producer into the agricultural economy. The plan permitted smallholders to produce cash crops such as coffee, tea, and pyrethrum and market them through cooperatives. At the same time, land titling was coupled with public investments in research and extension.

All this was a key part of the colonial legacy that formed a template for development in the post-independence period. However, institutions put in place to serve the needs of a predominantly large-farm sector—much of which was transferred intact in the post-independence period to members of the policy-making African elite—proved ineffective in serving the needs of a predominantly smallholder sector. Moreover, because of inadequate management and rent seeking, the high cost of sustaining agricultural marketing parastatals by the late 1980s was threatening overall macroeconomic stability, contributing significantly to the budget deficit and inflation.

Policy and public expenditure have not been equally beneficial to producers in all parts of the country and have had rather little to offer the producers and production systems of the low-elevation and drier areas where Europeans never wanted to live. This bias has been evident in public expenditure and programs in agricultural research, where, since the introduction of hybrid maize in the mid-1960s, few significant technological innovations were successful. Kenya's agriculture in the first decade after independence did achieve remarkable progress through increasing the area under high-valued production of coffee, tea, and hybrid maize. However, the reduction in national per capita income in the 1990s can be traced partly to weakness in the agricultural sector. Particularly for the lower, drier areas, little agricultural development is visible. Even in the higher-potential areas, failures in service provision by public-sector agencies are evident. In the agricultural credit system, for example, the Agricultural Finance Corporation (AFC) lends to only 1 percent of rural households. Some 85 percent of AFC loans are made in the Rift Valley compared to only 15 percent in the central highlands. Loans were made to farms averaging 19 acres, compared to a national average farm size of 4.3 acres, and 73 percent of borrowers had off-farm sources of income (Argwings-Kodhek 1998).

A recent study (Gautam 1999) on awareness and smallholder adoption of technological recommendations, generated by research and extended by the extension service, shows how factors outside the control of research can affect its impact. Lack of funds was cited most often as the reason for nonadoption or discontinuation of recommended practices. Similar examples of poor performance by public agencies in the seed industry_quality control and competition, market information, agricultural research, extension, and overall sector policy making—are the subjects of other chapters of this book.

The Policy Environment

Kenya is a decade into a process of macroeconomic reforms, liberalizing input and output markets, dismantling or privatizing parastatals, and moving government toward a smaller, largely regulatory, role. These changes have important implications for the agricultural sector and provide a backdrop to the management of agricultural research.

Agriculture forms a large, but decreasing, portion of gross domestic product (GDP), and changes in national GDP figures directly reflect changes in agricultural GDP (table 2.1), particularly because of periodic droughts and instability in world prices for coffee and tea. However, the different commodities and sectors that make up agricultural GDP have been experiencing widely differing levels of performance, as detailed in a later section.

Variable agricultural performance was not the only factor in the historical picture of unstable macroeconomic performance. Outside of agriculture, the performance and management of the public sector has played an important role. Government revenue has remained high, at up to 28 percent of GDP in 1994 as compared to about 17 percent for the rest of sub-Saharan Africa. Moreover, a large proportion of these funds is used to pay the recurrent and salary costs of a huge, nonteaching civil service of 270,000 and an additional 250,000 teachers. Over 2 percent of the population is on the government payroll—a payroll that was allowed to grow in an extraordinary manner, especially when the temporary increases in government revenue following the two coffee booms of the 1970s were treated as being permanent. The 1979 oil shocks and droughts in 1980–82 and 1984–85 exacerbated the fiscal imbalances brought about by the increasing public payrolls.

The poorly implemented 1986 Sessional Paper No. 1 on "Economic Management for Renewed Growth" recognized the causes and some solutions to the economic problems that were evident at the time. This document, together with a series of structural adjustment loans supported by the World Bank and the International Monetary Fund (IMF), set the macroeconomic framework for the next decade or so. Among the

---

Table 2.1   Agriculture in the Kenyan Economy, 1963–98

Period	Annual Change in Real GDP[a] (%)	Annual Change in Real AgGDP[b] (%)	Share of Agriculture in GDP[a] (%)
1963–75	4.5	4.7	37.0
1976–80	5.5	2.9	36.0
1981–85	3.2	2.2	31.0
1986–90	5.0	2.7	31.0
1991–95	2.2	0.3	28.0
1991	2.1	−0.7	30.0
1992	0.5	−3.3	28.0
1993	0.5	−3.3	27.0
1994	3.0	3.1	27.0
1995	4.8	4.9	27.0
1996	4.6	4.4	25.0
1997	2.4	1.0	24.6
1998	1.8	1.5	24.6

Source: GoK 1999. a. GDP = gross domestic product.   b. AgGDP = agricultural GDP.

27

key recent macroeconomic trends were the rationalization of public expenditure, limiting the budget deficit to no more than 2 percent of GDP, civil service reform aimed at reducing staff numbers, and the restructuring or privatization of parastatals. Monetary measures focused on controlling inflation by limiting monetary growth to GDP growth rates and allowing market forces to determine interest rates. The exchange rate also was allowed to float, and exchange controls were lifted, as were import licensing and controls over time on the movement of agricultural produce. Concurrent with economic reforms, the constitutional provisions barring the formation of competing political parties and multiparty democracy were rescinded.

The more liberalized macroeconomic environment, together with government fiscal constraints, has had some direct impact on agriculture. Liberalization of price controls set by the marketing boards, of interest rates, and of trade and exchange rate regimes has allowed the sector to respond to the incentives offered by a market economy. This has helped the growing horticultural export sector. Yet liberalization has joined the rest of agriculture, and indeed the whole economy, suffered high real interest rates (over 20 percent) and a shortage of credit. Increased competition and private-sector involvement in the importation of fertilizer, machinery and spare parts, seeds, and agrochemicals have benefited producers. Private imports of maize, wheat, sugar, and rice have brought benefits to consumers, but hurt inefficient producers and led to government-imposed import duties. However, the country's ability to use tariffs is limited by the World Trade Organization (WTO) agreement and suggests that investment in increasing the productive capacity of the agricultural sector will be a more certain method of increasing agricultural incomes.

Liberalized marketing has found some producers and sectors not fully equipped to deal directly with market forces. Investments in on-farm grain storage are lagging since the National Cereals and Produce Board (NCPB) reduced its role in providing intertemporal storage to producers and processors. Some commodity boards (e.g., in dairy produce and coffee) are responding too slowly to the new regime, resulting in court battles between producers and management. The agricultural sector is in a state of flux brought about by the change in orientation from government-provided services and policy leadership to groups of stakeholders being called upon to provide services and leadership for themselves, as detailed in the following section.

A Review of Commodity Performance

Maize

The area under maize has stagnated at 1.4 million hectares, and annual production averages 30 million bags. Figure 2.1 shows maize production compared with that of wheat from 1970 to 1998. The production systems are associated with the three major production environments: the high-potential systems typified by the surplus-producing areas of the Rift Valley, the mid-altitude zones typified by Embu and parts of western Kenya, and the more marginal production environments of eastern Kenya and the areas around Lake Victoria.

Figure 2.1   Maize and Wheat Production in Kenya, 1970–98

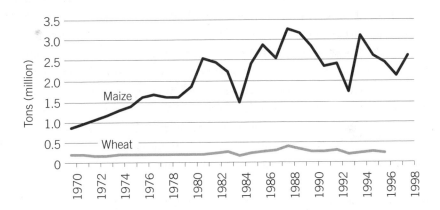

National average maize yields of 8.5 bags per acre (1.9 t ha⁻¹) are low by international standards, but differ markedly both across the main agroclimatic zones and
among different farmers within each zone. In the marginal environments (30 percent
of area), maize yields range from 0 to 8 bags per acre, depending primarily on weather.
The bulk of maize production in this zone involves intercrops with beans, cowpeas,
pigeon peas, sorghum, or millet. Sixty percent of maize area is planted to local,
unimproved seed, and 40 percent of farms use improved, open-pollinated varieties
(Argwings-Kodhek 1998). Fertilizer use is minimal.

In more than three out of ten years the maize crop in the marginal environments
fails because of drought. Producers persist in marginal production because maize is a
major food source and is cheaper to produce than to acquire from the market in those
years when they do get a crop. Maize also becomes a major cash crop in good rainfall
years. The risky production environment and the relative poverty of producers in
these areas partly explain the low levels of inputs used.

In the mid-altitude zones, which cover 55 percent of the maize area, intercrops
with beans dominate. Yields range from seven to twelve bags per acre. Here the yield
is less dependent on rainfall and reflects more agronomic practices used by farmers.
The use of early planting, the use of the appropriate hybrid seed (500 series), and the
quantity of fertilizer used are reflected in yields.

Yields in the prime production areas of the lower highlands range from twelve to
thirty bags per acre in normal years. Yields reflect production practices—the quality
and timeliness of land preparation and weed control, the use of certified seed, and the
quantity of fertilizer used. Cash flow constraints, and the almost complete lack of production credit, mean that those who can invest in optimal production practices are
those with large tracts of land or off-farm sources of income. Reforms in maize marketing mean that prices are relatively low immediately after harvest, and rise
significantly toward the middle of the following year. Those who can hold out until
mid-year to sell get a much higher return from their maize production than does the

typical smallholder, who must sell immediately to meet pressing cash needs such as December ceremonies and January school fees. Higher yields in Kenya are associated with higher costs of production per acre, but with lower costs per bag produced.

The National Cereals and Produce Board (NCPB), which used to dominate maize marketing through a system of pan-seasonal and pan-territorial prices, movement permits, and limits on how many bags could be moved without a permit, has become a peripheral player in the market. Purchases peaked at six million bags in 1990, and fell gradually to zero in 1998. The NCPB used to be a huge drain on the Treasury, but now operates commercially without government support. The government is charged for any noncommercial "social functions" undertaken, such as distributing famine relief or intervening to stabilize (usually raise) producer prices as happened in early 1999.

Maize market liberalization has had a variety of positive results. Wholesale market prices in the post-liberalization period are 15 percent lower than in the pre-liberalization period (Karanja, Jayne, and Strasberg 1998). Most producers prefer the current marketing system and find it easier to market their production. Consumers have benefited through lower prices for sifted flour and whole maize, as well as more convenient access to the "posho" mills that serve mainly the poor (Argwings-Kodhek and Jayne 1996). Private-sector imports now meet any production shortfall without recourse to government. However, Kenya is pursuing a policy of protecting the relatively poorer, inefficient producers and boosting the profits of the relatively well

Figure 2.2   Maize Trading Status of Households in Kenya

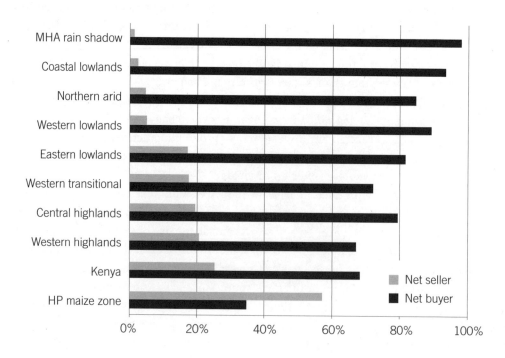

endowed, efficient producers through import bans and an import duty on maize. In a country where over 90 percent of the population are maize consumers, mostly living below the poverty line, and where 67 percent of maize producers buy more maize in a year than they sell (Argwings-Kodhek 1998; figure 2.2) using trade policy to raise maize prices seems an inequitable policy to follow. Kenya's maize sector—producers as well as consumers—would be better off if, rather than trying to use tariffs to protect local producers, investments were made in trying to make production systems more efficient.

Wheat

Domestic production of wheat meets less than 40 percent of domestic needs. Kenya produces mainly soft wheat and must depend on imports of both soft and hard wheat to meet the shortfall. Kenya can never meet its wheat needs from domestic production in the face of stagnating production and increasing demand. Government policy has consistently come down on the side of protecting a few producers rather than the millions of consumers. Import tariffs are used to raise domestic prices and keep some of the more inefficient producers in business while large-scale producers earn excess profits.

The cost of wheat production varies between different production scales and environments. Kenya's most efficient wheat production systems are the large-scale systems in Narok, Uasin, Gishu, and Nakuru whose production costs are lower than in the corresponding small-scale systems, mainly because of higher yields. Higher yields mainly depend upon weather and the timeliness of operations (Nyoro 1995). The timeliness of operations depends on access to, or ownership of, machinery. Some of the small-scale systems suffer because of lack of machinery—especially combine harvesters. However, buying and maintaining machinery is extremely costly, particularly as the interest costs associated with such purchases are high, and government taxes raise the cost of spare parts and fuel.

The quality of certified seed available to wheat producers also has been a cause of concern. This has led most producers to use retained seed. Some large producers are investing in dryers and seed preparation equipment, and a market is developing in uncertified, but treated, seed. Improvements in seed quality could help make Kenyan wheat systems more competitive. Wheat producers have already demonstrated a willingness to contribute funds toward research programs at the Kenya Agricultural Research Institute (KARI) wheat research station at Njoro in return for some control over the research agenda. Administrative obstacles have made this difficult to get off the ground.

Sugar

Kenya consumes over 600,000 tons of white sugar, but barely produces 400,000 tons in a good year (figure 2.3). For the foreseeable future, Kenya will import sugar as investments in new production schemes, such as those proposed for Busia and Siaya, lag behind growing domestic demand.

31

Figure 2.3 Kenya Sugar Production, Consumption, and Imports (in Tons), 1976–96

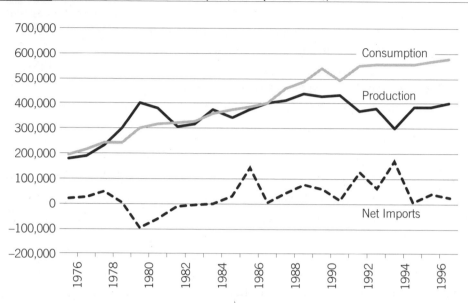

Kenyan consumers pay up to three times the world price of sugar due to a domestic pricing system that pegs prices to the production costs of the most inefficient producers, high taxes on imports, and 95 percent duties and taxes—the maximum allowed under the WTO, to which Kenya is a signatory. These maxima are to be reduced over the next few years, meaning that some of Kenya's more costly production zones may go out of business unless they become more efficient. The Mumias Company can make money selling sugar at up to Ksh 20,000 per ton less than the most inefficient factories. If the relative efficiency of the western production zone also were taken into account, then the bulk of Kenyan sugar production could be competitive with imports. The Mumias, the Sony, the Nzoia (if more efficiently run), and the relatively well-run Chemilil Companies (table 2.2), can compete if some efficiency-enhancing measures are undertaken.

Some measures to enhance efficiency:

- Efficiency on the farm can be increased through investments in research on cane varieties with a high-sucrose content. Recent steps by the sugar industry to take over the management and financing of sugar research are a step in the right direction.
- Sugar farmers need strong out-grower organizations to help small-scale farms produce sugar under contract to a sugar-processing factory. Optimal input use, combined with timely harvesting, could make Kenya's rain-fed cane production among the most efficient in the world.
- Farmers need to be able to enforce contracts with factories with regard to date of harvesting. Currently only the farmers lose when the crop is harvested late.

Table 2.2 Costs (Ksh) of Producing Sugar for Some Kenyan Companies

Company	Tons cane	Cost to produce 1 t cane	Costs per ton sugar		
			Cane	Processing	Production
Mumias	9.82	979	16,989	9,820	26,809
Sony	10.54	979	18,234	10,540	28,774
Chemilil	11.23	1497	19,428	11,230	30,658
Western	11.74	979	20,310	11,740	32,050
Nzoia	11.78	979	20,379	11,780	32,159
Muhoroni	14.86	1497	25,708	14,860	40,568
Miwani	16.65	1497	28,805	16,650	45,455

Post-farm efficiency can be enhanced most directly if:

- Canes are purchased on the basis of sucrose content, and
- Factories are privatized. This will eliminate some of the inefficiencies associated with the parastatal-run factories. Yet privatization already is proving difficult, as the government struggles to make the process transparent and politically acceptable.

Kenya could have a larger sugar industry, providing income and employment to thousands of people in the western part of the country, if investments could be made in efforts to improve the efficiency of farm production and post-farm processing. However, Kenya has yet to articulate its long-run policy with regard to import competition, nor has it explained to the sugar industry the implications of the WTO agreement that will reduce the level of duty that can be charged on imports. Investment in research will be key to keeping the sugar industry alive.

Tea, Coffee, and Horticulture

Coffee production in Kenya is on a severe downward trend. Production peaked at 130,000 tons in 1988 and fell to 50,000 tons in 1998. Low prices following the suspension of the international coffee agreement, and high input and marketing costs, led to the reduction among farmers of input use. Coffee berry disease, leaf rust, leached soils, and increased inter-cropping reduced production, as did fairly widespread uprooting and neglect of coffee trees in both the smallholder and estate sectors. High operational costs in the organizations serving farmers exacerbated the problems caused by low world prices. Management problems—low capacity utilization, overemployment, and poor investments including nonperforming loans—afflicted producer cooperatives as well as the major millers, the Kenya Planters Cooperative Union (KPCU), the Coffee Board, and the Coffee Research Foundation. These problems have resulted in institutional struggles within the industry that center on the role of the Coffee Board in a liberalized industry. The board is simultaneously a major player and an industry regulator.

33

Figure 2.4 Tea and Coffee Production in Kenya, 1970–97

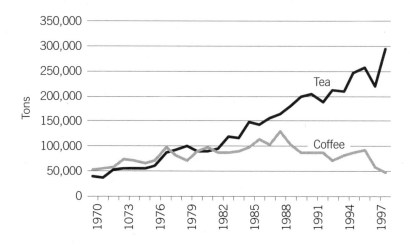

The tea industry, however, is enjoying record production levels (figure 2.4). Prices are high and recent investments in increasing processing capacity are reducing factory congestion that used to limit area expansion, the quality of tea produced, and thus also farmer payments. However, a growing number of smallholders, together with their members of parliament through the Coffee and Tea Parliamentary Association (COTEPA)—are expressing displeasure with the institutional arrangements in the sector. These center around the role of the Kenya Tea Development Authority (KTDA), which has a legal monopoly and exclusive control over the provision of extension services, planting materials, fertilizers, green leaf collection, quality control, processing, and marketing of smallholder tea. In its role as managing agent, KTDA holds up to three-quarters of farmers' payments for anywhere from four to sixteen months. This results in unhappy, cash-strapped farmers, a highly liquid KTDA, and allegations of corruption and overcharging on purchases that ultimately are charged to farmers.

The coffee and tea industries finance their own research organizations through self-imposed levies. These industries also have gone further than most in having a system of representative democracy and delegates running their main organizations. Yet these organizations have been slow to respond to liberalization and they retain much of their historical government-dominated parastatal character. The industries need better information on what roles different institutions play, what they cost, and whether the same or more important functions can be performed under more accountable and cost-effective institutional arrangements. In both industries the process of liberalization is being slowed by outdated pieces of still-enforced legislation, and by managements that have been able to co-opt farmer-elected directors through large sitting, travel, and personal allowances. The key issue in both industries is how to ensure that farmer representatives do indeed represent farmers,' rather than personal, interests.

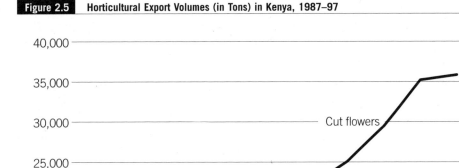

| Figure 2.5 | Horticultural Export Volumes (in Tons) in Kenya, 1987–97 |

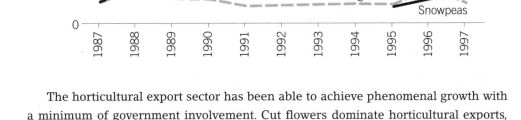

The horticultural export sector has been able to achieve phenomenal growth with a minimum of government involvement. Cut flowers dominate horticultural exports, followed by French beans and a variety of fruits and Asian vegetables (figure 2.5).

Small-scale producers dominate the production of French beans, Asian vegetables, and fruit. In the vegetable sector, strict limits on pesticide residues in European markets have tended to favor larger producers and exporters who are able to organize to have some control over the production practices of their suppliers, particularly with regard to the interval between pesticide sprays and picking. Larger producers also are favored by a move toward value-added prepacks, where French beans in particular are packaged ready for the supermarket shelf and immediate cooking. The high cost of airfreight out of Kenya means that the value-added prepacks can outcompete the traditional 3-kg box for limited and costly airspace. Smallholders also suffer from reduced access to credit and technical information, which often is tied to contracts with particular exporters or embodied in costly, often expatriate, consultants. The contributions of the research and extension systems to leveling the information "playing field" between large- and small-scale producers have been insufficient, leaving most producers to a process of trial and error or consultation with neighbors for technical information. Credit through exporters or farmer-organized groups has largely failed because of the difficulties experienced in trying to enforce contracts. The recent introduction of sea freight for fruits is increasing exports of sea-borne avocados and mangoes.

Large-scale producers of carnations, statice, and roses dominate cut flower exports. Large firms, which are integrated right from experimental farm trials through production and aircraft leasing, dominate the market. Some are multinationals or belong to well-endowed members of the elite. Technical advice, quality planting material, and market information are available to these large producers. Smallholders grow some of the less capital-intensive flowers, such as *alstroemeria, arabicum,* and a wide variety of other low-value flowers. The role of smallholders is shrinking because of the lower value-to-weight ratio of their production, and because of problems related to exploitation by, or disagreements with, middlemen.

The horticultural export industry has a dual structure, with the large, well-endowed, or well-organized producers doing well and the small, poor, and unorganized doing relatively badly. Many of the smaller producers graduated from producing for the domestic market, which utilizes over 95 percent of horticultural production. However, little attention by public sector research or by extension is paid to this important sector, where there is some expectation that private research will service the smallholder producer. For most smallholders, forays into producing for the domestic horticultural market for fruits and vegetables are an important route to raising rural farm incomes. However, research and extension information for horticultural products, both for domestic production and for export, is severely limited. The horticultural industries provide an interesting challenge to both agricultural research and extension. The sector requires research information, is relatively able to contribute toward the costs, and is fairly organized so it can collect levies. Even domestic horticultural production can be levied through the limited market channels through which it passes—for example, through local council road tolls or market fees. At the large-scale end of the market, growers already conduct much of their own research. The challenge to the agricultural research system is to tap into this reservoir of need, organization, and ability to pay. By demonstrating the possibilities of and the problems that can be solved through research to the export and domestic horticulture industries, KARI will be making the transition toward the flexible, market-oriented research system that Kenya will need in the twenty-first century. Furthermore, lessons learned in this relatively advanced and organized sector can be applied to other, less well endowed, sectors.

In both the food and cash crop industries, more minor commodities provide grist for the research mill. The pyrethrum industry has benefited from having an umbrella body that collects funds to finance research and produces and distributes high-pyrethrin-content cultivars using tissue culture techniques. The oilseed industries—soybean, sunflower, coconut, and cotton—would all benefit from having such an industry-responsive research infrastructure in place. Among the food crops, sorghum and millet, cassava, sweet and Irish potato, and upland rice all have specific research needs that may not have been adequately translated into specific research activities. Yet many of these minor crop sectors suffer from the lack of an organized stakeholder group able to articulate industry needs to the research system. Such groups also could organize to contribute funds or actually pay for research to be undertaken. This is the future context within which agricultural research in Kenya will be managed, and suggests major new orientations within both agricultural research and the functioning of the Agricultural Ministry. This Ministry has had various names at different times in the history of Kenya. Currently, Kenya has a Ministry of Agriculture and a Ministry of Livestock and Fisheries Development.

More emphasis should be placed on socioeconomic research, seeking and reaching out to stakeholders, and adopting a more responsive private sector and marketing orientation.

The Livestock Industries

Livestock contributes 42 percent of agricultural GDP, but gets limited attention from policy makers and policy research. As a result, much of the information on which planning for the sector is based is outdated. Kenya is long overdue for a livestock census, projections of supply and demand for animals and animal products, and studies of costs, competitiveness, and constraints facing the different production and marketing systems. The literature suggests that per capita consumption of most livestock products is low by world standards, and much lower in rural than in urban areas. Each year Kenyans consume about 10 kg of beef, 2 kg of sheep and goat meat, 0.71 to 2.4 kg of chicken (rural vs. urban), and 37 to 84 eggs (rural vs. urban) (MoALDM 1995). Urban demand is 150 percent of rural demand, and the urban population is growing. Incomes in both the urban and rural sectors are also expected to grow. This will lead to large increases in demand for animal products. The key policy question facing Kenya is whether this demand (as well as demand in neighboring countries) will be met from domestic production or from imports, primarily from neighboring countries to the north.

Kenya needs to improve the productive potential of its animal industries if they are to meet this challenge. The productive potential of the animal industries can best be addressed by studies of the following:

- Feeds, feeding, and general management,
- Disease control and the mix of private and government roles,
- Genetic potential of the flocks and herds,
- Arid and semi-arid lands (ASAL) issues, and
- The evolution of marketing systems.

Beef cattle are the biggest animal industry, and much of the production occurs in the ASAL, which face some particular constraints on marketing and feed supply. Restrictive disease control regulations make it difficult to market animals. Marketing infrastructure—roads, watering points, and pasture along the way—have been encroached upon or are in poor condition. These factors are limiting development of the livestock industry and the incomes of pastoralists, as off-take (percent slaughtered each year) is low because many animals, particularly those far from roads and

37

marketing infrastructure, are not marketed. Those that are marketed arrive in poor condition and receive low prices in the Nairobi market. The poor condition of animals and presence of foot-and-mouth disease also make it difficult to break into remunerative export markets.

Encroachment by sedentary farmers is denying the pastoralists access to what traditionally were the best-watered dry-season grazing pastures. Access to water has become more of a problem as watering points have failed and county council holding grounds have deteriorated. Insecurity, too, continues to be a problem, particularly in the border regions. The practice of transporting animals on the hoof for hundreds of miles, or truck, to abattoirs also encourages the spread of diseases. Investments in roads, rural electrification, and telecommunications may allow slaughter to be undertaken closer to the production point rather than near the market, if refrigerated transport modes can be developed. The concentration of slaughterhouses near urban markets—Nairobi and Mombassa—reflects previous controls put in place to protect the now defunct Kenya Meat Commission (KMC).

Policy related to the beef industry has dealt only with disease control and treatment. The large costs involved, together with the lack of cost recovery and the declining resources available through government, undermined vaccination and control programs and accelerated the transfer of dips to communities unable or unwilling to run them. In tandem with reduced enforcement of the Animal Diseases Act, compulsory vaccinations, and prompt communication and action in the event of an outbreak of communicable disease, this has led to a resurgence in cattle disease affecting both the beef and dairy sectors. Losses due to disease are estimated at an annual Ksh 1 billion, 45 percent of which is from the vector-borne East Coast fever (ticks) and tsetse fly-borne trypanosomiasis, and 30 percent from the viral rinderpest, foot-and-mouth disease, and contagious bovine pleuropneumonia (CBPP).

The disease problems of beef cattle, especially rinderpest, CBPP, and foot-and-mouth disease, are not as contained as they once were, because government funding for vaccination campaigns declined before the private services could be developed. Kenya has yet to come up with sustainable ways of funding infectious disease prevention and control. How this issue is addressed will determine future production trends.

In the dairy industry, many of the disease management issues are being handled through the privatization of veterinary, clinical, and artificial insemination (AI) services. The performance of these systems needs to be monitored, and government still has a role to play in those regions where private cattle owners may underinvest, particularly in tick control. Kenya has yet to find a formula for the sustainable operation of communally owned dips. Private and communal AI services are taking off, but not all farmers will be able to afford the imported semen that is replacing Kenya's own centralized production and distribution of disease-free semen. The centralized milk-recording service, so important in raising the genetic potential of the national herd, is also failing. Both systems may need to be taken over by some industry stakeholder group if they wish to remain viable in the face of reduced government funding.

Both the beef and dairy industries suffer from seasonal shortages of fodder. The animal-feeding regime, whether based on pasture or on concentrates, is an essential element in the competitiveness of the cattle systems and the poultry and pig industries. Beyond improved pasture management, silage making, and oilseed cake from a revitalized oil crops industry, the Kenyan animal industry will benefit greatly from

---

Box 2.1   **Kenya Cooperative Creameries (KCC) and the Dairy Industry**

1931   KCC established as a private producer-controlled organization formed from the merger of district-based European co-ops to coordinate marketing of butter and cheese for the export market in the deteriorating economic conditions of the great depression.

1954   Swynnerton Plan opened up the commercial market to African smallholders who marketed to KCC through cooperatives.

Three-tier quota pricing system introduced where highest prices went to producers able to guarantee supplies all year, lowest prices to those not able to guarantee any quantity in any season. Corresponded to large-scale Europeans vs. small-scale Africans.

1958   Dairy Industry Act set up the Kenya Dairy Board (KDB), which was progressively dominated by KCC. KCC processing monopoly was legalized in scheduled areas and able to limit new entrants to processing or raw milk marketing. KCC became KDB agent in collecting dairy development cess.

1965   Dairy Commission of Inquiry charged with finding a pricing structure in the interests of all producers.

1970   Pan-seasonal and pan-territorial pool pricing system replaced quotas based on past production. Guaranteed minimum price. All non-KCC dairies and sales to institutions discontinued.

1979   School Milk Program raised national demand by 30 percent—financially unsustainable.

1983   Introduction of January–April dry season bonus.

1980s–92 Increasingly high costs to KCC, especially for TetraPak processing material. Twenty percent real reduction in producer prices. Rising input prices. Cost squeeze reduced farmer intensification. Consumer shortages occurred because KCC was unable to reconstitute sufficient quantities of imported milk powder. Delayed payments to producers.

1992   Milk market liberalized. Declining sales to KCC as well as increased competition at the consumer level from raw milk. Eventually forty other processors were licensed, and the KCC struggled to survive in the face of producer price competition, an inability to pay producers and other suppliers, and disagreements with the government.

Late 1990s Dual dairy sector. Efficient producers near Nairobi market supplying raw milk. High and competitive prices. Services such as artificial insemination (AI) and credit availed, private, self-help groups. Some cooperatives are setting up processing facilities. Rift Valley further from big markets. Delayed KCC payments, weak farmer organizations providing no services, such as AI or treatment and drugs on credit. Reduced tick control and government-supported veterinary services. Cash-strapped farmers reducing production.

Source: Ngigi (2003).

---

reductions in the cost of maize, the main processed feed ingredient. Recent investors in the fast-food business were importing chicken from southern Africa. These inter-sectoral linkages strengthen the argument that, on the whole, Kenya is better off with lower maize prices.

A number of marketing and policy issues have the potential to either strengthen or severely weaken the livestock industries. In the dairy industry, the future role of the Kenya Cooperative Creameries (KCC) will have wide implications. Box 2.1. shows the history of the KCC from its inception in 1931 up to the late 1990s. The market for milk, particularly for producers near Nairobi, is increasing with the rapid develop-ment of new processors and raw milk marketing. Yet producers in the western parts of the country do not have the benefit of a large market for raw milk. This implies the need for some organized forms of marketing and processing to make those supplies available for sale nationwide, or even in neighboring countries. Producers in the northern Rift Valley may need to strengthen their producer cooperatives in order to make it easier to arrange collection, marketing, and payments for their milk, as well as services such as AI.

Experience from central Kenya suggests that, were the KCC to collapse, northern Rift producers would go through a painful period enforcing contracts with new mar-keting firms who collect milk but ultimately fail to pay. Whether the KCC should be saved, what form a restructured KCC should take, and how farmers might best pre-pare in case of its demise are some of the issues needing further research. How best to remove politics from the discussion of the future of this farmers' organization is perhaps the most pressing issue of all. A meeting of KCC shareholders is the only way the organization can begin to shape its future.

In the meat and dairy industries, up-to-date information on production and mar-keting costs, the nature of competition in marketing, regional comparative advantage, imports, and exports is lacking. Such information would help identify constraints, avenues for higher-value production and processing activities, and new avenues for local or foreign investment that provide context for the planning of agricultural research. Demand for animal products is set to increase dramatically. Yet investment in producing for that demand is discouraged by lack of information and lack of a clear and conducive government policy. Beneficiary participation in running industry serv-ices, including agricultural research, is likely part of the solution. This research area— how best to organize cost-recovery where externalities are high and beneficiaries are poor and widely dispersed—will challenge the research system.

Administrative Context

As the agricultural sector has been liberalized, the functions of the Ministry of Agriculture have been reduced to a virtual concentration on the extension service. Institutional change for the ministry has not been easy, and in the process it has abrogated its remaining role of defining the policy and regulatory framework within which the sector operates. That overall policy framework would help agricultural research managers understand the key elements of the policy environment that must be taken into account in determining the role of a public research organization. Currently it is difficult to discern what direction agricultural policy will take, leaving research managers to undertake their research independently of a coherent, sectoral policy framework.

If the the Ministry of Agriculture is to take the lead in setting the policy framework for the sector it must have access to good quality, relevant policy analysis. Attempts at building capacity in policy analysis within the ministry have not succeeded. Moreover, the capacity to collect reliable data on the sector has also deteriorated within both the ministry and the Central Bureau of Statistics. At the same time, several independent policy research institutes have been developed, having agriculture as only one element of their program. However, they have not been well linked to the policy formulation process and they in general have not had the resources to invest in primary data collection at a national level. Similarly, KARI itself has had other demands on its limited capacity in socioeconomics and has not been able to develop its own capacity in policy research or systematic, primary data collection—the maize database was one attempt to do so (Hassan 1998). To move toward a more coherent policy framework, both KARI and the ministry need to consider how to develop partnerships in the collection, generation, and analysis of policy-relevant data. This information and analysis need to be used to inform both sector policy makers and stakeholders. Ongoing discussions in the various commodity subsectors currently have little technical input from the ministry, KARI, or the policy research institutes.

Although government documents recognize the importance of agriculture in overall economic growth, expenditure on the sector as a percentage of the government budget has declined from 8–9 percent of the budget in the 1970s and 1980s to under 5 percent in recent years. This reflects partly the shedding of loss-making agricultural parastatals from the agriculture budget, and partly the failure of the ministry to develop and justify new policy initiatives in the national budgeting process. Lack of a policy research-based ministry and the ministry's focus on meeting the salary costs of an inordinately large but largely ineffective (Gautam 1999) extension service are largely responsible for the difficulty it has in pushing its agenda with the Treasury and with donors. The ministry provides little guidance on the policy issues of the day, such as the setting or removal of tariffs on imports. In the stakeholder-involved sector that the government is moving toward, the ministry needs to inform and to interact more with stakeholders. Some of the questions that the sector needs the ministry to address include:

- Who wins and who loses from the imposition of import tariffs, and why are these tariffs needed, at what level, and for how long?
- What will be the import parity and farm-gate prices for various commodities at harvest, and what kind of marketing conditions can farmers anticipate, based on the area under production of various commodities, the growing conditions, expected yields, and the cost of production?

41

- How can more effective farmer participation in the running of sector institutions, including agricultural research and extension, be encouraged?
- What has been the impact of various government- and donor-funded programs, and what lessons does this information provide for future sector planning and resource allocation?

It is encouraging that the ministry has begun to ask sector participants to prepare and forward policy suggestions, but the dialogue needs to go beyond the presentation of memoranda to the minister, permanent secretary, or director. Stakeholders need ministry involvement at the subpolitical level in an iterative and inclusive process of consultation, research, and analysis. As industries come together to define their future institutional arrangements, a revamped ministry can play the critically important role of adviser and impartial referee. The ministry also has great convening power—no other group or body in the sector has as great authority—and moral obligation to bring sector stakeholders together.

As the public agricultural research system looks to the future, a similar convening role might be envisioned. Greater stakeholder participation can allow KARI to make its limited resources go further. So many of the future needs of Kenyan agriculture can be met by only the research system. Global agricultural competition will be tipped in favor of those countries with the most cost-effective and productive agricultural research and extension—that is, agricultural knowledge—systems. A key element of those systems will be the manner in which stakeholders are able to organize to collectively solve emerging problems as farm sizes decrease, government resources become limited, and markets are liberalized (Jayne, Minde, and Agrwings-Kodhek 2002).

Conclusions

Agricultural research is critical in increasing agricultural productivity. Yet it is only one piece of an interlocking chain of drivers of agricultural development. Alain de Janvry reported at a workshop that the principles for achieving rural development in sub-Saharan Africa were as follows:

- The institutional gaps created by government contraction are the most serious hurdle to smallholder response.
- Rural poverty is fundamentally a result of insufficient control by the poor over income-generating assets.
- Because the rural poor are highly heterogeneous, multiple solutions must be found to alleviate rural poverty.
- Rural development programs must be demand-driven by the poor with appropriate technical assistance.
- This approach to rural development implies a strong and redefined role for the state to complement civil society.
- Problems of rural poverty cannot be solved by agriculture alone (World Bank 1997).

Kenya needs more agricultural research in an environment of declining public funds. Some of the better-organized stakeholders are demonstrating a willingness to contribute toward the funding of agricultural research. The challenge for agricultural research is to be able to demonstrate stakeholder-level benefits to funds invested in an environment where research must compete for limited resources with roads, water supply systems, and rural electrification.

Strategic clarity concerning the role of agricultural research in Kenya is important in maximizing the agricultural research share of the declining funding available. Strategic vision will revolve around the numerous issues that will be laid out in the rest of this book. A key example is demonstrating that the research system in Kenya consists of more than just the national agricultural research institute. To this end, increasing university involvement in the agricultural research system is the topic of chapter 10, increasing farmer-extension-research interfaces is the topic of chapter 11, and increasing the role of the private sector is the topic of chapter 14. Priority setting and ways of meeting the needs of the relatively lesser studied commodities and regions are topics that also need to be addressed, as well as the incentive and reward structures facing agricultural researchers. Kenya needs to decide what type of agricultural system it wants, how it will be funded, and the role of the various stakeholders in it. This book is aimed at furthering that agenda.

REFERENCES

Argwings-Kodhek, Gem. 1998. Monitoring for improved agricultural sector policy making. Tegemeo Institute Conference Working Paper. Nairobi: Tegemeo Institute for Agricultural Policy and Development.

Argwings-Kodhek, Gem, and T. S. Jayne. 1996. Maize market liberalization and food consumption patterns in urban Kenya. Tegemeo Institute Working Paper No. 2. Nairobi: Tegemeo Institute for Agricultural Policy and Development.

Bates, R. 1989. *Beyond the miracle of the market: The political economy of agrarian development in Kenya.* Cambridge, UK: Cambridge University Press.

Gautam, Madhur. 1999. *World Bank agricultural extension projects in Kenya: An impact evaluation.* Operations Evaluation Department Report No. 19523. Washington, D.C.: World Bank.

Government of Kenya (GoK). 1999. *Statistical abstract and economic surveys, various years.* Nairobi: Central Bureau of Statistics, Government of the Republic of Kenya.

Hassan, Rashid M., ed. 1998. *Maize technology development and transfer: A GIS application for research planning in Kenya.* Wallingford, UK: CAB International.

Heyer, Judith. 1981. Agricultural development policy in Kenya from the colonial period to 1975. In *Rural development in tropical Africa,* ed. Judith Heyer, P. Roberts, and G. Williams, 90–120. New York: St Martin's Press.

Jayne, T. S., Isaac J. Minde, and Gem Agrwings-Kodhek, eds. 2002. *Perspectives on agricultural transformation: A view from Africa.* New York: Nova Science.

Karanja, Daniel D., T. S. Jayne, and P. Strasberg. 1998. *Maize productivity and the impact of market liberalization in Kenya.* Tegemeo Institute Working Paper. Nairobi: Tegemeo Institute for Agricultural Policy and Development.

Lele, Uma. 1989. *Agricultural growth, domestic policies, the external environment, and assistance to Africa: Lessons of a quarter century.* MADIA Discussion Paper No. 1. Washington, D.C.: World Bank.

Lele, Uma, and Richard Meyers. 1987. Growth and structural change in East Africa: Domestic policies, agricultural performance, and World Bank assistance, 1963–86. Parts 1 and 2. Discussion Papers No. 273 and 274. Washington, D.C.: World Bank.

Ministry of Agriculture, Livestock Development, and Marketing (MoALDM). 1995. *Agricultural sector review.* Nairobi: MoALDM.

Ngigi, Margaret. 2003. Successes in African agriculture: The case of smallholder dairying in Eastern Africa. Paper presented at the InWEnt, IFPRI, NEPAD, CTA Conference, "Successes in African Agriculture," Pretoria, South Africa, 1–3 December 2003.

Nyoro, J. K. 1995. *Impacts of market reform on wheat production, processing and marketing in Kenya.* Proceedings of the Conference on Improving Agricultural Performance, September 1995, Nairobi, Kenya. Nairobi: Tegemeo Institute.

Winter-Nelson, A. 1995. A history of agricultural policy in Kenya. In *Agricultural policy in Kenya: Applications of the policy analysis matrix,* ed. Scott Pearson, Eric A. Monke, Gem Argwings-Kodhek, Francisco Avillez, Mulinge Mukumbu, Stefano Pagiola, D. Sellen, and A. Winter-Nelson, 31–48. Ithaca, N.Y.: Cornell University Press.

World Bank. 1997. *Taking action to reduce poverty in sub-Saharan Africa.* Washington, D.C.: World Bank.

3

Diversity and Dynamics in Kenyan Agriculture: The Challenge for Agricultural Research Policy and Management

STEVEN WERE OMAMO, MARKUS WALSH,
AND GEM ARGWINGS-KODHEK

Introduction

Agricultural technologies integrate both biological and socioeconomic processes. Technology design, which is at the heart of the agricultural research process, is thus a function both of the agroclimatic conditions in which the crop or animal is grown and the economic, cultural, and social conditions in which the farmer manages crops or livestock. Developing appropriate technologies for African conditions is a complex process, because farming systems are essentially rain-fed with minimal use of inputs, rely on ecological services to maintain productivity, and are complex in structure, involving a range of crop, tree, and animal components in complex arrangements. Moreover, the research institute must accommodate extraordinary spatial heterogeneity and temporal variability in the design of its technologies. The experience of postwar agricultural research on the continent has shown that borrowing technologies or research processes from either temperate or irrigated agriculture is limited in effectiveness and that African agricultural research generally must develop its own approaches and methods.

Several factors determine and reflect variations over space and time in Kenyan agriculture. In this chapter, these joint influences are analyzed by classifying them into three broad categories—agro-ecological, demographic, and market-related. Agro-ecological conditions reflect the influences of climate, soils, and biotic influences on crop choice and performance. Rural demographic factors, which vary significantly, influence the relative size and intensity of the farming operation, while market-access factors determine farmers' relative balance between subsistence and income-generating activities. The central questions explored are how, and to what extent, these three broad groupings condition and characterize the diversity and dynamics of Kenyan agriculture.

Agro-Ecological Diversity

The diversity and complexity of crop growing conditions in Kenya is well documented (Heyer, Maitha, and Senga 1976; Pearson et al. 1995). Classification criteria used to

45

Box 3.1 Rules for Determining Length of Photosynthetically Active Period (LPAP) and Aboveground Net Primary Productivity (AGNPP) for Normalized Difference Vegetation Index (NDVI) Time Series

---

LPAP calculations

- A threshold (T) of 66% of the difference between the maximum and minimum values observed in the profile (T = 0.66 × (NDVI$_{max}$ − NDVI$_{min}$) is calculated. All decadal entries falling above this threshold are classified as "green."

- For each decade (d), the increment I is calculated as I = NDVI$_{(d +1)}$ − NDVI$_{(d)}$. All positive values of I are classified as "greening up."

- Photosynthetically active decades (PAD) are then classified via a probabilistic Noisy OR relationship as: p(PAD|"green", "greening-up") = NoisyORDist(0.05, "green" = 0.9, "greening-up" = 0.7).

- LPAP is represented as the fraction of decades over the course of the entire time series that are photosynthetically active as: LPAP = $\Sigma n(f$PAD.365/n), where n is the number of recorded years.

AGNPP calculations

- For each year, the positive photosynthetically active increment (PPAI) is assessed using the following heuristic: SUM I IF PAD = "active" AND I > 0.

- The expected AGNPP (EAGNPP) in year n is then calculated linearly according to: EAGNPP$_n$ = {(PPAI$_n$ − PPAI$_{min}$)/(PPAI$_{max}$ − PPAI$_{min}$) × 1200}, where PPAI$_{min}$ is the average minimum NDVI value of the profile recorded over n years, PPAI$_{max}$ is the average maximum, and 1200 is a scaling parameter representing the maximum expected level of AGNPP (in gCm^{-2}y^{-1}) in Kenya from literature sources.

---

assess agro-ecological potential typically include long-term estimates of precipitation, potential evapotranspiration, and major limiting soil or terrain conditions in relation to crop requirements (Jaetzold and Schmidt 1984). In the absence of high-quality information about on-ground conditions, empirically derived relationships between total seasonal precipitation, seasonal potential evapotranspiration, elevation, and temperature are usually used as proxy variables for estimating the lengths and reliabilities of growing periods for various crops. However, such relationships tend to be crude. Recent developments in remote sensing permit more refined definitions of "agricultural potential" that integrate light, moisture, and nutrient-related constraints on agricultural productivity. For this chapter, the length of photosynthetically active period (LPAP, in days) and the average aboveground net primary productivity (AGNPP, in grams of carbon m^{-2}y^{-1}) were identified as the central indicators of agricultural potential. Relatively long LPAP and high AGNPP were hypothesized to confer high agricultural potential, independent of actual land use.

Neither the LPAP nor the AGNPP can be measured directly. However, they can be inferred via the normalized difference vegetation index (NDVI), which is strongly

Figure 3.1   Spatial Distributions of Agro-Ecological Zones in Kenya

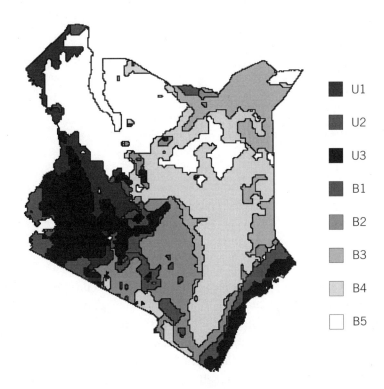

U1
U2
U3
B1
B2
B3
B4
B5

associated with the amount of on-ground, photosynthetically active vegetation (PAV) over a wide range of conditions. A reasonably long time series (1982–98) of advanced very high-resolution radiometer (AVHRR) images of these variables was used to estimate the LPAP and AGNPP for different parts of Kenya (see box 3.1 for the rule base).

Eight zones were identified based on distinct long-term average seasonal timings of the onset and duration of photosynthetically active periods, modalities of growing seasons, and estimated overall levels of ecosystem productivity. Figure 3.1 shows the geographic spread of the zones across the country. Table 3.1 shows the distributions of LPAP and AGNPP across the eight zones. The zoning scheme relates remarkably well to a number of other independently assessed geographical descriptors broadly related to agro-ecological potential, such as elevation and slope.

The zones U1, U2, and U3 are characterized by a unimodal NDVI profile, the others, B1 through B5, have bimodal profiles. The fall in LPAP from U1 to B5 is quite clear. However, because both the level and variability of the NDVI matters, the AGNPP profile across zones is more jagged, with two of the bimodal zones (B2 and B3) registering higher averages than zone U3, despite the latter's having a higher LPAP. Zone U1, which contains Kenya's cool, wet highland areas, thus may be considered as having the highest agro-ecological potential in terms of growing season length and overall levels of primary productivity. Conversely, zone B5, comprising the arid and semi-arid zones in the eastern and northern parts of the country, may be considered as having the lowest potential in terms of these variables. The AGNPP

47

Table 3.1   Selected Characteristics of Agro-Ecological Zones in Kenya

Zone	Area (1,000 ha)	LPAP[a]	AGNPP[b] (rank)	Elevation[c]	Slope[d]
U1	8,059	201	929 (1)	1,612	2.0
U2	3,798	188	635 (3)	1,553	2.1
U3	1,723	176	307 (6)	1,248	1.7
B1	2,986	179	643 (2)	861	0.8
B2	7,285	167	400 (4)	892	1.4
B3	6,038	149	352 (5)	461	0.4
B4	14,855	147	125 (7)	415	0.5
B5	12,754	144	89 (8)	671	1.0

a. LPAP = length of photosynthetically active period in days.
b. AGNPP = aboveground net primary productivity in grams of carbon m^{-2} y^{-1}.
c. Elevation (meters above sea level).
d. Slope over 1-km grid (degrees).

captures the agricultural carrying capacity of a region. Based on this parameter, zone B1, the high-rainfall, mid-altitude zone, ranks second in terms of potential, followed by the humid and subhumid zones U2, B2, and B3 and the relatively dry highland areas captured by U3 and the semi-arid zone B4, in that order. Between them, the five zones with the highest potential account for less than 50 percent of total area in the country. This has important implications for population dynamics and natural resource use across the country.

Population Dynamics on a Constrained Resource Base

Between 1960 and 1990, Kenya's rural population more than doubled, from 7.9 million to 17.8 million people, and at current growth rates it is expected to top 24.5 million by

Table 3.2   Aboveground Net Primary Productivity (AGNPP; in g-C-m^{-2}y^{-1}) and Population Density by Agro-Ecological Zone

Zone[a]	AGNPP	Population Density (PD)[b]	AGNPP/PD
U1	929	541	1.72
U2	635	374	1.70
U3	307	345	0.89
B1	643	99	6.50
B2	400	1	400.00
B3	352	78	4.51
B4	125	4	31.25
B5	89	2	44.50

a. See Table 3.1 for characteristics. b. People per square kilometer.

2020 (FAO 1999). While the total number of rural inhabitants has increased, the distribution of this increase has not been uniform. The areas with the largest numbers of people to begin with have registered the highest rates of population growth. This has important implications for the dynamics of natural resource use and availability in the country.

As argued in the previous section, the AGNPP of a region can be interpreted as a long-term measure of its agricultural carrying capacity. The ratio of AGNPP to population density thus provides a compact representation of long-term stress on natural resources. Table 3.2 shows this ratio for the eight agro-ecological zones.

Population pressure in the highlands (zone U1) implies considerably higher pressure on resources than in less well-endowed regions of the country (e.g., zones B1, B2, and B3). This continuum clearly reflects the tendency for human settlement to mirror underlying production potential. Pockets of extreme stress are found despite relatively low production potential (e.g., in zone U3), and of low stress despite relatively low potential (e.g., in zone B2). However, overall, the higher the inherent potential, then the higher the population density, and the higher the demonstrable stress on the natural resource base.

Historical evidence indicates that production decisions generally reflect technical choices that facilitate or catalyze the substitution of relatively abundant (hence cheap) factors of production for relatively scarce (hence expensive) ones (Hayami and Ruttan 1985). Population increase renders some resources, such as land, more dear while increasing the availability of others, such as labor, and has been identified as an important source of pressure for technical change through factor substitution (Boserup 1981; Tomich, Kilby, and Johnston 1995). The data in table 3.2 suggest that these pressures for change are likely to be important in Kenya. Lynam (1978) and Pearson et al. (1995) identified them as crucial to technology choice in a key region in eastern Kenya. The geographical patterns of agricultural production and value added reflect these considerations.

The Spatial Configuration of Agricultural Production and Income

Unfortunately, data on actual production practices (land use on farm) and farming incomes in Kenya are not available in a form that permits full and consistent integration with the eight zones. Typically, major farming systems are distinguished on the basis of extant output mixes, broad input-output relationships, geographic location (often including administrative unit), and, where possible, variables such as recorded rainfall, temperature, elevation, and soil type. Box 3.2 shows such a classification, which was used in a 1997 survey of 1,540 farming households in twenty-four districts in Kenya. The zoning scheme is a hybrid of broad agro-ecological zones (Jaetzold and Schmidt 1984) and administrative and political boundaries (Argwings-Kodhek 1998).

The point made earlier about the crudeness of such zoning methods is confirmed. Based on variability in LPAP and AGNPP, these nine agricultural zones do not span the full range of ecological zones outlined previously. However, this is a meaningful

49

Box 3.2	Nine Agricultural Production Zones in Kenya and Corresponding Agro-Ecological Zones

Agricultural production zone	Most representative ecological zone
Coastal lowlands	B3
Marginal rain shadow	U3
Northern arid	B5
Western lowlands	B2
Western highlands	U1
Eastern lowlands	B3
Western transitional	B1
Central highlands	U1
High-potential maize zone	U1

failing because it serves to illustrate the fact that actual production systems (land-use practices) reflect not only ecological potential but other factors, too. It is also meaningful because it conforms to the reality in Kenya, in which the bulk of arable farming occurs in a small percentage of the country. However, even within this relatively small area, commodities produced, and the production systems in which they appear, are numerous and diverse.

Table 3.3 shows the range of major crops produced in Kenya. Whereas some crops are reasonably widely produced (e.g., maize, sorghum, and pulses) others are concentrated in particular agro-ecological zones (e.g., tea and coffee in the western and central highlands). Specialized growing conditions imply sharp concentrations within particular zones of production of a number of crops (e.g., sugarcane, wheat, barley, sorghum, cotton, pyrethrum, pineapples, rice, tobacco, and sunflowers). A large share of root-crop production occurs in western Kenya, and along with sorghum, these products appear most prominently in lowland areas. Relatively more high-value products are grown and raised in areas with comparatively high agricultural potential. This distribution of production has important implications for the spatial configuration of agricultural income.

The high potential maize zone contributes the most to gross domestic product from agriculture (AgGDP), has the highest household incomes from agriculture, and has the highest returns per hectare under production (table 3.4). Agricultural incomes generated in the central highlands, while significantly below those in the high-potential maize zone, are still well above incomes in other zones, particularly in terms of returns to area under production. The figures suggest something of a dichotomy in Kenyan agriculture, between regions with relatively high potential and thus high incomes on the one hand, and those with comparatively low potential and correspondingly low incomes on the other.

Table 3.3   Distribution (%) of Major Crops Across Agricultural Production Zones in Kenya

Crop[a]	Agricultural Production Zone[b]								
	NA	CL	EL	WL	WT	HPM	WH	CH	MRS
Maize	1	5	15	12	10	19	14	19	5
Tea						22	24	54	
Coffee			8	2	1	3	33	53	
Sugarcane	2		10	13	58	5	2	10	0
Pulses		1	17	9	10	21	13	23	6
Irish potatoes			7	1	1	17		61	14
Wheat						94			6
Barley						100			
Sorghum	6	1	17	48	7	6	13		2
Millet			6	6	19	40	24	3	1
Cotton	24		3	73					
Pyrethrum						100			
Pineapples		19			63	16		3	
Paddy rice		58	4	38					
Root crops	1	14	24	20	20	9	5	7	1
Tobacco			50		6			44	
Sunflowers				11		78	11		

Source: Argwings-Kodhek (1998).
a. This listing is not intended to be exhaustive, but rather to capture the distribution of major commodities. For instance, livestock products and some horticultural commodities are not represented.
b. NA = northern arid, CL = coastal lowlands, EL = eastern lowlands, WL = western lowlands, WT = western transitional, HPM = high-potential maize, WH = western highlands, CH = central highlands, and MRS = marginal rain shadow.

Table 3.4   Agricultural Gross Domestic Product (AgGDP) and Household Incomes from Agriculture Across Agro-Ecological Zones in Kenya

Zone	AgGDP (Ksh million y^{-1})	Household Agricultural Income (HAI) (Ksh y^{-1})	HAI per ha (Ksh y^{-1})	Share of HAI in Total Household Income (%)
High-potential maize	75,921	61,530	22,789	38.28
Central highlands	37,728	46,029	14,384	36.00
Western transitional	15,367	28,995	6,066	44.37
Marginal rain shadow	3,655	23,068	6,610	37.31
Northern arid	4,851	21,013	6,162	51.22
Eastern lowlands	10,234	20,000	3,766	21.74
Western highlands	8,423	16,989	6,715	28.85
Coastal lowlands	3,173	13,470	3,318	6.22
Western lowlands	6,778	11,182	3,994	18.26
National averages	18,459	26,920	8,200	31.36

Source: Argwings-Kodhek (1998).

Annual incomes from agriculture of three or four thousand shillings, as in the lowland areas, would condemn families to starvation unless supplemented from other sources of income or subsistence. However, the relationship between the share of household income from agriculture and total household income is not clear (table 3.4). Whereas low income from agriculture in the coastal lowlands is supplemented by large off-farm inflows that render total incomes in this zone higher than they are in any other, comparable levels of agricultural income in the eastern and western lowlands make up about one-fifth of total household earnings. Yet in the western transitional, marginal rain shadow, and northern arid zones, where agricultural incomes are double those at the coast, shares of agricultural incomes in total household income are as high as 50 percent, on the average well above comparable shares in the zones where agricultural incomes are highest. Farmer choices with regard to production technology and market orientation underpin these differences.

Market Development and Farmer Incentives for Specialization and Intensification

Tomich, Kilby, and Johnston (1995) argue that the mechanism of economic progress in agriculture is the same one that operates in every other segment of the economy, namely specialization. More specialized agricultural production typically reflects more intensive use of inputs (Timmer, Falcon, and Pearson 1983). Considerable empirical evidence now exists that farmers' decisions to apply more and better inputs into their production activities are influenced importantly by the economic returns to such intensification (Binswanger et al. 1978; Capalbo and Antle 1988; Singh, Squire, and Strauss 1986). Ceteris paribus, the better developed agricultural input and output markets are, the greater the access is to trading points, the smaller farm-to-market transaction costs are, the lower farm-gate input prices are, and the higher corresponding output prices are. The cheaper improved inputs are, and the more valuable the commodities are into whose production they are being employed, then the more likely farmers are to adopt input-intensive practices.

In Kenya, the density and quality of rural roads are particularly important as influences on farm-to-market transaction costs and have been linked to differences in smallholder cropping patterns and farm income (Omamo 1998). Poor rural infrastructure raises farm-to-market transaction costs and lowers farm income by increasing the costs of using markets to acquire and dispose of goods and services. A recent study of fertilizer marketing in Kenya, Ethiopia, and Zambia found that domestic marketing costs accounted for 50 percent or more of farm-gate prices of fertilizer (Jayne et al. 2003). The lower farm incomes are, the lower the demand for and use of improved inputs are, the lower associated incomes are, and so on in a self-reinforcing downward spiral

The average road density in Kenya is just above 11 km per 100 km[2] (MTC 1998).[1] The comparable figure for India is 90 km per 100 km[2] (Heisey and Mwangi 1996). The key point, however, is that the pattern of road density mirrors that of agro-ecological potential (table 3.5). It is highest in districts with relatively high rainfall and agro-

Figure 3.2 **Commercialization of Crop Production in Kenya**

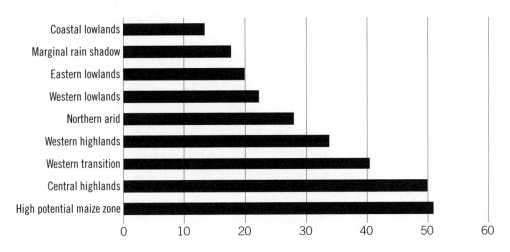

Source: Argwings-Kodhek (1998).

Table 3.5 **Road Lengths and Densities in Selected Districts in Kenya**

District	Relevant ecological zones	Road length (km)	Road density (km 100 km^{-2})
Kwale	B3	1,546	18.7
Kitui	B3, B4	1,967	6.7
Machakos	B3, B4	1,579	11.1
Kiambu	U1	2,296	93.8
Muranga	U1	1,520	61.4
Uasin Gishu	U1	1,243	32.8

Source: MTC (1998).

ecological potential (e.g., Muranga and Kiambu) and lowest in those with low rainfall and potential (e.g., Kitui and Machakos). These differences across zones interact with underlying agro-ecological potential to imply sharp distinctions in production practices, most notably in the degree of commercialization, which, according to Tomich, Kilby, and Johnston (1995), should be positively related with agricultural income.

Taking the ratio of sales to production of major crops as a measure of degree of commercialization, figure 3.2 reveals that Tomich, Kilby, and Johnston's (1995) logic is broadly supported by the data. Commercialization clearly increases as agro-ecological potential increases. The level and intensity of use of improved inputs follows a similar pattern across regions (table 3.6). Not only does the geographical pattern of fertilizer adoption rates generally mirror that of aggregate and household value added

53

Table 3.6   Fertilizer Use by Smallholders in Kenya

Zone	Fertilizer adoption (%)	Nutrient use intensity (kg ha^{-1})
High-potential maize zone	85.9	14.80
Central highlands	99.3	20.83
Western transitional	57.6	9.46
Marginal rain shadow	20.3	9.14
Northern arid	18.5	3.03
Eastern lowlands	33.7	3.25
Western highlands	82.7	7.89
Coastal lowlands	3.8	9.42
Western lowlands	5.3	4.42
National	61.1	14.04

Source: Argwings-Kodhek (1998).

Figure 3.3   Share of Maize Crop Produced Using Improved Seed

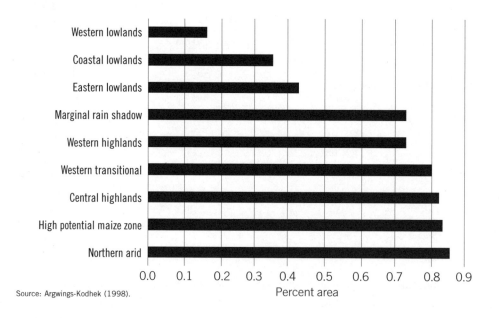

Source: Argwings-Kodhek (1998).

in agriculture, but also, to a large extent, so does the spatial configuration of nutrient use intensity. Indeed, the extremely high adoption rates in the central and western highlands and in the high-potential maize zones alongside low rates in the lowland zones further reinforce the picture of a dichotomous rural economy.[2] The relatively high nutrient use intensity in the coastal lowlands alongside extremely low levels of fertilizer adoption rates is deceptive. A few sampled farmers applied relatively high doses of fertilizer to very small parcels of land (Argwings-Kodhek 1998).

54

Maize is grown throughout Kenya, but relatively high incidence of use of improved maize seed around the country (figure 3.3) alongside generally low nutrient use intensity (table 3.6) suggests that whereas many farmers purchase improved seed, they are unable to apply sufficient fertilizer to realize the full genetic potential of these inputs. Even the highest rates of fertilizer use imply nutrient applications well below recommended rates for most chemical fertilizers. It is not mere coincidence that in the lowland areas where the degree of commercialization is low (figure 3.2), so, too, are fertilizer adoption rates, nutrient use intensity, and use of improved seed.

Farmers' output mixes and production methods both expose and condition the intensity and commercialization of their technical choices. Farmers in higher-potential zones thus tend to devote fewer resources to staples and more to cash crops than do those elsewhere in the country (table 3.7). The former group also intercrops less of its cash crops with staples than does the latter, and instead produces more in pure stands.

Clearly, agro-ecological potential influences the range of commodities from which farmers can select. More cash crops are suited to conditions in the higher-potential areas than they are to conditions in lower-potential areas (table 3.3). In addition, because rural road networks are more extensive and of higher quality in high- than in low-potential areas (table 3.5), purchased inputs and household consumption items are relatively less costly to acquire, and farm produce more valuable in the former zones. Together, these factors raise returns to specialization, intensification, and thus commercialization in the high-potential areas while having the opposite effects in the low-potential areas.

Table 3.7   Household Output Mixes and Production Methods

Zone	Household Income from Agriculture (Ksh y^{-1})	Staples	Cash crops	Intercropped Cash Crops	Pure Stand Cash Crops
High-potential maize	61,530	59	41	36	64
Central highlands	46,029	58	42	54	46
Western transitional	28,995	49	51	32	68
Marginal rain shadow	23,068	78	22	68	32
Northern arid	21,013	82	18	25	75
Eastern lowlands	20,000	91	9	78	22
Western highlands	16,989	73	27	54	46
Coastal lowlands	13,470	74	26	77	23
Western lowlands	11,182	79	21	59	41

Share (%) of Farmland Under[a]

Source: Argwings-Kodhek (1998).
a. Staple = a commodity with a relatively large share in household expenditures (e.g., maize, sorghum, or potatoes); cash crop = a commodity with a relatively small share in household expenditures (e.g., coffee, tea, or cotton).

Implications for Agricultural Research Policy and Management

The analysis in this chapter indicates that while Kenyan agriculture is indeed diverse in terms of agro-ecological potential, with respect to population trends, and with regard to market infrastructure and farmer access to regional trading points, it is largely dichotomous. There is a split between relatively productive, well-off, commercialized farmers with good market access residing in high-rainfall areas, on the one hand, and relatively unproductive, poor, subsistence-oriented farmers with poor market access situated in low-rainfall areas, on the other hand. This split raises important challenges for the design and management of research in the Kenyan agricultural research system.

Toward which of these segments of the farming sector should the bulk of research resources be directed? (Byerlee and Morris 1993). Will national production and income growth potential be better achieved by seeking to raise yields in the lower-potential areas via research interventions aimed at releasing technological and institutional constraints in these areas? Or will potential be better achieved by perhaps less uncertain, simpler measures suited to the higher-potential zones? The distribution of benefits to agricultural research in Kenya often closely matches that of value added in agriculture (Mills 1997; Mills and Karanja 1997). Thus, because the largest efficiency gains from research are likely to accrue from investment in high-rainfall areas, and because these areas evidence the highest levels of resource stress, perhaps research resources should be concentrated in these zones? Equity considerations complicate the decision, however. A large and increasing proportion of Kenya's rural population resides not in these high-potential areas but in the lower-potential zones. Here, however, yield gains are likely to translate into smaller aggregate and per capita economic returns, where stresses on natural resources are relatively less severe. Such concerns for equity in the allocation of research resources can easily overwhelm resource availability, to the detriment of the overall economic impact of research investments. Yet efficiency-based estimates of the research impacts can provide crucial information on the opportunity costs of resource allocations motivated by equity concerns, and thus should be formally incorporated into research planning (Mills 1997).

Additional challenges for research policy and management are raised upon recognition that, once identified, research priorities must be institutionalized. Put differently, management structures and processes must reflect established priorities. This is a major challenge in the Kenyan context. For example, structures and processes appropriate for demand-led research conducted in the multicommodity, adaptive, participatory mode, increasingly viewed as most effective for smallholder agricultural development in Kenya, are likely to be different from those suited to guiding research of a strategic, applied nature, which is typically focused on single commodities.

The analysis in this chapter suggests that the choice of institutional structure is crucial, but unlikely to be clear-cut. For instance, maize, Kenya's staple food, is produced throughout the country in several agro-ecological zones and under diverse socioeconomic conditions (table 3.3). Maize research programs and projects thus must

56

be attentive to both "national" and site-specific constraints on productivity growth. Clearly, both strategic applied and problem-solving, adaptive modes of research are appropriate. Cash crops like tea, coffee, and pyrethrum are crucial generators of rural income, but only in certain parts of the country where very often they are produced using relatively specialized and intensive production methods. On the surface, it might appear that a sharper focus on commodity-based strategic research interventions may be warranted. Yet when, as typically is the case, staples and cash crops appear together in production systems, outputs can be complementary to both broad, commodity-based research and region-specific, farming system research. The challenge facing individual organizations within Kenyan agricultural research and the system as a whole is to design institutional arrangements that permit an efficient and equitable balance of research resources across agro-ecological regions, farmer types, and commodities, while addressing key adaptive and strategic research issues (Karanja, Renkow, and Crawford 2003).

NOTES

1. The comparable figure for India is 90 km per 100 km^2 (Heisey and Mwangi 1996).
2. The relatively high nutrient use intensity in the coastal lowlands alongside extremely low levels of fertilizer adoption rates is deceptive. A few sampled farmers applied relatively high doses of fertilizer to very small parcels of land (Argwings-Kodhek 1998).

REFERENCES

Argwings-Kodhek, Gem. 1998. Monitoring for improved agricultural sector policy making. Nairobi: Tegemeo Institute for Agricultural Policy and Development.

Binswanger, Hans P., Vernon W. Ruttan, U. Ben-Zion, and others. 1978. *Induced innovation: Technology, institutions, and development.* Baltimore: Johns Hopkins University Press.

Boserup, Ester. 1981. *Population and technological change.* Chicago: University of Chicago Press.

Byerlee, Derek, and Michael Morris. 1993. Research for marginal environments: Are we underinvesting? *Food Policy* 18 (5): 381–93.

Capalbo, Susan M., and John M. Antle, eds. 1988. *Agricultural productivity: Measurement and explanation.* Washington: Resources for the Future, distributed by Johns Hopkins University Press.

Food and Agriculture Organization of the United Nations (FAO). 1999. *Statistics database of the United Nations FAO.* Internet Web site, *http://www.fao.org.*

Hayami, Yujiro, and Vernon W. Ruttan. 1985. *Agricultural development: An international perspective.* Revised edition. Baltimore: Johns Hopkins University Press.

Heisey, Paul W., and Wilfred Mwangi. 1996. Fertilizer use and maize production in sub-Saharan Africa. International Maize and Wheat Improvement Center (CIMMYT) Economics Working Paper 96–01. Mexico: CIMMYT.

Heyer, Judith, J. Maitha, and W. Senga, eds. 1976. *Agricultural development in Kenya: An economic assessment.* Nairobi: Oxford University Press.

Jaetzold, Ralph, and Helmut Schmidt. 1984. *Farm management handbook of Kenya.* Volume 3A, West Kenya (Nyanza and Western Provinces). Nairobi: Ministry of Agriculture.

Karanja, Daniel, M. Renkow, and E. W. Crawford. 2003. Welfare effects of maize technologies in marginal and high potential areas. *Agricultural Economics* 29:331–41.

Jayne, T. S., M. Govereh, M. Wanzala, and M. Demeke. 2003. Fertilizer market development: A comparative analysis of Ethiopia, Kenya, and Zambia. *Food Policy* 28:293–316.

Lynam, John. 1978. *An analysis of population, technical change, and risk in peasant semi-arid farming systems: A case study of Machakos District, Kenya.* Ph.D. diss., Stanford University.

Mills, Bradford F. 1997. Ex ante agricultural research evaluation with site-specific technology generation: The case of sorghum in Kenya. *Agricultural Economics* 16:125–38.

Mills, Bradford F., and Daniel D. Karanja. 1997. Processes and methods for research program priority setting: The experience of the Kenya Agricultural Research Institute Wheat Program. *Food Policy* 22:63–79.

Ministry of Transport and Communication (MTC). 1998. *Official unpublished data on road length and density in Kenya.* Nairobi: MTC of the Government of Kenya.

Omamo, Steven W. 1998. Transport costs and smallholder cropping choices: An application to Siaya District, Kenya. *American Journal of Agricultural Economics* 80:116–23.

Pearson, Scott, Eric A. Monke, Gem Argwings-Kodhek, Francisco Avillez, Mulinge Mukumbu, Stefano Pagiola, D. Sellen, and A. Winter-Nelson. 1995. *Agricultural policy in Kenya: An application of the policy analysis matrix.* Ithaca, N.Y.: Cornell University.

Singh, Inderjit, Lyn Squire, and John Strauss. 1986. *Agricultural household models: Empirical findings and policy implications.* Baltimore: Johns Hopkins University Press.

Timmer, C. Peter, Walter P. Falcon, and Scott R. Pearson. 1983. *Food policy analysis.* Baltimore: Johns Hopkins University Press.

Tomich, Thomas, Peter Kilby, and Bruce Johnston. 1995. *Transforming agrarian economies: Opportunities seized, opportunities missed.* Ithaca, N.Y.: Cornell University Press.

4

The Kenyan Farmer: Characterizing the Client

STEPHEN M. NANDWA

The African Farmer through the Lens of Agricultural Research

Introduction

Agricultural research institutes in sub-Saharan Africa (SSA) as major constituents of national agricultural research systems (NARS) are responsible for conducting research on agro-ecologies, systems, and commodities, and for helping meet the needs of farmers and farming communities. This entails helping clients or communities to increase productivity. Largely, this function is implemented through public- and private-sector funding. The funding agencies of today, more so than in the past, expect agricultural research to help resolve agricultural production problems and create opportunities for both farmers and clients. As a concept, farmer characterization by the researcher is a process of grouping heterogeneous and spatially distributed farming systems and communities into homogenous units. In this premise, farmers' needs are generally recognized as inherently related to their attributes. This implies that the researcher must at the onset have a clear perception of the farmers' attributes and their potential influence on the adoption of the formulated technologies. Apparently, this does not seem to be true with some NARS in SSA. This is evident from a recent review of the significance of agricultural research in eastern and southern Africa (Braun et al. 1997) showing that the long-term impact of such agricultural research has not been commensurate with investment (AHI 1997). Hypotheses have been proposed to try and explain this anomaly; one such hypothesis is that of client characterization. In this chapter, we examine the rationale for adopting the concept, process, and methods used in farmer characterization.

Rationale for Characterizing Farmers

In the review linking investment in agricultural research to return (AHI 1997), the authors attempted to explain the causes of low return to investment. Five reasons cited for this are:

1. Lack of adequate alternative technologies for the farmers' various microenviron-mental and socioeconomic circumstances. This is because most studies tend to be reductionist and hence address only one or a few components of a larger problem, such that resulting research outputs are of limited validity for the generally complex and dynamic farming systems and their exogenous environment.
2. The researcher lacks the participatory approach for involving the African farmer (the client).
3. The farmer is unable to adopt full recommendations because of inability to absorb initial investment cost, and because supplies of inputs are often unreliable.
4. Solutions based on individual technologies have not been sufficient to prevent land degradation.
5. Impact assessment of ex-ante and ex-post technology so as to fit lessons learned in the research cycle is lacking.

All these reasons to some extent imply the lack of identification and characterization of the researchers' clients and their circumstances. The review concludes that the challenge of generating technologies appropriate for the diverse farming system in SSA, regardless of the spatial scale (e.g., continental, national, district, and farm levels), requires major changes in research approaches, including wide adoption of the concept of farmer characterization. The two most important merits and justification of the farmer characterization approach are:

1. Better targeting of technology development, especially with the participatory technology development (PTD) approach, and
2. Focused farmer participation in the research process or cycle.

The approach enables the researcher to identify likely nonadopters (laggards), potential adopters, and innovators among the farming system targeted, so as to concentrate on the last two for significant impacts from the research planned.

Opportunities and Constraints in Characterizing Farmers

Despite recognition of the importance of client stratification, and the valuable information "farmer outliers" may provide, this concept is largely still treated with marginal significance in many NARS in SSA. An intriguing issue faced in characterizing Kenyan farmers and farming communities is their extreme diversity and dynamism (see chapter 3). This has been attributed primarily to the country's heterogeneous and complex agro-ecological conditions, which are responsible for widely varied agricultural production practices. Second, high population and diverse exogenous and endogenous markets and demand for agricultural products also influence this diversity. Third, farmers' socioeconomic circumstances vary widely. The Kenya Agricultural Research Institute (KARI) has faced up to this challenge of diversity through its comprehensive network of twenty-four research centers across many agro-ecologies. This can and often does lead to considerable transaction costs, thereby jeopardizing the financial

Table 4.1 Agro-Ecozoning of Sub-Saharan African Environments as Influenced by Altitude and Latitude, with Particular Reference to Kenya's Farming Systems

Main Zones/Belts of Zones	AGRO-ECOZONE			
	Subhumid	Semi-humid	Transitional	Semi-arid
TA - tropical alpine, annual mean 2–10°C	Sheep	Sheep	Sheep	Sheep
UH - upper highland, annual mean 10–15°C	Pyrethrum-wheat	Wheat-barley	UH ranching	UH nomadism
LH - lower highland, annual mean 18–11°C, normally no frost	Wheat-maize-pyrethrum	Wheat-maize-barley	Cattle-sheep-barley	LH ranching
UM - upper midland, annual mean 18–21°C, mean min 11–14°C	Main coffee	Marginal coffee	Sunflower-maize	Livestock-sorghum/ranching/nomadism
LM - lower midland, annual mean 21–24°C, mean min >14°C	Marginal sugar	LM cotton	Marginal cotton	Livestock-millet/ranching/ nomadism
L - lowland - inner lowland, annual mean > 24°C, mean max. > 31°C	L sugar	L cotton	Groundnut	Livestock-millet/ranching/nomadism
CL - coastal lowlands, annual mean 24°C, mean max < 31°C	L sugar	Coconut-cassava	Cashew nut-cassava	Livestock-millet

sustainability of the NARS. This is perhaps a good reason why NARS research networks must be rationalized into multidisciplinary or multicommodity and factor-based research programs to address the key clients' needs. This underscores the importance of and hence the opportunity for client characterization in KARI research programs, in the context of diverse farming systems.

In Kenya, farming or production systems or zones have been identified as the basic units of characterization through analysis of farming communities at the national scale, primarily on the basis of altitude and latitude (table 4.1) (Jaetzold and Schmidt 1984). The authors delineated twenty-eight farming systems. In addition, two recent farmer characterization schemes have been developed for setting priorities for soil fertility and plant nutrition research (Kilambya, Nandwa, and Omamo 1998) and for maize technology transfer research (Hassan, Onyango, and Rutto 1998).

In the priority setting of KARI's Soil Fertility and Plant Nutrition Research Program (SFPNRP), three criteria or determinants (annual precipitation, elevation, and population density) were used to stratify the country into five major target zones (table 4.2). Table 4.3 shows soil fertility-related constraints in each zone. The process involved eight steps: sensitization of research scientists, review of mandate area, zoning of mandate area, identifying and analyzing constraints and opportunities, specifying research themes, quantifying potential for technology generation and adoption, computing research benefits, ranking of research alternatives, and a stakeholder workshop for consensus building. Further stratification resulted in varied numbers of major production systems commonly found in the zones (table 4.4). In stratifying maize research, ten target zones were identified (table 4.5). Table 4.6 shows the diverse

Table 4.2 Research Target Zones of the National Soil Fertility and Plant Nutrition Research Program under the Kenya Agricultural Research Institute

Zone[a]		Agricultural Potential	Elevation (m)	Rainfall (mm y^{-1})	Population Density (people per km^2)	Districts[b]
I		Medium	<400	>900	>20	Kwale, Kilifi, Lamu
II	ASAL, low population density	Low	400–900	200–900	20–80	Kitui, Machakos, Laikipia, Nakuru, West Pokot
III	ASAL, high population density	Low/medium	400–1,200	>900	>80	Machakos, Meru, Kitui, Nakuru, Kiambu, Embu
IV	Medium rainfall, high population density	Medium/high	400–1,800	>900	>80	S. Nyanza, Siaya, Kakamega, Kisumu, Busia, Bungoma, Trans Nzoia, Muranga, Nyeri, Kirinyaga, Meru
V	High rainfall, low and high population density	High	1,800–3,000	>900	>20	Kericho, Nakuru, Uasin Gishu, Nyandarua

a. ASAL = arid and semi-arid lands. b. District names and boundaries as known and defined in 1992.

Table 4.3 Major Soil Fertility Problems Encountered under each Research Theme Ranked Across the Target Zones of the National Soil Fertility and Plant Nutrition Research Program

Research Themes	Zone I	Zone II	Zone III	Zone IV	Zone V
Problem soils:					
Salinity/sodicity	xxx	xxx	—	—	—
Low pH	—	—	—	xxx	xxx
Physical factors	xxx leaching (L)	xxx crusting	xxx hard setting	xxx L	xxx L hard pans
Al/Mn toxicity	—	—	—	xxx	xxx
P-fixation	—	—	—	xxx	xxx
High pH	xxx	xxx	xxx	—	—
Management of mineral fertilizer	xxx L	xxx low soil water	xxx low soil water nutrient mining	xxx L, acidity, erosion P-absorption, nutrient mining	xxx erosion, nutrient imbalance
Management of organic matter	xxx	xxx -------(low-quantity and low-quality organics)-------	xxx	xxx	xxx (surplus quantity organics burnt)
Technology transfer		-------------Socioeconomic constraints-------------			

Note: xxx = major; — = not applicable

Table 4.4   Principal Production Systems in Kenya

Production Systems (PS) (Farming System)	PS Share in Target Zone (%)	Commodities
Zone I: Coastal parts		
PS-1 Coconut based	35	Coconut (40), mango (30), citrus (10), cashews (10), cassava (5), groundnuts (5, bixa [1])
PS-2 Maize based	20	Maize/beans (40), cassava (30), mango (15), livestock (10), cowpea (5)
PS-3 Citrus based	15	Citrus (40), maize/beans (30), livestock (10), sesame (10), cowpeas (10)
PS-4 Cotton based	8	Cotton (25), maize (25), beans (15), cassava (15), groundnut (10), cowpea (5), livestock (5)
PS-5 Pure rice	6	Rice (100)
PS-6 Pure sisal	5	Sisal (100)
PS-7 Livestock based	7	Livestock (90), millet (10)
PS-8 Pure bixa	2	Bixa (100)
PS-9 Pure citrus	2	Citrus (100)
Zone II (typical arid and semi-arid lands): low population density		
PS-1 Maize based	50	Maize (40), beans (30), pigeon peas (20), livestock (10)
PS-2 Maize based	20	Maize (35), pigeon peas (35), livestock (15), cowpea (5), sorghum (5), millet (5)
PS-3 Pure livestock	15	Livestock (100)
PS-4 Maize based	5	Maize (90), livestock (10)
Zone III (arid and semi-arid lands and hilly masses): high population density		
PS-1 Coffee based	40	Coffee (40), maize (30), beans (15), horticulture (10), livestock (5)
PS-2 Maize based	35	Maize (40), beans (30), horticulture (20), livestock (10)
PS-3 Horticulture based	25	Horticulture (60), maize/beans (20), livestock (20)
Zone IV (western Kenya and central Kenya highlands): medium rainfall-high population density		
PS-1 Maize based	30	Maize (45), beans (15), tea (10), bananas (8), dairy (7), horticulture (5), cassava (5), millet (5)
PS-2 Coffee based	20	Coffee (50), maize (20), dairy (15), beans (8), bananas (5), potato (2)
PS-3 Tea based	15	Tea (60), Irish potato (15), dairy (10), horticulture (10), maize (5)
PS-4 Sugarcane based	10	Sugarcane (45), maize (30), dairy (8), beans (8), bananas (4), groundnut (3), soybean (2)
PS-5 Sorghum based	8	Sorghum (23), cassava (20), maize (15), livestock (11), millet (8), beans (8), sweet potato (5), groundnut (4), sunflower (4), horticulture (2), tobacco[a]
PS-6 Horticulture based	7	Horticulture (50), dairy (20), Irish potato (20), flowers (10)
PS-7 Dairy based	7	Dairy (80), horticulture (20)
PS-8 Coffee based	2	Coffee (90), flowers (10)
PS-9 Pure sugarcane	1	Sugarcane (100)
Zone V (former White Highlands in the Rift Valley): high rainfall-low and high population density		
PS-1 Maize based	30	Maize (50), dairy (35), maize/beans (10), potatoes (5)
PS-2 Wheat based	30	Wheat (50), barley (20), dairy (20), maize (5), horticulture (5), oats[a]
PS-3 Tea based	10	Tea (50), maize (20), dairy (20), pyrethrum (5), horticulture (5)
PS-4 Dairy based	8	Dairy (60), maize (30), maize/beans (8), horticulture (2)
PS-5 Potato based	5	Potatoes (50), horticulture (20), dairy (18), pyrethrum (8), sheep (4)
PS-6 Pure tea	5	Tea (100)
PS-7 Pure wheat	2	Wheat (100)

Note: Production system in zone VI (arid lands, mainly occupied by pastoralists) is not included because it does not lie in the mandate area of the National Soil Fertility and Plant Nutrition Research Program, but is in that of the National Arid Land Research Centers, Marsabit and Kiboko.
a. Crop recognized, but estimates not available.

Table 4.5   Maize Research Target Zones in Kenya

Zone	Elevation (m)	Total Precipitation Mar–Aug (mm)	Average Temperature (°C), Mar–Aug			Maize Area, 1990[a] (1000 ha)	% of Total Maize Area	% of Farmers in Sample
			Min	Max	Mean			
Lowland tropics	—	—	—	—	—	**33**	**3.2**	**7.1**
Dry	**>700**	**300–500**	**20.0**	**30.0**	25.4	12	1.2	2.8
Moist mid-altitude	**<400**	**>550**	**20.0**	**31.0**	25.8	21	2.0	4.3
Mid-altitude	—	—	—	—	—	**197**	**19.0**	**20.2**
Dry	**700–1,400**	**300–550**	**14.0**	**33.0**	22.0	79	7.7	7.2
Moist	**1,110–1,500**	**>550**	**13.0**	**30.0**	22.1	118	11.3	13.0
Transitional	—	—	—	—	—	**461**	**44.5**	**35.0**
Dry	**1,100–1,700**	**<550**	**11.0**	**27.0**	19.7	37	3.6	5.7
Moist	**1,200–2,000**	**>550**	**11.0**	**29.0**	19.7	424	40.9	29.3
Highland tropics	—	—	—	—	—	**307**	**29.6**	**32.0**
Dry	1,600–2,300	**<550**	**8.0**	**26.0**	16.6	33	3.1	6.0
Moist	1,600–2,700	**>550**	**7.0**	**27.0**	16.7	238	23.0	21.6
Cool	2,000–2,900	**<1,000**	**5.0**	**22.0**	13.8	36	3.5	4.4
Extreme H$_2$O stress	**400–1,100**	**<400**	**16.0**	**32.0**	23.8	**39**	**3.7**	**5.7**
TOTAL[b]	—	—	—	—	—	**1,037**	**100.0**	**100.0**

Note: Entries (figures) in boldface type represent criteria applied, whereas those not in bold represent average value of respective attributes in the zones.
a. From Otichillo and Sinange (1991). b. Totals of criteria applied.

Table 4.6   Maize Production Problems Ranked (Figure in Parentheses) for Each Research Zone (Numbers Not in Parentheses Indicate Gross Efficiency Index [G$_1$ = P$_1$ × G$_1$])

Problem		Zone I (coastal lowlands)	Zones II & III (ASAL[a] and hilly masses)	Zone IV (midaltitude)	Zone IV (transition)	Zone V (highland tropics)
Low soil fertility		—	8.8 (6)	24.1 (3)	7.1 (5)	30.0 (5)
Inadequate and erratically distributed rains		4.7 (2)	25.1 (2)	25.1 (2)	14.4 (2)	132.1 (1)
Hail		—	—	—	—	106.9 (2)
Stalk lodging		—	—	—	3.8 (7)	79.2 (3)
Weeds		14.4 (1)	39.1 (1)	24.1 (3)	9.6 (3)	—
Striga		—	—	47.8 (1)	—	—
Pests:	Stalk borer	2.6 (4)	11.1 (5)	19.9 (5)	3.8 (7)	46.1 (4)
	Chafer grubs	1.0 (6)	13.2 (4)	—	7.5 (4)	—
	Other	4.5 (3)	14.0 (3)	18.2 (6)	6.0 (6)	14.0 (7)
Diseases:	Headsmut	—	—	—	16.9 (1)	29.0 (6)
	Streak virus	—	1.7 (7)	16.1 (7)	—	—
	Other	2.4 (5)	—	—	—	—

a. Arid and semi-arid lands.

constraints to increased agricultural productivity for each target zone in the Maize Research Program. This clearly demonstrates the value of client characterization, in that it helps to target the research agenda.

Besides these approaches, the country's geographical and political delineations into provinces and districts can be used as a starting point for the characterization exercise. The smallest operational unit in a district is that of village or watershed, in most cases constituting a land use system (LUS). The LUS may, in turn, be composed of identifiable areas for farming activities, such as fishing, communal grazing, or fuel wood collection areas. The farming component of the LUS often fully or partially consists of three farm subtypes: primary production unit (PPU) or cropping production, secondary production unit (SPU) or livestock keeping, and the household or *manyatta* unit (HHU). In formulating a targeted research agenda for the cropping subtype system, NARS are or should be concerned with interaction between crops, soils, and pests, while in the livestock subsystem the focus is on herds, pastures and feeds, animal health, and manure. In the household subsystem the concern is with household members, food, household use and waste of resources, and decisions made on allocation of labor, capital, land, and on-farm management. Existence of this structure also provides opportunities and a basis for characterizing farmers as research clients. Farm components and farm types constitute the farming system, which is the commonly used unit of agricultural production analysis.

Farming Systems as an Analytical Structure

The term "farming systems" implies all forms of natural resource utilization including crops, agroforestry and woodlots, bee-keeping, fish farming, livestock production, range management, hunting and gathering, and all combinations of these. According to Okigbo (1979), a farming system consists of farms, agricultural enterprises, or business in which sets of inputs of resources are uniquely managed in such a way as to satisfy needs and to achieve desired objectives in a given environmental setting. In SSA, especially in rural areas, farming systems comprise activities of one or more individuals, usually a family unit or community group, where some or all members of the unit participate in part- or full-time farm work. Thus, the farming system functions as a decision-making unit in transforming land, resources, capital, and knowledge into useful products that can be consumed, or sold, or both.

To address these issues requires structural analysis of the farming systems of local communities. Comparative analyses of the farming systems help us understand the adaptation process of the different types of farmers in a given agro-ecosystem. This is of interest to people or institutions that are involved in farming systems research. Farming systems analysis involves defining the spatial-temporal scales of the system and its subsystems, and identifying problems and their potential solutions.

The process is iterative and cyclical and fits into the learning cycle of the farming systems' approach to research, extension, and training (FSA-RET). Analysis of farming systems has to particularly emphasize the main constraints facing different farming communities. Applications of the farming systems approach require participatory

65

analysis of the project sites, and promising interventions under farm conditions, while also pursuing necessary component research outside the system. This is a contribution to systems research and systems development. The approach subordinates the work undertaken on research stations to farming systems research and development undertaken directly in farming areas. The latter should dictate the former, and not the reverse. Focusing on the farming system as an analytical structure, we identify two major issues:

1. The actual research cycle and approaches, and
2. The stratification of the system into subunits at different spatial scales that entails identification of various enterprises and their relationships, from which stem opportunities for technology development.

Farming systems approach to research, extension, and training

In NARS such as KARI, FSAs in agro-ecology, research structures, and programs are organized to meet the needs of the principal farming systems, using interdisciplinary teams.

Integration of gender analysis in FSA-RET

The conundrum of gender is one of the most equivocal and popular, much advocated as a topic in FSA-RET in general, and in the discipline of social sciences generally. It is argued that gender (defined as a sociocultural construct that refers to roles, responsibilities, characteristics, attitudes, and beliefs about men and women) has a significant impact on the rate of adoption of technology. Therefore researchers are being encouraged to include gender analysis in their research projects in an effort to understand how men and women relate to each other in terms of their respective roles and responsibilities, and their access to and control of resources. The purpose of gender analysis is to ensure that research and extension activities incorporate the roles and needs of both women and men and enlist the participation of both as clients. This requires researchers to separate data by both gender and age. In this context, the gender analysis matrix (GAM) is a specific tool commonly used for gender analysis with client or target groups in planning, monitoring, and evaluating research and extension activities in order to analyze the impact of these activities on women, men, boys, and girls. In the planning of a research project, a GAM is made to assess the potential effects of promising solutions both as ex-ante and ex-post impact assessment.

Criteria and approaches for stratifying farming systems

The foregoing review emphasizes that a clear identification of the researcher's clients in terms of definite homogenous groups of farmers is a prerequisite for a high rate of technology adoption. Yet, so far, little attention has been given to the delineation of farmer target groups in the conducting of on-farm research (Tripp 1991). Recent examination of recommendations based on farming systems show that they are often too broad or too uniform to result in high returns to research investment. To overcome this, attempts are now being made to stratify the farming system into farm typologies, sometimes called "recommendation domains," each of which essentially consists of a group of farmers homogenous within the cluster, but heterogeneous between clusters (Hair et al. 1992). Approaches, tools, and models are currently being developed and applied in agro-ecosystems for this purpose. One general approach entails the grouping of easy-to-determine factors such as LUS or cropping system, followed by sub-grouping using a mix of factor analysis and self-grouping. A second option entails self-grouping by farmers within an LUS into wealth groups. A third approach has to do with farm comparison studies within "homogenous groups." The latter approach entails the comparison of many agronomic, management, social, and economic factors, and the use of discriminant or factor analysis to define subgroups according to major distinguishing factors. The first and second approaches have been widely used in Kenya in nutrient monitoring (NUTMON) projects. In projects monitoring nutrient flows and other resources in Kakamega, Kisii, Embu, and Kilifi (de Jager, Nandwa, and Okoth 1998) and Machakos, Makueni, Kitui, and Mwingi Districts (KARI 1996a, 1996b), farm typologies have been derived from LUS. They were arrived at mainly by using land use maps and satellite images, in consultation with experts, and combined with participatory rural appraisals (PRAs), rapid rural appraisal (RRAs).

Moving Beyond Analysis to Participation

The primary objective of participatory research is to obtain knowledge of the social structure from the perspective of the different wealth classes and to explore the needs of, problems of, and opportunities available to the intended beneficiaries or clients. The second objective is to work out methods and approaches to resolve the problems that have been identified jointly by the development agency and the local project participants. This process allows a higher degree of understanding of project objectives and commitment to project activities on the part of the intended beneficiaries. The degree of farmer participation in research primarily depends on the type of research conducted. Examples of participatory research are contract (researcher designed and researcher managed on farmers' fields), consultative or collaborative (researcher designed and farmer managed), collegial (researcher and farmer designed and managed), and farmer experimentation (farmer designed and managed). Research tools and approaches have been developed to facilitate the varied degrees of farmer involvement and participation in each type of agricultural research.

Tools commonly applied in participatory research include the Participatory Learning Action Research (PLAR) approach, also called the Participatory Agro-ecosystem Management (PAM) approach, and RRA and PRA, which are actively applied in the planning and implementation of research and development. It is interesting to speculate on what the relationship will be between the researcher and the farmer in this context. How will indigenous knowledge and modern scientific knowledge mesh in these approaches? These are questions that the agricultural researcher will have to answer to ensure successful adoption of the "farmer-led research" or client-oriented research approaches.

At present, participatory research has been developed or is being developed in NARS to strengthen resource-poor farmers' participation in research. However, the question being asked by financial backers of the research is to what extent farmer participation in research has been achieved. Tripp, Anandajayasekeram, and Saín (1990) have shown that on-farm research has succeeded in increasing scientists' understanding of and interest in the priorities and needs of farmers, particularly resource-poor farmers. In all cases, however, researchers found that organizing and sustaining farmer participation beyond the initial diagnosis stage was more demanding than they had anticipated. This suggests that the degree of farmer involvement and participation should be rationalized to suit the type of research that is being conducted.

Of the types of research listed above, Biggs (1989) reported that the dominant mode of research, found in more than half of the twenty-five case study efforts analyzed, was consultative, where farmers play essentially a passive role. In only one-third of the cases had researchers set up mechanisms for more direct, intensive, and continuous farmer participation. Only a handful of examples were found of the collegial type of research. There are a number of reasons for this finding. First, the lack of active farmer participation partly reflects a lack of training among researchers in skills required for productive interaction with clients (Chambers and Jiggins 1986). Second, it also reflects logistical constraints and managers' concerns that intensive farmer participation is expensive, beyond the resources of many national research systems. Third, at the root of much of the problem is researchers' hesitance to expose their work to clients for fear of interference by farmers or of losing control over the research agenda. Fourth, capacity building is needed to address this issue; for example, better linkage between farmers and researchers is required, which implies that multidisciplinary researchers must be trained in the skills necessary for collaborative work.

Further, the farming community and local leadership must be involved in designing and maintaining development efforts. Indeed, participation in the development process is what is required, not just systems analysis or farmers' consultation. Participation requires a positive approach to building farmers' social groups and community-based organizations and networks (bearing in mind equity and power) that can exercise increasing influence on local resource management and development. The first step in implementing farmer participation is identifying or creating and supporting local bodies that are representative of the farmers at the level at which the development initiative will be implemented. The local bodies are required as points of contact in planning the development initiative, and as recipient bodies and partners in the initiative. Within these local bodies, management capability and responsibility can be fostered.

The bodies to be identified or created should be involved from the outset in dialogue and decision making regarding the whole of the development process. A great degree of management responsibility should be vested in the local bodies concerned, and special efforts should be made to provide training in management skills to individuals nominated by the farmers' community. An environment of trust and cooperation needs to be established between local bodies and those fostering the research initiative. However, the diverse forms of participatory research need to be carefully considered with a view to adopting those most suitable for the farming systems targeted. Another question requiring attention is whether the scientists need more knowledge, or whether farmers should be more involved in the planning process and have opportunities to express their needs and constraints,. We shall use case studies of some selected Kenyan farming systems to explore the extent of adoption of participatory research and outcomes, as one agenda toward transforming Kenya's NARS. A classic example of successful client characterization and involvement in participatory research is that of the Western Kenya Soil Fertility Recapitalization and Replenishment Project (Niang et al. 1998; Sanchez et al. 1997).

The Dilemma of Participatory Research: Meeting Farmer Needs When Every Farmer Is Unique

The limitations of studies at higher spatial scales are many, as discussed by Stoorvogel and Smaling (1998) and Scoones and Toulmin (1998). Results at the subnational level, for example, may conceal the wide variation around the mean when individual farms are taken into account. The "positive outliers" may in fact provide valuable information on preconditions and driving forces for sound resource management. For example, in Kisii District in Kenya (SFPNRP target zone IV), with reliable rainfall and deep, relatively fertile soils, more options are available to safeguard soil fertility than in Machakos District (SFPNRP target zone II), with less and erratic rainfall and sandy soils. At household level, however, the farmer can modify the microclimate and soil fertility of individual plots. Individual households can be active and innovative, making use of indigenous knowledge to adjust their farming practices to changing agroecological and economic conditions.

Soil fertility of individual niches and plots in farm and village settings can also differ considerably (Chege 2000; Ojiem, Odendo, and Nandwa 1995; Ojiem and Odendo 1997). Reasons for this variation range from differences in soil texture and land use/ fallow history to microclimatic differences. Smallholder farmers exploit microvariability, because for each weather condition there are some pieces of land where crops perform well (Brouwers 1993). Hence, those who are seeking adequate subsistence levels rather than bumper harvests often regard farm and field heterogeneity as an asset. A striking example of farm-level variation lies in the ring management systems in semi-arid west Africa, where inner circles near the farms and village are much more intensively used and managed (table 4.7). Similarly, in the banana-based cropping systems of eastern Africa, there is higher fertility in fields near homesteads than in those far away. The "homestead fields" represent the plots just around the homestead, receiving substantial amounts of nutrients from animal manure and household wastes. As a consequence, soil productivity in this part of the farm remains at a relatively high level. One way of solving the use of microscale data to extrapolate to macroscale may be through use of appropriate data upscaling tools, such as geographic information systems or modeling.

| Table 4.7 | Nutrient Stocks of Different Subsystems in a Typical Upland Farm in the Sudan-Savanna Zone |

Field location	pH-H₂O	Organic C (g kg⁻¹)	Total N (g kg⁻¹)	Available P (mg kg⁻¹)	Exch. K (mmol kg⁻¹)
Homestead	6.7–8.3	11–21	0.9–1.8	20-20	4–24
Village	5.7–7.0	5–10	0.5–0.9	13–16	4–11
Bush	5.7–6.2	2–5	0.2–0.5	5–16	0.6–1

Source: Sedong 1993.

Case Studies of Kenyan Farming Systems

Dairy-Based System in Embu District

Introduction

Embu District lies in SFPNRP target zone IV, in the Central Kenya Highlands. Dairy production is the second-most important subsector (next to beef) in the livestock sector of Kenya and also in Embu District. Main livestock types in Embu District include cattle, shoats (sheep and goats), poultry, pigs, and rabbits. In 1993, of a population of nearly 140,000 cattle, over 37 percent were dairy cattle (MoALDM 1993). A rapid growth in the dairy industry in the district is partly attributed to the National Dairy Development Project (NDDP) established in 1980. This project aimed to develop appropriate technologies for smallholders, based on KARI's adaptive research component of NDDP, and to extend the technologies for smallholders as an extension component of the NDDP.

Spatial stratification, and analysis and results of dairy-based systems

In defining land use systems at the national level, nine production systems were identified in SFPNRP zone IV (table 4.4) where Embu District is located (Kilambya, Nandwa, and Omamo 1998). One of the production systems is a dairy-based system in which 80 percent of the farm is given to pasture and the remaining 20 percent is allocated to horticulture. Yet such a system is rare in Embu District. In characterizing the LUS by the NUTMON project, dairy cattle were identified mainly in LUS I and II, and only a few in LUS III (table 4.8). Thus, relatively few farmers practice zero grazing. Further stratification of each LUS by researchers resulted in three types of dairy-based farm types, each with distinct livestock breed types and management systems. For instance, while the Friesians are common in the tea/dairy LUS, the Ayrshires and Guernseys are dominant in the coffee/dairy LUS, and crossbreed cattle are mostly found in the coffee/maize LUS.

Farmers carried out their own participatory stratification into various wealth categories with the guidance of the researchers and extension staff. A methodology of sort cards (PLAR or PAM) was the main tool used for this exercise. Apparently the criteria that the farmers used culminated in the delineation of farmers and farm types in terms of resource endowments or wealth groups. These criteria encompassed biophysical

70

Table 4.8	Characterization of Embu District, Kenya into Major Land Use Systems and Farm Typologies

Characteristics	LAND USE SYSTEM		
	Tea/dairy	Tea/coffee/dairy	Coffee/maize
Altitude (m)	1,770–2,070	1,590–1,830	1280–1830
Mean temperature (°C)	15.8–17.7	17.5–18.9	18.9–20.7
Annual rainfall (mm)	1,750–2,000	1,400–1,800	1280–1830
Main soil types	Andosols	Nitisols, Andosols	Nitisols, Cambisols, Ferralsols
Crops	Tea (50% farm area), maize/bean, napier (25%), passion fruit, Irish potatoes, cabbages	Coffee, tea, napier, maize/bean, bananas	Coffee, maize/bean, napier, bananas
Livestock	Dairy cattle (Friesians), hair sheep, pigs, rabbits, chickens	Dairy cattle (Ayrshires/Guernseys), hair sheep, sheep, rabbits, chickens	Dairy cattle (cross-bred), meat goats, pigs, rabbits, chickens
Farm typologies:	1. Farmers raise grade dairy cattle in conventional zero-grazing unit.	Farmers zero-graze grade dairy cows within own farmland with a high level of fertilizer and manure on farm.	70% of the farmer's land under coffee and 30% under maize and other food crops. Farmers have conventional zero-grazing unit containing grade cattle.
	2. Farmers graze grade cows on natural pastures and feed napier in the night boma.	Farmers free graze crossbred dairy cows with medium level of fertilizer and manure input on farm.	50% of the farmer's land under coffee and 50% under maize and other food crops. Farmers practice semi-zero grazing using crossbreed cattle.
	3. Tethering of crossbred cows within homestead compound, roadside pastures, etc.	Farmers free graze crossbred cows within own farmland. Low levels of manure and fertilizer applied on crops.	30% of the farmer's land under coffee and 70% under maize and other food crops. Farmers practice zero grazing by mainly feeding crop by-products and residues to zebu cattle.

characteristics and socioeconomic circumstances. Coincidentally this characterization also resulted in the classification of the tea/dairy, coffee/dairy, and coffee/maize LUS into three farm types each, as shown in the wealth group indicators (box 4.1). Assuming the participating farmers to be a random sample, the categorization suggested the proportions shown in table 4.9.

The proportions of farmers in each wealth categorgy within each land use system are similar, but the level of production intensity and market orientation vary (table 4.9). High-wealth groups are more intensive in terms of production for all the enterprises, whereas the low-wealth group is mostly low in intensity of production, with the medium-wealth group being average in the level of production intensity for both crops and livestock. In all the land use systems there is a high level of use of inputs such as fertilizers and animal feeds, and a high level of credit availability among the high-wealth group, with levels of input use and credit availability decreasing through

Box 4.1	Wealth Group Indicators as Defined by Farmers	

High-Wealth Group	Medium-Wealth Group	Low-Wealth Group
3,500 tea stumps and over	1,500–3,500 tea stumps	Less then 1,500 tea stumps
Elaborate or permanent zero-grazing with high level of management	Good zero-grazing unit, but lack some facilities with medium level of management	Have cattle, but not on zero grazing, with low level of management
Permanent house	Semi-permanent house	Mud-made house
Relatively few family members	Big family sizes compared to the former category	Large family size
Ability to educate all children	Difficulties in educating all the children at times	Afford school education for their children up to primary level
Able to produce enough for household consumption with minimum purchases	Occasionally not able to produce enough for the household, and purchase from the market	Frequent food scarcity

The coffee/dairy land use system

High-Wealth Group	Medium-Wealth Group	Low-Wealth Group
At least one member of the family has formal employment.	At least one member of the family may have informal/or self-employment.	No off-farm employment except when supplying labor to the high-wealth group for wages.
Have 500 coffee trees and over	Have 200–500 coffee trees	Have 50–200 coffee trees
Land size of 1 acre and over	Land size of 0.5–1 acre	Land size of 0.5 acres and less
One to two dairy cows, mostly Friesian and Ayrshire	Mostly have one dairy cow of either Guernsey or a good crossbreed	Most do not have cattle and those who do, have a poor crossbreed
Have a conventional zero-grazing unit	Semipermanent zero grazing	No zero grazing—if there is a cow, it is managed through the tethering system
Small family sizes (3–4 children per household)	Bigger family sizes (5–8 children per household)	Large family sizes (most households have more than 8 children)
Well-educated children	Few children go beyond primary level education	Most children do not complete primary education
Take fried food with high beans:maize ratio	Take fried food with low beans:maize ratio	Main meal is maize mixed with bananas without beans.
Purchase new clothes for family often	Good secondhand (mitumba) clothes for family members	Family members use very cheap secondhand clothes.
Often purchase farm inputs from traders	Rely on cooperative societies for farm inputs such as fertilizers	Use very little fertilizer if any (1–2kg) purchased by use of labor wages because they are not credit worthy in the cooperative societies

The marginal coffee/maize land use system

High-Wealth Group	Medium-Wealth Group	Low-Wealth Group
Land size: more than 8 acres	Land size: 5–8 acres	Land size: below 5 acres
500 coffee trees and over	Between 200–500 coffee trees	Fewer than 200 coffee trees
Livestock type: Guernsey	Livestock type: Jersey	Livestock types: crossbreed or goats
Commercial feed for pigs	Commercial and homemade feed for pigs	Napier and banana pseudostems used as feed
Hire labor	Can hire labor at times	Depend on family labor and at times provide labor for wages
Most trained in farmer training centers (FTCs) and demonstration plots	Trained	No training
Formal employment or personal business	Very few have formal employment or personal business	No formal employment or education beyond primary school level
Children educated to and beyond form four level	Children mostly not educated beyond form four level	Children mostly not educated beyond primary school level
Credit readily available	Credit available, but with difficulty at times	Limited or no credit
Produce enough for household consumption and surplus for market	Produce enough for household consumption with occasional surplus for market	Do not produce enough for household consumption; purchase deficits from the market

Table 4.9 Proportion of Farmers in Various Farmer Categories or Wealth Groups Across Land Use Systems (Lus) in Embu District, Kenya

LUS	Proportion (%) of LUS farmers in various categories		
	High-wealth group	Medium-wealth group	Low-wealth group
Tea/dairy	31	32	37
Coffee/dairy/tea	17	44	39
Marginal coffee/maize	26	35	39

the medium- and low-wealth groups. Conventional zero-grazing is also an indication of production intensity. High-wealth groups are highly market oriented, and thus allocate most of their resources to cash-oriented enterprises such as tea, coffee, and .intensified dairy production. On the other hand, low-wealth groups are mainly subsistent producers with limited cash enterprises and high levels of food insecurity.

Implications of farmer characterization for livestock and other researchers under KARI

The stratification and delineation exercise described in the previous section made it possible to produce an inventory of KARI researchers' clients in dairy production in the Embu District. This indicates the innovators, potential adopters, and likely nonadopters (laggards), and gives a spatial representation of the dairy-based production system in the district that livestock researchers can use to organize research. This analysis shows that livestock researchers under KARI confront significant biophysical and socioeconomic diversity even at short geographical distances.

Lessons learned and conclusion

A well-defined characterization of the dairy-based system helped delineate the system into nine distinct farm typologies, contrasting in resource availability and utilization, and in income. Although the wealthy farmers are clear candidates for adopting a conventional zero-grazing technology, the poorest farmers are likely nonadopters. Farmer innovation is more important in dictating technology adoption than are the biophysical attributes of the farming system. Other important factors influencing technology adoption include off-farm income, family size, and access to extension knowledge.

Horticulture in Kiambu and Murang'a Districts

Introduction

Geographically, Kiambu and Murang'a Districts are located in the central province of Kenya, and were recently divided into two districts each—Kiambu and Thika, and Murang'a and Maragua. Both districts are in the Central Kenya Highlands. Kiambu lies between 1,400 and 2,400 m in elevation and receives an annual rainfall varying between 1,500 mm in the north and 500 mm in the southeast (Kiambu District). Murang'a lies between 914 and 3,353 m and has a rainfall range of 500 to 1,600 mm

73

annually. In both districts, rivers are an important source of irrigation water, especially for horticultural development. Horticulture in the two districts is both diverse and dynamic because of the proximity of the Nairobi market and the productivity of horticultural crops such as kale, cabbage, spinach, and fruit. Increased earnings from horticultural farming are used to buy food for rural households.

Spatial stratification, and analysis and results of horticultural systems

Both districts are located in Zone IV of the SFPNRP, which consists of nine production systems of which the horticulture-based system is more predominantly established in the Central Kenya Highlands (table 4.4). Horticulture is also an important enterprise in the dairy-based production system (with 20 percent share), tea-based system (with 10 percent share), and maize-based system (with 5 percent share).

Murang'a has in the recent past experienced diversity in terms of crops grown and market dynamics. The district previously was mainly a cash crop and food crop producer, especially of bananas. The opening of the new road to Sagana increased the number of middlemen, who began encouraging farmers to grow various crops. Some encouraged contract farming because of the proximity to the market, especially for French beans. Because of land scarcity in the high agro-ecological zones, a marked migration also occurred to the lower marginal areas, and farmers were eager to try out new crops such as French beans during the rains. Most farmers in Kiambu District grow vegetables in the valley bottoms because of the scarcity of land and the ability to grow crops there throughout the year. Farmers usually practice bucket irrigation. However, the land portions in the valley bottoms are relatively small and only limited growing can be achieved. The crops grown in the valley bottoms are mainly kale and cabbage.

The farmers who grow crops for the export market are in the drier parts of the Kiambu District and in the current Thika District. They rely on rainfall to grow vegetables, mainly French beans, to sell to middlemen, who in turn sell them to exporters. Farmers who have land in the vicinity of rivers use bucket and furrow irrigation for the production of tomatoes, onions, kale, and spinach. Vegetable production has been increasing steadily over the past five years. Flower production is mainly in the hands of large-scale farmers and for the export market. Most of the flowers are grown for sale to Europe between July and September. Other flowers are grown throughout the year both for export and for local markets. Flower production has greatly increased over the last five years because of good earnings, especially from the European market. The fruit trees are mainly temperate fruits such as peaches, apples, pears, plums, and more recently passion fruit. Some farmers in the Limuru and Tigoni areas of the district planted temperate fruit trees because of the area's similarity in climatic conditions to the Mediterranean. However, farmers grow the trees as a side activity. Passion fruit production is expanding in response to local and export demand. Because of the proximity of the Thika Horticultural Research Station, farmers are able to obtain planting material and technical information.

The preceding inventory can help KARI scientists reorient their research agenda. The dynamic nature of the horticultural industry implies that priorities need to be frequently reviewed in order to meet clients' expectations.

Lessons learned and conclusion

A detailed characterization of the horticulture-based farming system in Murang'a and Kiambu Districts is required in order to identify client categories, constraints, and solutions. At present, KARI's research agenda does not seem to be clearly coordinated, especially from the participatory, multidisciplinary, and multi-institutional points of view.

Mixed Crop-Livestock Systems in Machakos District

Introduction

Machakos District covers some 14,178 km^2 (GoK 1995), with about 896,000 ha lying within the high- to medium-potential areas, and about 454,000 ha in the low-potential category. The agro-ecological zones in this region range from LH2 just north of Machakos to LM4–6 where agriculture is only possible through the use of runoff catchment techniques. Most of the district lies within the UM4/LM5 zones. The geology of the district is largely of the Precambrian Basement Complex, which is crystalline rocks, but pockets of Quaternary volcanic and tertiary sedimentation are found within the area. These mainly give rise to Ferralsols, Luvisols, and Acrisols occupying most of the district. The soils are generally poor in essential nutrients, and farmers use minimal fertilizer. Except for hill masses, slopes lie between 2 and 8 percent (Kilambya, Nandwa, and Omamo 1998). The district has two rainy seasons, the second, in October, being the more reliable. The rains received in four out of five years range between 250 and 500 mm, peaking in April and November. Temperatures are high with a maximum of 25–30°C. Sporadic downpours lead to erosion hazards as vegetation becomes scanty after dry periods.

Table 4.10 Characterization of Semi-Arid Lands (SAL) or Districts of Eastern Province of Kenya into Major Land Use Systems (LUS) in the Hilly Masses

LUS	Farm Typologies	Area (%)
Coffee/dairy/subsistence	1. Coffee/dairy/horticulture/subsistence	4
	2. Coffee/dairy/subsistence	4
Coffee/horticulture/subsistence	1. Coffee/horticulture/subsistence	19
	2. Coffee/subsistence	30
Dairy/horticulture/subsistence	1. Dairy/horticulture/subsistence	1
	2. Dairy/subsistence	6
Subsistence	1. Horticulture/subsistence	10
	2. Subsistence	26

Box 4.2	Main Crop-Livestock Production Systems in Semi-Arid Land Use System (LUS), Target Zone II

No.	LUS (defined by crops/livestock that occupy >70% of farm land)
1.	Maize/bean-based
2.	Maize/pigeon peas-based
3.	Pure livestock
4.	Predominantly pure maize/livestock

Spatial stratification and analysis, and results of crop-livestock systems

In defining LUS at the national level, the arid and semi-arid lands (ASALs) were stratified into two SFPNRP target zones (II and III) ,as shown in table 4.10 and box 4.2, both found in Machakos District (Kilambya, Nandwa, and Omamo 1998). At the national level, zones II and III had the fewest number of production systems (between three and five), thus showing the negative impact of low rainfall and low fertility on agricultural potential diversity. Table 4.10 gives the LUS for the hilly areas of target zone II; and box 4.2 shows LUS for the semi-arid region.

Implications of farmer characterization for KARI arid and semi-arid land research

Production systems in the two ASAL zones (II and III) are fewer in number and less varied than those in other zones. Maize and livestock appear in most systems, dominating all but a few, suggesting that the focus for KARI research in the area should be on mixed crop-livestock interaction. A major difference between the two target zones, however, is that whereas cowpea- and pigeon pea–based systems are important in zone II, the slightly higher agro-ecological potential in zone III permits coffee and horticultural production in addition to maize, beans, and livestock (some on zero grazing). In the hilly masses, the coffee/horticultural/subsistence LUS and the subsistence LUS together cover more than 85 percent of the area. The National Dryland Farming Research Center, or other research centers that cover ASALs, need to make a major investment of their research effort on these enterprises.

Lessons learned and conclusion

A well-defined criterion for characterizing farmers in the hilly masses has been attained, but the criterion for the typical ASAL is less clear. Each commodity-based and factor-based research program needs to develop criteria for defining the core research targets in clients in the ASAL.

Smallholder Tea Cultivation in Kisii District
Introduction

Before its subdivision into Kisii and Nyamira Districts, Kisii District consisted of an area of 2,196 km², of which 861 km² was carved out to form Nyamira District. The Kisii

District has high potential for agricultural activities. South Nyanza (now Migori and Homa Bay Districts) borders it to the west, Kisumu to the north, Kericho to the east, and Narok to the south. The district has a highland type of topography and is mainly hilly with a few flat areas. The altitude in Nyamira ranges from 1,250 to 2,100 m. Because of local convergence of the daily lake winds with the easterlies, rainy seasons are extended, leading to continuous rainfall and water availability throughout the year. In the new Kisii District, the distribution of the two rainy seasons of the year is not easy to distinguish because there is normally no real dry season. In general, the long rainy season lasts from February to June, while the short one is between August and November. Nyamira has a long rainy season from December to June and a short rainy season from August to December, with a mean daily temperature of 19.4°C. Rainfall in Nyamira may be as high as 1,200–2,100 mm annually, and that in Kisii may reach 1,500–2,100 mm annually. Nitisols are the most predominant soils in the two districts, while other soil types represented in the district include Phaeozems, Ferralsols, Cambisols, and Lithosols.

According to the 1979 census, Nyamira District had a population of 441,480 (567 persons per km^2). In 1994 Kisii District had a population of nearly one million. Kisii District falls predominantly (over 75 percent) in UM1, with the rest of the district covered by lower highlands LH1 and LH2. On the other hand, LH1 and LH2 largely cover Nyamira District, and pockets of UM1–3 are also found.

Spatial stratification, and analysis and results of tea systems

Many commodities appear in the tea-based production systems that are complex in composition and present complications in formulating appropriate technologies. According to Soil Fertility Research zonation, Kisii District falls in target zone IV with some nine production systems (table 4.4). Of the nine systems, at least seven are found in Kisii District. For the purpose of this case study, only the tea/dairy, tea/coffee, and pyrethrum and pasture LUS can strictly be termed as part of the smallholder tea farming systems (table 4.11). This is because in most of these LUS, the percentage of farmland under tea is 10% and above. From the foregoing, we may conclude that the smallholder, tea-based farming system predominates in the district, because it is found in four of the seven land use zones (tea/dairy, pasture, pyrethrum, and tea/coffee LUS).

The tea/dairy LUS, which is a predominantly tea zone, lies in the agro-ecological zone LH1 of Nyamira District, and covers a relatively small area, which is characterized by high rainfall (>2,050 mm per annum), and also accommodates Tombe and Kebirigo tea factories. Next in importance to tea growing are pasture (dairy) and pyrethrum. Maize/beans, wheat, and finger millet are also grown. The zone has relatively large farm sizes (5–35 ha), allowing some farmers in the highlands to leave part of their land fallow during the short rainy seasons. This is in contrast to the lowlands, where a second crop of maize, wheat, beans, and finger millet is grown during the short rainy season. Here, farmers also keep cattle, sheep, goats, and poultry. Most farmers own an ox-plow, although many use hoes. Many farmers use family labor, few use hired labor, and mineral fertilizers are mainly used on the tea and maize crops.

Table 4.11 Descriptions of Defined Farm Types and Land Use Systems in Kisii/Nyamira District, Kenya

No.	Land Use System (LUS)[a]	Farm Type
I	Tea (40%)/dairy (10%) zone; crops also consists of pyrethrum (4%), and maize and beans. AEZ: LH1 (humid), LH2 (subhumid)	1. Fallow/ zero grazing 2. Fallow/ tether grazing 3. No fallow/ extensive grazing
II	Tea (10%)/dairy (35%)/pyrethrum (5%) zone; other crops are maize and beans (5%). AEZ: as LUS I	1. Paddocking/ some fish ponds 2. Paddocking/ some fish ponds 3. Paddocking/ zero grazing
III	Pyrethrum (30%) zone; other crops include tea (10%), pasture (3%), maize, and beans. AEZ: as LUS I	1. Pyrethrum/zero grazing 2. Pyrethrum/tether grazing 3. Pyrethrum/extensive grazing
IV	Tea (21%)/coffee (10%)/pyrethrum (10%) zone; other crops include maize and beans (3%). AEZ: Humid upper midland (UM1)	1. Farm size less than 4 acres 2. Farm size less than 4–6 acres 3. Farm size more than 6 acres
V	Coffee (5%)/banana (40%) zone; other crops include maize, beans, and pasture. AEZ: as LUS IV	1. Banana/zero grazing 2. Banana/tether grazing 3. Sugarcane/banana/extensive grazing
VI	Coffee (5%)/extensive grazing (10%)zone; other crops include pasture (5%), maize, and beans	1. Farmyard farm plus two other plots owned 2. Farmyard farm plus two other plots owned plus one rented 3. Farmyard farm plus three other plots owned plus one rented
VII	Sugarcane (40%)/extensive grazing (10%) zone; other crops include maize, beans, and pasture (15%). AEZ: as LUS IV	1. Non-contracted sugarcane 2. Contracted sugarcane 3. Contracted and non-contracted sugarcane

a. AEZ = agro-ecological zone.

Cattle manure and slurry are also applied on napier grass. Both certified seed (maize) and noncertified seed (beans, sorghum, finger millet) are used. Tea is the main source of income in this zone, and crops and products such as millet, beans, maize, and milk may be sold to supplement family income. Other sources of income include tea picking, brick making, timber splitting, weeding, and other forms of off-farm labor.

The tea/coffee LUS lies in AEZ UM1 and receives an annual mean precipitation of 1,700–1,900 mm. Most farms are from three to four acres in size. The farmers also practice double cropping in the lowlands, but plant one crop in the highlands. No striking differences are observable between the soil management and livestock pro-

78

duction subsystem in this zone and the tea/dairy system. Other sources of income are from bananas, horticulture, and chewing sugarcane. In further stratifying all the LUS of the district into farm types, the researchers found that each LUS had three distinct farm types.

Themes in Smallholder Farming Systems in Kenya

Household Factors Influencing Technology Needs

In the foregoing review of case studies, it has been implied that the functioning and strength of smallholder farming systems strongly depend on household settings. In several farm types occurring in the same region (biophysically), high, moderate, and low farm productivity may be observed, reflecting the role of the households and their decision-making process. Important factors on which farm performance may depend include:

- Short- and long-term production objectives,
- Diversity and dynamism in production enterprises,
- Degree of intensification in production and market orientation,
- Access to and control of resource endowments (land, capital from within and off-farm, sectoral organization, and gender division of labor), and
- Land tenure.

The extent to which these factors influence technology needs is examined later.

Agricultural and household income diversification

The primary goal of agricultural research and extension is generating and disseminating technologies that help farmers increase their production of food, fiber, fuel, and so on to meet their production objective and other goals such as food security and generation of off-farm income. In high-potential areas with fertile soils and good marketing infrastructure, diversification poses a challenge to the researcher. In the SFP-NRP target zone, one farm or field plot in each of the Kisii, Kakamega, and Embu Districts was found to be growing nearly twenty crops in highly varied proportion, making it difficult to prescribe recommendations.

Labor organization and gender division of labor

Availability and organization of labor under smallholder farming systems is an important determinant of the extent to which technology is adopted. Also linked to this is the gender division of labor. Labor can be differentiated in terms of productive, reproductive, and community tasks, which can be specified for sectors such as cropping, livestock and forestry husbandry, and income-generating and community activities. Women and men in Africa are known to have differing access to resources and this seemingly affects their ability to participate in research activities at any level. In most parts of Kenya, women depend on men to access resources. Women do not control

79

their own labor and income; they cannot obtain credit without their husband's signature. Lack of access to most resources limits their contribution to development. These gender issues, together with farmers' indigenous knowledge, are of prime importance for technology development.

Plant breeding is an important area where gender issues need to be considered in research. The criteria important to users of crops should be considered when describing desirable characteristics. Pwani Hybrid 1 and Coast Composite are recommended maize varieties for lowland coastal Kenya. Although aware that the improved varieties give higher yields, farmers grow Mudzihana, a local variety, whose grain recovery after pounding is higher for Mudzihana than that of the improved varieties. Breeders did not consider this trait initially.

Food security in rural households

In Kenya, as in many countries of sub-Saharan Africa, grain accounts for more than 50 percent of food expenditures among poor members of society, if they do not produce it themselves. In SSA, the per capita cereal production fell by 17 percent between 1970 and 1990 (Singer 1997). Currently, smallholders in many parts of Kenya suffer from food insecurity (especially for grains). In the western part of Kenya, smallholders have sufficient food to last only three out of twelve months of the year. Paradoxically, such households have the largest numbers of household members and also the smallest plots of land, with almost no cash crops (except where tea, sugarcane, and coffee are grown). Many of these people (70 percent of the households in the Vihiga/ Kakamega Districts) live below the poverty line (they earn less than US$1 per day, or a gross margin of less than 500 Ksh per household per annum). In developing options for replenishing soil fertility in the area, researchers addressed the issue of food security, and consequently farmers involved in the project are achieving a jump in maize yields from 0.8 to over 2.8 tons per hectare. Besides the socioeconomic and biophysical factors discussed previously, lack of food security may often result from sociopolitical factors such as war and ethnic conflicts creating an environment that is not conducive to agricultural growth.

Organizing the Production System

Diversification of the Production System

An objective of transforming NARS should be to facilitate the attainment of productive and sustainable agricultural systems. In this context, the advent of the market economy is seen as a stimulus to diversification of the agricultural sector. Agricultural diversification helps farmers to adjust to changes in both biophysical and socioeconomic factors.

Cash Cropping and Market Participation

The shift to cash cropping will require a revision of land tenure, because the demand for land for planting cash or tree crops is likely to exert stress on subsistence farms. Cash cropping and market participation will require research, extension, and other essential services to farmers, in the areas of harvest, storage, marketing and market information, transport and supplies of inputs, and access to credit and banking facilities. Who assumes the responsibility for delivering such services? National authorities, with substantial input from local farming communities, have to collaborate in identifying local needs and in ensuring implementation of initiatives. Rural service centers are essential for marketing of crops and livestock, input services, banking and rural credit facilities.

Managing Soil Nutrients

Soil fertility management is of great importance in all farming systems. Low soil nutrient levels constitute a serious constraint on agricultural production; hence, soil nutrient management is of great concern. This is particularly true for the resource-poor, small-scale farmers who depend on the natural processes of native soil nutrient releases and on-farm available plant nutrient materials rather than on external (off-farm) sources of nutrients. Today, the decline in soil fertility is the single most important factor responsible for declining per capita food production.

Recent literature reviews on managing soil nutrients and soil fertility status have aimed at highlighting the causes of soil fertility decline. Strategies for restoring and maintaining the productivity of soils in Kenya include those reported by Braun et al. (1997), CAB International (1994), Nandwa and Bekunda (1998), and Padwick (1983). A quantitative assessment of the reviews indicates that soil chemical properties and processes have been studied far more than have biophysical properties and processes (table 4.12). Despite the available research data on agricultural production and natural resource management, the adoption of technologies for soil fertility restoration is low among most smallholders in the region. It has been reported that outputs from research on enhancing soil productivity in east and central Africa during the last four or five decades have not been commensurate with investment (AHI 1997). Also, it has been reported that a considerable percentage of the data used in technology formulation is either absolute (Braun et al. 1997) or based on poorly conceived, executed, and synthesized field trials, with limited representativeness of recommendation domains (FURP 1994).

Little integration occurs between systems and process research, nor are the different spatial and temporal scales of soil fertility decline considered. Moreover,

Table 4.12 Proportion of Farmers in Various Farmer Categories and Wealth Groups Across Land Use Systems (LUS) in Embu District, Kenya

LUS	Proportion (%) of LUS farmers in various wealth groups		
	High	Medium	Low
Tea/dairy	31	32	37
Coffee/dairy/tea	17	44	39
Marginal coffee/maize	26	35	39

although most small farms are practicing integrated nutrient management (INM)-based technologies, the preceding reviews of past research show that limited attention has been given to soil fertility maintenance. Integrated nutrient management can be defined as the judicious manipulation of nutrient stocks and flows for sustainable agricultural production both environmentally and economically. The technologies should fit the existing sociocultural context and take into account local resources available to farmers. Only more recently has INM gained momentum as a holistic approach to farming system diagnosis, characterization, and development (Smaling, Fresco, and de Jager 1996). Both INM and related approaches are now required and geared toward provision of solutions and technologies that are widely adopted to combat soil fertility decline. In view of the foregoing, and of the apparent lack of adoption of soil fertility management practices, more research is needed in many areas. It must also be emphasized that identification of technologies and management practices that are most likely to be adopted by farmers will also depend on good basic research as well as adaptive research.

To organize or reorganize production systems in Kenya will require the implementation of the following actions in agricultural research:

1. Inventory of research efforts to identify gaps: This will entail conducting a comprehensive review and synthesis of unpublished and published research on the subject of maintenance and improvement of soil productivity so as to identify areas that have been overlooked or neglected. This will help focus future research efforts and avoid the costs of duplicating past work while underplaying the impact of untouched research. Lack of coordination among agricultural research organizations has been cited as a cause of insignificant impact of research because of undue duplication and overlapping of projects and overburdening of the client in the recipient countries (Braun et al. 1997).

2. Soil fertility and quality decline indicators: The value of monitoring nutrient flows, stocks, and balances is increasingly being appreciated. Therefore part of the organization of the production system will require a deepening understanding of NUTMON studies as a land quality indicator (de Jager, Nandwa, and Okoth 1998) and also methods of soil analysis such as nutrient release trials to allow rapid insight into soil fertility processes. Experiences from a pilot NUTMON project in Kenya (Van den Bosch, de Jager, and Vlaming 1998; Van den Bosch et al. 1998) have shown that for successful assessment of the system to occur, multidisciplinary teams must conduct investigations on representative sites of well-characterized agro-ecosystems.

3. Optimization of nutrient use efficiency of scarce nutrient sources: To increase the recovery efficiency of mineral fertilizer (hardly affordable by small-scale farmers) requires a deepened understanding of how to use organic methods and various management techniques in combination with inorganic fertilizers. Braun et al. (1997) reported that fertilizer recommendations based on limiting nutrients are superior to blanket recommendations.

Zone- and crop-specific fertilizer recommendations, if adopted judiciously, can mitigate nutrient depletion in four ways. First, substantial increases in harvestable products go together with increases in crop residues and roots, which contribute to soil organic matter (SOM). Second, targeted yields can be obtained on a relatively small proportion of land and thereby result in an increased area left to recuperate through improved fallow. Third, relatively immobile nutrients such as phosphorus are built up in the soil, and can be made available for subsequent crops. Fourth, application of fertilizer according to limiting nutrients results in savings in fertilizer materials. Mineral fertilizers have a bad name in the environmental circuit. However, if used judiciously, they merely feed the plant and contribute to yield increases. Also, they are real nutrient additions, whereas recycling of crop residues and manure is often no more than preventing nutrients from leaving the system. However, use of high amounts of fertilizer may lead to induced deficiencies of nutrients that were not contained in the fertilizer. In Fertilizer Use Recommendation Project (FURP) trials reviewed (FURP 1994), continuous application of nitrogen and/or phosphorus also resulted in scenarios where calcium and potassium began to limit the production of maize, indicating that NP fertilizer recommendations needed to be supplemented with recommendations for calcium- or potassium-containing materials.

The use of rock phosphate as a source of P and Ca is intensively being investigated in eastern, central, and southern Africa. In Kenya, several studies were conducted on the effectiveness and efficiency of rock phosphate in comparison to processed P fertilizers (Woomer and Muchena 1996; Okalebo and Nandwa 1997). The first overall conclusion from past studies is that among east African rocks, Minjingu on the average reaches 65 percent of the effectiveness of processed P fertilizers (triple super phosphate [TSP]), but costs only about 50 percent of what TSP costs on an elemental P basis (Woomer, Okalebo, and Sanchez 1997). The second conclusion is that application of rock phosphate with organics helps hasten its becoming soluble. For example, application of 400 kg per hectare of Minjingu rock phosphate was shown to improve maize yield by one to three tons per hectare when applied in combination with organic sources of nitrogen. The third conclusion is that the benefits of phosphate rock application are greater and much more likely only on low pH and P limiting soils (Okalebo and Nandwa 1997). These encouraging results triggered the formulation of several projects and proposals in eastern, central, and southern Africa on large-scale soil fertility recapitalization or replenishment of phosphorus with rock phosphate (Woomer and Muchena 1996; Woomer, Okalebo, and Sanchez 1997).

Lime and liming material are often applied to reduce soil acidity, so as to enhance the availability of nutrients. Soil acidity may also be ameliorated through better soil organic matter (SOM) management practices. Several researchers have reported on the comparative advantages and disadvantages of the use of lime and dolomite to correct soil acidity. However, the widespread adoption of liming technology is hampered by various factors:

- Its bulkiness (like phosphate rocks), and hence difficulty in transport and application;
- High leaching, especially under high rainfall conditions and in sandy soils; and
- General unavailability to the resource-poor farmers.

These problems may be overcome by applying comparatively small amounts of dressing at a time, well mixed into the soil. This has been reported as a more efficient method of lime application (FURP 1994). Other sources of nutrients requiring further research include manures (Palm, Myers, and Nandwa 1997), deep soil nutrient capture (Hartemink et al. 1996; Mekkonen, Buresh, and Jama 1997), biomass transfer (AHI 1997), agro-industrial by-product wastes (Palm, Myers, and Nandwa 1997), and biological nitrogen fixation (Giller et al. 1997). Other factors hampering adoption of liming technology are:

- Fertilizer recommendation extrapolation tools; and
- Integrated nutrient management. This is perceived as the judicious manipulation entirely or partly of nutrient inputs, outputs, and internal flows. Integrated nutrient management is being recognized as strategy for achieving productive and sustainable agricultural systems in SSA (Smaling, Fresco, and de Jager 1996).

Hitherto, research on the quantification of the impact of INM practices on soil fertility and productivity and the sustainability of agro-ecosystems has been ranked high in SSA (Palm, Myers, and Nandwa 1997; Smaling and Braun 1996). However, past research on this subject has focused on a narrow definition of INM, namely the combination of organic and inorganic sources of plant nutrients. There is a serious lack of data on the impact on soil productivity of the diverse INM components found in different farming systems in SSA. The NUTMON project was designed to address this knowledge gap. The NUTMON approach promotes farmer participation at all stages of the research process, where possible.

Internalizing Common Resources: Trees, Water, and Grazing
Trees, water, and grazing land are natural resources that are under pressure of overuse or misuse. The need for users to understand the importance of these resources beyond the farm boundary is critical. This is because on-site effects on these resources have a great bearing on off-site effects (e.g., common grazing land, water points, forests, and reserves). Sustainable farm productivity may depend on common grasslands (nutrient imports), just as forestland influences rainfall. Therefore, care of these resources is highly important.

Managing Pests and Diseases
Plant protection research in Kenya has been and is targeted at reducing crop losses caused by a range of biotic stresses that are constraints on sustainable farm productivity. These stresses are caused by a wide range of organisms, notably insect pests,

nematodes, fungi, bacteria, viruses, and weeds, which are traditionally studied by researchers in entomology, mycology, bacteriology, virology, and weed science, respectively. Nevertheless, interdisciplinary collaborators are increasingly involved in studies integrating a wide range of disciplines (e.g., breeding of varieties against diseases and pests). Similarly, the roles of agronomists and socioeconomists are becoming pivotal in the development and implementation of integrated pest and disease management (IPM-DM) strategies. Other disciplines of significance in this research include microclimatology, crop modeling, and cell molecular biology.

A weakness of crop protection research in Kenya has to do with the limited relationship between the impact of research undertaken and crop loss studies. Therefore, in order to reorganize production systems, researchers will need to address the following issues:

1. Research inventory to identify gaps: The identification and quantification of crop damage and yield loss is a basic prerequisite to defining research priorities and subsequently achieving the goals, purposes, and objectives of crop protection research and development in Kenya.
2. Optimization of crop management as a strategy for pest and disease control: Increasing evidence shows that cultural control methods (e.g., those that involve manipulation of sowing and harvesting dates, crop combinations and cropping patterns, and crop residue management), used successfully in the past, are rarely integrated into new research. This opens a new window for plant protection research that combines well with the need for crop protection recommendation packages that are environmentally friendly.
3. Other noninsecticidal control strategies: These include use of the phenomena technology and botanical insecticides, although this area remains relatively undeveloped.

Overall, future plant protection research should be concentrated on these scant areas, along with the development of genetically improved cultivars and parental material, and the integration of an array of control options into IPM-DM packages. The major challenges facing crop protection researchers in Kenya include:

- Identifying and controlling new pests, especially those that evade enforcement of regulations;
- Identifying management practices that are environmentally friendly and exist effectively within the clients' circumstances;
- Coping with increasing numbers of pests and diseases resistant to conventional control pesticides; and
- Evaluating and integrating indigenous technologies developed through farmers' own initiatives.

At present these challenges are being met through several "pest" management options that include host-plant resistance, pesticides, cultural and environmental manipulation, biological control, quarantine, and biotechnology. The research program investigates problems on the basis of agro-ecological distribution of the "pests" (e.g., those of medium- to high-potential areas, semi-arid systems, and crop protection in the peri-urban environments in high-potential areas). Moths, borers, thrips, aphids, smuts, wilts, streaks, and blights are of major concern, and most of these pests are also encountered in peri-urban environments. In the semi-arid areas, borers and storage pests of grain legumes and cereals are being addressed as priority problems.

Implications for Research and Extension

Ordering the Technology Design Problem

In most parts of sub-Saharan Africa, population growth is rapid and is predicted to increase to the year 2025. Population densities in some places are already high and will soon increase more. Nevertheless, it does not seem logical to jump to the conclusion that high population growth is the root cause of food deficits and degradation in the sub-Saharan African countries. Indeed, the notion of overpopulation is relative, and in some cases an increase in population represents an increase in the available labor force that can be deployed to conserve and develop the environmental resources (soils, vegetation, and others) of an area. Hence, a straightforward direct relationship cannot be drawn between population size and the intensity of the demands made on the environmental resources.

However, the intensity of resource use has become more and more dependant on external variables, and most particularly on the amount of money needed by each individual to survive physically and live in a globalized and liberalized economy. So, for any particular activity, be it farming or other, the environmental impact will depend on the technology adopted. Hence, agricultural research cannot bypass the technology design problem if it is to help the small-scale farmer in sustaining land use and productivity. Because human beings are not just cogs in a system of physical and chemical interactions, agricultural research must take into account the complexity of the relationship between the farmers' societies and their environment when designing technology. This means that the research will have to pay increased attention to social, cultural, economic, and even political dynamics that order the relationship between farmers and their natural environment.

Decentralization as a Response to Farmer Diversity

Environmental settings do not present a single phenomenon that may be apprehended and treated in a unique way. By carefully analyzing the relationship between local societies and their environmental settings, it can be seen that different farmers experience different combinations of demographic, sociocultural, historical, economic, technical, and environmental factors. This emphasizes the need for decentralization of agricultural research approaches in response to diversity. Decentralization seeks to strengthen farmers' management of their resources. It offers social accountability at their level, and an opportunity for them to define their own priorities, reassert their autonomy vis-à-vis researchers, and make their own decisions within their organizations. In the context of decentralization, researchers should not ignore the skillfulness of farmers. Tiffen (1996) said:

> A greater appreciation of the skill with which farmers, male or female, juggle resources, weigh opportunities and manage and negotiate family inputs, might lead to greater acceptance of the view that they are the senior partners in rural development. There will always be the unskillful or the unfortunate, who need special help, but they should not be conceived of as the majority.

Building Adaptive Research Capacity

Agricultural production using only local inputs may reach its limits. By that time, the recommendation that might be brought in is once again the use of external inputs. What will happen if small-scale farmers are still unable to purchase such inputs or if climatic conditions, such as those of dry lands, are strong limiting factors to their use? There is here a need for building an adaptive research capacity within the farmers' sphere. Agricultural research must evolve to a point that it makes farmers aware of increasing yields not only through the use of external inputs, but also through making more efficient use of locally available inputs (Budelman and Defoer 2000).

Although farmers may have tried everything within their knowledge, some factors may have escaped their notice, simply because of their lack of scientific background (Balakrishnaraj 2000). For instance, what happens underground? They may need to look at microbial activity and nutrient dynamics. What happens at night when certain pests are active? What is too small for their eyes to see, and what are the relationships between soil components that are beyond their understanding? These facts and processes may be difficult for farmers to follow. Knowing what a farmer cannot see or easily understand, measuring what he does not measure, and combining this with that farmer's know-how may provide a means by which agricultural scientists can build up the adaptive research capacity of farmers, and together with them increase the efficiency of low external input agriculture. By such an approach, agricultural scientists will be able to open a flow of access to other technologies that may have succeeded in similar ecological environments elsewhere.

Extension Technology as Information Flow

Sub-Saharan Africa possesses a large number of small-scale farmers who are faced with the challenge of making their production systems profitable and sustainable. Knowledge and technology generated by NARS institutes can be an important source of ideas for farmers. Hence technology transmitted through the extension services of NARS can be used as a means of information flow, provided this technology is brought to farmers using an active learning approach, such as PLAR. However, it is well known that many agricultural research institutes experience problems in responding to farmers' needs. This explains why efforts have to be undertaken to build partnerships and linkages with farmers and NARS extension services. The process calls for promotion and advocacy of the participatory methodologies as a strategy to involve farmers or their representatives in decision making on research priorities. It also calls for improving the linkages between research and its clients, while research effectiveness is enhanced as projects and technologies are better targeted to local needs.

However, the use of technology as a means of information flow in farmer-led agricultural research raises some problems. Farmer-led research tends to be short term in focus and highly applied in content, while longer-term, strategic research provides the basis for understanding the underlying constraints within agricultural systems. Thus some balance needs to be achieved between the two research approaches. Consequently, new skills and ways of working will be required in order for researchers to address the priorities set by farmers rather than by their own scientific aspirations, including the areas of technology and information transfer.

REFERENCES

African Highlands Initiative (AHI). 1997. *African Highlands Initiatives, cultivating the future, annual report.* Nairobi: AHI.

Balakrishnaraj, Neerchal. 2000. Can farmers think like researchers? Experience gained while studying indigenous technological knowledge. *Indigenous Knowledge and Development Monitor* 8 (3): 20–21.

Biggs, Stephen D. 1989. Resource-poor farmer participation in research: A synthesis of experiences from nine national agricultural research systems. On-farm client-oriented research (OFCOR) Comparative Study Paper 3. The Hague: International Service for National Agricultural Research (ISNAR).

Braun, Ann R., Eric M. A. Smaling, E. I. Muchugu, K. D. Shepherd, and John D. Corbett. 1997. *Maintenance and improvement of soil productivity in the highlands of Ethiopia, Kenya, Madagascar and Uganda: An inventory of spatial and non-spatial survey and research data on natural resources and land productivity.* African Highlands Initiative (AHI) Technical Report Series No. 6. Nairobi: International Centre for Research in Agroforestry (ICRAF).

Brouwers, Jan H. A. M. 1993. Rural people's response to soil fertility decline. The Adja case (Benin). Ph.D. diss. Wageningen University, The Netherlands.

Budelman, A., and T. Defoer. 2000. Not by nutrients alone: A call to broaden the soil fertility initiative. *Natural Resources Forum* 24:173–84.

CAB International. 1994. *Soil fertility research in East Africa.* Wallingford, UK: CAB International.

Chambers, Robert, and Janice Jiggins. 1986. Agricultural research for resource-poor farmers: The farmer-first-and-last model. Institute for Development Studies (IDS) Discussion Paper No. 220, UK: IDS.

Chege, A. G. 2000. Management of plant nutrients in smallholder farming systems of western Kenya. Ph.D. diss., University of Exeter, United Kingdom.

Fertilizer Use Recommendation Project (FURP). 1994. *FURP recommendations. National Agricultural Research Laboratories, vol. 1–23.* Nairobi: Kenya Agricultural Research Institute (KARI)-FURP.

Giller, Ken E., George C. Gadisch, C. Eholiotis, E. Adams, D. W. Sakala, and Paramu L. Mafongoya. 1997. Building soil nitrogen capital in Africa. *Soil Science Society of America Special Number* 51:151–92.

Government of Kenya (GoK). 1995. *Economic Survey 1995.* Nairobi: Central Bureau of Statistics, Government of the Republic of Kenya.

Hair, Joseph F., Rolph E. Anderson, Ronald L. Tatham, and William C. Black. 1992. *Multivariate data analysis with readings*. New York: Macmillan.

Hartemink, Alfred E., Roland J. Buresh, Bahir Jama, and Bert H. Janssen. 1996. Soil nitrate and water dynamics in sesbania fallows, weed fallows and maize. *Soil Science and Society of America Journal* 60:568–74.

Hassan, Rashid M., R. Onyango, and J. K. Rutto. 1998. Relevance of maize research in Kenya to maize production problems perceived by farmers. In *Maize technology development and transfer: A GIS application for research planning in Kenya,* ed. Rashid M. Hassan, 71–88. Wallingford, U.K.: CAB International.

Jaetzold, Ralph, and Helmut Schmidt. 1984. *Farm management handbook of Kenya. Volume 3A, West Kenya (Nyanza and Western Provinces)*. Nairobi: Ministry of Agriculture.

de Jager, Andre, Stephen M. Nandwa, and P. F. Okoth. 1998. Monitoring nutrient flows and economic performance in African farming systems (NUTMON). I. Concepts and methodologies *Agriculture, Ecosystems and Environment* 71:37–48.

Kenya Agricultural Research Institute (KARI). 1992. *Information Bulletin No. 7*. Nairobi: KARI.

———. 1996a. *A participatory study of farmers' constraints. Opportunities and research needs in the hilly masses of Eastern Kenya*. Nairobi: KARI.

———. 1996b. *PRA: A case study of Kasikeu sub-location, Makueni District, Kenya*. Nairobi: KARI.

Kilambya, Daniel, Stephen M. Nandwa, and Steven W. Omamo. 1998. Priority setting in a production-factor research programme (Soil Fertility and Plant Nutrition Research Programme). In *Agricultural research priority setting: Information investments for improved use of resources,* ed. Bradford Mills, 137–49. The Hague: International Service for National Agricultural Research (ISNAR).

Mekkonen, Kindu, Roland J. Buresh, and Bashir Jama. 1997. Root and inorganic nitrogen distribution in sesbania fallow, natural fallow, and maize fields. *Plant and Soil* 188:319–27.

Ministry of Agriculture, Livestock Development and Marketing (MoALDM). 1993. *MoALDM Annual Report*. Nairobi: MoALDM.

Nandwa, Stephen M., and M. A. Bekunda. 1998. Research on nutrient flows and balances in East and Southern Africa: State-of-the-art. *Agricultural Ecosystems* 71:5–18.

Niang, Abdoulaye, Jan De Wolf, K. Mwendwa, T. Hansen, M. Nyasimi, T. Defour, V. N. Ogaro, S. Obaga, and D. Rotich. 1998. Soil fertility replenishment and recapitalization in Western Kenya: Methodologies, approaches, and challenges. Pilot Project Report No. 7. Maseno, Kenya: Regional Agroforestry Research Centre.

Ojiem, J. O, and M. O. Odendo. 1997. Farmers' perceptions of spatial heterogeneity and its influence on soil management in small-scale farms in Western Kenya. *African Crop Science Journal* 3:283–87.

Ojiem, J. O, M. O. Odendo, and Stephen M. Nandwa. 1995. *Biological management of soil fertility in small-scale farming systems in Kakamega District*. Annual Report. Nairobi: Kenya Agricultural Research Institute (KARI).

Okalebo, J. R., and Stephen M. Nandwa. 1997. *Effect of organic resources with and without inorganic fertilizers on maize yields, mainly on P deficient soils in Kenya*. National Soil Fertility Plant Nutrition Research Programme Technical Report Series No. 12. Nairobi: Kenya Agricultural Research Institute (KARI).

Okigbo, Bede N. 1979. Cropping systems in the humid tropics of West Africa and their improvement. Paper presented at the International Institute of Tropical Agriculture (IITA), Ibadan, Nigeria.

Otichillo, W. K., and R. K. Sinange. 1991. Long rains maize and wheat production in 1990. Technical Report No. 140. Nairobi: Department of Resource Surveys and Remote Sensing, Ministry of Planning and National Development.

Padwick, G. Watts. 1983. Fifty years of experimental agriculture II. The maintenance of soil fertility in tropical Africa: A review. *Experimental Agriculture* 19:293–310.

Palm, Cheryl A., R. J. K. Myers, and Stephen M. Nandwa. 1997. Combined use of organic and inorganic nutrient sources for soil fertility maintenance and replenishment. *Soil Science Society of America Special Number* 51:193–217.

Sanchez, Pedro A., K. D. Shepherd, M. J. Soule, F. M. Place, Roland J. Buresh, Anne-Marie Izac, A. U. Mokwunye, F. B. Kwesiga, Cyrus G. Ndiritu, and Paul L. Woomer. 1997. Soil fertility replenishment in Africa: An investment in natural resource capital. *Soil Science Society of America Special Number* 51:1–46.

Scoones, Ian, and C. Toulmin. 1998. *Soil nutrient budgets and balances: What use for policy?* Managing Africa's Soils No. 6. The Hague: Ministry of Foreign Affairs.

Sedong, M. P. 1993. Evolution des sols ferrugineux lessives sous culture: Influence des modes de gestion sur la fertilité. Ph.D. diss., Université Nationale de Côte d'Ivoire, Abidjan.

Singer, Hans W. 1997. A global view of food security. *Agriculture and Rural Development* 4 (1): 3–6.

Smaling, Eric M. A., and Ann R. Braun. 1996. Soil fertility research in sub-Saharan Africa: New dimensions, new challenges. *Communications in Soil Science and Plant Analysis* 27:365–86.

Smaling, Eric M. A., Louise O. Fresco, and Andre de Jager. 1996. Classifying and monitoring soil nutrient stocks and flows in African agriculture. *Ambio* 25:492–96.

Stoorvogel, Jetze J., and Eric M. A. Smaling. 1998. Research on soil fertility decline in tropical environments: Integration of spatial scales. *Nutrient Cycling in Agroecosystems* 50:151–58.

Tiffen, Mary. 1996. Land and capital: Blind spots in the study of the resource-poor farmer. In *The lie of the land: Challenging received wisdom on the African environment,* ed. Melissa Leach and Robin Mearns. London, England: International African Institute, James Curry and Heinemann.

Tripp, Robert. 1991. The limitations of on-farm research. In *Planned change in farming systems: Progress in on-farm research,* ed. Robert Tripp, 247–57. Chichester, England: John Wiley and Sons.

Tripp, Robert, Ponniah Anandajayasekeram, and Gustavo E. Saín. 1990. *Diseño y manejo de los cursos del sistema de llamadas sobre la investigación en fincas.* Mexico: International Maize and Wheat Improvement Center (CIMMYT).

Van den Bosch, Heleen, Andre de Jager, and J. Vlaming. 1998. Monitoring nutrient flows and economic performance in African farming systems (NUTMON). II. Tool development. *Agriculture, Ecosystems and Environment* 71:49–62.

Van den Bosch, Heleen, J. N. Gitari, V. N. Ogaro, S. N. Maobe, and J. Vlaming. 1998. Monitoring nutrient flows and balances on three districts in Kenya. *Agriculture, Ecosystems and Environment* 71:63–80.

Woomer, Paul L., and F. N. Muchena. 1996. Overcoming soil constraints in crop production in tropical Africa. *African Crop Science Journal* 4:503–18.

Woomer, Paul L., J. R. Okalebo, and Pedro A. Sanchez. 1997. Phosphorus replenishment in Western Kenya: From field experiments to an operational strategy. In *Phosphorus Exploratory Project (PREP) for Western Kenya,* ed. J. J. Kapkiyai, J. R. Okalebo, and H. K. Maritim, 28–40. Initial Workshop Proceedings 12–15 May 1997. Eldoret, Kenya: Department of Soil Science, Moi University.

PART 2

The Transformation

REORGANIZATION OF RESEARCH SYSTEMS

5

Evolution of Kenya's Agricultural Research Systems in Response to Client Needs

ADIEL N. MBABU, MATT DAGG,
JOHN CURRY, AND MERCY KAMAU

Background

Kenya's agriculture has developed over a long period, with improvements and modifications introduced into the production and marketing systems for the benefit of all involved in agriculture. Long before the European settler agriculture altered the landscape, many of the indigenous inhabitants of Kenya had transformed their subsistence systems from food procurement to food production by adding crop cultivation and livestock husbandry to the existing hunting and foraging activities. An agropastoralism complex based on grain crops and herding of domestic stock developed in northeast Africa around 6000 B.C. and spread southward to Kenya, Uganda, and the Serengeti plains (Vansina 1996, 15). This spread was gradual. Pastoralists appear to have first entered Kenya during the first millennium B.C. (Robertshaw 1993, 358). Archaeological evidence from the Neolithic period (3300 to 1300 B.P.) indicates that groups of hunter/gatherers, pastoralists, and those who were possibly agropastoralists coexisted, exploiting different eco-niches in the Rift Valley (Ambrose 1984, 239). Robertshaw (1990) gives a recent treatment of the archaeological evidence for the development of pastoralism in Kenya:

> Introduction of new species and development of better varieties of plants and animals through selective crossing were most likely the early methods used, for food production systems developed throughout the region. In the first millennium A.D., farmers in eastern and southern Africa experimented with the proportions of the three main grain crops until they found the combination best adapted to local soils and rainfall (Vansina 1996, 24). Sorghum, one of these grains, was an early and important food staple: carbonized sorghum is found at all stratigraphic levels of the Engaruka site in Tanzania that dates from the fourth to the nineteenth century, A.D. (Shaw 1976, 114). Evidence shows that these early migrants also devised techniques for storage and protection of products from predators.

The primary production goals of early agricultural systems were the satisfaction of subsistence needs and local trading opportunities. However, evidence suggests the development of long-distance trade routes in many parts of the region, probably arising from what Vansina calls overlapping networks of local exchange (Vansina 1996, 24). Such trading opportunities served as a source of new ideas, improved varieties of seed, new breeds of animals, and new tools. Later innovations consisted of enriching and modifying parts of already well-honed farming systems or of adapting them to new conditions such as the rise of cities (Vansina 1996, 25). By the close of the precolonial era in Kenya, evidence suggests that agricultural systems in a few areas were responding to opportunities resulting from long-distance trade. Anderson's study of the precolonial irrigation systems of the pastoral Jemmus at Lake Baringo in the mid-nineteenth century is a case in point (Anderson 1989).

By the time Europeans settled in Kenya, they found many crops and animals that they were later to incorporate into their farming systems. These crops and animals had already been introduced experimentally and adapted to local conditions by the indigenous farmers. Earliest surviving descriptions of cultivation on the east African coast and islands date back to the early tenth century. These include Abu Zaid's descriptions of indigenous cultivation of sorghum and sugarcane, and al-Masudi's mention of sorghum, banana, coconut, and a ground plant that was most likely taro (Wigboldus 1996). The Portuguese first introduced maize to the region in Zanzibar and Pemba in 1643, growing the crop to supply the garrison at Mombassa. The adoption of maize as a staple crop was a gradual process, however. In 1848 the food of the Wakamba was described as consisting of a thick porridge made out of Indian corn prepared by boiling in water, but maize did not become a widely accepted staple in Africa until the twentieth century.

However, conditions have changed drastically over the years. The marketing opportunities for food and raw materials have expanded enormously, production systems have become more specialized and complex, and economic expectations from agriculture have expanded greatly. Experimentation and research have also become much more specialized, with a complex organization to supervise national investment in research for the public good. The range of beneficiaries (stakeholders) has also increased, with the inevitable concern for which clients will benefit most from society's investment. Meanwhile, many of the overall objectives of research remain similar to those of the early phases. These include best use of natural resources (including labor), plant and animal improvement to give desired products, protection of plants and animals from predators, and the satisfaction of markets with surpluses for the benefit of the stakeholders. However, these objectives must include intensification by the addition of chemical resources and machinery.

Consequently, the national agricultural research system in Kenya has evolved into a large and complex organization. However, it can still be analyzed in terms of how it meets research challenges arising from the needs of its clients and from marketing opportunities, in terms of the institutional and organizational arrangements necessary to meet these challenges, and in terms of the financial provision for, and efficient management of, the institutions. The evolution of the Kenyan agricultural research system will be reviewed in the following with respect to these terms within the framework of the economic and political circumstances of four distinct periods. Management issues to be addressed will include dominant clients in time and space; appropriateness of planning, monitoring, and evaluation processes; research priorities and types; organization and structure; funding strategies; and strategies for economies of scale.

Pereira (1997) has provided an important account of the role of agricultural research in the development of Kenya up to independence. His paper is a major source of information for the early sections of this chapter. However, our treatment of agricultural research at the various time periods in Kenya's history will focus more on the management and organizational issues, in order to examine the emerging institutional lessons rather than technical ones.

Agricultural Research in Kenya: 1890–1945

Background

Agricultural development policies in the period between 1895 and 1945 focused on providing the European settlers with land, financial resources (Cone and Lispcomb 1972), and cheap labor (Mutiso 1975; Wolff 1974). Yet, the same period also witnessed the creation of overcrowded African reserves (Ochieng 1977) and a limited commercialization of African agriculture (Mutiso 1975; Nganga 1981). Following the declaration of British Protectorate status for Kenya in 1895, a series of legislative procedures led to the establishment of a settler economy. Indeed, the 1899 Unoccupied Land Regulations converted all unoccupied land in Kenya to Crown land (Cone and Lipscomb 1972; KNA 1962). The 1902 Crown Lands Ordinance, which converted both occupied and unoccupied land to the ownership of the British Crown, further consolidated this claim (Gutto 1981). Soon after World War I, the Crown Lands Ordinance was modified to reduce the minimum requirements for improvements on alienated land and to extend land leases from 99 to 999 years.

By 1924, European settlers occupied 4.5 million acres of land, each settler owning an average of 1,285 acres (Cone and Lipscomb 1972). As of 1930, the White Highlands covered 19 percent of the forty thousand square miles of Kenyan land receiving over thirty inches of rain per annum (Wolff 1974). The Carter report on land situation in Kenya indicated that Europeans occupied 6.5 million acres of an estimated 40–45 million acres of arable land in Kenya. In the same year (1934), the average population density in the Kikuyu districts of Kiambu, Fort Hall/Muranga, and Nyeri was 283 persons per square mile (Ochieng 1977). During this period, political organizations took root in an effort to resist enforcement of labor laws, overcrowding, overstocking, and the corresponding overgrazing (Odinga 1967; Cone and Lipscomb 1972; Mbithi and Barnes 1975). Thus, in 1921, the Young Kavirondo Association was formed in western Kenya and the Young Kikuyu Association in central Kenya.

In the midst of this political activism, an "elite African group" was also emerging in the African reserves in close association with the European establishment. European missionaries converted followers to Christianity, teaching them how to read and write and how to function in monetary economies (Mutiso 1975). This elite group was encouraged to isolate and enclose formerly communal land for their exclusive private use (Mutiso 1975; Nganga 1981). This same group served the colonial state as local chiefs, court interpreters and clerks, teachers, and nurses, and also served as Christian preachers. Every development project was first given to the emerging elite group. As early as 1921, the Native Trust Fund was initiated to finance local development projects in the African reserves (Cone and Lipscomb 1972). In 1922, selected Africans were allowed to produce for the market. In support of this policy, the government funded the training of agricultural extension staff for African areas to enhance demonstration of improved farming methods and use of good quality seeds. By 1935, the elite group had crystallized sufficiently to justify the enactment of the Marketing of the Native Produce Ordinance to streamline marketing facilities for the smallholder African commodity producers.

The arrival and settlement of Europeans in Kenya brought a profound shift in the perception of farming that was to dominate the outlook on research for a long time to come. They brought with them the concepts of large-scale farming and ranching, in contrast to the array of smallholder peasant cultivation and pastoralist systems that they had found on arrival. Large-scale European farming could readily produce surpluses as markets developed. This type of European farming can be contrasted in many ways to indigenous African agrarian systems. Harlan, De Wet, and Stemler (1976, 17) have characterized African agriculture as a mosaic of crop (and livestock) and (primarily hand labor) technique combinations that through time have penetrated savanna and forest successively. Such technical systems can be viewed as an integral part of the social and political systems of the populations they sustain (Hakansson 1989, 12), possibly even more so than agriculture in capitalist systems. Perhaps the most striking feature of African agrarian systems is their resilience through time. Sutton (1989, 6) notes that the success of African agriculture reflects not so much an adherence to an unchanging traditional system and maintenance of an ecological equilibrium (a more European logic of production), but rather a constant adaptation in the face of ecological stresses and population growth.

In due course, research became focused on solving the problems of large-scale farming systems that were reasonably well capitalized. The early European settlers saw the temperate highland areas as being sufficiently similar to European conditions to introduce European crops and livestock breeds (e.g., wheat, barley, cattle, and sheep) and their attendant European methods of husbandry to supply familiar markets that were accessible. Government policy was to support white settlers, both on the Kenya coast, where they practiced tropical plantation agriculture, and in the high-potential White Highlands. The settlers rapidly discovered, however, that the tropical conditions at the coast and in the highlands were sufficiently different from those in Europe to cause serious production problems that required research to adapt the European systems, crops, and animals to local conditions. This remained a major focus of research in Kenya for many years, but additional tropical crops and animals were introduced as new marketing opportunities opened—as they did dramatically with the opening of the new railway line joining Mombassa with Kampala in 1901. The line not only improved the prospects for exports, but also greatly reduced the costs of import-ing machinery and other inputs to farming areas upcountry.

The Agricultural Research System

Initially, settlers and the private sector carried out research and experimentation, in partnership with the Department of Agriculture (DOA) of British East Africa (later the Kenya Colony and Protectorate). The British government at the time was encouraging settlement from Britain and elsewhere in Kenya, and recognized the importance of providing some support services to new farmers in Kenya. In the first decade of the twentieth century, the protectorate government, no doubt at the urging of the Euro-pean farming community, established the basis of a formal research service. Soon after the DOA came into being in 1903, its officers worked on testing sites and farms to develop a more systematic scrutiny of crop and livestock introductions to existing (and would-be) settler and planter farming operations. The DOA at this time used sev-eral terms to refer to European farmers—"planter" for a large-scale European farmer at the coast cultivating tropical crops (e.g., sisal, rubber, citrus, or coconut), "settler" for a farmer in the highlands, and "pastoralist" for large-scale European ranchers in semi-arid areas. The terms were sometimes used interchangeably.

Adjustments to this emerging research agenda were needed rather quickly. In a 1906 report, the DOA director recommended that the department be reorganized along the lines of the agriculture departments of the United States and of the Trans-vaal in South Africa. The dominant form of experimentation would be that of the cooperative system, the condition being that full reports of each experiment were to be furnished, and if results were satisfactory the farmers were to get twice the seed originally supplied to them (DOA 1908, 3). The first government farms were estab-lished about 1903 in Nairobi for crop testing and at Naivasha, near Lord Delamere's estate, for livestock improvement. In 1905, experiment stations were added at Meri-hini to investigate crops for the coastal belt and at Kibos, near Lake Victoria, to test cotton varieties. By 1907, the Nairobi and Merihini sites had been closed and replaced by the Mazeras Experiment Station near Mariakani and the Kabete Experiment Farm, situated between Nairobi and the Kikuyu Native Reserve. In 1908, an entomological laboratory was established in Nairobi that was later moved to Kabete. A veterinary pathology laboratory was set up at Kabete about 1911 to diagnose and study East Coast fever, rinderpest, and trypanosomiasis, and to develop vaccines for their con-trol. The farms at Mazeras, Kabete, Kibos, and Naivasha formed the core of the exper-iment system from 1908 until after World War I. Located close to rail stations for easy access by Europeans, the farms served two primary purposes. These were to test the suitability of crop varieties for the broad farming zone of their area (e.g., coast, high-lands, lake districts), and to propagate and supply planting materials to planters, set-tlers, and to a far lesser extent, native farmers. On-station trials were often supplemented by experiments conducted primarily on large-scale farms.

World War I disrupted this rather small-scale and straightforward agricultural research system. During the war, agricultural exports virtually ceased and surplus production was absorbed by the military, which purchased large amounts of maize, livestock, and other products as provision for the troops. Many European farmers joined the forces, and much African farm labor was diverted into military service via the Carrier Corps. Research activities virtually ceased as those officers not on active service were seconded to other duties in the department. At the beginning of the war, the entire Veterinary Department was pressed into service, becoming the East African Veterinary Corps, and charged with securing and maintaining draft animals and remounts for the Army. Following the war, agricultural research underwent considerable change. The Kabete Experiment Farm was closed in 1922 and a multidisciplinary agricultural research and advisory laboratory, the Scott Agricultural Laboratories, took over its research in entomology, mycology, and plant breeding on the same site. Pereira (1997) gives an account of some of the early work from these laboratories. At this point the department no longer relied on government farms for much of its field experiment work. In his 1922 report, the director remarked that the necessary experiment work could be undertaken in cooperation with farmers on their farms (DOA 1922, 40). The farms at Mazeras and Kibos are not mentioned in the annual reports of the period after 1921. However, a plant breeding station was established at Njoro in 1927 and began experiment work on cereals in 1928, with substations at Mau Summit and Scott Laboratories, continuing the work begun on Lord Delamere's Njoro farm earlier in the century. An agricultural chemist and a chemical officer appeared on the staff lists and were charged with assaying soil fertility and dips to control tick-borne diseases. Tea, which was first grown in Kenya in Limuru in 1904 (Owuor 1999), had become by this time a growing industry, so that in 1928, when the first factory-prepared tea consignment was exported, 4,809 acres were under cultivation (DOA 1928). Coffee was by this time well established as an important export crop. In response to the Coffee Board's demand for specialized research services and a separate research station, the department extended work on the crop at Scott Laboratories in 1928 (DOA 1928). By the end of the decade, on-station crop research had become consolidated at Scott Laboratories and the Plant Breeding Station at Njoro. Animal husbandry research was carried out at Naivasha Stock Farm (in collaboration with Rowett Research Institute, Scotland) and livestock disease research was conducted at the Veterinary Research Laboratory at Kabete.

The department was further changed during the 1930s. In 1931, the various sections of the department were reorganized into the Divisions of Plant Industry and Livestock Industry, replacing the system that had evolved in the 1920s. By 1929, these had become Administration and General, Division of Native Agriculture, Scott Agricultural Laboratories, Coffee and Sisal Services, Grading and Inspection, Cool Stores Services, Veterinary Division, and Division of Veterinary Research (DOA 1929). A further separation of the agriculture and veterinary departments occurred in 1937. In the same year, the agriculture department, at the request of the Coffee Board, created a multidisciplinary Coffee Team to address the many issues with coffee cultivation and pest control. This team consisted of an officer in charge (a former senior plant breeder), a soil chemist, a plant pathologist, two entomologists, an officer for white borer campaigns, an agricultural officer and an assistant from Scott Laboratories, an assistant vegetative propagator, officers in charge of Karimani and Nandi Stations, and the Coffee Board biochemist (DOA 1937). This redeployment of staff to an exclusive service placed considerable strain on the programs at the Plant Breeding Station, and on Njoro and Scott Laboratories. Work was also begun to establish supporting stations for coffee research at Thika, Makuyu, Karimani, Nandi, Sotik, and Mount Elgon. An experiment plot at Kitale was established in 1933 and had become a Research Station by 1937. Funds were voted in 1938 for a high-level Sisal Research Station at Thika to supplement research work at the main lowland site in Tanganyika. In the native reserves, two experiment sites that would become research stations by the end of the decade were also established—Bukura (in 1931) in Nyanza Province, and Kibarini (in 1935) in Coast Province.

Despite the expansion of major research sites, the department's research staff remained virtually constant at about forty, including about twenty-five full-time researchers and the remainder part-time researchers, agricultural officers (AOs), and laboratory staff. Researchers were closely linked with advisory services, and they, in turn, were in close contact with the relatively small contingent of settler farmers. Despite relatively poor roads, the network of communications was good, reinforced by social contacts. Researchers were therefore well aware of farmers' problems, which were addressed in research programs within the government's emphasis on exports and the severe limits of staff available. The settler farmers carried out essential research steps by testing new modifications in production systems for profitability and suitability to farmers, on relatively large farms, and at their own risk, as was the common practice in agricultural research in Britain. In essence, farmers did their own microeconomic analysis. The researcher did not need to do it, although an agricultural economist was appointed to the department in 1931. Judging from DOA reports of the period, his major duties were market analyses and production surveys. These latter included a survey of native production and a study of traditional land tenure in the reserves, and a comparison of Kikuyu smallholder production with farming systems in Denmark (DOA 1931; DOA 1933). The perspective of farmers doing their own research lasted a long time, to the detriment of smallholders who could not afford their own trials. Full-time researchers in the DOA were designated in scientific disciplinary terms (e.g., entomologist, soil chemist), while part-time researchers were designated as agricultural officers and experimentalists, or simply agricultural officers. In the Veterinary Department, researchers were designated as veterinary research officers. Most had degrees, many had additional diplomas, and some had postgraduate degrees. Contacts were maintained with research centers in the UK and South Africa, and with the Commonwealth Agricultural Bureaus when they were established in the late 1920s.

Although the dominant client group for agricultural research was the European farmers, throughout the period the department's research officers showed interest in African smallholder farming. As early as 1907, the manager of the Kibos Experiment Farm was devoting considerable time as plant instructor to working with farmers in the native reserves near Lake Victoria. These efforts included distribution of improved seed, native instruction in improved agricultural techniques, and establishment of crop suitability trials on experiment plots on the *shambas* (land) of local chiefs (DOA 1912). A plant instructor based at Mazeras conducted similar work prior to World War I in the native reserves on the coast. Most of this work was instructional, as was the instruction program at Kabete Farm, where the sons of local chiefs could come to be trained in improved farming methods in anticipation of either finding employment on settler farms or returning to the native reserves as progressive farmers. In the 1920s this task was taken over by Scott Laboratories, and by 1928 a new Native Agriculture School had been established at Bukura in Nyanza, along with 106 demonstration plots throughout the reserves that could also serve as sites for rudimentary investigative work. In 1929, work began at Scott Laboratories on a short-season maize variety, Muratha, which, as the director noted, would be of great value in the Kikuyu Reserve and in the short-season areas (DOA 1929, 46). In 1930, a census of native production was conducted in the reserves and included in the annual agricultural census of the colony. Smallholder mixed farming was promoted in the reserves, and field experiments using native methods as opposed to separate cropping were conducted at Scott Laboratories in 1931. The native reserve stations at Bukura and Kibarini were established and fully operational by 1937. Field experiments were also conducted at local native council seed farms (nineteen by 1938) and at a number of small plots throughout the reserves, mostly of a temporary nature, that were maintained with departmental funds and used for a variety of research, as required (DOA 1938, 96). Although the department placed most of its emphasis on instruction and extension, it used agricultural research as part of its strategy to transform native reserves into native estates, a vision put forward by the director in the 1920s.

Meanwhile, the British government was giving some thought to a regional approach to the governance of east Africa; indeed, plans for such a system were well in hand when the advent of World War II caused them to be set aside. However, the old German agricultural research laboratories at Amani in Tanganyika were renovated in 1927 as the East African Agricultural Research Institute (EAARI) (Story 1954) with a small team of specialists who were to work on problems common to the three countries of Kenya, Uganda, and Tanzania. Basic work on plant viruses was carried out, and the first soil map of east Africa was produced, with seminal work done on the concept of the soil catena. New strains of cassava resistant to mosaic virus were bred in pioneering research on that crop, some of which were tested out for Kenya in the 1930s at the Kabirini Station at the coast. The advent of World War II put a stop to many lines of research in Kenya, but the need to produce food to supply troops in northeast Africa gave rise to some shift of emphasis in research.

To summarize, the period between 1895 and 1945 witnessed the establishment of a dominant European large-scale and commercially oriented production system in Kenya's agricultural sector. This became the driving force behind the evolution of the agricultural research system in Kenya and the east African region. The same period also witnessed the emergence of a subservient African progressive farmer who benefited, albeit in a limited way, from the evolving agricultural research system. During this period, the bulk of the African farmers continued to adhere to subsistence production systems with minimal interaction with the emerging agricultural research system.

Agricultural Research in Kenya: 1945–63

Background

Following the outbreak of World War II, the Increased Production of Crops Ordinance was passed in Kenya to boost European settler production for war purposes. The ordinance provided for importation of machinery at subsidized prices and offered soft loans for operational expenses (Cone and Lipscomb 1972). Soon after the war, the European Agricultural Settlement Board (EASB) was established to facilitate subdivisions of large-scale farms to create room for European soldiers returning from the war. Further support for the European farmers was provided in 1950 through the European Revolving Settlement Fund. These measures, along with technological advances, land subdivisions, and capital ingestion greatly enhanced production efficiencies in European farms, consequently leading to a large-scale layoff of the African labor force. Subsequent return of these people to the African reserves further aggravated pressure on land and led to consequent political agitation (Odinga 1967).

In response to the tension building in the African reserves, the first ten-year development plan for African areas was launched in 1946 (KNA 1954; Cone and Lipscomb 1972). The plan undertook to establish an agricultural investigation center in each of the main provinces, and to develop a pasture research scheme for the colony. Local funds and the Colonial Development and Welfare Fund jointly financed the plan.

Political agitation in the African reserves intensified through the 1950s. Indeed, in 1952 a state of emergency was declared in response to the Mau-Mau rebellion. The following year, the colonial government appointed the East African Royal Commission to look into the problems of the African areas (Ochieng 1977). In its report, the commission noted that poverty prevailed in the African territories, and recommended that an agrarian revolution be launched within the African areas to alleviate the deteriorating conditions (Odinga 1967).

The recommended revolution came in 1954 in the form of the Swynnerton Plan (Cone and Lipscomb 1972; KNA 1953; KNA 1954). The plan marked a turning point in Kenya's agriculture by providing loans for individual African farmers to invest in agricultural production. The plan also provided for consolidation and registration of land, thus legitimizing the land enclosure process that had started as early as the 1920s in the African reserves (Swynnerton 1954).

On the political front, important constitutional changes took place between 1955 and 1960, paving the way for political independence and a new economic structure that was color-blind. In 1955, the colonial government lifted the ban on all African political activities (Bienen 1974); the following year the Coutts Report established voting qualifications for the Africans (Odinga 1967). In 1957, the Lyttelton Constitution

101

was passed to provide a multiracial government (Cone and Lipscomb 1972). The 1960 Macleod Constitution provided a common electoral roll for all races for the first time in Kenya's history (Cone and Lipscomb 1972; Odinga 1967). This plan gave Africans a majority in the Legislative Council.

In 1960, the Lancaster House Agreement resolved to dissolve European mixed farms and to sell them to the government for eventual subdivision and distribution to the Africans. This agreement also resolved to leave large-scale European farms relatively intact (Bienen 1974). This marked the dissolution of the color bar that had preserved the White Highlands for the exclusive use of Europeans. Thus, the African "progressive" farmer that had been evolving since the 1920s eventually joined the category of the privileged farmer in the eyes of the state.

The Agricultural Research System

Between 1946 and 1960, agricultural development policies in Kenya systematically moved to integrate African agriculture into the market, and to break racial restrictions in the White Highlands. This largely explains the extensive restructuring of the agricultural research system during this period. These changes in Kenya reflected the severe food shortages endured during the war. Thus, Britain launched a massive plant-breeding program to produce materials that could take advantage of chemicals and machinery. In the same vein, the British government set out to strengthen research in Kenya. Many of the recruits for research had basic science degrees with a subsequent diploma in agriculture from Cambridge or a diploma in tropical agriculture from Trinidad, or both. The few who had first degrees in agriculture were designated AOs working on the theme of general husbandry.

The ten-year development plan from 1946 to 1955, and the Swynnerton Plan (Swynnerton 1954) defined the character of the agricultural research system in Kenya. By the end of 1951, two new posts (development and research) at the assistant director level had been provided to accelerate the spread of cash cropping among smallholders. A team of district experiment officers (DEOs) worked in support of these offices. The organization of agricultural research in Kenya was fairly informal in the 1940s, with most of the central research based at the Scott Laboratories, but with a substantial amount of testing in the out-stations established in the previous two decades. A major step toward improving the organization was taken in 1952 with the establishment of a separate Research Division, headed by a chief research officer (CRO) and only thirty-four research officers at the time.

During this period, education among Kenyan nationals continued to lag; by 1956 only about 130 indigenous Kenyans had gained school certificates. Only in the 1960s did local university graduates begin to become available for recruitment as research officers. This was largely as a result of the establishment of Makerere University (1949) and of constituent faculties of agriculture in Kampala and veterinary medicine in Kabete (1956).

Research programming procedures were set out and all proposals were scrutinized in a meeting with all section heads and most of the research staff, together with policy guidance from senior Ministry of Agriculture (MoA) officials. Provincial assistant directors of agriculture (PADA) retained control of limited funds for district agricultural officers' (DAOs) experiments, but any larger proposals had to be referred to the CRO.

The Coffee Research Station remained under the MoA until 1963, but with strong association with the Coffee Board that provided a substantial part of the research funding from a levy on coffee exports. Linkage to both settler farmers and processors was very strong through specialized extension officers, ensuring close research attention to their technical problems. As smallholder coffee production grew, intensive advisory linkages were developed to new growers to maintain high standards. This meant that their problems also were presented to researchers.

The Tea Research Institute at Kericho was funded from its incorporation in 1951 (Owuor 1999) through the Tea Research Foundation by the combined tea industry of east Africa (and had substations in Tanzania and Uganda). Its relatively small research program, for the relatively few production problems in tea, was closely scrutinized by the Tea Research Council, and was almost entirely directed to large plantation systems of production. However, the Kenya Tea Development Authority (KTDA), after its formation in 1964 (Owuor 1999), was instrumental in ensuring that production methods were adapted to small-scale farming conditions. Coffee, tea, and pyrethrum were all well suited to intensive cultivation by smallholders.

During this period, the bulk of research investments were still directed to the needs of the settler farmers. In 1944, the government purchased a coffee estate at Ruiru to be a separate research station for coffee, and this was promptly staffed and opened in 1949. The Pyrethrum Board built laboratories at Nakuru to assess pyrethrin contents, and established a Pyrethrum Research Station at Molo for the improvement of crop materials and cultivation practices. Grassland research was moved in 1952 from its headquarters at Kabete to a Grassland Research Station at Kitale to service the important livestock sector. In 1955, a comprehensive maize research program was initiated at Kitale, after earlier intermittent work at Njoro, the Scott laboratories, and elsewhere.

The research program in the African reserves, begun in the 1930s, was primarily focused on determining good husbandry practices under different conditions, with survey programs of soils, vegetation, and rainfall used to help define those conditions. Building on the traditional trial plots at the local native council seed-farms and elsewhere in the reserves, land was acquired for General Investigation Centers (GICs) operating under the DAOs and used by extension, research, and other agencies. Housing and facilities were provided initially through the Ten-Year Development Plan, and later through Swynnerton Plan funds and the Colonial Development Fund. The GICs were established initially in the coast, central, and lake regions, and later in other areas such as Embu, Kisii, and Katumani.

Research staffing remained modest during this period. In 1945, the total full-time equivalent research staff was only about twenty-five at five stations, with a few substations in the White Highlands. However, personnel were rapidly boosted after the war. By 1947, the research staff was thirty-three, with a further nineteen AOs involved in some experiment work. By independence in 1963, seventy-seven researchers were working in agriculture and veterinary research within the MoA, of whom fourteen were nationals and the rest expatriate. Thirteen researchers were working in coffee and tea research, of whom two were nationals. Research at the young University of Nairobi was just beginning, with only about 1.5 person-years in applied research (Roseboom and Pardey 1993).

By independence, the research system had expanded substantially within the MoA. The Research Division had twenty-three research stations and GICs, while the Department of Veterinary Services (DVS) had only three research stations, plus four Veterinary Investigation Laboratories (VILs) (Pereira 1997). Compared to other African countries, this was a large number of research stations under the jurisdiction of the Research Division.

This period also witnessed the growth of regional research organizations intended to complement the efforts of the national research systems. Following World War II, the British government resumed its plans to develop regional east African facilities to serve the interests of Kenya, Uganda, and Tanzania. The East African High Commission (EAHC) was constituted in 1948. Among many other actions, it set up the East African Agriculture and Fisheries Council (EAA&FC) to coordinate and reinforce research in agriculture, animal industry, forestry, and fisheries (Pereira 1997). In particular, common specialist research services were established for agriculture, forestry, and animal diseases. In 1949, the East African Agriculture and Forestry Research Organization (EAAFRO) was set up at Muguga, near Nairobi, and absorbed the former EAARI from Amani. The East African Veterinary Research Organization (EAVRO) was also sited at Muguga. The British government bore all the capital costs and agreed to support half the recurrent costs; the other half came from a cess on taxes collected by the EAHC for the three countries.

These organizations were designed to supplement the national research services, and the key members of the reviewing body were the three senior research officers (later CROs) of the three countries, who joined in policy direction, approved programs, and were the main recipients of reports. In general, EAAFRO and EAVRO were staffed with specialists that the country services could not justify or afford separately at the time (such as virologists, forest entomologists, and agrometeorologists) and worked on problems common to at least two countries. They did not usually work directly with farmers or extension staff. This contrasted with the regional research organizations set up in West Africa that were focused on research on major commodities such as cocoa and oil palm. The research-oriented scheme of service for these organizations followed that of the British Scientific Civil Service. By the time of Kenya's independence in 1963, EAAFRO had twenty-five research staff, of whom three were nationals and the rest expatriate, and EAVRO had fourteen, all expatriate (Roseboom and Pardey 1993).

The EAAFRO and EAVRO were organized into disciplinary divisions and facilitated by east Africa–wide specialist committees. The main focuses of the program were agreed upon by research coordinating committees; with some considerable flexibility left for divisions to respond to emergencies and opportunities for collaboration with national or international research institutions. The detailed programs were worked out in the divisions. The organizations maintained their own research facilities at their headquarters. However, their experiment activities off-station relied on the facilities provided by the collaborating agencies.

In summary, this period saw a shift of research emphasis toward the farmers in the reserves, but mainly with respect to cash crops. The establishment of many GICs, later to become research stations, expressed this physically. Linkages between the national research services, extension, and large-scale settler farmers continued to be good, but in the reserves they were poor. Indeed, there were very many smallholder farmers, no trials directly on farms, and generally poor social contacts. The legacy of working with large-scale farmers, the researchers' dependence on stations for test sites, the traditional focus on variability of physical and biological rather than socioeconomic conditions, and the disciplinary mixes of the research staff may go a long way toward explaining why research work with smallholder farming systems lagged in Kenya. During the same period, the EAHC research organizations were set up. In both the national and regional organizations, an African scientific cadre was beginning to take root.

Agricultural Research in Kenya: 1963–78

Background

Kenya gained independence in 1963 and became a Republic in 1964. The period between 1963 and 1978 witnessed the consolidation of African commercial farming fully supported by the new independent state. The large-scale European farming subsector remained substantial throughout the period. Through the Land Development and Settlement Board (LDSB) and the agreements made at the Lancaster House Conference in 1961, a plan was laid out to facilitate African smallholder commercial farmers entering the former White Highlands (Leys 1975). In 1963, the Registered Land Act was passed to legally institutionalize African occupation of the former White Highlands (Gutto 1981). In 1966, the Mismanagement Land Order was passed, enabling the government to take over any large-scale farms considered mismanaged. The following year, Land Control Act 36 was passed to restrain land accumulation in the already adjudicated agricultural lands and to prevent fragmentation of land. In reality, however, this law neither checked land accumulation nor stopped unofficial subdivisions of land (Mbithi and Barnes 1975). In 1968, the Group Ranch Act was passed to facilitate funding for commercial ranching in the high-potential rangelands (Gutto 1981), serving the same purpose here as the Swynnerton Plan did for the high-rainfall areas of Kenya.

The 1970–73 Development Plan, recognizing the importance of exports, maintained a policy of supporting cash-crop production, while it committed itself to increasing resources for peasant and pastoral farming systems (Kenya Republic 1973).

105

During the plan period, the government committed itself to intensifying research for the smallholder farmers. In the 1974–78 Development Plan, the government further committed itself to supporting smallholder commercial production (Kenya Republic 1978). This subsector was viewed as an important source of employment. However, resource allocation would particularly favor those who produced high-value commodities. Agricultural research was expressly asked to cater to the needs of such commodities as tea, coffee, hybrid maize, pyrethrum, horticultural crops, sugar, and dairy goods.

The development policy of the new state was therefore completely consistent with the blueprint laid out in the last decade of colonial rule. An African commercial farmer category was well consolidated, joining the ranks of the European large-scale farmers. The two dominant social categories with highly similar interests would influence the character of the research system during the period under review.

The Agricultural Research System

Given the helpful policy environment, the research system grew rapidly in the 1970s. The big impact of the improved hybrid and synthetic maize had demonstrated the value of research. Elsewhere, great successes for agricultural research were being registered. In the Green Revolution in Asia, the massive benefits of research for wheat and rice production were being recognized. In Kenya, the economy was booming and government funds for research were available. Thus, the research system expanded, with an increasing danger of disjointed activities.

Most of the crops research was conducted in the MoA, with national research stations having responsibility for research on specific commodities such as maize, wheat, sugar, and horticulture. In 1963, the Coffee Research Foundation was set up as a parastatal research organization (funded by the coffee industry) with its own board of directors, but under the authority of the MoA. The Ministry of Livestock Development had its own Veterinary Research Division for research on animal diseases and animal production. The EAAFRO and EAVRO operated independently within the East African Common Services Organization (EACSO) in a supportive mode to the national services. The universities' research capabilities were embryonic in 1963, but grew steadily in strength throughout the period to 1978. However, staff members were primarily occupied with teaching. No institutional mechanism was in place to promote collaboration or joint research planning, apart from the disciplinary specialist research committees of EACSO. The MoA had by far the biggest research establishment and perhaps some responsibility for promoting coordination, but it had its own problems of research coordination among its dispersed stations. The number of research staff increased considerably over the period, from 137 in 1963 to 408 in 1978 (figure 5.1, table 5.1, Roseboom and Pardey 1993).

By far the biggest absolute increase (from 57 to 199) was in the Scientific Research Division (SRD) of the MoA. This presented the greatest management challenge to the system (NCST-ISNAR 1982). Figure 5.1 shows the same details for the Veterinary Research Division (VRD) and EAAFRO-EAVRO. In 1963, 86 percent of the research

Figure 5.1 Agricultural Research Staffing in the East African Agriculture and Forestry Research Organization (EAAFRO), East African Veterinary Research Organization (EAVRO), and Kenya Agricultural Research Institute (KARI), Muguga, 1961–85

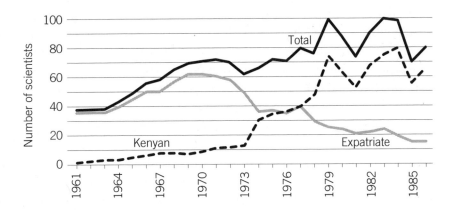

Table 5.1 Number of Research Staff in Research Organizations, 1963–78

Research Organization[a]	1963	1978	Increase (%)
Officers SRD	57	199	142
VRD	22	48	26
Forestry	4	6	2
Fisheries	1	24	23
CRF-TRF	13	29	16
NIB	0	11	11
EAAFRO	25	46	21
EAVRO	14	30	16
Academic	1	15	14
Total research staff	137	408	271

a. SRD = Scientific Research Division, VRD = Veterinary Research Division, CRF-TRF = Coffee Research Foundation Kenya - Tea Research Foundation Malawi, NIB = National Irrigation Board, EAAFRO = East African Agriculture and Forestry Research Organization, and EAVRO = East African Veterinary Research Organization.

staff was expatriate. Despite an urgent drive to replace expatriate staff, only a small supply of graduates was available from Makerere and from overseas universities. The number of research staff crept up slowly to 74 in SRD in 1968. Thereafter, the number rose sharply to 192 in 1973, after which numbers remained more or less steady until 1978.

Although most of the new recruits to the VRD had veterinary degrees from the relatively long-established Veterinary Faculty in Nairobi, most of the increase in the SRD was by recruitment of graduates with B.Sc. degrees in disciplines other than agriculture. Some of the rise was due to a relaxation of the rules on staff qualifications. At

107

independence, appointment to the position of agricultural research officer required an Honors degree in agriculture; appointment to a lower grade of assistant agricultural officer (AO-R) was possible with an Honors degree in an appropriate science. As with the former colonial government, promotion to agricultural research officer (ARO) required a postgraduate degree or diploma. This rule was relaxed in 1968 (Wapakala, personal communication, 1997), resulting in a surge in the numbers of research officers. Postgraduate training was still regarded as necessary to attain competence in research. Most of the new staff in the SRD were posted to the main national research stations. The 1981 Review found 188 researchers at ten national stations, with 55 researchers at eleven regional stations (NCST-ISNAR 1981).

Despite the increase in national staff, expatriate numbers continued to rise until 1972, before declining slowly. The raw numbers concealed a significant loss of research experience. As experienced expatriate researchers left, short-term contract officers replaced them that could not necessarily be relied upon to have tropical experience or knowledge of Kenyan conditions, particularly of smallholder farming systems. Similarly, the apparently steady numbers of national research staff do not reflect the very high rate of turnover of national staff as young postgraduates responded to better opportunities elsewhere in a competitive market (NCST-ISNAR 1982).

The rapid increase in numbers in the SRD, especially at more than twenty dispersed centers, imposed strains on the management and organization, particularly on the efficiency and focus of the formulation of the research program to be in line with national priorities and farmer requirements. The division continued to be directed by the CRO (later, director of research) with two senior officers at ministry headquarters, through the directors and officers in charge at stations. Although headquarters staff controlled the allocation of funds to stations, recruitment, and financial operations, they had little chance to give guidance on research programs, which were left to the station directors to devise in line with broad national policy, with or without coordination with other directors. To compound organizational problems, donor support ceased to be budgetary, and was provided for specific short-term projects, often in line with donor priorities.

As early as 1968, the minister for agriculture, recognizing the difficulties in managing agricultural research, appointed a team (headed by Rodenhiser) to study the situation. Among other things, the team observed that, "the present organization is not geared to meet the manifold current and projected needs of Kenya's growing agricultural industry" (Kenya Republic 1968). The report recommended creating a research department headed by a director, creating a research policy committee to advise the minister, better assessing research priorities for programs, more strongly coordinating within the system and with foreign donors, and a better scheme of service to attract and retain qualified and experienced scientists. It also recommended that all general investigation stations, except the coastal station at Mtwapa, be handed back to the Extension Service with the main emphasis on demonstrations, but remain available for experiments. Research funding was not perceived to be a major problem at the time. Indeed, throughout the period from 1963 to 1978, increases in funding kept pace with increases in research staff, maintaining a reasonable level of funding per scientist (Roseboom and Pardey 1993).

In response, the minister for agriculture established an Agricultural Research Advisory Council in 1969. At its inaugural and only meeting in 1969 (Kenya Republic 1969), the council endorsed many of the recommendations of the Rodenhiser Report and made several constructive and far-reaching recommendations, but few were adopted. This council did not become an effective body, partly because of its ad hoc nature. In any case, the council was created in the midst of an ongoing debate on the need for a wider national science and technology policy, and a need for a government institution to ensure close coordination among technical departments for the rational utilization of the available resources. This debate continued for another eight years before the enactment of the 1977 Science and Technology Act, which eventually created the National Council for Science and Technology (NCST) for that purpose. This closure was greatly enhanced by the collapse of the East African Community (EAC).

Following the EAC's collapse in 1977, regional research facilities and staff had to return to their respective countries. The Kenyan system had to absorb the Muguga establishment of EAAFRO and EAVRO. The mode of operation of the former EAC institutes had to change to match the new circumstances, with specialist functions shared with the Kenya centers at Kabete in particular. There was some uncertainty as to where the organizations would be placed in the government services, hence, the enactment of the 1977 Science and Technology Act. It took a further two years before the act was amended to facilitate establishment of statutory research institutes, which eventually changed the structure of the agricultural research system considerably (see chapter 6).

In this period, the role of international donors and international agricultural research centers (IARCs) increased considerably compared to previous periods. From 1963 to 1978 it was estimated that external technical assistance helped finance 329 projects. Close liaison was established with the International Laboratory for Research on Animal Diseases (ILRAD), the International Centre of Insect Physiology and Ecology (ICIPE), and the International Centre for Research in Agroforestry (ICRAF) after they were established in Kenya, but also with other IARCs as they expanded their international activities. The International Maize and Wheat Improvement Center (CIMMYT) and the International Potato Center (CIP) are good cases in point (NCST-ISNAR 1981).

In summary, the research services expanded considerably in this period, still concentrating closely on high-value commercial crops. Expatriate staff that dominated the establishment at independence was slowly replaced with national staff as they became available from the universities. The expansion of staff in coffee and tea research was relatively small and easy to manage on earlier patterns. The rise in numbers of research staff in the VRD, the EAAFRO, and the EAVRO was more extensive, but still manageable on existing patterns. However, the very rapid and large rise in staff numbers in many dispersed stations of the SRD required a radical reorganization that was

109

recognized as early as 1968. However, no effective changes were made during this period. Consequently, the whole system became unwieldy and uncoordinated as far as research programming and priority setting was concerned.

Agricultural Research in the Context of a Declining Agricultural Sector, 1978–86

Background

Following a long period of economic growth, the 1979–83 Development Plan (Kenya Republic 1983) aimed to spread the benefits of this growth to the rural population, while continuing to raise productivity in the intensive cash-crop sector. The basic strategy was poverty alleviation. This plan raised concern for the formerly marginalized regions (arid and semi-arid lands) and marginalized people (subsistence producers). The plan envisaged a Program of Action directed at Kenya's 1.7 million farms to achieve more productive farming across a broad field. Agricultural research was expected to play an unprecedented role in assisting these marginalized populations, bringing a sharp emphasis to a "farming systems' approach." This entailed conducting research with particular target groups in mind, taking into account their respective socioeconomic constraints as well as the physical and biological constraints of their environments. This approach recognized that technologies developed in the high-potential areas, assuming access to abundant resources, were not appropriate for subsistence producers and that research breakthroughs or technological innovations adaptable to smallholder mixed farming were not yet available for immediate adoption (NCST-ISNAR 1981).

This posed serious challenges to the organization of the research system, which had been focused on the cash crops of the high-potential areas, with almost all of its research staff and stations in those areas. Only the National Dry-land Research Station at Katumani specifically addressed crop and mixed farming in dry areas, with specialist help from Kitale, the National Agricultural Research Laboratory (NARL), and Muguga. The National Range Research Station at Kiboko addressed range management issues. In this period, moves were made to strengthen both stations with major projects funded by the Food and Agriculture Organization (FAO) and the United States Agency for International Development (USAID).

Considering the complexities of the new challenge—impacting on predominantly subsistence production systems of smallholders with mixed farming—the need for a stronger socioeconomic research program became more pronounced. To introduce this element into the research system, twelve new B.Sc. (agriculture) graduates who had taken the agricultural economics option were recruited into the SRD in 1978–79. The new recruits were posted to national and regional stations, with professional guidance in farming systems research from CIMMYT personnel based in Kenya (Collinson 2000). Despite successful training of most of them to Masters degree level, eleven had resigned by 1983. The complement of socioeconomists on the research staff remained small for a considerable period. This experience illustrates the difficulty of introducing a new perspective (FSA) in agricultural research with long-standing traditions. In the Kenya case, the tradition was based on a biophysical paradigm closely linked to the UK model and further reinforced by working closely with the European settler farmers, who subjected all new technologies to economic analysis on their own.

The Agricultural Research System

As the demand increased for agricultural research support to the subsistence producers in marginal areas, the system responded by increasing the numbers of research scientists. Given the apparently supportive environment, it was assumed that the total funding for agricultural research would increase from 1.1 percent agricultural gross domestic product (AgGDP) in 1979 to 1.5 percent AgGDP for the period 1983–93. It was also anticipated that the AgGDP would itself increase at 4 percent per annum, faster than the 3.5 percent achieved in the previous decade. In the circumstances, from 1978 to 1981 the number of research staff in the SRD rose from 199 to 288, and by 1986 to 419 (NCST-ISNAR 1982). The VRD, the Coffee Research Foundation (CRF), and KARI-Muguga experienced no such rise in numbers.

The increased numbers in the SRD further aggravated management problems already identified in the previous period. This problem was particularly acute in the context of the unexpected slowdown in the country's economy, as a result of which real funding for research was effectively frozen at its peak in 1978. The resultant rapid decline in funding per researcher in the SRD from about Ksh 860,000 in 1978, to Ksh 610,000 in 1981, to Ksh 367,000 in 1986 (all estimates at 1985 Ksh), was a serious problem for research efficiency (Roseboom and Pardey 1993). The consequent squeeze on operational funds for experiments, maintenance, and travel was inevitably more severe as total personal emoluments did not fall. Thus, the research system had to increasingly become more dependent on external donor funding for research operations with the consequent implications in management.

As noted earlier, the Amendment to the Science and Technology Act established KARI in 1979 to accommodate the EAC institutions in the first instance, with a view to including other agricultural research organizations. Yet the Ministry of Agriculture and Livestock Development (MoALD) resisted any such amalgamation of the SRD and the VRD into a semi-autonomous body. Moreover, the Agricultural Sciences Advisory Research Committee established at the same time, with a wide range of reviewing and coordinating functions, was not given adequate staff to make an impact. Thus, agricultural research proceeded in a relatively uncoordinated manner in several agencies, with no national plan derived from a national research strategy. The NCST wished to have a reference level for future planning, and in 1981 invited the International Service for National Agricultural Research (ISNAR) to assist in a review of the agricultural research system with wide-ranging terms of reference.

The review (NCST-ISNAR 1981) highlighted many of the same difficulties that needed resolution. These included the need for a unified system of governance and for a clear system for research planning and priority setting among and within programs, stronger socioeconomic research, rationalized research center mandates, and

111

stronger linkages between researchers, extension workers, and farmers. Difficulties to be resolved also included the need for postgraduate training for new recruits, an attractive scientific scheme of service, and improved resource allocation procedures to the centers.

As a follow-up to this report, ISNAR was requested in 1982 to help prepare a manpower and training plan, but no action was taken. The severe drought in 1984 appears to have rekindled interest in research and development. Thus, in 1985, the MoALD requested ISNAR to assist in formulating an agricultural research strategy and plan for Kenya. Many senior research staff from the ministry and KARI-Muguga took part in this comprehensive study, which eventually formed the basis for the National Agricultural Research Programme (NARP) in 1986.

In sum, a number of pressures from 1978 to 1986 forced Kenya's agricultural research system to restructure itself. First the new government chose to address the plight of African farmers in marginal areas, particularly in the arid and semi-arid areas. Second, the agricultural system continued to hire more scientists and staff in the hope that the economy would continue to grow and finance an expanded agricultural research program. Yet with reduced funding and the drought in 1984, there was no choice but to restructure the research system.

Research Impacts

The following section reviews methods and findings of studies on the adoption and impact of technologies. It also reviews studies of changes in productivity in the agricultural sector.

Maize

Maize was introduced into Kenya at the turn of the twentieth century. By 1903 it occupied 20 percent of the total food crop area, and by 1990 it covered 79 percent of the cereal crop area. Secondary data by Karanja (1990) show that area and yields more than doubled and production increased fivefold in the periods 1955–59 and 1985–88. The increase in maize production has been mainly attributed to the availability and adoption of modern technologies, especially hybrid seed and fertilizer.

The earliest maize breeding program began in Kitale when a full-time breeder was posted there in 1955 to develop late-maturing varieties for the wet highland tropics. The first hybrid was released in 1961. The second program to be initiated was based at Katumani, with the objective of developing improved varieties suitable for semi-arid conditions. The program in Embu was initiated to develop varieties suited to the mid-altitude zones. Research on cultivars for the hot and humid environment in the lowland tropics is based in Mtwapa, on the Kenya coast. A breeding program was recently initiated at Kakamega Center, to develop suitable cultivars for the zone referred to as moist transitional. The greatest achievement of the maize research team has therefore been in its provision of improved maize varieties suited for diverse agro-ecozones in Kenya.

Using a production function to estimate rates of return (ROR) to investments in Kenyan maize research in the period 1955–88, Karanja (1990) found that increases in research and extension expenditures and the spread of hybrid seed explain improvements in maize yield and the expansion of maize area. Fertilizers and higher producer prices also influenced maize area expansion. Maize research and extension and seed programs were shown to have contributed positively to higher maize yields and expanded production. Karanja (1990) further showed that a 1 percent increase in maize expenditure led to a 0.25 percent increase in yield and a 0.49 percent expansion in area. The resultant impact of research on output was reduced by about 0.35 percent because of the effect of area on yield and vice versa. After adjustments, he showed that a 1 percent increase in research expenditure raised output by almost 0.40 percent ten years later and this translated into an annual ROR of 68 percent in value terms. When estimated at the sample mean, the ROR was reduced to 53.5 percent. An ROR between 53.5 percent and 68 percent is excellent compared to alternative investments.

Karanja (1990) also estimated the effect of extension on research impact by creating a scenario that contained an effective seed program and a half-effective service, by halving the estimated effects of extension on yield and area. The effects of extension on research are felt through diminished impact on area and yield, which limits research impact. A half-effective extension system resulted in a reduced ROR of 46 percent. In another scenario, Karanja assumed a half-effective seed system with a fully effective one where the impact of seed on yield and area was halved. The resultant increase in output attributed to 1 percent increase in research expenditure had a 39 percent ROR. The results of the two scenarios indicate that both the extension and the seed programs in Kenya have contributed positively to the success of the maize research program, as is demonstrated by the fall in ROR any time the effectiveness of either of them slackened. The estimated ROR in the period 1955–88 shows a high payoff to investments in maize research. This productivity was made possible by complementarity between the research system, the seed industry, and the agricultural extension program.

Authors in Hassan (1998) analyzed the extent of diffusion of improved maize in Kenyan high- and low-rainfall areas and studied patterns of adoption of improved maize by agro-ecozone and farm-size group. They examined the efficiency of varietal turnover and the diffusion of hybrids and open pollinated varieties (OPVs), compared suitability performance and adoption of improved maize across agroclimatic zones and farmer groups, and assessed factors affecting the adoption of improved seed.

Authors in Hassan (1998) found adoption higher and more rapid in high-rainfall zones as compared to the semi-arid zones and lowland tropics. Large-scale farmers were the early adopters of new varieties of hybrid seeds, which were adopted more rapidly compared to OPVs. Adoption of hybrids in low-potential zones was much lower. The varied rates at which farmers in different agro-ecological zones adopted improved maize varieties and hybrids was attributed to the relatively later introduction of some kinds of improved seeds, information supplied about them to farmers, their actual availability, the economic gains they provided, and other seed qualities.

113

The lag period between release and 10 percent adoption by large-scale farmer groups was much shorter (two years) than that for farmers with smallholdings (eight years). However, even with the slow pace of adoption, small-scale farmers eventually achieved the same adoption rates as large-scale farmers. This difference was explained by accessibility of information, extension services, and credit. Adoption rates were much lower in high-potential zones where only hybrids are planted. About 37 percent of farmers who plant OPVs plant advance generations of the varieties, while only 3 percent of hybrid users did not buy new seed.

The late-maturing varieties (600 series) had small, weighted average age (WAA) index, indicating a rapid varietal turnover. This was attributed to the larger number of varieties released for the high-potential areas compared to medium- and low-potential areas, and the better seed supply system, transportation network, and extension services. Large-scale farmers also had faster replacement rates because of better access to information extension, and credit and risk-bearing capacity. The almost complete adoption of improved maize varieties in high-potential zones, coupled with the rapid replacement of varieties, indicates that the zones are in the post–Green Revolution phase of change, where yield gains are increased or stabilized through continued replacement of older varieties by newer improved germplasm. It was further found that the probability of adoption of improved maize was higher in favorable environments. This would be attributed to the relatively higher education levels, greater access to information, access to credit and markets, larger farms, and involvement of relatively younger farmers. Karanja, Renkow, and Crawford (2003) found that maize technology adoption in high-potential regions is likely to have substantially greater positive impacts on aggregate real incomes, but inferior income distribution outcomes compared to technology adoption in marginal areas.

Unlike the success story of hybrid seed, fertilizer use has remained low, especially in smallholder farms and in marginal areas. For this reason, the use of fertilizers on maize is considered to have potential for productivity growth in Kenya. Hassan (1998) examined the current state and determinants of fertilizer use on maize. Results indicate that fertilizers were adopted either at the same time as, or after the adoption of, seed. Indeed, fertilizers were found to have spread rapidly in zones favorable to maize production, and very slowly in unsuitable environments. This was because of the high risk associated with fertilizer use in marginal areas.

The study also found that Kenyan farmers apply lower amounts of organic fertilizer on maize crops than what is considered to be the economic optimum. Intensive farming, the low amounts of fertilizers applied, and the imbalance of nitrogen to phosphorous has led to mining of soil nitrogen. Despite the fact that levels of nutrients applied in smallholder farms have risen by 83 percent during the past decade, fertilizer application rates are still lower than optimum. Yield levels achieved under farmers' current practice were compared with economically optimum yield levels to derive the gap in maize yields. Results indicated that attainment of optimal fertilizer levels can potentially increase production by one million tons, and this will be mainly from the moist transitional and highland tropics zones.

In the early 1990s the government reformed its fertilizer marketing system. By 1993 prices were decontrolled and small-scale farms relied almost exclusively on the private sector and cooperatives for fertilizer. Even though domestic marketing costs of fertilizer were cut by 24 percent between Mombasa and Nakuru from 1990–95 to 1996–2000, fertilizer application rates are below levels recommended by the National Extension Service (Jayne et al. 2003).

Tea

Tea is an important cash crop in Kenya and is grown in high-altitude areas (1,400–2,700 m) with rainfall ranging between 1,800 and 2,500 mm. Commercial tea farming in Kenya started around 1925 by European settlers. In 1950, Kenyans were allowed to grow tea in high-potential areas (Kericho and Nyeri) on an experimental basis. In 1964, the Kenya Tea Development Authority (KTDA) was established to assist in expanding small-scale tea farming. The Tea Research Foundation (TRF) was established in 1980 to replace the Tea Research Institute of East Africa (TRIEA). Their research focus is mainly on the development of improved clones and appropriate production packages for improvement of yield and quality.

Since its inception, the smallholder tea sector has witnessed rapid growth in terms of area and production. Smallholders, with farms of less than 0.3 ha, account for 56 percent of total Kenyan tea production. In 1964, smallholders' tea production accounted for 16 percent of total area and 3 percent of production in the country. Today, it accounts for 70 percent of area and 56 percent of production. The annual growth rate in the smallholder sector compared to estates was much faster between 1964 and 1995. The area grew by 12.3 percent (compared to 3 percent) and production by 25 percent (compared to 6.4 percent). This dramatic growth in the smallholder tea sector is attributed to such factors as:

- The land expansion program,
- In-filling program to increase plant population per unit area (intensification program),
- The gradual replacement of unimproved seed with higher yielding clonal materials vegetatively propagated (the knowledge of propagating high-quality planting material was imparted to farmers for raising their own nurseries), and
- The fertilizer credit program.

Despite the rapid expansion of the smallholder sector, their yields have remained low compared to the estate sector.

Coffee

One of the biggest breakthroughs in coffee research was the release of an improved coffee hybrid, Ruiru 11 (R.11), by the Coffee Research Foundation (CRF), which gives higher yields and is resistant to two of the most important diseases in coffee—coffee berry disease and leaf rust. It was assumed that the new variety would be highly

115

attractive to coffee farmers who spend large amounts of money on chemicals to control diseases. Benefits accruing from adoption of R.11 are both in saving on costs of protection and in offering a crop assurance. Although 60 percent of estates (which produce 30 percent of Kenyan coffee) were eager to adopt the variety on a trial basis, the alternative modes of adoption pose problems in the takeoff of R.11. These include:

- Uprooting the older variety to replace it with R.11,
- Intercropping R.11 with old coffee stand, and
- Allocating new land to R11 (most preferred option).

The adoption rate was estimated at 36 percent, although estates located close to the CRF achieved adoption rates as high as 73 percent. Larger estates, particularly those under irrigation, tended to attain higher adoption rates. In all surveyed districts, the percentage of total sample area allocated to R11 ranged between 1.3 percent and 5.4 percent. Most estates (73 percent) had planted R.11 on new land, 28 percent had uprooted, and only 1 percent had interplanted. The future modes of establishment were 46 percent on new land, 34 percent uprooting old coffee, 18 percent interplanting, and 4 percent grafting (top working). The variety yielded 70–100 percent more than traditional varieties.

The Dairy Sector

Dairy production is second in importance after beef production. Dairy cattle are kept in almost all parts of the country (Ngigi 2003). The modern dairy industry dates back to the beginning of the twentieth century when exotic dairy bulls were imported into the country with a view to upgrading indigenous cattle through crossbreeding. The first attempts (by European settlers) were riddled with problems of disease and the choice of suitable breeds for the Kenyan environment. Their high mortality rates were reduced via crossbreeding and the discovery of acaricides to control tick-borne diseases. The 1954 Swynnerton Plan supported dairy production by African farmers. By the 1960s, dairy production had become an important source of income for Kenyan small-scale farmers. Currently, Kenya has a cattle population of fifteen million, of which only three million are of dairy type (Waithaka 1998). Smallholders own about 80 percent of the grade cattle for provision of milk, meat, draught power, and manure. The smallholders produce an estimated 1.8 billion liters of milk annually. Mean national yields of milk are between 1,200 and 1,500 kg per year per cow. The mean lactation yields for grade cattle are 1,500 L, and for zebu cattle, 1,501 L. Most of the milk from zebu cattle is consumed at home as compared to 37 percent of grade cattle milk.

Major achievements of past dairy research have been in animal health through the development of vaccines and curative drugs, crossbreeding of exotic and indigenous cattle, and improvement of the quality of animal feeds (Mwendia 1996). In an evaluation of dairy cattle fertility research in 1977, one of the conclusions was that dairy technologies were not accessible to smallholder farms, yet these farms contributed 82 percent of the national demand for milk. It was because of these findings

116

that the National Dairy Development Project (NDDP) was initiated in 1980 with the purpose of increasing dairy cattle productivity in smallholdings in high-potential areas. The NDDP was formulated in two parts: an adaptive research component to develop appropriate technologies for smallholders, and an extension component to extend these technologies to smallholders. The project was implemented in five phases, covering twenty-one districts in Kenya. Fifteen years after initiation of the first phase, a study was commissioned to check on the diffusion of dairy technologies in five leading districts in milk production. Kakamega district was also included. Two hundred households were sampled in each district. Twenty dairy technologies were defined and their adoption recorded qualitatively. The results showed that technologies were not adopted as a package, but as components of the package in all the districts, and that adoption varied widely with the technology as well as by district.

In a study carried out on the coastal belt (Nicholson et al. 1999), fifteen households participated in the elicitation process of the perceived impacts by households adopting the dairy technologies. Comparisons between adopting and nonadopting households were carried out on various issues. Ranking by the interviewed households indicated that the most important perceived impact resulting from adoption of grade cattle was increased milk consumption, followed by increased milk sales. The average cash income per month received from dairying was fifty-four times higher for adopting than nonadopting households. Dairy income in adopting households constituted more than one-third of total cash income, whereas dairy income from nonadopting households was less than 3 percent of total cash income. Adopting households hired more permanent labor to help in the increased workload. Results of the study showed no significant difference between the mean weight for height z score between adopting and nonadopting households. However, the mean z score for height for age was higher in children from adopting households. Moderate to severe stunting was more common in households without grade cattle.

Nyoro and Jayne (1999) carried out a study to assess the direction and magnitude of changes in agricultural productivity during the last twenty-five years in five regions of Kenya. They also examined the major factors affecting the changes in productivity. Their findings indicated that expansion in area has slowed down except in French beans, which suggests sources of future growth in production will be from intensification and the rising value of agricultural production due to the cultivating of higher-value crops. The authors also show growth rates in yields over different periods. Yields of most crops decline; they attribute this to stagnation in fertilizer use and the decline in fertility and quality of hybrid maize seed, among others.

Between 1970 and 1995, labor productivity is observed to have stagnated at Ksh 3,000 (1991–95 prices), and is shown to have increased between 1970 and 1979, but slightly declined in the 1980–85 period. A slight increase occurred in the period between 1985 and 1990, only to fall by as much as 23 percent in the period 1990–95. Land productivity increased by 12 percent in the period 1970–79, declined slightly in the following period, then recovered after 1985. In the period from 1985 to 1990, land productivity fell by 12 percent. The increased land productivity from 1970 to 1980 was a response to the adoption of high-yielding varieties of maize, increased use of fertilizers, and other yield-enhancing inputs. The slight drop in the period 1980–85 is attributed to the two droughts that occurred within that period. Nyoro and Jayne demonstrate that productivity of both factors varied across the regions, a fact that they attribute to the crop mixes in each region.

Owuor (1999) studied the determinants of agricultural productivity in Kenya. The study observed that fertilizers are used minimally in the coastal lowlands, the eastern lowlands, the western lowlands, and the marginal rain shadows. He attributes this to the production risk associated with erratic rainfall regions. Higher levels of fertilizer use are observed in four regions and this is translated to higher crop revenues. High levels of fertilizer use were observed in households growing horticultural and industrial crops. The study concludes that agricultural productivity varies with degree of commercialization, fertilizer use, and crop mix.

Lessons Learned

In this brief review of nearly a century of agricultural research in Kenya, the principal concern has been the evolution of public sector–based institutions in response to the changing needs of client groups, both dominant and subordinate, as well as changes in the relative power positions of the groups themselves. From this experience, several general themes can be identified. First, when viewed through the lens of history, clients for agricultural research and their needs appear dynamic, rather than static, in nature. Therefore, identifying and providing for the needs of these clients is an equally dynamic process.

Second, the application of models to solve problems for a changing clientele and to define and manage the research agenda developed in earlier times for other clients will be largely unsuccessful. Moreover, this lack of success will further exacerbate an already difficult research management situation, leading to crisis that can be resolved only through reorientation of the agenda to new client needs, and restructuring of the research system itself.

Third, in Kenya, agricultural research has responded to a changing clientele and its needs for most of the twentieth century by increasing the numbers of researchers and research facilities to cope with increases in the size of the client population. When the dominant client group for research was the small European-settler farm population, this strategy appeared to be successful in many instances. However, with the inclusion of the African smallholder in this clientele, the problem became one of accommodating more farmers, and of addressing an increasing complexity in farming systems and socioeconomic circumstances of the farm population. Therefore, the old solution of attempting to solve problems through staff increase could not cope with this growing complexity.

Fourth, the strategy of increasing staff numbers in anticipation of growth in the agricultural sector and AgGDP reached a crisis stage in the 1970s, as agricultural growth declined and the system had to cope with meeting new challenges from new clients with dwindling resources. Thus, a new dimension in management issues was added. Priorities shifted from addressing the possible range of scientific and technical problems to solving a limited number of prioritized research agendas with the limited resources.

Fifth, the inevitable change in clientele and the corresponding responses of the agricultural research system explains the need for a paradigm shift in agricultural research and management in Kenya. This shift is based upon more awareness of the dynamics of client circumstances and needs, and seeks to offer more flexibility in response by agricultural research to those needs.

Thus, in contrast to traditional responses of more staff and more facilities, future agricultural research and management will need to become visionary and analytical to respond to the changing circumstances and needs of the clients. This will require not only an appropriate disciplinary mix that effectively taps biophysical and social science knowledge, but also a suitable balance in simultaneously addressing the immediate and long-term needs of the clients. To sustain this balance, the system needs an effective organization and structure. This is the subject of the following chapter.

REFERENCES

Ambrose, S. H. 1984. The introduction of pastoral adaptations to the highlands of East Africa. In *From hunters to farmers. The causes and consequences of food production in Africa,* ed. J. Desmond Clark and Stephen A. Brandt, 212–39. Berkeley: University of California Press.

Anderson, Dennis M. 1989. Agriculture and irrigation technology at Lake Baringo. *Azania* 24:85–98.

Bienen, Henry. 1974. *Kenya: The politics of participation and control.* Princeton, N.J.: Princeton University Press.

Collinson, M. P., ed. 2000. *A history of farming systems research.* Wallingford, UK: CAB International and FAO.

Cone, L. Winston, and J. F. Lipscomb. 1972. *The history of Kenyan agriculture.* Nairobi: University Press of Africa.

Department of Agriculture, Colony and Protectorate of Kenya (DOA). 1908. *Annual report.* Nairobi and London: DOA.

———. 1912. *Annual report.* Nairobi and London: DOA.

———. 1922. *Annual report.* Nairobi and London: DOA.

———. 1928. *Annual report.* Nairobi and London: DOA.

———. 1929. *Annual report.* Nairobi and London: DOA.

———. 1931. *Annual report.* Nairobi and London: DOA.

———. 1933. *Annual report.* Nairobi and London: DOA.

———. 1937. *Annual report.* Nairobi and London: DOA.

———. 1938. *Annual report.* Nairobi and London: DOA.

Gutto, Shadrack B. O. 1981. Law, rangelands, the peasantry and social classes in Kenya. *Review of African Political Economy* 20:41–55.

Hakansson, T. 1989. Social and political aspects of intensive agriculture in East Africa. In *History of*

119

African agricultural technology and field systems, ed. John E. G. Sutton. Special Volume *Azania* 24:12–20.

Harlan, Jack R., Jan M. J. De Wet, and Ann B. L. Stemler. 1976. Plant domestication and African agriculture. In *Origins of African plant domestication,* ed. Jack R. Harlan, Jan M. J. De Wet, and Ann B. L. Stemler, 3–19. Netherlands: Mouton Publishers.

Hassan, Rashid M., ed. 1998. *Maize technology development and transfer: A GIS application for research planning in Kenya.* Wallingford, UK: CAB International.

Jayne, T. S., J. Govereh, M. Wanzala, and M. Demeke. 2003. Fertilizer market development: A comparative analysis of Ethiopia, Kenya, and Zambia. *Food Policy* 28:293–316.

Karanja, Daniel D.1990. The rate of returns to maize research in Kenya (1955–88). Master's thesis, Michigan State University.

Karanja, D. D., M. Renkow, and E. W. Crawford. 2003. Welfare effects of maize technology in marginal and high potential regions of Kenya. *Agricultural Economics* 29:331–41.

Kenya National Archives (KNA). 1953. *Agriculture Department. Policies.* AGR/KSM/1/499. Nairobi: Government Printer.

———. 1954. *Agriculture Department: Plan to intensify the development of African agriculture.* AGR./KSM./1/525. Nairobi: Government Printer.

———. 1962. *Memorandum on the Masai land question and the London Constitution Conference.* Mac/Ken/100/1. Nairobi: Government Printer.

Kenya Republic. 1968. *A critical review and recommendations by the agricultural research survey team.* Nairobi: Government Printer.

———. 1969. *A report of the first meeting of the Agricultural Research Advisory Council.* Nairobi: Government Printer.

———. 1973. *Development plans 1970–73.* Nairobi: Government Printer.

———. 1978. *Development plans 1974–78.* Nairobi: Government Printer.

———. 1983. *Development plans 1979–83.* Nairobi: Government Printer.

Leys, Colin. 1975. *Underdevelopment in Kenya. The political economy of neo-colonialism.* Berkeley: University of California Press.

Mbithi, Philip, and Carolyn Barnes. 1975. *Spontaneous settlement problem in Kenya.* Nairobi: East African Literature Bureau.

Mutiso, Gideon-Cyrus. 1975. *Kenya politics, policy and society.* Nairobi: East African Literature Bureau.

Mwendia, C. W. 1996. Past dairy research in Kenya: Success and failures. In *Priority setting for the KARI Dairy Program,* ed. KARI. Nairobi: KARI.

National Council for Science and Technology-International Service for National Agricultural Research (NCST-ISNAR). 1981. *Kenya's agricultural research system: A report to the government of Kenya.* The Hague: NCST-ISNAR.

———. 1982. *A manpower and training plan for the agricultural research system in Kenya, 1983–1987.* The Hague: NCST-ISNAR.

Nganga, D. K. 1981. What is happening to the Kenyan peasantry? *Review of African Political Economy* 20:7–14.

Ngigi, Margaret. 2003. Successes in African agriculture: The case of smallholder dairying in Eastern Africa. Paper presented at the InWEnt, IFPRI, NEPAD, CTA Conference, Successes in African Agriculture, Pretoria, 1–3 December 2003.

Nicholson, Charles F., Philip K. Thornton, L. Mohammed, R. W. Muinga, D. M. Muwamachi, E. H. Elbasha, S. J. Staal, and W. Thorpe. 1999. *Smallholder dairy technology in Coastal Kenya: An adoption and impact study.* International Livestock and Research Institute (ILRI) Impact Assessment Series No. 5. Nairobi: ILRI.

Nyoro, J. K. 1985. *Economic implications of introducing new hybrid variety of Arabica coffee in Kenya.* Vol. 51. Nairobi: Kenya Coffee.

Nyoro, J. K., and T. S. Jayne. 1999. *Trends in regional agricultural productivity in Kenya.* Proceedings of the conference on strategies for raising productivity in agriculture, May 1999, Kenya Agricultural Monitoring and Policy Analysis Project (KAMPAP), Tegemeo Institute, Egerton University.

Ochieng, William R. 1977. *The second word. More essays on Kenyan history.* Nairobi: East African Literature Bureau.

Odinga, Oginda. 1967. *Not yet Uhuru. The autobiography of Oginda Odinga.* New York: Hill and Wang.

Owuor, P. O. 1999. Agrotechnology of tea in East Africa (Kenya, Uganda and Tanzania). In *Global advances in tea science,* ed. N. K. Jain. Delhi: Aravali Books International.

Pereira, C. 1997. *The role of agricultural research in the development of Kenya before independence.* Bangor-Kenya Agricultural Research Institute (KARI) Review of Kenyan Agricultural Research Vol. 1, June. Nairobi: KARI.

Robertshaw, Peter. 1990. *Early pastoralists of south-western Kenya.* Memoir No. 11. Nairobi: British Institute in Eastern Africa.

———. 1993. The beginnings of food production in southwestern Kenya. In *The archaeology of Africa. Food, metals and towns,* ed. Thurstan Shaw, P. Sinclair, Andah, A. Bassey, and A. Okpoko, 358–71. London: Routledge.

Roseboom, Johannes, and Philip G. Pardey. 1993. *Statistical brief on the national agricultural research system of Kenya.* International Service for National Agricultural Research (ISNAR) Statistical Brief No. 5. The Hague: ISNAR.

Shaw, Timothy. 1976. Early crops in Africa: a review of the evidence. In *Origins of African plant domestication,* ed. Jack R. Harlan, Jan M. J. De Wet, and Ann B. L. Stemler, 107–53. Netherlands: Mouton Publishers.

Story, H. H. 1954. *Basic research in agriculture: A brief history of research at Amani, 1928 to 1947.* Nairobi: East African Standard.

Sutton, John E. G. 1989. Editor's introduction: Fields, farming and history in Africa. In *History of African agricultural technology and field systems,* ed. John E. G. Sutton. Special Volume *Azania* 24:6–11.

Swynnerton, R. J. M. 1954. *A plan to intensify the development of African agriculture in Kenya.* Nairobi: Kenya Department of Agriculture.

Vansina, Jan. 1996. A slow revolution: Farming in subequatorial Africa. In *The growth of farming in Africa from the equator southwards,* ed. John E.G. Sutton. Special Volume *Azania* 29–30:15–26.

Waithaka, Michael. 1998. *Integration of a user perspective in research priority setting: The case of dairy technology adoption in Meru, Kenya.* Kommunikations und Beratung 22. Weikersheim, Germany: Margraf Verlag.

Wigboldus, J. S. 1996. The spread of crops into sub-equatorial Africa during the Early Iron Age. In *The growth of farming in Africa from the equator southwards,* ed. John E. G. Sutton. Special Volume, *Azania,* 121–29.

Wolff, Richard D. 1974. *Britain and Kenya, 1870–1930. The economics of colonialism.* Nairobi: Transafrica Publishers Ltd.

6

Building Agricultural Research Systems in Africa

CYRUS G. NDIRITU, FRED J. WANGATI,
AND JACOB KAMPEN

Introduction

Most agricultural research in Kenya is carried out within government institutions, including universities, research foundations, and other facilities sponsored by agro-industry. The basic structure of the larger research institutions comprises a directorate, central laboratories, information and administrative services, and a network of research centers and trial sites located within major commodity-growing areas or ecological zones.

In this chapter, we use the term "restructuring" to describe the changes made in the various organs of an institution, in their roles and responsibilities, and in the way they interact internally and externally. "Rationale" relates to the purpose and objectives of restructuring. The "process" includes the methods used, the procedures followed, and the time frame in which changes are implemented. The "practice" is the way in which the new structure operates and its achievements in relation to the objectives of the restructuring. The historical evolution of agricultural research in Kenya is described and analyzed in detail in chapter 5. This chapter will therefore concentrate on the rationale, process, and results of the restructuring that took place soon after the collapse of the East African Community (EAC) in 1967.

Background to the Restructuring of the National Agricultural Research System (NARS) in Kenya

The purpose and focus of agricultural research in Kenya up to the late 1950s was to support the production of export crops, such as coffee, tea, and pyrethrum, which were produced on European-owned large farms. The basic research structure at this stage was comprised of a small administrative unit in the Ministry of Agriculture (MoA), a central research laboratory for specialized analysis, and some experiment sites located in the main production zones for the major commodities. The initial restructuring of agricultural research in Kenya was carried out shortly after independence in 1963, when research emphasis shifted from large farms to smallholder agriculture. This shift made it necessary to expand publicly funded agricultural research in order to

123

support the larger variety of crops and livestock enterprises that characterize small-holder agriculture. Research divisions were set up in the Ministries of Agriculture and of Livestock Development. The experiment sites and research subcenters already operational were formalized into research stations and substations and increased in size to cover the major agro-ecologies.

As the research agenda and hence the research infrastructure expanded, dissatisfaction grew among scientists and research managers with the bureaucracy necessitated by civil service procedures. Rules governing procurement of goods and services, and staff recruitment and promotion, and the way in which they were applied made it increasingly difficult to efficiently operate field and laboratory experiments and to retain the more productive scientists and technicians. In this respect, the apparent simplicity and efficiency of research management in the coffee and tea research facilities, which had been accorded the status of semiautonomous research foundations under the sponsorship of the respective commodity marketing boards, were the envy of research managers operating under the civil service. The initial motive for the subsequent restructuring was more a desire to reduce bureaucracy and simplify administration rather than a strongly felt need to improve the relationship between research and potential users of research results, or the efficiency of research in terms of priority setting and resource use. The need for autonomy was felt especially at the higher levels of institutional management, and they strongly advocated change. Although pressure for change had been building up for a long time, the second restructuring was basically triggered by the EAC's collapse.

The EAC

The EAC was created in 1967 as a political organization to replace the East African Common Services Organization (EACSO). The most important change brought about by the creation of the EAC was the institution of a higher political forum, the "Authority," through which the presidents of Kenya, Tanzania, and Uganda would meet periodically to give policy direction and endorse any major decisions of the Ministerial Council, which guided the operation of the EAC. For about a decade, this forum worked well, elevating the status of EAC cooperation to the level of an intergovernmental organization. The regional agricultural research programs of the EAC were organized and carried out under the East African Agriculture and Forestry Research Organization (EAAFRO) and the East African Veterinary Research Organization (EAVRO). These organizations had their headquarters and main specialized laboratories located at Muguga in Kenya, but EAAFRO had a large sorghum and millet research program based in Uganda, and a sugarcane research program based in Tanzania.

The sharing of research responsibilities between the national and regional programs worked well because the research agendas of the EAC institutions were determined in consultation with the national research services on the basis of complementarity and comparative advantage. For example, plant virology research was assigned to EAAFRO and vaccine development to EAVRO to facilitate joint use by the three member states of the expensive equipment and the few specialized personnel available. In the same spirit, extension activities remained the responsibility of national programs. On behalf of the region, the EAC institutions achieved high-quality research, and some of the most classical research on natural resources was carried out regionally, using experiment catchments located in the partner states. An international journal was also published by the regional institutions. However, in due course, relationships among the three member countries became strained by perceived differences in economic and social-political benefits of the common services to the individual countries and, to some extent, because of some basic differences in political and economic policies. The collapse of the EAC was triggered by changes in political leadership in one of the countries, rendering the apex institution, the EAC Authority, totally inoperative in 1977.

The sudden breakup of the EAC created considerable confusion at the national level. Although it was relatively easy to nationalize the institutions and physical infrastructures located in the respective countries pending the division of EAC assets and liabilities, regional programs ceased to exist and staff had to be accommodated within the national public services. The resulting need to integrate the services, and to absorb the now redundant Kenyan personnel into the Government of Kenya (GoK) public services, created a sense of urgency in dealing with the organizational structure for research. In Kenya, where the headquarters of EAAFRO and EAVRO existed alongside strong national agricultural research services and infrastructure under the Ministries of Agriculture and of Livestock Development, converting EAAFRO facilities into the Agriculture Department, and EAVRO facilities into the Veterinary Research Division (VRD), alleviated the immediate problem.

Although the interim measures taken lessened, or at least postponed, the immediate problem of staff integration into the national public service, the operation of a dual research system with a component restricted to the facilities at Muguga proved unworkable and resulted in undesirable duplication of effort. Fortunately, a major debate had already been initiated under the National Council for Science and Technology (NCST) on the merits of reorganizing all research into semiautonomous parastatal institutions operating outside the mainstream civil service, along the models of the already well established Coffee and Tea Research Foundations.

The Coffee Research Foundation (CRF)

The CRF is a private commodity research organization run by coffee farmers and financed by a parastatal marketing organization, the Coffee Board of Kenya (CBK). However, the CRF has a strong link with the government, which is represented on the Board of Management. Research at CRF is mission-oriented, with farmers determining the problems to be researched through their representatives on the CRF Board. The board is empowered and makes decisions on the activities and management of CRF affairs quickly and independently. Where necessary, government approval on policy matters is facilitated by government representatives as members of the board and its standing committees. The Coffee Research Advisory Committee (CRAC) has additional farmer representation and advises the board on matters of research planning, execution, and evaluation.

The CRF model of management has succeeded for a variety of reasons, the main one being that a core of assured funds is provided through a levy on coffee. Although this levy has increased from 1 to 3 percent during the past few years, it does not provide enough funds to cover all CRF expenditure requirements.

Originally, the coffee research services had an Advisory Section, which rendered direct technical advice to both large- and small-scale growers. The advisory services were taken over by the MoA in 1967. The foundation has instead a Research Liaison, Training, and Public Relations Section through which contact with the ministry and the coffee industry is maintained. In response to increasing demand for extension services, the CRF built a training center in 1979 that was later expanded and finally completed in 1996. The CRF reaches coffee farmers in many ways, including training of farmers and their agents, publications, field and open days, advisory visits, and weekly radio programs.

The Tea Research Foundation of Kenya (TRFK)

Brooke Bond Kenya (BBK) started tea research in Kenya in 1949. As the tea industry flourished, the research department expanded its services to cover the whole of the tea industry in Kenya, and later Uganda and Tanzania. In 1951, the research department was renamed the Tea Research Institute of East Africa (TRIEA). The institute was registered in Uganda in 1957 and in Tanzania in 1959, with one station in each country. When research collaboration among the three east African countries collapsed, the Kenya government, through its Tea Board, took over the tea research station in Kericho and established the present TRFK in 1980 as a public limited company (PLC).

The TRFK is a parastatal organization managed by a board of directors comprising representatives of tea farmers and other stakeholders including the relevant government ministries. The board makes all major decisions, such as approval of budget and capital expenditure for development. It has also established two committees that meet more frequently and can be assembled quickly to deal with urgent matters. The Staff and Finance Committee (SFC) monitors implementation of policy guidelines in administration and financial management. The Research Advisory Committee (RAC) is responsible to, and assists, the board in formulating research strategies, and guides implementation of research programs through planning, monitoring, and evaluation through meetings held twice annually. Membership of the RAC includes experienced representatives of the tea industry, academicians from universities, and representatives of other stakeholder organizations. A board member or a senior representative from the tea industry, with long experience in corporate culture and management skills in plantation crops, chairs the committee.

The Field Advisory Services Department disseminates proven technology to the tea industry, advises on specific problems encountered in tea production, and provides feedback to researchers. The department also organizes regular field visits to the tea growers to advise on tea management. Seminars and workshops addressing specific problems are held regularly both at the foundation estate and on the growers' or producers' premises. Training is also organized for foundation and tea industry personnel in close liaison with other foundation departments.

Unlike most agricultural enterprises, tea farming in east Africa is relatively free from problems of disease and pests. It has therefore been possible to take care of the crop with a relatively small research outfit, concentrating mainly on breeding, selection, and multiplication of clones that yield more and better quality tea, and improvement of agronomic techniques. However, the processes of tea curing, drying, and milling are critical for attaining the desired quality in processed tea. The research institute therefore works closely with the tea factories in monitoring and modifying as necessary the various stages of manufacturing processes.

The TRF model is interesting from a resource provision and management viewpoint in that the tea industry started and maintains the research through cess levied on tea growers. In 1997, cess was levied at the rate of 46 Kenyan cents (US$0.06) per kilogram of processed tea. The cess is collected and controlled by the Tea Board of Kenya. In addition to the cess, the foundation also generates 30 percent of total expenditure through the sale of green leaf produced from its own commercial/demonstration tea estate.

Although the TRF is small and reasonably efficient, it also has some weaknesses that limit its capacity to serve the large tea industry effectively. For example, the small infrastructure of substations does not allow adequate regional adaptability trials of released technology and assessment of region-specific client needs. The TRF model has nevertheless served the tea industry well. The strong representation of the industry's stakeholders on the governing board and operational committees allows them to set the research agenda, to monitor both the administrative and financial aspects of management of the TRF, and hence to build confidence in the industry in order to ensure sustainable funding of the organization.

Restructuring Solutions

The problem of integration of the ex-EAC and GoK research systems and allocation of research responsibilities was therefore passed on to the Agricultural Sciences Advisory Research Committee (ASARC), established under the 1997 Science and Technology Act. This act was eventually amended in 1979 to provide for the establishment of semiautonomous research institutes. Each institute would have a board of management drawn from stakeholders and would operate under the supervision of the most relevant government ministry, through which it would be funded. The act also provided for the transfer of research resources and programs from relevant government ministries to the newly created research institutes. The NCST and the relevant advisory research committees were given the responsibility of assessing the programs and financing priorities of each institute and of advising the government on the budgets required to execute the programs. As semiautonomous government institutions, the research institutes were expected to provide:

- Management independence combined with assured government financial support required for the execution of short- and long-range research programs in response to present and future needs, and the flexibility to ensure continuous improvement of the research management systems;
- A research environment in which creative research could be undertaken through an effective management structure; and
- Capacity to attract and retain research personnel of outstanding caliber, capable of finding solutions to national development problems.

The perceived advantages of the parastatal as opposed to the management structure of the civil service were:

- The replacement of inefficient bureaucracy associated with government departments by an independent board of management. The board was expected to have sufficient authority to formulate and implement rules and regulations governing all aspects of institute operations, taking into consideration the particular needs of an efficient agricultural research organization. These included the hiring, promotion, discipline, and even dismissal of staff, and procurement of other goods and services essential to the organization.
- The board of management could be mobilized at short notice to deal with urgent issues that might affect timely execution of research programs.
- The board would facilitate participation of farmers and other stakeholders in research priority setting and evaluation of the usefulness of research results.
- The board would have authority to generate and utilize revenues and to negotiate directly with donors and the private sector for financial support for research programs.

Formation of Kenya Agricultural Research Institute (KARI)

The Process

After several meetings and consultations with the main stakeholders, the ASARC recommended that all national agricultural (including livestock and forestry) research programs and facilities operating under government ministries should be reorganized under a new semiautonomous government research institution to be known as the Kenya Agricultural Research Organization. The NCST endorsed the ASARC recommendations, but believed that the title "organization" would encourage the establishment of a large amorphous institution with limited opportunity for integrating and coordinating program planning and execution. Thus the NCST recommended that the name of the proposed institution should be KARI. In addition to taking over the facilities of the Agricultural Research Division (ARD) and the Veterinary Research Division (VRD) at Muguga, KARI would also coordinate all agricultural research carried out by government departments.

However, serious difficulties emerged in the course of transferring research services to a parastatal structure. The first major issue concerned the future operation of the extensive network of research stations that were also used by the concerned ministries for plant, seed, and livestock multiplication, and extension activities. In 1981, the MoA, which was then responsible for KARI, and the NCST commissioned a major study with the help of the International Service for National Agricultural Research (ISNAR) on the content and structure of the research to be undertaken under KARI. A study on human resources development (ISNAR 1981) recommended that KARI should not simply take over all the agricultural research functions, stations, and responsibilities of the ministries; rather it was argued that amalgamation of agricultural research functions and division of responsibilities should be mutually agreed upon among the main stakeholders. The study also recommended rationalization of research facilities under KARI in which a limited number of key national and regional (ecoregional) research centers, each with a critical mass of scientists, would be identified, leaving the smaller stations to serve as trial and extension sites.

The second major issue was the decision by the KARI board that it would fill all positions in the new structure on a competitive basis, thus blocking automatic transfer of staff from the existing research services. This created insecurity among research staff, many of them having attained senior positions through experience rather than formal qualifications. The government was also duty bound to retain all staff until they reached retirement age.

The rationalization exercise therefore proved difficult to implement and KARI in its early days failed to develop as envisaged. The KARI's research activities remained confined to Muguga despite its intention to relocate its headquarters.

The Practice and Rationale

During the first seven years of KARI's existence, its research activities remained minimal while most of the agricultural research activities in Kenya continued to be managed under the Scientific Research Division (SRD) and the Veterinary Research Division (VRD). Research was also carried out by research foundations (e.g., for coffee and tea), and by several private-sector enterprises such as the East African Industries (oilseeds), and the Kenya Seed Company. Research in forestry and agroforestry, wildlife, and range management also continued under the Ministry of Environment and Natural Resources. Hydrology and irrigation research was carried out under the Ministry of Water Development. Linkages among, and coordination of, the different components remained entirely inadequate. Other issues of concern were that:

- The proliferation of small donor-financed projects, each with different management systems, research priorities, and objectives, resulted in duplication of efforts between centers and programs, and inefficient use of national scientists and technical assistance.
- Without comprehensive management systems, appropriate allocation and effective utilization of all available research resources and facilities could not be assured. This was exacerbated by insufficient delegation of responsibility and

129

hence inadequate design, and the implementation of research programs for key commodities, factors, and disciplines. Procedures for research management to supervise, monitor, and evaluate research programs and research staff needed improvement. Research-farmer linkages and information dissemination were inadequate.

- Staff recruitment and deployment was not related to research needs because of lack of a rational policy for establishing agricultural research facilities. Inadequate career development opportunities and training caused scientists to lose motivation, resulting in a high turnover of staff.
- The proportion of the operating budget for agricultural research needed to pay staff (76 percent in 1985) was too high, leaving an insufficient budget for the execution of programs and for the maintenance of research infrastructure.
- Linkages were weak and improved contacts were required within the MoA, particularly with extension, input supply, credit, and animal health; and with outside institutions such as the universities, International Agricultural Research Centers (IARCs), and the private sector.
- The formulation of research programs failed to adequately recognize the site-specific demands for new technologies by extension, farmers, and private enterprise.

To deal with these problems, the GoK in 1984 developed a new research strategy, prepared a proposal to consolidate the several agricultural research institutions and numerous projects into one single manageable institute, and set long-term priorities for research. A study in 1985 identified major issues facing agricultural research and recommended solutions; and in 1986 the government restated its policies on agriculture (GoK 1986). Following these recommendations, the government then organized a task force to prepare a detailed outline of actions that would need to be taken to revitalize the Kenya agricultural research system. This work culminated in a report, entitled "Kenya National Agricultural Research Project" (NARP), which has been a key instrument for restructuring KARI. The report described the vision and strategy for the long-term development of the Kenya Agricultural Research Program, and the immediate requirements for implementing the first phase of this program (NARP-I). Agricultural research requires long-term support in order to yield results and respond effectively to consumer demands. Several research activities, such as breeding programs, often need a time frame of ten years or more to produce results. Thus, the strategic planning of research programs was viewed with a ten- to fifteen-year time horizon. However, considering that planning research activities over a long period involves many uncertainties, the NARP-I Project was therefore designed as the first five-year time slice of a much longer commitment to support the national program. The main objectives of NARP-I were to:

- Focus on priority research programs with a significant likelihood of high and early returns to investments,

130

- Develop technologies that contribute to increased productivity, particularly of small holdings,
- Intensify producer participation in research program formulation, and
- Strengthen linkages between research and other agricultural services, such as extension, and between the new agricultural research establishment and other institutions involved in agricultural research, particularly the universities, private enterprise, and international organizations.

All donors participating in the NARP understood and accepted the implications of a long-term program. Thus at this early stage the need was clearly understood of distinguishing between the long-term development of Kenya's agricultural research and a first phase attempt or "project" to begin implementation, which subsequent projects would follow. However, some confusion remained between the long-term "program" objectives and the necessarily more modest goals of its first phase (NARP-I).

The GoK, KARI, and donors therefore agreed that NARP-I would be implemented as an integrated program rather than as isolated single-commodity projects. Ensuring such implementation of the separately appraised donor-supported projects, which are all part of NARP, required strengthened mechanisms for donor coordination. The GoK, through KARI, was expected to:

- Establish clear research priorities and adhere to these while coordinating external aid.
- Develop a long-term strategy, consisting of a KARI corporate plan and appropriate crop, livestock, factor, and disciplinary research programs.
- Develop and introduce improved management systems from headquarters to field research activities. These improved systems would lead to better supervision of individual research programs, stations, and staff; more stringent budgeting and financial management; and more meaningful reporting, monitoring, and evaluation.

The NARP-I Action Plan

The major components of the NARP-I action plan are given in the following.

Organization and management

All research functions and activities scattered between the former EAC establishments, the SRD, and the VRD were integrated into a single management organization—the new KARI—governed by a board of management with statutory functions as defined in the amended Science and Technology Act. The board's Research and Technical Committee and that on Finance and Administration were to oversee the institute's management. The KARI budget and accounting system were rationalized so as to provide up-to-date management information on budgets, expenses, and funding per research center and program.

131

Rationalization of Research Centers

The existing research centers were reorganized into National (NRC) and Regional (RRC) Research Centers. The RRCs were assigned zonal responsibility on a district and agroclimatic basis to identify production constraints and devise, test, and apply technological packages suited to these zones. The NRCs were charged with commodity, factor, and disciplinary research, covering the national territory; they also maintained links with other national and international research institutes.

Research Priorities

A systematic procedure of arriving at priorities in research activities was developed. It took into account:

- Relative farm-gate value of commodities,
- Area cultivated and probability of expansion,
- Present and potential contribution to economic development, food security, nutrition, employment, and market potential,
- Probability of success, including the state of knowledge and the scope for transfer of results in Kenya and internationally, and
- Research scale, costs, and time horizon.

"Specialist Committees" were to periodically review the long-term program strategies in close cooperation with the program coordinators and KARI management. Responsibility for implementation of agreed upon research programs was, however, assigned to the relevant research centers.

New Funding Arrangements

An Agricultural Research Fund (ARF) was established in order to create more competitiveness, to bring in the full capacity of the Kenya national agricultural research systems (NARS; including the universities and private sector), to contribute to agricultural technology development and ensure more dependability and timeliness of funding for applied agricultural research. Peer-review assessments were used to select research projects to be supported, and an independent ARF Management Committee made the award of grants.

Human Resource Management

The KARI initiated training programs for various cadres of staff, and introduced an improved, although inadequate, Scheme of Service in order to attract and retain qualified staff.

External Financial Support

External support was sought in order to speed up restructuring of the agricultural research system to help Kenya meet its future role in a rapidly changing technological environment. The KARI developed procedures for coordination of external assistance with a view to supporting priority programs. The main components of donor support under NARP-I included:

- Assistance for the restructuring of KARI as a semiautonomous government agency to undertake research planning, management, budgeting, supervision, reporting, and training.
- The development of KARI's management and research capacity through staff training and external expert assistance in selected areas (funded by bilateral donors).
- Support for the execution of adaptive research programs covering all of Kenya's agroclimatic zones, and for equipment and rehabilitation of the RRCs.
- Assistance to implement critical nationally coordinated commodity, factor, and disciplinary research programs for applied research and to rehabilitate the NRCs from which such programs were managed. All major donors were involved, with the United States Agency for International Development (USAID) particularly supporting major cereal programs, Overseas Development Administration (ODA) animal health, the Netherlands animal production, and the European Economic Community (EEC) soil fertility management programs. The International Development Association (IDA) component also assisted key programs in terms of non-salary operating costs, equipment, and civil works.

Achievements under NARP-I

Progress was made toward meeting all project (and program) objectives under NARP-I, although none were achieved fully. Delays in project processing and meeting conditions for project effectiveness postponed project commencement by over one year. Problems encountered in restructuring KARI that were compounded by changes in the parent ministry for agricultural research were not finally resolved until 1991. Responsibility for KARI was moved three times between the MoA and the Ministry of Research, Technical Training, and Technology (MRTTT) during 1988–91. The time lag in transferring KARI's budget to the Ministry-in-Charge created considerable logistical problems. These delays slowed release of GoK funds, leading to technical and logistical problems that arose in the establishment and operation of KARI's research management and financial systems. The institutionalization of better-functioning management and administration systems was resolved only toward the end of the first-phase project; and further actions to improve KARI's accounting system are still underway. However, if fairly evaluated on the basis of the more modest "de facto" goals of the first phase, the overall impact of NARP-I in the domain of Kenyan agricultural research was substantial.

In 1991, KARI produced a major research policy statement (KARI 1991) that identified priorities on the basis of commodities and factors of production. A refinement of priorities on the basis of agro-ecological zones was produced in 1995, together with strategies for maize, sorghum/millet, wheat, and dairy products. Overall, the focus on

133

commodity research was widened to embrace farming systems' research. Significant progress was made on improving the contribution of the RRCs to the research programs and to supporting extension activities. The need to match resources with prioritized programs and to actively involve extension agents in the process from the start was better understood. The focus of on-farm trials on specific production constraints was facilitated and enhanced by the adoption of the Farming Systems' Approach to Research, Extension, and Training (FSA-RET). The operational procedures developed in the area of research-extension coordination are readily replicable and sustainable, and a channel of funding was devised to improve timely release and continuity of fieldwork. The farming systems' approach has been fully institutionalized at the RRCs. The NRCs have also started to adopt this strategy to ensure relevance and appropriateness of their program objectives. However, a fully coordinated research system has yet to be attained.

Lessons Learned during NARP-I

Objectives and Their Time Frame

The de facto objectives of NARP-I focused on the broad themes of restructuring and institutional development. With the benefit of hindsight, it would have been better if program objectives had been expressed in terms of specific targets on a stated time scale. This would have made it clear that rationalization of the total research network and prioritization of research themes was required before final commitments were made to developing physical infrastructure. The first-phase project attempted to achieve progress on too many fronts in the initial time slice: reorganize KARI, rationalize centers, improve the research priority-setting process, develop coordinated programs, institute farming systems' research, put into operation links with extension, and coordinate the donors.

These major tasks, together with the substantial civil works program, proved rather ambitious, and set a tall order for the first-phase initiative, which ideally should have focused primarily on building and strengthening the requisite institutional foundations.

Assumptions on Availability and Allocation of Resources

Nine principal donors supported NARP-I, with additional contributions to the research effort coming from sources external to NARP. Apart from the fact that donor support was not always forthcoming at the rate anticipated, for KARI to develop subprojects and manage contributions from so many sources was an immensely complex task. Moreover, the inputs made by ISNAR in advising on restructuring and prioritization did not fully acknowledge issues of ecological diversity and population pressure in Kenya. Thus, the methodological deficiencies in KARI's first attempt at prioritization in research are attributable more to the "state of the art" than to KARI capacity itself.

The GoK financial commitment to the project was to cover salaries and other operating costs of research and a minor proportion of the capital expenditure. However, funding for research operations was not maintained at effective levels or released on time, which led to serious financial difficulties that affected all activities. By the end of the fifth year, the original closing date for NARP-I, GoK expenditure was only about 65 percent of the amount forecast in Ksh terms, or only about 42 percent in US$ terms. By the end of June 1995, GoK expenditure was estimated at about 120 percent of the Staff Appraisal Report (SAR) projection in Ksh terms, or about 60 percent in US$ terms.

It was expected that, as a result of increased GoK funding as well as utilization of savings from staff reductions, the proportion of salaries in the total government budget contribution would fall progressively during NARP-I from the 83 percent of total recurrent costs at project commencement. In the event, although salaries accounted for 50 percent in the first and 75 percent in the second year of the project, the proportion they later consumed increased to an average of about 87 percent of total budget releases.

In June 1990, a special account was established for the World Bank–assisted components of the project, which should have helped implementation by providing adequate finances in a timely manner. However, the treasury managed the special account—that is to say, it was outside KARI control and was largely ineffective in alleviating its financial exigencies. As a result of the delayed availability of funds (in a period of considerable inflation) the implementation program was disrupted, with civil works being particularly severely affected. Inadequate budget releases also led to a situation of financial shortages, which KARI spent much effort on resolving.

Had KARI streamlined operations by reducing the number of research centers and staff, the effects of the financial problems would have been reduced. However, it must be recognized that even for a semiautonomous institution such as KARI, laying off staff is not easy in Kenya, or in any other country where public service employment serves as a form of social security. Because of these difficulties, however, KARI seriously began to review the program-staff ratios with a view to rationalizing them. This particular matter received broad donor support, with the European Union (EU) finally undertaking to commit 10 million ECU from the Stablising Export Earnings (STABEX) funds of the European Community.

Financial Sustainability

The momentum evident in farmer-oriented research was likely to be maintained if adequate operating budget was provided. The GoK, however, appears to have difficulty in funding KARI at its present size. Although several responsibilities have been divested to the private sector and to the agricultural extension service, the total annual cost of KARI is still around Ksh 1.3 billion (US$27 million). The GoK is meeting about US$12 million (44 percent) and donors meet the remainder (about US$15 million). Salaries accounted for most of the government contribution—88 percent in the 1995–96 financial year. The KARI's board has approved a staff retrenchment plan that includes redeploying staff in accordance with research priorities, and rationalization of the network of research centers. The GoK has reached agreement with bilateral

135

donors of the EU regarding the financing of this plan, and the first phase has already been completed successfully.

KARI's Legal Structure, Effectiveness, and Sustainability

In terms of the efficiency of its operations and the effectiveness of its research programs, KARI has greatly benefited from the organizational structure of a semiautonomous institute under its own board. The current KARI board provides for significant stakeholder participation from both the public and private sector and from the broader Kenyan NARS. The board has played a proactive role in the development of the national agricultural research strategy and in the priority-setting process. The board has specifically directed KARI's efforts toward early and significant achievements in terms of increased productivity of smallholder enterprises and management and conservation of the natural resource base. The board has also protected KARI management from undue political pressure in the restructuring of the research network.

However, KARI's semi-autonomy has not progressed to a full autonomy and independence in financial matters, as was originally envisaged. The monthly budget releases from the Treasury remain unpredictable and often lack timeliness. It has not been possible to achieve a situation where, once an annual work program and budget have been agreed upon, the required budget is released to KARI in full at the beginning of the financial year, with proper implementation being KARI's sole responsibility. This has resulted in a lack of continuity in several research programs, particularly those that comprise significant on-farm activities. In turn, this has caused much loss of faith among the real stakeholders at the district level. Much remains to be done to make KARI a research organization with full autonomy and responsibility to implement research programs that are responsive to client needs and market demand. Some disadvantages of the parastatal structure were also noted:

- Research and the extension services departments operating under different government ministries are administratively separated.
- The research services, having lost the financial cushion usually available in a large government ministry, therefore have become more susceptible to budgetary deficits.

The Challenge of Linking Research with Extension Service

Concerns remain, however, with regard to the adequacy of KARI's provisions for stakeholder involvement at the central and, more especially, the regional level. The KARI has not yet developed sufficient capacity, either within the institute or through collaborative programs with other institutions, to ensure that research programs remain ahead of market developments and orientation. With research increasingly being funded in a "research project mode," there appears to be insufficient provision, particularly at the regional level, to respond to these opportunities and needs.

At board level, significantly stronger representation of the private sector, including especially farmers and their organizations, is considered desirable. This is even more important at the level of the CRACs, where, so far, real client (farmer) participation in priority setting and resource allocation has remained weak. Opportunities to substantially involve nongovernmental organizations (NGOs) have also been insufficiently utilized. To create more incentive for beneficiary participation, KARI could benefit from Tanzania's experience with "Zonal ARFs," which provide opportunity for local organizations to propose contract research for funding.

Linkage between research and extension functions has always been problematic in Kenya. The problem can probably be traced to two issues. The first is the separation of functions and responsibilities within ministries. The second issue is that of a research culture that rewards scientists for scientific excellence as measured by acceptance of their work for publication in journals rather than the demonstration of relevance and impact of such work in solving production constraints on farm. The recruitment and rise of a cadre of research scientists with narrow specialization and often no agricultural background could also have contributed to lack of orientation and skills to relate to farming situations. Also, for a long time, appreciation was lacking of the need to recruit high-caliber scientists and to train them for leadership in extension. As a result, a serious intellectual gap existed between research and extension services, to the point where extension was considered a lower-level activity. Some efforts were made to address this issue, including:

- Establishing ecoregional research centers charged with responsibility for acquiring, developing, and adapting technologies to specific farming systems and ecologies, and extension liaison committees as formal mechanisms to link research and extension personnel at the regional centers.
- Strengthening socioeconomic capacity and the inputs of this discipline in planning and conducting agricultural research.
- Establishing a senior position in the MoA with responsibility for research-extension liaison.
- Recruitment of agriculture graduates to head extension services at the district level.

The Second Phase of NARP (NARP-II)

In order to consolidate and build on experiences gained in NARP-I, plans for a second phase of NARP (NARP-II) were initiated (KARI 1995). In addition to continuing the institution-building process initiated under NARP-I, important elements of NARP-II were research management and programming, financial management, further development of the ARF, integrated information systems, human resource development, and monitoring and evaluation as well as impact assessment. The transfer of research responsibility to the private sector, especially for industrial crops, such as sugarcane and pyrethrum, continues to be actively pursued. The NARP-II phase became effective in 1997. Its focus was on technology development and adaptation to specific agro-ecological and socioeconomic environments; improvement of technology

137

delivery systems, particularly through more effective collaboration with the MoA and the universities; and active participation of smallholder farmers in technology development and adaptation. The three main components of NARP-II are:

1. *Institution Building,* which supports KARI's transformation into a leaner, more efficient organization focused on carrying out adaptive research in accordance with the highest national priorities, and promoting the dissemination of proven technologies to farmers, especially smallholders, who are often women. As part of improved research management, KARI's financial and accounting systems are being strengthened to ensure that all financial resources are mobilized and allocated efficiently in accordance with the agreed upon priorities. All information support is handled through an "Information Technology Unit," which is establishing a new management information system.

2. *The Research Program Implementation,* which finances high-priority adaptive research programs implemented through the RRCs, and commodity and factor (of production) research implemented through the NRCs. It also finances research in natural resource management, socioeconomic research, collaborative research with universities, IARCs, and NARS of the eastern Africa region. It co-finances research proposals with the private sector for selected research topics on a competitive basis through the ARF. The KARI's management of research programs is being strengthened to focus on the highest national priorities and to raise the efficiency of program implementation. Authority and responsibility for implementing the research programs, including financial operations, is being progressively decentralized to the Research Centers. As part of human resource development, a new performance appraisal system is being implemented that will ensure that rewards (including promotions) are closely linked to research output and impact.

3. *The Seeds Program,* which finances a pilot scheme to develop a sustainable national seed system through the establishment of "Foundation Seed Units" that can help ensure the availability of the quantity and quality of seeds required by farmers in a timely manner.

An important aspect of NARP-II is its emphasis on establishing appropriate procedures for the timely and effective use of all available financial and human resources, and the strengthening of KARI's capacity for assessing research impact. More broadly, the sustainability of agricultural research in Kenya depends on continuation toward a market-oriented economy and concomitant realignment of the roles of the public and private sectors in research. As envisaged under the second-phase project, agricultural research in the public sector will focus on the highest national priorities and be implemented by a leaner, more efficient institution (KARI). The viability of KARI will depend on the quality of its management and systems, to be strengthened under the follow-up project, and commitments by government on financing operating costs. Sustainability will also depend on continuing support from donors, on a declining basis.

An essential component is a growing role for the private sector, such as assuming responsibility for research on industrial crops, and participation in the joint design and implementation of research on other commodities (under appropriate cost-sharing arrangements). It is expected that, in the future, agricultural research could be sustained on the basis of a partnership between public and private sectors without donor support. However, the basic premise is that KARI's operations and organization will be significantly restructured, with the private sector assuming much greater responsibility.

Kenya's Experience Compared with Other Countries in the Region

Other governments in the region, for example those of Ethiopia, Uganda, Tanzania, Zambia, and Zimbabwe, have also made large investments in their NARS during the

---

Box 6.1   **Achievements and Shortfalls of Donor-Assisted Agricultural Research Projects in Sub-Saharan African (SSA) Countries**

Listed below are some achievements and shortfalls of donor-assisted agricultural research projects in SSA.

- Human resource development and training (impressive achievements; however, many of the best scientists are leaving the national systems).
- Agricultural research organization and management (significant improvement, but frequent policy change, financial uncertainty, and rapid staff turnover often place managers in an impossible position).
- Rehabilitation of infrastructure (reasonably successful, but many empty shells).
- Closer client participation in priority setting (progress made and much more needed).
- Research output in terms of technology adoption and increased, more efficient production (some evidence of success, particularly in genetic improvement, but lacking in many areas).
- Improved donor coordination (limited progress by some countries).
- Allocation by governments of a dependable budget for nonsalary operating costs (remaining extremely difficult).
- Identification of alternative financing for agricultural research, including through the private sector (achievements by some countries through competitive funds and by producer involvement in tea and coffee, but much greater effort required).
- Attaining a rational salary/operational costs balance (deteriorating in many countries).
- Improved staff service conditions (largely unsuccessful and in some cases getting worse).

Evidently, although some progress has been made, especially in the first six areas, much remains to be done in putting agricultural research on a sound, sustainable basis. More effort is also required to make the NARS more effective in addressing the technology demands to generate more productive and sustainable agricultural systems that conserve the natural resource base.

last two decades. Similar to the case in Kenya, bilateral donors, the World Bank, and other multilateral agencies have provided considerable assistance to facilitate agricultural technology generation and transfer, particularly through improving research infrastructure and the development of the human resource base. The results of this support have been successful to varying degrees (box 6.1), but the overall impact on the NARS in terms of increased productivity and incomes has been less than expected.

The shortfall in research productivity in SSA countries is explained partly by:

- Over-reliance on technical assistance in a project context (which cannot effectively replace national staff);
- Lack of continuity of research in earlier "integrated rural development" projects under which small project-specific research initiatives were encouraged rather than the strengthening of national programs; and
- Limitations in available staff, physical facilities, management quality, and finance.

Direction is lacking in many National Agricultural Research Master Plans. These documents are supposed to set the broad, long-term priorities for agricultural research, but many of them are incomplete, or were not adhered to during the implementation period. Many of the national plans were also prepared with little real beneficiary participation. They are often not followed up with specific research action plans focusing on the most important technical questions that require urgent resolution in specific agro-ecological zones, within each identified priority commodity or factor area. Donor coordination has remained weak, often leading to lack of a shared vision in the development of agricultural research and common implementation arrangements.

In many countries, agricultural research is too centralized, with insufficient delegation resulting in a "top-down" approach that fails to understand and take account of actual client needs. Insufficient progress has been made in improving the exchange of information on agricultural technology within and between countries, and linkages with research systems outside the region remain inadequate. Governments have not provided adequate salaries, appropriate incentives, and essential operating funds in a consistent and timely manner, particularly during implementation of structural adjustment programs. This has resulted in a lack of commitment, frequent disruption of activities, and decreased resource use efficiency; relevance and applicability of research results have been severely affected. In almost all countries, a serious imbalance continues in the ratio between budgets for staff salaries and the provisions for operational costs of research that causes low productivity; this is caused in part by very high numbers of support staff compared to scientific staff. Insufficient progress has been made to involve the private sector in financing agricultural research, especially in the cash/export crop subsectors. Notwithstanding considerable effort, the linkages between research and extension remain inadequate in most countries. This overall state of affairs, along with haphazard government funding arrangements, has led to waste and inefficient use of the limited resources available for agricultural research; the NARS in many countries of the region therefore remain in a "state of crisis" (Chema, Gilbert, and Roseboom 2003).

KARI's Performance and Lessons Learned

KARI has performed reasonably well compared with research organizations in other countries in the region. However, there is a problem in providing adequate and reliable operating funds for KARI's approved work programs. Ethiopia is probably the only country in the region where the level of government commitment to agricultural technology development and dissemination is most solidly demonstrated through sustained financial support for nearly the entire nonsalary operating cost budget. The essential importance of dialogue between the NARS and national decision makers, especially in Ministries of Planning and Treasury, with strong emphasis on the linkages between agricultural (and national) development, and the generation and adoption of new technology, cannot be overemphasized.

Another lesson that can be drawn from the regional experience is the importance of revised scientist-support staff ratios, and relating the number of scientists in different areas to the identified priorities and the likely available resources in the medium term. Uganda, where the National Agricultural Research Organization (NARO) earlier went through a restructuring and downsizing effort, has developed a better balanced, more efficient, and publicly financed system. The most important lesson to be drawn from developments in the different countries of the region is probably the significance of autonomy (even if limited) for an improved enabling environment conducive to research achievement. The Tanzania experience (box 6.2) is similar to that of Kenya.

The Tanzania experience differs from that of Kenya in that:

- The pressure to create a separate livestock research institute succeeded in Tanzania.
- The semiautonomous research infrastructure was disbanded before it had time to become fully established and to demonstrate its advantages, hence the renewed desire to revive it.
- Instability of the national research system is likely to persist as the donor-assisted NARP-II enters the second phase while the system remains under a cloud of restructuring.

The Ugandan experience (box 6.3) is rather different. Although, like Kenya, Uganda had a well-established research system, it was totally devastated by civil war. However, with strong government and donor support and in the absence of competing institutions, the newly constructed NARO has developed faster than KARI and has been able to incorporate relevant research efforts at the universities. It has been suggested that NARO should also take responsibility for technology transfer—a new arrangement whose feasibility is yet to be evaluated.

Those countries where publicly financed agricultural research continues to be managed through a ministerial department (often agriculture) as part of the regular civil service, such as Tanzania, Zambia, and Zimbabwe, seem to have fared considerably

| Box 6.2 | The Tanzania Experience |

Tanzania, a partner with Uganda and Kenya in the East African Community (EAC), also had a national agricultural research system (NARS) under the Ministry of Agriculture (MoA) operating parallel to, and complemented by, research under the EAC. The country was therefore faced with an urgent need for restructuring to accommodate changes resulting from the EAC's collapse. This led to the enactment of a number of semiautonomous research parastatals between 1977 and 1980, including the Tanzania Agricultural Research Organization (TARO) and the Tanzania Livestock Research Organization (TALIRO).

In addition to the urgent need to attract and retain competent scientific staff, especially those coming from the defunct EAC institutions, establishment of the semiautonomous research parastatals was also a response to a general feeling among different stakeholders that agricultural and livestock research directly under the ministries was not effective because of too much government bureaucracy. It was therefore expected that the new structure would help ensure a committed and dedicated research staff by providing special schemes of service and would institute appropriate incentive packages not possible under government ministries.

The steps and actions required to strengthen the national agricultural and livestock research systems were reiterated in several reports and fora, among them the National Agricultural Policy (1982), the Tanzania Agricultural Research Resource Assessment (1985), and United Nations Development Programme (UNDP)/Food and Agriculture Organization (FAO), and World Bank Mission reports and Aide Memoires (1982 to 1988). Most of these recommended, among others, consolidating the existing research institutions to establish one semiautonomous research parastatal or bringing back research under the MoA as a department. Following these recommendations, and under pressure from various stakeholders, TARO and TALIRO were dissolved in 1989 and agricultural and livestock research reverted to the combined Ministry of Agriculture and Livestock Development (MoALD) as a Department of Research and Training (DRT). A National Agricultural Research Master Plan (NARM) was prepared and approved in 1992. During the National Agricultural Research Program phase I (NARP-I), efforts were made by the MoALD to improve its linkages with other components of the NARS.

The restructuring from semiautonomous, research parastatals to DRT led to instability and uncertainty. Re-categorization of the research staff took too long, and when it was done the salary entry point was lower than under the parastatal organization. This, coupled with attempts to rationalize the system, caused some research scientists to leave the system. Inadequate and untimely funding was a further major limitation. Despite the dissolution of TARO and TALIRO, key stakeholders are of the view that the DRT has not provided solutions to key problems of research management. A third phase of restructuring is therefore proposed in which agricultural research programs will be integrated under a semiautonomous National Agricultural Research Institute (NARI) operating under the existing National Agricultural Research Council (NARC).

Box 6.3   The Uganda Experience

Uganda, a partner with Tanzania and Kenya in the defunct East African Community (EAC), also had to restructure its agricultural research system after the EAC's collapse. However, in the case of Uganda, delay was considerable and the task has involved rebuilding of the research service after many years of civil unrest and almost complete destruction of the original infrastructure.

As part of the economic recovery program, the government in 1987 established an agricultural task force to formulate recommendations for strengthening the agricultural services sector. A working group consisting of top scientists from key institutions in the country prepared the National Agricultural Research Strategy and Plan with financial and technical support from the World Bank and the International Service for National Agricultural Research (ISNAR), respectively. The Plan was to encompass a range of objectives, a structure, and implementation procedures that would ensure sustainable progress. It was also aimed at attracting support from policy makers and financiers and ensuring the effective transformation of the research system into a client-responsive organization. A first phase, World Bank–financed Agricultural Research and Training Project (ARTP) to support implementation of the strategy and plan, became effective in 1992, and a follow-up project has been designed. The government approved the plan and later used it as a basis for establishing the National Agricultural Research Organization (NARO) by an Act of Parliament in 1992. The organization consists of the board, the secretariat, eight research institutes, and associated institutes. The main objective of NARO is to undertake, promote, and streamline research in crops, livestock, fisheries, and forestry.

The NARO has become a model for agricultural research in sub-Saharan Africa in organizational management, priority setting, improved technology generation, and so on. It has retained most of its technical and support staff with relatively good salaries and privileges compared to prevailing opportunities elsewhere. It has also made and maintained a good name with national, regional, and international organizations. However, it also has some shortcomings. For example, many potential end-users of technologies generated by NARO have not yet benefited from NARO's output, mainly because research and extension in Uganda have not yet addressed this subject seriously and jointly.

---

worse than those, such as Kenya, Uganda, and Ethiopia, that opted for semi-autonomy. Countries that have been successful in "hiving off" significant research responsibility to the private sector (while maintaining the full resource allocation, then focused on fewer "subsistence" commodities) have a better chance of impact and sustainability. Finally, those countries that have succeeded in developing strong donor coordination arrangements are better able to ensure a well-balanced, holistic national program.

REFERENCES

Chema, Sam, Elon Gilbert, and Johannes Roseboom. 2003. *A review of key issues and recent experiences in reforming agricultural research in Africa.* Research Report 24. The Hague: ISNAR.

Government of Kenya (GoK). 1986. Economic management for renewed growth. Sessional Paper No. 1. Nairobi: Government Printers.

International Service for National Agricultural Research (ISNAR). 1981. *Report to the government of Kenya: Kenya's national agricultural research system.* ISNAR Document No. R2. The Hague: ISNAR.

Kenya Agricultural Research Institute (KARI). 1991. *Kenya's agricultural research priorities to the year 2000.* Nairobi: KARI.

———. 1995. *National Agricultural Research Project: Phase II Project Proposal.* Nairobi: KARI.

7

Organizing Agricultural Research: Fitting Institutional Structure to the Research Agenda

J O H N   L Y N A M   A N D   H O W A R D   E L L I O T T

The organization and structure of agricultural research systems in Africa has been driven by a need to match severely limited resources to highly complex research problems, or as Eyzaguirre (1996) has termed it, "matching the scope of research with the scale of available resources." Colonial governments, which established the original structural features of African research systems, tended to have highly focused systems, most often concentrating on just export crops. Independence brought with it the political necessity of expanding the research scope to address more directly the diverse needs of often subsistence-based farmers, and the rapidly expanding food needs of these countries. African national agricultural research systems (NARS) have had to continuously adapt to expanding research mandates, some from domestic quarters, others coming from the expanding international agricultural research system and the evolution in agricultural and biological sciences themselves. Often, organizational structures did not keep pace with these changes, resulting in overextended systems that were particularly weakened during the economic stagnation of the 1980s. The 1990s was a decade of assessing organizational structure as a key component of developing more effective agricultural research systems on the continent.

The Evolution of the Organization of Research

The colonial agricultural research system evolved over about a fifty-year period. Agricultural research stations were established in some parts of Africa prior to World War I, and continued to expand through the interwar period. They were individual stations funded by the different colonies (e.g., the Kitale research station in Kenya established in 1937) mixed with stations based more on export commodities, often organized on a regional basis. The West African Oil Palm Research Institute, the Empire Cotton Research Corporation, and the cocoa and coffee research centers are all examples of such regionally based research organizations. The policy of the colonial government during this period was one of limiting financial support to the colonies and moving them toward economic self-sufficiency. Agricultural research was supported by either the colonies, cesses on export crops, or funds generated by the research institute itself. The research agenda was, therefore, closely linked to commercial producers and interests, as dictated by the financing arrangements. The structure of the research system was based on relatively autonomous research stations, whose overheads were kept small and where limited mobility and communications restricted the administrative burden on scientists' time. This, together with a highly focused research program and a limited number of well-trained staff, produced effective research programs, although limited in scope.

The period following World War II witnessed an increase in support by the Colonial Office for agricultural research, an expansion in the scope of research, and the establishment of mechanisms to link country research stations through regional programs. The East African Agricultural and Forestry Research Organization expanded the scale of agricultural research in east Africa. A division of labor was effected between research institutes in the region, and scale economies in programs, such as sugarcane breeding, were developed. Disciplinary programs in soil science, crop protection, and the newer science of biometrics were developed within the East African Agriculture and Forestry Research Organization (EAAFRO), and the research body both developed regional programs and linked to national research programs. The additional financing provided by the Colonial Office was essential to the development of this structure, as it funded increased administrative overheads and the transaction costs associated with joint program planning within the region. This was an extraordinarily productive period for agricultural research, producing both a firm knowledge base for succeeding research and most of the improved crop varieties that led to the first generation of productivity increase in African agriculture.

Independence halted this evolution of agricultural research on the continent—that is, toward an interdependent system of regional and national capacities based on both an evolving division of labor and exploitation of scale economies at a regional level. Independence brought with it the dismantling of the regional system, which occurred almost immediately in West Africa but was delayed until 1977 in east Africa with the demise of the East African Community. Efforts to build an agricultural research system at the regional level were replaced by a focus on the national level, which brought with it several decades of institutional and organizational experimentation during a period when trained scientific personnel and financial resources were highly constrained. This was also a period when donors effectively bypassed national systems by concentrating on expanding the Consultative Group on International Agricultural Research (CGIAR) centers in Africa, and investing in integrated rural development and extension programs, with the International Agricultural Research Centers (IARCs) viewed as principal sources of technology (Eicher 1990). As the 1974 National Academy of Sciences report noted:

> Donor agencies have been reluctant to support national research programs that stand alone administratively but that may, nevertheless, have international potential through the quality

and relevance of the research. They have opted to support those research programs that fit in an international administrative network involving two or more countries. (168)

The building of NARS for the first twenty years or so after independence—that is, before the increase in donor funding for African NARS in the mid-1980s, had several characteristics. These included expansion in both the size of NARS and the number of research institutes, rapid change from expatriate to indigenous staffing, and considerable fluidity in organizational structures focused on better coordination of agricultural research. Pardey, Roseboom, and Beintema (1997) note that the number of mid-sized NARS in sub-Saharan Africa (those employing one hundred to four hundred researchers) increased from three in 1961 to eighteen in 1991. Idachaba (1980) points out that the number of national agricultural research institutes in Nigeria increased from four at independence to eighteen by 1980. Drivers of this expansion are less easy to identify. Eicher (1990) attributes this inflationary process to four factors:

1. The more general expansion in state bureaucracy,
2. Commitment of the research system to hiring science graduates from the expanding university system,
3. The recent increase in donor funding for agricultural research, and
4. The expansion of the scope of research in relation to the declining ability to access or borrow technologies from outside the country.

This process led to overstaffing of experiment stations, illustrated by the increase in senior staff at the Nigerian Institute for Oil Palm Research from 15 in 1970–71 to 283 in 1985 (Eicher 1990). The interaction between donors and the expanding scope of research is illustrated by the upgrading of the Food and Agriculture Organization's (FAO's) Hides and Skins Demonstration and Training Project to the Leather Research Institute of Nigeria (Idachaba 1980). In most respects, expansion in agricultural research capacity in Africa was not effectively managed in relation to clear research priorities and strategies for technology borrowing. As described in the following, there was little effective capacity to manage and coordinate this process, because research elements were added among competing government departments in relation to narrowly defined interests. Once added, government employment policies restricted any ability to reduce, eliminate, or change staffing and research programs, thus creating only forward momentum.

Agricultural research in Africa tended to expand within the bureaucratic framework of Ministries of Agriculture (MoAs). Different divisions tended to develop their own research capacities, with competition between departments driving expansion. Particularly pronounced was the competition between livestock and agriculture, each usually representing different geographical, ethnic, and therefore political interests. Several factors contributed to a search for more effective organizational structures, producing cycles of frequent reorganizations. These factors included the centralization

147

of decision making away from provincial and district offices; separation of function between state-controlled agricultural marketing, extension, and research departments; and declining administrative efficiency with expanding size. Roseboom and Pardey (1993) describe the process in Kenya. In 1974, all crop and livestock research scattered throughout the various divisions within the Department of Agriculture was brought together within a Scientific Research Division. In 1979, crop and livestock researchers were again separated when the ministry was divided into a Ministry of Agriculture and a Ministry of Livestock Development. In 1983, the two were reunited, only to be divided again in 1984. Today Kenya has a Ministry of Agriculture and a Ministry of Livestock and Fisheries Development.

Unstable institutional structures naturally led to a period of relatively unproductive research output from national research systems. It was not until the mid-1970s that such impacts began to appear, with cassava in Nigeria (Nweke, Spencer, and Lynam 2002), and maize in eastern and southern Africa (Byerlee and Eicher 1997). The 1980s marked a shift to farming systems research and donors' renewed interest in investing in NARS. In many cases, a whole new agenda was added to still weakly articulated systems, such as those of Zambia and Malawi. Institutionalization of farming systems research during the 1980s in African NARS largely failed—some of the most effective programs were developed in Ethiopia (Franzel and van Houten 1992). However, this process did provide legitimacy for an additional stage within the research process, namely adaptive research. How to organize applied and adaptive research within African NARS would become a central feature of NARS organizational debates in the 1990s.

Universities and the faculties of agriculture within them developed independently of the research system. Establishment of universities did not occur until after independence, with a focus on establishing a few high-quality institutions who were defined more as vehicles for development than as centers of research excellence. University staff development became the focus for overseas Ph.D. training. Some faculties of agriculture developed their own experiment stations, but research tended to have a disciplinary focus and to be restricted to trials on stations. Ongoing, sustained agricultural research capacity rarely developed within the universities; nor were many attempts made to link to the public agricultural research system, a separation usually reinforced by the fact that the two research systems were overseen by separate ministries. Faculties of agriculture thus developed as another independent component of a fragmented agricultural research system.

Economic stagnation and the shift to structural adjustment in the 1980s halted expansion in research systems and produced a marked decline in operational support to research scientists (Pardey, Roseboom, and Beintema 1997). Any prospects for developing an effective agricultural research capacity were dissipated by declining public-sector budgets, the maintenance of staffing at the expense of capital and operational budgets, and a resultant institutional crisis that undermined any attempts to sustain research programs. Rather, the impetus for restructuring came from the World Bank and the new mechanism of conditionality associated with structural adjustment.

The World Bank also assumed effective leadership of the Special Program for African Agricultural Research (SPAAR) as a forum for linking other donors to this process. In most countries with World Bank loans for agricultural research, the strategy was to consolidate agricultural research capacity in a parastatal authority, largely independent of the MoA and legally mandated as responsible for agricultural research in the country. The search for how best to organize agricultural research is being played out in these parastatal National Agricultural Research Organizations (NAROs). The first-order decisions on institutional structure have now been made, while a host of second-order decisions remain to be specified.

Principles of Efficient Organizational Forms

Given the amount of literature on the subject of agricultural research, very little is available on the topic of efficiency in alternative organizational forms, and certainly nothing approaching a theory of research organization. Ruttan (1982) focuses on two elements in agricultural research organization and notes that, "little formal knowledge about the economics of location and scale is available to help in decision making either at the level of the individual experiment station or research center or at the level of the national or international agricultural research system." Much of the literature focuses on the resource allocation problem (Alston, Norton, and Pardey 1995) — that is, the issue of the scope of the research enterprise. Scale and internal organization usually remain outside formal analysis (Pardey, Roseboom, and Anderson 1991), yet are viewed as critical to the efficient management of agricultural research. This section briefly reviews principles that underlie efficient organization of agricultural research in Africa.

Organizational Principles

Eyzaguirre (1996) defines the scale concept as "the institutionalized research capacity of a national system; it is a combination of a system's human and financial resources, its knowledge base, and its infrastructure." The human and physical capital and the annual budgetary resources define scale. However, when research output is evaluated in relation to increasing such resources, Alston and Pardey (1996) make a distinction between economies of size and economies of scale. Economies of size relate to investments in large capital items, such as laboratories, vehicles, and equipment. Thus, the ability to invest in laboratory and analytical services and some strategic research capacity significantly increases the effectiveness of applied and adaptive research. The development of analytical laboratories with sufficient quality standards has been a continuing problem in African NAROs and derives partially from the inability to realize size economies. On the other hand, economies of scale internal to the research process "arise simply from being large enough to allow appropriate specialization and division of labor" (Alston and Pardey 1996, 236). Economies of scale are apparent, although virtually no empirical evidence exists on size, internal organization, and research productivity. Economies of scale are often assumed in breeding as

149

practiced at IARCs, where large germplasm collections, specialized breeding nurseries, and specialization in screening methodologies, reinforced by biotechnological
techniques such as marker-assisted selection, disproportionately increase the range
and characteristics of varietal development. Finally, economies of scale external to the
research process relate to economic benefits, as opposed to efficiency in producing
research products, derived from the research investment. Such economies are realized with larger output markets, more homogeneous production conditions, and bet-
ter-structured input markets. These conditions rarely apply in Africa.

The other principal organizational element in agricultural research is that of scope.
Eyzaguirre (1996) defines scope as the research agenda of the system, consisting of
"the range of research programs, meaning the commodities and topics covered, and
the level of research, meaning whether it is strategic, applied, or adaptive." Scope is
obviously related to the diversity within the agricultural sector, the relation between
research priorities and government policy, and the ability to borrow technology or
research results. Economies of scope derive explicitly from diversification in the
research portfolio. Alston and Pardey (1996) note that such economies derive in part
from "the intellectual spill-over effects between scientists from the same or different
disciplines working on the same or different projects." This has provided the
justification for interdisciplinary research teams and the notion of critical mass within
research programs. Within adaptive research, possible economies of scope also arise
from complementarity between system components, such as the application that
research on a legume might have on striga control in maize. Given the expansion in
the research portfolio over the last few decades, in many African NAROs the question
of how to define and organize the scope of the research portfolio is critical to the
efficiency of research systems, because management and transaction costs may actually introduce diseconomies of scope.

Organization of the scope of agricultural research consistent with constraints on
scale forms the principle basis for the search for efficiency gains in the research
enterprise. Institutional structures, number and type of research programs, location of
experiment stations, level of decentralization, and disciplinary staffing are all components in effective organization of agricultural research institutes. As noted, no well-
developed theory guides this process, with organizational and programmatic elements
(i.e., soft elements) being adapted to infrastructural, locational, and other fixed investments. Thus, institutional changes tend to be more marginal, cumulative, and aggrega-
tive, with a tendency to focus on improved coordination and complementarity between
programmatic elements. The current trend in sub-Saharan Africa for more radical
institutional reorganization is thus historically unique because it attempts to consolidate the atomistic expansion in the post-independence period and to provide a structure around which future development will build. Because restructuring is so
disruptive, it can be considered only relatively rarely, so that current restructuring
within the framework of autonomous parastatals provides opportunities but brings
with it high costs if not done correctly. Clarity about the principal forces and elements
that enter into this restructuring process is thus important.

Organizing Applied and Adaptive Research

In Africa, the complexity of multiple-enterprise farming systems has precipitated the development of an often-extensive, adaptive research capacity, reinforced by the farming systems research movement of the 1980s (Collinson 2000). This supports a more decentralized and dispersed institutional structure, which is also consistent with the heterogeneity in agro-ecologies. However, it constrains any movement toward size or scale economies. Moreover, development of such adaptive research capacity depends critically on a consistent flow of new techniques and knowledge from applied research programs. Yet the scope of the research problems at an adaptive research level cannot be matched by similar scope at an applied level. How to organize applied and adaptive research within African NARS is a central structural and organizational issue. How much to invest in adaptive research relative to applied research, how to define the scope of applied research, and how to develop appropriate linkages between the two are tensions in this restructuring process.

Defining the Scope of Applied Research

Applied research generates varieties, pest and disease control strategies, soil management techniques, mechanical innovations, livestock breeds, and grazing or pasture systems on which increases in agricultural productivity are based. In agricultural economies where markets are well integrated, markets drive a search for regional comparative advantage that induces specialization at the level of agro-ecologies and farming systems and usually input-based production practices. This allows an effective setting of priorities and targeting of applied research, and the realization of external economies of scale. However, in Africa significant heterogeneity in agro-ecologies (especially in east Africa), underdeveloped market infrastructure (Spencer 1996; Omamo 1998), highly limited input use, and often variable rainfall regimes lead to an extraordinary level of diversification and risk-reducing strategies at all scales of African agriculture. To this complexity in defining the research agenda is added a continuing expansion in the objectives of agricultural policy, particularly as compared to research policy in developed countries where the focus is principally commercial interests. In Africa, policy objectives include food production and food security, rural poverty alleviation, and resource management and agricultural sustainability. These have provided political legitimacy to an extensive portfolio for applied research. However, policy pressure, pressure from adaptive research, and the diverse nature of African agriculture make the scope of the applied research portfolio difficult to contain.

To the problem of how to bound the applied research portfolio is added the problem of how best to organize applied research programs, especially if possible economies of scope can be gained through appropriate organizational configurations. Applied research has tended to be organized within the framework of commodity research programs. The notions of critical mass, multidisciplinary research teams, research strategies defined across a range of ecologies, and appropriate linkages to international research capacity all tend to expand the staff and operational resources needed to reach a sufficient scale of operation. With some bounds on resource availability, real

151

trade-offs occur between the size of commodity research programs and the number of research programs included in the portfolio. These internal cost trade-offs (i.e., within the research process itself) are rarely addressed because such decisions are usually evaluated at the margin rather than within the framework of some sense of an optimum organizational structure and nonlinear returns on investment.

Organizing Adaptive Research

Adaptive research was in many respects a creation of farming systems research (FSR), and in Africa it has evolved from an FSR framework. The creation of FSR units within experiment stations largely failed in the 1980s. This was followed by a second generation of experience that is not as well documented and is not as explicitly donor driven. In the 1990s FSR contributed to the development of farmer participatory research (FPR) methods and practice. The question of how best to organize adaptive research in African NARS is still wide open. Smaller systems with fewer experiment stations, such as the NARO in Uganda, began by attempting to integrate an adaptive research capacity into applied commodity research programs, and have most recently moved to posting adaptive research teams in the twelve principal agro-ecologies. For larger systems, such as the Kenya Agricultural Research Institute (KARI), the country is divided into zones of contiguous administrative districts, and particular stations are given mandates to develop adaptive research programs for particular zones.

Adaptive research works within the context of the whole farming system—something that FSR actually rarely achieved. Such systems research is both sophisticated and challenging, requiring experienced researchers that combine varying disciplines and knowledge of a range of crops and livestock. Achieving scope economies through appropriate team formation and division of work remains an ad hoc process. There is even less experience with achieving sufficient scale economies in adaptive research—that is, assuring a sufficient scale of adoption for techniques arising from adaptive research. Thus, organization of adaptive research has several critical features, including the number and density of stations, research team composition, and taking adaptive research results to scale.

Location Specificity

African agricultural research must balance a significant degree of agroclimatic heterogeneity, a large component of location specificity in biological research, and financial constraints limiting the number of research sites. Locational decisions are critical to effective agricultural research, influencing the number and distribution of research stations, the balance between on- and off-station research, the design of technology testing systems, and the potential for spill-ins from technology. Research stations are very much a fixed investment, and most African NARS are locked into locational decisions made in the colonial period. The needs of export agriculture, proximity to principal administrative centers, and the needs of crop breeding influenced decisions at that time. Thus, research stations tended to be located on more fertile soils, in better agroclimatic zones, and near capital cities. For example, four of NARO's six principal research stations are concentrated around Kampala in the southern part of Uganda. Much of the trend in the postcolonial period has been to try to correct for these inherent biases in the location of research stations, while accepting the fixed investments that have already been made.

Heterogeneity is a justification to decentralize research. Definition of an optimum level of decentralization is made more difficult by the location specificity of both applied and adaptive research. Adaptive research in any particular station, because it is organized around contiguous mandate areas, will often—at least in east Africa—operate across different agroclimatic zones, so that a one-to-one correspondence is difficult between agro-ecological zone and specific research stations. Thus, there may be gains from information flows between adaptive research teams operating in similar agro-ecological zones. On the other hand, applied research programs tend to be centralized in order to achieve some economies of scope, yet must deal with agro-ecological heterogeneity. Thus, Kenya's maize-breeding program targets five different environments, requiring maize-breeding capacity in each of those zones, and yet with gains from sharing both early breeding materials and capacity in pathology and entomology. Given such needs in most applied research programs, there are real organizational questions of how to rationalize applied research within an environmental matrix, balancing travel and operational costs with location of personnel at particular sites.

A research agenda therefore underlies locational decision making in agricultural research. Research systems must understand the agro-ecological heterogeneity within the agricultural sector, the biological response across agroclimatic domains, the variability in biotic and abiotic constraints, and the distribution of crops, livestock, and principal agricultural systems (Hassan 1998). This type of characterization can then be linked to resource allocation decisions (Wood and Pardey 1994), and then to locational decisions. However, this requires the creation of a spatial database capability, often within the framework of a geographical information system, and to date these are rare in African NARS.

Internal and External Linkages

The integration of agricultural research activities into a single system, the distribution of research activities across a significant number of research stations, the development of adaptive research as a complement to applied research, and the resultant matrix of coordinated, linked, and joint activities has created a system where undertaking research involves large transactions costs. These are costs in researcher time, in travel and operational costs, in administrative costs, and in loss of focus and continuity of effort. The efficiency of research systems is to a significant degree based on the extent to which transaction costs can be kept to a reasonable level, and this is largely a function of organization and the cost of information flows. Agricultural research systems in Africa are developing e-mail and Internet connectivity. This is now possible for stations based in capital cities. Phone lines to often-remote research

153

stations are in many cases not sufficiently reliable. The impact of e-mail on reducing transaction costs thus still remains in the (hopefully short-term) future.

The dimensions of internal research linkages are many. Applied research programs must usually coordinate across breeding and testing sites, across different disciplinary research programs, and to adaptive research programs. The latter, on the other hand, must link to a range of technology and research sources, depending on principal activities and constraints in the farming systems, and might take advantage of common problems shared with other adaptive research sites. The communication channels needed to access multiple sources of technological innovation are difficult to establish, given periodicity of requests, demands on researchers' time at the source, and the time needed for joint planning of research. Finally, disciplinary based, cross-cutting programs, such as social science, crop protection, and to a certain extent soil science, often have a distributed set of researchers but operate at least partially within a divisional research agenda. Research planning, techniques and material flow, and budgetary allocation all form part of this matrix of internal transactions. Decentralization of decision making does not address what is much more of an intersecting set of linkages within the institution.

The complexity of internal linkages is matched only by the increasing demand for external linkages. These are covered more fully in other chapters, but include both upstream and downstream linkages. The former would include the capacity needed to link to the rapid expansion in biotechnological research (chapter 13). Networks of more applied research, in the past organized as a part of IARC research programs, have greatly expanded recently with the creation of regional research consortia, such as the Association for the Strengthening of Agricultural Research in Eastern and Central Africa (ASARECA) and the Southern Africa Center for Coordination of Agricultural Research (SACCAR) (chapter 12). This allows applied research programs to devolve some of the research activities to regional networks, and allows adaptive research programs access to a wider array of technologies and expertise. Nevertheless, it also increases the transaction costs, some of which are provided through donor funds to the networks. How to best internally organize NARS to make these linkages, while at the same time increasing research efficiency, has only recently been added to the organizational agenda for African research systems.

The downstream linkages also offer their own complexities. The links between research and extension programs have never been strong in Africa, and have in general suffered from countercyclical donor funding of either research or extension (chapter 11). The recent development of adaptive research capacity has raised even more questions about both the relative roles of extension and adaptive research and the links between the two. Added to this is the potential role of nongovernmental organizations (NGOs) in extension (Farrington et al. 1993). Although NGO capacity has been increasing over the last two decades, how to form effective linkages to a highly dispersed community with often highly differing capacities remains an open issue. All in all, African NARS have to work within a far more complex internal and external environment than was the case with the relatively simple systems in the colonial period.

KARI Organization of National Commodity Programs

The creation of KARI provided a framework for integrating most of the agricultural research scattered across various ministries into one institution. Forestry, fisheries, and trypanosomiasis remained in separate, publicly funded research institutes, and coffee and tea remained in privately funded ones. The KARI absorbed all the research personnel, research stations, and fixed capital equipment that had previously existed in various divisions of various ministries. In one sense, the scope of the agricultural research enterprise was largely defined for KARI in this amalgamation process. The KARI is the third-largest NARS in sub-Saharan Africa after Nigeria and South Africa, and thus in comparison to either the population or the agricultural gross domestic product (GDP) of other African countries, KARI worked within a far larger scope of activities. The challenge over KARI's decade of existence has been how to efficiently manage this scope within the constraints of the financial base provided for agricultural research.

Managing Scope in Agricultural Research

The basic organizational structure was put in place at KARI's inception. An organizational framework was imposed on the existing set of research stations, whereby programmatic responsibilities were assigned to each center for either regional, adaptive research (Regional Research Centers [RRCs]) or a subset of national commodity programs (National Research Centers [NRCs]). In a few cases, centers were given joint responsibility for both regional and national research. The separation of crops and livestock research was at least administratively maintained by the creation of a deputy director for each, although crops and livestock programs were often combined in some of the national research centers, allowing the possibility of some joint research planning.

Defining a manageable number of research programs is difficult given the multispecies nature of Kenyan farming systems. In many ways, the scope of research programs in the whole CGIAR is telescoped into a single national system. The KARI programmatic structure covers the principal range of both tropical and temperate crops and the wide range of livestock species and livestock diseases (box 7.1). The question is whether maintaining a capacity in each of these areas is necessary. There are two arguments for such a broad scope in research programs. The first is that a minimal capacity is needed to borrow research results or techniques from other sources, to link to networks, or to adapt technologies to Kenyan conditions. What constitutes a minimal capacity will depend on what constitutes the main productivity constraints. The second argument is that almost any commodity will be at least regionally important, and to maintain an effective adaptive research program will require some minimal capacity in a broad scope of activities. For some commodity research programs, this minimal, "national" capacity is developed solely within the framework of the adaptive research programs. This might be said to apply to such programs as banana and rice.

155

Box 7.1 The KARI Programmatic Structure

Crops Department

Cereals	Root and tuber	Grain legumes	Horticultural	Industrial
Maize	Cassava	Beans	Vegetables	Oil crops
Wheat	Sweet potato	Cowpeas	Fruits	Fiber and cotton
Sorghum and millets	Irish potato		Herbs and spices	Sugarcane
Rainfed rice			Macadamia nuts	Pyrethrum
			Floriculture	

Livestock Research Department

Arid and semi-arid rangelands	Animal health	Animal production
Range resource management	Bacterial diseases	Dairy
Range animal production	Healminth diseases	Poultry
Arid range resource management	Ticks and tick-borne diseases	Beef
Livestock ecology and production	Viral diseases	Pasture and fodder
Animal health in arid-lands livestock	Wildlife diseases	
Modeling of range productivity and climatic factors	Veterinary epidemiology and economics	
Socioeconomics		

Scope is therefore managed in terms of program distribution across the research centers and the relative size of each research program. Box 7.2 presents their distribution. The location of the program largely depends on the relative distribution of the commodity or the location specificity of the research. However, many programs are an amalgamation of different commodities, for example, root and tubers, grain legumes, and horticulture. In this case, the program must make the decision on the relative scope of research activities and the location, because cassava and potatoes or beans and cowpeas have almost no overlap in terms of agro-ecological distribution. Moreover, basing several national commodity programs in a particular center does not necessarily lead to systems work between those programs. The adaptive research program is the framework by which this occurs, as the work of the commodity program is usually to link research efforts across research centers into a national program.

National Commodity Programs

The hypothesis is that managing scope in African NARS is not a function of the number of research programs, but of their relative size and resource deployment across them, again principally to maintain some capacity in each program for technology borrowing. Program size will determine their function, because small programs will focus much more on external linkages, technology borrowing, and adaptive research. Investments beyond this minimum capacity are then oriented to applied research directed toward technology development itself. However, limiting the scope of applied research programs is by no means straightforward, because these programs must also address the agro-ecological heterogeneity under which the commodities are produced and draw on the potential for economies of scope within centralized multidisciplinary teams. Obviously, the two tendencies pull in different directions, the first toward decentralization and separate research projects, and the second toward centralization, coordination of overall efforts, and priority assessment. The development of national commodity research programs within KARI very much reflects movement between these two poles.

Given that African economies are still primarily agrarian in structure and staples are important in production and consumption patterns, NARS will need to maintain

---

Box 7.2   **National Research Centers and Their Mandates**

National Research Centers	Crop/Commodity Factor (Mandates)
1. National Maize and Pasture Research Center, Kitale	Maize and pastures/fodder
2. National Wheat and Oilseeds Research Center, Njoro	Maize and oilseeds
3. National Horticultural Research Center, Thika	Horticultural crops (fruits, vegetables, beans)
4. National Potato Research Center, Tigoni	Potatoes, flowers
5. National Agricultural Research Center, Muguga	Animal nutrition and management, plant introduction and quarantine, genetics, soil and water conservation, plant physiology, agricultural engineering, agrometeorology, plant virology
6. National Veterinary Research Center, Muguga	Veterinary protozoology, virology, bacteriology, and helminthology
7. National Agricultural Research Laboratories, Nairobi	Soil chemistry and soil fertility, soil survey and land capability, postharvest technology, plant pathology, entomology, insect and pathogen taxonomy and surveys, pesticide analysis
8. National Animal Husbandry Research Center, Naivasha	Dairy and beef cattle, sheep and goats, pigs, poultry
9. National Dryland Farming Research Center, Katumani	Soil and water management, crop and animal production systems in dry areas
10. National Range Research Center, Kiboko	Range ecology management, agrometeorology, watershed management, range animal production
11. Veterinary laboratories, Kabete	Wildlife diseases, animal health component of Collaborative Research Support Project (CRSP) and veterinary virology
12. National Fiber Research Center, Mwea Tebere	Cotton and kenaf
13. National Seed Quality Research Center, Lanet	Seed research and technology, seed research-related services
14. National Pyrethrum Research Center, Njoro	Pyrethrum (including research-extension liaison)
15. National Sugar Research Center, Kibos	Sugar (including research-extension liaison)
16. National Irrigation and Drainage Research Center, Ahero (medium to long term)	Irrigation and drainage development
17. National Arid Lands Research Center, Marsabit	Range management and arid lands research

research capacity in their basic staple food crops. The KARI is no exception, and it maintains a large maize research program. The program will be used as an example of issues inherent in organizing national commodity programs. The KARI inherited the maize research structure put in place in the colonial period during the period 1955 to 1964. Four quite separate maize breeding programs were established in that period, one at Kitale breeding for highland environments, one at Embu breeding for mid-altitude environments, one at Katumani breeding for semi-arid environments, and one at

Table 7.1   Improved Maize Varieties Released in Kenya

Variety/Hybrid	Year Released	Age in 1992	Percentage of Area Planted to Variety/ Hybrid in 1992–93[a]	Weighted Average Age of Variety/ Hybrid[b]
Used in 1992–93:				
Coast composite	1974	18	0.95	0.17
Katumani composite B	1968	24	5.33	1.28
Makueni composite	1989	3	0.24	0.01
Hybrid Pwani	1989	3	0.59	0.02
Hybrid H511	1968	24	7.23	1.17
Hybrid H512	1970	22	3.67	0.81
Hybrid H632	1965	27	0.36	0.10
Hybrid H622	1965	27	2.13	0.58
Hybrid H613 D	1986	6	2.13	0.13
Hybrid H614 D	1986	6	41.83	2.51
Hybrid H525	1981	11	22.87	2.50
Hybrid H626	1989	3	12.80	0.38
Not used in 1992:				
Kitale synthetic II	1961	31	0.00	na
Katumani synthetic II	1963	29	0.00	na
Katumani composite A	1966	26	0.00	na
Hybrid H611	1964	28	0.00	na
Hybrid H621	1964	28	0.00	na
Hybrid H631	1964	28	0.00	na
Hybrid H611 C	1971	21	0.00	na
Hybrid H612 C	1966	26	0.00	na
Hybrid H613 C	1972	20	0.00	na
Hybrid H614 C	1976	16	0.00	na
Hybrid H612 D	1986	6	0.00	na
Total			100.00	10

Source: Kenya Agricultural Research Institute, Maize database records of crop improvement experiments, and farmer survey (1992–93).
a. These figures represent the percentage share of area sown to improved varieties and hybrids only, which occupy 73 percent of the area planted to maize in Kenya.
b. na = data not available.

Mtwapa breeding for lowland tropical environments. By the mid- to late 1960s, varieties were produced from each of these programs (table 7.1) that were the basis for relatively widespread adoption by both the large and small farm sectors (Hassan 1998). The challenge for the KARI maize program has been how to move to the next generation of maize technologies.

Over the last decade, KARI has faced a number of issues in developing a national maize program, the most important of which are:

1. Integrating the four programs into a national maize program;
2. Assessing the validity of the structure inherited in the reorganization;
3. Integrating breeding, crop protection, and agronomy so as to achieve better synergy between disciplines; and
4. Identifying the sources of economies of scope, in order to justify the formation of a national program.

Past success created a certain inertia, in that the widespread adoption of the new varieties made it difficult to challenge the underlying hypotheses governing the structure of the maize research effort. Breeding remained the core activity around which the program was organized. The original populations formed for the production of the first generation of varieties were maintained as the core of the breeding programs. Agronomy and crop protection scientists were attached to the individual regional programs, but usually with quite independent research agendas. The task was how to make the whole more than the sum of the parts.

Three elements have provided impetus for the movement toward a national program. The first, begun in 1992, was the development of a national research planning framework, the Kenya Maize Database (Hassan 1998). This national planning framework provided a quantitative basis for assessing breeding targets, agro-ecologies, and constraints on maize productivity. The exercise identified an agro-ecology—the transitional zone—for which there was no current breeding program, and yet which represented 45 percent of Kenyan maize production. This resulted in the creation of a breeding project for this ecology. It also provided a framework for priority assessment, and particularly showed the large differences in returns across ecologies (table 7.2). Thus, potential returns from maize research for the lowland tropics were only 0.3 percent of the returns to research in the moist transitional zone. However, adjustment of scope in relation to these findings was limited by the constraints on reallocating personnel between centers that were primarily under the jurisdiction of the center directors.

The second element began in 1997 and focused on developing the breeding program within a mutually interacting framework (Ochieng 1997). The components of this approach were:

1. A move away from a pure focus on breeding for yield to incorporating resistance to the principal biotic and abiotic constraints,

2. Specialization across stations in the development of source populations for resistance to specific constraints,
3. Close integration of pathology and entomology into the breeding program, and
4. A clearer specification of breeding targets for each of the maize ecologies.

Table 7.2   Net Potential Economic Surplus (million Kshs, real discount rate = 5%) Generated by Potential Kenya Agricultural Research Institute (KARI) Maize Program Research

Type of research/ surplus	Lowland Tropics	Dry Mid- altitude	Moist Mid- altitude	Dry Transitional	Moist Transitional	Highland Tropics	All Zones
Varietal development:							
Producer surplus	97.5	0	400.0	808.7	27,435.9	2,609.7	30,968.7
Consumer surplus	53.6	0	292.1	531.4	17,988.1	1,751.5	20,758.8
Total surplus	151.1	0	692.1	1,340.1	45,424.0	4,361.2	51,727.5
Crop management:							
Producer surplus	110.8	1,448.5	1,166.3	912.3	1,610.2	59.5	5,730,2
Consumer surplus	60.7	893.6	840.2	602.8	1,142.3	108.8	3,663.0
Total surplus	171.5	2,342.1	2,006.5	1,515.1	2,752.5	268.3	9,393.2
Technology environment:							
Producer surplus	59.6	490.0	934.1	265.6	2,534.7	2974.9	7,185.4
Consumer surplus	33.0	311.4	669.4	182.7	1,785.2	1,992.5	4,999.0
Total surplus	92.6	801.4	1,603.5	448.3	4,319.9	4,967.4	12,184.4

The focus was on achieving some returns to specialization while at the same time ensuring more integration of activities across the different sites.

The third element was the liberalization of the Kenyan maize seed market in the mid-1990s, allowing international seed companies to compete in a market previously reserved for the Kenyan Seed Company, which in turn relied on the production of KARI varieties. These companies particularly targeted the mid-altitude and transitional zones, where KARI had been least effective, with materials that had been developed primarily in southern Africa. Although increased competition had some natural impact, seed liberalization brought the issue of division of labor between private and public research to the fore. Seed liberalization reinforced the coordinated ecosystem breeding framework, in that public sector research would be focused on yield constraints where the private sector would likely not invest; and opened the avenue for alternative channels by which to disseminate KARI varieties and research, particularly through royalty arrangements.

The maize program closely tracked experience with other national commodity research programs. Although programs were given the mandate to develop applied research within a national framework, they had difficulty reconceptualizing research that achieved economies of scale or scope while at the same time working within a decentralized program structure. The latter was necessary (e.g., in Nigeria, commodity research remains centralized in national commodity research centers), but it limited achievement of the former. Detailed characterization of maize production within Kenya was necessary to provide a framework for planning at a national level, but it was not sufficient, in that a research strategy had to be developed around it. Moreover, the program was not given the overall responsibility for managing the scope of activities because it could deploy operational funds in relation to priorities, but there were constraints on redeploying scientific personnel.

Cross-Cutting, Disciplinary-Based Programs

Another approach to achieving economies of scope is to focus on intradisciplinary rather than interdisciplinary interaction. Alston and Pardey (1996) even hypothesize that "the potential is greater for intradisciplinary spillovers than for interdisciplinary spillovers," although their perspective was framed in the context of a university. The KARI has attempted to exploit such scope economies in social science and crop protection by creating structures that link scientists within these disciplines, but scattered across research centers and programs. Given that demand for these disciplines comes from virtually all commodity and adaptive research programs, the deployment of these disciplines needs to be rationalized across research programs.

Much of the agricultural research during the colonial period in the EAAFRO was organized along disciplinary lines, and this structure was maintained in incorporating research into the Kenyan MoA. The KARI thus inherited some centralized elements in pathology, entomology, and biological control, as well as many crop protection scientists distributed across commodity research programs. The central crop protection program at the National Agricultural Research Laboratory (NARL) has been searching for a framework for its own research, as well as for the coordination or linkage of research across the programs and centers. Given that more than ninety scientific staff work in the area of crop protection, the transactions costs in such an endeavor are large and the potential for conflicts in authority over research planning are also significant.

The research framework that has been created over the last three decades for research in crop protection is that of integrated pest management—that is, the integration of host plant resistance, biological control, cultural practices, and only when necessary the use of pesticides. Commodity breeding programs work on resistance, the biological control program develops such eponymous programs for a few targeted pests, and most of the crop protection scientists focus on the latter two components. Thus, the crop protection program has adopted an approach of identifying a priority set of pests and diseases on which to undertake research. Given the huge array of pests and diseases affecting the complex of crops on which KARI does research, priority setting has remained problematic, particularly given the limited database on which to make such judgments. The applied research program in the first five years thus tended to be spread across a range of studies, with little basis for judging the relative priority of the research. In the following five years these decisions were made in the context of either the crop program or the field-based, adaptive research

161

program, and the role of the central unit was therefore one of a backstopping, service function, providing analytical services and specialized research on request. Such a readjustment, however, is not easy, and organization of crop protection remains caught between the two positions.

Social science research, on the other hand, was not a feature of agricultural research in either the colonial period or the MoA. Rather, demand for social scientists evolved in relation to the development of both farming systems research and adaptive research programs, and social scientists were slowly added to center research programs. Demands from other quarters came for expertise in priority setting, impact assessment, and directed policy research, each requiring relatively specialized skills. Thus, a socioeconomic division was created in the mid-1990s to plan and allocate limited social science research staff. When the division was formed, there were only twenty-two staff in the socioeconomic division, only one of whom had a Ph.D. Thus, building social science capacity within KARI has been a principal feature of the internal organization of the institute.

The work of the social scientists was focused on farming systems characterization, technology assessment, and planning of adaptive research at the research centers and was principally based on farmer surveys. The issue was whether economies were possible in a more systematic approach to such work, particularly drawing on the experience of the maize database and on some specialization of function between technology assessment, impact evaluation, priority setting, and policy research. The database would require some capacity for coordination, and specialization would require some focused training. Given the demand for social scientists from the expanding adaptive research programs and the center directors' authority over their work, some centralized capacity was needed for social science. Assessing priorities for deployment of limited social science staff remains a difficult enterprise, not just for KARI but for virtually all agricultural research institutions.

Integrating Natural Resource Management

The organization of research on natural resource management (NRM) is a more recent issue, partly driven by the increasing attention to it within the CGIAR and partly driven by the increasing recognition of the problem within Kenya itself. Natural resource management research was difficult to structure within a commodity-based structure, divided as it was between crop and livestock research and where NRM cut across and integrated both components. In part natural resource management had some characteristics of a crosscutting research area, where much of the research was organized around the soil science discipline. On the other hand, the NRM research agenda was greatly defined by agro-ecology, being very different for the arid and semi-arid areas, compared to the well-watered, upland areas. This argued for a more decentralized approach to the research, but at the same time they needed to try to capture some scale and scope economies. Similar to the CGIAR, KARI has found no easy formula for the effective organization of NRM research.

When KARI was created it pulled in some of the seminal research programs on soil, water, watershed, and agrometeorology that had been developed under EAAFRO in the 1950s and 1960s. However, unlike NARO in Uganda, research on forestry and fisheries in Kenya was maintained in separate research organizations, and not incorporated into KARI, creating some problems in mandate and capacity in the evolving area of agroforestry. Thus, the restructuring led to the creation of several national programs distributed across different centers and agro-ecologies. The national agricultural research laboratory at Kabete maintained a national capacity in soils and land capability mapping, soil chemistry, and plant nutrition. Muguga developed a research program on soil and water conservation in the upland areas, and Katumani in the semi-arid areas. Kiboko was responsible for range ecology in the semi-arid areas, and Marsabit for range management in the arid areas. Each program developed quite independently and in the first five years focused principally on process studies carried out on the research stations. The potential scale and scope economies of integrating the centralized capacity at the NARL in soil science with the soil management work in the other centers were not realized in this period.

In the late 1990s NRM was decentralized or "mainstreamed" across the different centers. The NRM research shifted from a more applied to a more adaptive focus (see next section). This allowed a more whole farm, systems focus, the integration of a wider array of disciplines, and further specificity in agro-ecologies. This shift was in part backstopped by CGIAR centers, especially the International Centre for Research in Agroforestry (ICRAF), and networks both within Kenya (e.g., the legume research network managed from NARL) and within ASARECA, particularly the African Highlands Initiative (AHI). This shift started with the centers in the highland areas and has more slowly taken hold in the arid and semi-arid areas. The NRM research is still evolving and the actual impacts of the change in organization on resource management are yet to be seen on a wide scale. If anything, what have been lost are the more rigorous process studies, especially longer-term instrumentation and monitoring of watersheds, as was done in EAAFRO in the 1950s. The NRM research demonstrates many of the issues in defining a relative balance between adaptive and applied research and how to maintain effective linkages between the two. This issue is turned to in the next section.

Organizing Adaptive Research

The KARI is relatively unique in sub-Saharan Africa in the structure it has adopted in organizing agricultural research, attempting to integrate a national commodity research program framework into a decentralized structure of regional research centers that focus on more systems and adaptive research. The NARO in Uganda and the Nigerian agricultural research system are organized purely in terms of national commodity research programs and centers. However, the recent and dominant trend is to organize research within the framework of decentralized, regional centers. Thus, the Tanzanian research system has recently adopted this model, and the Ethiopian system, the Ethiopian Agricultural Research Organization (EARO), is also moving in this direction, compounded by the simultaneous development of a federal-province type of system. Before evaluating KARI's regional research system, a consideration of the forces driving the movement to a more decentralized system is necessary to set the stage.

Demand-Responsive Research Systems

Different streams of thinking on why agricultural research investment has had such little apparent impact in Africa have converged on the idea that technologies remain inappropriate to the needs of African farmers and that national research systems need to be more responsive to those needs. This book explores the complexity of organizing the technology supply side. It argues that just making agricultural research more demand-responsive will not in and of itself fill the breach, without also addressing many of the other institutional issues. In fact, the trend toward making research structures more demand-responsive started with the farming systems movement of the 1970s, which exposed the limitations of station-bound agricultural research. Two decades of work followed on how to target the technology development process more precisely to the needs of farmers. This has primarily focused on on-farm research and development of better information databases and methods for research planning. However, a series of more recent developments has raised even further the profile of farmer integration into the research process.

The leading element in this process has been the transformation of farming systems research into farmer participatory research (FPR) (Chambers, Pacey, and Thrupp 1989; Scoones and Thompson 1994). This has brought with it an agenda for institutional reform that is usually framed in terms of a reversal or reform of what is termed the transfer of technology model of organizing agricultural research (Chambers 1989). Ashby and Sperling (1995) best summarized the elements of this agenda: research "is client-driven, requires decentralized technology development, devolves to farmers the responsibility for adaptive testing, and requires institutions and individuals to become accountable for the relevance and quality of technology on offer."

Decentralization of agricultural research, so that each center defines its research agenda in terms of its subregional mandate area, has some congruence with the trend to administrative decentralization of public services in which health, extension, and livestock services are financed and managed at a district level. Donors, administrative structures, and agricultural research seem to be converging on a district focus, although with the distinct potential for loss of economies of scope or scale.

Two other factors reinforce a move toward autonomous, regional research institutes. The first is the creation of a range of commodity research networks within regional bodies, such as ASARECA and SACCAR (Eicher and Rukuni 2003). These regional frameworks are intended to rationalize applied research across countries and to integrate that capacity with research within the IARCs. In theory, a movement to subregional adaptive research institutes would build demand linkages with farmers and rely on the networks for technologies, techniques, and applied research needs to feed into them. However, the transactions costs for each network to build links to each research station in a country are large, and in the end shift the costs of applied research to other NARS or IARCs. The second factor is the recent emphasis put on systems research, such as agroforestry, integrated pest management, integrated nutrient management, or NRM. Systems research entails such components as research on processes, modeling, monitoring, and research in situ in what are termed benchmark sites. The organization of regional research stations lends itself to such a systems research focus.

Engineering agricultural research structures so that technology development is more responsive to farmer requirements has been on the African agricultural research agenda for two decades. Field methods have played a large part, but some experimentation has also been undertaken with institutional models. Most of this experience rests with regionally based Adaptive Research Teams, which are based on extension models rather than on research models, and which have been instituted in such countries as Nigeria, Zambia, and Malawi. Links back to research in general have remained weak. During the farming systems period, adaptive research units were created in research stations with a mandate for on-farm research. Such a model was probably most effective in Ethiopia, but because the teams were often staffed with young economists and agronomists, interaction with principal research programs was limited. The move to use adaptive research to organize the whole research center is thus an attempt to do away with administrative divisions between on-station and on-farm research and to create a research environment that encourages solutions to farmers' problems. However, Tanzania's approach of creating independent zonal centers is very different from the KARI approach of locating regional centers in a matrix of applied research programs.

Organizing Adaptive Research

Adaptive research at KARI is done through RRCs. There are ten such centers, six of which have only an adaptive research mandate, and four of which combine both regional and national mandates (box 7.3). Contiguous districts have been identified as mandate zones and allocated to each of the centers so that the whole country is covered. A deputy director oversees adaptive research, but the principal research decisions are decentralized to the research stations through the Center Research Appraisal Committee (CRAC). No structured mechanisms are in place for interaction across the RRCs. As such, they provide a relatively dense coverage of agricultural and livestock production in the country.

Although RRCs were embodied in the original structure of KARI, only in the last five years have adaptive research programs been actively developed at the centers, mostly with directed support from a range of donors. The focus has been on developing an on-farm research capacity, with much less emphasis on the on-station component. Because district boundaries created the zones, each center faces significant heterogeneity in agro-ecological conditions and must divide up its mandate area into recommendation domains. In each, village-based benchmark sites are identified within which the on-farm research is carried out, usually within an FPR framework. The research is done within the context of the whole farming system, and is backstopped

Box 7.3	Regional Research Centers (RRCs) and Mandate Districts in Kenya
Center	**Mandate District**
RRC Embu	Embu, Kirinyaga, Nyeri, Tharaka-Nithi, and Nyambene
Garissa	Garissa, Wajir, Mandera, and Marsabit
RRC Kakamega	Kakamega, Bungoma, Busia, Nandi, Siaya, Vihiga, and Mt. Elgon
National Dryland Farming Research Centre (NDFRC)	Katumani, Machakos, Kajiado, Makueni, Mwingi, and Kitui
RRC Kisii	Kisii, Nyamira, Kericho, Kisumu, Homa Bay, Migori, Bomet, and Kuria
National Agricultural Research Council (NARC)	Kitale, Trans Nzoia, West Pokot, Uasin Gishu, Keiyo, Marakwet
NARC Muguga	Kiambu, Murang'a, Thika, and Greater Nairobi
RRC Mtwapa	Kilifi, Kwale, Mombasa, Taita Taveta, Lamu, and Tana River
National Plant Breeding Research Centre (NPBRC) Njoro	Nakuru, Narok Nyandarua, and Laikipia
RRC Perkerra	Baringo, Samburu, and Turkana

by a multidisciplinary team of scientists. There has been a sense of long-term commitment to each of the sites, which usually number about ten to fifteen for each of the centers. Several years are required to make a program such as this operational, so that most of researchers' time and operational budgets have gone into establishing a system of on-farm research sites.

Adaptive research at KARI represents a substantial investment of staff and funds. It is too early to evaluate the return on that investment, but several emerging issues can be identified. The first, and critical point, is that progress in adaptive research depends on a steady flow of research products and information into the process. Improved varieties in most cases provide the entry point in terms of capturing farmer interest, allowing, in turn, the introduction of more complex technologies in such areas as pest control, soil erosion control, or soil fertility management. However, success here depends on a steady flow of germplasm into the program from breeding programs. Adaptive research programs have the ability to select and evaluate relatively advanced populations, but have little capacity to create those populations or make the crosses. Thus, systematic links to applied research programs (particularly breeding programs) are critical, yet these links remain underdeveloped.

Given the number of crop and livestock components in Kenyan mixed farming systems, and the number of potential constraints on each, the scope of possible research topics even at this level remains large. Moreover, the expertise to manage such topics as striga, stem borer, micronutrient deficiencies, or viruses is significant and in many centers requires links back to that expertise somewhere else in the KARI system. Establishing those links, identifying whether the need is for information, products, or joint research, and adjusting respective time commitments all make the process of effective interaction between adaptive and applied research organizationally complex.

The linkage problem has an attendant secondary issue, which is the decision to undertake on-station research. Optimally there should be an iterative process of on-farm and on-station research. The question of what types of on-station research should be pursued is a difficult one, especially in relation to the wide range of possible topics identified in the on-farm research. Factors involved include researcher time commitments to the on-farm research, transactions costs in establishing links to specialists on the problem, difficulties inherent in establishing what research has already been done on the problem, and scientist research experience on the topic.

Finally, the density of the on-farm research effort in Kenya raises the question of the functional division of labor with extension. Each RRC will have a center research extension liaison officer from the extension system, who will be the point of contact with the research system. However, the adoption of an FPR approach, the relative density of on-farm research capacity throughout the country, and the seamless weaving of demonstration plots, farmer field days, farmer-to-farmer exchange, on-farm, farmer-managed research trials, and on-farm, researcher-managed trials in the benchmark villages combine both the adaptive research and extension functions. Also, productivity change in low-input African systems may be based as much on improved management as on the adoption of inputs. Therefore the scaling-up process may not be so much the extension of particular technologies—often within relatively narrow domains—as the expansion of the adaptive research process (Farrington 1998). Thus, the overall structure of agricultural research and extension systems in Kenya and other African systems over the next decade will depend critically on how adaptive research is organized and evolves.

Conclusions

The vocabulary of today's debates about agricultural research is phrased in terms of farmer demand and participation and of restructuring research organizations to be more demand responsive. The view is forward-looking and is based on restructuring on the basis of key principles. The debate misses virtually all of the issues developed in this chapter, namely the history and evolution of research systems, the complexity of the research task, the organizational trade-offs in the search for efficiencies and economies of scale and scope, the balance of adaptive and applied research structures, and the continuous need to adjust to limited resources. The NAROs have changed significantly in the last decade, particularly from their nadir in the institutional crises of the 1980s. The current debate essentially argues that effective demand, if allowed to express itself, will bring forth its own supply of research products. The argument in this chapter is that it is not necessarily so. Just as market liberalization did not bring forth a huge response by the private sector, so increasing farmer voice in the development of agricultural technologies—although inarguably useful—does not necessarily guarantee that the best research products will be forthcoming. The organizational, institutional, and structural constraints on that must also be addressed, just as those constraints must be addressed in developing effective agricultural markets on the continent.

167

REFERENCES

Alston, Julian M., and Philip G. Pardey. 1996. *Making science pay: The economics of agricultural R&D policy.* Washington, D.C.: NEI Press.

Alston, Julian M., George W. Norton, and Philip G. Pardey. 1995. *Science under scarcity. Principles and practise for agricultural research evaluation and priority setting.* Ithaca, N.Y.: Cornell University Press.

Ashby, Jacqueline A., and Louise Sperling. 1995. Institutionalizing participatory, client-driven research and technology development in agriculture. *Development and Change* 26:753–70.

Byerlee, Derek, and Carl K. Eicher, eds. 1997. *Africa's emerging maize revolution.* Boulder, Colo.: Lynne Rienner.

Chambers, Robert. 1989. *The state and rural development: Ideologies and an agenda for the 1990s.* Brighton, UK: Institute of Development Studies at the University of Sussex.

Chambers, Robert, Arnold Pacey, and Lori Ann Thrupp, eds. 1989. *Farmer first. Farmer innovation and agricultural research.* London: Intermediate Technology Publications.

Collinson, M. P., ed. 2000. *A history of farming systems research.* Wallingford, UK: CABI International

Eicher, Carl K. 1990. Building African scientific capacity for agricultural development. *Agricultural Economics* 4:117–43.

Eicher, Carl K., and Mandivamba Rukuni. 2003. *The CGIAR in Africa: Past, present, and future.* Washington, D.C.: World Bank Operations Evaluation Department.

Eyzaguirre, Pablo. 1996. *Agricultural and environmental research in small countries: Innovative approaches to strategic planning.* Chichester, UK: John Wiley.

Farrington, John. 1998. *Organisational roles in farmer participatory research and extension: Lessons learned from the last decade.* Natural Resource Perspectives No. 27. London: Overseas Development Institute (ODI).

Farrington, John, Anthony Bebbington, Kate Wellard, and David Lewis. 1993. *Reluctant partners? Nongovernmental organizations, the state and sustainable agricultural development.* New York: Routledge.

Franzel, Steven, and Helen van Houten, eds. 1992. *Research with farmers: Lessons from Ethiopia.* Wallingford, UK: CAB International.

Hassan, Rashid M, ed. 1998. *Maize technology development and transfer: A GIS application for research planning in Kenya.* Wallingford, UK: CAB International.

Idachaba, Francis. 1980. *Agricultural research policy in Nigeria.* Washington, D.C.: International Food Policy Research Institute (IFPRI).

National Academy of Sciences. 1974. *Food science in developing countries: A selection of unsolved problems.* Washington, D.C.: National Academy of Science National Public Research Council and U.S. Department of Commerce and National Technical Information Service.

Nweke, Felix, Dunstan D. C. Spencer, and John Lynam, eds. 2002. *The cassava transformation: Africa's best-kept secret.* East Lansing: Michigan State University Press.

Ochieng, Ondolo H. A. 1997. A study of regional determinants of mortality differentials in children (Kenya). Ph.D. diss., University of London.

Omamo, Steven W. 1998. Transport costs and smallholder cropping choices: An application to Siaya District, Kenya. *American Journal of Agricultural Economics* 80:116–23.

Pardey, Philip G., Johannes Roseboom, and Jock R. Anderson. 1991. *Agricultural research policy: International quantitative perspectives.* Cambridge, UK: Press Syndicate of the University of Cambridge.

168

Pardey, Philip G., Johannes Roseboom, and Nienke M. Beintema. 1997. Investments in African agricultural research. *World Development* 25:409–23.

Roseboom, Johannes, and Philip G. Pardey. 1993. *Statistical brief on the national agricultural research system of Kenya.* International Service for National Agricultural Research (ISNAR) Statistical Brief No. 5. The Hague: ISNAR.

Ruttan, Vernon W. 1982. *Agricultural research policy.* Minneapolis: University of Minnesota Press.

Scoones, Ian, and John Thompson, eds. 1994. *Beyond farmer first: Rural people's knowledge, agricultural research and extension practice.* London: Intermediate Technology Publications.

Spencer, Dunstan S. C. 1996. Infrastructure and technology constraints to agricultural development in the humid and subhumid tropics of Africa. *African Development Review* 8:68–93.

Wood, Stanley, and Phillip G. Pardey. 1994. Supporting agricultural research policy decisions: An econometric-ecologic systems approach. In *Opportunities, use and transfer of systems research methods in agriculture into developing countries,* ed. Peter G. Goldsworthy and Frits Penning de Vries. Dordrecht, the Netherlands: Kluwer Academic Publishers.

8

Toward an Institutional Planning, Monitoring, and Evaluation System

ADIEL N. MBABU AND DOUGLAS HORTON

Introduction

Planning, monitoring, and evaluation (PM&E) are generally agreed to be relatively weak areas in agricultural research management that need improvement. At the International Service for National Agricultural Research (ISNAR) and elsewhere much time and effort has gone into developing, refining, and adapting PM&E tools and methods for application in national agricultural research organizations. Substantial technical support has been provided and numerous training courses organized. Yet, the introduction and sustained use of these tools and methods has often been far less than anticipated. Relatively few agricultural research organizations have achieved the goal of establishing PM&E systems that effectively support management decision making and accountability. In this chapter we attempt to explain why efforts to strengthen PM&E often fail, and to identify some promising avenues for capacity building in this strategic area of management.

What Is an Institutional PM&E System?

An institutional system for PM&E can be thought of as the "central nervous system" of an agricultural research organization. Such a system keeps managers in touch with all parts of the organization and with the external environment. It provides top managers with information needed to set broad goals, chart appropriate courses of action, and send consistent signals to the organization's members, who stimulate appropriate responses to opportunities and threats as they arise. An institutional PM&E system also allows decision makers throughout the organization to keep in touch with one another and to coordinate their activities efficiently, within the framework of a coherent overall strategy. An institutional system continuously monitors the organization's activities as well as its internal and external environment. It also records information on experiences that aid in reflection, analysis, and organizational learning.

The Agricultural Research Organization as a Production System

An agricultural research organization can be viewed as a type of production system that operates within a given physical, economic, and institutional environment. It captures resources, or inputs, from the environment and carries out research and related activities to transform them into useful information and technologies. These research outputs flow back to, and impact upon, the environment (figure 8.1).

Let us consider the Kenya Agricultural Research Institute (KARI), established to generate information and technology (outputs) that contribute to agricultural development and the well-being of the Kenyan people (impact). The institute operates within a dynamic environment with a multiplicity of physical, social, economic, and institutional dimensions. To produce the outputs expected of it, KARI employs a range of scientific, physical, and financial inputs and engages in a wide range of research and research-related activities (internal processes). These are organized in projects and programs, and are executed in decentralized research centers and laboratories, coordinated from its headquarters on the outskirts of Nairobi.

Management Systems and Functions

In order to provide direction and to ensure the adequate use of resources in the pursuit of desired goals, complex organizations such as KARI develop management systems. In earlier times, when research organizations were smaller, their mandates and research processes were simpler; and when they had fewer clients and stakeholder groups, management systems were correspondingly simple. However, as modern research organizations have become more complex, so have their management systems.

Management systems vary considerably from organization to organization, but effective systems all perform certain basic functions. They obtain resources and control their use. They provide direction and supervise ongoing operations. They provide conditions necessary for internal specialization and the coordination of activities in order to meet client needs. An organization without an effective management system

Figure 8.1   The Agricultural Research Organization as a Production System

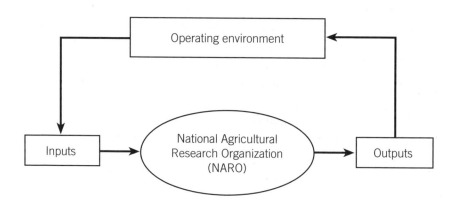

that performs these functions has little chance of survival in the current era of organizational and institutional dislocations (Drucker 1989; Meyer 1995; Gálvez et al. 1995).

Agricultural research organizations have hierarchical structures with at least three decision-making levels. Top-level managers are concerned with decisions that affect the entire organization and its activities. Mid-level managers are responsible for individual research units, such as divisions, programs, or centers that carry out research in specific areas or on specific problem areas. At the base of the hierarchy, scientists carry out individual research activities, often grouped into projects.

The terms "project" and "program" are often confused. In this chapter, we use the following definitions, drawn from the general management literature. A project is a set of research activities designed to achieve specific objectives within a specified period of time; it is composed of interrelated research activities or experiments that share a rationale, objectives, plan of action, schedule for completion, budget, inputs, outputs, and intended beneficiaries. A program is a broader set of research projects or activities that is oriented toward the attainment of higher-level objectives; programs generally have longer planning horizons than do projects (Horton et al. 1993; Dale 1998).

In agricultural research organizations, projects and activities can be viewed as falling within the cells of a "management matrix" formed by the spheres of influence of crosscutting programs and research centers (figure 8.2). In such a management matrix, a researcher may report to both a center director and a program leader. The center-program matrix has built-in tensions concerning the control of operating funds and resources. In such cases as the Instituto Nacional de Tecnología Agropecuária (INTA), Argentina, and the Empresa Brasileira de Pesquisa Agropecuária (EMBRAPA), Brazil, center directors control operating funds, and program leaders play scientific and coordinating roles. In other cases, such as the Instituto Nacional de

Figure 8.2 The Center-Program Management Matrix

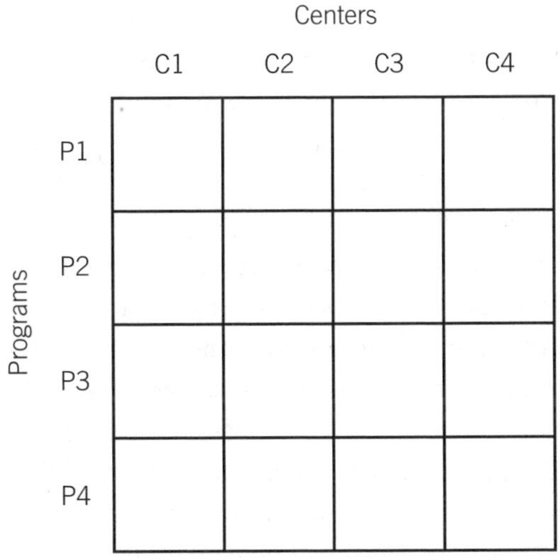

Investigacíon Agraria (INIA), Uruguay, and KARI, program leaders control operating funds and center directors play essentially administrative and facilitating roles.

In organizations such as KARI, where external donors fund specific projects or programs, the management structure is much more complex. To the extent that individual researchers receive funds from, and are hence accountable to, a number of different donors, internal management and accountability can be seriously weakened.

Planning, Monitoring, and Evaluation as Strategic Management Functions

Planning, monitoring, and evaluation are strategic functions of a management system, in that they affect the performance of other management functions.

Planning is a periodic process for assessing needs and opportunities, establishing goals, setting priorities, and deciding on courses of action for achieving goals. Planning can help build a consensus and commitment to the mandate, direction, and priorities of a research program or organization. It is often said that a well-orchestrated planning process is more useful than an excellent planning document produced through a faulty process (i.e., without appropriate involvement of organizational members and other key stakeholders).

Monitoring involves a process of continuous or frequent observation and checking. Originally, in Latin, to monitor was to warn. In current usage, research monitoring involves observation and collection of information about activities to ensure they are proceeding according to plan, to warn of deviations from initial goals, and to provide a record of input use, activities, and results. For monitoring to serve as a useful management function, data gathering and analysis must be coupled with reflection, consultation with peers and supervisors, feedback, decisions, and actions that improve research processes.

Evaluation, often confused with monitoring, is a more thorough and reflective analytical process undertaken at specified points in time in order to judge, appraise, or determine the worth or value of something. In an agricultural research organization, an evaluation may involve determining the relevance and quality of proposed research, the efficiency and effectiveness of ongoing research, the quality of research outputs, or the impact of completed research. An evaluation may also judge the replicability of a research approach or finding, or the sustainability of a development effort or of its results (Horton et al. 1993; Dale 1998).

The Need for Integration and Harmonization of PM&E Activities

In an integrated, institutional PM&E system, planning, monitoring, and evaluation operate as linked phases in a management cycle that is implemented at each decision-making level. The linking of planning, monitoring, and evaluation at a given decision-making level is referred to as *horizontal integration*. At the beginning of the management cycle, planning is carried out to assess client needs and research opportunities, to establish goals and set priorities, and to identify courses of action to achieve goals. Plans contain milestones and targets that are used as reference points in subsequent monitoring and evaluation. During implementation of planned work, progress toward goals is monitored, to permit adjustments to be made in planned activities; key information on activities, resource use, and results is recorded for use in later, more in-depth, evaluation. Toward the end of the management cycle, results are evaluated in relation to plans, and findings are fed forward into the next cycle to improve planning and the design of future research activities (figure 8.3).

The management cycle is generally longest at the institute level, a little shorter at the center and program levels, and shorter yet at the project and activity levels. In the Consultative Group on International Agricultural Research (CGIAR), for example, system reviews are carried out about every ten years; individual centers prepare strategic plans every five years; programs are reviewed about every three years; and projects are often reviewed annually. KARI's long-term planning horizon is twenty years; program planning has a five-year horizon; projects and activities are reviewed annually.

In addition to horizontal integration—at a given decision-making level—integrated PM&E systems are characterized by *vertical integration* between decision-making levels. An organization's strategic planning should inform, and be informed by, planning carried out for research centers, programs, projects, and activities. Similarly, progress reports prepared for research projects should form the basis for program and institute reports. Such vertical integration requires the use of standardized and compatible procedures for PM&E at all levels of the organization.

Planning, monitoring, and evaluation at any level require information on four classes of variables:

Figure 8.3   The Management Cycle

Revise plans

Planning
• Assess needs
• Set goals
• Develop plans
• Identify monitoring and evaluation indicators

Evaluation

STOP

Continue research

Implementation/Monitoring
• Carry out research
• Adjust plans

175

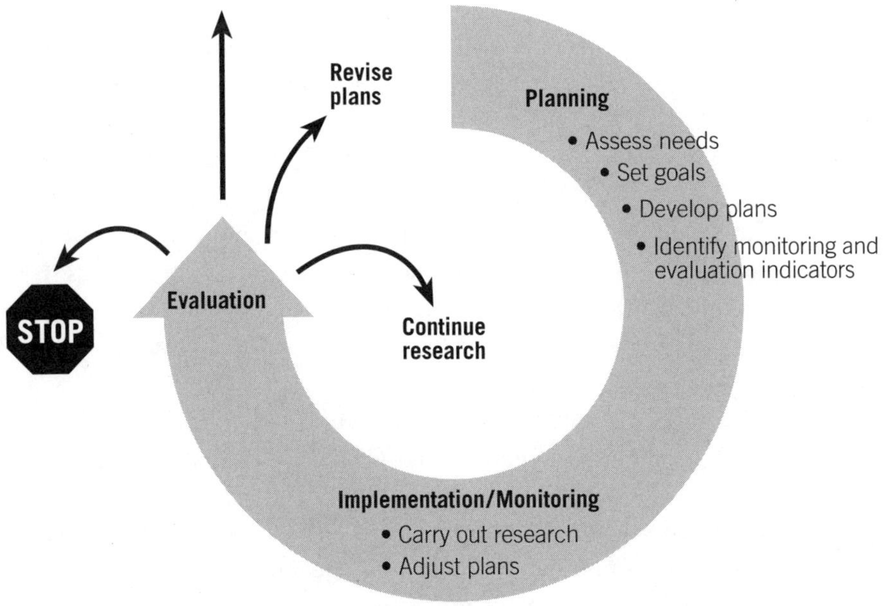

Figure 8.4 Ideal Model of an Institutional Planning, Monitoring, and Evaluation (PM&E) System for a Research Organization

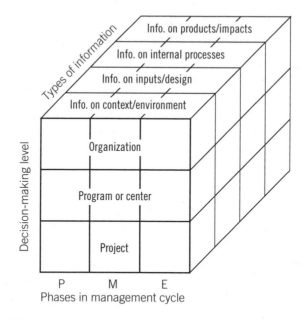

Based on Gálvez et al. 1995 and Stufflebeam 1985.

1. The context of research (e.g., client needs and existing knowledge in the field);
2. Research inputs (e.g., physical, financial, and human);
3. Research processes (e.g., objectives, designs, and implementation procedures); and
4. Research products (e.g., their characteristics, use, and impact).

In research plans, much of this information is based on assumptions and expectations. In monitoring, estimates are gradually made firm. In evaluations, an attempt is made to document actual results.

Figure 8.4 illustrates the three main dimensions of an institutional PM&E system as discussed previously, where planning, monitoring, and evaluation take place at all decision-making levels. Activities of PM&E at each level and phase in the management cycle inform, and are informed by, those at other levels and phases. They are concerned with information on four aspects of research: the context or environment in which it is carried out, research inputs (e.g., designs and plans), research processes, and research products and impacts.

Integration requires a minimum of standardization and compatibility of the information provided by each of the organization's divisions, centers, programs, and projects. It also requires the coordination and synchronization of PM&E processes, to ensure that information required for decision making and reporting is available to the person needing it, at the time needed, and in a useable form. These requirements imply the need for harmonized PM&E procedures and processes.

Utility of an Institutional PM&E System

An institutional PM&E system supports three crucial organizational functions, as outlined in the following.

Fund-Raising and Accountability

Perhaps the most widely appreciated use of PM&E is to ensure that the organization is able to obtain and account for the resources it needs to operate. The term "accountability," much in vogue nowadays, refers to the obligation of an organization or its members to account for, report on, explain, or justify their actions or the use of resources entrusted to them. In practical terms, it refers to the responsibility of a research organization and its staff to account for research expenditures and provide evidence of performance to those who have provided resources (e.g., taxpayers, the Ministry of Finance, producer groups, external donors, or financial agencies).

Concerns for "transparency" and "governance" are closely associated with accountability. In recent years, demands have risen for organizations, particularly in the public sector, to upgrade their governance and management, to be transparent in their decision making and actions, and to be accountable to their stakeholders. The scope of accountability has broadened to cover not only the use of resources in conformity with established norms, but also the attainment of high levels of performance, in terms of goal achievement and benefits for society.

Recently, a strong trend has been to reduce "core" resources for research, from the public treasury or from donor grants, in favor of "project" funding from competitive sources that is earmarked for use in specific research or development projects designed to achieve specific objectives and produce specific predefined research products or services. In this context, planning, monitoring, and evaluation are essential. Those who provide core funds expect organizations to possess modern management systems that incorporate such components as strategic and operational planning, management information systems, quality assurance procedures, and performance measurement and enhancement systems. Those who offer project funding through competitive schemes are yet more demanding. Access to funding is based on the submission of well-crafted, competitive projects that offer useful outputs in defined time periods with defined budgets. Management of external project funding requires careful monitoring. Evaluation of results is essential for learning the lessons that can help improve future project activities.

Management Decision Making

Institutional PM&E processes support decision making in several ways. Through strategic planning, an organization builds a sense of organizational purpose, direction, and cohesion. A strategic plan provides the broad framework within which meaningful programs and projects can be developed that contribute to a common goal (Collion 1989; Mintzberg 1994). Operational plans for programs and projects translate broad organizational goals and strategies into concrete targets and implementation plans.

177

Monitoring allows researchers and managers to keep abreast of "current events" inside and outside of the organization, to check on work, and to reflect on the progress being made. Regular field visits and preparation and review of progress reports and other monitoring tools can play a valuable role in research management by motivating staff members and their supervisors to reflect on work, to provide and receive feedback, and to take corrective measures where needed. The hallmarks of effective institutional monitoring are individual reflection and suggestions from clients, peers, and supervisors that lead to useful action. Unfortunately, monitoring often becomes a mechanistic administrative activity with a one-way flow of information. In such a case, individuals hastily complete forms, supervisors provide little or no feedback on substantive issues, and monitoring ceases to contribute to the improvement of research activities.

Research activities, by their nature, involve numerous types of evaluation. In planning and executing their work, scientists routinely evaluate such areas as researchability of topics, quality of research designs, effects of research treatments, validity of findings, and quality of research publications. These types of evaluations, which are seen as part and parcel of the scientific method, are usually carried out with a minimum of organizational oversight, through the use of expert or peer judgments, and are necessary for the conduct of high-quality research. However, they do not suffice for the management of an agricultural research organization. Periodic evaluations of projects, programs, centers, and staff members are also required, as are occasional reviews of the organization as a whole.

The value of evaluation is that it serves to "close the loop" in the management cycle, bringing closure to one cycle and preparing the way for the next. Evaluations provide opportunities for the organization's members, in consort with external stakeholders and external peers or evaluation specialists, to take stock of what has been accomplished during the management cycle in relation to the initial objectives. An evaluation can provide a wealth of information on client needs, the continuing relevance of research objectives, the quality of research designs, the adequacy of management procedures, the efficiency and effectiveness of research work carried out, and the outcomes and impacts produced. (Effectiveness refers to the extent to which research achieves its objectives; efficiency refers to cost-effectiveness.) At their best, evaluations involve organizational members, clients, and stakeholders in ways that produce new insights for each group on research problems and approaches (for methods, see Patton 1997).

Organizational Learning and Improvement
Although discrete PM&E activities can be valuable in and of themselves, the benefits for individual and organizational learning are far greater when they are carried out as intimately related parts of an institutional management system. When the notion of the management cycle and the fundamentals of PM&E become ingrained in the thinking and actions of an organization's members, it leads to a valuable process of continuous learning and improvement.

178

An institutional PM&E system is an essential feature of what has recently come to be known as organizational learning–the process by which an organization continuously expands its capacity to "create its future" (Senge 1994). Organizational learning goes beyond individual learning by incorporating lessons from experience into the organization's values, norms, and operating procedures (Kline and Saunders 1993; Mabey and Iles 1994). In the management cycle, the PM&E phases are analogous to the phases in an effective learning process—presentation of concepts and information, practical application of the concepts and information imparted, and review of performance and feedback from peers and facilitators (Zapata 1992). The management cycle presented here is also essentially the same as the total quality management cycle, with four steps—plan, do, check, and act (Tribus 1987; Roberts 1991).

To the extent that PM&E becomes institutionalized—embedded in the operations and culture of an organization—the organization in question becomes a "learning organization" that continuously learns from its experiences and applies that learning to the improvement of its operations, thereby enhancing its performance. Some key issues of institutionalization are discussed in the following section.

From Theory to Practice: Experiences with PM&E in KARI

Up to this point, we have discussed the key features, characteristics, and uses of an ideal type of institutional PM&E system. Being an ideal, what we have described cannot be found in practice in any agricultural research organization. In most organizations, in fact, the practice of PM&E is far removed from the ideal. In this regard, KARI is the norm, not the exception. However, well-functioning, high-performance organizations usually have many of the PM&E system elements we have described, and over time they are moving in the direction of the ideal system. Organizational change processes have been poorly documented and are little understood, particularly in agricultural research organizations. In this section we describe and assess recent KARI experiences with strengthening PM&E.

Since the time that KARI was created, the importance of PM&E has been acknowledged, to ensure efficient and effective research management and to account for the use of resources. However, until recently, this realization has not been accompanied by a coherent strategy for building an institutional PM&E system. Nor have resources been made available to carry out PM&E as institutional processes in support of KARI management. Some different initiatives at different points in time have aimed at achieving different objectives. There have been, for example, a number of planning exercises at different organizational levels. Many of these have been carried out in conjunction with negotiations for external funding. Funding agencies have also required extensive monitoring and evaluation of the work they have funded. KARI researchers commonly prepare quarterly reports for donor agencies, and donor projects are typically reviewed at midterm and evaluated upon completion. Donors have also arranged for a number of assessments of the impact of KARI research. The result is that a multiplicity of PM&E activities have been carried out by, for, or with KARI

179

staff members. Yet these activities have often been in isolation, and sometimes they have worked at cross-purposes. The need to harmonize the different procedures and activities and to integrate them into a comprehensive institutional system is only now being realized and put into practice.

In this section, we describe some experiences with PM&E in KARI. The discussion is structured around ten propositions drawn from KARI experience and that of other agricultural research organizations with which we are familiar. The experiences with PM&E outside of KARI are principally in Latin America and the Caribbean, where ISNAR has worked with some organizations to strengthen their PM&E over a number of years (Novoa and Horton 1994; Andersen et al. 1998; Horton and Borges-Andrade 1999; Horton and Novoa, 1998). We have phrased the propositions in such a way as to provoke reflection and to provide a sense of direction for future efforts to strengthen PM&E. As the propositions are drawn from a rather limited base of experience, they should be considered as potentially useful ideas to be subject to further verification rather than as well-established principles.

Proposition 1: There is a tendency to overemphasize the importance of planning and to divorce it from "M&E"

In this section, we draw heavily on Taylor (1991) and Majisu and Wapakala (1994). KARI has considerable experience with the planning of agricultural research. In 1981, the Kenyan government commissioned ISNAR to carry out a diagnostic review of the national agricultural research system (ISNAR 1981). The review was carried out as a joint effort of ISNAR staff members (two), consultants (three), and Kenyan professionals (three) who were familiar with the country's research system.

In organizing the review and subsequent activities, ISNAR employed what it called the "D-P-I framework" for institutional strengthening, which includes diagnostic review, followed by planning, and later implementation. In this framework, ISNAR provided leadership for the diagnostic phase, worked jointly with agricultural leaders in the planning phase, and played a supporting or backstopping role during implementation of planned activities. The Kenya review was significant for ISNAR, because it was the first of forty such reviews to be carried out over the next decade (on ISNAR experience with diagnostic reviews, see Reijmerinck and Uribe [1991]). Usually such reviews were requested by countries in the context of preparing a large-scale project to be funded by an external donor or financial agency, aimed at strengthening agricultural research capacity in the country.

The emphasis in the D-P-I sequence is on planning for institutional strengthening. The review phase was designed to lead into planning. Implementation, monitoring, and evaluation were left to local authorities and those who funded the plan. There was no explicit mechanism for linking planning, monitoring, and evaluation. The Kenya-ISNAR review assessed some key aspects of the research system (ISNAR 1981):

- System structure, organization, and management;
- Research policies, programs, and priorities;
- Generation and application of research knowledge;
- Gaps in the current research, services, and training; and
- General requirements for strengthening the system.

The report noted the absence of a functional system for research planning and priority setting. It found that although valuable research had been carried out in the past, research efforts were fragmented among several organizations that lacked coordination. The review team concluded (ISNAR 1981, vii):

> The most crucial and fundamental conclusion is that there is needed a functional, semi-autonomous, comprehensive, and cohesive organization charged with the responsibility of planning, executing, and supervising a coordinated agricultural research program for the nation.

This conclusion led to the creation of KARI in 1986.

After the agricultural system review, a dialogue was established between Kenya's National Council for Science and Technology (NCST), the Ministry of Agriculture, and ISNAR. In 1982, NCST directed a second review, to analyze the human resource requirements of the Kenyan agricultural research system and to develop a training plan to meet the identified needs (NCST-ISNAR 1982). Conducted by a team of professionals from ISNAR and the Kenyan government, this exercise identified gaps in the technical training and scientific capabilities of Kenyan organizations engaged in agricultural research. It outlined a human resource development plan that was carried out during the remainder of the decade with the support of external donors, the United States Agency for International Development (USAID) in particular (Kimani 1990). As in most training programs for agricultural researchers at that time, the bulk of the training was in technical research fields, such as plant and animal breeding, pathology, physiology, and agronomy; virtually no formal training was provided in management or the social sciences (Debela 1998).

In 1985, the Kenyan government commissioned ISNAR to work with a national team in developing a national agricultural research strategy and plan (ISNAR 1985). The result was a blueprint for the creation of KARI, and provided the basis for launching what has become known as the National Agricultural Research Program (NARP). The NARP highlighted the need to plan and set priorities for KARI's research programs and projects; it also suggested mechanisms for monitoring and evaluation. However, the planning processes were viewed as separate and distinct from "M&E," which was termed a "watchdog" function (MoALD 1986, 22).

This tradition of separating planning from M&E has persisted in KARI, and is common elsewhere. In INTA, Argentina, for example, separate directorates were established for planning and M&E in the 1980s. This separation is also common in development projects funded by international agencies. An internal study in the World

181

Bank identified a preoccupation with new lending and the lack of integration of planning, implementation, monitoring, and evaluation as major causes of declining project performance (World Bank 1992).

Proposition 2: Doing PM&E to satisfy external demands contributes little to development of institutional capacity; in fact, excessive external pressure for PM&E may undermine capacity development.

During the early years of review and planning in KARI, in-house planning capacity was relatively limited (Majisu and Wapakala 1994). Consequently, reliance was heavy on experts from ISNAR and other agencies. Planning efforts at this time were intended to produce specific planning documents that were necessary to establish KARI and obtain funding for its programs. It was assumed that participation of KARI personnel in such exercises would contribute to KARI's planning capacity, but there is little indication that this in fact occurred. One reason is that local professionals were often assigned support roles in the project preparation (e.g., data gathering and processing), which did not contribute much to their planning or managing skills. Another reason is that preparing plans for external funding agencies requires quite different skills from those needed to plan and manage ongoing research programs and projects. A third, higher-order reason is that by focusing on the needs and requirements of external agencies, the attention of KARI's most able staff members may have been diverted from the task of managing KARI's research.

The NARP was designed essentially to serve as a framework within which external funding could be negotiated. Kenya has enjoyed the support of many donors as well as that of the World Bank. National funding for agricultural research, the limited funding that KARI receives from Kenya's public treasury, has in many years covered little more than the salaries of KARI staff members. As a result, KARI has depended heavily on external donors for its operating budget.

Over the years, KARI has been the recipient of funding from more than a dozen external agencies via scores of discrete agreements or projects. An important feature of this complex funding pattern is that each donor requires KARI to comply with its own procedures for PM&E. KARI has been literally "overrun" with donor representatives engaged in planning, inspection, review, and evaluation missions of one sort or another. KARI's top managers and its best researchers spend a considerable amount of their time attending to such missions. Many researchers are required to complete multiple quarterly plans and reports to satisfy the accountability needs of different donors.

The multiplicity of PM&E activities oriented to external needs may have resulted in adequate PM&E for discrete projects and programs. Yet it may have deprived KARI of the opportunity to develop its own, internal, PM&E system. Another likely result is that donor demands, which focus on administrative accountability, may have diverted researchers and managers from developing more appropriate procedures for planning, monitoring, and evaluating their research activities. A recent study of aid dependence in Tanzania reaches a similar conclusion (Catterson and Lindahl 1998, 3):

Aid coordination, logical framework analysis, promotion ownership through partnership [and other efforts] . . . though well-intentioned, are being made within an aid system which thwarts sound development. This is because the system is highly supply-driven and public-sector-focused, and because the supplier (the donor) bases his decisions on administrative concerns rather than on knowledge about what makes for success, and sustainability.

Proposition 3: Avoid specialized units for planning or policing activities

When planning, monitoring, and evaluation are viewed essentially as procedures for obtaining and accounting for external funds, PM&E units tend to be created and staffed by administrators or specialists in technical aspects of planning or information management. Such units may be able to provide useful information for funding agencies, to coordinate PM&E activities, or to provide technical backstopping to researchers and managers. Yet they seldom succeed in planning, monitoring, or evaluating research activities.

In 1990, KARI created a "Program Monitoring and Evaluation Unit" (PMEU) under the direction of an experienced biometrician. In addition to project-level monitoring and evaluation, the PMEU was responsible for statistical analysis in the institute and for overseeing KARI's library and publications unit. USAID provided a modest amount of funding for computer hardware and software and for developing data-collecting instruments. Formats were designed to capture information on research projects, and a database was set up for storage and manipulation of this information. Preliminary data collection was initiated by sending out questionnaires to the centers. Some of these questionnaires were duly completed and returned to headquarters for processing. However, this effort did not gain momentum, because of resistance from scientists, who viewed it as a top-down control mechanism of little or no use to them. After several months, the unit's head decided to return to biometrics work, and the unit collapsed.

Experience in Latin American agricultural research organizations mirrors the KARI case. Executing units are often established to coordinate PM&E activities for large-scale investment projects aimed at strengthening agricultural research organizations. This has led to what the Inter-American Development Bank refers to as the "Executing Unit Syndrome." During the planning and disbursement of the loan, the unit operates as a sort of PM&E unit for the organization. Yet when the loan terminates, the unit is closed, leaving the organization with no institutional PM&E mechanism.

Proposition 4: For training in PM&E to have an impact on management processes, it must go hand in hand with an organizational development plan

In the 1985 strategy and plan, the need for management training was noted, but no resources were provided for formal training. In the next few years, the need to strengthen managerial capacity became viewed as a priority. In 1989, with financial support from the European Union, KARI entered into a "linkage project" with ISNAR to provide short-term training and related support needed to improve the organization and management capabilities of KARI research managers (IAC 1994). Between

183

1990 and 1996, thirty workshops and conferences were held, addressing (Ananda-jayasekeram 1996; Debela 1998):

- Program planning and priority setting (three workshops);
- Commodity and factor program reviews (three workshops);
- Scientific writing and presentation skills (seven workshops);
- Participatory rural appraisal and farming systems research (five workshops);
- Monitoring and evaluation (two workshops);
- Management information systems (two workshops);
- Agricultural research policy (five workshops); and
- Human resource development, data processing, and general management.

Topics for this training effort were selected on the basis of discussions between KARI and ISNAR staff members, usually on the basis of requests from KARI. The project was expected to contribute to improving performance in the institute and its research programs, but no explicit strategy was in place for employing training within a broader organizational development effort. Training was provided through a series of stand-alone courses and workshops organized by KARI's Training Unit. Usually, these events lasted five days; ISNAR staff members and Kenyan specialists generally served as instructors. The training events aimed to sensitize managers to a range of management issues and to present basic management concepts and tools. There was seldom time to explore how these concepts and tools could be applied in the specific situation of the participants to improve management in KARI.

A midterm review of the KARI-ISNAR linkage project was carried out in 1994, and a final review in 1996. These concluded that the KARI-ISNAR training had been relevant and useful. It had helped sensitize KARI managers on major research management issues, provided them with valuable management concepts, and helped KARI managers develop skills in some important areas. Through the commodity and factor program reviews, the project had contributed directly to identifying research priorities for some key commodities. However, the reviews found that the overall impact of the workshops on KARI management had been limited. The principal shortcoming of the project was seen to be the lack of a strategy or "master plan" to guide KARI's training activities toward the achievement of institutional goals (Anandajayasekeram 1996, 4, 16):

> ISNAR and KARI need to look beyond the workshops and develop a long-term vision for institution building. . . . Training should be viewed within the context of long-term capacity building and institutional development.

The second major shortcoming of the project was seen as the lack of integration and institutionalization of PM&E-related activities (Anandajayasekeram 1996, 4):

184

Limited progress has been made in the area of integration of training activities and institutionalization. . . . ISNAR should play a catalytic role in the process of integrating planning,
priority setting, program formulation, M&E, and INFORM, and in ensuring that a training
strategy is developed and implemented as an integral part of institutionalization.

In essence, while the training seems to have provided useful concepts and tools for
PM&E, the individuals trained were faced with a dual challenge of:

1. Discovering how the various concepts and tools presented in different workshops
   related to one another and could be applied in a coherent systematic fashion, and
2. Devising a strategy for applying what was learned to improve management in
   KARI.

In most agricultural research organizations, such as KARI, the key constraint to
effective PM&E is not the inadequate use of one or another specific tool, but the lack
of appropriate institutional processes. Within a strategy for institutionalizing PM&E
processes, training can play an essential role. Yet in the absence of such a strategy,
training is bound to have little impact. Based on the recommendations of the midterm
and final reviews, a formal assessment on training needs was carried out and a training master plan was developed in 1998. The needs assessment identified PM&E as the
highest-priority area for short-course training for research scientists (KARI-ISNAR
1998, 39).

Proposition 5: Tools and systems for PM&E need to be carefully selected and adapted to meet local needs under local circumstances

Many tools for PM&E have been tried out in KARI over the years. Some, like the logical framework, have gained widespread use; others have not. Experience with the
introduction of an ISNAR-developed information management tool known as Information for Research Management (INFORM) is especially rich and informative.
ISNAR developed INFORM to provide managers with up-to-date and easy-to-access
information on their research activities and the costs associated with them. INFORM
is a computer application built around a database that allows users to sort and group
individual research activities (experiments or studies) according to a number of their
features. For example, activities can be readily grouped by project, program, center,
disciplinary focus, research problem (e.g., plant pathology vs. livestock breeding) and
type of research (basic, applied, etc.). One of INFORM's main strengths is its ability to
allocate associate research budgets with discrete research activities, which can in turn
be aggregated to the level of projects and programs.

Workshops on INFORM were organized in 1992 and 1994 to introduce the system
to selected KARI managers and donor representatives. The initial workshops were
organized under the ISNAR-KARI linkage project and funded by the European
Union. Subsequent training for INFORM operators was supported by USAID. Based

on participants' interest in the system, ISNAR was requested to work with KARI to install INFORM at each of the institute's research centers.

A series of two-week workshops was organized to train staff members to operate INFORM at headquarters and in research centers; several hundred individuals were trained. Center directors were brought in for the last two days of each INFORM workshop to familiarize themselves with INFORM and to learn how they could use its outputs. In conjunction with the INFORM training, data were gathered on research activities being carried out in each of the centers. After the training, the INFORM software (a specialized application developed in a commercial database known as "Reflex") was installed in each center. INFORM specialists from ISNAR or KARI headquarters visited the centers to ensure that the system was operational. It was expected that, based on the INFORM training and follow-up, KARI would begin to use INFORM as a management tool. So far, however, this has not occurred, for several reasons. First, there must be a demand for the information it can provide managers. Peterson (1990, 308) coincides with this point, stating, "significance is the most important variable influencing institutionalization" (see also Peterson et al. 1995; Hobbs 1997). In the case of INFORM, it was assumed that managers needed systematic, detailed, project-based information for decision making and for meeting accountability requirements. Prior to the INFORM training, however, managers' information needs were not thoroughly assessed, and this assumption may not have been valid.

KARI managers have shown little interest in the information provided by INFORM. This may reflect the institute's rather traditional management culture, in which decisions are based largely on experience and intuition. It may also reflect managers' inexperience with computers or information-based management. Alternatively, the information provided by INFORM—a generic tool that was not specifically designed for KARI or adapted to its conditions—may be of little value to managers in the performance of their tasks. This is what many managers report.

A second problem seems to be that the magnitude of the challenge of introducing a management information system into an organization such as KARI was underestimated. The introduction and sustained use of a management information system requires numerous, coordinated changes in management practices. As Peterson (1998, 58) states:

> Information technology reform in African bureaucracies is a highly contingent process. It is a craft not a science and requires committed and creative individuals who can overcome formidable constraints. It requires a firm commitment to reforming an organization, appropriate technical assistance that combines a technical design with the socio-technical system, and political support that allow its virtues to be recognized and its detractors to be managed.

In KARI, the introduction and use of a comprehensive management information system would be especially complex because of the many research activities that are carried out by different individuals in different research programs and centers scattered throughout the country. Many of the centers have few computers or computer-literate staff members, severe budget limitations, and inadequate electrical and telecommunications infrastructures. While training provided individuals with technical skills for operating the INFORM software, no parallel effort was made to establish adequate management processes for implementing INFORM as an institutional system. INFORM cannot be used effectively by an individual; it must be used by the entire organization, or at least by an entire center or program. For institutionalization to occur, a well-coordinated effort would be needed to:

- Determine the information needs of managers at different decision-making levels and different points in time;
- Assign responsibilities for data collection, analysis, and reporting;
- Establish and enforce schedules for these same tasks;
- Design and produce reports tailored to specific managers' needs;
- Provide technical support for center operators; and
- Continuously improve and upgrade the system.

In the effort to install INFORM, these process issues apparently received inadequate attention (Anandajayasekeram 1996; Mbabu, Omamo, and Ondatto 1998). For the various reasons outlined previously, most center managers have been unable or unwilling to make the investments of time and resources necessary to implement INFORM. Although many managers (and donor representatives) still recognize the potential value of an information system, for the time being INFORM has been shelved. Similar experiences have been encountered with other attempts to introduce computerized accounting or information systems in KARI and elsewhere. In the early 1990s, with support from USAID, Price Waterhouse was contracted to install a computerized accounting system in KARI. After several years and an outlay of several hundred thousand dollars, the system was abandoned. More recently, another system has been installed. Although promising to be user-friendly and to provide accounting reports that will meet the requirements of KARI's diverse managers and donors, the system has proven difficult to operate and the outputs fall far short of expectations.

Experience indicates that managers need to select tools and systems for PM&E with great care, to ensure that they meet real information needs in ways that are feasible and cost-effective in the local setting. Often, tools imported from elsewhere do not meet local needs, are too complex or costly to use, or do not mesh well with existing management practices. For this reason, successful introduction of new tools for PM&E requires a careful assessment of managers' needs and a significant period of development or adaptation.

Proposition 6: Demands for improved PM&E lead to demands for social science expertise

A few agricultural economists were involved in agricultural research in Kenya long before the creation of KARI. They normally worked at the project level, studying production costs and the costs and benefits of technologies under development or being extended to farmers. Little socioeconomic work was being carried out to address policy issues of relevance to the design or evaluation of research programs. A review of agricultural research capabilities and effectiveness carried out in 1977 recommended the establishment of a central economics service, on the following grounds (Desrosiers, Rose, and Matata 1977, 32):

> Several research officers expressed the feeling that the services of an economist should be made available to study the costs and returns on investment to be expected from new practices being developed at the research stations. . . . Such a service would be useful in encouraging the adoption of new practices and would also be helpful in anticipating problems in this regard.

In 1981, when the Kenyan agricultural research system was reviewed, the need to strengthen research planning, priority setting, and program formulation was identified as a top priority (ISNAR 1981, ix). In this context, it was recommended that a social science division be created in KARI (ISNAR 1981, xi). Over time, demands have intensified for KARI to strengthen its planning capacity in order to focus its work while responding to the multiple needs and demands of Kenyan producers, national policymakers, and financial agencies.

In KARI's predecessor organizations, as in most public-sector agricultural research organizations, biological scientists had considerable freedom to pursue their own research interests at their own pace. Scientific performance was gauged by research output, not necessarily by its applicability or use in practice. The KARI management, with support and encouragement from the government of Kenya and external funding agencies, wished to shift from such a "supply paradigm" to a "demand paradigm," in which research activities are targeted to solving the specific problems of defined user groups. Such a shift in paradigm implies a broader role for the social sciences, beyond economic studies at the project level. The complex task of managing a process of organizational change—from supply to demand focus—creates new demands for social science skills and inputs. Introducing and sustaining a demand focus necessitates close interaction between KARI and its clients, which social scientists can facilitate. Social science perspectives, frameworks, skills, and information are also needed for policy analysis and dialogue, for assessment of technology needs and opportunities at farm and market levels, for strategic planning and priority setting among and within programs, and for designing and conducting evaluations of various types.

As part of the institutional effort to strengthen its social science capacity, KARI trained more than twenty social scientists in the fledgling Social Sciences Division. It also arranged for ISNAR to assign three postdoctoral fellows to the institute (one sociologist and two economists, funded by the Rockefeller Foundation under its postdoctoral fellowship program for the social sciences). From 1992 to 1998, each of these postdoctoral fellows was based at KARI for a two-year term. During the same period, KARI worked with the International Maize and Wheat Improvement Center

(CIMMYT) and the Rockefeller Foundation to place a senior economist in KARI. The Overseas Development Authority of the U.K. (now known as the Department for International Development, DFID) also placed three technical advisors—an economist, an anthropologist, and an economic epidemiologist—to help strengthen the institute's social science research capacity.

The expanding team of social scientists has defined an agenda for social sciences in KARI that seeks to provide support to decision making at all major levels in the institute. The Socioeconomics Division is now charged with the responsibility of carrying out necessary research to support the institute's policy dialogue, strategic planning, priority setting, evaluation, and impact assessment. In addition to research, this division is currently responsible for spearheading and coordinating PM&E as a management function.

Proposition 7: Ultimate responsibility for PM&E must reside with the appropriate managers

Since its establishment, KARI has grappled with the thorny issue of priority setting. In 1991, an exercise was carried out to set priorities among major research programs, with technical support from ISNAR (KARI 1991). A relatively simple scoring model was employed to develop a prioritized list of commodities on which research should be carried out. The resulting priorities were incorporated into the second phase of the NARP. A great challenge to the analysts, and a principal limitation of the study, was the paucity of relevant and reasonably accurate data on essential variables such as the value of production of each commodity, present and potential yield levels, numbers of farm households producing each commodity, and main uses of the commodities. The other challenge was to identify skilled resource persons within the institute to undertake priority-setting work in the future. These two challenges remained until KARI assigned responsibility for priority setting to the social science division.

To complement the 1991 exercise, which set priorities among different commodity and factor programs, the focus of recent work has been on methods for setting priorities within programs. The goal was to identify priority research thrusts for each program. As already stated, specialized databases with relevant and accurate information need to be developed for such exercises. Skills need to be acquired for conducting the analyses. Priority setting is not a once-off exercise; it needs to be done on a regular basis. For all of these reasons, KARI resolved to build in-house capacity for priority setting and to institutionalize a priority-setting process. . In this context, ISNAR outposted two research fellows to help KARI scientists develop a practical process for targeting available resources to meet client needs.

The process was conducted in three phases. First, a commodity or factor working group develops a consensus on program target zones and the potential for development and adoption of technology in each zone. Second, the working group assumptions are combined with economic data to estimate potential program impacts (in terms of economic surplus measures). Third, the results are presented to a larger group of stakeholders that reviews the working group's assumptions, establishes

189

research priorities, and translates them into guidelines for resource allocation decisions (Mills and Karanja 1997; Mills 1998; Kamau, Kilambya, and Mills 1997).

By mid-1998, most of the commodity and factor research programs had completed, or were in advanced stages of completing, priority-setting exercises. Priority-setting methods for regional adaptive research programs had been tested, and plans were well advanced for prioritizing research thrusts in the remaining regional research programs. Training in priority-setting methods had been given to senior economists in KARI, and three had been appointed to coordinate and facilitate priority-setting processes in commodity, factor, and adaptive research programs.

One common error is to view priority setting as a technical exercise that can be left to economists or other social scientists. On the contrary, although social scientists can provide useful frameworks and perspectives for priority setting, and have certain skills for assembling and managing relevant socioeconomic data, they alone cannot do the job. Biological scientists and others familiar with the technical subjects in question must also be involved, to provide their own perspectives and relevant information. Furthermore, those with a stake in allocation decisions should also be involved, to ensure that they will be informed about, and committed to, the conclusions reached during the exercise. A second error is to confuse priority setting with decision making concerning the allocation of resources among activities, projects, or programs. A priority-setting exercise can inform, or provide useful information for, decision making. However, a priority-setting group generally does not have the authority to make or implement decisions concerning resource allocations.

To institutionalize priority setting, some institutional mechanisms were created. At the apex, an executive priority-setting committee was established, convened by the assistant director for the Socioeconomics Division, and including as members the assistant directors responsible for various research programs. The main responsibility of this organ is to provide overall guidance in the process and to avail necessary resources. A working group consisting of senior socioeconomists and selected program leaders was established to provide technical advice to the executive committee. Program Priority-Setting Working Groups were created to guide the process at the program level. Program socioeconomists were assigned to synthesize available information on farm-level constraints and relevant agricultural statistical data, and to facilitate priority-setting exercises within the programs (Mills 1998).

Proposition 8: A PM&E system should ensure high standards of scientific work

PM&E systems often focus on institutional and administrative processes and pay little attention to ensuring the quality of research processes and outputs. In the case of KARI, this issue is partly addressed through a series of biennial scientific conferences initiated in 1988. The conference serves as an important opportunity for Kenyan agricultural research scientists to present their scientific findings to a diverse audience, mainly from KARI; it also provides an opportunity to honor outstanding scientists whose findings have the greatest scientific merit. Usually key government officials, such as ministers or permanent secretaries of the Ministries of Research

190

and Technology or of Agriculture and Livestock Development (MoALD), officiate at the opening and closing ceremonies. This serves to link research processes with policy making. Participants at conferences are mainly those scientists whose papers or posters are accepted for presentation. A multidisciplinary panel of scientists representing various biophysical, social science, and biometric traditions select the papers and posters. Participants also include board members, KARI management, members of MoALD, collaborating national and international research and development organizations, and donor representatives.

Conferences are generally dedicated to themes that reflect scientific challenges in the country. For example, the themes for the conferences held in 1994 and 1996 were agricultural research for intensifying rural and industrial development, and agricultural research for sustainable development in a changing economic environment. Considering that only a limited number of presentations can be made, the organizing committee prescreens proposals to identify the best papers and posters. A multidisciplinary panel of distinguished scientists representing various traditions in biophysical sciences, social sciences, and biometrics does the prescreening. These scientists are selected from within and outside KARI, based on their scientific recognition. To assist in improving skills, the organizing committee of the biennial scientific conference has organized several workshops on scientific writing and presentation skills.

To set the tone of the conference, a special guest is invited to present a keynote address on issues relating to the theme of the conference. To determine the quality of scientific writing and presentation, a panel of judges, selected in advance and working with well-established criteria, evaluate each presentation and enter individual scores. These are subsequently averaged to identify the best presentations in various categories and the overall winners. In a colorful ceremony officiated by top KARI management, the board of management, and government representatives, the winners are presented with trophies and cash awards. This high-profile reward system has created great enthusiasm among scientists, and has led to great demand for participation.

Proposition 9: Evaluation can be empowering for managers and researchers

The following two cases of project and center evaluations in KARI present instances where the management had as much to learn and gain as the scientists themselves from reflective and consultative evaluation processes.

Project evaluation

Soon after each KARI biennial scientific conference, the organizing committee, on behalf of KARI management, convenes to discuss experiences and document lessons learned for future improvements in organizing the conference. At the postconference meeting held in 1994, it was noted that some of the judges were unhappy with the criteria used to select winners for the conference. They were heavily tilted to scientific methodology and less sensitive to efforts and strategies geared toward impacting on households and communities. This criticism was particularly relevant in the context

191

of the emerging dominance of the adaptive research thrust in the institute. In this light, the organizing committee resolved to establish a second area for competition that would recognize the projects most responsive to client needs.

Project evaluations were introduced in KARI in 1996 and are intended to be carried out every two years to coincide with the biennial scientific conferences. The purpose of project evaluations is to assess the value of research projects with respect to client needs. A multidisciplinary team of distinguished scientists representing the main research programs in the institute—animal production, animal health, range management, food crops (cereals), horticulture and industrial crops, soil and water, adaptive research programs, socioeconomics, and biometrics—carry out the evaluations. To compose the team, the organizing committee of the biennial scientific conference solicits nominations from the program directors in the institute. It is emphasized that only outstanding scientists should be nominated for this purpose. The organizing committee of the biennial scientific conference appoints the secretary to the evaluation team, and the evaluation team elects the chairperson.

To initiate the evaluation process, the secretary to the evaluation team writes to all KARI research centers, inviting entries to the competition. In the invitation letter, project leaders are requested to submit the project title, a list of the involved researchers and collaborators, the date of commencement of the project and the experimental term, the source and level of funding of the project, and the program to which the project is affiliated. The review team uses this information to plan for the evaluation visits. Each center is allowed up to three submissions to the competition. The purpose of this prescreening effort is to compel each center to go through a preliminary internal evaluation process, which ensures that all projects within a center are subjected to a form of evaluation, whether or not the project leaders intend to compete in the KARI-wide competition.

Once the nominated projects are submitted to the secretariat of the project evaluation committee, further correspondence is sent to the project leaders informing them of the evaluation date and providing them with a checklist of issues to guide the evaluation process. This checklist is based on the full evaluation criteria, which are built on the extent to which the project reflects KARI's mission—meeting clients' and stakeholders' needs. More specifically, questions address:

- How the client's and stakeholders' needs were identified,
- How the client and stakeholders are involved in the project implementation,
- Why the project was considered a priority,
- How gender issues are addressed,
- Whether environmental concerns are incorporated,
- Whether the project's products are affordable and acceptable,
- How much collaborating institutions and individuals are actively involved throughout the project life, and
- How responsive the project is to various reviews.

Each criterion is assigned a weight, depending upon its perceived importance. The winning project is the one that scores the most points. Procedures are outlined in KARI (1996, 794–800) and detailed in KARI (1998).

To cut down on travel costs, center visits are planned following the most direct routes in a given direction. An approximate cost to cover all the projects reviewed in 1998 was Ksh 500,000—a modest sum considering the value of the activity to the institution. The top three winners are invited to make presentations at a special session of the biennial KARI scientific conference. At the closing ceremony of the conference they are presented with trophies and cash awards.

Center evaluations

Following the first cycle of project evaluations in 1996, the organizing committee of the KARI biennial scientific conference received comments from the centers requiring consideration for evaluation of management support to scientific research processes. Center evaluations were introduced in KARI in 1998 and are intended to be carried out every two years to coincide with the biennial scientific conferences. The purpose of the center evaluations is to assess the extent to which management processes support or hinder scientific research activities. KARI centers are basically the home of research scientists and research programs, projects, and activities; center directors head them, assisted by deputy directors. The center management is basically responsible for administrative support and scientific leadership.

A team of representatives from the planning, finance, and administration department (i.e., administration, accounts, supplies, estate management, training, and personnel) and the two research departments (i.e., crops, soil, and water; and livestock) carried out the center evaluation. To determine the team, the organizing committee of the biennial scientific conference contacted departmental heads and asked for nominations. The need for the nominations to include both headquarters and center-based staff was emphasized. The organizing committee of the biennial scientific conference appointed the secretary to the evaluation team, which in turn elected the chairperson.

To initiate the evaluation process, the evaluation team wrote to all KARI center directors informing them of the planned evaluation visits. In the letter, the rationale for the exercise was articulated and the evaluation process explained. For this first center evaluation, the checklist intended to be included in the information package to the centers was not ready by the time of dispatch. The checklist captured the management issues at stake, and was based on the evaluation criteria. It was eventually prepared and used during the evaluation process.

The evaluation criteria were designed to specifically address the respective management fields—finance, supplies, personnel and administration, training, and estate management. Weights were assigned to the various criteria depending on their perceived importance. The winning center was the one that scored the most points. The top three winners were invited to make presentations at a special session at the sixth KARI biennial scientific conference and were presented with trophies and cash awards at the conference's closing ceremony.

193

Thus, experience shows that, in instances where the views of those being evaluated are incorporated in the planning and execution of the evaluation, the process becomes educative and supportive to both operators and supervisors.

Proposition 10: Staff appraisal and rewards are essential components of an integrated PM&E system

One of the most contentious issues in personnel management in KARI has been the criteria used for promotions. At the time KARI was launched, it was expected that research scientists would be operating above the normal ranks of the equivalent civil servants, and that the terms of service for scientists would be closely comparable with those of local university staff. In practice, this has not been so. A particular constraint in this process has been an apparent lack of suitable criteria for promotions; thus KARI appointed a task force to remedy this deficiency and develop such criteria. This led to a shift from the traditional criteria, based mainly on the time spent in the institute, to one based on performance. The new approach proposed moving scientific staff evaluation from the personnel division and placing it under the scientific divisions. The new procedure basically relied on self-evaluation and peer reviews. A similar system is being considered for the support divisions.

To facilitate performance-based evaluation, activities and anticipated outputs were specified for all scientific cadre—deputy directors, assistant directors, center directors, program coordinators, project leaders, and scientists. Differential scores were assigned to respective outputs depending on their perceived importance in contributing to KARI's mission. The scores are counted cumulatively, allowing productivity in the course of time to define the rate at which one rises in the institutional ranks. Theoretically, therefore, one could bypass those who were hired earlier, but who may not have been as productive. So far, this system has been used once in KARI. The results appeared to give an equal chance for recognition to all scientists, irrespective of the type of research they did (strategic or adaptive) or the discipline to which they subscribed. The message behind this system is clear—productivity rather than time spent in the institute is the basis for upward mobility in the institute. The means for driving and capturing this productivity lies squarely in the institutional PM&E system.

Proposition 11: Given the multiplicity of stakeholders, crafting a PM&E system requires extensive consultation and negotiation

KARI enjoys support from many bilateral donors and financiers (DFID, USAID, the Netherlands' government, the European Union, and the World Bank). Many of these donors and financiers manage the research portfolio they support through independent units. This creates a multiplicity of management systems that could be potentially disruptive to the mainstream KARI management. Harmonizing approaches among such diversity calls for a conscious and deliberate negotiation process. A series of workshops was held in KARI to facilitate this process, culminating in an institutional task force charged with the responsibility of institutionalizing a harmonized PM&E system.

M&E workshops

Within the schedule of workshops conducted in the KARI-ISNAR linkage project, M&E was toward the end. Because M&E was perceived at the time as a tool for meeting accountability requirements, rather than as a means of learning from experience in order to improve research programs, the workshop was put off until late in the project. The workshop was designed to review KARI's current M&E activities and identify gaps in procedures, to relate planning to M&E, and to introduce principles and methods for evaluation. It focused mainly on M&E at the project level, but an integrated framework was introduced showing how project management needed to fit into a hierarchical structure and how M&E needed to fit into a broader management cycle, including planning. Major conclusions reached by participants during the workshop were that planning, monitoring, and evaluation should be perceived as logically sequential processes, and that PM&E should be linked vertically to integrate research activities, projects, programs, and the research agenda of the entire institute (Reed et al. 1994).

During the first M&E workshop it was also realized that institutionalizing an M&E system would require more than a one-week training event. In 1994, a World Bank mission to plan for NARP-II made some recommendations for agricultural research management. Thus another workshop was organized in November 1994 to integrate recommendations of the 1993 M&E workshop and those of the World Bank mission, and to develop a project proposal for institutionalizing M&E at KARI (Cheaz Peláez et al. 1995). The proposal aimed to integrate the activities heretofore treated separately as planning, M&E, and INFORM in more global management decision-making processes. The proposal had a strong bias in favor of training and a rather hefty budget (US$850,000). These two factors discouraged donors from supporting the project.

To develop a more workable and acceptable approach, a third workshop was held in 1996 to develop a uniform schedule for PM&E events across different programs, to link such events with the generation of relevant information from INFORM, and to synchronize them with KARI's annual budgeting calendar. By the end of the workshop, it was recognized that the issues at stake were so bound up with existing administrative procedures in KARI and in donor organizations that they could not be resolved without extensive negotiations with KARI managers and with key donor representatives. It was recommended that a task force be formed to further debate these issues and to conduct needed negotiations.

PM&E Task Force

The PM&E Task Force was established, including representatives from different departments and levels of decision making in KARI, as well as donor representatives. Its main objective is to guide the development of an institutional PM&E system in KARI. In consultation with key stakeholders, both within KARI and in the donor community, the task force has developed a working paper that has been endorsed by KARI management for implementation. This document is intended to lay a blueprint for institutionalization of a harmonized PM&E system in KARI. A significant feature of this effort is the belief that the process is as important as the product. In this case, the task force provided a forum for diverse representation and intensive negotiations, and provided a mechanism for wide consultations and effective consensus building. Because PM&E is such a central feature in decision making, it was necessary that the system be credible and acceptable to potential users.

Conclusions

Experience shows that it is inadvisable to attempt to design a complete and fully functional institutional PM&E system and then to install it in an agricultural research organization. The ideal model presented earlier in this chapter should not be viewed as something to install or adopt, but as something to aspire to and move toward over time. As learning occurs, the ideal model is bound to change.

Experience also indicates that it is inadvisable to attempt to "borrow" PM&E systems or to "transfer" them from one organization to another. To meet an organization's needs in an efficient manner, its PM&E system must be crafted over time through a process of learning and improvement. Gradually, PM&E processes should be refined to match decision-making levels and structures and to merge seamlessly with other management processes. Because each organization has a unique set of structures and processes, so must it also have a unique PM&E system.

We do not wish to leave the impression that nothing can be learned from theory or from the experiences of other organizations. On the contrary, successful institutional PM&E conforms to general principles. Yet each organization needs to develop its own management systems, in order to apply general principles in unique ways. The result is a system that conforms to general principles but is unique in its implementation procedures.

Organizational development and strengthening efforts in the past have tended to emphasize the introduction of management tools or techniques developed elsewhere. Tools are undeniably important, yet tools alone seldom produce significant improvements in management and organizational performance. The KARI case, and others with which we are familiar, indicates that tools are not the logical starting point. When seeking to improve PM&E, the initial priority issues relate to linking planning, monitoring, and evaluation to organizational strategy, structure, and existing management processes. Selection of specific PM&E tools and techniques is more appropriately treated as a "second generation" issue.

The functioning of an institutional PM&E system presupposes that management decisions are made throughout the organization. This implies a management culture in which authority and responsibility for many types of decisions are delegated. It implies a culture of "management for results." In the past, the culture of most agricultural research organizations has been hierarchical and control-oriented, rather than learning- and performance-oriented. In such situations, institutionalizing PM&E as a means of enhancing accountability, management, and organizational learning implies profound changes in the organizational culture. External agents cannot bring about such a cultural change. For this reason, managers and staff members must craft their own PM&E systems.

REFERENCES

Anandajayasekeram, Ponniah. 1996. *Report of the internally commissioned external review of KARI/ISNAR agricultural research management linkage project in Kenya.* Final draft. Nairobi: Kenya Agricultural Research Institute (KARI).

Andersen, Anders, Juan Cheaz Peláez, Douglas Horton, and José de Souza Silva. 1998. Introduction to the PM&E Project. Paper presented at the review and synthesis workshop Assessment of Organizational Impacts of ISNAR's PM&E Project, CGIAR Secretariat, Washington, D.C., 4–6 August 1998. The Hague: International Service for National Agricultural Research (ISNAR).

Catterson, Julie, and Claes Lindahl. 1998. *The sustainable enigma.* SIDA Evaluations Newsletter No. 4/98. Stockholm: Swedish International Development Agency (SIDA).

Cheaz Peláez, Juan, Adiel N. Mbabu, Douglas Horton, and Hilary Ondatto, eds. 1995. *Monitoring and evaluating agricultural research: Report of the second KARI-ISNAR workshop.* Workshop held in Mbagathi, Kenya, 9–11 November 1994. The Hague: International Service for National Agricultural Research (ISNAR).

Collion, Marie-Hélène. 1989. Strategic planning for national agricultural research systems: An overview. ISNAR Working Paper No. 26. The Hague: International Service for National Agricultural Research (ISNAR).

Dale, Reidar. 1998. *Evaluation frameworks for development programs and projects.* New Delhi: Sage Publications.

Debela, Seme. 1998. ISNAR's impacts in Kenya: Case study results. In: *ISNAR's achievements, impacts, and constraints: An assessment of organizational performance and institutional impact,* ed. Ronald Mackay, Seme Debela, Terry Smutylo, Jairo Borges-Andrade, and Charles Lusthaus, 73–96. The Hague: International Service for National Agricultural Research (ISNAR).

Desrosiers, Ronald, T. Rose, and James Matata. 1977. *Agricultural research in Kenya: Review and assessment of the agricultural research capabilities and effectiveness of the scientific research division, Ministry of Agriculture.* Nairobi: Ministry of Agriculture, Republic of Kenya.

Drucker, Peter F. 1989. *The new realities: In government and politics, in economics and business, in society and world view.* New York: Harper and Row.

Gálvez, Silvia, Andres R. Novoa, José de Souza Silva, and Marta Villegas. 1995. *The strategic approach to agricultural research management.* Manual N0.1 of the series Training in Planning Monitoring and Evaluation for Agricultural Research Management. The Hague: International Service for National Agricultural Research (ISNAR).

Hobbs, Huntington. 1997. Strengthening the use of information tools in NAROs: The implementation triangle. Unpublished mss. The Hague: International Service for National Agricultural Research (ISNAR).

Horton, Douglas, Peter Ballantyne, Warren Peterson, Beatriz Uribe, Dely Gapasin, and Kathleen Sheridan. 1993. *Monitoring and evaluating agricultural research: A sourcebook.* Wallingford, U.K.: CAB International.

Horton, Douglas, and Jairo Borges-Andrade. 1999. Evaluation of agricultural research in Latin America and the Caribbean. *Knowledge, Technology and Policy* 11 (4): 42–68.

Horton, Douglas, and Andres R. Novoa. 1998. Dynamics of PM&E in LAC: A study of 9 cases. Paper presented at the review and synthesis workshop Assessment of Organizational Impacts of ISNAR's PM&E Project, CGIAR Secretariat, Washington, D.C., 4–6 August 1998. The Hague: International Service for National Agricultural Research (ISNAR).

International Agricultural Center (IAC). 1994. *Final evaluation of Kenya national agricultural and livestock research project.* Phase 1, Volume 1: Main report, final draft. Wageningen, The Netherlands: IAC.

International Service for National Agricultural Research (ISNAR). 1981. *Report to the government of Kenya: Kenya's national agricultural research system.* ISNAR Document No. R2. The Hague: ISNAR.

———. 1985. *Report to the government of Kenya: Kenya agricultural research strategy and plan.* ISNAR Document No. R24. The Hague: ISNAR.

Kamau, Mercy W., Daniel Kilambya, and Bradford Mills. 1997. Commodity program priority setting: The experience of the Kenya Agricultural Research Institute. International Service for National Agricultural Research (ISNAR) Briefing Paper No. 34. The Hague: ISNAR.

Kenya Agricultural Research Institute (KARI). 1991. *Kenya's agricultural research priorities to the year 2000.* Nairobi: KARI.

———. 1996. *Focus on agricultural research for sustainable development in a changing economic environment.* Proceedings of the 5th KARI Scientific Conference, held in Nairobi, 15–16 October 1996. Nairobi: KARI.

———. 1998. *Sixth KARI Scientific Conference, project evaluation guidelines, procedures, and score sheets—processed 1998.* Internal Document. Nairobi: KARI.

Kenya Agricultural Research Institute-International Service for National Agricultural Research (KARI-ISNAR). 1998. *KARI training master plan 1997/1998–2001/02.* Nairobi: KARI-ISNAR.

Kimani, Lilian W. 1990. Human resource management and development: Introduction to issue 3. In *Proceedings of a workshop on issues in the reorganization of KARI and the implementation of the NARP,* ed. Robert Raab. Nairobi: Kenya Agricultural Research Institute (KARI).

Kline, Peter, and Bernard Saunders. 1993. *Ten steps to a learning organization.* Arlington, Va.: Great Ocean Publishers.

Liebenthal, Andres, Osvaldo N. Feinstein, and Gregory K. Ingram. 2004. *Evaluation and development: The partnership dimension.* World Bank Series on Evaluation and Development, volume 6. New Brunswick, N.J.: Transaction Publishers.

Mabey, Christopher, and Paul Iles, eds. 1994. *Managing learning.* London: Routledge.

Majisu, B. N., and W. W. Wapakala. 1994. *Case studies: Agricultural research planning in Kenya.* Nairobi: Kenya Agricultural Research Institute (KARI).

Mbabu, Adiel N., Steven W. Omamo, and Hilary N. Ondatto. 1998. *Reflections on sixteen years of collaboration between KARI and ISNAR.* A discussion paper prepared for the ISNAR Board of Trustees visit to KARI on 16 February 1998. Nairobi: Kenya Agricultural Research Institute (KARI).

Meyer, N. Dean. 1995. *Structural cybernetics: An overview.* Ridgefield, Conn.: N. Dean Meyer and Associates, Inc.

Mills, Bradford, ed. 1998. *Agricultural research priority setting: Information, investments for the improved use of research resources.* The Hague: International Service for National Agricultural Research (ISNAR).

Mills, Bradford, and Daniel D. Karanja. 1997. Processes and methods for research program priority setting: The experience of the Kenya Agricultural Research Institute Wheat Program. *Food Policy* 22 (1): 63–79.

Mintzberg, Henry. 1994. The fall and rise of strategic planning. *Harvard Business Review* 72 (1): 107–14.

Ministry of Agriculture and Livestock Development (MoALD). 1986. *National agriculture research project proposal.* Nairobi: Republic of Kenya.

National Council for Science and Technology-International Service for National Agricultural Research (NCST-ISNAR). 1982. *A manpower and training plan for the agricultural research system in Kenya, 1983–1987.* The Hague: NCST-ISNAR.

Novoa, Andres R., and Douglas Horton, eds. 1994. *Administración de la investigación agropecuaria: Experiencia en las américas.* Santa Fe de Bogotá, Colombia: Tercer Mundo Editores.

Patton, Michael Q. 1997. *Utilization-focused evaluation.* 3d ed. Thousand Oaks, Calif.: Sage Publications.

Peterson, Stephen B. 1990. Institutionalising microcomputers in developing bureaucracies: Theory and practice from Kenya. *Information Technology for Development* 5 (3): 277–324.

———. 1998. Saints, demons, wizards and systems: Why do information technology reforms fail or underperform in public bureaucracies in Africa? *Public Administration and Development* 18:37–60.

Peterson, Stephen B., C. Kinyeky, J. Mutai, and C. Ndungu. 1995. Computerising accounting systems in development bureaucracies: Lessons from Kenya. Development Discussion Paper No. 500. Cambridge, Mass.: Harvard Institute for International Development.

Reed, Mark, Lilian K. Kimani, Douglas Horton, Dely P. Gapasin, and Hilary N. K. Ondatto, eds. 1994. *Monitoring and evaluating agricultural research: Proceedings of a workshop.* Muguga, Kenya, 25–29 October 1993. The Hague: International Service for National Agricultural Research (ISNAR).

Reijmerinck, J., and Beatriz Uribe. 1991. ISNAR diagnostic reviews: An analysis of recommendations. Report prepared for the external review panel, Background Paper No. 4. The Hague: International Service for National Agricultural Research (ISNAR).

Roberts, George W. 1991. Managing research quality. *Research Technology Management* 34 (1): 28–34.

Senge, Peter M. 1994. *The fifth discipline: The art and practice of the learning organization.* New York: Doubleday Dell Publishing Group.

Stufflebeam, Daniel. 1985. *Systematic evaluation: A self-instructional guide to theory and practice.* Boston: Kluwer.

Taylor, T. Ajibola. 1991. ISNAR in collaboration with Kenya's National Agricultural Research System: Policy implications. In *Agricultural research policy in Kenya: Proceedings of a workshop held in November 1991 in Nairobi, Kenya,* ed. KARI. Nairobi: Kenya Agricultural Research Institute (KARI).

Tribus, Myron. 1987. Quality in R&D. Applying quality management principles. *Research Management* 30 (6): 1–21.

World Bank. 1992. *Effective implementation: Key to development impact.* Report of the Portfolio Management Task Force, 22 September 1992. Washington, D.C.: World Bank.

Zapata, Vicente. 1992. *Manual para formación de capacitadores. Sección de desarrollo de materiales para capacitación.* Cali, Colombia: Centro Internacional de Agricultura Tropical (CIAT).

9

Human Resources for Agricultural Research and Development

KITHINJI KIRAGU, HILLARY N. K. ONDATTO, AND LILIAN KIMANI

Introduction

As smallholders entered the market economy in the 1970s and 1980s, agricultural researchers were charged with developing new technology to meet their diverse needs. Migrants in the arid and semi-arid areas of Kenya also needed new technology. Because the farmers were of mixed types, Kenya adopted a farming systems approach to research in the 1980s.

Kenya's research system was reorganized in 1986, with the formation of the Kenya Agricultural Research Institute (KARI). At the time of KARI's inception, the economy was on a downward trend and public-sector institutions were under stress. Therefore KARI's decision to build its scientific capacity to meet the new challenges required a human resource (HR) strategy. The extent to which this was achieved is the subject of this chapter.

Human resources represent the most valuable part of any organization. Agricultural research is an HR-intensive enterprise. Human resources are the basic determinant of the rate of development of science and technology institutions. Scientists provide the knowledge and expertise for scientific development in research organizations. The most important function of a National Agricultural Research Organization (NARO) such as KARI is the development, retention, and continued motivation of its staff. It is therefore of critical importance that the leaders and managers of NAROs pay careful attention to HR activities such as manpower, recruitment, training and development, performance management, motivation, and utilization (Marcotte, Stave, and Valverde 1989, 6).

Human resources for agricultural research are expensive both to develop and to maintain. Human resource development is a long-term undertaking that should cover both managerial and technical knowledge and skills, as KARI confirmed in 1996 during the Training Needs and Constraints Assessment (Franca et al. 1996). Such HR development entails inculcation of problem-solving abilities, command of relevant factual information, and technical, managerial, and entrepreneurial skills. These skills are acquired through learning by doing (Ridker 1994). It takes about twenty years of intensive education and experience beyond a researcher's first university degree for him or her to qualify as a breeder.

A report on strengthening national agricultural research systems (NARS) in eastern and central Africa revealed the following problems (Kampen et al. 1995):

- A few disciplines were overstaffed, while others were understaffed.
- Research programs were grossly underfunded, which gave rise to a supply-driven national flow of funds.
- Recruitment was curtailed and a lack of funds made it difficult to retain competent scientists.
- Overstaffing with support staff reduced the availability of funds for operating expenditures.
- Local and regional university capacity was inadequate for postgraduate training, particularly with respect to the retraining of scientists to improve the skill mix.
- Collaboration was lacking among agricultural research institutions and universities in the sharing of human resources and facilities.

Some problematic issues that historically have affected HR at KARI are examined, and a brief summary of ideal policies and practice follow. After covering the best practice from a theoretical perspective, the rest of the chapter examines three key HR elements—(1) HR planning and rationalization, (2) HR training and development, and (3) performance management and reward system. The analysis of these three elements looks at the policies and ideals that have been guiding KARI, the contextual factors, and KARI's achievements in these areas. The chapter concludes by looking at lessons learned and the way forward.

Issues Facing Human Resource Management at KARI

Staff Numbers and Institutional and Organizational Issues

KARI began as a very large organization with 6,200 staff on its payroll. KARI acquired staff from:

1. The Scientific Research Division (SRD) of the Ministry of Agriculture and Livestock Development (MoALD);
2. The Kenya staff that served in the East African Community under the East African Agriculture and Forestry Research Organization (EAAFRO) and the East African Veterinary Research Organization (EAVRO); and
3. New KARI employees.

KARI was shaped by its historical background, especially in terms of staff numbers and quality, with most staff coming from the Ministry of Agriculture and Livestock and many lacking the skills needed to handle the research demands that lay ahead. However, KARI could not just lay off employees to enable it to hire scientists with the right skills. Staff numbers were also high because of the indiscriminate hiring that had taken place between 1970 and 1980 when the economy was booming. The organization was very large and complex to manage. Personnel and financial management systems were a necessity to enable the new organization to begin functioning. "Compared with where it had come from, the new institute seemed to be on the run before it could walk" (Kimani 1998, 49). Several research projects, construction works, and capacity-building and training projects were behind schedule. On the HR side, tacit power struggles occurred as the diverse staff from the three different origins settled down. These power struggles would continue for some time. As Kimani (1998) observed, the *new* KARI experienced transitional problems that were economic, institutional, organizational, and managerial. The support staff was overly large, but there was a shortage of professionals in some key areas, particularly in senior posts in the finance and administrative and the livestock departments. Significant staffing gaps were also evident in such support areas as telephone operators, secretarial staff, and technical assistants (Mulandi 1998). Yet for many years, because of bureaucratic and budgetary constraints, KARI could neither recruit to fill the vacancies nor lay off redundant staff.

Training

The problems of HR development at the time of KARI's inception were pervasive. Lack of trained manpower for agricultural research continues to be an important constraint on the planning, organization, and management of research in Kenya. A 1981 review of the system highlighted this constraint and identified lack of adequate manpower and planned manpower development as major weaknesses in the system. Not only were the numbers of research scientists inadequate in relation to the priority and urgent problems of agricultural research and development, but also a large proportion of these scientists were inadequately trained or not trained at all for research functions (ISNAR 1985, 37). For example, most scientists had only an undergraduate-level (B.Sc.) education, which was not sufficient to enable them to independently and reliably conduct research. The ISNAR study showed that of 566 research staff, only 192 had research-oriented training at the postgraduate level (M.Sc. equivalent diploma or Ph.D.)—14 percent for crop commodities, 23 percent for animal production and veterinary science, and 22 percent for forestry. The total number of inexperienced staff was 374. An appropriate disciplinary mix of scientists was lacking to facilitate a multidisciplinary approach to research (ISNAR 1981, 57–58).

The ISNAR study pointed out that the situation was worsened by:

- Recruitment of many first-degree graduates in agriculture and science to research positions;
- Loss of some trained and experienced research staff to the private sector; and
- The growing need to staff the increasing subcenters and testing sites as they were upgraded to research station status.

Over time, sustainability of graduate training has become a major issue for KARI, the extension service, and other agriculture-related industries. Over the past ten years, 80–90 percent of graduate training has taken place overseas, mainly in the United States, Canada, the United Kingdom, Australia, and the Netherlands. The institute had hoped that over time the local universities would expand to allow 80 percent of training to be done locally, with only 20 percent of training occurring overseas. However, the loss of senior scholars has crippled the ability of local universities to build strong graduate programs and to undertake research.

Funding

As described in chapter 5, funding for research was not a problem between 1963 and 1978. However, the situation changed during the economic slowdown between 1983 and 1993, the period in which KARI was formed. The increase in public-sector employment in the 1970s and 1980s resulted in an untenable paradox whereby HR costs crowded out operational expenditures in the budget, while compensation levels for public servants either remained stagnant or declined. In the case of public expenditures on agricultural research in Kenya, the proportion of salaries to total expenditure rose from about 50 percent in the late 1970s to about 75 percent in the mid-1980s. The Ministry of Agriculture's target ratio in 1988 was 55 percent, which was then considered to be consistent with the government's ability to pay for salaries, facilities, and operational costs (Simons and Gitu 1989, 21–25).

Low Staff Motivation

In 1986 KARI staff motivation was very low, turnover was relatively high, and many senior research posts remained vacant, for various reasons. KARI lacked progressive career pathways that would have allowed a research scientist's career to grow without having to move to the more lucrative administrative positions in the respective ministries. Research scientists were therefore lured to compete with their extension counterparts for more senior administrative posts, and thereby abandoned research functions.

The KARI research centers in the 1980s and early 1990s experienced high research staff loss to institutions such as the International Agricultural Research Centers (IARCs), universities, and the commercial sector. The 50 percent turnover rate of scientists at KARI National Agricultural Center at Kitale caused instability in the national maize research program (ISNAR 1981). Staff mobility was attributable to the relatively unattractive terms and conditions of service at KARI and to a lack of adequate operating budgets. Also, the institute had no provision for scientists to advance as scientists. In such circumstances, KARI could not build a sustainable capacity for research. Simons and Gitu (1989, 80) commented that "the Scientific Research Division has been used as a training ground for young graduates who then seek jobs elsewhere." Pay levels for researchers were low and based on a scheme for civil servants. The key facets contributing to low staff motivation were the physical, social, remunerative, organizational, managerial, and intellectual conditions under which the scientists worked (Simons and Gitu 1989).

Human Resource Policies and Practice: An Ideal Situation

Many HR theories set benchmarks to guide organizations such as KARI. The extent to which such ideals are met or practiced in real organizational life will largely depend on contextual parameters, including socioeconomic, political, cultural, and top management's leadership philosophy. To be effective, both HR management and development policies and practice should be guided by the overall organizational policy (vision and mission). Organizational policy sets the broad direction, determining implementation through organizational objectives (Thomson and Mabey 1994, 7). Further, such HR policies and practice recognize that the achievement of corporate objectives depends on the quality, effort, and cooperation of its staff. They also recognize that the organization has a responsibility toward its staff to provide high standards of employment and working conditions, to treat them fairly, to provide them with opportunities to develop and to obtain a sense of satisfaction from their work. In accordance with these principles, the HR policy objectives are to ensure that (Armstrong 1984, 376):

- The organization develops and maintains an effectively and efficiently performing system.
- The organization obtains, develops, and retains the quantity and quality of staff it requires to meet its present and future needs.
- The best use is made of staff so that maximum degree of effective effort is obtained.
- Constructive and harmonious relationships are established and maintained with staff that will encourage the highest degree of cooperation.
- The staff is provided with the maximum scope to use its capacities to the full and to develop within the organization.
- Equal opportunities are provided to potential or existing employees for employment or promotion.
- Conditions of employment, employee benefits, and working conditions are established that will help achieve its objectives and ensure that the organization meets its social and legal responsibilities toward its employees.

Over the years, KARI has adopted pragmatic HR management policies and practices. Particularly significant has been the institute's policies and practice in relation to hiring and rationalization, staff training and development, performance management, and sustainable research funding. Having looked at ideal policies and practice, how then did KARI proceed in handling the key HR elements: HR planning, training and development, and performance management? For these three HR elements we shall examine policies and practice, contextual factors, and KARI's achievements.

Human Resource Planning and Staff Rationalization

Human resource planning is a process of determining an agricultural research organization's or a system's overall staff size and number, discipline, and level of staff required in its research programs (Brush 1993). A remarkable feature of this has been the extensive and sustained support of ISNAR. In 1982, ISNAR assisted the National Council for Science and Technology (NCST) in developing the first national HR development and training plan. By the time KARI was constituted in 1987, most of the plan for increased intake at both universities and agricultural colleges was in operation (ISNAR 1981).

When KARI was set up it had 6,200 employees on its payroll that it needed to utilize in the best possible way. A new organization would ideally have begun by conducting a job analysis, followed by hiring of the right skills, and then by giving the new employees their job descriptions. Output targets would then have been set for each employee for performance management and appraisal. But this did not happen at ISNAR. First, ISNAR absorbed staff from other government research organizations. However, since their tenure of service was protected by government civil service regulations, KARI was not empowered to dismiss them. Second, institutional support systems had other priorities. Third, the newly created Personnel and Training Divisions needed strengthening in order to implement the HR strategy.

Manpower plans were prepared in 1986 and 1994. The 1986 plan had projected the need for about 8,600 staff by the year 2000, more than double the actual number (3,920) in April 2001. The corporate planning exercise of late 1994, which facilitated an in-depth, program-by-program reassessment of the institute's HR needs, projected a need for 4,800 staff. In the corporate planning exercise of 1994, KARI applied the recommended International Labor Office (ILO) and ISNAR staffing norm ratio of five support staff to one research scientist. The aim was to reduce the number of support staff on KARI's payroll by nearly 2,000. The corporate planning exercise determined that KARI's staff should ultimately stabilize at 4,800 (including 800 research scientists and 4,000 support staff) (KARI 1995, 319). Looking back, the plan did not examine or quantify jobs as such. The situation has since changed and the staff has been further reduced to below the 1994 target.

KARI's large staff was claiming over 70 percent and later 80 percent in personnel emoluments, thus reducing operational funds. To reverse the situation, and therefore increase operational funds, KARI adopted a staff reduction policy through:

- Normal staff attrition (through retirement, death, resignation, etc.) without replacement of nonessential staff;
- Transfer of services and related staff to other organizations; and
- Retrenchment of nonessential staff.

The policy of nonreplacement of staff has had the risk of creating an aging institution. Figure 9.1 shows KARI staff age profiles for different years. Scientists in the age

Figure 9.1   Age Profiles for Scientists of the Kenya Agricultural Research Institute (KARI)

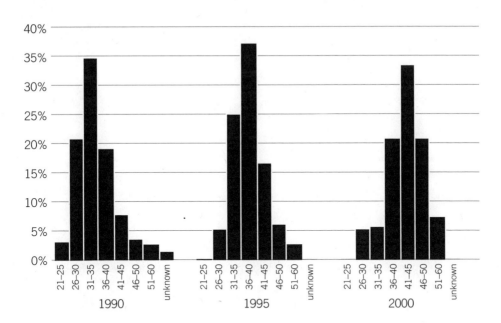

bracket 46–50 have been rising from 47 (7 percent) in 1990, to 51 (10 percent) in 1995, to 125 (29 percent) in year 2000. This is a serious concern for an organization, because through retirement it loses essential skills and talent that have taken resources and many years to develop. Losing talent risks creating gaps in essential services and in critical research programs.

In 1999, KARI transferred a total of 273 staff from Lanet, Kitale, the National Agricultural Research Center (NARC) Muguga, and the National Agricultural Research Laboratory (NARL]), and chief graders and inspectors at the Mombassa Port to the Kenya Plant Health Inspection Service (KEPHIS). A further 42 staff members were transferred from Kibos Sugar to the newly created Kenya Sugar Research Foundation (KESREF) in February 2001.

The rationalization process began in earnest in 1995. Table 9.1 provides a summary of the staff reduction measures. The investment in staff rationalization was estimated at about US$20 million and projected to yield an attractive 14.3 to 6.9 percent real rate of financial return in the medium to long term. This could also be viewed from the viewpoint of salary savings. Of the Ksh 48 million total budget that the institute spends per month, a saving of Ksh 4.8 million (10 percent) was realized through the retrenchment. This saving enabled the institute to implement increased staff house allowances in 2001. The implementation of the staff rationalization program did not begin until July 1998 because of delays in procuring the necessary funds. The European Union (EU) provided US$10 million to fund the first phase of the program, and a team of consultants was recruited to support KARI in its implementation. Nonetheless, it is significant that in the short interval between adoption of the staff

207

Table 9.1	Summary of Planned Staff Reduction Measures, Kenya Agricultural Research Institute, July 1995	
Planned reduction measures	**Target occupation/ function group**	**Total estimated staff reductions**
Offload noncore functions and staff at:	All nonscientists deployed in these functions	204
• Chief graders unit		
• Lanet Seed Center		
• Kitale Seed Center		
Contract out services, including: maintenance (50% staff reduction)	Maintenance functions in nontechnical functions	154
Reduce auxiliaries by 40% through increased reliance on temporary labor	Auxiliaries	908
Other sundry measures	Technical, administrative, secretarial, and clerical staff, and drivers	198
Total estimated staff reductions		1,464

rationalization program and the launch of its implementation, the KARI establishment was reduced considerably.

The rationalization exercise was implemented by using both top-down and bottom-up approaches. Although KARI used internationally derived norms, they were not applied blindly because conditions in the developing world are quite different from those of industrialized countries. The use of staffing norms was restricted to determining the long-term ratio of technical assistants to research scientists. To accomplish the rationalization, a process-oriented approach was adopted, with two prongs: top-down processes for rationalization of role and functions, and bottom-up processes for rationalization of operations, and improving efficiency and effectiveness of operations.

The top-down processes involved the global examination of organizational roles, policies, priorities, and objectives, and broadly reaching out for opportunities for efficiency gains and reducing staff redundancies. The processes entailed identifying and assessing alternative forms of service delivery, such as ownership and own-production, management contracting, outsourcing joint public-private ventures, and divestiture. Changes in the organization's role, mandate policies, rules, and regulations were also considered. As of June 2001, the institute had adopted outsourcing of motor vehicle repair and servicing, buildings and equipment maintenance, and most security services.

In the bottom-up processes, KARI management recognized the need to institute measures for improving the organizational environment in order to implement the staff rationalization. Ensuring the necessary cooperation of most of the senior staff was important; otherwise the rationalization would be superficial and disruptive. This entailed consulting with all senior officers, and especially the heads of departments and the center directors, to obtain some consensus on the objectives of, targets of, and strategies for rationalization, and to enlist their participation in and support of the rationalization program. Measures were also initiated to encourage a change of attitude toward work among the senior officers, especially the research officers. At the same time, plans were made to improve working conditions of staff, by, for example, availing transport and computers. Other measures contemplated included decentralization of authority in the hiring of of support services and decentralization of funds management to research centers, coupled with improved fund availability.

The process culminated in the identification of cases of overstaffing and low-priority functions. The results of the top-down processes were generally reflected in the KARI Strategic Plan to the Year 2000, as well as the policies and strategic measures adopted for the Second National Agricultural Research Project (NARP-II). In other words, the strategic thrusts and policies thereby developed were the starting points for the staff rationalization process (KK Consulting Associates 1995, 15).

By the year 2000, an estimated 1,464 staff would be retrenched (table 9.1). The retrenching was to be implemented in two phases. Phase I, which retrenched 663 staff, took ten months, from February to October 2000, because staff had to be prepared and counseled for retirement. Phase II will be implemented after a further staff evaluation and the number retrenched will depend on funds availability. In May 2001, the staff complement was 3,572 (table 9.2).

One of the objectives of the staff rationalization program was to facilitate recruitment of new staff, maintaining the right mix of staff and effectively implementing planned programs. However, staff recruitment has not attained the required momentum to maintain a suitable staffing balance for all programs. Table 9.3 summarizes staff by category for 1995, 1997, and 2001.

The phased program of staff rationalization adopted in 1995 entails reducing total staff numbers by 1,464 (equivalent to 28 percent total establishment in June 1995). As part of the staff rationalization program, KARI would have to recruit new staff from Kenya's labor market to maintain the right mix of staff to facilitate effective implementation of planned programs. Recruitment would be based strictly on identified needs of the planned programs and activities and KARI staff establishment. The supply of funds for research limits the size of the research workforce and activities (KARI 1998).

Human Resource Training and Development

In 1963 the government was keen to Africanize agricultural research by reducing the percentage of expatriates, which stood at 86 percent at the time. However, the capacity for training graduates in agriculture was limited in the region because Makerere, the only university with an agricultural faculty at that time, was able to admit only a few Kenyan scientists. However, the situation changed after 1973 when Nairobi University opened an agricultural faculty and, in the mid 1970s, the number of expatriates at KARI began to decline. By the early 1990s, less than 10 percent of researchers were expatriate (Roseboom and Pardey 1993, 12). Table 9.4 shows the progress that Kenyan NARS have made over the past three decades. Today, less than 5 percent of researchers are expatriates, excluding the relatively strong presence of IARCs in the country. The latter include the International Livestock Research Institute (ILRI), International

Table 9.2 Distribution of Kenya Agricultural Research Institute (KARI) Staff by Center and Staff Category, May 2001

Center name[a]	Senior Managers	Research Scientists	Technical Support Staff	Administrative Support Staff	Auxiliary Support Staff	Total
KARI Headquarters	18	22	22	217	55	334
NARC Kitale	—	29	78	55	86	248
NFRC Kibos	1	11	18	19	26	75
NPRC Molo	1	2	14	14	17	48
NPBRC Njoro	—	33	49	39	27	148
NPRC Tigoni	1	9	15	17	28	70
NARC Muguga	1	29	60	64	97	251
NARL Kabete	1	67	70	100	59	297
NHRC Thika	1	30	60	70	51	212
NFRC Mwea-Tabere	1	4	13	18	12	48
NDFRC Katumani	1	42	53	58	96	250
NVRC Muguga	1	22	59	40	138	260
NAHRC Naivasha	1	11	30	50	102	194
NALRC Marsabit	1	9	8	11	65	94
NRRC Kiboko	1	11	16	26	77	131
RRC Kakamega	1	24	51	46	46	168
RRC Kisii	1	17	39	52	55	164
RRC Embu	1	21	47	44	33	146
RRC Garissa	—	2	4	8	9	23
RRC Mtwapa	1	14	34	18	26	93
RRC Perkerra	1	5	12	11	30	59
ARSC Alupe	—	1	5	3	10	19
BRC Lanet	1	9	24	27	14	75
ARSC Ol Joro Orok	—	1	13	16	13	43
VRSC Trans Mara	—	—	7	4	10	21
RRSC Buchuma	—	—	2	3	19	24
AHRSC Mariakani	—	—	6	8	24	38
ARSC Matuga	1	1	4	8	16	30
ARSC Msabaha	—	—	5	2	2	9
Total	37	426	818	1,048	1,243	3,572

a. AHRSC = Animal Husbandry Research Sub-Centre, ARSC = Agricultural Research Sub-Centre, BRC = Beef Research Centre, NAHRC = National Animal Husbandry Research Centre, NALRC = National Arid Lands Research Centre, NARC = National Agricultural Research Centre, NARL = National Agricultural Research Laboratory, NDFRC = National Dryland Farming Research Centre, NFRC = National Fibre Research Centre, NHRC = National Horticultural Research Centre, NPBRC = National Plant Breeding Research Centre, NPRC = National Potato Research Centre, NRRC = National Range Research Centre, NVRC = National Veterinary Research Centre, RRC = Regional Research Centre, RRSC = Range Research Sub-Centre, and VRSC = Veterinary Research Sub-Centre.

Table 9.3   Distribution of Kenya Agricultural Research Institute (KARI) Staff Numbers by Grade

Staff grade category	June 1995	November 1997	May 2001
Top managers	40	42	37
Research scientists	544	464	426
Administrative support staff	1,473	1,521	1,048
Technical support staff	1,016	986	818
Auxiliary support staff	2,271	1,948	1,243
Total	5,344	4,961	3,572

Centre of Insect Physiology and Ecology (ICIPE), and the International Centre for Research in Agroforestry (ICRAF). While in the earlier years the expatriates were almost all British nationals, they now represent nationalities from every continent.

In 1985, KARI undertook the preparation of the first agricultural research strategy and plan, which formed the basis for the reorganization and rationalization of the public research system in 1986. In the strategy and plan (ISNAR 1985, 37–48), information on the previously assessed training needs was updated, with emphasis on the urgent need for a training program that would upgrade the research capacity of the staff over the period 1985 to 1995. The most important and urgent training requirements were for the scientific staff members who were to spearhead the implementation of the strategy and plan. Kenya became one of the first few countries in sub-Saharan Africa to develop a formal strategic plan and national program for agricultural research institution building and program development (Taylor 1991, 164–74). The plan projected that 504 M.Sc. and 126 Ph.D. fellowships would be required over a ten-year period (ISNAR 1985, 43). The report further projected that, of these, 304 M.Sc. and 42 Ph.D. would be tenable at the University of Nairobi, while the balance of 200 M.Sc. and 84 Ph.D. would be tenable in overseas institutions. Three hundred short-term training opportunities were planned for technical support staff through the National Agricultural Research Programme, Phase I (NARP-I). The training policy in NARP-I was to increase the critical mass of scientists with Masters and Doctorate degrees to arrive at a ratio of 20:60:20 for B.Sc.: M.Sc.: Ph.D. The short-term training plans included technical and managerial courses for both support and scientific staff. The plan was not based on a detailed gap analysis of HR requirements and training needs. As a result, research support staff did not receive adequate attention with regard to training. This omission was addressed in the KARI Training Master Plan of 1997–98 to 2001–2, which more comprehensively assessed the training needs of the various categories of staff.

Training Policy

By 1995, when some of the NARP-II projects began, the training policy for KARI was still evolving. In the second half of the 1990s, KARI's training policy tried to provide a mix of technical and managerial skills and knowledge, as guided by the organizational vision. The forces behind the change were:

211

Table 9.4 Educational Status and Nationality of Agricultural Researchers, Select Periods 1961–91, Kenya National Agricultural Research System (NARS)

Institutional Category[a]	Researcher Status	Period						
		1961–65	1966–70	1971–75	1976–80	1981–85	1986–90	1991
Government	Ph.D.	2.6	2.2	8.8	13.6	10.8	27.8	39.0
	M.Sc.	3.9	22.0	60.1	95.7	159.8	242.4	279.0
	B.Sc.	9.4	36.1	83.2	145.0	275.8	308.0	361.0
	Subtotal	15.9	60.3	152.1	254.3	446.4	578.2	679.0
	Expatriate	65.6	71.1	98.1	74.8	67.4	63.4	65.0
	Total	81.5	131.4	250.2	329.1	513.8	641.6	744.0
Semi-public	Ph.D.	0.6	1.6	3.0	3.4	3.5	4.0	5.0
	M.Sc.	0.2	0.6	4.8	9.9	16.0	21.9	26.0
	B.Sc.	0.8	4.0	7.8	9.3	10.3	13.8	12.0
	Subtotal	1.6	6.2	15.6	22.6	29.8	39.7	43.0
	Expatriate	12.5	25.4	24.0	13.3	6.3	2.2	2.0
	Total	14.1	31.6	39.6	35.9	36.1	41.9	45.0
Regional	Ph.D.	0.2	2.0	5.4	7.0	—	—	—
	M.Sc.	0.1	2.6	5.4	13.0	—	—	—
	B.Sc.	2.6	3.0	10.2	17.5	—	—	—
	Subtotal	2.9	7.6	21.0	37.5	—	—	—
	Expatriate	38.4	56.2	48.2	37.5	—	—	—
	Total	41.3	63.8	69.2	75.0	—	—	—
Academic	Ph.D.	0.1	0.6	1.9	5.3	9.5	11.6	—
	M.Sc.	0.0	0.5	1.2	3.2	8.5	12.9	—
	B.Sc.	0.1	0.4	0.3	0.9	2.1	2.4	—
	Subtotal	0.2	1.5	3.4	9.4	20.1	26.9	—
	Expatriate	0.8	2.5	3.5	2.3	3.2	2.8	—
	Total	1.0	4.0	6.9	11.7	23.3	29.7	—
Total	Ph.D.	3.5	6.4	19.1	29.3	23.8	43.4	44.0
	M.Sc.	4.2	25.7	71.5	121.8	184.3	277.2	305.0
	B.Sc.	12.9	43.5	101.5	172.7	288.2	324.2	373.0
	Subtotal	20.6	75.6	192.1	323.8	496.3	644.8	722.0
	Expatriate	117.3	155.2	173.8	127.9	76.9	68.4	67.0
	Total	137.9	230.8	365.9	451.7	573.2	713.2	789.0

Source: Adapted from Roseboom and Pardey 1993.
a. With the collapse of the East African Community in 1977, the Kenyan facilities and staff of the East African Agriculture and Forestry Research Organization (EAAFRO) and the East African Veterinary Research Organization (EAVRO) were absorbed into the government sector. The 1976–80 average for the "regional" category relates only to the years 1976–77.

- A strong desire to improve the organization and management of research (NARP-I);
- Adaptation and adoption of ideas from the various collaborators, development partners, and farmers;
- Sensitivity to the client (the farming communities), who at times rejected KARI technology; and
- A strong desire for KARI to be relevant in economic development.

These changes in training policy were guided by the shift in the research paradigm in the 1980s and 1990s (Kimani 2000a):

- In the 1980s there was a commitment to serving the small-scale farmer, but technology development was researcher-led. The scientists' motivating factor was to publish and contribute to the field of knowledge. Because farmers were not involved in this process, technology adoption rates were often low.
- In the 1990s, KARI researchers became more client-responsive and they moved toward adaptive research—the Farming Systems' Approach to Research, Extension, and Training (FSA-RET), participatory research, and gender sensitivity—and HR development provided training in these areas. For example, KARI introduced training in gender analysis and leadership for change.
- Today there is pressure to justify KARI's role to its public, private, and non-governmental organization (NGO) partners. Currently, the special project known as the Agricultural Technology and Information Response Initiative (ATIRI) is offering training in leadership and team building, proposal writing, business management, and participatory methodologies.

New training needs and policies are emerging as the ATIRI is implemented. Management and commercialization of research will be important areas for training. To win the goodwill of private-sector partners, KARI staff will have to produce research products of the required quality in a timely manner, improve their reputation and image, improve communication, and promote the services available (Disney 2000, 6). In summary, scientists will have to excel at salesmanship—a quality that requires training.

Training Achievements

There was an overlap in degree training between the two NARP project periods from 1988 to 1997. The KARI began implementing its 1985–95 training plan with multidonor development partners including the United States Agency for International Development (USAID), the Canadian International Development Agency (CIDA), the Overseas Development Administration (ODA), the European Economic Community (EEC), the Japan International Cooperation Agency (JICA), and the Swedish International Development Agency (SIDA), among others. The many administrative issues affecting the new institute delayed most training projects. However, table 9.5 shows the significant achievements made in postgraduate training of KARI scientists during this period.

213

Table 9.5   Degree Levels of Kenya Agricultural Research Institute (KARI) Scientists, 1986–97

Year	Type of Degree			Total
	B.Sc.	M.Sc.	Ph.D.	
1986	223	215	16	454
1987	214	215	16	445
1988	234	230	16	480
1989	221	243	16	480
1990	192	260	23	475
1991	258	281	30	569
1992	245	287	37	569
1993	231	293	44	568
1994	189	308	51	548
1995	131	338	58	527
1996	144	287	92	523
1997	114	287	103	504

Short courses undertaken during NARP-I included:

- Over twenty-five short-term research management training courses in collaboration with ISNAR and funded by the EU. The courses, mainly for scientists, included priority setting, scientific writing and presentation, HR management, program reviews and management, research policy review, and so on.
- The EU, the Netherlands, and the Department for International Development (DFID) supported courses in gender sensitization and participatory research.

Table 9.6 gives details of long-term training and table 9.7 of short-term training during NARP-II.

Institutionalization of Gender in Technology Development

KARI decided to institutionalize gender in the technology development process in 1995 in order to speed up technology adoption by farmers. Prior to 1995, both technology development and dissemination were gender blind, and it was often assumed that the male head of the household was also "the farmer." However, it is now widely known that many women are farmers; they contribute immensely to the farming process and should not be ignored. The literature is replete with information on women's important role in agricultural production. Women contribute 80 percent of labor for food production, 50 percent of labor for cash crop production, but receive only 7 percent of extension service information (Kooijman and Mbabu 1998, cited by Kimani 2000b, 4). Women manage 40 percent of the farms in Kenya (Kimenye 1998, 203). In research, therefore, gender should be considered an essential variable in

214

Table 9.6   Summary of Academic and Professional Long-term Training of Kenya Agricultural Research Institute (KARI) Staff, 1997–98 to 2001–2

Subject Area of Training	Type of Certificate	Planned Number to Be Trained	Number Trained
Senior management:			
Human resource development	M.Sc.	1	1
Research scientists:			
Crop improvement and management	Ph.D.	20	2
	M.Sc.	22	15
Plant protection	Ph.D.	2	5
	M.Sc.	3	4
Soil and water management	Ph.D.	7	6
	M.Sc.	6	3
Animal production and health	Ph.D.	5	6
	M.Sc.	2	5
Socioeconomics, biometrics, farming systems research, and others to be determined	Ph.D.	5	3
	M.Sc.	13	17
	P.G. Diploma	5	0
	P.G. Certificate	6	0
Technical support staff:			
Crop production	B.Sc.	2	3
	Diploma	29	10
	Certificate	32	0
Soil and water management	B.Sc.	1	1
Socioeconomics, biometrics, farming systems, and others to be determined	B.Sc.	1	4
	Diploma	12	1
	Certificate	6	0
Animal production and health	M.Sc.	0	1
	B.Sc.	6	6
	Diploma	7	4
	Certificate	0	7
Laboratory technology	H.N. Diploma	13	2
	O.N. Diploma	17	0
Administrative support staff:			
Human resource development	M.Sc.	3	3
Human resource management	M.B.A.	2	1
	Diploma	10	10
	Certificate	40	2
Accounts	Certificate	52	13
Supplies management	M.B.A.	0	1
	Diploma	10	2
	Certificate	10	4
Catering and institutional management	Diploma	6	6
Computer and information technology	M.Sc.	0	1
	B.Sc.	1	1
	Diploma	2	2
	Certificate	4	2
Information and library science	Diploma	7	7
	Certificate	6	1
Facility maintenance	Diploma	10	1
	Certificate	13	0
Secretarial	Certificate	46	9
Security	Certificate	15	1
Telephone operation	Certificate	13	6

Table 9.7 Short-Course Training of Kenya Agricultural Research Institute (KARI) Staff, 1997–98 to 2001–2

Staff Category	Type of Short Course	Number Planned to be Trained	Number Trained
Senior management	Management courses	175	207
	Study tours, workshops, and conferences	20	92
Research scientists	Management courses	260	339
	Technical courses	441	104
	Postdoctoral and attachment fellowships	3	6
	Study tours, workshops, and conferences	875	390
	Induction courses	80	0
Technical support staff	Management courses	200	84
	Technical courses	186	101
	Study tours, workshops, and conferences	0	7
	Induction courses	80	0
Administrative support staff	Management courses	120	480
	Technical courses	287	93
	Induction courses	80	0

characterizing the clients (farmers), who comprise both men and women playing complementary roles on the farm (Kimani 2000b).

In 1995, KARI formed the Gender Task Force (GTF), which was responsible for the work plan (box 9.1) and implementation. The GTF was an efficient management tool in overcoming interdepartmental bureaucracy. Its composition was representative of

Box 9.1 The Gender Task Force (GTF) Work Plan

- Sensitize top management and researchers
- Identify a suitable gender consultant/facilitator
- Ensure that suitable training materials with relevant case studies are developed
- Select two scientists per center who are good in communication and have them trained as Gender Advisors (GAs); select a few to be trained as trainers
- Collect relevant literature on gender and create a computer database
- Organize a gender conference to review status of progress
- Send a few scientists for graduate training so that they could back up the process
- Encourage GTF members to attend Center Research Advisory Committee (CRAC) meetings in order to evaluate research projects for gender sensitivity
- Incorporate gender perspective in planning Monitoring and Evaluation Manual

Source: Modified from Koojiman and Mbabu 1998, cited by Kimani 2000a.

both technical departments and development partners. The change of policy had the full support of top KARI management.

By April 2001, remarkable achievements had been realized (updated from Kimani 2000a, 7–8):

- Over 410 officers had been gender sensitized, including scientists, a few extension officers, and KARI managers.
- Twenty-eight Gender Advisors (GAs) had been trained in two courses to assist their fellow scientists to understand the gender concept as well as to prepare gender-sensitive research proposals.
- Six scientists of the 28 were trained as trainers and participated in training GAs. This is one area in which KARI has built training capacity.
- Scientists have begun to change their attitudes about gender. At the start, resistance and cynicism were common because scientists, like most people, thought, "gender means women." Scientists are also collecting gender-disaggregated data, and projects are beginning to be gender responsive. This information is assessed through the Center Research Advisory Committee (CRAC) meetings, which many of the GTF members attend.
- scientists have been trained at the Master's level in gender, or anthropology with a gender bias. For the initial sensitization workshops, the GTF could not identify a trainer who was versed in agricultural research, so KARI hired one who specialized in community development. Later, it was possible to hire a consultant who was agricultural research oriented. The challenge now is to facilitate the GAs at the center with resources so that they may assist the scientists.

A Universal Threat That Cannot Be Ignored

Acquired Immunodeficiency Syndrome (AIDS) has become a serious health problem worldwide. Since its discovery twenty years ago, scientists have learned about many aspects of the disease (Barnett and Rugalema 2001). The Kenyan government developed a policy framework for fighting HIV/AIDS in Sessional Paper No. 4, which was adopted by Parliament in September 1997 (MOH 1998). The report acknowledges that AIDS affects Kenya's development and security and calls for, among other things, a multisectoral AIDS prevention program. The National AIDS and Sexually Transmitted Disease (STD) Control Programme (NASCOP) of Kenya's Ministry of Health is charged with spearheading and coordinating key activities for the multisectoral approach (MOH 1998, 1).

The government of Kenya recently declared HIV/AIDS "a national disaster," and with the support of development partners has started an intensified community education campaign. As an organization charged with technology development, KARI approaches AIDS morbidity and mortality from two perspectives. The first is that the loss of lives can nullify the gains and impact of agricultural technology. The second

217

is that HIV/AIDS morbidity and mortality also affect food security by reducing house-holds' ability to produce and buy food, by depleting assets, and by reducing the insur-ance value of social networks as the household calls in favors. Morbidity affects agricultural productivity by affecting labor availability, forcing households to reallocate labor from agriculture to patient care. AIDS mortality permanently removes adult labor from the household. This combination of adult morbidity and mortality and the asso-ciated reallocation and withdrawal of labor has led to the following adverse changes (Barnett and Rugalema 2001):

- Downgraded crops and loss of livestock,
- Loss of farm management resources and skill,
- Inability to earn income,
- Loss of assets,
- Disruption of social networks, and
- Increasing dependency.

A study on the impact of HIV/AIDS in five commercial agro-estates in three provinces of Kenya revealed that cumulative cases of AIDS account for as much as 45 percent of the workforce (30 percent Nyanza, 12 percent Rift Valley, and 3 percent Eastern Provinces [NASCOP 1999, 38]). A study of 1,422 households in 1977 and again in 2000 in twenty-two districts in rural Kenya found that premature adult death is indeed eroding the livelihood of many households, particularly those that are already poor (Yamano and Jayne 2004). The authors point out that the long-term effects of AIDS remain unknown and that follow-up long-term research is needed.

As an employer of about four thousand workers, KARI is directly threatened with losing its workers and their respective skills through the disease. Similar to the case with other organizations, KARI employees fall within the most vulnerable age bracket of twenty to forty-nine years (NASCOP 1999, 16). This report further says that, in Kenya, more than 75 percent of AIDS deaths occur in adults between the ages of twenty and forty-five, and that the peak ages for AIDS cases are twenty-five to twenty-nine for females and thirty to thirty-four for males. KARI has introduced training pro-grams to inform and educate its employees. Since 1995, all in-house training programs have included an HIV/AIDS awareness course. About one thousand employees have gone through awareness training.

Summary of Training

Training is costly and KARI has invested heavily in staff training. In its first ten years of existence, the institute has achieved the following successes:

- Academic training, especially for scientists, is considered a great success, as pre-viously mentioned.
- Capacity building and skill development have advanced in participatory research methodologies, gender awareness and use of gender analysis tools, scientific

writing and presentation, proposal writing, priority setting, project planning, project cycle management, field experimentation, enhancing linkages with partners, computer software packages, and leadership and management courses, among others. All these skill-enhancing courses have evolved to meet perceived needs of the organization.

The effectiveness of the KARI training program in recent years is underpinned by the institute's training cycle (box 9.2). This is a systematic method of planning, implementing, and evaluating training activities. It is a continuous process that involves all the relevant stakeholders in the diagnosis, design, implementation, monitoring, and evaluation of training activities.

However, the success of KARI training has not been without challenges, many of which are frequently mentioned:

- The main challenge has been retaining and motivating trained staff through an attractive reward system and job satisfaction.
- Training funds are becoming more rare now, with declining donor support. Many of KARI's partners do not favor professional training for support staff. Therefore, support staff development needs new sources of funding.

Box 9.2   KARI's Training Cycle

The training cycle involves six major components.

1. Organizational constraints and the overall human resource requirements are diagnosed and analyzed.
2. Training needs are assessed where gaps in managerial and technical knowledge and skills are identified.
3. Training plans are formulated and include three types: the training master plan, annual plans, and detailed course plans. The training master plan is formulated every five years to facilitate forward planning and national allocation of resources.
4. Training based on detailed plans for each course is implemented. For academic and professional courses this involves final selection of three trainees and the training institution as well as disbursement of funds. For short courses, it involves the delivery of the training activity by subject matter and training specialists.
5. The implementation of training activities is monitored. This entails continuous assessment of trainees involved in academic and professional courses through progress reports, interviews with relevant line managers, and visits to and observations of the trainees as applicable.
6. All stages of the training cycle are evaluated. This includes pre-training evaluation through ex-ante analysis of the planned activities. Evaluation during training includes self-assessment of the course and trainers.

- In the absence of attractive pay packages, staff members look at training as the main avenue to career advancement.
- The process of HR planning with job specification that leads to a balanced staff establishment has not been harmonized yet.
- It is necessary that officers achieve optimum output through an objective performance management system.
- The sustainability of graduate training is threatened because local universities lack facilities and they face major challenges of the brain drain.
- There is a need to keep up with the shifting research paradigm in the direction that the rest of the world is moving.
- Training in biotechnology is a major challenge.

Biotechnology

Biotechnology application in agricultural development is a new field in Africa. Many governments have not formulated policies for promoting the use of and investment in biotechnology. Fortunately, Kenya has done so, although the process is very much in an early phase. The route to biotechnology development begins with well-trained scientists. New trainees must be hired and trained at the Master's level in Molecular Biology. One of the challenges is in the cost of training such people outside Kenya. Molecular biologists are very rare in SSA. Currently there are fewer than ten molecular biologists in Kenya. The other challenge is that of retaining them long enough to make an impact. Can KARI's terms and conditions of service attract enough such highly specialized professionals to make an impact?

Currently, only one or two scientists are working on plant and animal transformation at the laboratory level in Kenya, using gene constructs borrowed from advanced laboratories in the United States. This should change with time. In the developed world, science and technology are making use of bio-informatics, which is a new discipline encompassing information technology and biotechnology. Agricultural development is being aided by bio-informatics to speed up plant and animal transformation. For this to happen, the science of bio-informatics needs to be adopted in Africa. The process calls upon a critical mass of well-trained scientists in biological, genomic, and bio-informatics sciences. The latter entails training the scientists in the use of computer software for managing biotechnology techniques. This is a major challenge in that it further lengthens the chain of HR training and development in both time and resources. Backup services and effective computer connectivity among colleagues within and outside the KARI system need to be in place. The NARS and KARI also need to have a strong Intermediate Technology (IT) backup and training service. There is a major challenge in providing training, retaining trained professionals, providing hardware and software, and having a strong backup IT service. Planning and investing in IT is the only way forward. For SSA countries to benefit from one another's knowledge of bio-informatics and to create synergy within the region, they need to employ virtual networking.

Performance Management

Performance management is broader than performance appraisal and involves three main stages (Thomson and Mabey 1994):

1. Planning performance, which requires that the manager and the individual employee agree on job description, targets, and standards of performance. The process involves sharing the mission statement and translating it into individual activities.
2. Supporting performance, which refers to the provision of resources, facilities, information, training leadership, and so on.
3. Measuring performance, which is the stage where the appraisal tool is applied. Most organizations concentrate on this stage and tend to ignore the first two. The measurement is designed to assess the achieved performance against the agreed-upon criteria and then provide reward or promotion to the individual accordingly. The assessment evaluates the effectiveness of the whole process and its contribution to the organizational goal.

The performance management system integrates effective planning, identification of standards, performance review, prioritization of development needs, and measurement of improvements. It's specific objectives are to:

- Ensure that employee output contributes to the overall goal of the organization.
- Provide an objective basis for rewarding (promoting, recognizing) and disciplining employees. It thus contributes to motivating staff and hence enhancing staff retention.
- Help the organization assess skills gaps and hence indicate areas where the staff needs career development and training.

In the past, performance management usually has been restricted to highly subjective annual staff performance appraisal, which also has been confidential. In that system, the organizational vision and mission was out of focus. Besides filling in their biodata, employees did not play any role in their own assessment. In such a system, managers often have insufficient understanding of the potential that may be derived from an objective performance appraisal scheme. Consequently, research managers and research scientists fail to understand the dynamics of the process wherein the manager and employee talk meaningfully about performance improvement, about measures, and about how the individual can grow in his or her capability and career (Bennell 1989, 3).

One reason why KARI was formed was to improve the terms and conditions of service of agricultural researchers and support staff. A suitable incentive framework for researchers to perform well was necessary if investments in agricultural research facilities, HR, and systems were to yield the expected dividends. However, for a long

Table 9.8   Number of Kenya Agricultural Research Institute (KARI) Research Scientists at Different Levels before and after Promotion in January 2001

Staff Position	Number in Post Before Promotion	Number Promoted January 2001	Number in Post After Promotion
Chief research officer	7	3	9[a]
Senior principal research officer	0	10	8[b]
Principal research officer	6	27	33
Senior research officer I	0	62	62
Senior research officer II	0	44	44
Senior research officer	72	—	40
Research officer I	235	—	123
Research officer II	76	1	74
Assistant research officer	34	—	34
Total	430	147	427

a. One scientist left for another organization soon after promotion.
b. One scientist retired; one became center director.

time the attainment of KARI's autonomy did not result in any significant enhancement of the compensation levels of its staff above those prevailing in the government sector. The rigor of building the essential institutional systems of the new organization was highly demanding on KARI. An objective appraisal system that would assess scientists based on quantifiable output was introduced in 1995. A task force was appointed by the KARI director to work on the criteria and eventually prepare an appropriate tool. This was necessary because since the institute's inception it had based scientists' promotion on academic performance rather than output that would contribute to scientific productivity. A main purpose of this appraisal was to promote scientists according to output. Owing to a lack of funds to pay the scientists as per their new status, the process was held up for a long time. After the initial assessment was finalized in September 2000, scientists began to be promoted based on output. The appraisal tool was circulated widely to all scientists for revision before the second evaluation in 2001. Table 9.8 shows the analysis of the research scientists' status before and after promotion in January 2001. The promotion moved 147 scientists from the grades of senior research officers and research officers I to higher positions.

The appraisal elicited mixed reactions. A few center directors reported that it was encouraging to note that scientists were highly motivated to work hard after realizing that this would be recognized. The raises they received may have motivated half of the scientists. However, some felt they were not well evaluated, while others who never believed in the exercise failed to fill in the forms properly. However, the process having begun, there is room for its improvement, and both staff and management have an opportunity for learning.

Box 9.3 compares two job grades between KARI and the Kenyan government. These are for Research Officer II (job group L), which is the entry point for fresh

---

Box 9.3   Comparative Compensation Levels for Selected Professional Jobs Grades in the Kenya Agricultural Research Institute (KARI) and the Government of Kenya, 1997 and 2001

In KARI (1997)			In Government (1997)		
Job Title / Grade	Gross Annual Salary/Allowance		Job Title / Grade	Gross Annual Salary/Allowance	
	Ksh	US$		Ksh	US$
Assistant Director / Job Group Q	326,400	$5,446	Head of Division / Job Group P	323,160	$5,400
Research Officer II / Job Group L	194,496	$3,250	Graduate Professional / Job Group K	176,700	$2,950
In KARI (2001)			**In Government (2001)**		
Assistant Director / Job Group RI.3 (Q)	484,800	$6,060	Head of Division / Job Group P	425,820	$5,323
Research Officer II / Job Group RI.7 (L)	236,520	$2,956	Graduate Professional / Job Group K	190,440	$2,380

graduate research scientists, and Assistant Director (job group Q), which is the apex of a professional career for a research scientist in KARI as of 1997. However, with changes as of 2001, both scales have risen in KARI and government service, as indicated in box 9.3. The salary scale difference in 2001 is 13 percent for assistant director and 24 percent for the graduate professional. However, the salary raises from the appraisal may not adequately compensate for the rise in cost of living.

In sub-Saharan Africa, in response to the severe erosion in real pay levels of government employees over the past three decades, the adoption of an autonomous institute arrangement has achieved some limited success in obtaining more attractive salary levels for researchers. However, in others, the adoption of a semiautonomous status has been neither sufficient to guarantee improved compensation nor adequate to introduce compensation and promotion systems based on performance, which in reality may be achievable only under completely autonomous arrangements (Purcell and Anderson 1997, 12–13).

Despite its autonomous status, KARI still needs the government (the Ministries of Agriculture and Treasury) to approve and fund its annual HR budget. In this context, the government has insisted that the compensation levels for KARI staff be pegged to those prevailing in the government, except that KARI staff salaries can be fixed at two job groups higher than those of civil servants. Yet civil servants' compensation levels for professional and technical staff are estimated to be 300 to 450 percent below those prevailing in Kenya's private sector (Republic of Kenya 1998). In the circumstances, therefore, KARI's technical and professional staff members remain at comparatively low compensation levels. This situation generally applies to all public institutions in the NARS.

KARI is aware that salary, with its terms and conditions of service, is not the only motivating factor for employees. According to management theorists, this falls under extrinsic motivating factors or what is also referred to as the hygiene factor. Therefore, all other means for motivating staff should be employed. However, with the current high cost of living that has eroded staff net earnings, no organization can afford to ignore the remuneration package of its HR.

Lessons Learned and the Way Forward

Managing Change

What is the way forward? KARI has learned that being proactive and holistic are essential elements for managing change. Whenever change was needed and KARI lacked the know-how, it engaged outside assistance. Having a willingness to change and taking a bold step to do so is important in managing change. KARI is to be commended for involving its scientists and center directors in the change process. This is currently happening with the review of center research mandates and networks. It is also happening in interpreting the Strategic Plan. KARI has managed change by forming temporary structures such as task forces that have the authority of the top management to perform certain specific tasks. Task forces were used to institutionalize gender in technology development, to prepare project proposals, and to prepare the appraisal system for scientists.

Retention of Trained Staff

HR is important to an organization. Yet the development of HR is also an expensive process in terms of time, funds, and facilities. The main challenge now is how to retain the trained staff members by ensuring that they are motivated with attractive pay, research facilities, and funds to enable them to give their optimal output according to the institute's objectives. Bennel and Zuidema (1988, 16) state that the "retention, motivation, and performance of well-trained agricultural research staff depend critically on compensation policies and procedures." Idachaba (1998, 19–21) reports that low pay for research scientists is common in most SSA countries (figure 9.2). Many years of inflation followed by structural adjustment programs and the drastic devaluation of the foreign exchange rate often make salaries of NARS scientists noncompetitive in dollar terms, resulting in significant emigration abroad.

ISNAR-SPAAR (1987) reports that attrition rates in excess of 7 percent among research staff are the norm rather than the exception in Africa, as compared with 3 to 4 percent in research services in industrialized countries. These high rates of attrition imply that the entire pool of researchers and technicians in many NAROs will have to be replaced every fourteen to sixteen years. These turnover rates obviously undermine the productivity of research programs where continuity is required, and increase the need for training, with the consequent heavy costs. At KARI, staff attrition varied from 3 percent in 1998 to 9 percent in 1996. The large attrition rates of 13 percent (1997) and 21 percent (2000) coincide with staff transfers to the newly created organizations of KEPHIS and KESREF. If staff on leave of absence without pay is added, this raises the percentages. Staff members on leave of absence usually do

Figure 9.2 Attrition of Scientists in the Kenya Agricultural Research Institute, 1995–2000

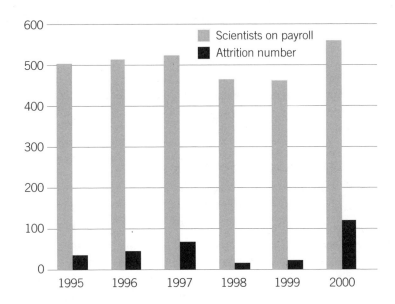

not wish to return to the institute if they can find permanent employment elsewhere; and even when they do return, they find the low pay discouraging.

Idachaba (1998, 20) states that countries "differ in their responses to changes in the structure of local domestic wages and salaries of scientists relative to the international wages of scientists abroad. Those countries that are slow in responding tend to have the most chronic-systemic staff instability in their NARS, resulting in the mass exodus of their researchers." Idachaba (1998, 21) further argues that

> Research staff instability has negative consequences on the effectiveness of NARS' research programs, building a knowledge pool for NARS, and stability of remaining staff, some of whom may be just immovable for failure of a better alternative.

Faced with low compensation levels, improved facilities and postgraduate training opportunities have probably provided the most important incentive for most research scientists to stay in KARI (Purcell and Anderson 1997, 12–13). Over the past five years, about 30 percent of KARI research scientists have had the opportunity to pursue postgraduate training. The short skill-enhancement courses also have had a positive effect on staff morale.

Enhanced Partnerships and Collaboration

Another incentive is increased partnerships with private-sector and other key stakeholders. This process has already begun with ATIRI. Scientists who are able to create business through research collaboration need to be compensated in order to encourage them to remain with KARI. KARI scientists need to be more proactive in reaching

225

out for opportunities with partners, especially in the private sector. Partners insist that KARI scientists need to sell their capabilities and products to potential customers. In this regard, KARI professionals need be more commercially oriented and also more creative in finding alternative sources of funding.

Sabbatical Leave

The KARI has been thinking of introducing a sabbatical leave policy so that scientists can pursue opportunities for career growth without losing their position or jeopardizing their research programs.

Raising the Retirement Age from Fifty-Five to Sixty

Developing and then losing staff is a costly affair for KARI. One way to overcome this is to delay staff retirement by five years. The mandatory retirement age for employees in all of Kenya's public institutions is fifty-five. KARI is not yet exempt from this public-sector-wide policy. Yet, senior professionals are adept at training and developing subordinates and shaping the future direction of the organization (Marcotte 1991, 2). Therefore, KARI continues to retain on contract terms some highly experienced Kenyans past the mandatory retirement age. This needs to be institutionalized.

Enhancing Performance through Leadership Style

Many organizational and managerial factors have been cited as important in improving organizational performance. Such factors include the manager's style of leadership (e.g., personality, confidence, values, motivation; researchers' motivation, education, experience, commitment, understanding of organizational goals and the organization itself) (Bennel and Zuidema 1998, 25). An earlier study by the government of Kenya and USAID (in 1978) found that management skills were needed in improved leadership, motivating, and coordinating skills combined with less authoritarian leadership styles and improved communication. The study recommended that training in leadership and human relations be given to all officers carrying direct and indirect supervisory responsibilities (Ellington, Olsen, and Baker 1982, 87).

Agricultural research organizations require a style of leadership and management that will allow a diverse group of well trained and potentially creative individuals to work alone and in teams to achieve organizational goals and objectives (Bennel and Zuidema 1998, 25). The leadership and organizational climate of the new KARI has played a significant role in mitigating the staff instability associated with low pay. KARI has enabled scientists to work in teams and allowed them to make decisions on their work. Consequently, intrinsic motivation has been enhanced through doing challenging work and having some autonomy in decision making within KARI. The institute proposes to continue to provide its staff with leadership skills in teamwork, leadership, problem solving, conflict management, and communication. It also plans to cement the corporate culture among all staff.

The Effect of Bureaucracy in Organizational Effectiveness

Some experts claim that the climate and leadership behavior in the hierarchical structures prevailing in the NARS institutions are not conducive to the motivation and performance of research scientists. Most NARS tend to be highly centralized and bureaucratic (Jain 1989, 5). Formal bureaucracies that are the norm in most public-sector institutions are typically in contrast to the features of an effective research institution. Research management can be an extremely challenging undertaking. Traditional bureaucracies exert formal authority in a manner that differs from the ideal authority system of a research organization. The term that has been used to characterize this ideal system is a "matrix organization," reflecting the complex flow of information and authority in coordinating research programs. Effective communication occurs laterally as well as vertically, so that lines of authority extend in all directions. Then teams are formed from different parts of the organization for a common research activity. Thus, in matrix fashion, communication and authority flow upward, downward, and laterally. Even describing such an arrangement can be complex and confusing, but when it works it can combine the benefits of organizational diversity with commonality of purpose. What is often lost in the process, however, is the classical bureaucratic model of hierarchy and control.

Bureaucracy is here used as a neutral technical term for formal organizations configured in the Weberian model of a hierarchical pyramid with delineated functions. Contemporary vernacular use of the term "bureaucracy" often conveys a negative connotation associated with organizational dysfunctions. Bureaucracies formalize rules and procedures and rely upon their repeated application to get things done. Generalists are more effective bureaucrats than technicians and professionals posted to such roles. In matrix organizations, however, where the appropriate institutional roles are catalytic, expert leadership is the answer. Management and coordination cannot be routine, regulated, or formalized; it is an adaptive process requiring flexibility and creativity in key leadership roles. KARI has circumvented the issue of bureaucracy by forming clearly focused "task forces" to achieve changes, as has been mentioned. The case for gender institutionalization in the research process is a good example. Task forces have been charged with institutionalizing planning, monitoring, and evaluation, and preparation of the various five-year NARP phases. KARI had the will to change, and sought assistance on how to change as need arose. In order for realistic change to occur and in order to build internal capacity, the institute has always ensured that partners and consultants have worked with its staff through the change process. The institute has also emphasized teamwork and consultative leadership, and gradually is working toward decentralization of functions. This leadership style and organizational climate have been critical for relative staff stability and high performance. This is the climate that is needed to cope with the many challenges that lie ahead, and is most important in managing change. Herein lies the secret behind KARI's ability to manage the change process.

In retrospect, one would say that KARI has been experiencing the Chinese proverb "a journey of a thousand miles begins with one step." There have been many challenges, but the institute has been learning from mistakes and challenges and will continue to do so. As a learning organization it has been steadily pursuing the ideal— to achieve the unattainable—and the quest is important, not the arrival. To have arrived is the equivalent of saying, "We've done it! There is nothing left for us to learn" (Pearn, Roderick, and Mulrooney 1995, 9).

REFERENCES

Armstrong, Michael. 1984. *A handbook of personnel management practice.* 2d ed. London: Kogan Page.

Barnett, Anthony, and Gabriel Rugalema. 2001. *Health and nutrition: Emerging and re-emerging issues in developing countries.* Focus 5, Brief 3 of 11 HIV/AIDS. Washington, D.C.: International Food Policy Research Institute (IFPRI).

Bennell, Paul. 1989. Annual performance appraisal schemes in agricultural research organization. Working Paper No. 24. The Hague: International Service for National Agricultural Research (ISNAR).

Bennell, Paul, and Larry Zuidema. 1998. Human resource management for agricultural research: Overview and issues. Working Paper No. 15. The Hague: International Service for National Agricultural Research (ISNAR).

Brush, Edwin G. 1993. Human resource planning. In: *Monitoring and evaluating agricultural research: A source book,* ed. Horton Douglas, Peter Ballantyne, Warren Peterson, Beatriz Uribe, Dely P. Gapasin, and Kathleen Sheridan, 92–99. Wallingford, UK: CAB International.

Disney, John. 2000. *Commercialization of agricultural research at KARI.* Proceedings of a workshop held in April 2000 at KARI Headquarters, Nairobi, Kenya. Nairobi: KARI.

Ellington, Earl F., Duane A. Olsen, and E. Kirk Baker. 1982. *Professional and subprofessional agricultural human resource in Kenya.* Mid-American International Consortium (MIAC) team report to United States Agency for International Development (USAID) and Government of Kenya (GoK). Washington, D.C.: USAID.

Franca, Zenete P., Joseph Wachira, Lilian W. Kimani, Hilary N. K. Ondatto, and Jorg Edsen. 1996. *Training needs and organizational constraints. Assessment in Kenya Agricultural Research Institute (KARI).* The Hague: International Service for National Agricultural Research (ISNAR).

Idachaba, Francis S. 1998. *Instability of national agricultural research systems in sub-Saharan Africa: Lessons from Nigeria.* Research Report 13. The Hague: International Service for National Agricultural Research (ISNAR).

International Service for National Agricultural Research (ISNAR). 1981. *Report to the government of Kenya: Kenya's national agricultural research system.* ISNAR Document No. R2. The Hague: ISNAR.

———. 1985. *Kenya agricultural strategy and plan. Volume 1: Organization and structure.* The Hague: ISNAR.

International Service for National Agricultural Research-Special Program for African Agricultural Research (ISNAR-SPAAR). 1987. *Guidelines for strengthening National Agricultural Research Systems in sub-Saharan Africa.* Washington, D.C.: World Bank.

Jain, H. Krishan. 1989. Organization and structure in NARS. International Service for National Agricultural Research (ISNAR) Working Paper No. 21. The Hague: ISNAR.

Kampen, Jacob, Jan Weijenberg, Matthew Dagg, and Maurice Kalunda. 1995. Strengthening national agricultural research systems in eastern Africa: A framework for action. Technical Paper No. 290. Washington, D.C.: World Bank.

Kenya Agricultural Research Institute (KARI). 1995. *National Agricultural Research Program Phase II Project Proposal.* Nairobi: KARI.

———. 1998. *Training master plan 1997/98–2001/02.* The Hague: International Service for National Agricultural Research (ISNAR).

KK Consulting Associates. 1995. *Staff rationalization study.* Consultants' report to Kenya Agricultural Research Institute (KARI). Nairobi: KARI.

Kimani, Lilian W. 1998. Human resource strategies for organizational change. The case of the Kenya Agriculture Research Institute. Master's thesis, University of Manchester, UK.

———. 2000a. Human resource development by the Netherlands Government in NARP II. Paper presented in a workshop at the end of the Netherlands program support to Kenya Agricultural Research Institute (KARI), 29 November 2000, KARI Headquarters, Nairobi, Kenya.

———. 2000b. Women in agricultural research policy and management today. The Case of the Kenya Agricultural Research Institute (KARI). Paper presented in the workshop on Gender and Agriculture in Africa: Effective Strategies for Moving Forward, 3–5 May 2000, Serena Hotel, Nairobi, Kenya. Available at *www.cgiar.org/isnar.*

Kimenye, Lydia N. 1998. Assessment of technology dissemination and utilization by women and men farmers: A case study from Embu and Mbeere Districts. In *Institutionalizing gender in agricultural research: Experiences from Kenya,* ed. John Curry, Margo Kooijman, and Helga Recke, 201–14. Nairobi: Kenya Agricultural Research Institute (KARI).

Marcotte, Paul. 1991. *Careers and career development.* Proceedings of a workshop on Human Resource Management and Development. Nairobi: Kenya Agricultural Research Institute (KARI)-International Service for National Agricultural Research (ISNAR).

Marcotte, Paul, Krystyna Stave, and Carlos Valverde. 1989. An analysis of human resource capabilities and constraints in INIAP, Ecuador. Working Paper No. 25. The Hague: International Service for National Agricultural Research (ISNAR).

Ministry of Health (MOH). 1998. *Proceedings of the Second National HIV/AIDS/STD Conference Report: Lessons Learned.* Held 28–30 October 1998, Nairobi, Kenya. MOH, NASCOP (National Acquired Immunodeficiency Syndrome [AIDS]/ Sexually Transmitted Diseases [STDs] Control Programme), Nairobi, Kenya.

Mulandi, Juliana C. 1998. Recruitment: The KARI case. In *Proceedings of a Workshop on Human Resources Development and Management,* ed. ISNAR and KARI. The Hague: International Service for National Agricultural Research (ISNAR).

National AIDS/STDs Control Programme (NASCOP). 1999. *Background, projections, impact, and interventions.* Nairobi: Ministry of Health.

Pearn, Michael, Ceri Roderick, and Chris Mulrooney. 1995. *Learning organizations in practice.* London: McGraw Hill.

Purcell, Dennis L, and Jock R. Anderson. 1997. *Agricultural extension and research: Achievements and problems in national systems.* A World Bank Operations Evaluation Study. Washington, D.C.: World Bank.

Republic of Kenya. 1998. *Office of the President/Directorate of Personnel Management Civil Service Reform medium term strategy 1998–2001.* Kenya: Government Printers.

229

Ridker, Ronald G. 1994. *The World Bank's role in human resource development in sub-Saharan Africa.* A World Bank Operations Evaluation Study. Washington, D.C.: World Bank.

Roseboom, Johannes, and Phillip G. Pardey. 1993. *Statistical brief on the national agricultural research system of Kenya.* Indicator series project (Phase II), Statistical Brief No. 5. The Hague: International Service for National Agricultural Research (ISNAR).

Simons, Scott, and Kangethe W. Gitu. 1989. Funding agricultural research and extension: The implications for growth. Long-range Planning Unit Technical Paper 89. The Hague: International Service for National Agricultural Research (ISNAR).

Taylor, T. Ajibola. 1991. ISNAR's collaboration with Kenya's National Agricultural Research System: Policy implications. In: *Agricultural research policy in Kenya: Proceedings of a workshop held in November 1991 in Nairobi, Kenya,* ed. KARI. Nairobi: Kenya Agricultural Research Institute (KARI).

Thomson, Rosemary, and Christopher Mabey. 1994. *Developing human resources.* Institute of Management Diploma Series. Oxford, UK: Butterworth-Heinemann Ltd.

UNAIDS (United Nations Report on acquired immunodeficiency syndrome [AIDS]). 1999. Available at *http//www.unaids.org.epidemic.*

Yamano, Takashi, and T. S. Jayne. 2004. Measuring the impacts of working age adult mortality on small-scale farm households in Kenya. *World Development* 32 (1): 91–119.

Universities and Agricultural Development in Africa: Insights from Kenya

RUTH ONIANG'O AND CARL K. EICHER

The vision of a new society will need to be developed in Africa, born out of the African historical experience and the sense of continuity of African history (Ajayi 1982, 8).

Background

The pioneering research on human capital by Nobel Laureate T. W. Schultz (1981) has spawned the conventional wisdom that investments in human capital (education, health, nutrition) can make a major contribution to economic growth and improved living standards. The problem is that poor countries cannot afford to invest as much in education as rich countries can. As a result, poor countries have to establish much clearer educational priorities in terms both of quantity and quality. The hard choices surrounding the debate over quantity and quality are especially difficult for contemporary universities in sub-Saharan Africa (hereafter Africa) because many universities have overexpanded, and the quality of higher education has fallen, especially in the last decade (Ajayi, Goma, and Johnson 1996). The African Development Bank (1998) reports that because of the low life expectancy of Africans and the low level of combined educational enrollments in African institutions, Africa has the lowest level of human development of any region in the world.

Great strides were made in increasing the number of universities in Africa (from about 20 in 1960 to 160 by 1996) and students (from 120,000 to over 2,000,000 during the same period) (Beintema, Pardey, and Roseboom 1998). However, universities throughout the continent are facing severe financial problems, a decline in the quality of the educational experience, and an exodus of senior academics to other well-endowed universities, such as those in South Africa, to nongovernmental organizations (NGOs), and to the private sector. The loss of senior scholars has been especially crippling for universities that are trying to build research capacity and graduate programs, because senior scholars set the research direction and the intellectual tone for their departments and they are ultimately responsible for the quality of local master's and doctorate programs (Eicher 2004).

Kenya has been independent for over forty years, and it now has six public universities and seven private universities, with a total enrollment of more than forty thousand students, up from eight thousand in 1970. This expansion represents a glowing achievement, but there is a strong belief in Kenyan society and in donor circles that Kenya's universities are not making a significant contribution to the national agricultural research agenda. These concerns have been echoed across the continent. Odour-Okelo and Taylor (1991), Hoste et al. (1995), Byerlee and Alex (1998), and others have suggested ways to tap the latent research potential of universities. Kenya's academic staff members are well aware of the criticism and they generally counter this assertion with two compelling arguments. First, they point out that Kenya's universities are having difficulty in financing undergraduate education, let alone taking on an expanded role in financing research and graduate degree programs. Second, they argue that because of low academic salaries, expanded teaching loads, and the lack of core funding from university budgets for research, most academics are forced to moonlight and pursue multiple careers. The reduction in university support for research is common throughout Africa. In 1997, the University of Zimbabwe's core budget allocated 98 percent of its recurrent budget to its teaching program and 2 percent to research activities (Thulstrup, Jagner, and Campbell 1997).

Several important reasons explain why it is timely to address the contribution of universities to agricultural research in Kenya. First, the brain drain of the 1990s has reduced the number of senior academics who have historically provided leadership in university research and graduate training. Second, the decline in the quality of university graduates is manifested in less well trained graduates for the extension service and the various research organizations in Kenya. Third, there is uncertainty over the respective roles of the government, the universities, and the private sector in capturing the benefits of information technology and agricultural biotechnology from the global research system. Finally, many donor-financed projects for universities have been unproductive.

This chapter aims to contribute to the debate over the role of African universities in agricultural research and human capital development. The following two questions are addressed:

1. What are the major barriers to increasing the agricultural research output of Kenya's universities?
2. What lessons can other countries in Africa draw from the experience of Kenya's universities in building agricultural research capacity and graduate training programs in agriculture?

Without question, human capital degradation in food and agriculture in Kenya is especially troubling because it is jeopardizing Kenya's ability to take advantage of the worldwide advances in science and technology. The thesis of this chapter is that universities are the weak link in Kenya's agricultural knowledge triangle, which embraces teaching, research, and extension. Many reasons account for why agricultural universities and faculties of agriculture are weak in Kenya and in other countries in Africa. First and foremost is their infancy relative to their counterparts in Europe, Asia, and

Latin America. Consider the following situation in Africa (Beintema, Pardey, and Rose-boom 1998):

- Most faculties of agriculture were established in the past thirty years.
- Most new universities of agriculture were established in the last twenty to thirty years.
- Most postgraduate programs in agriculture in Africa were established in the past decade.

Despite their early stage of scientific and institutional development, African universities represent the only sustainable institution that, in the long run, can break the cycle of dependency on overseas training (Eicher 1989, 1990, 1999, 2004). The managers of agricultural research and extension systems in Africa should be deeply concerned about improving the quality of local postgraduate programs. This is because, after donors phase out scholarships for overseas training, African universities will be the primary source of human capital for agricultural research and extension agencies and the source of future academic staff members.

Why Invest in Universities and Agricultural Higher Education?

A decade ago, the then World Bank vice president, Edward Jaycox (1989), identified the lack of administrative, managerial, and scientific capacity as the weak link in African development and urged the World Bank and other donors to launch capacity-building initiatives (Wai 1995). Yet, in historical terms, the current concern over capacity building represents old wine in new bottles. Three decades ago, Julius Nyerere (1967) brilliantly laid out the role of education as a contributor to capacity building and national development in his elaborate thesis of Education for Self-Reliance. Nyerere dissected the shortcomings of Tanzania's colonial education system and called for a new model—one of education for self-reliance and development. In the same year, Thomas Odhiambo (1967) published his visionary article, "East Africa: Science for Development." The present concern about increasing the research output of Kenya's universities is a reiteration of the vision of Nyerere and Odhiambo (see also Court 1987).

Nevertheless, after much discussion of education and capacity building in Africa, the role of universities in capacity building remains a hotly debated issue. There are as many advocates as critics of universities in promoting development. The advocates believe that African universities should be encouraged to play a bigger role in research, graduate training, and capacity building, because:

- Many universities in Africa have a large stock of agricultural scientists with M.Sc. and Ph.D. degrees. For example, in 1995, 547 African scientists with a Ph.D. in agriculture were employed by universities, and 357 were employed in the national agricultural research systems (NARS) in eastern and southern Africa (Mrema 1997).

- The failure of policy reforms to speed economic recovery in Africa has created a growing awareness that efficient, reliable, and relevant institutions matter as much as policies in accelerating economic growth (see Burki and Perry 1998). Because African universities are a core institution in the agricultural knowledge triangle, it is important to nurture and enhance their contribution to national development.
- Empirical support is growing for the proposition that the accretionary process of learning by doing is an efficient way to build scientific and managerial capacity (Solow 1997; Appleton 1998). Gerald Helleiner (1979, 240) sums up the problem of relying on foreign experts for research and advisory roles: "A succession of expatriates learn more and more about developmental decision making while the Africans below them in the hierarchy become progressively more alienated and discontented. Thus foreigners appropriate the experience and collective memory that is accumulated during the process of development then leave the country, carrying these invaluable assets with them."
- Graduate students represent a valuable and cost-effective source of agricultural research output.
- A human capital renewal system that is indigenous and cost-effective is central to the long-run sustainability of universities and national research and extension systems. Because of the cutback in foreign aid for overseas training over the past decade, it follows that African universities represent the only sustainable institution to replace overseas training in agriculture, science, and related fields. The government of Botswana is an exception because it has ample foreign exchange from mineral exports to pay the full cost of overseas graduate training of its agriculturists.

Despite this growing support for the proposition that universities have a strategic role to play in research and national capacity building, several influential critics have argued that African universities are bloated, inefficient, and in need of downsizing. Critics have also pointed out that the annual cost of higher education per student is substantially higher in Africa than in Asia or Latin America (see Coleman and Court 1993, 354). This has led to intense political and policy debates throughout Africa on how to reduce the unit public cost of higher education. Cost recovery is now being addressed in many universities by privatizing some operations such as catering, charging tuition, introducing student loan schemes, and offering evening classes.

The critics of higher education often cite a study by Psacharopoulos (1994), who marshaled evidence to show that primary education in Africa has generated a higher social rate of return to society than has secondary and higher education. However, Bennell (1996) re-examined seventeen of the eighteen original African studies on which Psacharopoulos based his conclusion on the high payoff to primary education and found that only seven countries in the sample had reliable data for primary schooling. Some scholars argue that the microdatabase for comparisons between primary, secondary, and university education is shaky and an unreliable guide for making decisions on how much to invest in specific levels of education in Africa. The challenge is to carry out country-by-country assessments of the payoff to specific out-

234

puts of higher education, such as undergraduate education, graduate education, and research. The payoff to these investments should then be compared with that to investments in other activities, such as health care and roads.

Many donors reduced their support for agricultural higher education in Africa because of the poor performance of universities and the belief that investments in primary education, extension, and research would have more impact on agricultural production and economic growth. The donors' ambivalence to supporting universities is partially attributed to the long gestation of and uncertain payoff to investments in universities and faculties of agriculture. Also, donor experience was lacking in the design and supervision of projects to strengthen universities and build national research and development (R&D) capacity (AID 1989; Purcell and Anderson 1997). How do we reconcile these criticisms of universities with the plea for agricultural universities and faculties of agriculture to increase their agricultural research output (Byerlee and Alex 1998)? Is there a case for maintaining and even increasing public spending on agricultural higher education, especially if these expenditures can be directed toward public goods activities (research and graduate education) instead of undergraduate training? Private returns in the latter are high, and many of the users (undergraduates) can pay a greater share of the cost of tuition, room, and books. The answer depends on the benefits associated with graduate education, such as research, building national scientific capacity, and reducing the dependence on foreign aid. This question should be pursued in case studies of the economics of agricultural higher education in Africa.

The Agricultural Knowledge Triangle

Over the past ten to fifteen years, there has been an ongoing debate over the need to move beyond the project-by-project approach to a systems approach to coordinating and sequencing interlinked investments in agricultural research, extension, and education (for examples see USAID 1985; Eponou 1996; and Michelsen and Shapiro 1998). For a synthesis of the evolution of the World Bank's support for agricultural services (mainly extension and research) in Africa, see Venkatesan and Kampen (1998). Various scholars have articulated this approach under the rubric of agricultural knowledge system, agricultural knowledge information system (AKIS), and the agricultural knowledge triangle (Eicher 1999). Röling (1988) discusses the evolution of the agricultural knowledge system and reports that this approach has been adopted by Wageningen University in the Netherlands. Basically, these approaches argue that public and private managers of separately governed institutions should coordinate decisions on the size and sequencing of public investments in research, extension, and education. The reason is that the returns on investments in these three activities have been found to be higher if they are planned and executed as a joint activity rather than pursued as freestanding extension, research, or education projects (Evenson, Waggoner, and Ruttan 1979; Bonnen 1998; Boughton et al. 1995).

The policy implication is that the returns to investment in research will be low if public extension agents and seed and fertilizer companies do not diffuse research and

235

turn it into commercial success. Likewise the returns to investment in extension will be low if extension agents are not continuously recharged with new technology from public and private research organizations. Finally, because the quality of scientific human capital is the main determinant of research productivity, the returns to investment in national research services will be low if the research agency is not recharged with a flow of well-trained university graduates. These examples point out the strategic role of crafting agricultural research triangles that promote interaction and cooperation between research and extension organizations and faculties of agriculture.

Despite the documented high returns to joint research, extension, and education projects in industrial countries, most donors prepare separate projects for research, extension, and universities. The first and most important reason for the separate project approach is the historical priorities of colonial governments. Because colonial governments gave priority to extracting the agricultural surplus from Africa, they established export crop research stations between 1900 and 1920, followed by a time lag of fifty to seventy years before faculties of agriculture and veterinary science were established. The documented high rates of return to research help explain why many NARS have received generous donor support over the past twenty to thirty years (Oehmke and Crawford 1996). Second, donor-financed projects often include research and extension activities in the same project because both are often based in the Ministry of Agriculture. Third, joint research, extension, and higher education projects have proven difficult to coordinate and implement because the administrators of universities and those of extension and research services typically report to different ministries. Fourth, African scientists are well aware that many of the institution-building projects, which include research, extension, and higher education, (e.g., the U.S. land-grant model and the state [Indian] agricultural university model) have not performed well in Africa (Johnson and Okigbo 1989; Hansen 1990; Francis Idachaba, personal communication, 1998). The fifth reason for the fragmented approach to investment in the agricultural knowledge triangle stems from the bureaucracy of donor and international organizations. A former extension specialist in the World Bank describes the bureaucratic difficulties in preparing and implementing joint research, extension, and agricultural higher education projects:

> The Bank's involvement with the development of higher agricultural education at the university level in Africa has been minimal . . . within the Bank, the Agriculture Divisions have no responsibility for universities, which are the responsibility of the Education Divisions. . . . It is not therefore surprising that the Bank projects in extension and research do not provide support to higher agricultural education. (Venkatesan 1991)

What has been the result of sprinkling separate extension, research, and higher education projects across the African landscape? Has this approach resulted in an underinvestment in one of the three components of the triangle? A recent World Bank review of its global expenditures on research, extension, and education sheds light on this question. The review found that agricultural higher education received about 2

Table 10.1 World Bank Global Support for Agricultural Research, Extension, and Agricultural Higher Education, 1987–97

	Million US$	Percentage
Agricultural research	2,482	51.50
Agricultural extension	2,229	46.25
Agricultural higher education	108	2.25
Total	4,819	100.00

Source: Willett 1998.

percent of expenditures, while agricultural research and extension received roughly 98 percent of the Bank's $4.8 billion of global investments in agricultural education, research, and training over the 1987–97 period (table 10.1).

How did Africa fare in this $4.8 billion package? During the 1987–97 period, the Bank made six loans to agricultural higher education totaling $108 million; three of the six were for Africa—Ghana, Uganda, and Ethiopia.

The Evolution of Higher Education in Africa

The Colonial Period

In most African countries, higher education is new relative to its inception in Latin America and Asia. Brazil had been independent for 138 years before Nigeria achieved its independence in 1960. The University of Buenos Aires was established in 1820. The University of Bombay conferred its first Ph.D. in economics in 1935, some eleven years before Makerere University was established in Uganda.

By contrast, the British government established four universities in Africa after World War II. Each had strong links to the University of London: Gordon College in Khartoum, Sudan, and Makerere College in Kampala, Uganda were both established in 1946, and the University College in Ibadan, Nigeria, and the University of Gold Coast in Ghana were established in 1948. The University College at Salisbury in Rhodesia (now Zimbabwe) was established in 1953. Entrants to these colleges were relatively few, but they were destined to become senior civil servants, directors of public corporations, headmasters of schools, and doctors. The French trained an elite cadre of students exclusively in France, but this policy left the Francophone African countries deeply dependent on France in the pre-independence period, a trend that continued in the 1960s and 1970s (Orivel 1995). French scientists managed the NARS in Senegal for ten years after its independence and for fifteen years after the Ivory Coast's independence.

The Golden Era of the 1960s and 1970s

Without question, the 1960s and 1970s can be described as the golden age of higher education in Africa because education enjoyed political support that was embodied in a generous flow of resources used to train thousands of undergraduates to replace expatriates in the civil service and parastatals. During this period, many African governments converted agricultural colleges into faculties of agriculture, established new agricultural faculties, and sent many academic staff members overseas for postgraduate training (Lynam and Blackie 1994).

The Financial and Quality Crises of the 1980s and 1990s

University development in Africa in the 1980s and 1990s was marked by an increase in the number of public universities, a dramatic increase in student enrollment, a reduction in public financial support per student, political turbulence, and a slowdown in donor support for higher education (World Bank 1994). Beintema, Pardey, and Roseboom (1998) report that real (inflation-adjusted) spending per university student in Africa declined from an average of US$6,300 in 1980 to US$1,500 in 1988. Also, the real salaries of academic staff members fell by 30 percent during the period 1980–88 (Blair and Jordan 1994). The combined effects of these forces led to a marked decline in the quality of education and student and faculty morale, an increase in faculty moonlighting, and an exodus of academic staff. For an exchange of views on the problems facing higher education in the 1980s and 1990s, see Ajayi, Goma, and Johnson (1996), World Bank (1992, 1994), King (1995), Saint (1992), and Blair and Jordan (1994).

Duplication of Effort among Faculties of Agriculture, Forestry, and Veterinary Medicine

The bread and butter issues in strengthening agricultural knowledge triangles in eastern and central Africa are extremely complex because of the colonial legacy, the large number of universities in the region, and the fragmentation of teaching and research on agriculture and natural resources. The latter arises from the creation of separate faculties of agriculture, forestry, and environmental sciences (Norman 1998). There are thirty-five faculties of agriculture, forestry, and veterinary medicine in the ten countries in eastern and central Africa (table 10.2), obviously a duplication of effort in the region. The merger of faculties of agriculture and forestry could reduce administrative costs and promote cooperation in research on agroforestry. Because of the many faculties of agriculture and forestry in eastern and central Africa, most donors do not have an adequate information base upon which to decide which faculty or faculties to support in the region.

However, the fragmentation and duplication of B.Sc. and M.Sc. degree programs in eastern Africa is also a pervasive problem in developing countries. Argentina, a nation of thirty-five million people, currently has twenty-eight faculties of agronomy (agriculture). Kenya, a nation of twenty-eight million people, has six public universities, with five having a faculty of agriculture. Yet with the unfolding global information revolution, and the reduction in the cost of information exchange, many countries in Africa should be able to close some of their agricultural experiment stations, merge some faculties of agriculture and forestry, and phase out redundant faculties of agriculture. At the same time, the research required to develop, borrow, and adapt biotechnology to local agro-ecologies will require research inputs from university

Table 10.2 Universities in the Ten Eastern and Central African Countries with Faculties of Agriculture, Forestry, and Veterinary Medicine

Country	University	Agriculture	Forestry	Vet. Med
Burundi	Université du Burundi	✔	—	—
Eritrea	University of Asmara	✔	—	—
Ethiopia	Alemaya University of Agriculture	✔	✔	—
	Addis Ababa University	—	—	✔
Kenya	University of Nairobi	✔	—	✔
	Egerton University	✔	—	—
	Moi University	✔	✔	—
	Jomo Kenyatta University of S&T	✔	✔	—
	University of Eastern Africa, Baraton	✔	—	—
Madagascar	Université d'Atananarivo	✔	—	—
Rwanda	Université Nationale du Rwanda	✔	—	—
Sudan	University of Khartoum	✔	✔	✔
	University of Juba	—	✔	—
	University of Gezira	✔	—	—
	Bahr El Ghazal University	✔	✔	—
	Dongola University	✔	—	—
	El—Gadarif University	✔	✔	—
	Upper Nile University	—	✔	—
Tanzania	Sokoine University of Agriculture	✔	✔	✔
Uganda	Makerere University	✔	✔	✔
Zaire	Université de Kinshasa	✔	✔	—
	Université de Lubumbashi	—	—	✔
TOTAL		18	11	6

Source: Mrema 1997.

scholars in agriculture as well as disciplines such as law, business administration, and molecular biology.

Evolution of Universities in Kenya

Education Policy in the 1960s and 1970s

After the attainment of independence in 1963, the government of Kenya expanded its education system to provide qualified persons to replace expatriates in the civil service and to undertake reforms to reflect the aspirations of an independent state. Immediately after independence, the Ministry of Education appointed a Commission of Education to survey the educational resources in Kenya and to advise the government on the formulation of national policies for education. Members of the commission looked to education as a primary means to unite people of different racial and ethnic groups. Apart from training high-level manpower, the reform and expansion of the education system was motivated by political pressures and promises such as universal primary education, free education, and the Africanization of syllabi and teaching staff.

The socioeconomic and political pressures in the 1960s and 1970s, coupled with external support, fueled a rapid expansion of all levels of the education system:

- Primary enrollment increased almost fourfold from 1963 to 1983.
- Secondary enrollment at independence was about thirty thousand pupils and 1,600 teachers, most of whom were expatriates or foreign trained. Twenty years later, in 1983, secondary school enrollment was over half a million, with most teachers being Kenyans.
- University enrollment rose from eight thousand undergraduates in 1970 to forty-one thousand in 1990.

In 1970, the University of Nairobi was established by an Act of Parliament; the university enjoyed political and financial support and maintained high standards in the 1970s and 1980s. New universities were launched in Kenya over the period from 1984 to 1994 in response to communities who petitioned the president to open a university or university college in their region. Moi University was opened in 1984, followed by Kenyatta University in 1985, Egerton University in 1988, Jomo Kenyatta University of Agriculture and Technology in 1994, and Maseno University in 2001.

The Double Intake Decision and the Decline in Quality

In 1987, the government decided to double the intake of first-year students in public universities in order to clear the backlog of applicants created by a long period of university closure because of the alleged participation of some students and academic staff in the attempted coup of 1982. Initially, the double intake decision made political sense because it relieved the government of pressure from parents who were tired of having their university-qualified students delay their education by a year or more. Also, from an academic perspective, it seemed as though the transition to the 8:4:4[1] system would have experienced great difficulty if the double intake decision had not been made because it would have meant running two parallel systems in universities for a number of years (Wandiga 1997). Yet the decision to double the intake of first-year students in 1986–87 and again in 1990–91 increased the enrollment of students in the five public universities from 8,800 in 1986–87 to 38,848 in 1990–91, and pushed university facilities to the brink of collapse.

The political decision to quadruple the number of university students in four years (between 1987 and 1991) without a commensurate increase in funding imposed a nightmare on university administrators and lecturers alike. University facilities were swamped, and both student and academic staff morale plummeted. Today, many nations in Africa are saddled with overexpanded and low-quality educational systems (Blaug 1992). This is the case of higher education in Kenya today.

From Centers of Excellence to General-Purpose Universities

The University of Nairobi is Kenya's oldest university and it offers virtually all disciplines, both science and arts based, professional and nonprofessional. When four new public universities were established over the period from 1984 to 1994, the strategy called for each new university to specialize in one or two academic disciplines and become a national center of excellence. Yet political forces and internal academic politics coalesced to turn these new universities into general-purpose schools. Moi University, for example, was established with an initial emphasis on information sciences and forestry, but other disciplines were added to accommodate qualified high school graduates. Initially, Kenyatta University specialized in training secondary school teachers, but it too has broadened its range of degree programs under political pressure. Egerton University was established in 1988 and given a mandate to become a national center of excellence in agriculture, but it has evolved into a general-purpose university. Jomo Kenyatta University of Agriculture and Technology, with substantial financing from the government of Japan, has remained a small science and technology-based university.

Male enrollment is higher than female enrollment in almost all of the departments in Kenya's five public universities. The disciplines with the highest female enrollments are home science, nursing, information science, dental science, education, law, arts, anthropology, social science, pharmacy, and commerce. Female enrollment in agriculture at the University of Nairobi increased from 12 percent in the 1973–74 academic year, to 20 percent by 1979–80, and to 25 percent by the 1993–94 academic year (table 10.3).

In 1994, the president appointed a Committee on University Education in Kenya to assist the government in working out how to implement remedial measures to finance higher education. The committee had a challenging task of making the public aware of the constraints that the government was experiencing in financing higher education in an era of structural adjustment, retrenchment, and low academic staff morale. Although some of the committee's recommendations, especially the loan scheme, are being implemented, most have yet to see the light of day (Republic of

Table 10.3 Undergraduate Enrollment by Gender in the Faculty of Agriculture, University of Nairobi, Selected Years

Academic year	Male	Female	Total	Percentage female
1972–74	130	17	147	12
1979–80	274	70	344	20
1980–81	290	77	367	21
1986–87	445	122	567	22
1987–88	679	166	845	20
1993–94	839	273	1,112	25

Source: Enrolment Records, University of Nairobi.

241

Kenya 1995). The recommendations in the report have partly been undertaken and produced by another commission appointed by the government to evaluate the entire educational system in the country. This commission made recommendations that would affect higher education, if implemented.

The Evolution of Faculties of Agriculture in Kenya

In Kenya, most faculties of agriculture and graduate degree programs in agriculture are relatively young. When the University of Nairobi was created in 1970 it included a faculty of agriculture. The Egerton College of Agriculture was upgraded in 1988 to a full-fledged university (Egerton University). Moi University was established in 1984 with a specialization in forestry and information science, and a faculty of agriculture was added in 1997. Jomo Kenyatta University of Agriculture and Technology established its faculty of agriculture when it attained full university status in 1994. The newer faculties of agriculture are slowly developing an intellectual and research identity. Egerton University is trying to make a name for itself in agricultural research circles, but its staff is primarily committed to teaching undergraduates. It takes time and sustained research activity and publications to garner a reputation for excellence in research. The Tegemeo Institute has enhanced Egerton's reputation as a policy research center, but the faculties of agriculture at Moi and Jomo Kenyatta Universities will need time to identify their niche and generate a steady flow of research output.

The ability of academic staff members to control their time has been a major attraction of a university career. Before the double intake of students in the late 1980s, the academic workload was divided between teaching (60 percent) and research (40 percent). Staff members would teach one or two classes per semester, pursue research, participate in departmental and university committees, attend seminars and interviews, and prepare papers for publication. However, the double intake decision increased teaching loads and left little time and few resources for research. As a result, academic staff members were forced to look outside the university for research support.

Agricultural research in Kenya's universities is at a crossroads. Kenya has five underfunded faculties of agriculture, and its universities do not have a clear division of labor in agricultural higher education. The deans of agriculture need to come together and discuss harmonization and coordination of programs, quality assurance, research cooperation, and partnerships. Academic entrepreneurship is desperately needed to strengthen the quality of research and graduate programs. Research capacity is currently underutilized in Kenya's universities. Yet stable core funding is also lacking to underwrite the cost of high-quality graduate training programs, to rebuild libraries (the total 1998 library budget for the University of Nairobi was US$50,000) and computer support services, and to purchase laboratory equipment and new vehicles. Creative senior academics are frustrated in an academic environment that does not provide visionary leadership, intellectual stimulation, and administrative backstopping. As a result, many professors have gone on leave for periods of up to four

242

years, thus undermining the continuity of teaching, research, and graduate programs. While on leave, many faculty members resign when they realize that little change is likely to take place in their universities.

The lack of incentives for academic staff is a core issue that is undermining creativity, continuity, and a commitment to building world-class scientific leadership. Basic salaries in Kenyan public universities have stagnated to a level where some cadres of senior civil servants in government ministries are now enjoying higher basic salaries and allowances than professors.

Kenya's Universities: An Agenda for Renewal

Human Capital Degradation

Kenya's thirty-five years of independence have generated a mixed record of success and failure in higher education. The golden era of the expansion of higher education in the 1960s and 1970s was followed by overexpansion, financial stress, a decline in quality of the educational experience in the 1980s, and noticeable human capital degradation in the 1990s. Turning to agriculture, Kenya now has five poorly funded faculties of agriculture. Each is facing serious financial and quality problems. Each is facing a brain drain of senior academics that are crucial to providing mentorship to junior academics, as well as research direction for graduate students and the generation of peer-reviewed research output. Because these issues have an impact on the quality of university graduates who are hired by the Kenya Agricultural Research Institute (KARI), the extension service, and agribusiness firms, it behooves members of Kenya's agricultural establishment to come together and discuss the following issues:

- How can universities do a better job in recruiting the best minds from secondary schools to pursue a career in agriculture?
- How should universities revise their curriculum to address the changing demand for B.Sc. graduates in agriculture in a rapidly changing global economy?
- How can local graduate degree programs in agriculture be revitalized and the relevance and quality of M.Sc. theses increased?
- What changes in the incentive structure are needed to encourage academics to pursue long-term university careers and carry out joint research programs with KARI scientists?
- What changes in KARI's incentive structures are needed to encourage KARI scientists to teach graduate courses, supervise local graduate students, and communicate the research output from M.Sc. theses to farmers, traders, agribusiness firms, and the people of Kenya?

Because graduate training and research are complementary and symbiotic activities, we first explore how to attack human capital degradation and improve the quality of M.Sc. degree programs, then discuss how to strengthen university-KARI research linkages and increase the agricultural research output of Kenya's universities.

243

Although discussion is underway in eastern and southern Africa about adding new Ph.D. programs in agriculture, we believe that Kenya should give first priority to shoring up the quality of existing M.Sc. programs in agriculture over the next five to ten years (and perhaps longer). Priority should be given to improving the quality of M.Sc. training for two reasons. First, the development of high-quality and effective M.Sc. programs will serve as the foundation for Ph.D. programs. Second, rigorously supervised M.Sc. theses can make a valuable and cost-effective contribution to the local knowledge base. To summarize, the first priority is to revitalize existing M.Sc. programs.

Revitalizing M.Sc. Training Programs in Agriculture

There is broad agreement in Kenya and throughout Africa that high-quality local graduate training programs are essential to the long-term productivity and sustainability of NARS (Jones and Blackie 1991). However, the database on the strengths, weaknesses, and performance of Kenya's graduate programs in agriculture is weak. We know that 10 percent of KARI's scientists with graduate degrees have received them from local universities. Yet little information is available on the cost and quality of local versus regional and overseas graduate training, and the quantity and quality of the research output of faculties of agriculture in Kenya (BIFAD 2003).

The leaders of Kenya's agricultural establishment should be deeply concerned about the decline in quality of local M.Sc. training programs because the most important factor affecting the quality of KARI research is the quality of its scientific human capital. Because Kenya's universities will be the major training institution for the next generation of agricultural scientists, KARI scientists with low-quality B.Sc. degrees will have difficulty in being admitted to M.Sc. programs in Kenya. This phenomenon is already unfolding in eastern Africa, where World Bank and European Union (EU) scholarships for local M.Sc. training have not been utilized because of the poor quality of local B.Sc. degrees in agriculture. KARI scientists with low-quality M.Sc. degrees also will have difficulty in gaining admission to high-quality Ph.D. programs in overseas universities. Human capital degradation in agriculture jeopardizes Kenya's long-run ability to take advantage of the worldwide advances in science and technology.

What can be done to shore up the quality of local M.Sc. programs in agriculture? The first step is to analyze the causes of human capital degradation. Evidence is growing that Kenya is experiencing a meltdown in graduate teaching and research capacity that was laboriously assembled and nurtured in its faculties of agriculture in the 1970s and 1980s. Donors and foundations played a major role in building this capacity over the past thirty-five years. The U.S. Agency for International Development (USAID) invested heavily in strengthening Egerton University, and the Rockefeller Foundation helped strengthen the University of Nairobi. Coleman and Court (1993) give an analysis of the Rockefeller Foundation's university development program. The University of Nairobi was one of the fifteen universities in twelve developing countries that received support from this program from 1961 to 1981. Likewise, the German academic exchange program initially offered generous financial support to the

University of Nairobi, and it subsequently extended aid to the other public universities in Kenya.

The following factors are contributing to the meltdown in Kenya's graduate teaching and research capacity:

1. The exodus of Kenyan senior academic staff to universities in southern Africa and the private/NGO sectors, and the prevalence of moonlighting have crippled the capacity of faculties of agriculture to supervise M.Sc. and Ph.D. student research and carry out high-quality and timely public goods research. In 1998 the University of Nairobi's Faculty of Agriculture had only four senior academic staff with a Ph.D. degree (two associate professors and two professors) for its six departments (Ekwamu et al. 1998). In 1998 Egerton University's Department of Agricultural Economics had one Ph.D. in residence out of twenty-five members of its academic staff (Table 10.4).

2. The number of donor-financed agricultural scholarships for overseas training has fallen in the 1990s. In many cases, donors have increased their support for training in local universities, but Norman (1998) reports that the number of graduate students in agriculture is falling in universities in eastern Africa.

3. Agricultural policy circles in Kenya and eastern Africa are perceiving that local M.Sc. programs in agriculture (and related fields) are of lower quality, longer in duration, and riskier (because of turnover of senior academics and civil strife) than those in universities in industrial countries.

4. Universities have been unable to develop an incentive structure to reward both university and KARI staff who excel in the supervision of local graduate student research. Because of delays in reading student theses, it sometimes takes three to six years for students to complete local M.Sc. degrees in the various fields of agriculture.

To summarize, the capacity of Kenya's faculties of agriculture to offer high-quality M.Sc. degrees in agriculture on a timely basis appears to be weaker than it was

Table 10.4   Academic Staff Numbers in the Faculty of Agriculture, Egerton University, Kenya, 1998

Department	Assistant Lecturer	Lecturer	Senior Lecturer	Associate Professor	Professor Professor	Total
Ag. economy/business mgmt.	9	13	3	—	—	25
Agronomy	5	11	11	1	—	28
Animal science	11	6	9	1	—	27
Dairy food science/technology	2	8	—	—	—	10
Horticulture	17	6	1	—	2	26
Natural resources	6	8	3	2		19
TOTAL	50	52	27	4	2	135

Source: Ekwamu et al. 1998.

a decade ago. The departure of local associate professors and professors from Kenya's universities, coupled with a loss of long-term technical assistance from overseas universities, political disturbances, and financial stress have ominous implications for a country trying to develop the capacity to contribute to and benefit from the global biological and information revolutions.

Regional M.Sc. programs

Regionalization of training is frequently mentioned as a way to drive down the unit cost of graduate programs. Yet there is a large gap between the theory and the practice of recruiting and training M.Sc. degree students from a region such as eastern Africa. The sobering experience of the University of Nairobi's M.Sc. Regional Program in Agricultural Economics illustrates this point (Eicher 1999). With financial assistance from the government of Germany, the University of Nairobi launched an M.Sc. degree program in 1974 with a specialization in agricultural marketing for students from eastern Africa (Thimm 1992). The program was subsequently broadened to include a full range of courses in agricultural economics (Amann and Kriesel 1976). The two-year M.Sc. program in agricultural economics consisted of coursework during the first year and thesis research in the student's home country during the second year. Members of the academic staff were excited about teaching courses to students from eastern Africa, but it was difficult for them to find the time and resources to travel to Uganda and Tanzania to supervise the research of M.Sc. students from these countries. Also, the University of Nairobi's Department of Agricultural Economics lost eight doctoral staff from 1985 to 1995 (Ackello-Ogutu and Mwangi 1995) because of low salaries, funding constraints (i.e., a budget of US$532 for supplies in 1993–94), and frequent university closures. Finally, the intake of students from eastern Africa dried up in the early 1990s, and then the intake of Kenyan students fell from twenty in 1989, to twelve in 1991, to five in 1993, and to three in 1997. This case study of a twenty-five-year effort to mount and sustain a regional M.Sc. program reveals that it was easy to garner foreign aid to launch a local M.Sc. program, but difficult to sustain the regional program, decade after decade. Additional case studies of regional training programs should be carried out and the results made available to governments, universities, and donors.

M.Sc. training: The costs and benefits of national, regional, and overseas programs

The economics of graduate training in agriculture remain a mystery after forty years of African independence. Little is known about the comparative cost and direct and indirect benefits of local, regional, and overseas M.Sc. and Ph.D. programs. Several examples illustrate this point. Zeller, Mataya, and Islam (1997) report that the total cost of a two-year M.Sc. degree in agricultural economics at the University of Malawi is US$11,000. However, closer examination reveals that this does not include the salaries of two part-time international staff that, if included, would increase the cost per M.Sc. degree to US$18,000 per student (Manfred Zeller, personal communication, 1998). Also, the quality issue should be examined because Malawian M.Sc. candidates reported that they perceived the quality of training at overseas universities to be higher than that of local training and that overseas training includes a range of perks and hidden income (Zeller, Mataya, and Islam 1997).

The annual cost of an M.Sc. degree in agriculture at Makerere University is $10,800, or about $25,000 for an M.Sc. degree lasting an average of 2.5 years (Ekwamu et al. 1998, 24). Anandajayasekeram et al. (1996) report that the average cost per M.Sc. degree in southern Africa's four regional specializations (agronomy, animal sciences, land and water management, and agricultural economics) and in Australia, North America, and the Philippines was as follows:

- Southern Africa, US$21,983 per M.Sc. degree (includes local salaries of teachers).
- Southern Africa, US$31,189 per M.Sc. degree (includes cost of local teachers and German teachers on technical assistance contracts).
- Australia, US$32,000 per M.Sc. degree.
- North America, US$56,800 per M.Sc. degree (two years) (BIFAD 2003).
- The University of the Philippines at Los Baños estimates that the cost for an M.Sc. degree in agriculture is US$12,000 per year, or $24,000 for two years, including a thesis (Edith C. Cedicol, personal communication, 1999).

The variation in the preceding estimates of the cost of M.Sc. programs in various African universities points out the need for a study of the full costs and benefits of local, regional, and international training (Ponniah Anandajayasekeram, personal communication, 1998). The cost of training must be supplemented with additional information on the monetary and nonmonetary benefits of local versus regional and overseas training. For example, even if donors paid the full cost of overseas training and it was of higher quality than local training, local M.Sc. and Ph.D. training programs have important benefits. First, the coursework in local degree programs is likely to better prepare students for careers in research and extension because the courses are grounded in national agricultural policies and local agro-ecologies, institutions, and farming systems. Second, the research of students in local M.Sc. and Ph.D. programs is more likely to focus on local and national problems than would that of African students in overseas universities who often have no alternative but to pursue research on problems of industrial agriculture. Third, the incremental buildup of the quality of local graduate programs will serve as an insurance scheme if a donor discontinues scholarships for overseas study. These direct and indirect benefits of local graduate training should be factored into comparative studies of the costs and benefits of local versus regional and overseas training.

Ph.D. training

Undergraduate education is the bread and butter of African university education, and the political pressure to increase undergraduate enrollment is relentless. Nevertheless, the urgency of setting up African-based M.Sc. and Ph.D. programs is dramatized by two sobering facts. First, as few as twenty Africans a year currently receive doctorates in economics from all sources, both within the continent (including South

Africa) and outside of it (Fine 1997). Second, Ghana has been independent for four decades and no Ghanaian university has ever produced a Ph.D. in economics (Jebuni 1998). When the African Economic Research Consortium (AERC) was launched in 1988, it carried out a study of graduate education in economics in Africa and found that graduate training in any meaningful sense appeared to have collapsed in most universities. The study attributed this to the systemic causes of lack of funds, civil disorder, loss of capable staff, deteriorating faculties and equipment, and a massive expansion of undergraduate enrollment (Fine 1997).

Without question, building Ph.D. training programs in Africa is a more complex, costly, and lengthy enterprise than building up local M.Sc. degree programs. For example, it took Michigan State University seventy years (from 1855 to 1925) before it awarded its first Ph.D. degree! The recent experience of Makerere University in Uganda illustrates the complexity of the enterprise and the difficulty of securing funding and experienced academics to teach up-to-date courses, mentor students, supervise Ph.D. theses, and mobilize local financial support to replace donor support over time. In 1996, Makerere launched an alternative Ph.D. program in agricultural economics whereby eight American professors were recruited to volunteer their time and travel to Makerere to teach a one-month Ph.D. course on an accelerated basis (Wessell 1998). Eight Ph.D. courses were taught to nine Ugandan Ph.D. students, but funds were not available under the World Bank and USAID projects to recruit visiting professors to oversee the nine students during their research, data analysis, and write-up of their Ph.D. dissertations in Uganda. The easy task in Ph.D. training programs is to teach courses. The challenge is to mobilize financial support to recruit, reward, and retain a cadre of dedicated indigenous academic staff who enjoy the challenge of recruiting, mentoring, supervising research, and mobilizing an assured base of local financial support to sustain the program, decade after decade. Innovations are urgently needed in Ph.D. programs in Africa. Because of the sharp difference in the resource intensity and length of time required for a Masters (two years on the average) and a Ph.D. program (four to six years), it is easy to underestimate the time, resources, and funding required to implement and sustain a high-quality Ph.D. program.

The problem of developing and maintaining high-quality Ph.D. programs also plagues many industrial countries. Finland, a nation of seventeen million people with an annual per capita gross national product of $US24,000 in 1997 has taken steps to face up to the quality problem in the teaching of economics. Finland currently has thirteen departments of economics in Finnish universities, and most of them are too small to offer a competitive doctoral program. In 1990, a joint Ph.D. program was introduced to teach core courses to graduate students, irrespective of their base institution. Courses offered under the Finnish Post-Graduate Program in Economics (FPPE) supplement courses that students take in one of the thirteen departments of economics in the country (FPPE 1999).

The Agricultural Research Fund: Competitive Grants

What can be done to extract more research output from academic staff members and graduate students? We turn to the Agricultural Research Fund (ARF) because this type of competitive grant mechanism has been successful in Latin America. In Chile, for example, university researchers are implementing about half of the total value of competitive grants financed by research foundations in the country (Echeverria, Trigo, and Byerlee 1996). The ARF is being promoted in numerous African countries as a mechanism to generate more research output from universities. In Kenya, KARI developed the ARF in 1990 as an integral part of the National Agricultural Research Program (NARP) in order to fund innovations or high-risk research, cooperative or team research, or research that could not be funded within the KARI system. In 1991, USAID provided a grant to support research by non-KARI scientists, followed by a World Bank grant to enable the fund to be opened to the wider scientific community. With additional support from the UK, and the World Bank in 1998, the fund has US$4 million to be disbursed over the next five years in the form of competitive grants. The fund is open to researchers from universities, the private sector, and NGOs. Donors provide foreign currency and the government provides personnel, a secretariat, and motor vehicles.

Every June, the ARF issues an invitation for research proposals in daily newspapers and at local workshops. The number of applications to the fund has increased dramatically, from 16 in 1991 to 163 in 1996, with the bulk coming from universities, followed by KARI and the private sector (KARI 1996). To date, most recipients of the awards have been academic personnel from universities. The fund has brought researchers from KARI, the universities, and the private sector together, and has helped develop local capacity in operating a competitive funding program. Because of the strict review and monitoring process in place with the fund, only three researchers have defaulted from 1990 to 1996. The fund secretariat has imposed strict financial practices, which KARI closely monitors. What can be done to strengthen the ARF? The committee for awards should figure out how to develop more ongoing joint KARI-university research projects. It should analyze what type of incentives are needed in order to encourage mutual collaboration in the design and execution of projects, including giving preference to joint proposals from a team of university and KARI researchers. The processing of grants and the rate of grant disbursements should be accelerated. An annual report should be published, including the name of grant recipients, research topics, and progress. The ARF spending guidelines should be broadened to allow grant recipients to secure access to vehicles and the Internet, and support to attend regional and overseas scientific meetings. Ways should be found to utilize the fund to finance sabbatical leaves of local academics at KARI research stations. This program would strengthen KARI-university research linkages and help integrate local M.Sc., Ph.D., and postdoctorates in KARI's research program.

A transparent national R&D policy is needed to spell out the working relationships between KARI and local universities. Each one needs the other; each can reinforce the other. The national R&D policy should also lay down guidelines and priorities in developing indigenous capacity in biotechnology and information technology. Two major issues that should be resolved soon are:

1. Where should a national biotechnology laboratory be constructed—at KARI or at a university?
2. What are the ingredients of a memorandum of understanding to ensure that members of the KARI, universities, and the private sector have access to a central biotechnology laboratory?

In addition to the faculties of agriculture, numerous research institutes and university centers have played an important role in national development. These include the University of Nairobi's Institute of Development Studies, Egerton University's Agricultural Resource Center (ARC), and Tegemeo Institute. The Tegemeo Institute of Agricultural Policy and Development was established in 1988 at Egerton University through a collaborative research project between Egerton, the University of Arizona, and Stanford University, with financial support from USAID. The institute was affiliated with a university because it was assumed that policy-oriented research could be better addressed from a university than from a government department. Tegemeo's objective was to carry out applied research in order to provide an improved information base on policy issues. The institute supplements its core staff with part-time staff from the University of Nairobi, Kenyatta University, and KARI. Members of the Tegemeo Institute feel they could complement KARI's work by pooling university expertise to carry out multidisciplinary research on the critical policy problems facing Kenya's agricultural sector. After three years of operation, the Tegemeo headquarters was moved from Egerton to Nairobi in order to be in closer physical proximity to the policy arms of the government.

Looking Ahead

Four decades of independence have shown that the continent of Africa is too big, complex, and variable in terms of stages of development to yield to simple blueprints for building national agricultural knowledge triangles, an African extension model (witness the rise and demise of the Training and Visit extension model), or a university model that can be replicated throughout Africa. For these reasons we quickly reviewed the evolution of higher education in eastern and central Africa and then turned to an in-depth analysis of the evolution of agricultural higher education in Kenya during its first forty-one years of independence. We have stressed the need to examine universities as one of the three core public organizations in the agricultural knowledge triangle. The triangle provides a framework for encouraging debate at the national level on the appropriate levels and sequencing of investments in research, extension, and agricultural higher education, partnerships with commodity research networks, the Consultative Group on International Agricultural Research (CGIAR), and private firms. Without question, Kenya's universities have made a major contribution to training thousands of undergraduates for the civil service, the extension service, and society at large. Yet the concept of the university as a seat of innovation and a birthplace of "new knowledge" was not endorsed by political leaders in the 1960s and 1970s. As a result, political interference, financial constraints, internal academic struggles, and the brain drain from universities have rendered Kenya ill-prepared to address the second-generation challenge of mobilizing science and technology to attack the fundamental problem of the scarcity of resources—land, pastures, drinking water, and so on. "New knowledge" is needed to meet this challenge. The creation of "new knowledge" raises the standard of scholarship. With little innovation and new knowledge generated through research, the standards in Kenyan universities have fallen. It is time for the leaders of Kenya's universities, research agencies, and scientists to launch a vigorous public debate on what needs to be done to reverse the downward spiral in the quality of its faculties of agriculture. The next step is to figure out what Kenya's faculties of agriculture should do to increase their ability to meet the demand for training and research in the emerging areas of agribusiness, information technology, food safety, marketing, intellectual property rights, and agricultural sustainability. Special attention should be paid to the major reforms now underway at Makerere University in Uganda (Musisi and Muwanga 2003) and in Tanzania (Mkudu, Cooksey, and Levy 2003).

Taking the long view of development, we have identified five capacity-building issues that are central to improving the contribution of Kenya's universities to agricultural development. The five issues are outlined in the following.

A Productive and Sustainable Agricultural Knowledge Triangle

The first issue is the need for the leaders of Kenya's agricultural establishment to come together and work out how to build a productive and sustainable agricultural knowledge triangles. The challenge is to focus on ensuring that the core institutions communicate, cooperate, and reinforce each other. The national level is the appropriate level for focusing on the coordination issue because, after donors phase out their support for national research institutions, regional organizations, and commodity networks, then national governments will have to shoulder the fiscal burden of financing the continued participation of KARI scientists in such regional organizations as ASARECA and commodity networks. Looking ahead, a time span of twenty-five to thirty-five years is the appropriate time horizon to use in developing a national agricultural knowledge triangle that is staffed by indigenous scientists, teachers, and extension agents, and financed primarily from national sources. This time period is needed to pursue a trial and error process of crafting a demand-driven triangle that generates local political and financial support, sequential continuity in investments, and effective programs of work in each of the three organizations in the triangle (Rukuni, Blackie, and Eicher 1998).

The Balance Between Short- and Long-Term Investments

The second capacity-building issue to resolve is the conflict between short-term gains of expanded undergraduate education programs and the longer-term gains in promoting research and knowledge creation through postgraduate training. This is reflected in apparent conflicts in the time frames and priorities of politicians, parents of university students, teachers, researchers, extension agents, and donors. Kenya's political leaders are primarily concerned about the short- term issue of expanding access to undergraduate education and turning out thousands of B.Sc. graduates rather than building postgraduate education. Parents are primarily interested in the short-term issue of access of their children to undergraduate education, but with the decline in quality and the frequent closure of universities, many are sending their children overseas for undergraduate degrees. Donors purport to be interested in the long-term task of building scientific capacity, but most have difficulty in staying the course for the twenty- to twenty-five-year time frame of successful institution-building projects.

The KARI and leading academics in Kenya are concerned with the long-term issue of acquiring more financial support for postgraduate education and research to build the agricultural science base for a modern agriculture. Basically, the political leadership of Kenya will have to develop a national agricultural development strategy to build a modern agriculture.

Rebuilding the Capacity of Local Faculties of Agriculture

The third issue in building the scientific capacity and research output of universities is the need to address the meltdown in the capacity of local faculties of agriculture to offer high-quality M.Sc. degree programs in agriculture and to deliver more research output. The exodus of Kenya's senior academics to the private sector, NGOs, and consulting firms has created a private superstructure of NGOs, consulting firms, and policy networks around deteriorating public institutions (universities, extension services, and NARS). The end result is human capital degradation in three public organizations in the triangle that further contributes to the false belief that the private sector and the NGOs are needed to replace public research and extension services. In short, the policy reforms supported by donors are distorting the economic incentive structure and undermining the public institutions in the agricultural research triangle. Finally, the meltdown limits the research output of faculties of agriculture and contributes to a reduction in the quality of B.Sc. and M.Sc. graduates, many of whom are eventually hired by KARI and other research agencies.

In the final analysis one can see that policy reforms and privatization are unwittingly contributing to the decay of public institutions. It should be clearly understood that graduate programs in agriculture are "research programs," and the quality of the graduate teachers affects the quality of the graduates. Because of the lack of senior academic personnel to supervise graduate students, national policymakers working with university administrators must develop schemes for promoting the development of centers of specialization in Kenyan universities. This involves not only the recruitment of qualified and experiences personnel to staff these centers, but also a highly determined effort by the national government to provide the infrastructure and equipment for research and innovation. The private sector must become involved in this venture, as must the Kenyan top scientists and academics that have left the country. The idea is not to call them back, but to involve them in the new exercise of rebuilding their old institutions. They should develop links between their present centers of learning and their old centers in Kenya. In this way they will contribute to the removal of isolation that afflicts most African scientists in the local universities. The sustainability issue of centers of excellence has been referred to earlier.

Global Information and Biological Revolutions

The fourth capacity-building issue is sorting out what Kenya's faculties of agriculture, science, and law need to do to contribute to and benefit from the global information and biological revolutions. To cope with these revolutions, farmers, agribusiness firms, and rural and urban consumers will demand new types of university courses, new knowledge, and new technology. The issue boils down to relevant teaching and research.

Part of the challenge is to determine the type of scientists that will be needed by KARI, the extension service, and the private sector in the coming decades. With the advent of the global biological and information revolutions, the dividing line between agricultural and nonagricultural sciences is becoming blurred. One thing is certain— faculties of agriculture will be unable by themselves to satisfy the broadened research and training agendas. For example, if KARI wants to acquire information on intellectual property rights, it will likely turn to the Faculty of Law rather than to the Faculty of Agriculture at the University of Nairobi. The faculties of agriculture cannot become the "jack-of-all-trades." Although new courses must be developed to meet the emerging demands of clients, what is most needed is the application of "new science" to solve seemingly intractable problems. The university should always behave as one entity, and there should be free flow of information among and between faculties and departments. This avoids duplication. As has been pointed out, the challenge for Kenya's agricultural establishment is to work out how its separately governed teaching, research, and extension organizations can cooperate and mutually reinforce one another. In this way they will be able to generate new knowledge, improve the relevance and quality of local graduate training programs, and develop the scientific capacity to become intelligent borrowers of new knowledge and technology from the dual information and biotechnology revolutions.

Research Contribution of Faculties of Agriculture

The fifth capacity-building issue is that of increasing the research contribution of members of faculties of agriculture, science, social science, law, and commerce. Funding for university research is highly important, and we have discussed the evolution of the ARF, the many achievements of the fund to date, and the steps that need to be taken to improve its performance. Equally important is the program of work that should be set out by the Kenyan researchers. University scientists must be challenged to:

253

- Apply science and technology to add value to the nation's primary products with an eye on new regional and global markets for value added export commodities;
- Develop the capacity to link scientific knowledge on natural resources to policy, problem solving, and long-term planning processes; and
- Educate and train young scientists in cutting-edge science, agribusiness, and information technology.

NOTE

1. Kenya's educational system had changed from 7:3:2:3 to 8:4:4 (eight years of primary education, four years secondary, and four years nonprofessional undergraduate degree).

REFERENCES

Ackello-Ogutu, Christopher, and Wilfred Mwangi. 1995. Training of agricultural economists in Eastern and Southern Africa. In *Agricultural competitiveness: Market forces and policy choice. Proceedings 22nd International Conference of Agricultural Economists, 22–29 August 1994, Harare, Zimbabwe,* ed. George H. Peters and Douglas D. Hedley, 591–604. Aldershot, U.K.: Dartmouth Publishers.

African Development Bank. 1998. *African development report.* Abidjan, Ivory Coast: African Development Bank.

Agency for International Development (AID). 1989. *Impact of investments in agricultural higher education.* AID Evaluation Highlights No. 5. Washington, D.C.: AID.

Ajayi, J. F. Ade. 1982. Expectations of independence. *Daedalus* 3:1–9.

Ajayi, J. F. Ade, Lameck K. H. Goma, and G. Ampah Johnson, eds. 1996. *The African experience with higher education.* With a contribution by Wanjiku Mwotia. Athens: Ohio University Press.

Amann, Victor F., and Herbert Kriesel. 1976. Postgraduate training in agricultural economics, economics and commerce in eastern Africa universities. In *International training in agricultural economic development,* ed. L. P. Schertz, A. R. Stevenson, and A. M. Weisblat, 83–88. New York: Agricultural Development Council.

Anandajayasekeram, Ponniah, J. Woodend, M. Rukuni, R. Rose, and A. Kashuliza. 1996. *Report on the impact assessment, costing and tracer study of the (SADC)/GTZ project on strengthening postgraduate training in agriculture.* Gaborone, Botswana: Southern Africa Development Community (SADC), Southern African Center for Cooperation in Agricultural Research (SACCAR).

Appleton, Simon. 1998. Human development in sub-Saharan Africa. *Brown Journal of World Affairs* 5:117–36.

Beintema, Nienke M., Philip G. Pardey, and Johannes Rosebook. 1998. Educating agricultural researchers: A review of the role of African universities. Environment and Productivity Technology Division (EPTD) Discussion Paper No. 36. The Hague: International Food Policy Research Institute (IFPRI) and International Service for National Agricultural Research, Netherlands (ISNAR).

Bennell, Paul. 1996. Rates of return to education: Does the conventional pattern prevail in sub-Saharan Africa? *World Development* 24:183–99.

Blair, Robert, and Josephine Jordan. 1994. *Staff loss and retention at selected African Universities: A synthesis report.* Technical Note No. 18. Washington, D.C.: World Bank.

Blaug, Mark. 1992. The overexpansion of higher education in the third world. In *Equity and efficiency in economic development: Essays in honor of Benjamin Higgins,* ed. Donald J. Savoie and Irving Brecher, 232–43. Montreal and Kingston: McGill-Queen's University Press.

Board for International Food and Agricultural Development (BIFAD). 2003. Renewing USAID investment in global long-term training and capacity building in agriculture and rural development. Washington, D.C.: BIFAD.

Bonnen, James T. 1998. Agricultural development: Transforming human capital, technology and institutions. In *International agricultural development,* 3d ed., ed. Carl K. Eicher and John M. Staatz, 271–86. Baltimore: Johns Hopkins University Press.

Boughton, Duncan, Eric W. Crawford, Julie Howard, James Oehmke, James Shaffer, and John Staatz. 1995. A strategic approach to agricultural research program planning in sub-Saharan Africa. Michigan State University International Development Working Paper No. 49. East Lansing: Michigan State University.

Burki, Shahid Javed, and Guillermo E. Perry. 1998. *Beyond the Washington consensus: Institutions matter.* Latin American and the Caribbean (LAC) Studies. Washington, D.C.: World Bank.

Byerlee, Derek, and Gary E. Alex. 1998. *Strengthening national agricultural research systems: Policy issues and good practice.* Washington, D.C.: World Bank.

Coleman, James S., and David Court. 1993. *University development in the Third World: The Rockefeller Foundation experience.* Oxford: Pergamon Press.

Court, David. 1987. Education and socioeconomic development in Africa: The search for the missing link. *Rural Africana* 28–29 (Spring-Fall): 61–76.

Echeverria, Rubén G., Eduardo J. Trigo, and Derek Byerlee. 1996. Institutional change and effective financing of agricultural research in Latin America. Technical Paper No. 330. Washington, D.C.: World Bank.

Eicher, Carl K. 1989. Sustainable institutions for African agricultural development. Working Paper No. 19. The Hague: International Service for National Agricultural Research (ISNAR).

——. 1990. Building African scientific capacity for agricultural development. *Agricultural Economics* 4:117–43.

——.1999. *Institutions and the African farmer.* Third distinguished economist lecture. Mexico: International Maize and Wheat Improvement Center (CIMMYT).

——. 2004. Rebuilding Africa's scientific capacity in food and agriculture. Background Paper No. 4 commissioned by the InterAcademy Council Study Panel on Science and Technology Strategies for Improving Agricultural Productivity and Food Security in Africa. Amsterdam: Inter Academy Council.

Ekwamu, Adipala, George Kanyama-Phiri, Nancy Karanja, Sheunesu Mpepereki, and David Norman. 1998. *Evaluation of the forum programme supported by the Rockefeller Foundation.* Nairobi: Rockefeller Foundation.

Eponou, Thomas. 1996. *Partners in technology generation and transfer: Linkages between research and farmers' organizations in three selected African countries.* Research Report No. 9. The Hague: International Service for National Agricultural Research (ISNAR).

Evenson, Robert E., Paul E. Waggoner, and Vernon W. Ruttan. 1979. Economic benefits from research: An example from agriculture. *Science* 205:1101–7.

Fine, Jeffrey C. 1997. *An African based doctoral program in economics: Summary report.* Nairobi: African

255

Economic Research Consortium.

Finnish Post-Graduate Program in Economics (FPPE). 1999. Available from FPPE Web page at *http:// www.valt.helsinki.fi/fppe/fppe.htm.*

Hansen, Gary E. 1990. *Beyond the neoclassical university: Agricultural higher education in the developing world—An interpretive essay.* Agency for International Development (AID) Program Evaluation Report No. 20. Washington, D.C.: AID.

Helleiner, Gerald K. 1979. Aid and dependence in Africa: Issues for recipients. In *The politics of Africa: Dependence and development,* ed. Timothy Shaw and Kenneth Heard, 221–45. New York: African Publishing Co.

Hoste, C. H., Heike Michelsen, H. F. Nouwakpo, L. B. Olugbemi, and Larry W. Zuidema. 1995. A framework to strengthen the role of universities in national agricultural research systems. International Service for National Agricultural Research (ISNAR) Briefing Paper No. 24. The Hague: ISNAR.

Jaycox, Edward V. K. 1989. Capacity building in Africa: Challenge of the decade. Remarks presented at a roundtable on the challenge of capacity building and human resource development in Africa. Halifax, Nova Scotia: Dalhousie University.

Jebuni, Charles D. 1998. The study of doctoral education in economics: Ghana case study. African Economic Research Consortium (AERC) Special Paper 29. Nairobi: AERC.

Johnson, Glenn L., and Bede N. Okigbo. 1989. Institution-building lessons from the USAID's agricultural faculty development projects in Nigeria. *American Journal of Agricultural Economics* 71:1211–18.

Jones, Richard B., and Malcolm J. Blackie. 1991. An approach to the development of expanded postgraduate training for agricultural scientists within the Southern African Development Coordination Conference Region. *Agricultural Systems* 35:251–64.

Kenya Agricultural Research Institute (KARI). 1996. *Harambee: Pulling together.* Nairobi: KARI.

King, Kenneth. 1995. World Bank traditions of support to higher education and capacity building: Reflections on higher education: The lessons of experience. In *Learning from experience: Policy and practice in aid to higher education,* ed. Lene Buchert and Kenneth King, 19–40. The Hague: Centre for the Study of Education in Developing Countries.

Lynam, John K., and Malcolm J. Blackie. 1994. Building effective agricultural research capacity: The African challenge. In *Agricultural technology: Policy issues for the international community,* ed. Jock R. Anderson, 106–34. Wallingford, U.K.: CAB International.

Michelsen, Heike, and D. Shapiro, eds. 1998. *Strengthening the role of universities in the national agricultural research systems in sub-Saharan Africa.* International Service for National Agricultural Research (ISNAR)-German Foundation for International Development (DSE)-Technical Centre for Agriculture and Rural Cooperation. The Hague: ISNAR.

Mkudu, Daniel, Brian Cooksey, and Lisbeth Levy. 2003. *Higher education in Tanzania: A case study.* Oxford: James Currey.

Mrema, Geoffrey C. 1997. Agricultural research systems in the ECA sub-region. In *Development of a long-term strategic plan for agricultural research in the eastern and central African region,* ed. Geoffrey C. Mrema. Kampala, Uganda: Association for the Strengthening of Agricultural Research in Eastern and Central Africa (ASARECA).

Musisi, Nakanyike, and Nansozi K. Muwanga. 2003. *Makerere University in transition, 1993–2000: Opportunities and challenges.* Oxford: James Currey.

Norman, David. 1998. *Institutional capacity with reference to applied microeconomics in eastern and southern Africa.* Nairobi: Rockefeller Foundation.

Nyerere, Julius K. 1967. *Education for self-reliance.* Dar es Salaam, Tanzania: Ministry of Information and Tourism.

Odhiambo, Thomas R. 1967. East Africa: Science for development. *Science* 158:876–81.

Odour-Okelo, D., and T. Ajibola Taylor. 1991. Universities in Kenya national agricultural research systems (NARS). In *Agricultural research policy in Kenya,* 114–23. Proceedings KARI-ISNAR workshop, 25–28 November 1991, Silver Springs Hotel, Nairobi, Kenya. Nairobi: KARI.

Oehmke, James F., and Eric W. Crawford. 1996. The impact of agricultural technology in sub-Saharan Africa. *Journal of African Economies* 5:271–92.

Orivel, François. 1995. French aid and the crisis of higher education in Francophone Africa. In *Learning from experience: Policy and practice in aid to higher education,* ed. Lene Buchert and Kenneth King, 247–56. The Hague: Center for the Study of Education in Developing Countries.

Psacharopoulos, George. 1994. Returns to investment in education: A global update. *World Development* 22:1325–44.

Purcell, Dennis L., and Jock R. Anderson. 1997. *Agricultural extension and research: Achievements and problems in national systems.* World Bank Operations Evaluation Study. Washington, D.C.: World Bank.

Republic of Kenya. 1995. *Committee on university education: Final report.* Nairobi: Commission for Higher Education in Kenya.

Röling, Niels. 1988. *Extension science: Information systems in agricultural development.* New York: Cambridge University Press.

Rukuni, Mandivamba, Malcolm J. Blackie, and Carl K. Eicher. 1998. Crafting smallholder-driven agricultural research systems in southern Africa. *World Development* 26 (June): 1073–87.

Saint, William S. 1992. Universities in Africa: Strategies for stabilization and revitalization. World Bank Technical Paper No. 194. Washington, D.C.: World Bank.

Schultz, Theodore W. 1981. *Investing in people: The economics of population quality.* Berkeley: University of California Press.

Solow, Robert M. 1997. *Learning from Learning By Doing: Lessons for economic growth.* Stanford: Stanford University Press.

Thimm, Heinz-Ulrich. 1992. Professional manpower for agricultural development in SADC countries. *Agricultural Economics and Rural Development* 2:37–44.

Thulstrup, Eric W., Daniel Jagner, and Peter N. Campbell. 1997. *Natural science research in Zimbabwe: An evaluation of SAREC support for research capacity building.* Sweden: Swedish International Development Agency (SIDA).

United States Agency for International Development (USAID). 1985. *Plan for supporting agricultural research and faculties of agriculture in Africa.* Washington, D.C.: USAID.

Venkatesan, Venkatchalam. 1991. World Bank's agricultural services initiative in Africa: Main issues and future strategy. *Journal of Extension Systems,* December: 28–43.

Venkatesan, Venkatchalam, and Jacob Kampen. 1998. Evolution of agricultural services in sub-Saharan Africa: Trends and prospects. Discussion Paper No. 390, Africa Region Series. Washington, D.C.: World Bank.

Wai, Dunstan M. 1995. *The essence of capacity building in Africa.* James Smoot Coleman Memorial

Lecture. California: African Studies Center, University of California at Los Angeles.

Wandiga, O. Shem. 1997. *Capacity building and institutional development in higher education in Kenya.* Paris: International Institute for Educational Planning, United Nations Educational, Scientific, and Cultural Organization (UNESCO).

Wessell, Kelso L. 1998. *End of term report (1995–97).* Ohio: Agricultural Research and Training Project and Department of Agricultural Economics, Makerere University, Kampala, Uganda and Ohio State University, Columbus.

Willett, Anthony. 1998. *Agricultural education review: Support for agricultural education in the bank and by other donors. Executive summary.* Washington, D.C.: World Bank.

World Bank. 1992. *World Bank assistance to agricultural higher education, 1964–90.* Washington, D.C.: Operations Evaluation Department, World Bank.

———. 1994. *Higher education: The lessons of experience.* Washington, D.C.: World Bank.

Zeller, Manfred, C. Mataya, and Y. Islam. 1997. Strengthening capacity for food, agricultural, and nutrition policy analysis in sub-Saharan Africa: An overview of the literature, and lessons learnt from Malawi. Outreach Discussion Paper No. 15. Washington, D.C.: International Food Policy Research Institute (IFPRI).

PART 3

Strategic Alliances

Farmer–Extension–Research Interfaces

JOSEPH MUREITHI AND JOCK R. ANDERSON

Introduction

A Typical African Scene?

An eroded field in southeast Kenya is being prepared for the next maize crop. The soil-conserving terraces are in bad repair, reflecting the perceived unprofitability of the labor-intensive effort required for maintaining them.

The Player

A young, female front-line extension worker (FEW) is speaking to a group of women, farmer members of a church-based women's group. They have discussed many things, including the weather, farm activity alternatives, and prospects for the family food-sustaining crop that must soon be sown into the remaining topsoil.

The Action

They are focusing now on the fertilizer that might be used, and how to acquire it, because the past crop failure has left them short of cash, and their immediate first priority is payment of school fees. The FEW is not too sure about the fertilizer question, because her primary expertise is in child nutrition, a topic they have discussed many times, and about which all now have good working knowledge. The FEW is cash-strapped herself, having not been paid her field allowances for four months. She has been told that small amounts of "fertilizer" should be becoming available, as part of an external aid program. But apparently it will be a compound mix of imported materials, high in nitrogen (suitable for assisting crop growth later in the season, should it rain), but low in phosphorus (most needed now for the establishment of the crop).

Unfortunately for the immediate conversations and ensuing decisions, the FEW must seek more information from her subject matter specialist (SMS) on soil management, but it has been many months since she has seen him, because of his remoteness from her site. He has been unable to reach the FEW's location for a long time because he has had no petrol for travel in his designated field vehicle (due to a lack of operating funds). He has also been unable to keep up adequately with the work the research service has been doing to synthesize fertilizer recommendations for the diverse ecologies of this and nearby districts. In the meantime, all those in the group discussion in the field are agreed that what they need are more profitable alternatives to some of the maize crops on which they are presently concentrated. Yet how are they to diversify into, say, fruits and vegetables without effective market access, or into horticulture without the credit to make the investment in the trees? This, too, is beyond the experience of the FEW.

And so it goes, here and elsewhere on the continent, the problems of the group, and the extension staff generally, of course not ending there. Perhaps, however, we have sufficient grasp of the anecdote to glimpse something of the difficulties and challenges facing agricultural development and contemporary extension services in many parts of the world (Eicher 2002). These challenges range from educational preparation of field staff, to fiscal sustainability of public extension services, to mechanisms for getting better technical and economic information into the hands of those who most need it, involving as it does the links between farmers, extension workers, and researchers. The latter theme of linkage is the focus of this chapter on the Kenyan extension experience.

The Role of Extension in the Agricultural Knowledge System

The Traditional Technology Development and Transfer Model

Traditionally, the major role of agricultural research systems has been to generate technologies that provide better means for overcoming existing agricultural production constraints (Arnon 1987). Agricultural research can be grouped into four categories (Okali, Sumberg, and Farrington 1994):

1. Basic research that develops new knowledge,
2. Strategic research that solves specific problems,
3. Applied research that develops technologies based on knowledge generated from basic and applied research, and
4. Adaptive research that effects changes in the technologies to adapt them to specific regions and producer groups.

Traditionally, once generated, the technologies were passed on to the agricultural extension service to transfer and spread to farming communities (box 11.1). Several methods were used for their transfer, including the training of farmers through organized courses, mass media, meetings (*barazas*), individual farm visits, group extension methods (e.g., training and visits), demonstrations, and agricultural shows.

On the other hand, beyond transfer of technology and information, extension staff had many tasks to perform that typically included agricultural administration, credit administration, and input supply (Mettrick 1993). Extension staff were not adequately endowed with resources and had little formal technical education (Arnon 1987). Most of their extension methods focused on progressive farmers and neglected the so-called laggards. For agricultural research to be useful to agricultural development,

---

Box 11.1   The Traditional Model of Technology Generation and Transfer

The traditional model of technology generation and transfer was seen as a one-way process where researchers generated technologies and passed them to extension staff, who, in turn, extended them to farmers. This model emphasized a "top-down" approach of information flow from researchers to extension and then to the target client (Röling 1988). However, research technologies developed through this model often had rather limited success, especially in developing countries where farming is largely in the hands of resource-poor farm families (Röling 1988; Chambers, Pacey, and Thrupp 1989). Such limited success has been blamed largely on the way research and extension systems operated. Researchers have been accused of conducting fragmented research largely along narrow disciplinary lines, and driven by the professional and intellectual attraction of pure science (Arnon 1987). They usually paid little attention to agricultural indigenous knowledge (AIK) and tended to neglect traditional food crops. According to Bonitatibus (1995), researchers were generally more satisfied with the publication of scientific papers that carry status and lead to promotion and recognition.

---

researchers must understand the farming systems and socioeconomic background of their client groups. This will increase the likelihood that the technologies being generated are appropriate to the circumstances of the client groups and are actually able to contribute to their economic development.

An alternative to the traditional technology development and transfer model is the linkage model, where information flows two ways between each of the major subsystems: research, extension, and farmers (Mettrick 1993). For the model to be effective, cooperation should begin among the players at the planning stage and should be formalized. In this way, farmers are assured that research workers address their constraints and that farmers are consulted in searching for solutions to their problems. The extension workers feel that they are full partners in the research process and have a say in what innovations should be adopted and on when and how this should be done. Farmer Participatory Research (FPR) is an approach that aims at involving all players in all stages of the agricultural research process—that is, diagnosis and analysis, planning, experimentation, evaluation, and dissemination (Bently 1994; Okali, Sumberg, and Farrington 1994; Ashby and Sperling 1995).

Changing Paradigms of Extension

The vantage point of the late 1990s is probably unprecedented in its purview of great and rapid change in approaches to agricultural extension. Updating an earlier review by Schwartz and Kampen (1992), Venkatesan and Kampen (1998) recently described the changing scene in sub-Saharan Africa (SSA). In tracing the history of agricultural extension in SSA, they emphasize the rich diversity and the dynamism of approaches to extension that have been taken, often with the active support of the World Bank. Their typology includes institutional, organizational, managerial, and methodological dimensions of extension programs. Another relevant review is Umali-Deininger's (1997) wide-ranging discussion of the market for extension activities of various forms.

263

She nicely opens our eyes to the diversity of informational niches that might be better serviced by suppliers other than public extension systems of the traditional or even reformed type. Development agencies must consider nontraditional forms if they are to bring the urgently needed efficiency and economy to such interventions. The pilot experiences in Nicaragua reported by Keynan, Olin, and Dinar (1997) represent just a few of many recent interesting attempts to break from the shackles of convention in a quest to overcome the manifold difficulties of public funding and delivery of extension advice. These difficulties are now well analyzed and diagnosed in, for instance, many World Bank reports, and broadly summarized by Purcell and Anderson (1997). The focus here on World Bank operations is justified by the fact that the World Bank has been the major source for external assistance in implementing extension in the developing world. Especially in Africa, the Training and Visit (T&V) model has been the dominant one deployed.

Under T&V, agricultural extension was expected to forge the link between agricultural research establishments and millions of small-scale farmers. The agricultural extension system was reoriented from a bureaucratic, desk-bound focus to a disciplined, field-based, professionally motivated occupation. It was closely connected to research and geared to the systematic promotion of improved cultural practices through a strict calendar of visits and regular training sessions (initially with designated contact farmers, later usually with contact groups). This amounted to a major public-sector reform effort, albeit one largely driven by top-down perspectives as to what it was good for farmers to be trying to do.

Three challenges underlie the need for a major revision of approach and past practice. First, the governments of developing countries are under continuing, and in many cases increasingly severe, strain. They can ill afford to employ large numbers of extension workers on a permanent basis. Also, their administrative capacities are greatly stressed by the demands of an increasingly far-flung and sophisticated technical establishment, which they are not always competent to adequately train, reward, and motivate (Antholt 1994, 28). A new role for the state is emerging that gives pride of place to the creation of enabling environments for private and voluntary action rather than to the direct provision of services. Even in India, for long the major national-level implementer of "classical" T&V, significant changes are being made to modify the various state agricultural extension schemes and to modernize the planning and management of such services.

Second, the perception of agricultural development potentials and constraints has changed. In many situations, the dissemination of standard packages of inputs and practices is no longer relevant, if indeed it ever was (Simmonds 1988). What is increasingly required is a farming systems approach capable of generating tailor-made, environmentally friendly solutions based on full farmer involvement and overt concern for better natural resource management (Anderson 1991; Axinn 1991; Eponou 1996; Purcell and Anderson 1997).

Third, the spread of education and modern communication, the rise of commercial farming, and the associated agricultural developments have created opportunities for alliances between the public, private, and voluntary sectors. More open and liberalized agricultural markets are bringing the knowledge and skills of private agribusiness to farmers, without involving public-sector intermediaries. In both more- and less-developed countries, farmer-led approaches to extension are spreading, while farmers' associations, cooperatives, self-help agencies, and other local-level institutions are contributing handsomely to mechanisms for the diffusion of modern technology.

The "reform" experiences around the world are diverse, but generally encouraging. According to Tendler (1997), informal performance contracting between Brazilian farmers and extension agents has led to increased commitment of extension workers to the job, greater customization of advice, and improved productivity. Integrated pest management programs centered on farmer field schools in Indonesia and sponsored by the Food and Agriculture Organization (FAO) (Kingsley and Musante 1996) show the value of turning farmers into extension agents, and extension agents into farmers. Such programs also show the diffusion potential implicit in group learning and the use of farmers as trainers.

Although a total shift from public funding to client funding may not be in the public interest, given the externalities of technology diffusion and legitimate equity concerns (Dinar 1996), obvious benefits, above all value for money, are associated with a more demand-driven approach. In some settings, public extension systems are still needed pending the emergence of alternative channels of technology diffusion. In others, divestiture of government support services can and should be actively pursued. Everywhere, ways should be sought to enhance the "voice" of farmers and the cost-effectiveness of service delivery. Unbundling of the previously twinned government roles of public financing of extension to resource-poor farmers and actual service delivery has become increasingly essential to progress.

Thus, it is argued here and elsewhere (Lindner 1993; Umali-Deininger and Schwartz 1994; Rivera 1996; Picciotto and Anderson 1997), centralized mainline extension services must continue to give way to a variety of hybrid solutions, combining public support with private delivery methods. Cost-sharing and voucher systems can increase the voice of farmers in the management of extension systems (World Bank 1990; Antholt 1994). Contract extension, long practiced in China, can increase responsiveness. In Ecuador, extension agents sharecrop with farmers for a profit. Costa Rica has experimented with promoting private technical assistance to small- and medium-scale producers through the provision of vouchers. Guidelines for preparing extension contracts have recently been assembled to help reduce the learning costs of World Bank clients (Rivera 1998).

Chile publicly finances 70 percent of the costs of private technology-transfer firms, which contract with small-scale producers directly or through their new Management Centers. Similar services are operative in Mexico and Venezuela. In New Zealand, gradually rising cost-recovery targets were set for the public extension service and were easily exceeded over the adjustment phase of 1988–94, when profitability was achieved and the service was fully privatized (Milligan 1997). Our review is anything but comprehensive. Rather, it is intended to point to a rapidly changing

265

and still evolving situation for agricultural extension around the world. Considering the Kenyan situation and relevant options for its future seems to make sense to us against such a backdrop.

Going beyond these private dimensions of a more pluralistic extension service are analogous important developments in the research and education subsectors. The complex of such changes constitutes a new paradigm for the agricultural knowledge information system (AKIS), conceived as having empowered rural dwellers such as farmers at its heart. The complementarities to be realized through more effective integration of these reformed elements—working interactively with rural folk and concern with improving their lots through more productive problem solving—are judged to be considerable (Crowder et al. 1998). Many obstacles and sources of inertia will impede the achievement of such benefits, however, given the entrenched interests involved. The centerpiece of client empowerment is in itself a major challenge to be met before all the actors in the system can play their needed roles (Crowder and Anderson 1998). Major changes in "mind-sets" about the processes of learning and change, such as fostering explicit creative reflection on experience, are necessary features of the way forward to energizing the actors, but the difficulty of bringing these changes to the fore should not be underestimated (Rogers 1996).

Institutional Arrangements for Extension in Kenya

This section gives a historical overview of agriculture extension in Kenya. Mureithi (1981) and Kandie (1997) have previously provided detailed reviews of this. The overview is presented in two phases: the pre-independence era from 1900 to 1962, and the post-independence era from 1963 to the 1990s.

Pre-Independence Era

The extension system was developed to serve the white farmers, who were settled in the Kenyan highlands and owned large tracts of land, and the small-scale peasant African farmers, who were settled or relocated to areas referred to as "reserves or nonscheduled areas." Most agricultural extension and all agricultural research efforts were concentrated on serving the large-scale farming sector, which was seen as the backbone of the Kenyan economy (Mureithi 1981). Efforts were taken to boost the profitability of enterprises such as coffee, tea, pyrethrum, wheat, barley, dairying, and sheep farming. These enterprises were exclusively in the hands of white settler farmers. However, in the early 1930s, some agricultural extension officers were appointed to serve African farmers in the reserve areas, and multiplication farms for improved seeds were established. Because of high population densities in the reserve areas and high stocking rates, soil erosion became a major concern and extension efforts were directed to soil conservation.

In 1946, the colonial government implemented a ten-year plan aimed at enabling African communities to increase food production to meet food demand for the increasing population. The plan had two strategies: to obtain more land for the

African farmers, and to intensify soil conservation efforts. The plan removed restrictions on crops that African farmers could grow, but farmers had to meet several conditions before they were allowed to grow cash crops or keep dairy cows. This meant that only progressive farmers were receiving attention from the extension workers. The initial extension work to promote production of cash crops was done through strict enforcement of agronomic recommendations for each crop. Similarly, soil conservation measures were implemented by the use of harsh regulations. This strict top-down approach made the African farmers fear the extension agents and developed a measure of mistrust (Kandie 1997).

After the declaration of the "state of emergency" because of the Mau Mau uprising of 1952–53, the government decided to develop agriculture for African farmers. The assistant director of agriculture, R. J. M. Swynnerton, compiled a plan in 1953 that became a policy allowing agricultural development in African lands. The plan hypothesized that sound agricultural development would be more likely to occur by having a system of land tenure making land available to the African farmer, and a farming system where production would support a family at a level comparable with other occupations (Swynnerton 1954, quoted by Mureithi 1981). Implementation of this plan meant that additional extension officers were to be recruited to provide the required service. A shortage of trained manpower and the absence of agricultural training institutions hampered staff recruitment. By 1962, the agricultural field staff had increased to 179 agricultural officers, 1,107 assistant agricultural officers, and 2,347 agricultural instructors. The "instructors" were the front-line extension staff and had a background of insufficient training (Kandie 1997).

Post-Independence Era

After independence, many white farmers left the country and the government initiated programs to settle landless people on the vacated farms and encouraged the purchase of large-scale farms by groups of people. The government policy in this period emphasized the promotion of smallholder agriculture. A major constraint to implementation of this policy was the lack of trained manpower in the agricultural sector. Following several studies on manpower development, the government undertook to expand agricultural training institutions, which included universities, colleges, and institutes (Kandie 1997). As a result, well-trained extension staff were continuously recruited to provide extension advice from such diploma-offering institutes as Egerton.

The agricultural extension approach was dominated by individual farm visits, which tended to favor "progressive" farmers (i.e., those enterprising farmers with some education and who could afford some agricultural inputs) and neglected the majority of farmers, who were poor and earning something less than Ksh 2,000 per year (Mureithi 1981). The extension service was organized along three distinct specialized departments—veterinary, agriculture, and water. The extension workers extended messages to farmers within their narrow fields. A 1967 government-commissioned study by Weir highlighted the problems of a specialized extension approach and recommended a unified one focusing on groups rather than individuals (box 11.2). A system of agricultural information centers was established through British support in order to reach more farmers in the rural areas. Farmer training centers were strengthened so as to serve farmers better. The commodity extension approach originally introduced for promotion of cash crops continued to be used. This was strengthened by the formation of commodity boards for crops such as pyrethrum, sisal, cotton, and coffee as well as development authorities for horticultural crops, tea, and sugarcane.

In 1983, the first National Agricultural Extension Project (NEP) was set up to address the problems affecting smooth operation of the extension service. The project adopted the T&V extension approach. The intention was to enhance the operational efficiency of the extension system in servicing the needs of the full range of smallholder clients and to make the service more effective through a set of structured mechanisms for delivering agreed upon messages on a regular basis. It was also a design intention that information should flow from "contact farmers" (CFs) to other members of the rural communities. Local extension groups were managed from district headquarters. The World Bank designed this approach in the 1960s to introduce better production methods and new technologies at field level. It aims at closing the gap between the yields obtained using best-practice technologies and the yields that farmers actually achieve (Bindlish and Evenson 1997). The cogency of messages was supposed to be insured through a system of SMSs who would channel relevant information in terms of timing, seasonal appropriateness, being up-to-date with respect to research findings, and so on, to the FEWs, who would then reach the CFs on the agreed upon regular schedule. The introduction and operation of the project was facilitated by funds from the World Bank that were used to provide operational funds, improved transportation, training, adaptive research, technical assistance, monitoring, and evaluation (Kandie 1997). Initially the project was implemented in two pilot districts, and by 1985 it had expanded to cover thirty districts (about 90 percent of Kenya's arable lands), the remaining areas being covered under the second phase that came to an end in 1998 (Bindlish and Evenson 1997).

This structure, combined with the local administrative arrangements in each province and district, combined to yield a national extension system that is elaborately expensive but hardly sustainable in an era of tight and declining resources.

Box 11.2   **Specialized Extension Approaches**

In the late 1960s, "the farm management approach to extension" was introduced, primarily to assist farmers in securing agricultural loans or credit from the Agricultural Finance Corporation. The extension staff assisted farmers in developing feasible farm plans and realistic budgets for securing credit. This approach, however, disappeared when the credit program was discontinued. This was followed by the Integrated Agricultural Development Project (IADP), initiated in 1976, which was based on an integrated extension approach. The project organized provision of inputs to farmers through cooperative societies and supported construction of rural access roads. This project also was discontinued after the first phase, mainly because of administrative problems, poor coordination, and the problem of loan recovery (Kandie 1997).

The unfortunate result is that most of the available resources are absorbed in salaries. Also, the opportunity for extension workers to get out to work with their clients is highly constrained by lack of budgets for maintaining vehicles and bicycles, and the absence of funds for fuel and other per diem expenses associated with fieldwork.

In short, the T&V extension system introduced in the 1980s doubtless succeeded in getting relevant messages and materials to many smallholders (details are set out from recent survey data in the following) and boosted the productivity of their subsistence crop production and small-scale livestock management. However, the system is not now in good health. There is presently an inability within the extension system to reach effectively into the communities that should be serviced. The T&V system, as implemented, is simply too expensive for the government of Kenya (GoK) to sustain, despite support through a follow-up World Bank operation (NAEP II 1990). Anderson and Feder (2004) report that the cost of the T&V extension model was 25 percent higher than the public extension model it replaced. The whole question of extension reach into communities and the issue of cost recovery must be revisited, especially with those industries for which fees for service could still be recovered, such as is presently done for tea, sugar, and pyrethrum. Also, the links with the research service and with nongovernmental organizations (NGOs) working within rural communities need to be reassessed. Other matters such as the status and degree of training and education of extension personnel must also be further re-examined in working toward a more efficient and affordable system. Yet first we should review the existing linkage situation.

Contemporary Extension and Farmer-Researcher Links

Ministry of Agriculture, Livestock Development, and Marketing (MoALDM).

Kandie (1997) gives a good description of the structure, organization, and operation of MoALDM. Box 11.3 accordingly gives only highlights.

The objectives of the ministry's extension services closely follow the overall policy objectives in agriculture, which include to:

Box 11.3   **The Ministry of Agriculture, Livestock Development, and Marketing (MoALDM), Kenya**

The ministry is the major public institution charged with the responsibility for promoting agricultural development in Kenya. It is involved in extension services for crop and livestock production, soil and water conservation, farm management, and home economics. It also runs an agricultural program for rural youth to acquaint them with modern agricultural production techniques. The services cover the entire country and are delivered through three departments: Agriculture, Livestock, and Veterinary Services. Each department has its own technical extension personnel. They are managed as a hierarchy extending from headquarters through the provincial, to the district, to the divisional, and ultimately to the local level. The departments have independent facilities (e.g., offices, vehicles, and training institutions) and prepare separate budgets. A director heads each department, and the permanent secretary and the minister oversee the directors.

- Achieve food self-sufficiency,
- Generate additional agricultural production for export,
- Supply agricultural raw materials for local industries,
- Stimulate job creation in the rural areas,
- Stimulate economic growth of the entire community, and
- Stimulate the attainment of higher incomes in the rural areas.

In 1998, technical staff numbers of the ministry staff were approximately as follows:

University graduates	1,826
Diploma certificate holders	2,480
Front-line workers (nongraduates)	8,824
TOTAL	13,130

The three departments operate on a total budget of about US$50 million per annum. Although the government meets the costs of staff emoluments, the donor community provides the bulk of resources to support the actual delivery of extension services. For example, the International Development Association (World Bank) and the International Fund for Agricultural Development co-finance the National Extension Project. The Swedish International Development Authority (SIDA) supports the soil and water conservation project. The German Assistance Corporation supports the Farm Management Branch. The British Department for International Development (DFID) supports the Agricultural Information Center, and the European Union supports livestock development.

Parastatals for Specialized Extension Services

The government has set several commodity-based parastatals under different acts of Parliament:

1. Agricultural Act, Cap. 318 Sections 190 and 191
   - Kenya Tea Development Authority (KTDA), 1964
   - Horticultural Crops Development Authority (HCDA), 1967
   - Kenya Sugar Authority (KSA), 1973
2. Pyrethrum Board of Kenya (PBK) - Pyrethrum Act, Cap 340
3. Coffee Board of Kenya – Coffee Act, Cap 333
4. Cotton Board of Kenya – Cotton Act, Cap 335
5. Dairy Board of Kenya – Dairy Industry Act, Cap 336
6. Sisal Board (SB) – Sisal Industry Act, Cap 341
7. Pig Industry Board (PIB) – Pig Industry Act, Cap 361.

These parastatals provide a range of services to farmers, such as provision of inputs, processing, and marketing. The KTDA is the largest, with 525 extension staff, followed by the PBK, with 108, and the HCDA, with 17. Some parastatals, such as the KTDA, have extension staff seconded from the ministry. The salaries of extension workers in at least this parastatal are topped up to try to encourage them to be more efficient, although the extent of top-up is not clearly documented. The funding for these parastatals is derived from cesses levied on the produce they promote, and they are answerable to the respective producers through a board of directors.

Nongovernmental Organizations

In Kenya, many NGOs are undertaking agricultural extension as a major part of their work (Kandie 1997). Some are locally based while others are international secular organizations. The major goal of their work is to help smallholders to improve their crop production, and to do so in a sustainable manner. Kandie (1997) gives a comprehensive list of NGOs operating in Kenya, including religious and many secular NGOs. The religious NGOs primarily aim to promote spiritual matters, and their agricultural extension objectives are not usually very clear. Their extension agents operate rather like social workers, with a goal of empowering communities to help themselves and to seek extension information elsewhere as appropriate. They usually work closely with ministry extension staff when extending technical messages.

The secular NGOs, unlike the church-based ones, have more focused objectives, often with specific production targets. They target resource-poor smallholders, especially those in the more marginal areas. Extension contact is done through organized groups and, depending on the size of the organization, the beneficiary group could range fromtwo hundred to sixty-five thousand farm families. These organizations enjoy reliable donor support and are generally well equipped.

Kenya Agricultural Research Institute (KARI)

The KARI was established under the Science and Technology Act to undertake agricultural research in Kenya. Its broad goal is to generate research innovations that will enable farmers to produce adequate food and other farm produce and thereby raise the income and quality of life of rural people. In 1988, KARI reorganized and started planning its activities in five-year phases. This became known as the National Agricultural Research Project (NARP). The first phase, NARP I, was initiated in 1988 and the main focus was the creation of a strong institutional foundation for technology development and transfer. Major emphasis was put on the support of commodity and factor research, the development of human resources, and the rehabilitation of the infrastructure. However, the major limitation of NARP I was that the Regional Research Programs (RRPs) implemented by KARI's ten Regional Research Centers (RRCs) were not adequately supplied with necessary resources. Most research proposals implemented by the RRPs lacked client orientation and were presented in the form of adaptive commodity- and factor-oriented experiments. Beneficiaries of the research programs were not involved either in the prioritization of the research agenda or in the planning, implementation, and evaluation of research activities (KARI 1996a).

271

With the growing realization of these limitations, a major element of KARI strategy in NARP II (initiated in 1994) was to strengthen the RRPs so that they could be the means of:

- Analyzing the strengths and weaknesses of the existing production systems at regional level;
- Incorporating farmers' innovations (indigenous technical knowledge [ITK]) in technology development and testing;
- Assembling and testing different technologies by harnessing improved materials from applied and adaptive research results; and
- Establishing and maintaining strong and effective linkages with farmers, extension agents, and other stakeholders in technology development and transfer (KARI 1995).

The KARI adopted the Farming Systems' Approach to Research, Extension, and Training (FSA-RET) as a strategy for implementing national and regional research programs (MoALDM 1991). The FSA-RET has evolved from earlier farming systems' approaches and is defined as an interdisciplinary approach that seeks to generate and diffuse relevant technologies for a specific group of farmers, with their participation, focusing on identified priority problems, constraints, and opportunities of the production system under consideration (KARI 1996b). The approach seeks to improve the productivity and sustainability of the existing production systems under different agro-ecological and socioeconomic conditions with the involvement of all participants (researchers, extension agencies, trainers, farmers, policymakers, etc.) in the process of technology development and dissemination.

The KARI created an assistant director's office (AD-RRCs) to coordinate the RRPs and to provide support for their implementation. The office is responsible for building up expertise in FSA-RET in the RRCs, for ensuring that the RRP work plans are properly executed, and for promoting strong and effective linkages with relevant public and private institutions involved in agricultural technology development and transfer.

Linkages

The application of this FSA is intended to facilitate the establishment and maintenance of linkages between all the key participants in agricultural technology development and transfer. The basic concept of FSA is to foster greater research relevance by involving the relevant institutions and stakeholders. Although FSA is yet to be fully put into operation within the research and extension systems, some mechanisms for strengthening and maintaining research-extension-farmer linkages are in place and are highlighted in the following.

Research Extension Liaison Division (RELD)

The RELD of MoALDM was initiated in 1988 and put into operation in 1991. The division aims specifically at improving the flow of communication between all research

---

Box 11.4   **The Research Liaison and Regulatory Branch**
_____

The Research Extension Liaison Division has three functional branches, with the most relevant to research linkages being the Research Liaison and Regulatory Branch. The branch is responsible for enhancing linkages between research and extension services. It mainly focuses on promoting farmer and extension staff participation in research trials and demonstrations to enhance adoption of improved new technologies.

---

institutions in the country that generate agricultural technologies and the MoALDM extension personnel who disseminate these technologies to the farmers. It also collects views from the farmers and in this way provides feedback to researchers to assist in their research prioritization activities. The specific objectives of the RELD include to:

- Enhance liaison between interrelated ministries and agencies on technology development and verification and regulatory services (box 11.4);
- Collect, collate, and communicate research information; and
- Coordinate specialized agricultural research projects.

To date, the RELD has operated under the director of agriculture, and has been mainly involved in implementing the recommendations of the Memorandum of Understanding (MOU) between the MoALDM and the Ministry of Research, Technical Training, and Technology (MRTTT) signed in 1993 (MoALDM- MRTTT 1993). The MOU strives to strengthen linkages between researchers, extension agents, and farmers and to ensure that the FSA-RET approach is used effectively in promoting agricultural development. The joint activities to be undertaken by research and extension institutions have been clearly identified in the MOU, including the designated lead institution for each type of activity and the roles played by other participants. These activities include field visits, planning and review meetings, diagnostic surveys, on-farm trials and demonstrations, training courses, workshops, seminars and conferences, field days, and multiplication of genetic materials. The MOU established a committee at the regional level known as the Regional Research-Extension Advisory Committee (RREAC) to scrutinize and approve the work plans of the partners active in agricultural research and extension in the region. The committee is composed of provincial and district heads in MoALDM, the RRC director, and the research section heads. The committee, scheduled to meet quarterly, also supervises and monitors the implementation of the work plans and regularly reviews their progress.

The MOU created the National Research Extension Liaison Committee (NRELC), whose membership comprises senior extension and research managers (at the level of deputy and assistant director) from the MoALDM and the KARI. The chairmanship of the committee rotates annually among the members, except for the AD-RRC, who is the secretary to the committee. The NRELC meets quarterly, and its functions include to:

- Review and approve joint research-extension activities recommended by the RREAC;
- Supervise, monitor, and evaluate the implementation of research-extension activities;
- Solicit for and rationalize the allocation of resources to research-extension activities; and
- Oversee the functioning of RREACs and the full implementation of the FSA-RET approach.

Joint research-extension accounts were opened at KARI Headquarters and the RRCs to facilitate implementation of the joint activities. Initial funds came from NEP-II, supported by the World Bank. The implementation of the MOU has necessitated the appointment of research-extension liaison officers (RELOs) at the RRCs and at the offices of the provincial directors of agriculture (PDAs).

The RELD has worked reasonably well and fostered linkages with research institutions in the country. So far, the division has been involved in identifying farmers' constraints using District Farming Systems Teams, which combine researchers, agricultural extension personnel, and farmers, as well as personnel from NGOs. The division has participated in the implementation of joint activities such as field days, testing sites, and farmers' field days, multiplication of crop materials, and technology packaging and dissemination.

The division has, however, faced several constraints in implementing its activities. The main one has been poor interaction with the Departments of Veterinary Services and Livestock Development, and even on occasion with the Department of Agriculture. This has been blamed mainly on the shortage of research staff with appropriate training in those areas. The NRELC meetings have not been held as regularly as planned, and participation in RREAC meetings by heads of technical departments has been irregular. The RELOs cover gazetted mandate districts or areas of the RRCs that in many cases extend beyond provincial administrative boundaries. In some regions, these areas are too large for one RELO to effectively cover (e.g., eleven districts in Nyanza Province!). Because of poor coordination between the three departments, ministry funds have been disbursed to RRCs in piecemeal fashion. This has led to difficulties in KARI's apportionment of these funds to effectively cater for the planned joint activities. Even where funds have been apportioned, they have not been adequate to cover operational necessities such as transport.

Center Research Advisory Committee (CRAC)

The CRAC is an integral part of KARI's organizational and management structure. Each research Center has a CRAC for reviewing and approving research activities to be undertaken by the RRC's mandate area. Membership of CRAC comprises provincial and district heads from the mandate area covered by the RRC, senior scientists from the RRC, and representatives of training institutions, agribusiness firms, NGOs, and farmers' organizations. The chairmanship of the committee rotates annually among the provincial heads from the province where the RRC is located. The RRC director is the secretary to the committee.

Meetings of CRAC are held annually to review past activities and deliberate on new ones. Most KARI centers have been holding their CRAC meetings regularly, and most take their preparation seriously. They first hold pre-CRAC meetings where new proposals are presented to the researchers for comments. The proposals are then updated and forwarded to the Center Technical Committee, which ascertains their scientific merit. Comments from the committee are incorporated and then a CRAC document is compiled for circulation to members before the meeting is held.

The CRAC meetings are not mere formalities, as some people tend to think. Proposals that are not addressing real farmers' problems are rejected outright, and some are deferred for improvement. For example, the CRAC meeting of KARI's RRC-Kisii held on 16–17 September 1997 deferred three research proposals. The first, on replenishment of soil fertility, appeared to repeat work that was already ongoing. The second, on napier grass evaluation, was not addressing a felt need. The third, a livestock price data survey, did not have a clear methodology. Unfortunately, farmers were not included in the CRAC meetings because they were thought to be too technical for farmers to follow. Besides, it was assumed that their interests would be represented by farmers' organizations, such as the Kenya National Farmers' Union, that are members of the committee. However, some centers have decided on their own to include farmers in the CRAC membership because they are directly affected by what is discussed in these meetings and should be invited to contribute. For example, during the 1998 meeting of RRC-Mtwapa, farmers were invited and the meeting agreed to hold its deliberations in Kiswahili so that they could participate. This proved to be highly useful because farmers asked questions and made many suggestions. The CRAC decided to include farmers in all of its future meetings. All KARI centers are encouraged to follow suit if they have not done so already.

A major constraint to holding CRAC meetings regularly is the cost involved. For example RRC-Mtwapa spent about Ksh100,000 (US$1,700) in 1998 to hold the meeting in a Farmers' Training Center and to pay the transport and subsistence costs of the participants. Currently, donors support most meetings, and KARI has to devise ways of supporting them once the donor support comes to an end. One option is for KARI to encourage non-KARI members to meet their participation costs because it is assumed that they value this opportunity of vetting research proposals and are keen to receive progress reports of ongoing work.

Farmer Participatory Research (FPR) in KARI

Farmer participatory research is an important feature of the FSA-RET approach, because it enables farmers to have more influence on research priorities and ensures that more relevant research projects are undertaken (Okali, Sumberg, and Farrington 1994). In this approach, the participatory rural appraisal (PRA) method is the main diagnostic instrument for identifying priority problems. The KARI has undertaken to strengthen the capacity of RRPs in this approach and has so far trained most of its

275

scientists in PRA procedures. In collaboration with the International Service for National Agricultural Research (ISNAR), KARI has recently trained a core team of scientists on participatory research to become trainers of other scientists and has developed a comprehensive training module.

Several KARI RRPs are implementing participatory research, mainly with donor support. The main donors are DFID, the Dutch government, and the Rockefeller Foundation (RF). The RF is supporting FPR work in the Soil Management Project (SMP) implemented by two KARI centers at Kitale and Kisii. The project was initiated in 1994. The research is conducted mainly in farmers' fields by research teams that are multi-institutional (KARI researchers, extension staff, and NGOs) and multidisciplinary (socioeconomists, agronomists, soil scientists, agroforesters, livestock officers, horticulturists, pathologists, entomologists, and biometricians). The project began with a one-week training of the research teams on the FPR methodology by CIAT trainers and other trainers from local institutions. The training was heavily biased toward PRA methodologies. After the training, the teams selected four study sites and implemented the research activities using the FPR approach.

However, a review of the research work two years after initiation revealed that whereas farmers participated actively in the diagnostic stage, their participation in the subsequent stages (e.g., trial designs, monitoring, and evaluation) was low. In some sites, farmers' interest in the trial had diminished greatly. This was attributed to the low farmer participation in the subsequent stages of the research project beyond diagnosis. The research teams were not exposed to participatory methods of involving farmers in these stages and were merely using their own intuition. This is because FPR methods to effectively involve farmers beyond diagnosis are generally lacking or seemingly not well developed (Okali, Sumberg, and Farrington 1994).

To overcome this limitation, two FPR sites (Kisii and Kitale Research Centers) were initiated in 1997 to primarily focus on the development of postdiagnostic FPR methods. This was done in collaboration with another RF-funded project based at CIAT-Uganda. Work again began with a comprehensive training on the FPR approach that included elaborate field exercises. Unlike when the SMP was being initiated, more time was spent in the diagnostic phase and efforts were taken to involve farmers more in problem causal analysis. A farmers' workshop on experimentation in general was held to acquaint farmers with the research process. Areas covered during the workshop included choice of treatments, value of replications, determining plot sizes, value of keeping records, and evaluation of results. Participating farmers were asked to select a Farmer Research Committee (FRC) whose main role was to oversee trial implementation. The FRC was also to act as link between the participating farmers and the research teams.

Some positive results have been achieved. Because of the farmer workshop on experimentation, farmer confidence in conducting experiments and evaluating the results has been greatly boosted. They proudly show their trial records and some have even labeled their trial treatments. Farmers explain their trials and treatments being tested and tell of the observed differences between treatments. They actively participate in the evaluation of the trial results using their own criteria. The FRC has been active in overseeing trial implementation. Members of the committee reprimand those farmers lagging behind in accomplishing important trial activities, for example weeding. During evaluation of trials, the committee acts as an expert panel and leads other farmers in the exercise. They meet every two weeks to deliberate on the progress of the trials. The deliberations of the meetings are written in the local language or Kiswahili and communicated to the research teams. As expected, the FRC has been useful in providing feedback to the research teams. An important aspect of the approach is that it has resulted in a change of attitude among farmers, extension workers, and scientists, because they now see each other as equal partners in the research process.

However, a few shortcomings have been noted that might limit the value of the FPR approach. The PRA exercises conducted at the initiation of the research identified most problems affecting farming in the area and this raised community expectations that all problems would be addressed. The project concentrated on only soil fertility improvement and varietal evaluation of important food crops such as maize, millets, and beans. Because FPR requires that frequent contact with farmers be maintained to develop meaningful rapport, a lot of resources are required, especially of human time and transport. The approach requires committed and devoted scientists and farmers because it takes time to get conclusive research results (which may not be publishable in international journals because of their site specificity).

Currently the project is struggling with issues of scaling up technologies generated through the FPR approach so that many farmers in the region can benefit. Also, the project is developing exit strategies so that when it comes to an end, farmers will be able to analyze their own problems and decide on the appropriate action to take. Exiting does not mean complete withdrawal of research input in agricultural development of the area, but reducing the involvement of researchers in the FPR project so that farmers can take the lead role of initiating new research activities. The KARI scientists will always be available to provide their input whenever farmers demand it. Already farmers have an FRC that can be strengthened to provide research leadership in the area.

Although KARI is not enforcing the use of the FPR approach in all of its centers, the management is encouraging centers with experiences in the approach to share them with all other centers. This will ensure that most centers are exposed to the merits and demerits of the approach and make an informed decision on whether to adopt it or not. Needless to say, this is not the only approach that involves farmers in the research process, and others exist, including participatory learning and action research and farmer field schools.

Past Economic Analysis of Extension-Related Investments

In principle, the economic analysis of extension projects requires systematic comparison of costs and benefits with and without the project (Birkhaeuser, Evenson, and

Feder 1991). In practice, systematic social experiments comparing different methods of extension in similarly situated areas have not been executed. Where extension programs have been evaluated by comparing outcomes in similar contiguous areas, the results have been nuanced. Thus, careful work comparing productivity differentials in Haryana and Uttar Pradesh (Feder, Slade, and Lau 1985; Feder and Slade 1986; Feder, Lau, and Slade 1987) suggests that T&V had no significant impact on rice production, but yielded economic returns of at least 15 percent in wheat-growing areas. Similar work in Pakistan (Hussain, Byerlee, and Heisey 1994) found even smaller impacts in wheat areas, although the effect of T&V in increasing the quantity of extension contact was documented.

At first glance, we seem particularly fortunate in considering the experience of extension in Kenya because of the conduct of a major study in the early 1990s by the Africa region of the World Bank. This work was largely contracted to Robert Evenson of Yale University, who was assisted by Vishva Bindlish of the Bank's Africa region. However, the econometric studies summarized (Bindlish and Evenson 1993, 1997) are not without controversy. The extraordinarily high rates of return for expenditures on agricultural extension that they imply are, unfortunately, not robust. We regard the issues as sufficiently important to justify a separate treatment (see appendix 1). In this re-examination of the Bindlish-Evenson data and analysis, some alternative specifications of the estimations are made in order to explore the sensitivity of the earlier reported results to some reasonable and feasible modifications. Needless to say, the adjusted rates of return to such investment range from negative to only modestly positive. In short, because one cannot rely on the specific values previously estimated, the results regrettably do not throw much light on the dilemmas currently facing policy makers, but their skepticism about getting returns to investment in public extension that are actually rather low seems well justified. Further evaluative work on Kenyan extension was put in hand during 1998, and we now turn to a brief consideration of some of the early results from this work.

Recent Evaluation of the Effectiveness of Kenyan Extension Arrangements

The most recent and independent data on the effectiveness of Kenyan extension come from a study by Madhur Gautam (1998), of the Operations Evaluation Department, World Bank. We are grateful for access to these data from Gautam's survey of 596 rural households on household access to information on agricultural enterprises, including specific questions relating to the nature and extent of contact with the public extension service. The survey was an expanded version of the 1990 questionnaire used by the Bank's Africa Technical Department (ATD) for its previously noted evaluation of the T&V extension system in Kenya (Bindlish and Evenson 1993). A local university introduced the survey to the responding farmers as an exercise to determine the current state of agriculture in the farmers' locality, in order to distance it from any association with the extension service itself. Overall, 51 percent of the respondents said government extension (including veterinary services) is their primary source of information,

278

18 percent said friends and family, and almost 21 percent do not have a "normal" source of information. The responses by gender of household head and farm size also revealed government extension as the primary source for the majority in each category, although relatively more male-headed households appear to have access to government extension than their female counterparts. Other studies have tackled the same topic, although with somewhat different purpose and method, so the data are not fully comparable with those of Gautam that are given prominence here. One early study provides a rare insight into the alternative sources of information available to farmers in the early 1970s (Gerhart 1975). Based on a household survey of eleven districts (five of which were also included in the Gautam study), Gerhart found that over 35 percent of the households had received information on hybrid maize from the government extension service and about 45 percent from friends and family. The survey also showed an extension bias in favor of the more productive districts. Other early studies (Leonard 1972) also support an early bias of the extension efforts toward the more "progressive," wealthy, and large-scale farmers.

Gautam sought to determine whether the information that farmers need is more readily available now than it was ten to fifteen years ago, when T&V was introduced. Almost one-half of the 1998 respondents (47 percent) say that information is less available now than it was before; 28 percent think it is more available now; 17 percent think it is about the same; and 8 percent are not sure. By farmer characteristics, over one-half of the male farmers (51 percent) think it is less available now, while a lower proportion of women (39 percent) think so.

A little before the introduction of the T&V system, the Ministry of Agriculture started to expand its staff drastically, pursuant to the government's decision to hire all eligible agricultural graduates (Kandie 1997). In this process, the number of extension staff also increased. Data on the date of appointment of current staff from the recent skills inventory study, conducted by the Ministry of Agriculture, show that appointments grew at a rate of about 8.5 percent per year from 1982 to 1990.

Official statistics show that the number of farm families has also increased, from about 2.16 million in 1978 (CBS 1981) to 3.44 million in 1995 or at an annual rate of just under 3 percent. The growth rates of extension staff and farm families yield an annual growth rate for staff-farm ratio of about 3 percent (from 1982 to 1995). Gautam's data on outreach taken along with these figures thus suggest that the increase in outreach is only marginally higher than the increase in extension staff per farm, so that an improvement in the gross efficiency of extension delivery is not apparent from these data. In a Probit regression analysis of his survey data, Gautam found that while some of the biases of the old system have disappeared, new biases have entered. Most significantly, the bias against women has declined, as has that against younger farmers. However, no apparent bias showed against small-scale farmers after controlling for the other factors in the pre-1982 period.

A key design feature of T&V is its use of contact farmers (CFs). Although the concept has been used by the Kenyan extension service for a long time, in the earlier system it often targeted the more progressive and wealthy farmers (Gerhart

279

1975). Under T&V, the approach has been formalized to make the CFs strategic agents of intervention by the extension service. They are expected simultaneously to be role models, catalysts for the spread of new technology, and mentors to other or "follower" farmers. In the Kenyan context in particular, the approach was modified early on to include contact groups as the point of regular contact by the extension agent with the farmers in his or her area. The CF approach (henceforth here to be taken to include both individuals and groups) seeks to impart in-depth knowledge and specialized skills through regular and high-intensity contact between the extension agent and the CFs. At the same time, it allows an opportunity for the extension agent to deal with the nuances of local agro-ecological and socioeconomic circumstances, either by solving problems on the spot or bringing them back to the research establishment for solutions. The approach was also meant to deal with the problem of trying to reach too many farmers, thereby spreading the extension staff-farmer contact too thinly and missing out on the desired quality of extension contact. It relies on the fact that the farmers are likely to be well connected with other farmers, and thus to have open channels of communication through which to spread the "messages" and to have a strong demonstration effect. In short, the CF is an essential feature in the T&V system.

To establish the efficacy of the CF approach, farmers who knew a CF were further asked by Gautam's interviewers (a) if they had ever received any advice from the CF, and (b) if yes, if they received such advice on a regular basis. Of the noncontact farmers (NCFs) who know a CF, about 58 percent (18 percent of all NCFs) reported ever receiving advice from a CF, with the proportion being marginally higher for male-headed households. Further, of those who have ever received advice from a CF, only 37 percent have done so on a regular basis. That is, less than 8 percent of the NCFs have received advice from CFs on a regular basis.

Overall, Gautam's results clearly indicate that the current system of extension is not delivering advice either on a regular basis or with the intensity envisaged by the T&V design. It further appears that no improvement has occurred since 1990, the start of the Bank-supported NEP-II. What is perhaps of even more concern is that, even among the few CFs (in theory the "farmers of choice" for dissemination of information) meetings are infrequent and often held in an environment not conducive to effective learning or to a substantive exchange on problems of a technical nature. *Barazas* and other public meetings appear to be the dominant method used by the extension service, but these settings are more oriented to lecturing and broadcasting messages. Although such meetings have some benefits, for example, creating awareness about new techniques or technologies, they are not the intended outcome of the national extension projects, which sought to institutionalize a learning process more substantively. In fact, what the data suggest is that the pre-T&V methods of extension, such as relying on *barazas* and other public meetings rather than regular "face-to-face" contact, continue pretty much as the norm. Gautam's data also show the extension advice as having a strong subsistence orientation, especially to maize production, with one notable exception—that of advice on soil conservation. The latter has been well publicized by Kenyan political leaders for a long time and has also been aggressively pursued under a special program supported by SIDA.

A better test of the relevance of extension advice received by farmers should be the extent to which farmers have applied the recommendations. However, even though Gautam found that virtually all farmers consider the messages to be applicable, a much smaller number have actually applied the recommendations. He found that most (about 60 percent) of those farmers who "normally" receive advice at least once a year (some 240 sample members) report that they have not applied any of the recommendations. Just over one-half of the CFs have not applied the extension recommendations. As to the reasons, about 33 percent do not find the recommendations applicable and another 10 percent noted that they did not understand them. About 29 percent lack the funds and about 20 percent claim other input constraints prevent application. In summary, concerning applicability, farmers do consider extension meetings to be useful and the messages to be generally applicable, but most have not actually applied the recommendations. The pattern of responses thus constitutes something rather less than a positive client assessment, because the majority who respond favorably actually have no personal experience with the recommended practices. Further, the reasons cited for not applying the recommendations, either the lack of funds or shortage of other factors of production, indicate that the messages being received are either unsuitable or irrelevant to most farmers' circumstances.

Probably the most cost-effective method of delivering general information or simple messages is the use of radio. About 61 percent of farmers listen to agricultural programs on the radio, making this a particularly attractive dissemination medium. Gautam found that the proportion of male listeners is significantly higher than for females, as is the increase from 56 percent of small-farmer audience to 75 percent of the large farmers. A vast majority (93 percent, consistent across farmer categories) told Gautam's interviewers that they would like more time devoted to agricultural programs on the radio. This observation thus provides clear guidance for future activities, and is touched on in the following.

The Way Forward

Previous sections represent harsh, but we hope fair, commentary on the progress of extension and its links to research in Kenya. They lead us to some ideas about what might be a better way of doing business. Because they are to some extent revolutionary and involve radical change, these ideas should be considered as tentative, and they have yet to be shared with officials of the GoK and with other stakeholders in Kenya.

Embracing Rural Reality and Perspective in Research and Development Efforts

Kenya has made great progress in implementing farming systems' approaches to agricultural research and development. To be fair, it has been actively involved with such endeavors for a long time in one form or another. To have it as such a core procedure in KARI constitutes a significant institutional development in itself. But KARI must not

281

rest on its laurels in this regard, because the process must be recognized as being still incomplete relative to the wider and ever-growing needs of Kenyan rural communities. This incompleteness will require transfer of key skills around the country to enable KARI to initiate the process in those areas not yet covered in a substantive way. Thus KARI will be able to better connect those parts of the research system to the situation and needs of the farmers not yet adequately linked to it, and to the new and improved technologies it must deliver. The effective functioning of the existing arrangements for consultation at the local level, such as the CRACs set out previously, will require vigilant scrutiny and timely intervention and adaptation as necessary.

Folding Core Extension Functions into the Research Services

The inadequacy of the extension service as presently constituted has been noted at several points, despite (and perhaps because of) many different forms of external assistance. Some worthy progress was made through the MOU between the MoALD and KARI. Yet this limited success must thus be seen as a pointer to what is seemingly the only really sustainable way to getting cogent new agricultural technological information into the resource-poor households of rural Kenya. That way is to have the research system itself take a stronger lead in what has traditionally been regarded as the province of extension. All parties stand to benefit from a change in arrangements, but most of all farmers themselves do. This avoids the necessity for crafting understandings between disparate organizations with their different professional ethos and incentive structures. The intended feedback from farmer to scientist is an immediate and direct bonus of the closer contacts that are envisaged, and are being implemented in neighboring Uganda, for example.

One problem remains prominent, of course, and it cannot be avoided when making this suggestion for a major new direction in public support for agricultural services in Kenya. Resources to support a new combined research-extension service must be found, and the search will not be easy. Yet it should not be impossible, especially if some important guiding principles are kept in mind. First, high efficiency of provision must be the key principle. Having higher levels of skill among committed staff (responding to clear new incentive structures) is one element of this. Leveraging their skills and knowledge to a wider and more effective reach is also critical, as is noted in the two suggestions that follow. Reducing the leads and lags between problem definition and delivery of research product will be yet another vital element of a smarter and more agile agricultural knowledge information system (AKIS). Needless to say, Kenya will not be alone in taking such a fresh approach to explicitly integrating the research and extension sides of agricultural knowledge management. We do not, however, wish to understate the many difficulties of personnel management and assignment that would have to be addressed in moving to such a different system.

Unfolding Core Extension Functions into Civil Society Entities

With the millions of farms that must be serviced by an extension function in Kenya, clearly the nation will never be able to afford the staffing costs that were implicit in earlier attempts to reach all communities by direct or indirect contact with government extension officers. Accordingly, this suggestion and the one that follows are offered to point to possibly feasible solutions. Civil society, as has been noted, is already heavily involved in providing much of the face-to-face contact that occurs between farmers and advisory services in rural Kenya. Again, as we have noted, this is often less than ideal in its orientation to the low emphasis on technology and management per se, given the primary religious and other thrusts of the agencies concerned. Of the many changes that may be entertained, one is the need to persuade the authorities of the benefits that recipient households will derive from having better access to more productive information. This will enable the tithing and support of other social objectives, such as the provision of superior education.

We recognize that we cannot naively assume that all members of Kenyan rural society will be served adequately by such nongovernmental entities. There will always be a need for focused attention to those needy rural dwellers who are missed by other providers, and the government and its agricultural ministry surely have a role in seeking to address these needs in an effective manner, doubtless involving a plurality of novel arrangements. Research is urgently needed on feasibility of the farmer field school extension model (Feder, Murgai, and Quizon 2004).

Exploiting Low-Cost Modern Communication Methods for Residual Public Delivery

Mention has already been made of the surveyed farmers' positive attitude to receiving more and better agricultural information via the radio (and presumably also the TV for some of the wealthier households). The costs of passing on a unit of information are so much lower via electronic media relative to any sort of direct or face-to-face method that the underinvestment in such means is truly remarkable. It is not that there are not many important technical issues to be addressed and overcome in making such provisions. There are, and doing more in this domain will require considerable new investment in scarce skills and new linkage mechanisms to get existing and new information into forms suitable for transmission. The programming and broadcast facilities must also be enhanced to be able to do what is needed, especially to meet the special needs of women. Yet the pursuit of an efficient delivery system cannot proceed without such attention, and must happen early to start reaping the benefits. The KARI itself must be actively involved, and this will bring other major spillover benefits to the wider purpose of the institute.

In short, the change agenda proposed here in these several dimensions of the research-extension continuum will be challenging indeed to address, but failing to do so will oblige millions of potentially more productive households in Kenya to be denied the fruits of technical progress and economic advancement. Brave people must take up this challenge, which will fly in the face of stiff opposition from entrenched interests and bureaucratic inertia that will say it is all too hard.

REFERENCES

Anderson, Jock R. 1991. FSRE impact inquisition: Investor issues. *Journal of the Asian Farming Systems Association* 1:55–68.

Anderson, Jock, and Gershon Feder. 2003. Agricultural extension: Good intentions and hard realities. *World Bank Research Observer,* vol. 19.

Antholt, Charles H. 1994. Getting ready for the twenty-first century: Technical change and institutional modernization in agriculture. World Bank Technical Paper No. 217. Washington, D.C.: World Bank

Arnon, Isaac. 1987. *Modernization of agriculture in developing countries: Resources, potentials and problems.* Cirencester, U.K.: Wiley-Interscience.

Ashby, Jacqueline A., and Louise Sperling. 1995. Institutionalizing participatory, client-driven research and technology development in agriculture. *Development and Change* 26:753–70.

Axinn, George. 1991 Potential contribution of FSRE to institution development. *Journal of the Asian Farming Systems Association* 1:69–78.

Bently, Jeffery W. 1994. Facts, fantasies and failures of farmer participatory research. *Agriculture and Human Values* 2 (2/3): 140–50.

Bindlish, Vishva, and Robert E. Evenson. 1993. Evaluation of the performance of T&V extension in Kenya. World Bank Technical Paper No. 208, Africa Technical Department Series. Washington, D.C.: World Bank.

———. 1997. The impact of T&V extension in Africa: The experience of Kenya and Burkina Faso. *World Bank Research Observer* 12:183–201.

Birkhaeuser, Dean, Robert E. Evenson, and Gershon Feder. 1991. The economic impact of agricultural extension: A review. *Economic Development and Cultural Change* 39:607–50.

Bonitatibus, Ester. 1995. Research extension and training. *International Agricultural Development* 15:16–17.

Central Bureau of Statistics (CBS). 1981. *Integrated rural surveys, basic report.* Nairobi: CBS.

Chambers, Robert, Arnold Pacey, and Lori Ann Thrupp, eds. 1989. *Farmer first: Farmer innovation and agricultural research.* London: Intermediate Technology Publications.

Crowder, Loy V., and Jock Anderson. 1998. Linking research, extension and education: Why is the problem so persistent and pervasive? *European Journal of Education and Extension* 3:241–49.

Crowder, Loy V., W. I. Lindley, W. Truelove, and R. DelCastello. 1998. Knowledge and information for food security in Africa: From traditional media to the Internet. In *Telecoms in Africa: Tam Tam to Internet,* ed. Terrefe Ras-Work, 60–77. Johannesburg: Mafule.

Dinar, Ariel. 1996. Extension commercialization: How much to charge for extension services. *American Journal of Agricultural Economics* 78:1–12.

Eicher, Carl K. 2002. Building African models of agricultural extension: A case study of Mozambique. Paper presented at the workshop entitled "Extension and Rural Development: A Convergence of Views on International Approaches," 12–15 November. World Bank.

Eponou, Thomas. 1996. *Partners in technology generation and transfer: Linkages between research and farmers' organizations in three selected African countries.* Research Report No. 9. The Hague: International Service for National Agricultural Research (ISNAR).

Ewell, Peter T. 1989. *Linkages between on-farm research and extension in nine countries.* OFCOR Comparative Study No. 4. The Hague: International Service for National Agricultural Research. (ISNAR).

Feder, Gershon, Lawrence Lau, and Roger H. Slade. 1987. Does agricultural extension pay? The training and visit system in Northwest India. *American Journal of Agricultural Economics* 69:677–86.

Feder, Gershon, Rinku Murgai, and Jaime B. Quizon. 2004. Sending farmers back to school: The impact of farmer field schools in Indonesia. *Review of Agricultural Economics* 26 (1): 45–62.

Feder, Gershon, and Roger Slade. 1986. The impact of agricultural extension: The training and visit system in India. *World Bank Research Observer* 1 (2):139–61.

Feder, Gershon, Roger Slade, and Lawrence Lau. 1985. The impact of agricultural extension: The training and visit system in Haryana. World Bank Staff Working Paper No. 756. Washington, D.C.: World Bank.

Gautam, Madhur. 1998. The efficacy of the T&V system of agricultural extension in Kenya: Results from a household survey. Extension Study Working Paper No. 1, Operations Evaluation Department (OED). Washington, D.C.: World Bank.

Gerhart, John. 1975. *The diffusion of hybrid maize in western Kenya.* Mexico: International Maize and Wheat Improvement Center (CIMMYT).

Hussain, Syed S., Derek Byerlee, and Paul W. Heisey. 1994. Impacts of the training and visit extension system on farmers' knowledge and adoption of technology: Evidence from Pakistan. *Agricultural Economics* 10:39–47.

Kandie, Enock K. 1997. *Proposals to improve effectiveness of the agricultural extension services in Kenya.* Nairobi: Agricultural Extension Policy Project; Ministry of Agriculture, Livestock and Marketing; Government of Kenya; and the German Agency for Technical Cooperation in English (GTZ).

Kenya Agricultural Research Institute (KARI). 1995. *National Agricultural Research Program, Phase II. Project preparation report.* Nairobi: KARI.

———. 1996a. *Implementation guidelines for regional research programs.* Nairobi: KARI.

———. 1996b. *Strengthening regional research programs and AD-RRCs, revised plan of operations.* Nairobi: The Netherlands Support to National Agricultural Research Program II (NARP II).

Keynan, Gabriel, Manuel Olin, and Ariel Dinar. 1997. Co-financed public extension in Nicaragua. *World Bank Research Observer* 12:225–47.

Kingsley, M. A., and P. Musante. 1996. Activities for developing linkages and cooperative exchange among farmers' organizations, NGOs, GOs and researchers: Case study of an NGO-coordinated integrated pest management project in Indonesia. In *Farmer-led approaches to extension: Papers presented to a workshop in the Philippines, July 1995,* ed. Scarsborough, 5:5–13. London: Agricultural Research and Extension Network, Overseas Development Institute (ODI).

Leonard, David K. 1972. The social structure of the agricultural extension services in Western Province of Kenya. University of Nairobi Discussion Paper. Nairobi: Institute of Development Studies.

Lindner, Robert K. 1993. Privatizing the production of knowledge: Promise and pitfalls for agricultural research and extension. *Australian Journal of Agricultural Economics* 37:205–25.

Mettrick, Hal. 1993. Development oriented research in agriculture: An ICRA textbook. Wageningen: Netherlands: International Center for Development-Oriented Research in Agriculture (ICRA).

Milligan, Keith E. 1997. *Extension and technology transfer in New Zealand 1970–1996.* Canterbury, U.K.: Lincoln International Ltd.

Ministry of Agriculture, Livestock Development, and Marketing (MoALDM). 1991. *Guidelines on farming systems approach to research, extension and training.* Nairobi: MoALDM.

Ministry of Agriculture, Livestock Development - Marketing Ministry of Research, Technical Training, and Technology (MoALDM-MRTTT). 1993. *Memorandum of understanding between the Ministry of*

285

Agriculture, Livestock Development and Marketing and Ministry of Research, Technical Training and Technology. Nairobi: Republic of Kenya.

Mureithi, Erastus Kihara. 1981. The development of agricultural extension in Kenya: An historical review and assessment. Masters thesis, Wye College, University of London.

National Agricultural Extension Project II (NAEP II). 1990. Staff appraisal report. NAEP Report No. 9051 KE, World Bank document. Washington, D.C.: World Bank.

Okali, Christine, James Sumberg, and John Farrington. 1994. *Farmer participatory research: Rhetoric and reality.* London: Overseas Development Institute and Intermediate Technology Publications.

Picciotto, Robert, and Jock R. Anderson. 1997. Reconsidering agricultural extension. *World Bank Research Observer* 12:249–59.

Purcell, Dennis L., and Jock R. Anderson. 1997. *Agricultural extension and research: Achievements and problems in national systems.* World Bank Operations Evaluation Study. Washington, D.C.: World Bank.

Rivera, William M. 1996. Reinventing agricultural extension: Fiscal system reform, decentralization and privatization. *Journal of International Agricultural and Extension Education* 3:63–67.

———. 1998. *Contracting for extension services: A practitioner's guide.* Agricultural knowledge information system (AKIS) Thematic Team, Rural Sector Board. Washington, D.C.: World Bank.

Rogers, A. 1996. Participatory training: Using critical reflection on experience in agricultural extension training. In *Training for agriculture and rural development 1995–96,* ed. FAO, 86–103. Economic and Social Development Series No. 54, Food and Agriculture Organization (FAO). Rome: FAO.

Röling, Niels. 1988. *Extension science: Information systems in agricultural development.* New York: Cambridge University Press.

Schwartz, Lisa, and Jacob Kampen. 1992. Agricultural extension in East Africa. World Bank Technical Paper No. 164. Washington, D.C.: World Bank.

Simmonds, Norman W. 1988 Observations on induced diffusion of innovations as a component of tropical agricultural extension systems. *Agricultural Administration and Extension* 28:207–16.

Tendler, Judith. 1997. *Good government in the tropics.* Baltimore: Johns Hopkins University Press.

Umali-Deininger, Dina. 1997. Public and private agricultural extension: Partners or rivals? *World Bank Research Observer* 12:203–24.

Umali-Deininger, Dina, and Lisa Schwartz. 1994. Public and private agricultural extension: Beyond traditional frontiers. World Bank Discussion Paper No. 236. Washington, D.C.: World Bank.

Venkatesan, Venkatchalam, and Jacob Kampen. 1998. Evolution of agricultural services in sub-Saharan Africa: Trends and prospects. Discussion Paper No. 390, Africa Region Series. Washington, D.C.: World Bank.

World Bank. 1990. *Agricultural extension: The next step.* Washington, D.C.: Agriculture and Rural Development Department, World Bank.

Economies of Scale through Regional Cooperation in Agricultural Research in Africa

GEOFFREY C. MREMA, MOHAMOOD NOOR,
PABLO EYZAGUIRRE, AND MOCTAR TOURE

Introduction

Most national agricultural research systems (NARS) in Africa are, by world standards, comparatively small. Many of them employ fewer than two hundred full-time equivalent (FTE) scientists (e.g., the ten NARS in eastern and central Africa employed about 2,300 FTE scientists in 1997, compared to over 800 in Malaysia and 2,100 in Indonesia). Many of these NARS, however, are required to undertake research on a large number of commodities, factors, systems, and agro-ecologies. Consequently, they are overstretched because they do not have, individually, the critical mass and scientific capacity to excel in any particular field or commodity. The decline in government funding has exacerbated the situation even further. This has occurred in an increasingly globalized and competitive world economy.

The decline in funding from both the national treasuries and external donors has forced most NARS in Africa to adopt a two-pronged strategy. First, they have prioritized the programs they are undertaking nationally, and are increasingly forced to allocate their resources to the high-priority commodities or factors where the research is likely to have high impact in increasing productivity and overall production as well as economic growth. This has meant, in some cases, the closing down of research programs or stations and the redeployment of scientists to the higher-priority commodities and factors. Second, even with the priority commodity and factors, NARS are increasingly participating in regional and subregional research programs and networks. Many regional and subregional agricultural research programs have been started over the past decade through initiatives by scientists, International Agricultural Research Centers (IARCs), Advanced Research Institutions (ARIs), NARS leaders, donors, and governments.

Regional cooperation in agricultural research in Africa (as well as in other fields) is a well-trodden path. Indeed, sub-Saharan Africa countries at independence in the 1960s inherited a number of well-functioning regional agricultural research organizations. These, however, collapsed in the 1970s for a multiplicity of reasons. Since the mid-1980s, there has been a great deal of discussion on the modes of regional cooperation;

the linkages between the research efforts at national, regional, and international levels; the financing and management of the regional research programs and their impact; and the role of different partners in such endeavors.

This chapter deals with lessons learned from the regionalization of agricultural research in eastern and central Africa, in particular, and in other regions of Africa. It is also an attempt to analyze the future outlook, given the national, regional, and international trends in agricultural research and technology transfer.

The Rationale for Regional Cooperation

Economic development through regional economic cooperation and integration is a major objective of most of the regional groupings in the world, including those in Africa. Most NARS in Africa are small in size and are required to work with many commodities, factors of production, and agro-ecologies. This, coupled with a severe lack of both human and financial resources, makes it necessary for most countries to consider regional cooperation in planning for the expansion of their NARS. Indeed, as has been observed elsewhere:

> Given the size and diversity of the eastern and central African region, the diverse agro-ecological zones, the large number of commodities and factors of production (there are 101 such commodities/factors), and the small size of most NARS in the subregion, it is unlikely that any of the countries can individually set up and sustainably finance a NARS with the critical mass of scientists and facilities to adequately cover all the commodities/factors of production" (ASARECA 1997).

The spreading of human resources and other facilities across many commodities or factors appears to be relatively serious in the smaller National Agricultural Research Institutes (NARIs), for example those with fewer than two hundred full-time scientists in post (table 12.1). As many informed observers have noted, "Donors and the CG system tend to individually push poor countries into developing research systems for far more food commodities than they can support. Some of this is driven by a 'food first' type of mentality; some is driven by excessive emphasis on direct impact rather than indirect impact on poverty, nutritional status, and other ends of development" (Eyzaguirre 1996).

Although failures have occurred, regional and international collaboration in agricultural research has a good track record since the colonial era, and has contributed to the agricultural development of both developing and developed countries (Eicher and Rukuni 2003). A memory remains, if not a tradition, of scientists from different countries in the same region working together on common research problems. At present the impetus for regional collaboration is even greater, because of the ever-increasing cost of agricultural research. Strong reasons exist for regional and international collaboration to capture spill-ins and spillovers of technology at relatively reduced cost (Eyzaguirre 1996; Byerlee and Alex 1997; box 12.1). These reasons

Table 12.1 Number of Research Programs and Scientists in National Agricultural Research Institutes (NARIs) in Eastern and Central Africa, 1997

Country (NARI)	Total Number of Scientists Employed and In Post	Total Number of Scientists with M.Sc. or Ph.D	Research Programs
Burundi (ISABU)	51	9	13
Eritrea (DARES)	39	10	6
Ethiopia (IAR)	250	129	16
Kenya (KARI)	537	419	20
Madagascar(FOFIFA)	126	76	14
Rwanda (ISAR)	28	8	13
Sudan (ARC)	289	223	11
Tanzania (DRT)	349	241	9
Uganda (NARO)	207	156	27
D. R. Congo (INERA)	68	25	15

include scientific and technical developments in key areas that are beyond the reach of many countries (e.g., biotechnology and natural resource management), and the fact that some constraints, such as pests and diseases, cut across political boundaries.

Other outcomes include to:

- Create an enabling environment for scientists, by providing them with operational resources, training, and exchange of experience including the necessary critical mass working on a commodity or factor;
- Avail modalities for working on cross-border issues such as natural resource management and animal health, as well as on expensive and long-term research beyond the reach of individual countries (e.g., biotechnology);
- Facilitate a more rapid flow of germplasm, information, and technological innovations;

Box 12.1   Advantages of Regional Networking

- To exchange information and combine the collective experience of professionals in the same field.
- To achieve economies of scale and efficiency by concentrating scarce human, financial, and other resources on key national and regional problems.
- To minimize duplication.
- To capture research spillover/spill-in effects.
- To mobilize research efforts on transnational problems that require collaboration between countries.
- To enable countries to share in innovations and technical capacities that may not necessarily exist in some countries, for example, biotechnology and information communication technologies.
- To exploit a larger market for agricultural research products through regional cooperation (e.g., hybrid seeds, etc.)

- Foster increased visibility of research institutions and their enhanced influence on the agricultural policymaking process; and
- Facilitate improved response to the emerging research priorities of regional political groupings in Africa that are dictated by globalization and the emergence of new trading blocs.

These outcomes, while desirable, are predicated on having the resources available to build or manage the regional research institutions and programs. Regional research in Africa is predicated upon the NARS, hence this chapter emphasizes the relationship between the NARS and "regional research approaches." According to this viewpoint, a regional approach is a national research strategy that promotes active participation in regional research programs. It is also one that incorporates research conducted elsewhere in the region into national planning and priority setting. A growing body of experience now can be assessed to determine the particular mechanisms and structures that enable NARS to participate in and contribute to the success of regional networking and research collaboration.

For Web sites of interest, see: *http://www.egfar.org/nars/gateway/coraf.htm; http://www.egfar.org/nars/gateway/saccar.htm;* and *http://www.egfar.org/docs/RegionalPrioritysetting/FARA/SACCARstr.pdf.*

Regional Cooperation in Agricultural Research in Africa

Historical Perspective

As has been noted elsewhere (ASARECA 1997; Eyzaguirre 1996), for decades the idea of regional integration in agricultural research has been subject to opposing forces. The history of agricultural research in Africa is littered with many attempts at regional cooperation. Some of these were part of larger regional political and economic groupings, while others were geared specifically at cooperation in agricultural research. Before the 1960s (when most countries in Africa gained their political independence), agricultural research was organized at the regional level, with a number of imperial (based in the metropolitan countries) and subregional commodity research organizations from the countries in each subregion under a colonial power. Little cooperation occurred across the different colonial zones. Thus research systems in Belgium-governed Congo, Rwanda, and Urundi (under the Belgian colonial rule) were linked to the system in Belgium rather than to the one in eastern Africa.

Because of the increase in land degradation and soil erosion, the Inter Africa Conference convened to discuss soil conservation and land utilization problems in 1948 in the eastern Congo town of Goma. It was agreed that they would establish four regional Committees for the Conservation and Utilization of Soils (CCUS), SARCCUS for the Southern Africa Region, EARCCUS for the Eastern African Region, CROACCUS for the Western Africa Region, and CRACCUS for the Central Africa Region. These CCUS werte required to mobilize the scientific and agricultural extension community in developing and extending such technologies as then existed on soil and water conservation. Subsequent to the Goma Conference, a regional scientific conference on the same theme was held in Johannesburg in 1949, and a rural economy conference was held in Jos, Nigeria, in 1950.

The subregional committees established in 1948 were largely inspired by the resolutions of the Goma, Johannesburg, and Jos conferences. However, with the advent of independence in the 1960s, these were disbanded in 1963 when the Organization of African Unity (OAU) was formed and amalgamated into the latter's Scientific and Technology Commission with its headquarters in Lagos, Nigeria. However, SARC-CUS continued to operate until the 1980s and is credited with having developed the Soil Loss Estimation Method for Southern Africa (SLEMSA), which is sometimes compared to the U.S.-developed Universal Soil Loss Equation (USLE) (Kayombo and Mrema 1994). The apartheid-era South African regime strongly supported SARC-CUS and it was merged with the Southern Africa Center for Coordination of Agricultural Research (SACCAR) when the democratic elections were held in South Africa in 1994.

The Subregional Agricultural Research Organizations established by the colonial powers in the 1940s and 1950s continued to function after independence for some time. However, by 1978, all had been disbanded, for a multiplicity of reasons. Each country then set out to build its own NARS, independently or with assistance from donor and international development agencies. It soon dawned on the scientists and their leaders, however, that they did not have the critical mass nationally to undertake the required research. This realization began with the so-called minor or orphan commodities (e.g., potatoes, beans, and cassava). The establishment of the Consultative Group on International Agricultural Research (CGIAR) system, and its IARCs, led to the latter being instrumental in establishing regional networks on the commodities for which they were responsible. The IARCs, being neutral and nonpolitical, were thus able to establish, with donor assistance, a new generation of networks. Examples of these include the potato, cassava, and agroforestry research networks in eastern and central Africa that were established in the 1980s with the United States Agency for International Development (USAID) and Swiss assistance.

These networks were, however, initially what Eyzaguire (1996) has defined as "central source networks," in which the technology-generating institution uses the network as a mechanism for carrying out its programs and transferring the technology it generates. They were thus perceived as belonging to the IARCs and could be sustained only provided the latter had the resources to finance their activities. From the mid-1980s, both donor agencies (who were funding these networks through the IARCs) and the directors of the NARS began to press the IARCs for more regional ownership of these networks.

In some parts of Africa, where intergovernmental organizations (IGOs) had been established to coordinate regional economic cooperation (e.g., the Southern Africa Development Community, SADC) the networks were brought under the umbrella of these IGOs. In other parts, such as eastern Africa, where no IGOs were as yet established, informal mechanisms were established to superintend the activities of these networks (e.g., the informal Directors Committee in eastern Africa).

During the late 1970s and early 1980s several continent-wide famines occurred in Africa, the effects of which were beamed worldwide by television and other news media. Although these famines could partially be attributed to drought and civil wars, it was also apparent to most donors and government leaders that per capita food production had declined in most countries in Africa during the 1970s and 1980s, food imports had increased, agricultural exports had declined or stagnated, and environmental degradation had become more widespread. It was therefore necessary to reappraise the agricultural development policies pursued by most countries in Africa in the 1970s and 1980s.

Two schools of thought emerged from this reappraisal—pricism and structuralism—regarding the cause of and solution to the African agricultural development crisis. The proponents of pricism argued that Africa's agricultural development crisis stemmed primarily from artificially distorted price incentives. Macroeconomic policy reform, aimed at "getting prices right," was seen as the way to increase agricultural production and restore the macroeconomic equilibrium. The World Bank report (1981) commonly known as the Berg Report was instrumental in the subsequent adoption of policies based on this premise. These policies were initially directed at opening the economies to market forces and abolishing the monopoly enjoyed particularly by government-controlled parastatals in agricultural input supply and produce marketing. These policies had, however, limited success in reversing the decline in agricultural production in Africa.

When it became apparent that these policies were not reversing the decline in food production, there was a move toward structuralism. Advocates of this approach argued that production was hampered more by structural issues than by commodity prices, and that Africa's technological and structural backwardness had to be tackled first. Studies commissioned by the World Bank revealed the low levels of technological development in African agriculture and the weakness of the institutions responsible for this development. Emphasis then shifted, and the World Bank, which had largely funded projects in agricultural extension in Africa, began from the mid 1980s to consider in several countries relatively large-scale loans under the so-called National Agricultural Research Programs (NARPs), among others, KARI.

Other international efforts included the establishment of the Special Program for African Agricultural Research (SPAAR) in 1985. The CGIAR was concerned about the declining food production situation in Africa, despite the apparent success of the green revolution (spearheaded by the IARCs), which had reversed a similar situation in Asia a decade earlier. It was argued that the reason why no green revolution had occurred in Africa was largely because of the weakness of the NARS and the need to coordinate more closely the efforts of the IARCs with other donor-funded initiatives for strengthening the former. Regional mechanisms were seen as offering a potential for success in Africa. In collaboration with intergovernmental agencies, SPAAR therefore developed frameworks for action (FFA) for strengthening agricultural research through regional cooperation. These FFA were anchored in four subregions: eastern and central Africa, Sahel, western Africa, and southern Africa. Organizations such as ASARECA (*www .asareca.org*) owe their existence to these consultations on FFA in eastern Africa (SPAAR 1998).

Eastern and Central Africa

Regional collaboration in agricultural research in eastern and central Africa, as in other subregions of the continent (e.g., west and central Africa and southern Africa), dates back to the colonial era. In British East Africa there were regional research organizations (EAAFRO) for agriculture and forestry (Kenya), freshwater fisheries (Uganda), veterinary science (Kenya), trypanosomiasis (Uganda), tropical pesticides (Tanzania), virology (Uganda), and cotton (Uganda). Similarly, Belgium organized sub-regional agricultural research institutions in the Great Lakes, and Italy did so in Italian East Africa (Kampen et al. 1995). These colonial institutions were extensions of the research systems of the colonial power in the "metropole" and were part of a worldwide colonial network that facilitated the exchange of genetic materials and information. These organizational structures generated useful technologies mainly for commercial crops, as well as some important commodities for local consumption in the colonies.

Shortly after independence, with the collapse of the East African Community, which included Kenya, Tanzania, and Uganda, the regional research centers became national institutions. However, by the 1980s, regional collaboration was reinitiated in the form of regional networks that the IARCs managed and backstopped. These networks were involved in the generation of relevant technologies, the transfer of improved germplasm, the training of scientists, and the strengthening of the management of agricultural research (Kampen et al. 1995). Despite their success, these regional networks had some drawbacks:

1. They were top-down arrangements in which the IARCs were the dominant partner in the planning, management, analysis, and dissemination of the results of the collaborative research work. The national partners were responsible for the fieldwork and facilities.
2. The IARCs did not coordinate their activities, and this placed considerable demand on the time of the leaders of the national systems for meetings.
3. The networks lacked ownership by the national systems.

In 1992, the NARS in eastern and central Africa and SPAAR initiated the formulation of an FFA to strengthen agricultural research in the regional context. With wide support from the donor community and other development partners, this led to the establishment of the Assoication for the Strengthening of Agricultural Research in Eastern and Central Africa (ASARECA) by the NARS leaders in Addis Ababa, Ethiopia, in September 1994. The association is composed of the NARIs of Burundi, D.R. Congo, Ethiopia, Eritrea, Kenya, Madagascar, Rwanda, Sudan, Tanzania, and Uganda.

293

The association was established as a nonprofit, nonpolitical organization, largely taking cognizance of the rather fluid political situation in the eastern and central African region, as well as the experience of other subregional organizations in Africa. Its secretariat, which is kept small, is located in Entebbe, Uganda, and coordinates a number of regional agricultural research networks or programs (box 12.2). ASARECA is not formally linked to any regional intergovernmental organization, although it works closely in some of its networks or projects with such. Although the lack of formal linkages to regional intergovernmental organizations may constitute an institutional weakness, the experience of other subregional organizations (SRO) in Africa does show that such linkages may at times impede the development of regional cooperation in agricultural research. The ASARECA Committee of Directors has therefore adopted a cautious view on the issue of formal linkages with regional political bodies.

In its short history, ASARECA has made some progress:

1. The establishment of a lean secretariat and the formal adoption of the constitution and by-laws of the association;
2. The establishment of various working groups on priority setting and detailed planning of areas of collaboration;
3. The development and adoption of a strategic plan and a sustainable financing initiative that charts the orientation of the association over the next one to two decades;
4. The expansion (from four to nineteen) of the number of regional collaborative networks and programs and their alignment with the recommendations of the strategic plan (box 12.3); and
5. The contribution, in collaboration with other SROs in Africa, to the establishment of the Africa-wide Forum for Agricultural Research in Africa (FARA), as the African representative on the Global Forum on Agricultural Research (GFAR).

Southern Africa

In 1980, the newly independent countries of the region formed an intergovernmental organization that was known then as the Southern African Development Coordination Conference (SADCC) and in 1992 became the Southern African Development Community (SADC). This regional organization established SACCAR. The mandate of SACCAR was to assist and enhance the capacity of the NARS in the member states to cooperate in agricultural technology generation, dissemination, and promotion; information exchange; and human resource development. In 1993, SADC gave SACCAR the responsibility of coordinating regional research in food, agriculture, and natural resources.

In 1990, SACCAR, in collaboration with SPAAR, the NARS of the member countries, the IARCs, and donors, initiated a participatory process to formulate an FFA to strengthen agricultural research through regional collaboration. A four-person task force of SACCAR and SPAAR staff helped to develop the FFA, following intensive

---

Box 12.2   Regional Networks and Programs under the Association for the Strengthening of Agricultural Research in Eastern and Central Africa (ASARECA)

First generation of networks, established in the 1980s

AFRENA-ECA	Agroforestry Research Networks for Africa–Eastern and Central Africa.
	(Renamed the Trees on Farm Network [TOFNET] to differentiate this ASARECA network form the ICRAF-based AFRENA for east and central Africa.)
EARRNET	Eastern Africa Rootcrops Research Network
ECABREN	Eastern and Central Africa Bean Research Network
PRAPACE	Regional Potato and Sweet Potato Improvement Program in Eastern and Central Africa
FOODNET	Postharvest Processing Network

Second generation of Networks, established in the 1990s

BARNESA	Banana Research Network for Eastern and Southern Africa
ECARSAM	Eastern and Central Africa Regional Sorghum and Millet Research Network
A-AARNET	ASARECA Animal Agriculture Research Network
ECAMAW	Eastern and Central Africa Maize and Wheat Research Network

Networks established in 1998–99

ECSARRN	Eastern, Central and Southern Africa Rice Research Network
EAPGREN	Eastern Africa Plant Genetic Resources Network
SWMNet	Soil and Water Management Network
CORNET	Coffee Research Network
RAIN	Regional Agricultural Information Network

Projects, programs, and initiatives (operational)

AHI	African Highland Initiative
AfricaLink	Electronic Communication
ASARECA	Technology Transfer Project
ECAPAPA	Eastern and Central Africa Program for Agricultural Policy Analysis

---

consultations with all stakeholders (Spurling 1992). The SACCAR Board and the Eleventh SPAAR Plenary adopted the final document in 1991. The FFA encompassed the existing SACCAR collaborative regional agricultural research networks and programs and set the guiding principles for strengthening agricultural research at the national and regional levels. Tanzania was selected to be the pilot country for the implementation of the FFA principles. This pilot activity contributed to strategic planning, priority setting, donor coordination, the decentralization of agricultural research, and the introduction of a competitive research fund in Tanzania.

In 1997, SADC decided to transform SACCAR from a regional commission to a Sector Coordination Unit (SCU), supported and managed by the government of

Botswana on behalf of the region. It was anticipated that most of the current research activities, as well as planned initiatives, would be maintained. As an SCU, SACCAR will perform the overall coordination functions for agricultural and natural resource research and training. The most important achievements of the organization have been the release of a number of improved varieties of crops, postgraduate and in-service training within the region and abroad, and exchange of information and germplasm.

West and Central Africa

In the Francophone colonies, the Office de la recherche scientifique et technique d'outre mer (ORSTOM), today known as the Institut français de recherche pour le développement en coopération, carried out basic research in soil, water, and plant relations and socioeconomics. The Centre de coopération internationale en recherche agronomique pour le développement (CIRAD; *http://www.cirad.fr/agro_ct/ras/ coraf.html*) and its commodity research institutions carried out research involving the selection, breeding, and release of oil palm hybrids, high-yielding clones of rubber, robusta coffee, cotton, and maize, as well as on the agronomy of these crops. After independence, both institutions continued to operate regionally on behalf of the new states, in collaboration with national institutions. In some cases, these externally man-aged research institutions dwarfed the fledgling national research departments and institutes. The work of these institutes resulted in technological innovations in oil palm, rubber, robusta coffee, cotton, maize, farming systems, and animal production and health.

In what was the Belgian Congo in central Africa, the Institut national pour l'étude agronomique du Congo (INEAC) carried out considerable research on commercial export crops (Taylor 1996). In general, regional research collaboration in Francoph-one countries of west and central Africa has been stronger in the area of export crops than with food staples and natural resource management.

In the Anglophone countries, individual colonies took the lead for specific com-modity research, (e.g., Ghana for cocoa, Nigeria for oil palm, and Sierra Leone for rice). However, independence led to the breakup of the regional programs and the creation of individual country programs. In the 1970s, regional collaboration, mainly in food crops, was initiated with support from several donors. The IARCs coordinated this in collaboration with the NARS. Among the most important networks were those for:

- *Maize, cowpeas, root and tuber crops, and plantain:* International Institute of Trop-ical Agriculture (IITA),
- *Rice:* West Africa Rice Development Association (WARDA),
- *Livestock:* International Livestock Centre for Africa (ILCA), now the International Livestock Research Institute (ILRI),
- *Sorghum, millet, and groundnut:* International Crops Research Institute for the Semi-Arid Tropics (ICRISAT), and

- *Farming system research:* IITA, WARDA, and the International Centre for Research in Agroforestry (ICRAF).

Other networks and programs were coordinated by ARIs, sometimes on the same commodities and with counterpart scientists, resulting in unnecessary duplication. These research activities were managed mostly by the IARCs or the ARIs. The countries collaborated only indirectly, because of the absence of a regional collaboration mechanism. To overcome these constraints to the regionalization of agricultural research in west and central Africa, the Conférence des responsables de recherche agronomique en Afrique de l'oueste et du centre (CORAF; *www.coraf.org*) and the Institut du Sahel (INSAH) started a dialogue in 1995. Their aim was to strengthen cooperation with the approval of the NARS and other stakeholders within the SPAAR coalition. A process to harmonize regional collaboration in agricultural research was initiated. This process resulted in the transformation of CORAF into an African-led organization serving both Francophone and Anglophone countries, while maintaining strong linkages to external scientific partners.

In 1996, CORAF and INSAH reached an agreement to forge close linkages between the FFA for the Sahel and the humid and subhumid zones of west and central Africa, given the fact that the Sahelian and the humid zones cut across several countries. In this understanding, CORAF was given the mandate to coordinate collaborative regional research networks and programs. As a result, CORAF now has a membership of twenty-four western and central African countries, participating in about seventeen regional research networks, research poles, projects, and programs, technically back-stopped mostly by ARIs, and with financial support from the donor community (CORAF 1997b; SPAAR 1995, 1996, 1997).

However, a high degree of duplication remains among the four networks back-stopped by the IARCs and those coordinated by CORAF (USAID 1996a, 1996b). This indicates that more can be done at the regional policy level to coordinate research programs in line with regional needs and priorities as opposed to more externally driven networking initiatives. Box 12.3 shows the regional networks and programs coordinated by CORAF and managed by NARS, and those coordinated and back-stopped by the IARCs. With support from the European Union (EU), CORAF is preparing its strategic plan, which will provide the framework for priority setting, programming, and coordinating agricultural research activities in western and central Africa. The Inter-ministerial Meeting on Sustainable Financing of Agricultural Research and Development in Western and Central Africa, held in Abidjan, Côte d'Ivoire, in April 1998, endorsed the concept of sustainable financing at the national level. It mandated SPAAR, CORAF, and other co-sponsors of the meeting to establish a working group to review issues relevant to the establishment of a regional competitive fund for the development and transfer of agricultural technology.

Box 12.3   Regional Networks and Programs under Conférence des responsables de recherche agronomique en Afrique de l'oueste et du centre (CORAF)

CORAF: Ongoing Initiatives

R3S: The drought resistance research network.

                    The rice network.

                    The cotton network.

                    The livestock network.

                    The forest network.

                    The groundnut network.

                    The regional project for the improvement and management of fallow land in west Africa.

CERAAS: The centre d'étude regionale pour l'amelioration de l'adaptation a la secheresse.

PSI: The regional research pole for irrigated systems in the Sudano-Sahelian zone.

PRASAC: The regional pole of applied research for the development of the central Savanna

PRASAO: The regional pole of applied research for the development of the west African savanna

New Initiatives

                    Yams network

                    Regional plant genetic resources program

                    Research pole for small ruminants

                    Research pole for natural resources management

                    Research pole for sorghum

                    Technology transfer and impact assessment

International Agricultural Research Centers - International Crops Research Institute for the Semi-Arid Tropics, India (ICRISAT), West Africa Rice Development Association (WARDA), International Institute of Tropical Agriculture, Nigeria (IITA)]:

                    Maize network (WCAMRN)

                    Sorghum network (WCASRN)

                    Rice Task Force

                    Cowpeas network (RENACO)

                    Vegetables network

Governance of Regional Research Networks

Regional collaboration in agricultural research in Africa has developed along three pathways:

1. As part of an intergovernmental subregional agricultural research organization, such as SACCAR in southern Africa;

2. As an SRO, based on the association of NARS, such as ASARECA and CORAF; and

3. Through independent, professional soil scientists (e.g., Soil Science Society of East Africa).

In the first case, research collaboration and regional research policy making are embedded and supported by the regional body of member states. Within such an organization, an SRO for agricultural research may then exist (e.g., SACCAR and SADC). In the second case, the association of research institutions collectively petitions or convenes on behalf of its member institutes the requisite endorsement of national policymakers to collaborate in agricultural research to solve common problems. In both cases, the question of policy coordination among countries in the region is important, but in each case it is approached in a different way.

So far, both models of SRO-based research have been effective, but have relied on external support for the central coordination core budget. The sustainability of the SRO model will largely depend on securing ongoing support for the collaboration that has in both cases been devolved to the countries. This in and of itself is a major achievement in research collaboration among African NARS. In the third case, the professional societies are autonomous and independent and largely concentrate on convening workshops or seminars for information exchange and normally have weak linkages to governments and key policymakers.

The Intergovernmental Organization

An intergovernmental, regional organization (e.g., SADC, Intergovernmental Authority on Development [IGAD]) is a formal organization of governments with a mandate to enhance regional collaboration. Such organizations usually have a formal governance structure and decision-making process. The highest apex body is often the summit of heads of states, assisted by the council of ministers, technical committees, and a coordinating secretariat with a mandate in the sectors targeted for collaboration. Agreements are often approved by all the appropriate bodies of each government. They deal with political, security, economic, and social issues that are of common interest. Within such an organization, an SRO for agricultural research (e.g., SACCAR in SADC) may then exist.

The advantages of this form of organizational modality are:

- Political legitimacy that is based on formal agreement and consensus;
- Access to policymakers and therefore potential influence on national and regional policies; and
- The fact that collaborative activities and the secretariat can be funded from national budgets as well as from external sources.

On the other hand, such a form of collaboration has some negative features as well:

- The decision-making process within this type of organization is slow and time-consuming;

- It can be adversely affected by political events that are not related to the area of technical cooperation; and
- Bodies other than the implementing institutions often make the final decisions.

The NARS SROs

NARS-based subregional research organizations (SROs) are formal associations or organizations of NARIs with linkages to other partners, such as universities, extension services, NGOs, and the private sector in the cooperating countries. This mode of collaboration exists in eastern and central Africa, and in west and central Africa. Agreements are often reached among the collaborating institutions with the "blessings" of the ministries responsible for agricultural research in the respective countries. However, the most important decisions are made by the Committee of Directors, in the case of ASARECA, and the Plenary Conference assisted by the Executive Committee, in the case of CORAF (ASARECA 1997). Both organizations have a small executive secretariat that, with the help of scientific and technical committees and external partners, coordinates the technical activities of collaborative regional agricultural networks and programs.

This mode of cooperation has the following advantages:

- Cooperation focuses on agricultural research and thus involves institutions with similar backgrounds, mandates, and missions.
- There is less bureaucracy and therefore decision making is relatively fast.
- The cooperating institutions have the general support of their governments while enjoying an adequate degree of autonomy.
- The arrangement is acceptable to most donors and external scientific partners, such as the IARCs and the ARIs.

Among the disadvantages of this mode of cooperation are that the linkages to national and regional policymakers and bodies are informal and weak; and the legal status of the SROs is not adequately understood by all stakeholders.

Despite the differences between intergovernmental and NARS-based SROs, their missions, goals, and objectives are similar. They both:

- Plan, coordinate, and guide collaborative regional agricultural research in order to find solutions to identified common constraints in priority commodities and factors.
- Serve as regional forums that bring together all stakeholders in agricultural research and development.
- Align national and regional priorities in agricultural research.
- Enhance the level of scientific and resource accountability at the national and regional levels.
- Increase public- and private-sector support to agricultural research and development.
- Have the potential to positively influence national and regional agricultural policy.

The two models have evolved with cognizance of national and regional realities, and neither one can be considered to be more appropriate than the other. Each model has taken advantage of the status quo by exploiting existing national and regional systems (or the nonexistence of such systems) to build institutional structures for regional collaboration in agricultural research. Where an effective regional inter-governmental body pre-existed it was possible to nest within it and secure the policy support upon which to build collaboration in agricultural research. Where such bodies were nonexistent, as in eastern Africa, the NARS have banded together to increase their voice with their respective governments, with donors, and with external partners, and to secure support for new modes of research networking and collaboration. Most encouraging has been the initiative in national and regional governance of research that has in may ways secured greater visibility and self-reliance in setting priorities and coordination of activities among countries.

Below the SRO level, the organization and governance of the regional networks and programs is largely similar across the continent. Each regional network or pro-gram is governed by a technical Regional Steering Committee (RSC), which superin-tends the activities of the network or program under the overall guidance of the SRO Committee of Directors. The national coordinators of research for the particular com-modity or factor that the network is handling mostly dominate membership in the RSC. The IARCs or ARIs that are technically backstopping the network normally man-age the coordinating offices of these regional networks or programs. These IARCs or ARIs also disburse funds and other assistance to network members and are respon-sible for accounting for donor assistance for the collaborative programs.

These institutions have been used for this function largely because they have a better institutional infrastructure for handling resources across countries in the sub-region. Most of the NARS institutions do not have the capacity to coordinate and han-dle the resources of a network outside their own national boundaries. As regional collaboration is strengthened, it is conceivable that the coordinating functions may eventually be entrusted to one of the NARS institutions by the SROs. This, however, requires the development and approval of the legal and financial protocols that will enable a NARS institution such as the Kenya Agricultural Research Institute (KARI; *www.kari.org*) to coordinate the activities and account for the resources provided to a regional network within and outside its national borders.

Although the NARS (and their national governments) remain (and will continue to remain), the primary stakeholders of the SROs, there are also other stakeholders who remain quite important in the process of building regional cooperation for agri-cultural research. These include:

- Donor agencies who find the SROs to be important avenues for channeling their assistance, given the perceived wider regional impact of their aid programs.
- IARCs who expect the SROs to provide a forum or structure within which they can interact in a more systematic and harmonious way to fulfill their international,

301

regional, and national roles without dealing with each NARS separately, which can be quite expensive and time consuming. given the many NARS in Africa.

- Regional intergovernmental organizations who perceive the SROs as adding value to their primary mandate of regional economic and political cooperation at lower transaction costs.
- GFAR, which regards the SROs as an important building block to its efforts at the global level (see next section).
- Forum for Agricultural Research in Africa (FARA), whose role is to coordinate interregional cooperation in agricultural research in Africa, regarding the subregional organizations as the primary operation units.

Thus, cooperation at the regional level adds value not only to the national efforts, but also to the efforts of other important regional, international, and global stakeholders. A key factor in the coming two decades will be how each SRO in Africa will be able to involve its main stakeholders (who may at times have conflicting interests) in its priority setting and program implementation. Another important factor will be how each SRO in Africa will be able at the same time to attract stakeholder support and assistance and build an efficient, effective, and transparent system for superintending the portfolio of regional agricultural research networks and programs.

International Linkages

The IARCs and ARIs have been active and effective participants in collaborative regional agricultural research networks and programs throughout Africa. However, their efforts were not coordinated in the past. In addition, the external scientific partners that planned and managed the networks and made all the major decisions often dominated the cooperation. Although the in-kind contribution of NARS was substantial, the absence of a collective voice for these organizations reduced their influence in the decision-making process. As the management and scientific capacity of the NARS improved, their demand for effective participation in decision-making increased. This, in addition to the renewal process of the CGIAR and the establishment of SROs, has resulted in an increase of African participation in regional programs and the GFAR. Figure 12.1 shows the African linkage to the GFAR.

Financing of Regional Research and Scale Economies

Scale Economies through Regional Cooperation

The aggregate number of scientists employed in the NARS in the region has increased over the past thirty years (the average increase over the thirty-year period from 1961 to 1991 for the five countries Kenya, Uganda, Ethiopia, Tanzania, and Sudan was 1,228 percent [ASARECA 1997]). However, the number of scientists working on specific commodities on a per-country basis is still very low. This is largely because of the large number of commodities and factors that each NARS has to handle.

Figure 12.1   Global Forum on Agricultural Research

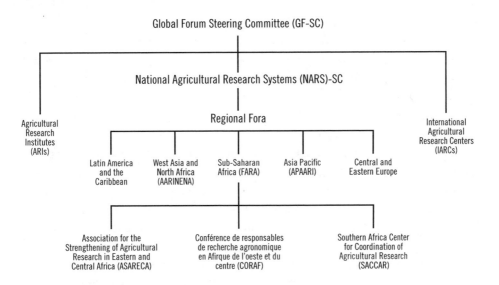

Table 12.2   Numbers of Researchers by Commodity in Eastern and Central Africa, March 1997

Country	Potatoes		Sweet Potatoes		Sorghum & Millet		Bananas	Coffee	
	With BSc	With MSc &/or PhD	With BSc	With MSc &/or PhD	With BSc	With MSc &/or PhD	With BSc, MSc or PhD	With BSc	With MSc
Burundi	2	—	—	—	1	2	7	—	8
D.R. Congo	3	5	4	—	—	—	12	—	—
Eritrea	—	8	—	—	4	1	—	—	—
Ethiopia	4	8	4	3	15	35	5	—	13
Kenya	—	4	7	10	4	14	4	2	27
Madagascar	—	—	—	—	—	—	4	na	na
Rwanda	3	—	3	—	3	—	4	2	1
Sudan	—	—	—	—	1	27	—	—	—
Tanzania	2	3	1	2	4	12	13	15	10
Uganda	1	6	1	7	9	6	20	—	8
SUBTOTAL	15	35	20	22	41	97	69	19	67
TOTAL	50		42		138		69	86	

Sources: Potatoes/sweet potatoes (PRAPACE 1998); Sorghum and millet (ECARSAM 1998; BARNESA 1998); Coffee (CORNET 1998).
Note: All figures are for total number of scientists working on a commodity (i.e., those who spend more than 30 percent of their time on a particular commodity, hence not full-time equivalent).

Table 12.2 displays the number of scientists with B.Sc. and higher qualifications working on six important commodities (potatoes, sweet potatoes, bananas, sorghum, millet, and coffee) in 1997 in the ASARECA region. With the exception of a few commodities, most national programs have ten or fewer scientists with M.Sc. and higher qualifications. There is therefore a lack of a critical mass working on these commodities in any of the countries in the region. Regionally, however, if mechanisms could be developed to make these scientists work together, a critical mass could be achieved. The same applies to many other commodities and factors of production. These scientists have to work on the plant breeding, crop protection, agronomy, socioeconomics, and processing of these commodities, among other areas.

As has been noted by Anderson (1992), considerable economies of size and scope can be achieved in technology generation and transfer. With the need for particular disciplinary skills (at world-class level, given the globalized market) to forge progress on the specialized aspects of research (e.g., coffee), in most cases a minimum of one fairly specialized person per research team is required to adequately cover the opportunities for scientific innovation. The economics of size in the national systems become quite important. Equally important is the issue of economies of scope, where, given the diverse commodity and factor mixes, small NARS are attempting to meet the required commodity and factor coverage with extremely thin resources. Such situations do therefore point to the need for the NARS to share their limited infrastructure and other resources with their neighbors in order to achieve economies of size and scope. The SROs avail to such NARS through institutional mechanisms of the regional networks or programs through which they can borrow or share innovative research findings and practices.

Funding of Regional Agricultural Research Networks and Programs

Networking, in agricultural research, is a cost-effective mode of collaboration. An evaluation team reviewing four ASARECA collaborative regional agricultural research networks found that three of these (bean, cassava, and potato and sweet potato) have already recouped the cost of their investment through successful technology development and transfer resulting in enhanced productivity at farm level (ASARECA 1997; USAID 1996a). The average donor-provided external expenditure for ASARECA networks and programs in recent years has been about US$450,000 per annum (USAID 1996a, 1996b). External resources are required for coordination activities, operational expenditures for research, training, publications, and information exchange. The hiring of networks and coordinators within the region leads to additional savings. The gradual introduction of NARS-managed networks with only scientific backstopping, from IARCs or ARIs, could result in further savings. The collaborating NARS also provide substantial support in the form of in-kind contributions consisting of professional and technical staff, research facilities, and some in-country operational funds. However, external funding for regional programs is essential. With assistance from donors and NARS, ASARECA is planning sustainable financing mechanisms, such as competitive research financing, and the possibility of an endowment fund to ensure the sustainability of regional collaboration.

Impact of Collaborative Research Networks and Programs

The collaborative regional networks have made significant contributions to the productivity of important commodities in the cooperating countries. The most important contributions in eastern and central Africa (ASARECA 1997) are:

- The development or introduction of improved varieties of crops, which include high-yielding varieties of climbing beans, African common mosaic virus (ACMV)-tolerant cassava varieties, and improved and adapted varieties of potatoes and sweet potatoes;
- Integrated pest management (IPM) in several crops;
- Improved agronomic practices of most crops;
- Training and exchange of information among scientists; and
- Enhanced capacity to respond to and deliver research and technology products in emergencies (e.g., the assistance extended to Rwanda through the USAID-supported Seeds of Hope project).

Looking Ahead

The success of regional cooperation in agricultural research in Africa will depend on a number of issues that the SROs and their NARS members need to tackle.

Network Devolution and Increased NARS Ownership

Regional research collaboration has been undergoing a process of devolution that began with the dissolution of the colonial research structures. In the process, a burgeoning of network activities (largely initiated and coordinated outside the structures of NARS and the subregional organizations in the continent) has led to some duplication of effort, network overload on NARS leaders and scientists, and lack of a sense of ownership and leadership by the NARS and national policymakers. The success of the regional networks will depend on, among other factors, increased ownership by NARS.

Increased Scale and Less Redundancy

The efforts undertaken since 1990 to build regional research collaboration between NARS and to make them share resources and benefits and increase their voice with policy and external partners are important achievements. The foundation has been established for integrating regional research with national and regional development policies to address shared research problems that are beyond the scale of a single country. As reliance on external partners as sources of technologies has declined, the capacity of NARS to generate and exchange technology and information has increased, at a time of declining funding to national research systems. The potential to achieve economies of scale and scope in the implementation of research through regional collaboration is high. However, this is only the first phase in building a true regional partnership based on and managed by the NARS.

Improved Governance and Lower Coordination Costs

One clear and demonstrable impact is the growing consolidation and streamlining of network coordination and management mechanism and transaction costs. The area of governance has improved as regional networking activities have become more account-able to national policies and national research programs. Only upon this basis can NARS activities expect support from both national governments and donors. Another demonstrable impact is in the priority-setting methods and the tools for programming of collaborative network activities. The SRO collaborative research networks are pro-viding opportunities, mechanisms, and training that enable NARS to incorporate regional priorities and sources of technology and information into their national plans.

Building on NARS Strengths

As NARS make better use of technology and information generated within the region, they are able to concentrate more on those areas in which they have comparative advantage vis-à-vis other partners in the region. This leads to economies of both scale and scope with potential for a much bigger impact in technical output and uptake by farmers as well as the ability to influence policymakers to provide more funds. The NARS are casting a wider net in their search for support. The regional partnership increases their visibility and avails to them mechanisms for demonstrating high-qual-ity research outputs while enhancing prospects for increasing support. Even in a donor environment of decreasing funds, one is constantly on the lookout for success stories because success attracts new investment.

Global Linkages

The SRO-based networks present an excellent opportunity to link research to such global issues as international trade. The new networking approach managed by NARS is making significant headway in reducing the barriers between export commodity research and research aimed at food security and natural resource management. This is likely to increase efficiency in the use of research resources and outputs as useful results, experience, and facilities are shared and underused capacity is mobilized.

Natural Resources Issues

All of the regions in Africa face major natural resource management issues that span national boundaries. The new networking modes are pursuing collaborative research on natural resource management.

Wider Participation

As noted in earlier sections, the SROs and NARS are in the early stages of an institu-tional experiment. However, there are indications that scientists in the region will be able to participate in professional associations. The growing visibility of research and development should also provide incentives for greater farmer participation through farmer organizations and producer groups. The dialogue between farmers and producer groups is already built into the culture and structure of the SRO-based networks.

Greater Voice in Policy

Finally, strengthening NARS through regional collaboration should strengthen the links between researchers and policymakers. The creation of FARA will enhance the ability of SROs to participate in the global forum of agricultural research. The vision of FARA is to work with the SROs and NARS of Africa to within a generation, enable Africa to achieve 6 percent growth rate in agriculture, through enhanced research, value adding, and marketing, with consequent food security and economic growth. FARA is aware that it will play the role of facilitator and that it will need to be linked to the continental policy-making body, the African Union (AU). FARA has taken cognizance of the fact that the AU intends to strengthen African agriculture because it is the primary industry for growth across most countries. The AU is therefore participating strongly in the New Partnership for Africa's Development (NEPAD; *www.nepad .org*) process.

The mission of NEPAD is to accelerate Africa's economic development, leading to a prosperous continent free of conflict in which all our people can fulfill their potential, that participates effectively in the global economy on an equal footing. The launch of the NEPAD process is based on the realization that Africa is currently marginalized in the global arena. The NEPAD is addressing the following issues:

- Bridging the infrastructure gap,
- Human resource development and reversing the brain drain,
- Agriculture,
- The environment,
- Culture, and
- Science and technology.

NEPAD is giving initial priority to the development of a Pan African cassava initiative.

REFERENCES

Anandajayasekeram, Ponniah, B. J. Ndunguru, and D. Martella. 1995. *Report on the impact assessment of the SADC ICRISAT Sorghum and Millet Improvement Program. Vol. 1.* Botswana: Southern Africa Center for Coordination of Agricultural Research (SACCAR).

———. 1996. *Evaluation of agricultural research: Current status and experiences in eastern, central and southern Africa.* Occasional Publication No. 1. Botswana: Southern Africa Center for Coordination of Agricultural Research (SACCAR).

Anderson, Jock. 1992. Difficulties in African agricultural systems enhancement: Ten hypotheses. *Agricultural Systems* 38:387–409.

Association for the Strengthening of Agricultural Research in Eastern and Central Africa (ASARECA). 1997. *Development of a long-term strategic plan for regional agricultural research in eastern and central African region.* Entebbe, Uganda: ASARECA.

Banana Research Network for Eastern and Southern Africa (BARNESA). 1998. *Annual progress report to the ASARECA Committee of Directors.* Entebbe, Uganda: BARNESA.

Byerlee, Derek, and Gary E. Alex. 1997. Strategic issues for agricultural research policy into the 21st century. Paper presented at the Study of New Investment Strategies for Agriculture and Natural Resources Research Workshop, 1–2 September 1997, London, U.K.

Coffee Research Network (CORNET). 1998. *Progress report to the ASARECA Committee of Directors.* Entebbe, Uganda: CORNET.

Conférence des responsables de recherche agronomique en Afrique de l'oueste et du centre (CORAF). 1996. *Annual report.* Dakar, Senegal: CORAF secretariat.

——. 1997a. *Annual report.* Dakar, Senegal: CORAF secretariat.

——. 1997b. *CORAF Action No. 2.* Dakar, Senegal: CORAF.

Eastern and Central Africa Regional Sorghum and Millet network (ECARSAM). 1998. *Project proposal for the establishment of ECARSAM to the ASARECA Committee of Directors.* Entebbe, Uganda: ECARSAM.

Eicher, Carl K., and Mandivamba Rukuni. 2003. *The CGIAR in Africa: Past, present, and future.* Washington, D.C.: World Bank Operations Evaluation Department.

Eyzaguirre, Pablo. 1996. *Agricultural and environmental research in small countries: Innovative approaches to strategic planning.* Chichester, U.K.: John Wiley and Sons.

Gates, J. D. 1996. *The sustainable financing of SACCAR: Understanding the cost and implications.* Consultants' report by ABT Associates to USAID-Africa Bureau, Washington D.C. (USAID-AFR-SD), July 1996. Washington, D.C.: USAID.

Kampen, Jacob, Jan Weijenberg, Matthew Dagg, and Mauric Kalunda. 1995. Strengthening national agricultural research systems in eastern Africa: A framework for action. World Bank Technical Paper No. 290. Washington, D.C.: World Bank.

Kayombo, B., and Geoffrey C. Mrema. 1994. Soil conservation, mechanization and sustainability of agricultural systems in Africa: A critical review. *Network for Agricultural Mechanisation in Africa (NAMA) Newsletter* 2:30–69.

New Partnership for Africa's Development (NEPAD). 2002. *Agriculture in new partnership for Africa's development.* Nairobi: NEPAD.

Programme régional d'amelioration de la culture de la pomme de terre et la patate douce en Afrique Centrale et de l'Est (PRAPACE). 1998. *Annual report to ASARECA Committee of Directors.* Entebbe, Uganda: ASARECA.

Southern Africa Center for Coordination of Agricultural Research (SACCAR). 1997. *SACCAR long-term strategy for regional agriculture and natural resources research and professional training.* Draft document. Gaborone, Botswana: SACCAR.

Special Program for African Agricultural Research (SPAAR). 1995. *Annual report.* Washington, D.C.: SPAAR Secretariat.

——. 1996. *Annual report.* Washington, D.C.: SPAAR Secretariat.

——. 1997. *Annual report.* Washington, D.C.: SPAAR Secretariat.

——. 1998. *The second External Programme and Management Review (EPMR).* Washington, D.C.: World Bank.

Spurling, Andrew. 1992. Agricultural research in southern Africa: A framework for action. World Bank Discussion Paper, Africa Technical Department Series No. 184. Washington, D.C.: World Bank.

Taylor, Ajibola. 1996. Strengthening national agricultural research systems in the humid and sub-humid zones of west and central Africa: A framework for action. World Bank Technical Paper, Africa Technical Department Series No. 318. Washington, D.C.: World Bank.

United States Agency for International Development (USAID). 1996a. *An evaluation of regional research networks for cassava, beans, agro-forestry, potatoes and sweet potatoes: A collaborative research program in east Africa among national and international research and development agencies.* Washington, D.C.: USAID-PARTS.

——.1996b. *An evaluation of regional research networks for rice, sorghum, maize and cowpea: A collaborative research program in west Africa among national and international research and development agencies.* Washington, D.C.: USAID-PARTS.

World Bank. 1981. *Accelerated development in sub-Saharan Africa: An agenda for action.* (The Berg Report.) Washington, D.C.: World Bank.

Strategic Technology Linkages: The Case of Biotechnology

JOHN S. WAFULA, JOEL I. COHEN,
AND SAMUEL WAKHUSAMA WANYANGU

Introduction

Since the 1960s, improved performance in agricultural production in Kenya has come about not only from the relative endowment with land, but also from the capacity to integrate land utilization with technological innovation in production through research and discovery. Science and technology have largely characterized the development of agriculture in Kenya and defined the distribution of its products.

With increased population, pressure has increased on natural resources, leading to continuing damage to the fragile ecosystems. Intensification of farming on the land under cultivation has therefore become central to ensuring sufficient food production and promoting rural development. Although improved seeds and the use of fertilizers and pesticides have constituted the major sources of productivity growth in agriculture in the past, biotechnology is a new tool that could help confront these challenges. Many countries in the north can increase agricultural productivity with biotechnology (James and Krattiger 1996). However, several important emerging issues need careful assessment. These include the limitations on the free exchange of research products, the high cost of some products of biotechnology, and potential environmental and food safety issues, as well as ethical and social concerns about some types of biotechnology. Finally, for developing countries such as Kenya, capacity must be built to help identify opportunities for cost-effective interventions, to gain access to appropriate techniques, to evaluate risks associated with biotechnology, and to create adequate mechanisms to regulate their use (Lele 2003; Alhassan 2003).

Potential of Biotechnology for Agricultural Development

Agricultural production is the most important indicator of economic performance in Africa. Unfortunately, except for a few countries such as South Africa and Egypt, the performance of the sector in the last half century has been discouraging (Ndiritu and Wafula 1994). The continent's population growth is potentially harmful to the environment because of excessive land degradation as well as land, air, and water pollution.

311

The results are unexpected climatic changes, such as those experienced in Sahel, and nonreversible loss of biodiversity.

Looking ahead, increased food production in Africa will have to come from area expansion, additional irrigation, and increased productivity per unit area of land. However, to achieve this increase will require increased use of science-based agricultural systems, fertilizers, better soil and water management, biodiversity utilization and conservation, improved disease and pest control, structural changes in land use, and the use of biotechnology applications. Biotechnology is defined as the integrated use of molecular genetics, biochemistry, microbiology, biology, and process technology employing whole or parts of microorganisms, or cells and tissues of higher organisms, to supply goods and services. It is neither a scientific discipline nor an industry by itself, but a continuum of technologies. In contrast to biotechnology research and development per se, many biotechnology applications are uncomplicated and inexpensive, because they do not require capital-intensive inputs. Biotechnology is expected to facilitate faster development of crops that are resistant to pests and diseases, enhanced food value, and the development of technologies for the control of postharvest losses. In addition, crops with resistance to pests and diseases will result in reduced use of toxic chemical pesticides, which will, in turn, lead to a safer environment. Biotechnology is expected to be the vehicle that will drive the agricultural sector in many countries in Africa, Asia, and Latin America

The following examples of developments in biotechnology can be applied readily in agriculture:

- *Microbial Inoculation of Plants*. This involves the selection and multiplication of microorganisms beneficial to plants, and their application to plants, seed, or soil. Some of these methods include biofertilizers, with agents such as *Rhizobium* inoculants for legumes and biological control agents such as *Bacillus thuringiensis* for control of pesticide-resistant disease vectors. Production of microbial inoculants is easy, requiring unsophisticated fermenters of modest volume. Application of microbial inoculants is therefore now commonplace in Africa (Sasson 1993).
- *Plant Cell and Tissue Culture*. This technology is based on the ability of many plant species to regenerate a whole plant from tissue or a single cell. The technique is simple and straightforward, requiring only a sterile workplace, nursery, greenhouse, and trained manpower. Many countries in Africa have now taken up plant tissue culture production at the commercial level (Wafula 1995).
- *Embryo Transfer*. As a technology, embryo transfer could be relatively costly because of the hormones involved, and because often embryos themselves have to be imported. Research on cows, however, has been highly successful, and many developing countries are now entering into the use of embryo transfer technologies in cattle and other species.
- *Monoclonal Antibody Technology*. The laboratory facilities required to produce monoclonal antibodies are modest, although the actual production could be laborious and costly compared with conventional production of polyclonal antiserum.

However, monoclonal antibody–based tests are highly relevant to African countries in plant and animal disease diagnosis and in animal reproduction.

- *Molecular Markers Technology*. DNA fingerprinting analysis is a powerful tool for identifying genetic linkages to qualitative and quantitative traits in plants and animals. The technique is based on the polymerase chain reaction (PCR), which is relatively simple and easy to acquire. It can be used to manage, monitor, and assess genetic resources (examples of its use include, monitoring the introgression of genes and gene flow between species, identifying valuable traits such as stress resistance and growth, monitoring the stability of genomes, and performing disease diagnosis). DNA marker technology can be an important tool in increasing the number of traits to be incorporated into new plant cultivars and animal breeds for increased yields and productivity.

- *Recombinant DNA Technology*. This powerful technology, which includes DNA probes, recombinant DNA vaccines, and transformation of plants and animals, is used for developing more stable and safer vaccines, and in rapid cross-breeding of species that are too far apart for normal sexual reproduction. Recombinant DNA technologies are much more expensive than conventional methods and are successfully performed only in well-staffed, fully equipped laboratories.

Global Application of Crop Biotechnology

Figure 13.1 shows the global trends in area cultivated with transgenic crops since 1995. The estimated global area cultivated with transgenic crops for 2001 was 52.6 million hectares (130 million acres) grown by 5.5 million farmers in fourteen countries, including the United States, Argentina, Canada, China, South Africa, Australia, Mexico, Bulgaria, Uruguay, Romania, Spain, Indonesia, Germany, and France (James 2001). More than one quarter, equivalent to 13.5 million hectares, of the global transgenic crop area in 2001 was located in six developing countries. Indonesia commercialized *Bacillus thuringiensis* (*Bt*) cotton for the first time in 2001 (James 2001). The United States grew 35.7 million hectares (68 percent of global total), followed by Argentina with 11.8 million hectares (22 percent), Canada with 3.2 million hectares (6 percent), and China with 1.5 million hectares (3 percent). China had the highest year-on-year percentage growth with a tripling of its *Bt* cotton area from 0.5 million hectares in 2000 to 1.5 million hectares in 2001—the first year when the global area of transgenic crops exceeded the historical milestone of 50 million hectares (Huang et al. 2003). The increase in area between 2000 and 2001 was 19 percent, equivalent to 8.4 million hectares, almost twice the corresponding increase of 4.3 million hectares between 1999 and 2000, equivalent to an 11 percent growth.

The use of biotechnology to develop virus-resistant tobacco in China has resulted in an increase of between 5 and 7 percent in leaf yield accompanied by savings of two to three insecticide applications. In the United States, benefits of *Bt* maize against the stem borer in 1996 included a 20 percent increase in yield, while the use of herbicide-tolerant soybean in the same period reduced herbicide usage by 10 to 40 percent. In addition, weed control and soil moisture conservation improved through reduced land

Figure 13.1 Global Trends in Area Cultivated with Transgenic Crops, 1995–2001

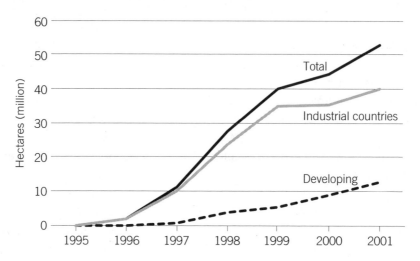

Source: James 2001

tillage. In 1996, planting of *Bt* potatoes in the United States resulted in reduced insecticide control costs of US$75–300 per hectare, with a net saving of US$25–50 per hectare. These and other benefits, from other agribiotech applications, such as the control of maize streak virus (MSV) and the development of GoldenRice™, which has a higher level of vitamin A, are among some of the notable examples of the benefits of biotechnology.

The Promise of Crop Biotechnology for Africa

Africa's crop production per unit area of land is the lowest in the world. Table 13.1 compares the yield trends of some common food crops in sub-Saharan Africa (SSA) with the average yields of developing and developed countries. Taking the example of sweet potato, a staple crop in many SSA countries, the current yield in Africa is almost four times lower than it is in China (18 tons per hectare). The potential exists to increase African agricultural production tremendously if biotic stresses such as viral diseases and pests are controlled using appropriate biotechnological applications.

Some successful examples of agribiotech applications in Africa include the use of *Bt* cotton in South Africa that not only showed over 40 percent increase in yield, but also resulted in increased farm incomes of US$150 per hectare (Clive James, personal communication, 2001). The growing of *Bt* cotton by farmers reduced exposure to insecticides thus reducing environmental pollution. South Africa is now commercializing the growing of *Bt* white maize.

In Kenya, farmers are already benefiting from the application of biotechnology by the International Service for the Acquisition of Agribiotech Applications (ISAAA) in maize, bananas, pyrethrum, sweet potatoes, sugarcane, and multipurpose trees. In Kenya, the projected effect of controlling the sweet potato feathery mottle virus is

314

Table 13.1 Yield (t ha⁻¹) Trends of Some Food Crops in Sub-Saharan Africa (SSA) Compared to Developing and Developed Country Yields

Crop	Average Yield		
	Current SSA Yield	Developing Country	Developed Country
Maize	1.7	2.4	4.0
Cassava	7.7	9.9	40.0
Rice	1.6	3.4	2.5
Millet	0.7	0.8	1.0
Sorghum	0.7	1.1	2.0
Sweet potato	4.8	13.5	14.0
Potato	6.0	12.4	33.0
Wheat	1.5	2.2	3.0

Source: Modified from Biotech Coordinator, November 1999.

estimated at US$5.4 million annually, while that of developing a weevil-resistant potato is estimated at US$9.9 million annually (Qaim 1999b). In Africa, with a subsistence grower's value of about $275 per ton, virus-tolerant sweet potatoes could potentially be worth an additional $495 million dollars per year for Africa (Qaim 1999b). More importantly, the extra sweet potato tonnage produced would supply half of the dietary needs of about ten million people, with no additional production costs. This would improve the living standards of rural families, particularly those living in marginal areas.

With regard to tissue culture banana technology, the average annual change in total economic surplus is expected to be in the range of US$1.6–12.8 million, depending on the price of tissue culture banana seedlings (Qaim 1999a). Currently, small-scale farmers growing tissue culture bananas are estimated to have increased their household incomes by up to 38 percent. In addition, the use of seed with resistance to MSV can potentially bring about significant economic impact and food security in Kenya. Based on the foregoing facts, it is likely that biotechnology could make a significant contribution to solving several problems of smallholder farmers in Africa.

Options for Biotechnology Research

Kenya, like many countries in Africa, has relied and continues to rely on agriculture as a base for economic growth and the major source of the country's food security. The Kenya Agricultural Research Institute (KARI) constitutes the main system for development of the country's agricultural research in response to the national development objectives. Before its reorganization in 1986, KARI did not have a comprehensive prioritization of research, but rather research managers were expected to interpret National Development Plans and policies and undertake research that was relevant to national development. With such vague guidelines, the research agenda and activities were driven by top-down scientific curiosity rather than by a problem-driven approach.

Thus, during the first phase of the National Agricultural Research Program (NARP), which began in 1987–88, the institute's research portfolio was large and unmanageable. It often included research on commodities and factor research programs such as animal health, soil and water, crop protection, range management, and socioeconomics (KARI-NARP I 1986). Within each of these areas both strategic and adaptive types of research were undertaken. Since 1991, the institute has evolved approaches and systems for priority setting within programs and projects that take into account agricultural problems at the farm level, the socioeconomic and technological demands of stakeholders, and the availability of resources. This has led to a reduced and more focused, demand-driven research portfolio, which is manageable within the available resources and capability, and which is able to deliver services and goods to the research client (World Bank 1996).

In the same spirit, the incorporation and use of biotechnology in agricultural research and development in Kenya did not start from a national policy or formal priority-setting background. Rather, it began from individual scientific and institutional curiosities arising from considerations of its ability to provide alternatives to conventional methodologies of conducting research and enhancing certain agricultural improvement needs. A review of the evolution of biotechnology in Kenya shows the emergence and application, in the early 1970s, of the simpler and cheaper techniques of microbial inoculation and tissue culture at the University of Nairobi and in a few research centers in KARI (Wafula and Falconi 1998).

With the advent of more complex biotechnology techniques and with an increasing number of scientists and institutions in Kenya entering the field, a desire arose to identify needs, consider options, and set priorities for incorporating biotechnology into the various sectors of the national economy (Mailu, Mugah, and Fungoh 1991).

It was agreed that the approach should include issues such as difficulties in improving desirable traits through conventional technologies and the ability of the national programs to carry out the proposed biotechnology research, taking into account the level of investment needed for developmental research in biotechnology versus the application of existing techniques. Consideration was also given to the time frame anticipated for developing a product in relation to the severity of the problem, national policy considerations (including presence and adequacy of national biosafety regulations and evaluation mechanisms), and structures for socioeconomic analysis of the proposed biotechnology applications. These aspirations led to the process for establishing national priorities and regulatory frameworks for biotechnology in Kenya during the early 1990s.

Priority Setting for Biotechnology in Kenya

Defining priorities for biotechnology research helps decision makers ensure that resources allocated to research are consistent with agreed upon national objectives such as efficiency, equity, food security, and environmental protection. The framework for making such decisions includes expected development costs, the need for integration with conventional research programs, potential opportunities for international collaboration, and challenges of public perception including biosafety and intellectual property rights (IPRs). Making such decisions requires interaction between technical, financial, and policy specialists. In addition, the need for periodic meetings with stakeholders is essential for selecting appropriate research activities. Decision makers can foster these interactions by encouraging scientists to focus their research on agreed upon priorities and by supporting policies that provide for the development and delivery of products. Choices for agricultural biotechnology in Kenya have therefore been defined within the framework of national agricultural research priorities guided by the need for improved agricultural production.

Two approaches were followed in identifying national priorities for biotechnology. The government, under the National Advisory Committee on Biotechnology Advances and their Applications (NACBAA 1990) commissioned the first approach, carried out between 1990 and 1991. The NACBAA was established in 1990 to develop a biotechnology strategy for Kenya to the year 2000 and beyond. The committee, which comprised directors of ten research institutes in the country, identified major national priorities for biotechnology on the basis of such considerations as:

- Biotechnology's comparative advantage and its ability to complement traditional methods of production in small-scale agriculture,
- Rapid access to new germplasm,
- Reduction in the high cost of agricultural inputs, and
- Access to cheaper and more environmentally friendly alternatives.

Through this process, NACBAA identified as the national priorities for biotechnology in Kenya:

- Application of tissue culture for mass propagation and disease elimination.
- Development of disease diagnostic tests and novel vaccines.
- Development and use of microbial inoculants.
- Plant genetic transformation for various biotic and abiotic stresses.
- Postharvest technology, environmental protection, and conservation of natural resources.
- Policy development on biosafety and capacity building at various levels in the country.

However, because the translation of the committee's recommendations into implementable programs was stalled for three years, institutions such as KARI undertook their own program reviews in order to determine and initiate activities in support of areas where biotechnological interventions offered comparative advantage. A key lesson that emerged from this process was that the top-down approach to priority setting, such as that taken by NACBAA, poses problems of communication and ownership and can stifle program implementation.

A different approach to NACBAA was thus initiated between 1992 and 1993. Taking into account the fact that 80 percent of Kenyan agriculture is comprised of small-scale farms, this approach took on a participatory, bottom-up method of problem identification, priority setting, and program formulation. In this process, two phases were undertaken. The first phase took two years and involved problem identification at the technical, policy, and farm levels, and the setting of priorities at the national level. The second phase focused on program formulation, taking into account national and international collaborative needs and opportunities for technology transfer and adoption. To accomplish both phases, a series of workshops was organized between 1993 and 1995 involving policymakers, researchers, extension workers, and farmers (KABP 1993). The process culminated in the identification of national priorities for biotechnology that were essentially similar to those identified by NACBAA. In addition, the process led to the establishment of the Kenya Agricultural Biotechnology Platform (KABP) as a body to provide advice on matters relating to the advancement of biotechnology in Kenya.

Although the priority-setting approach undertaken by NACBAA was more rapid and less costly, it did not constitute a multilevel decision-making framework incorporating all key stakeholders. Because linkages between the various beneficiary groups were lacking, implementation of the committee's recommendations did not take place. In contrast, significant advances were made under the multilevel participatory approach, and a number of technical, management, and institutional capacity-building initiatives were developed. Different institutions are implementing these through projects in biosafety policy, human capacity development through training, molecular-marker-assisted breeding, plant tissue culture, recombinant-DNA-based diagnostic tests and vaccine development, and technology transfer.

In assessing options for biotechnology in the national agricultural improvement strategy, a hierarchical approach should be taken in decision making so as to involve scientists, sectoral leaders, and national policymakers. This is because an analysis at each level ensures that a complete picture of biotechnology is created and that decision makers have a framework for implementing the identified biotechnology research.

Status of Agricultural Biotechnology in Kenya

A review of the status of biotechnology in Africa shows that, apart from Egypt, Kenya, Zimbabwe, and South Africa, few countries have developed national priorities for biotechnology. In most countries little investment has been made in genetic engineering activities, except microbial inoculation and tissue culture (Wafula 1995). Although priority setting for biotechnology in Kenya was carried out only recently, the evolution of modern biotechnology research in Kenya began in the 1970s with the development of biofertilizers in food legumes at the Department of Crop Science,

University of Nairobi. Following the setting of priorities for biotechnology in Kenya in 1995, a number of programs and projects were initiated in various institutions encompassing a diversity of biotechnology gradients that range from biofertilizers to recombinant DNA technologies.

Microbial Inoculation

In Kenya, the inoculation of food legumes, particularly of beans with rhizobium species, began in the early 1970s at the University of Nairobi. This program expanded during the 1990s into the current Microbiological Resource Center (MIRCEN) Project. Field inoculation trials have been conducted in various parts of the country, although, as yet, no full-scale production has been established because of lack of the necessary equipment.

Tissue Culture

The application of tissue culture biotechnology in Kenya began in the early 1980s with its incorporation into pyrethrum production in KARI's Muguga laboratory, and in the citrus research program at the University of Nairobi's Department of Crop Science in 1983. By 1986, tissue culture biotechnology was widely applied in mass-propagation of pyrethrum at KARI's National Pyrethrum Research Center, Molo. The Pyrethrum Board of Kenya entered into contractual arrangements with KARI to employ the technology in its pyrethrum seed multiplication program. Tissue culture activities in Muguga expanded over time and today cover other significant crops, including sweet potatoes and ornamentals. In addition, tissue culture has been integrated into improvement and mass production of crops in other centers in KARI and in other research institutions in the country. The technology is widely applied in the production of basic seed potatoes at KARI's National Potato Research Center, Tigoni, and in the production of macadamias, strawberries, and bananas in KARI's National Horticultural Research Center, Thika. The production of citrus at the University of Nairobi through tissue culture began in 1983, and since 1991 has expanded to cover sugarcane and pyrethrum. In 1995, the Jomo Kenyatta University of Agriculture and Technology incorporated the technology in mass production of bananas. The Coffee Research Foundation also applies tissue culture to coffee production and the Tea Research Foundation of Kenya (TRFK) to tea production. Although the demand for banana, potato, and coffee planting materials is high in the country, their rate of production by the institutions mentioned here is still at a very small, microcommercial level. Development in other crops such as citrus, strawberries, and tea is still experimental, being basically laboratory-based. The private firm Oserian Company was set up at Naivasha in the late 1980s, and that of Genetic Technology Limited (GTL) in Nairobi in 1994. They are involved in the commercial production of ornamental flowers for export (Oserian), and of bananas, pineapples, and sugarcane (GTL).

Molecular Markers

The application of molecular-marker-assisted technologies for selection and identification of markers in plants, pests, and other pathogens began in Kenya in 1995. At present, these activities are nested within the cereals breeding program in KARI, focusing on developing maize varieties and lines resistant to insect pests (especially stem borers), MSV, and drought tolerance. Genetic marker approaches are also being employed at the TRF in mapping, selection, and breeding of tea varieties, as well as in germplasm conservation.

Genetic Engineering of Crops

KARI initiated efforts to apply genetic engineering encompassing transformation and regeneration of crops in 1991, working in partnership with Monsanto Company Limited, USA, to develop transgenic sweet potatoes resistant to sweet potato feathery mottle virus (SPFMV). At Monsanto, KARI scientists using Kenyan sweet potato varieties carried out this work, successfully achieving transformed materials that were later transferred to KARI through a license agreement. Apart from genetic engineering of sweet potatoes, this technology has not been extended to other crops in Kenya, although ongoing efforts in the institute toward strengthening capacity in genetic engineering aim to see the extension of this technology to other crops. A license agreement has been completed between KARI and Monsanto to make available to KARI transformed plant materials, the transformation system, and processes, as well as gene constructs for transformation and evaluation of the technology in Kenya.

Novel Vaccines and Disease Diagnostics

Major advances in biotechnology in Kenya have been made in the area of livestock research. National agricultural research institutions, universities, the private sector, and International Agricultural Research Centers (IARCs), such as the International Livestock Research Institute (ILRI), are involved in animal biotechnology research and development. The main developments are in the area of cattle breeding and nutrition, development of animal vaccines, and disease diagnostic tests. Specific DNA probes have been developed for the diagnosis of heartwater disease and babesiosis in KARI and in ILRI. KARI is also developing diagnostic kits for contagious respiratory diseases of cattle and goats, particularly contagious bovine pleuropneumonia and contagious caprine pleuropneumonia. Similar activities are in process directed at protozoan diseases and viral conditions of livestock such as rinderpest. Multivalent recombinant vaccines for some of the common livestock diseases in the African region are also under development at KARI. These include vaccines against Rift Valley fever, rinderpest, sheep and goat pox, theileriasis, and lumpy skin disease. In animal breeding, Kenya has a long record of artificial insemination, especially for cattle, which has resulted in considerable improvement of the dairy industry. The technique of embryo transfer has the potential for improving local breeds of cattle, and this at present is being applied by progressive farmers and through local private veterinary firms such as the Nairobi Veterinary Center in Kenya.

320

Table 13.2 Agricultural Biotechnology Sources of Funding (%), Kenya

Source	Year		
	1989	**1993**	**1996**
Government	21	39	28
Donors	75	55	67
Sales products	4	4	3
Levies	0	2	2
TOTAL	100	100	100

Source: Wafula and Falconi 1998.

Financial Resources

Budgetary resources are tight and institutions must always be on a quest to secure additional support. Funds have been received from both government and bilateral and multilateral donors (table 13.2). Various institutions, especially KARI, have also sought to diversify their sourcing approaches through developing competitive programs and establishing contract and collaborative research linkages with international biotechnology research programs and private-sector firms (Wafula and Falconi 1998). International development assistance and loans have also been used as sources of funding for biotechnology and biosafety capacity building, including training and research.

In Kenya, public research institutions, universities, and private noncommercial research organizations are involved in biotechnology research programs ranging from crop improvement to tissue culture to genetic transformation of crops and recombinant

Table 13.3 Biotechnology Research Focus in Kenya, 1996

Technique	Commodity	Objective	Funding source[a]
Biofertilizers	Beans, soybean	Nitrogen fixation	DGIS, FAO, IAEA
Tissue culture	Bananas, sweet potatoes, flowers, potato, cassava, macadamias, pyrethrum	Micropropagation	WB, DGIS, RF, IDRC
Marker-assisted breeding	Maize	Drought tolerance	DGIS
		Insect resistance	DGIS
		Virus resistance	RF
	Tea	Gene mapping	Levies, taxes
DNA technology	Transgenic sweet potatoes	Virus resistance	USAID, Private firms.
	Animal vaccines	Disease control	USAID, DFID, DGIS
	Plant/animal diseases	Disease diagnosis	DGIS, WB, DFID, GoK

Source: Wafula and Falconi 1998.
a. DFID = Department for International Development, DGIS = Directorate General for Development Cooperation, Dutch Ministry, FAO = Food and Agriculture Organization, GoK = Government of Kenya, IAEA = International Atomic Energy Agency, IDRC = International Development Research Centre, RF = Rockefeller Foundation, USAID = United States Agency for International Development, and WB = the World Bank.

animal vaccines (table 13.3). The funding for these activities has been derived from a variety of sources ranging from those mentioned previously to levies and sale of products.

KARI, which is the main public institution carrying out biotechnology research in Kenya, accounted for almost 70 percent of the total national expenditures on biotechnology from 1989 to 1998. Different funding mechanisms and approaches have been employed in seeking support from different sources for different activities. Thus the Rockefeller Foundation (RF) funds the institute's MSV research and the International Development Research Center (IDRC) of Canada and RF support the Banana Tissue Culture Project jointly. KARI developed these activities as collaborative projects with other institutions and with the ISAAA as an honest broker and backstopping agency.

The institute's potato, cassava, sweet potato, and macadamia tissue culture projects, and some components of animal health (e.g., the project to develop maize lines with resistance to stem borer and with drought tolerance) are funded as components of the Netherlands' support to the Biotechnology Development Program for Africa, Asia, and Latin America. The funding is through the Directorate General for Development Cooperation (DGIS) of the Dutch Ministry. These projects were identified and formulated through the participatory, bottom-up, priority-setting approach elaborated previously. Funding for evaluating the adaptive research components of the animal health biotechnology program, some aspects of crop tissue culture improvement, and infrastructural development is provided through the multilateral World Bank support to NARP-II. The project to develop sweet potato varieties with resistance to viral diseases was established as a joint venture between KARI (a public-sector institution) and Monsanto Company (a private-sector commercial firm) through a royalty-free technology donation agreement. Although Monsanto has provided financial support to the activity since 1991, additional funding for this project has been given by the United States Agency for International Development (USAID) through the KARI-USAID bilateral support to NARP–I's Agricultural Biotechnology for Sustainable Productivity (ABSP). The ISAAA supports mainly training in biosafety aspects of the project and proprietary technology transfer negotiations.

Contract research with private commercial and noncommercial organizations has been established between KARI and companies such as the Oserian Flower Company and the Pyrethrum Board of Kenya to develop procedures for tissue culture production of the relevant crops. Similar ventures have been expanded to include joint field technology evaluation and crop management research with GTL in banana and sugarcane tissue culture.

Access to funding for biotechnology projects through bilateral support to the NARP has been realized in animal health projects, and to a small extent in horticultural research. The British Government's Department for International Development (DFID) and USAID have supported staff training in molecular biology disciplines, biotechnology infrastructural capacity building, and technical support to a number of animal health and horticultural biotechnology development activities, including the development of diagnostics and animal recombinant vaccines.

Joint program development and funding within the context of international biotechnology research programs has been pursued with American universities, British institutions of advanced research, and locally based IARCs. Thus the development and evaluation of the recombinant rinderpest, East Coast fever, and Rift Valley fever vaccines, and a biological control agent were carried out jointly by KARI, the University of California at Davis, the Institute for Animal Health in the UK, ILRI, and the Institute for Mycological Research, with funding from USAID and DFID.

The high proportion of KARI's research program devoted to biotechnology research can be attributed to the high level of funding that the institute has enjoyed. However, it must be noted that such funding has emanated from the establishment of mutual understanding between the institute and the various organizations. It has also emanated from the presence of scientists trained in the relevant biotechnology disciplines, and the existing enabling environment.

Universities accounted for about one-fourth of the total research expenditure during the period 1989–98, while the private, non-commercial-sector organizations commanded less than 6 percent of expenditures (Wafula and Falconi 1998). About 65 percent of funding for biotechnology activities in the universities has come from the government and the rest from donors including the International Atomic Energy Agency (IAEA), DGIS, the World Bank, and the United Nations Educational, Scientific, and Cultural Organization (UNESCO). On the other hand, private, noncommercial organizations are funded by levies (taxes) from their commercial commodities and sales of their products.

Given that donor support has formed the greatest proportion of funding for biotechnology, especially in KARI, where the bulk of the research is carried out,the national financial ministries and research institutions must determine how to develop greater responsibility for future program funding.

Human Capacity Development

The development of biotechnology capacity requires increased technical expertise among mid- and high-level positions in ministries and research institutes. Such capacity and competency in biotechnology is needed to provide technical input when analyzing program options and proposals, performing peer review of proposals, using the participatory approach for priority setting, analyzing applications for donor support or loans, reviewing implications regarding materials protected by IPRs, and convening panels for regulatory reviews.

In Kenya, the human resource dimension poses an urgent requirement. Fifty-six biotechnology scientists were involved in 80 percent of the country's biotechnology research in 1998, of which twenty-one were in public universities where they spent less than 10 percent of their time on biotechnology-related activities. This means that only thirty-five full-time equivalent researchers were engaged in the entire national

323

biotechnology research program. The challenges to establishing human capacity for biotechnology in Kenya have been compounded by the deficiency in both quantity and quality of trained experts in the various biotechnology-related disciplines, including molecular biology, molecular genetics, cell immunology, ecology, biosafety, and others that are crucial in national biotechnology development.

In building national capacity in biotechnology and biosafety, institutions such as KARI have incorporated their biotechnology research training needs within the framework of their individual project training strategies. This has enabled these institutes to seek support for capacity building from relevant international organizations and special programs. For example, KARI has linked its training requirements in tissue culture to its projects on bananas, macadamias, and roots and tubers under the support of RF, IDRC, and DGIS. The collaborative linkages of these activities with advanced tissue culture institutions in South Africa and India have enabled Kenyan researchers to undertake training in basic and advanced tissue culture methodologies in these countries. Similarly, KARI's linkages with the John Innes Centre and the International Maize and Wheat Improvement Center (CIMMYT) within the framework of the collaborative MSV and resistance to pest projects under RF and DGIS funding have enabled the institute to train five scientists in molecular-marker-assisted breeding technologies.

The institute has linked its training requirements in gene construction and crop transformation with private-sector firms such as Monsanto, and U.S. universities such as Michigan State University, the University of Missouri, and Texas A&M through collaborative programs on sweet potatoes and pest-resistant maize. Funding for these activities has come from USAID, ABSP, and the Government of Kenya. This approach has resulted in three KARI scientists being trained in crop genetic engineering technologies and biosafety development.

Table 13.4   Human Resource Deployment on Biotechnology Activities in Kenya, 1996

Technique	Number of Scientists at Institutions[a]						
	KARI	JKUA	UN/BIOCHEM	UNCS	CRF	TRF	Total
Biofertilizer	0	0	2	0	0	0	2
N_2 fixation	0	0	0	6	0	0	6
Tissue culture	12	4	0	7	3	2	28
DNA diagnosis	9	0	0	0	0	0	9
Genetic markers	2	0	0	0	0	2	4
Recombinant vaccines	5	0	0	0	0	0	5
Crop transformation	2	0	0	0	0	0	2
TOTAL	30	4	2	13	3	4	56

Source: Wafula and Falconi 1998.
a. CRF = Coffee Research Foundation, JKUA = Jomo Kenyatta University of Agriculture, KARI = Kenya Agricultural Research Institute, TRF = Tea Research Foundation, UN/BIOCHEM = University of Nairobi Biochemistry Department, and UNCS = University of Nairobi Crop Science Department.

Scientific and technical capacity building in recombinant DNA techniques in animal disease diagnostics and vaccinology has been developed through collaborative international animal health research programs with research institutions and universities in the United States, the United Kingdom, and Kenya supported by international funding agencies, notably USAID, DGIS, and DFID.

An overview of the agricultural biotechnology research focus of the six major Kenyan biotechnology organizations (table 13.4) shows that most activities are on biological nitrogen fixation, tissue culture, and DNA analysis. The former require less scientific knowledge, and less time and financial resources, than the latter.

Two-thirds of the scientists in biotechnology programs use less sophisticated techniques for crop improvement. The rest are employing more advanced techniques, including genetic engineering of plants, molecular markers, recombinant DNA vaccines, and diagnostics.

Although the number of researchers in biotechnology has risen over time, the country has not reached the critical mass needed to cultivate the necessary biotechnology environment and establish extensive international contacts for the enhancement of modern biotechnology. As stated previously, a good number of the scientists are found in the universities and spend most of their time teaching rather than on actual biotechnology research. Human resource development is therefore still required to ensure a strong base in the various biotechnology research initiatives.

Transfer and Delivery of New Technologies—Strategic Partnerships

International Cooperation

Collaborative research projects provide opportunities for international partnerships in research. Such collaboration expands the range of biotechnology applications relevant to African agriculture. Kenya and several other African countries have taken advantage of such collaborative partnerships (table 13.5). These projects range from animal and plant disease diagnostics to the development of transgenic crops and live recombinant vaccines. Some of the partnerships have provided opportunities for scientific and technical training as well as technology transfer avenues.

Decisions about the production and delivery of products to identified users must be considered in the early stages of research and development. Collaboration or joint ventures between the private, commercial-sector, and public institutes or universities is essential. In some cases, national or international intermediary organizations have facilitated technology transfer from public- to private-sector organizations. The strong relationship between the public and private sectors in product development has been emphasized, specifically in the areas of product price regulation and registration; offering on-farm demonstrations, pilot production facilities, and science parks for start-up companies; and procuring and distributing planting material. Issues that must be considered in this regard are:

- Do opportunities presented correspond with national or institutional priorities?
- Is the local research infrastructure adequate to apply the results of international collaboration?
- Are conditions in place for testing and diffusing products from collaboration?

In Kenya, ways of dealing with these questions are indicated by:

- The efforts and mechanisms initiated within the framework of the national priority-setting processes of the National Advisory Committee on Biotechnology Advances and their Applications (NACBAA) and the participatory bottom-up approach;
- The institutional as well as the human capacity development approaches taken by KARI;
- The collaborative and linkage program development and implementation options; and
- The financial sourcing and support approaches followed in the country.

Although public-funded research organizations have played, and will continue to play, a key role in the development, acquisition, and transfer of technologies in Africa, the private sector could also play an increasing role in the transfer of technology through affiliated or licensed marketing or research centers. This can be seen, for example, in the number and type of applications pending biosafety review in developing countries. However, this technology has not readily reached the public sector for further research because its proprietary developers restrict it.

In this regard, national and public institutions can also benefit from collaboration with international biotechnology programs that provide access to both public- and proprietary-domain technologies. Examples of commercial technology transfer originating from international programs are illustrated by KARI's sweet potato project involving Monsanto, AID, and KARI as well as the KARI-Oserian collaboration in commercial tissue culture flowers, and the KARI-GTL collaboration in banana production.

The traditional route of donor, IARC, and developing-country access to biotechnology through public institutions is being affected by the increasing trend toward privatization. This fact coupled with pressures on national agricultural programs to divest production and distribution responsibilities may reduce opportunities for public-sector technology transfer. Commercial producers may be encouraged to assume some of these responsibilities.

Enabling Environment: Safety and Social Concerns

Biosafety

Although tissue culture and some other components of biotechnology are widely accepted, many safety concerns have been raised about genetic engineering. One concern is that genetically modified organisms themselves, or other organisms that

326

Table 13.5 International Research and Development (R&D) Activities with Focus on Kenya

Program	R & D activity	Collaborating institutes
Agricultural Biotechnology for Sustainable Productivity (ABSP)	• Genetic engineering of sweet potato for insect resistance • Development of transgenic maize Agrobacterium-mediated system	Kenya Agricultural Research Institute (KARI)
Feathery mottle resistant sweet potato for African farmers through biotechnology (AID-1) Monsanto	• Transformation of sweet potato for resistance to feathery mottle virus	KARI
Centre de coopération internationale en recherche agronomique pour le dévelopement – Plant Breeding Division (CIRAD-MICAP)	• Genetic transformation of coffee with *Bt* toxin genes • Insect-resistant cotton through the transfer of *Bt* toxin genes or presence inhibitor genes • Coffee genome mapping • Mass propagation of coffee through somatic embryogenesis • Molecular tagging of sorghum genes controlling grain qualities corresponding to consumer demand	Coffee Research Foundation
Special Program Biotechnology and Development cooperation (DGIS-BIOTECH)	• Tissue culture banana, cassava, potato, sweet potato, macadamia, citrus • Animal health • Maize stalk borer and drought tolerance • Bio-pesticides • Biosafety	Kenya Agricultural Biotechnology Platform
International Centre of Insect Physiology and Ecology (ICIPE) Biotechnology Research Unit (ICIPE-BRU)	• Biological control through the use of *Bt*	KARI Kenya Trypanosomiasis Research Unit (KETRI)
International Institute of Tropical Agriculture (IITA) Biotechnology Research Unit (IITA-BRU)	• Biochemical and molecular markers for cassava, yam, cowpea, banana/plantain • Disease elimination of virus indexing in cassava, yam, cowpea, banana/plantain • Regeneration and transformation of cassava, yam, cowpea, banana/plantain	University of Nairobi KARI
International Laboratory of Molecular Biology for Tropical Disease Agents (ILAMB)	• Diagnostic kit for rinderpest • Recombinant rinderpest vaccine	KARI
ILRI Tick-borne Diseases Program (ILRI-1)	• Recombinant vaccine for East Coast fever • Diagnostic tests for tick-borne diseases	KARI
ILRI Trypanosomiasis Program (ILRI-2)	• Diagnostic tests for trypanosomiasis • Vaccine development for trypanosomiasis	KETRI
International Service for the Acquisition of Agribiotech Applications (ISAAA)	• Transformation of sweet potato • Maize streak virus	KARI
Small Ruminant Collaborative Research Support Project–Animal Health Component (SR-CRSP)	• Vaccines for Nairobi sheep disease and Rift Valley fever • Identify vaccine genes for *haemonchus contortus* • Vaccine for contagious caprine pleuropneumonia (CCPP)	KARI

Source: IBS 1997.

exchange genes with them, might spread spontaneously and have unforeseen negative impacts. For instance, crops engineered to tolerate pests, diseases, or herbicides might cross with their wild relatives, and create "super weeds" that are expensive to control. It has recently been shown that novel genes engineered into oilseed rape have been transferred in the field into a close weed relative, *Brassica campestris*. Although this is the first time that such an occurrence has been demonstrated, it could have substantial implications for the deployment of genetically engineered crops.

Another concern is whether crops engineered to kill certain pests might be harmful to other organisms, that is, escape from a genetically modified organism (GMO). A specific concern is related to *Bt*, which has been used to develop crops resistant to insect pests. *Bt* is a biopesticide used by organic farmers, so if insects develop resistance to *Bt* through widespread planting of GMOs, the *Bt* used by organic farmers would be rendered ineffective. For example, the diamond-back moth has developed resistance to four *Bt* toxins, based on single-gene action. This suggests that, in a much shorter time than anticipated, widespread exposure to crops engineered with *Bt* could lead to development of *Bt*-resistant insect populations, especially in the many areas of the developing world where implementation of integrated control measures (e.g., mixed plantings and refuges) is weak.

In the case of herbicide resistance, it is feared that herbicide use could increase and have adverse impacts on the environment and human health. For example, an important weed (*Striga* spp.) of maize can now be controlled using herbicide (imadizoline)-resistant maize. To ensure that *Striga* resistance to the herbicide does not evolve, strict integrated control measures would be needed. As in the case of insect pest control, such measures are often not implemented because of weak technology transfer capacities. Another concern is that agricultural biodiversity will decline as farmers replace numerous existing varieties with a handful of genetically improved superior varieties. There are, however, counterarguments in favor of these technologies. For example, mutations and gene flows between organisms occur in nature, and the possibility that weedy relatives could receive traits from improved varieties exists to some extent with conventional breeding. Maintenance of pest resistance is also a major concern of conventional breeding. Moreover, even where some adverse impacts exist, these need to be balanced against those created by current practice, which normally involves either pesticides or expanding the area under cultivation, with consequent environmental damage.

A major concern of some consumers is that GMOs and other biotechnological products may be harmful because of the possible inadvertent production of toxins and allergens (FAO-WHO 1995). The fact that genetic engineering can cause problems involving food allergies has been demonstrated by studies on a genetically engineered soybeans. Soy containing a gene from Brazil nut to enhance the nutritional profile of the soy for use as animal feed was tested against blood samples from people with known Brazil nut allergies. The modified soy was found to be allergenic and the project was abandoned. Other cases could be more difficult to test, especially if the proteins from other sources (e.g., bacteria) have not been available previously in food products.

The ultimate success of biotechnological applications depends on consumer response. Many European consumers, for example, are reluctant to buy genetically engineered foods. Studies indicate that reluctance is not only related to safety aspects, but also to general values about food and the environment. Many consumers perceive biotechnology as being oriented toward high-input, environmentally damaging agricultural practices. The GMOs may be better received when they clearly contribute to consumers' preferences and environmental conservation.

So far, little information is available on how consumers in developing countries will react to GMOs. However, developing countries exporting to sensitive markets in industrialized countries have to be aware of the possible effect on their market position when introducing GMOs. Much more work on preferences and perceptions of consumers in developing countries is required, and experience to date underlines the importance of engaging the public in a debate on these issues at an early stage. With regard to ethics, genetic engineering of crops and cloning of animals incite the strongest ethical debates. Some people object on moral grounds to the transfer of genes between taxonomic kingdoms or to patenting living organisms, sometimes based on religious beliefs—humans do not have the right to "play with nature." Some espouse caution, based on a sense that, given the uncertainty about the potential effects of genetic engineering, the risks of unforeseen damage to people and nature are too high. Others stress the virtues of individual and intellectual freedom and have a high tolerance for taking risks. Issues of individual freedom of choice sometimes conflict, for example the freedom of farmers to choose between sources of seed and the freedom of consumers to choose nontransgenic foods.

These ethical concerns differ from person to person, and among population groups and countries. Policymakers and politicians often face public concerns, opposing opinions, and conflicting values. Often, a clear right or wrong cannot be perceived, nor are these concerns something that can be "solved" only through education and information. Not only do these differences arise at the national level, but also in international negotiations about trade-related issues, especially on the adoption of standards for safety regulations, principles for IPR regulations, consumers' rights to choose, and standards for animal welfare.

Social issues are also at stake regarding who benefits from the new technologies. These issues may be important if they involve the use of high-cost seed (because of high investments by private firms in research) or have high management requirements that limit adoption to larger-scale farmers. Other social issues include potential dependence by farmers on one or a few technology suppliers, and potential changes in world commodity prices through the development of commodity substitutes (e.g., cocoa and vanilla). For example, one biotechnology currently under development that has raised considerable debate on both ethical and social grounds is the so-called seed terminator technology (or seed technology protection system) that seeks to protect IPRs by preventing seed germination. The Consultative Group on International Agricultural Research (CGIAR) system and many developing countries have decided that they will not incorporate into their breeding materials any genetic system designed to prevent seed germination.

Safety in biotechnology is therefore a sensitive issue, considering the potential short- and longer-term risks posed once organisms resulting from biotechnology application are released in the environment, for example through international trade. Many developing countries are concerned that some GMOs, if imported into their countries deliberately or unintentionally, might be harmful to humans and the environment. These concerns have led to calls for the establishment of national as well as regionally and internationally harmonized biosafety regimes to enhance control of intracountry and transboundary movements and use of GMOs. Most scientists now agree that instead of an outright ban on GMOs, the risks call for appropriate biosafety standards. Such standards include developing adequate biosafety regulations, risk assessments for biotechnological products, and mechanisms and instruments for monitoring use and compliance in order to minimize harmful effects on the environment and on people.

"Biosafety" means the policies and procedures adopted to ensure the environmentally safe application of biotechnology. Biosafety has been found to be a top policy concern of African countries considering the use of biotechnology (Cohen, Falconi, and Komen 1998). There are many reasons for this. One of these is the attention given to biosafety in international forums such as negotiations on an internationally binding "biosafety protocol" under the Convention for Biological Diversity.

Numerous examples can be found, especially from representatives of international research centers, emphasizing that biotechnology products are being introduced in a growing number of developing countries. Moreover, a range of products can be expected from international collaborative programs. Some of these products, for example transgenic plants and recombinant livestock vaccines, require biosafety reviews. Donors supporting international collaborative research programs therefore often request a formal biosafety review before technology transfer can take place. Although much experience has been gained in genetically improving crops in developing countries through conventional breeding, concern continues regarding the extent of knowledge available on transgenic products.

The three most important needs identified include developing biosafety guidelines, establishing a responsive national system, and increasing the capability to perform risk analysis of genetically modified organisms. However, discussions on potential benefits and environmental risks are hampered by lack of data. This is particularly true regarding the introduction of transgenic organisms into tropical ecosystems and centers of diversity.

Establishing a system for biosafety review has many facets and challenges in itself. These include formulation and adoption of safety guidelines, establishing national and institutional biosafety committees, and ensuring infrastructure for contained and large-scale field-testing of genetically modified organisms. As suggested by Traynor

(1998), an effective biosafety system is one that allows the environmentally responsible use of agricultural biotechnologies, a system that can be established when:

> The framework (policies, guidelines) defines clearly the structure of the biosafety system, the roles and responsibilities of those involved, and how the review process is to operate, the people involved are knowledgeable and well-trained, and have the support of their institutions, the review process is scientifically sound and uses available information to make decisions that balance benefits and risks, feedback mechanisms are used to incorporate new information and revise the system as needed.

In Africa, it has not been possible to separate the establishment of biosafety policies and procedures from national developments in gene technology. A system for safe, efficient, and knowledgeable development and use of GMOs is only essential if a country is involved in the development, or wishes to realize its benefits through technology transfer mechanisms. Many countries in Africa, for reasons of policy, and financial, institutional, and public perception, have not embarked on the development, importation, and use of GMOs. Those that have done so are South Africa, Egypt, Kenya, and Zimbabwe, and their research initiatives in gene technology include the development and evaluation of transgenic crops and animal recombinant vaccines (see following list, from Wafula [1995]).

Development of Genetically Modified Organisms in Africa

Country	Transgenic Plants and Microorganisms
Egypt	Cotton - stress and insect resistance
	Maize - insect and fungal resistance
	Faba bean - stress and virus resistance
Kenya	Sweet potato - virus resistance
	Capripox-Rift Valley fever - recombinant vaccine
South Africa	Potato, tomato, tobacco - virus and insect resistance
	Cotton - insect resistance
Zimbabwe	Cotton (only field-testing of imports) a
	Tobacco – insect resistance

Only a few countries have established regulatory frameworks and national capacities for biosafety (table 13.6). In the rest of the countries where biotechnology has not taken hold, their biosafety structures are either not available or are very weak.

Difficulties in establishing national capacity for biosafety in Africa begin with the fact that only a few activities drive biosafety developments. Deficiencies also occur in both the quantity and quality of trained expertise in molecular biology, ecology, and other disciplines that are crucial in national biosafety developments. Such trained experts are key to national planning for biotechnology and the development of biosafety oversight, and their absence severely limits the development of biosafety.

331

Table 13.6 Status of Biosafety in Selected African Countries

Stage	Country			
	Kenya	South Africa	Zimbabwe	Egypt
Writing team assembled	Yes	Yes	Yes	Yes
Guideline drafted	Yes	Yes	Yes	Yes
Guidelines promulgated	No	Yes	No	No
National Biosafety Committee established	Yes	Yes	Yes	Yes
Guidelines implemented	Yes	Yes	No	No
Institutional Biosafety Committee established	Yes	Yes	No	No
Reviewers trained	Yes	Yes	No	No
Applications received	Yes	Yes	No	No
Approvals given	Yes	Yes	No	No
Controlled environment experiments conducted	Yes	Yes	No	No
Field-tests conducted	No	Yes	No	No

Source: Traynor 1998.

Accessibility to biotechnology and biosafety information databases, appropriate facilities, and equipment to carry out monitoring and risk assessment, as well as finances to support implementation of safety issues is an important and integral part of a national biosafety development and implementation program.

In Africa, some countries such as Kenya have incorporated their biosafety needs within the framework of their national biotechnology research programs, thus enabling the government and research institutions to seek support for capacity building in biosafety from relevant funding agencies and special programs (Wafula and Ndiritu 1996).

The development of the biosafety oversight structure and capacity in Kenya went through various stages and different funding sources. Driven by its developments of recombinant DNA vaccines and transgenic sweet potatoes, KARI was the first national institution to establish Institutional Biosafety Guidelines and an Institutional Advisory Committee on Biotechnology, in 1993 (KARI 1994). These guidelines were mainly aimed at guiding the institute's biotechnology activities at the laboratory level. In anticipation of contained release and evaluation of these products in the near future, KARI initiated intensive negotiations with the relevant government authorities and donors to establish a national biosafety structure in the country. Meanwhile, during this period, some Kenyan scientists and policymakers were participating in various national, regional, and international seminars and workshops on biosafety in which they becamesensitized to and made aware of the need for establishment of a national biosafety oversight to foster development and application of biotechnology.

This sensitization resulted in the government establishing in 1995 a national task force to formulate biosafety guidelines for Kenya with financial support from the World Bank and the DGIS. Following a series of stakeholders' workshops to review and provide inputs, the guidelines were finally published in 1998 and a National

Biosafety Committee appointed under the National Council for Science and Technology (NCST 1998). As shown in table 13.6, although the guidelines are under implementation, with at least two applications having been reviewed, they are still to be promulgated and made into an Act of Parliament. However, they remain operational under ministerial decree.

Attempts have been made to establish harmonized, regional biosafety structures in east, central, and southern Africa since 1993, when the first Regional Conference for International Cooperation on Biosafety in Biotechnology was held in Harare, Zimbabwe, with the support of the Netherlands DGIS Biotechnology Program. The conference resulted in the establishment of a Regional Biosafety Coordination Committee comprising representatives of thirteen countries in eastern and southern Africa (Thitai and Wafula 1996). Although these efforts finally led to the establishment of a regional focal point, a harmonized regional biosafety structure has not been developed. This may be because various countries in the region are at different levels of development of their national biosafety guidelines.

In recent years, some meetings and workshops have been organized in an attempt to create an internationally agreed upon protocol on safety in biotechnology in the context of the Convention on Biodiversity (CBD). The first meeting in this respect was that of the open-ended, ad hoc working group on biosafety held in Aarhus, Denmark, in July 1996 in response to the decision by the Conference of the Parties to the CBD at its second meeting held in November 1996 in Jakarta, Indonesia. The decision was to start the process of developing, in the field of the safe transfer and the handling and use of GMOs, a protocol on biosafety. The protocol was to specifically focus on transboundary movement of any GMO resulting from modern biotechnology that has adverse effect on the conservation and sustainable use of biological diversity (Mulongoy 1997). The latest meeting seeking to establish the international protocol on biosafety was held in February 1999 in Cartagena, Colombia, but ended unsuccessfully. It is expected that continued efforts will be made toward the realization of these international objectives.

Intellectual Property Rights

"Intellectual property rights" is a broad term for the various rights granted by law for the protection of economic investment in creative effort. The main categories of intellectual property relevant to agricultural research are patents, plant variety rights, and trademarks. In most developing countries, policies for the application of IPR to biotechnology products are still under formulation. Some countries have never explicitly excluded living material from patent protection. Others have recently adopted an IPR for biotechnology, or are discussing IPR legislation in which the inclusion of living material is envisaged. Currently, African countries are exploring the options and implications for agricultural research as regards national policy decisions on IPR and biotechnology (Erbisch and Maredia 2003).

One reason that the topic of IPR receives such attention is that agricultural development, including the release of improved planting materials through formal breeding and production, has benefited from a long history of public-sector, "public-good" investment. At the core of this system has been the free availability of plant genetic resources. Thus, increased IPR protection in agricultural research does not always seem fully in line with either the longstanding tradition of public-sector investments, or innovations contributed by international agricultural research or by informal or indigenous communities. Many practitioners fear that invoking such protection destroys the public-good nature of agriculture, especially as it relates to the needs of the rural poor.

Most countries participating in the seminars are members of the World Trade Organization (WTO), and therefore are bound to introduce international standards for IPR protection. The extent to which changes in the IPR legislation of developing countries will, in fact, lead to accelerated technology transfer and to greater domestic innovation in advanced technology remains to be seen. Only limited studies exist regarding IPR in developing countries and their relationship to welfare and development. Considerations of stronger intellectual property protection will require an analysis of both costs and benefits, with costs involved being more foreseeable.

Lessons Learned

This chapter has summarized important findings on how to establish a viable biotechnology framework in an African country. The phases include identifying research priorities for which biotechnology application plays a key role, formulating and implementing an appropriate research agenda, establishing relevant national policies, and providing for transfer and delivery of research products.

Priorities, experiences, and methodologies have been presented primarily from Kenya's perspective, with some other countries' experience included as well. Undertaking a priority-setting exercise related to national agricultural objectives provides a first step toward creating an appropriate research agenda. Combined experiences have recognized the importance of stressing that when biotechnology is used to address agricultural objectives it must be built on a strong foundation of conventional research. The specific priorities identified prepare officials for the steps ahead and are used to justify these decisions to institutions, governments, and donors. Socioeconomics, priorities, and end-user relations have gained renewed importance, because they are means to ensure that broader segments of the agricultural sector benefit from biotechnology research. Strong participatory mechanisms have been stressed, to ensure relevance of research, and to mobilize both public and private sectors.

An enabling policy environment has been discussed, focusing on two examples, biosafety and IPR. As shown from the Kenyan experience, and from the experiences of others studied by the International Service for National Agricultural Research (ISNAR), time frames for developing biotechnology products, capabilities, and policies are long, with the development of these products often taking from ten to fifteen years. As seen in ISNAR's policy seminars, biosafety competence is of the highest national importance, regardless of the technological level of the country. Significant progress has been made in this area in Kenya, but other African nations have much preparatory work to do. However, managing the biosafety process in Kenya remains critical to its success, and links must be built between the framework (policies, guidelines), the people involved, the instillation of a scientifically sound review process, and the appropriate feedback mechanisms.

As Kenya's biotechnology research grows and it is confronted with requests to import genetically engineered seed, food, and livestock products, specific attention will need to be paid to food safety and public acceptance issues. The main challenge here will be to supply consumers and growers with information focused on their needs and interests, summarizing discussions and scientific facts regarding modified foods.

With regard to IPR, there is only limited evidence of the private sector's role in relation to research. Most efforts are still handled as traditional public goods, without invoking any form of intellectual property protection. Kenya has made progress in developing national IPR expertise, but clearly agriculture will not be a major factor in this regard for some time. These developments are more relevant with regard to deliberations regarding the WTO.

Funding was another factor mentioned. Here, a strong reliance on donor support was made evident. Thus, sustainable funding policies and mechanisms will be needed to ensure that the growth achieved thus far will be maintained. This is why building capacity and competency in biotechnology poses complex and difficult investment decisions for developing countries. With regard to implementing Kenya's research agenda, there is an increasing need for and demand on technical, financial, and managerial resources. Clearly, as these demands grow, further effort in regard to the specifics of managing biotechnology will be needed. This has also been emphasized in the policy seminars, where enhancing the management of biotechnology research has been given high importance. However, training opportunities are limited, with most support provided instead for fundamental research.

Providing for the transfer and delivery of products arising from biotechnology-based research requires special attention because of regulatory issues, product-quality standards, and difficulties with consumer acceptance. To meet such needs, institutional partnerships and collaboration are crucial. However, they are also complicated by the nature of the private sector, proprietary technologies, and regulatory concerns. The national programs can take advantage of research undertaken by international programs that have identified traits of potential utility to small-scale farmers and are advancing this work toward field trials. However, many issues regarding technology transfer will still exist, especially as the utility of biotechnology has been demonstrated in a wide range of crops that are important for developing-country food security.

REFERENCES

Alhassan, Walter S. 2003. *Agrobiotechnology application in West and Central Africa (2002 survey outcome)*. Ibadan, Nigeria: IITA.

Cohen, Joel I., César A. Falconi, and John Komen. 1998. Strategic decisions for agricultural biotechnology: Synthesis of four policy seminars. International Services for National Agricultural Research

(ISNAR) Briefing Paper No. 38. The Hague: ISNAR.

Erbisch, K. H., and K. M. Maredia, eds. 2003. *Intellectual property rights in agricultural biotechnology*. 2d. ed. New York: CABI Publishing.

Food and Agricultural Organization-World Health Organization (FAO-WHO). 1995. *Report of the FAO technical consultation on food allergies*. Rome: FAO.

Grindle, M. S., and J. W. Thomas. 1991. *Public choices and policy change: The political economy of reform in developing countries*. Baltimore: Johns Hopkins University Press.

Huang, Jikun, Ruifa Hu, Carl E. Pray, Fangbin Qiao, and Scott Rozell. 2003. Biotechnology as an alternative to chemical pesticides: A case study of *Bt* cotton in China. *Agricultural Economics* 29:55-67.

Intermediary Biotechnology Service (IBS). 1997. *BioServe database on international initiatives in agricultural biotechnology*. The Hague: International Service for National Agricultural Research (ISNAR)-IBS.

James, Clive. 2000. Global review of commercialized transgenic crops: 1999. International Service for the Acquisition of Agribiotech Applications (ISAAA) Briefs No. 17: Preview. Ithaca, N.Y.: ISAAA.

————. 2001. Global review of commercialized transgenic crops: 2001. International Service for the Acquisition of Agribiotech Applications (ISAAA) Briefs No. 24: Preview. Ithaca, N.Y.: ISAAA.

James, Clive, and Anatole F. Krattiger. 1996. Global review of the field-testing and commercialization of transgenic plants: 1986 to 1995. The first decade of crop biotechnology. International Service for the Acquisition of Agribiotech Applications (ISAAA) Briefs No. 1. Ithaca, N.Y.: ISAAA.

Kenya Agricultural Biotechnology Platform (KABP). 1993. *Proceedings of the National Agricultural Biotechnology Workshop*. ETC Kenya Consultants B.V., September 1993. Nairobi: KARI.

Kenya Agricultural Research Institute (KARI). 1994. *Guidelines for biosafety in biotechnology*. Nairobi: KARI.

Kenya Agricultural Research Institute-National Agricultural Research Program Phase I (KARI-NARP I). 1986. *The Kenya Agricultural Research Institute, National Agricultural Research Project Phase I. 1986.* Nairobi: KARI.

Lele, Uma J. 2003. *The CGIAR at 31: An independent meta-evaluation of the consultative group on international agricultural research*. Washington, D.C.: World Bank Operations Evaluation Department.

Mailu, Andrew M., Joseph O. Mugah, and Patrobah O. Fungoh, eds. 1991. *Biotechnology in Kenya. Proceedings of the National Conference on Plant and Animal Biotechnology*. Nairobi: Initiative Publishers.

Mulongoy, K. J. 1997. *Transboundary movement of living modified organisms resulting from modern biotechnology: Issues and opportunities for policymakers*. Geneva: International Academy of the Environment.

National Advisory Committee on Biotechnology Advances and their Applications (NACBAA). 1990. *National Advisory Committee on Biotechnology Advances and their Applications for the year 2000 and beyond*. Nairobi: Ministry of Research, Science, and Technology.

National Council for Science and Technology (NCST). 1998. *National regulations and guidelines on biosafety in biotechnology*. Nairobi: NCST.

Ndiritu, Cyrus, and John Wafula. 1994. Background on biotechnology. In *Biotechnology priorities, planning, and policies: A framework for decision making,* ed. Joal I. Cohen, 1–6. A Biotechnology Research Management Study, International Service for National Agricultural Research (ISNAR) Research Report No. 6. The Hague: ISNAR.

Qaim, Matin. 1999a. Assessing the impact of banana biotechnology in Kenya. International Service for the Acquisition of Agribiotech Applications (ISAAA) Briefs No. 10. Ithaca, N.Y.: ISAAA.

———. 1999b. The economic effects of genetically modified orphan commodities: Projections for sweet potato in Kenya. International Service for the Acquisition of Agribiotech Applications (ISAAA) Briefs No. 13. Ithaca, N.Y.: ISAAA.

Sasson, Albert. 1993. *Biotechnologies in developing countries: Present and future. Volume I.* France: UNESCO Publishing.

Thitai, Grace N. W., and John S. Wafula. 1996. Identified national needs and effects of biosafety workshops. In *Biosafety capacity building: Evaluation criteria development,* ed. Ivar Virgin and Robert Frederick. Stockholm: Biotechnology Advisory Commission, Stockholm Environmental Institute.

Traynor, Patricia Leslie. 1998. Biosafety management: Key to the environmentally responsible use of biotechnology. In *Managing agricultural biotechnology: Addressing research program needs and policy implications,* ed. Joel I. Cohen, 155–65. The Hague and Wallingford, U.K.: International Service for National Agricultural Research (ISNAR) and CAB International.

Wafula, John S. 1995. Opportunities for regional planning for biotechnology under ASARECA: Turning priorities into feasible programs. In *Proceedings of a Policy Seminar on Agricultural Biotechnology for East and Southern Africa,* April 1995, South Africa. Association for the Strengthening of Agricultural Research in Eastern and Central Africa (ASARECA).

Wafula, John S., and César A. Falconi. 1998. Agricultural biotechnology research indicators: Kenya. International Service for National Agricultural Research (ISNAR) Discussion Paper No. 98-9, September 1998. The Hague: ISNAR.

Wafula, John S., and Cyrus Ndiritu. 1996. Capacity building needs for assessment and management of risks posed by living modified organisms: Perspectives of a development country. In *Transboundary movement of living modified organisms resulting from biotechnology: Issues and opportunities for policymakers,* ed. K. J. Mulongoy, P. Van der Meer, and I. Zannoni, 63–70. Geneva: International Academy of the Environment.

World Bank. 1996. *Staff appraisal report for the Republic of Kenya National Agricultural Research Project (NARP) Phase II.* Report No. 14535-KE. Washington, D.C.: World Bank.

Realizing the Potential for Private-Sector Participation in Agricultural Research in Kenya

DAVID NDII AND DEREK BYERLEE

The Context: Shifting Public and Private Roles

The emerging crisis in public funding of agricultural research throughout Africa (see chapter 15) has led to a search for new ways of doing business. One response has been to look for a greater role for private-sector support to research and development (R&D). This movement is, of course, in line with the trend in all sectors in the 1990s away from dependence on the state. Governments everywhere are asking what activities currently being undertaken by the state could be devolved to the private sector (Byerlee and Echeverria 2002). Widespread market and trade liberalization is opening new opportunities for the private sector through the removal of barriers to private-sector participation in technology development and foreign investment, and the relaxation of rules on importation, approval, and release of new technologies. In addition, the strengthening of the legal framework for intellectual property is increasingly facilitating private appropriation of the benefits of investment in R&D. Especially notable is the upsurge in legislation on intellectual property rights (IPR) for biological technologies, mandated by international agreements. Finally, market liberalization has favored agricultural commercialization, including stimulation of both traditional and nontraditional exports. This, in turn, favors private investment in R&D for agricultural inputs and agricultural processing.

Interest in private-for-profit R&D has been matched by a burgeoning interest in private not-for-profit organizations, at both the national and the local level. These so-called nongovernmental organizations (NGOs) have become major players in developmental efforts, especially as donors have looked to new mechanisms to more effectively reach the rural poor. The NGOs, with their perceived grassroots support, flexibility, and orientation to emerging developmental paradigms, such as people's participation and environmental causes, are now seen by many as central actors in rural development efforts.

These changes are already well underway in most countries, including Kenya, which has always looked to the private sector as the main engine of growth, although often private-sector activities have been heavily regulated and trade and market entry

Figure 14.1 Private Research and Development (R&D) Share of Total Agricultural R&D in Industrial Countries

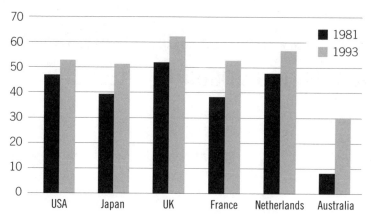

Source: Alston, Pardey, and Roseboom 1998; and Alston, Pardey, and Smith 1999.

controlled, allowing and even mandating the emergence of monopolies. Structural adjustment and market liberalization in the 1990s have changed the environment for the private sector in Kenya and led to a realigning of roles. This liberalization process is still incomplete and adjustments are ongoing.

The purpose of this chapter is to provide an overview of private investment in R&D in Kenya with a view to analyzing policy, marketing, and institutional issues that will help private R&D realize its potential in the future.

Global Trends in Private R&D

In the industrialized countries, rapid growth in private R&D has largely compensated for recent stagnation of funding in the public sector. Private funding for agricultural

Figure 14.2 Growth Rate of Public and Private Agricultural Research and Development Expenditure, 1981–93

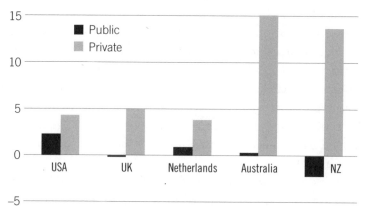

Source: Alston, Pardey, and Smith 1999.

Table 14.1 Private Agricultural Research and Development Expenditure

Country	1985	1995	Growth Rate (% per year)
Developing countries (millions 1995 US $):			
India	23.5	34.5	3.8
Indonesia	2.8	4.7	5.2
Malaysia	14.1	16.8	1.8
Philippines	6.2	10.5	5.3
Thailand	10.6	19.0	5.8
Colombia	36.5	52.8	3.7
Chile	0.4	0.3	−2.9
Industrialized countries (million 1985 US$):			
Australia	68.4	137.3	15.1
United Kingdom	471.8	614.8	4.8
United States	1966.7	2391.5	4.3

Source: Pray and Umali-Deininger (1998) for developing countries; Pardey, Roseboom, and Craig (1999) for industrialized countries.

Table 14.2 Estimated Shares of Agricultural Research Expenditure by Public Institutes, Universities, Private Companies, and Others, Various Years

Countries[a]	Public Institutes	Universities	Private Companies	Others[b]
Developing countries:				
Argentina	89	5	6	0
Brazil	63	29	8	0
Chile	75	20	4	1
Colombia	61	2	8	29
Ecuador	52	5	36	7
Mexico	50	17	28	5
Peru	65	20	5	10
Venezuela	80	10	9	1
India	43	33	16	8
The Philippines	46	18	32	4
Australia	76	14	10	0
Industrialized countries:				
Spain	48	28	24	0
United Kingdom	37	5	57	0
USA	15	31	54	0

Source: Pray and Umali-Deininger (1998).
a. Figures are from 1988 for India; from 1991 for Brazil and Spain; from 1992 for the USA; from 1993 for Colombia, the Philippines, and Australia; from 1994 for the United Kingdom; and from 1995 for Argentina, Chile, Ecuador, Mexico, Peru, and Venezuela.
b. Commodity groups, NGOs, etc.

341

research in these countries averaged half of total R&D spending in the agricultural sector in 1993, a sharp jump from 41 percent in 1981 (figure 14.1). This represents a growth rate of over 5 percent during this period, and more than double the growth in public funding (figure 14.2).

Data on private investment in R&D in developing countries are scarce and unreliable. However, to date, private R&D has played a relatively small role in developing countries, especially in Africa (Pray and Umali-Deininger 1998). Available evidence for a number of countries suggests that private investments average around 10 to 15 percent of total agricultural R&D expenditures (tables 14.1 and 14.2). Data for sub-Saharan Africa (SSA) are absent, but one estimate by the International Service for National Agricultural Research (ISNAR) puts it at 3 percent of total expenditures, although, as shown in the following, the percentage in Kenya is much above this figure.

Although private-sector investment in developing countries is expanding rapidly, the response by the private sector does not yet seem to be sufficient to fill the gap left by declining support from the public sector. In fact, including both public- and private-sector funding, research intensities in the industrialized world average 5 to 8 percent of agricultural gross domestic product (GDP), compared to an estimated 0.6 percent in developing countries. This implies a ratio of about 1:10 in relative spending on R&D between the developing and industrial countries, a gap that is widening.

General Principles for Analyzing the Role of Private R&D

The distinction between public and private research must begin with a distinction between the funding and execution of research. Traditionally, the public sector has funded research carried out in the public sector, while private companies have supported their own research. However, this distinction is no longer clear-cut, as public funding is sometimes used to support research carried out in the private sector, and public research organizations increasingly draw on private sources to support their activities. In practice there are many combinations of funding and execution of research are possible. These public-private interactions reflect a move away from the private sector being viewed as a competitor to public hegemony in agricultural R&D, to that sector being seen as complementary. Traditionally, public organizations have had a comparative advantage in upstream research, while private organizations usually have had specific skills in technology refinement and market development. This has led to various forms of joint public-private sector ventures.

A second distinction is between public and private goods. Public goods in agricultural research are those technologies and knowledge where benefits cannot be appropriated because benefits cannot be restricted to those who might pay for them, and where consumption of the good does not reduce its supply to others (Pray and Umali-Deininger 1998). Typically, knowledge that is embodied in new inputs is a private good, while "disembodied" knowledge, such as crop management information and basic scientific knowledge, is a public good. However, the boundaries between

342

public and private goods are shifting as new means (e.g., strengthening of IPRs) or technologies (e.g., hybrid seed) allow private actors to more cost-effectively appropriate benefits. Even management technologies that increasingly depend on computerized models and expert systems may be private goods in the future, because they are embodied in copyrighted computer software.

A third distinction is whether private R&D is supported by agribusiness corporations that can appropriate benefits through so-called proprietary technologies in which new knowledge is embodied in either inputs or processing, or whether R&D is supported by the collective action of farmers through a levy or check-off to fund research that they may or may not execute. In the case of collective action, the private sector can also support research on nonproprietary technologies, especially if contributions to research are made legally binding on all beneficiaries. All of the preceding concepts define the potential for private R&D. Private investment in practice depends on a host of other factors (Pray and Umali-Deininger 1998), such as:

- Market size,
- Overall business environment,
- Location specificity of technologies that determine revenues from R&D investments, and
- Factors such as access to strategic research, economies of size and scope, human capital, incentive systems, and IPR enforcement that determine costs of R&D.

Pray and Umali-Deininger (1998) combine these various factors to show how this is likely to affect private R&D investment in different types of technologies in developing countries. Private funding is concentrated in technology areas with opportunities to appropriate benefits, especially machinery, chemicals, and hybrid seed. However, in most developing countries, private funding of research on machinery and chemicals is low because these technologies are not highly location-specific, and developing countries use products of private R&D performed in industrial countries. That is, while agrochemical, machinery, and food processing industries continue to be largely located in North America, it is unlikely that private R&D in developing countries (and other countries such as Australia and New Zealand) will ever reach the high levels it has reached in Europe and North America.

For private R&D by multinationals, the share of investment in plant breeding and plantation agriculture, which are much more location-specific technologies than are chemicals, food processing, and machinery, is two-thirds. With changes in opportunities for intellectual property protection, private investment in biological technologies has increased especially rapidly. Factors affecting private not-for-profit investment in R&D by NGOs are much more difficult to characterize, in part because the motivation and support for NGOs is highly diverse. Most NGOs work at the local level, where involvement in research is likely to focus on adaptive research with immediate payoffs, and its scope will necessarily be limited by financing. However, some NGOs have much broader mandates, such as environmental conservation at a national or regional level, and may be able to support research on a broader scale. Finally, some NGOs are established with the primary objective of carrying out research, especially some foundations endowed for this purpose.

Overview of Private Agricultural R&D Financing in Kenya

In Kenya, as elsewhere, the actual and potential participants in agricultural R&D take various overlapping organizational forms that can be seen as a continuum ranging from pure public (tax-financed) research organizations at one end to commercialized R&D activity on the other. In between are various semipublic and collective interest organizational forms, including farmer and other producer associations, development NGOs, universities, and independent research institutes. Kenya is also host to some nonprofit international research institutes, which complement the national agricultural research system and increasingly collaborate with the private sector.

Farmer organizations and a few agribusiness concerns have been the dominant actors in private agricultural R&D in Kenya. Tea and coffee producers finance their respective national research institutes through levies on marketed output (Kangasniemi 2002). These two crops contribute half the gross value of marketed agricultural production and close to 40 percent of merchandise exports. The statutory boards responsible for sugar and pyrethrum also impose a research levy from the marketed output, but this is largely used to finance recurrent costs of research on these crops at Kenya Agricultural Research Institute (KARI). Individual private agribusiness concerns have been the principal actors in research on malting barley, pineapples, tobacco, and oilseed crops.

Only crude estimates of total private expenditures in agricultural R&D in Kenya are available. In a national survey of private R&D activity in all sectors, conducted by the National Council for Science and Technology, agricultural R&D accounted for 42 percent of private R&D outlays and 60 percent of the full-time research scientists engaged by private commercial enterprises (Makau 1988). This survey estimated annual agricultural R&D by commercial enterprises at US$1.25 million and farmer-financed agricultural research at US$2.2 million. By comparison, the government institutes spent US$20 million (average over 1985 and 1986 expenditures as reported by Roseboom and Pardey 1993). Combining the enterprise and farmer-financed outlays suggests a private share close to 15 percent, as estimated by Beynon et al. (1988). This is close to or higher than the developing world average and much higher than the average for SSA.

Agribusiness Investment in R&D

Agricultural Input Industries: Seed

Maize, Kenya's most important food crop, is largely produced by smallholders, who consume up to 80 percent of what they produce. Average maize yields increased from 0.87 tons per ha in the late 1950s to 1.85 tons per ha in the late 1980s, largely because of the expansion of hybrid maize, which accounted for 64 percent of the planted area in the late 1980s (Karanja and Oketch 1990). Credit for this impressive performance is due to public-sector breeding efforts, which have produced over twenty hybrids, combined with efficient seed production and dissemination by the Kenya Seed Company (KSC).

The KSC is one of a number of commercial entities hitherto owned and controlled by (mostly white) commercial farmers that the government of Kenya co-opted into the national agricultural development strategy after independence. Other examples are the Kenya Cooperative Creameries (KCC), the Kenya Farmers Association (KFA), and the Kenya Planters Cooperative Union (KPCU). The government acquired a 51 percent equity stake in KSC through the Agricultural Development Corporation (ADC) and granted it exclusive rights to multiplication and distribution of varieties and hybrids bred by KARI. The company was provided a national monopoly on certified maize seed until 1993, when import liberalization opened the domestic market to imported seed. The KSC initially used the distribution network of the KFA, which was then the main distributor of agricultural inputs, but over time, it built its own distributor network to over three thousand stockists. Recently, KSC has developed some breeding capability of its own.

Although KSC continues to have exclusive access to KARI breeding material, liberalization of the seed industry has attracted several national and multinational competitors. These include the Oil Crops Development Company, Cargill International, Pioneer Seeds, and Western Seed Company. Private entrants have also been influenced by the increased scope for commercial exploitation of R&D investment in plant varieties following the enactment of plant breeders' rights legislation in 1994 (Seed and Plant Varieties Act). The most significant entrant so far is Oil Crops Development Ltd. (OCD), which has made substantial investment in adapting imported breeding material to the local agro-ecological conditions. Previously, OCD was engaged in oilseed R&D for its parent company (East African Industries, a subsidiary of Unilever), which had a virtual monopoly in edible oils before liberalization. The OCD entry into the maize seed market was prompted in part by erosion of the parent company's edible oils monopoly following liberalization, because it has undermined the scope for recouping investment in the nonproprietary oilseed R&D. These market developments, as well as KARI's desire to earn revenues from its hybrid development program, have prompted an effort to redefine KARI-KSC informal collaboration. A memorandum of understanding signed in 1995 obliges the KSC to remit a royalty to KARI, but this is yet to be effected. A review of revenue-generating options commissioned by KARI (Delloite and Touche Consulting 1997) estimated seed royalties' potential at Ksh 60–80 million for 1995–96 (US$1–1.5 million), close to 8 percent of the KARI annual operating budget.

The considerable private-sector interest in the seed sector calls for rationalization of the regulatory framework. The KSC continues to have exclusive access to KARI breeding material. At the same time, there is a growing perception that the overall quality of KSC maize seed has declined, and claims of adulterated seeds have been

345

reported in the press (both vigorously denied by KSC). The National Seed Quality Control Services, a unit within KARI previously responsible for seed certification, has been transformed into an autonomous organization now known as the Kenya Plant Health Inspection Service (KEPHIS), answerable to the Ministry of Agriculture. Presently, the KEPHIS mandate is limited to ex ante seed quality certification, but these perceptions indicate that it should become more proactive (e.g., by investigating claims of seed adulteration and providing independent public information). Beyond that, a clear competition policy needs to be formulated for the industry. Researchers disagree on whether or not imported lines can form substitutes for domestic hybrids, although in the long run hybrids developed by the private sector likely will capture a significant share of a liberalized market. However, exclusive KARI licensing to KSC may be leading to an oligopolistic industry in which KSC competes with one or two large multinational firms. Experience elsewhere shows that a competitive seed industry often depends on equal access to public germplasm. This is especially important for small-scale, start-up seed companies that do not have the capacity to carry out their own R&D. For example, the public research corporation in Brazil has an agreement to supply maize inbreds to a consortium of small seed companies in return for royalties on seed sold (Garcia 1998). These small seed companies now command a significant share of the market and compete effectively against large companies, including multinationals. At the same time, the royalties earned pay a large share of the operating budget of the public maize research program.

High-Value Crops: The Horticulture Export Sector

Horticultural products, mainly cut flowers, vegetables, and fruits, have grown rapidly since the early 1970s, from 27,000 tons valued at US$10 million in 1973, to 300,000 tons valued at US$250 million in 1996. Kenya is one of the leading and most diversified horticultural product exporters in SSA, exporting seventy-five different products to more than a dozen markets. In 1992, Kenya accounted for 54 percent of SSA's cut flower exports to the European Community (EC), 30 percent of processed fruits and vegetables exports, and 5 percent of fresh fruits and vegetable exports (Jaffee 1995).

The private sector almost exclusively has developed the industry. It has received relatively little production, marketing, and infrastructure support services from the government, especially when compared with cereals, coffee, and tea. A National Horticultural Research Station existed prior to independence, but its activity level declined after independence as national policy objectives, and hence research resources, shifted to food (mostly maize and wheat) self-sufficiency. An oversight agency, the Horticultural Crops Development Authority (HCDA) was created in 1967, but whether it has actively promoted the industry or has been a passive follower is a contested issue. For instance, Jaffee (1995, 341) contends that, hampered by vague powers, little authority, inadequate funding, frequent management changes, and lack of policy guidance, the HCDA's support to the export trade was limited to "operating a small shed at the airport, convening meetings between exporters and airfreight suppliers, and instituting common standards for packaging." The HCDA vigorously contests this, arguing that the private sector has thrived in the industry precisely because it has pursued a policy of facilitating the private sector (as opposed to competing with or stifling it, as have other regulatory boards). The HCDA points to the fact that it organized and nurtured the Fresh Produce Exporters Association (FPEAK), including surrendering part of its levy funds to finance it (FPEAK operated out of HCDA's offices initially).

A 1991 survey found twenty-six horticultural exporting companies, but the six largest exporters accounted for 70 percent of total exports (Jaffee 1995). Foreign firms dominate processed fruits and vegetables and the cut-flower trade, while local firms dominate the fresh fruits and vegetable trade. Market concentration and foreign ownership is highest in processed fruits and vegetables, reflecting the predominance of canned pineapples by Del Monte, which invested heavily in an ailing Kenyan company in the 1970s. A similarly large investment in 1969 by a Danish firm, Dansk Chrysanthemum Kultur (DSK), transformed the cut-flower industry from a cottage industry into an important export industry. Although DSK divested in 1976, a substantial proportion of the cut-flower industry is a direct spin-off from the firm's operations and technical expertise.

The horticultural export industry demands mainly four types of research services—adaptation and field trials of planting material, pest and disease management, soil management, and postharvest handling. Western Europe is the main source of planting material, but increasingly Israel and South Africa are also suppliers. A large flower producer, Oserian Development Company, initially contracted the tissue culture for its planting material to KARI. However, Oserian has since established its own research facility and is now self-sufficient in both tissue culture and laboratory services.

Typically, floriculturists undertake soil, foliage, and water analysis three to four times a year. Expertise and laboratory facilities are available at KARI, as well as at Nairobi and Egerton Universities. However, most producers have their analysis done by laboratories in the Netherlands because of the faster turnaround time (4–7 days) and a superior service package, in terms of accuracy of diagnosis, results interpretation, prescription, and follow up.

Fertilizers and pesticides are by far the largest single component of horticultural production costs. Additionally, reducing chemical use and eliminating it altogether where feasible is now an imperative because of the growing market sensitivity to eco-friendliness and food safety concerns for horticultural products. This requires primary agronomic research of a largely nonproprietary nature to develop alternative methods of pest and disease control, particularly biological methods. This need prompted the industry in 1995, out of a levy by the HCDA of 20 cents per kg of fresh produce exported, to earmark 3 cents for research, amounting to US$40,000 per year on the average. The aim is to establish a research fund that will extend grants to researchers on a competitive basis. An R&D committee with HCDA and exporter representation was established to manage the fund, but has yet to prioritize the industry's research needs and to establish operational modalities.

The horticulture industry is also benefiting from pest management research conducted by the International Center of Insect Physiology and Ecology (ICIPE) in

347

Nairobi. Founded by a Kenyan scientist, Professor Thomas Odhiambo, in 1970, ICIPE has grown to be the premier center for tropical insect science. It employs over sixty scientists and has an annual budget of US$10 million. Collaboration of ICIPE with the horticultural export industry began under an International Fund for Agricultural Development (IFAD)-United States Agency for International Development (USAID)-funded project on participatory pest management. In the project, ICIPE and FPEAK jointly work with farmers to develop improved pest management practices. The ICIPE and the industry (FPEAK and the Flower Growers Council) are negotiating technical collaboration toward the cost of evaluating a fungal pathogen that has shown promise in the control of thrips, a pest that affects most horticultural crops.

Pineapples are a special case, where a single multinational company has established a monopoly position, and that company's market position is yet to be affected by liberalization. Del Monte Kenya has been active since 1964, but in the early 1970s it invested in a new factory after securing a lease on 10,000 ha for estate production from the government, a ten-year pineapple processing monopoly, and concessional freight charges. The company took over pineapple research from KARI in the mid-1970s after it had consolidated its monopoly position in the production, processing, and exporting of the crop. The company was initially staffed by scientists attracted from the public sector, and its research has focused on improving planting material, developing agronomic techniques, and controlling a major pest (mealy bug).

R&D for Contract Production of Industrial Inputs: Barley and Tobacco

Barley and tobacco represent cases where industrial corporations have secured their input supplies through establishing a system of contractual production with growers. The corporations generally provide all inputs and technical services, and back this with their own R&D capacity.

Kenya Breweries Limited (KBL) has been the sole buyer of malting barley in Kenya, with over 20,000 ha of the crop under cultivation by its contract farmers, to whom it supplies all inputs and extension services. Two-thirds of its contractees are medium-scale farmers with 30–50 ha, and the rest are large farms. Kenya Breweries established its own research station in 1975 with one agronomist, largely out of dissatisfaction with the low priority accorded to the crop by the public sector, and by 1978 it had effectively taken over all the research. However, an outbreak of barley yellow dwarf virus in 1989 prompted KBL to seek technical collaboration with KARI in which KBL agreed to contribute US$500,000 over six years. The KARI was successful in finding a variety to control the virus (Beynon et al. 1998).

The KBL monopoly in the beer market resulted from import protection. Following import liberalization in 1993, it has faced stiff competition, mainly from South African Breweries. However, while competition in the beer market may squeeze R&D investment, liberalization has also opened the way for KBL to commercialize its R&D directly by multiplying and distributing certified barley seed, which the KSC hitherto monopolized.

In the case of tobacco, BAT Kenya Ltd. has developed an outgrower network with over ten thousand small-scale farmers, each cultivating about 0.5 ha of the crop, who are provided a complete service package that includes seed, credit, and extension. The company's investment in tobacco production started in the mid-1970s in response to nationalization of BAT Tanzania, which had previously supplied Kenya. Research was initially focused on yield improvement with a view to attaining self-sufficiency. Once it became evident that production potential exceeded BAT's domestic demand, research shifted toward quality improvement with a view to developing exports. Between 20 and 30 percent of the crop is now exported.

The BAT tobacco-processing monopoly was broken in the early 1990s following the entry of Mastermind Tobacco, a new local company established by a former BAT employee. Mastermind's market position was subsequently strengthened by a strategic partnership with R. J. Reynolds, one of BAT's major international competitors. R. J. Reynolds entered the regional market by acquiring Tanzania's state-owned cigarette manufacturer, which was owned by BAT prior to nationalization.

Policies Influencing Corporate R&D Development and Public-Private Collaboration

The preceding review shows that private business R&D investment has been considerable in a number of crops, and there are now several success stories of payoffs to this investment. In the past, much of the corporate investment in agricultural R&D was motivated by the need to develop a reliable source of raw materials and the leverage provided by monopoly rents. Although liberalization has undermined both, it has also opened up opportunities to commercialize R&D where incumbency could confer "first mover advantage." Realizing the full potential of private R&D investment will require the government to strengthen institutions (particularly those concerned with property rights' enforcement), enhance incentives, and nurture public-private collaboration.

Under Kenya's income tax law, firms are allowed to charge all R&D outlays on current income—that is, capital assets are fully depreciated in the first year. The case for other financial concessions, to stimulate private R&D start-ups in particular, also needs to be evaluated. Experience with export incentive schemes in Kenya has shown that the financial incentive is easily offset by high compliance costs caused by unwieldy administration procedures. Direct subsidy schemes such as matching grants are an alternative to tax incentives. The Agricultural Research Fund (ARF), a competitive research grants scheme established in 1990 by KARI, is a vehicle that could be expanded to include matching investment grants or venture capital for private R&D.

The Kenya experience also shows growing public-private collaboration. The KARI actively seeks opportunities for cost recovery for its research products (see chapter 15). It also seeks various types of joint ventures with private companies to test promising technology in contractual arrangements with private firms. Such contracts exploit the highly specialized human and physical resources at KARI and the demand for a research product from the private sector. Although currently affecting only small segments of the overall research system, such schemes are bound to grow, as market mechanisms become more prevalent in guiding agricultural development and R&D activities. The main policy issue for such arrangements is to ensure that public-sector research remains, and is seen as being, motivated by broader societal objectives and is not perceived as having "sold out" to industry. For this reason, public-private ventures will need to be approached with caution, because they can quickly distort program priorities and attention. The KARI will need to develop a clear and transparent policy for ensuring that such collaboration is consistent with the public interest, applying IPRs to protect technologies developed fully or partly with public funds, providing free access to protected technologies to other researchers, and sharing revenues within KARI. It will also need to strengthen its legal and business skills to identify potential products to commercialize, to select private partners, and to negotiate contracts with them. This will involve some combination of in-house expertise and contracting of skills from outside. The costs of acquiring these skills can be considerable, and KARI's research managers need to carefully evaluate costs against expected benefits. Costs of establishing an office of technology commercialization might take several years to be recovered, especially because only a small proportion of products is ultimately commercially successful. Research managers and scientists will also need training in several aspects of joint ventures, including IPRs.

Finally, it remains to be seen whether the Treasury will see income earned by KARI through public-private collaboration as additional income or whether it will substitute for public appropriations. Evidence from China suggests that the income generation by public research corporations has largely been offset by a reduction in public funding support (Pray and Umali-Deininger 1998). This issue needs to be carefully monitored in KARI.

Farmer Financing of Research

The Coffee and Tea Research Foundations

The Kenya government established the Coffee Research Foundation (CRF) and the Tea Research Foundation of Kenya (TRFK) as autonomous parastatal organizations soon after independence. They fall under parent marketing boards, the Coffee Board and the Tea Board of Kenya, and are governed by boards of directors representing their parent body, the Ministry of Agriculture, and farmers. Their activities are financed primarily from statutory levies, but they also raise revenue from sale of seedlings and occasionally receive contributions from the government and external donors (usually less than 5 percent of their budgets). Both crops are marketed through a centralized auction managed by the parent bodies, which makes the levies easy to collect.

The coffee and tea industries have sustained higher levels of research funding than government-funded institutions even as donor support to the latter has increased. In the early 1990s, the CRF operating expenditure per full-time equivalent (FTE) scientist averaged US$60,000, and for the TRFK it was US$ 25,000, compared to KARI's US$8,000. Despite this relatively favorable resource situation, the industry structure on which it is based is in transition toward a more decentralized market-based system, and it remains unclear whether these changes will affect research financing and management positively, adversely, or not at all.

Coffee production has been falling since the mid-1980s because of weak international prices, poor weather, and management problems in the smallholder sector. Production in the 1990s has averaged 85,000 tons, down from a peak crop of 130,000 tons in 1983–84. To maintain the level of research funding in the face of declining revenue, the levy was increased from 1 percent to 3 percent of revenue in 1992 with the support of large-scale coffee farmers. Smallholders were largely against this increase, although this may be a reflection of their dissatisfaction with other aspects of the Coffee Board's performance. The industry is presently polarized between farmers who want oversight of the industry to remain with the Coffee Board and those who want the board abolished altogether. The latter case would require an alternative system of collecting the research levy, which may not be as cost-effective. At the same time, however, it could release resources to research from money currently absorbed by the board for marketing services (typically 10–15 percent of revenue).

The smallholder tea industry is under similar pressure to reorganize on account of farmer dissatisfaction with the performance of the Kenya Tea Development Authority (KTDA), a parastatal body that manages forty factories processing smallholder production, and markets the tea on their behalf.

Research Foundations for Other Commercial Crops

The overall success of the CRF and the TRFK has prompted consideration of the model for other commercial crops. Levies have been instituted for pyrethrum and sugar, but these go directly to the commodity boards, which then give a grant to KARI. Presently, up to 60 percent of the recurrent cost of KARI's sugar research, and 40 percent of the pyrethrum research, is financed by levy proceeds. A proposal by the sugar industry to establish a Sugar Research Foundation was adopted by the government, and all sugar research work previously carried out by KARI has been passed on to the now operational National Sugar Research Foundation based at Kibos near Kisumu. Similar proposals have been put forward for the pyrethrum, cotton, and oilseeds industries.

Yet even as the sugar industry begins to set up an autonomous research foundation, its survival is threatened by imported sugar. The industry is unable to compete with imports partly because of rampant duty evasion by importers and partly because of processing inefficiencies in the government-owned mills. Six out of seven sugar factories in the country are government owned and operated. Thus, although the scope for increasing farmer financing is considerable, farmer support for research could easily be undermined by overall policy uncertainty if the transition to privatization and liberalization is not properly managed. Conversely, greater accountability to stakeholders would enhance overall efficiency and profitability, thereby stimulating the demand for research.

351

The Emerging Policy Framework for Farmer Support to R&D

Direct funding of research in Africa through group action by farmers dates from colonial times, when regional research centers for export crops such as tea, coffee, and cocoa were often supported by levies. Most of these centers became national in scope after independence, and the use of levies declined. Levies are again receiving considerable attention in efforts to finance research in Africa. In today's climate of austerity, levies have obvious appeal for various reasons:

- Farmer contributions internalize funding to the initial beneficiaries of research products and reduce demands on public resources for research.
- Those who benefit most from research pay more and therefore the system is relatively equitable.
- Direct funding of research can be linked to greater farmer decision-making power on the type of research that is conducted, contributing to a demand-driven research system.

From an economics perspective, research levies can be an efficient way to fund research relative to the use of general tax revenues, and are also equitable because the cost of research is borne in direct proportion to those who benefit (Alston, Pardey, and Roseboom 1998). Of course, as the Kenya case shows, this form of funding works best for commercial products that pass through a concentrated marketing channel, making it administratively feasible and cost-effective to collect the contributions or levy. It is least appropriate for traditional food crops (e.g., cassava) that pass through informal marketing channels, and for noncommodity or factor research. Potential certainly exists to expand the levy system further in Kenya, even for basic food products, such as maize, wheat, and milk, because the marketed share of these products passes through a few processors.

In Kenya, little rationale is apparent for fixing the amount of the levy. In some cases, such as tea, the levy of 0.16 percent of the value of agricultural output is low by international standards, while in the case of coffee it is relatively high at 1.8 percent. International experience suggests that a levy of 0.5–1 percent can often be justified to pay largely for applied and adaptive research. The real value of a levy is realized only if farmers' contribution to funding is combined with farmers' participation in setting the research agenda. It is most effective when initiated and supported by farmers, who see it as in their interest, as beneficiaries, to invest in agricultural research, rather then seeing it as just another tax. However, legislation is usually needed to ensure that the levy is obligatory on all farmers in order to avoid "free riders." Thus levies for research should be encouraged only with appropriate institutional means to ensure farmer participation in determining the level of contribution as well as in setting priorities for the research to be funded.

In Kenya, although farmers have undoubtedly been represented in the commodity boards and research foundations supported by the levies, or on the research advisory councils to these bodies, it is time to revisit the governance of these funds. In the case of coffee and tea, a case may be made for separating the research foundation from the commodity boards in order to remove them from the political controversies surrounding the continuation of the boards. Farmer representation on the foundations could then be strengthened relative to the boards. Also, it is not clear if the automatic allocation of levies for pyrethrum and sugar through commodity boards can be justified relative to a more competitive allocation mechanism in which growers have more voice in setting priorities.

In several countries, notably Australia and Uruguay, levies are matched by government funds on a one-to-one ratio. This is because where farmers determine the levy amount and its allocation, they will typically focus on short-term research priorities and will not invest at socially optimal levels in more basic and longer-term research, or in research with broader societal benefits (e.g., protection of the environment). Government provision of matching funds can be justified in order to support this broader agenda. At present, government funding for the levied crops is minimal and suggests the need for wider policy debates on the merits of matching funds.

Finally, there is the issue of who should execute the research supported by the levies. In Kenya, following the example of coffee and tea, the trend is toward keeping funding and execution of research together by establishing commodity-specific research centers supported by farmer funds. Following the trend toward separation of research funding and research execution, there is no reason to expect commodity research foundations or producer organizations to be the most efficient suppliers of research services, except for adaptive research to test and refine technologies on-farm. Proliferation of commodity research foundations that undertake their own research raises efficiency issues on account of economies of scale and scope and research synergy that may be forgone, particularly in more strategic and basic research and for smaller industries. The pyrethrum and oilseeds industries may, for instance, be too small to sustain a comprehensive and independent research infrastructure without exploiting complementarities with related crops. Although setting up research funds to finance contract and collaborative research would be preferable for the smaller sectors, the responsiveness of public-sector organizations (KARI and the universities) to their research needs is an issue of concern to the industries. The most efficient option is likely to be some form of competitive grants fund, where all parties, including public research institutes and the private sector, can compete to supply research services, and where producers have considerable influence in the fund's governance and in setting demands for research services.

Role of NGOs in Research and Extension

The Kenyan Experience with NGOs in Research and Extension

Increasingly, NGOs are being looked upon to provide socially valuable, but commercially unrewarding, research and extension (R&E) to the rural poor and marginal agro-economic zones. These are zones where government services have failed, either because the beneficiaries constitute weak political interest groups or because of weak institutional capacity to respond to their demands. This contention would seem to be borne out in Kenya by the fact that NGO R&E projects are concentrated in the arid and semi-arid districts. The autonomy of NGOs has various advantages, including highly motivated staff prepared to work in difficult conditions, staff less prone to professional biases (e.g., agronomists' preoccupation with yield improvement through use of external inputs), and considerable flexibility to respond to local demands, which make them potentially highly effective community mobilizers (Kaimowitz 1993; Wiggins and Cromwell 1995).

The level of NGO activity in R&E-related projects in Kenya is relatively low in comparison with NGO presence in other sectors, such as the finance (microenterprise credit) and social sectors. As in other countries, the main focus of NGOs engaged in R&E activities is environmental management, through the promotion of agroforestry and wood-fuel energy conservation technologies. The Kenya Energy and Environmental Organization (KENGO) is the most active NGO in this area. It pursues its objectives through R&D on, and promotion of, improved wood fuel stoves, agroforestry research, and by supporting community afforestation initiatives. The Cooperative for American Relief Everywhere (CARE)-Kenya, an internationally based NGO, also has a large agroforestry extension project employing fifty-nine technical personnel in western Kenya. The project provides extension on agroforestry-based techniques of soil fertility improvement and on seed variety screening. Maize yields among participating farmers have increased by one-third using these practices. The R&E activities of other NGOs are mostly small, localized, and peripheral to the organization's core activities or competencies (see also chapter 10).

Increasing the Participation of NGOs in R&D

Various concerns are raised about the long-term viability of the NGO model. In Kenya, as elsewhere, NGOs are criticized for lack of focus, poor coordination among themselves and with others, and weak monitoring and evaluation (White and Eicher 1999). A case study of NGOs involved in soil and water conservation in Machakos District found more collaboration between NGOs and the technical personnel of the relevant government ministry than between NGOs themselves (Kaluli 1990). In 1993, the Kenyan government enacted much-resisted legislation to coordinate NGO activity through the establishment of a registration and coordination board in the Office of the President. This has prompted NGOs to give more attention to coordination, while by and large the government has not interfered with their program activities, as was earlier feared.

KENGO is an example of an institutional structure that has been able to overcome most of the criticisms regarding coordination and sustainability. Founded in 1981, KENGO is both a national stakeholder network and an operational NGO in its own right, which has enabled it to secure collaboration with other NGOs, with government ministries (including financial support), and with university research. The NGOs in Kenya have developed useful R&E programs at the local level, with a special focus on environmental concerns. This parallels experience in other countries, where success-

354

ful research activities of NGOs in natural resource management have been reported (Buckles, Triomphe, and Sain. 1998). However, their research activities are downstream, and tend to focus on participatory approaches to technology transfer rather than on formal research per se. Collaboration between formal research organizations and NGOs is needed to exploit complementary skills and provide needed technical backstopping to NGOs.

In a few countries, NGOs with a specific research mandate have been established, sometimes to carry out upstream-type agricultural research activities, including biotechnology research. However, these research-type NGOs are usually backed by heavy corporate support and sometimes an endowed foundation (e.g., the TATA corporation group in India [one of India's largest corporations with interests in many industries], and the Polar group in Venezuela [a beer producer]. Such NGOs are likely to develop in Africa, as industrial corporations grow and their need for an improved social image becomes more apparent.

Conclusions

This chapter reveals an active and growing private-sector participation in R&D in Kenya, together with public-sector efforts to facilitate and respond to these changes. The role of the private sector will necessarily change with the ongoing process of market liberalization. In some cases, this will reduce incentives for private investment in R&D, but on balance, liberalization is likely to increase private R&D efforts as existing firms seek to enhance their competitive position, and new firms enter.

Despite these gains, the public sector will play a lead role in research for many years to come. First, many products of research will continue to be public goods that do not attract private investment. These include crop, livestock, and resource management practices, where the major product of research is information (e.g., integrated pest management). Even with stronger IPRs, private-sector research will focus on certain aspects of commercial agriculture. For example, in plant-breeding research, it is difficult to see how it will be cost-effective for private firms to enforce plant varietal rights for self-pollinated crops in the smallholder sector, where seed can easily be passed from farmer to farmer. Private participation will also be limited by market size, a major determinant of private investment in R&D. This places small countries and secondary commodities at a disadvantage in attracting private R&D. Most countries still restrict technology imports (e.g., varietal release procedures, and regulations on imported seed). Thus, private R&D in small and medium-sized countries, such as Kenya, will prosper only where countries adopt open-border policies for technology flows within the region, so that private companies can target the region rather than a single country.

Developing private R&D is a long-term process that requires considerable input from public R&D, especially in basic and strategic research. Even proprietary hybrids are often based on pre-breeding and breeding research in the public sector. In the U.S. hybrid seed industry, public-sector inbreds accounted for one-half of the inbreds used

355

up to the 1960s, some thirty years after the initiation of private-sector R&D. In developing countries outside China, hybrids based on private R&D make up only 60 percent of the sales of hybrid maize seed by the private sector; the rest of the hybrid seed sold by the private sector is based on hybrids developed in the public sector. Also, the main initial source of scientific personnel for private-sector R&D efforts is the national agricultural research institute of the public sector.

Public-sector research organizations such as KARI must have long-run strategies to facilitate and respond to a growing private sector. These include:

- Backing private-sector R&D with strategic and basic research in the public sector;
- Focusing public-sector research in areas unlikely to attract the private sector because of the nature of the technology or the nature of the farmer (e.g., farmers in more marginal areas);
- Avoidance of activities that may undermine incentives for private R&D (e.g., hybrid maize research in the long run in Kenya); and
- Developing institutional mechanisms (e.g., specialized competitive funds) and appropriate legal frameworks for joint ventures between the public and private sectors.

Finally, the growing private-sector role in global research and the increasing tendency toward protection of biological technologies will soon pose new challenges for Kenya. Public organizations, such as KARI, will have to seek global alliances with the international public and private sector to maintain access to the latest technologies, many of which will be subject to patents on genes or processes. At the same time, the public sector will face new challenges in regulating these new technologies, whether in the public or private sectors, for potential biological and environmental risks, and in providing information to both farmers and consumers.

REFERENCES

Alston, Julian M., Phillip G. Pardey, and Johannes Roseboom. 1998. Financing agricultural research: International investment patterns and policy perspectives. *World Development* 26:1057–72.

Alston, Julian M., Phillip G. Pardey, and Vincent Smith, eds. 1999. *Paying for agricultural productivity.* Baltimore: Johns Hopkins University Press.

Beynon Jonathan, Stephen A. Ackroyd, Alex D. Duncan, and Stephen Jones. 1998. *Financing the future: Options for agricultural research and extension in sub-Saharan Africa.* Oxford, U.K.: Oxford Policy Management.

Buckles, Daniel, Bernard Triomphe, and Gustavo E. Sain. 1998. *Cover crops in hillside agriculture: Farmer innovation with Mucuna.* Ottawa: International Development Research Center-International Maize and Wheat Improvement Center (IDRC-CIMMYT).

Byerlee, Derek, and Rubén G. Echeverria, eds. 2002. *Agricultural research in an era of privatization.* New York: CABI Publishing.

Deloitte and Touche Consulting. 1997. *KARI–revenue generation strategic review.* Overseas Development Administration contract reference: cntr 96 1193A. Final report. Nairobi: KARI.

Echeverria, Rubén G., Eduardo J. Trigo, and Derek Byerlee. 1996. Institutional change and effective financing of agricultural research in Latin America. Technical Paper No. 330. Washington, D.C.: World Bank.

Garcia, J. C. 1998. Country case study: Brazil. In: *Maize seed industries in developing countries,* ed. Michael L. Morris. Boulder, Colo.: Lynne Reiner.

Jaffee, Steven. 1995. The many faces of success: The development of Kenya's horticultural exports. In *Marketing Africa's high-value foods: Comparative experiences of an emergent private sector,* ed. Steven Jaffee and J. Morton. Dubuque, Iowa: Kendall Hunt.

Kaimowitz, David. 1993. The role of nongovernmental organizations in agricultural research and technology transfer in Latin America. *World Development* 21:1131–50.

Kaluli, James W. 1990. NGOs and technical change. In *Environment change and dryland management in Machakos District, Kenya 1930–1990,* ed. Mary Tiffen. Overseas Development Institute (ODI) Working Paper No. 62. London: ODI.

Kangasniemi, Jaakko. 2002. Financing agricultural research by producers' organizations. In *Agricultural research in an era of privatization,* ed. Derek Byerlee and Ruben G. Echeverria, 81–104. New York: CARI Publishing.

Karanja, Daniel D., and O. G. Oketch. 1990. The impact of research on maize yields in Kenya 1955–1988. Paper presented at the KARI Maize Review Workshop, November 1990, Kakamega, Kenya.

Makau, B. F. 1988. *Survey on private sector research and development resources and activities in Kenya.* National Council of Science and Technology (NCST) Publication No. 26. Nairobi: NCST.

Pardey, Phillip G., Johannes Roseboom, and Barbara J. Craig. 1999. Agricultural R&D investments and impacts. In *Paying for agricultural productivity,* ed. Julian M. Alston, Phillip G. Pardey, and Vincent H. Smith. Baltimore: Johns Hopkins University Press.

Pray, Carl E., and Dina Umali-Deininger. 1998. The private sector in agricultural research systems: Will it fill the gap? *World Development* 26:1127–48.

Roseboom, Johannes, and Phillip G. Pardey. 1993. *Statistical brief on the national agricultural research system of Kenya.* Indicator series project (Phase II), Statistical Brief No. 5. The Hague: International Service for National Agricultural Research (ISNAR).

Wiggins, Stephen, and Elizabeth Cromwell. 1995. NGOs and seed provision to smallholders in developing countries. *World Development* 23:413–22.

White, Robert, and Carl K. Eicher. 1999. NGOs and the African farmer: A skeptical perspective. Staff Paper No. 99–01. East Lansing, Mich.: Department of Agricultural Economics, Michigan State University. (Website at *http:/agecon.lib.unm.edu/msu/sp99–01.pdf.*)

PART 4

Resource Mobilization

Financing Agricultural Research

S T E P H E N   A K R O Y D ,   R O M A N O   M .   K I O M E ,
A N D   C Y R U S   G .   N D I R I T U

Introduction

Following steady growth in worldwide public funding for national agricultural research systems (NARS) during the 1960s and 1970s, many NARS experienced funding difficulties in the 1980s and 1990s. This was particularly true in many African countries, where governments faced growing fiscal constraints, often associated with structural adjustment programs (Brinkerhoff, Gage, and Gavian 2002). African NARS are responding to this crisis in two ways. First, as discussed in chapter 14, closer attention is being paid to the role of the private sector in the finance and delivery of agricultural research, with the introduction of cost recovery measures and the state ultimately withdrawing from those activities that can be provided by the private sector. Second, improved cost-effectiveness is being sought through enhanced priority setting, greater user orientation, and innovative mechanisms to promote competition for research funds.

This chapter examines progress in the second of these reforms, drawing on experience from Kenya. Here, public-sector agricultural research in general, and Kenya Agricultural Research Institute (KARI) in particular, are facing a crisis of both limited and unreliable provision of operating funds, and a degree of dependence upon donors that is perceived as unsustainable.

The chapter begins with a review of global trends in agricultural research financing and assesses how sub-Saharan Africa (SSA) has fared in comparison with other regions. This is followed by a more detailed analysis of trends in Kenya, highlighting key issues for sustainable agricultural research financing. The third section examines the various options that have recently been introduced or are being considered by KARI as a means of alleviating financial constraints and making more effective use of existing resources. Access to and management of funds is critical to the development of a sustainable funding base for public-sector agricultural research in Africa. The fourth section of the chapter examines how KARI manages its funding sources and how funds are allocated according to research priorities agreed upon by KARI and its funding sources. The chapter concludes with a summary of the fiscal, efficiency, and equity implications of reforms to agricultural research financing, and makes recommendations for the development of sustainable financing mechanisms for other NARS in Africa.

Trends in Agricultural Research Expenditures

Global Trends

Considerable effort has been devoted to quantifying international agricultural research expenditures and personnel (e.g., Evenson 1987; Evenson and Kislev 1975; Oram and Bindlish 1981; and Pardey, Roseboom, and Anderson 1991). This task is made difficult because of increasing complexities in public and private roles in the funding and delivery of agricultural research, and the need to establish consistent criteria for definitions of "national," "agricultural," and "research."

The International Service for National Agricultural Research (ISNAR) has compiled a comprehensive set of data (the Indicator Series). It shows that global real agricultural research expenditures grew strongly over the period 1961–85, but that both the rate of growth of expenditures and the expenditures per researcher have been falling (see Pardey, Roseboom, and Anderson 1991). Table 15.1 reproduces a recent update (Alston, Pardey, and Roseboom 1998) of the same data series to 1991 (with the notable addition of South Africa). Although the data are not directly comparable with the earlier series, they support the conclusion that, in real terms, world agricultural research expenditure continued to grow during this period, but that rates of growth had declined by the early 1980s, with some recovery by 1991.

Between 1971 and 1991, global public expenditure on agricultural research more than doubled from $7.2 billion to $14.9 billion annually (1985 international dollars). During this period, the developing country share of expenditure increased from 41 to

Table 15.1   Public Agricultural Research Expenditures, Global Trends 1971–91

Area (Number of Countries)	Agricultural Research Expenditure (1985 $PPPm)[a]			Average Annual Growth Rates (%)		
	1971	1981	1991	1971	1981	1991
Developing countries (131)	2,984	5,503	8,009	6.4	3.9	5.1
Sub-Saharan Africa (44)	699	927	968	2.5	0.8	1.6
China	457	939	1,494	7.7	4.7	6.3
Asia/Pacific, excl. China (28)	861	1,922	3,502	8.7	6.2	7.3
Latin America/Caribbean (38)	507	981	944	7.0	−0.5	2.7
West Asia and North Africa (20)	459	733	1,100	4.3	4.1	4.8
Developed countries (22)	4,298	5,713	6,941	2.7	1.7	2.3
Global total (153)	7,281	11,215	14,949	4.3	2.9	3.6

Source: Alston, Pardey, and Roseboom (1998).
a. Purchasing power parity exchange rate.

54 percent. The declining contribution from the Organization for Economic Cooperation and Development (OECD) countries is explained by a rapid increase in privately funded research in these countries from $4 billion in 1981 to $6.6 billion in 1991 (and $7 billion in 1993). This compares with total public expenditure of developing countries on agricultural research in 1991 of $8 billion (Alston, Pardey, and Roseboom 1998).

A comparative analysis of the spending patterns of agricultural research is provided by agricultural research intensity (ARI) ratios, which show agricultural research expenditures of the public sector as a proportion of agricultural gross domestic product (AgGDP). In developed countries, public spending on agricultural research increased from 1.4 percent of AgGDP in the early 1970s to 2.4 percent in 1991. These figures are five times greater than those for developing countries, whose average ARIs increased more modestly from 0.4 to 0.5 percent of AgGDP over the same period (Alston, Pardey, and Roseboom 1998).

Analysis of ARIs across developing country regions shows that during the 1970s and 1980s, SSA spent more on agricultural research as a proportion of gross domestic product (GDP) than did any other region (figure 15.1). Although this lead was reduced during the 1980s, this suggests that SSA has not been as relatively underfunded as some assessments would suggest. Yet the value and effectiveness of agricultural research has been most questionable in SSA, probably because in absolute terms the agricultural research expenditure in SSA is still low. For example, in 1974 SSA obtained only 55 percent as many "standardized publications" per scientist-year (a proxy measure of "research output") as low-income South Asian countries. Furthermore, the cost of doing a comparable piece of research was widely reckoned to be at least three times as high in SSA as in South Asia in the mid 1980s (Lipton 1988). The following section provides a more detailed analysis of research expenditure trends in SSA.

Trends in Sub-Saharan Africa

More detailed data for nineteen SSA countries up to 1991 show that total agricultural research expenditures fell by a modest 2.4 percent in real terms between 1981 and 1991, having risen 35 percent in the previous decade (figure 15.2). However, this hides significant variation between countries, and is considerably distorted by a 60 percent collapse in research spending in Nigeria, which accounted for a major share of the regional total. Excluding Nigeria, total expenditures for the remaining eighteen countries rose by 22 percent in the 1980s, faster than the 15 percent of the previous decade. In fact, between 1981 and 1991, annual growth rates were positive in thirteen countries (Burkina Faso, Ethiopia, Ghana, Kenya, Madagascar, Malawi, Mauritius, Niger, Rwanda, South Africa, Swaziland, Zambia, and Zimbabwe) and negative in only six (Botswana, Ivory Coast, Lesotho, Nigeria, Senegal, and Sudan). Nine countries experienced faster growth during the 1980s than in the 1970s.

In 1981, ARIs for SSA rose steadily to a peak of about 0.9 percent, subsequently falling to 0.7 percent in 1991 (Pardey and Roseboom 1998). South Africa's research intensity ratio rose from 1.2 percent in 1961 to reach 2.6 percent by 1991. By contrast,

Figure 15.1 Agricultural Research Intensity Ratio Across Developing Regions, 1971–91

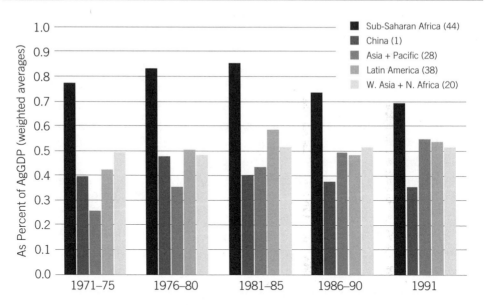

Figure 15.2 Agricultural Research Spending in Nineteen Sub-Saharan Countries, 1961–91, Puchasing Power Parity (PPP), 1985 Prices

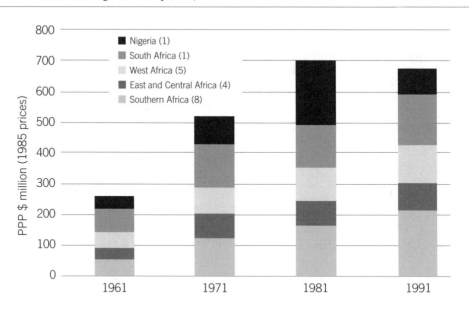

Nigeria's ratio collapsed from 0.8% in 1981 to just 0.2 percent in 1991, back to the level of 1961. Excluding these two countries, the 1991 figure rises to 0.9 percent—almost double the developing country average. However, cross-country differences remain large, With ARIs ranging from less than 0.5 percent in Nigeria, Sudan, and Ghana, to over 3 percent in Botswana and Cape Verde.

364

Data on agricultural research spending as a proportion of total government expenditures support the finding that SSA governments invest more intensively in agricultural research than do other developing countries. Despite a reduction from almost 1 percent in 1971 to 0.7 percent in 1991, SSA continued to spend proportionately more on agricultural research than did other regions. These figures compare with figures of about 0.2 percent in OECD countries, 0.2 percent in Latin America, and 0.6 percent in Asia (Tabor 1998). Within SSA, 1991 agricultural research spending as a proportion of public expenditures varied from over 2.5 percent in Zambia and Malawi to just 0.2 percent in Lesotho and Nigeria.

Although staff numbers increased in parallel with research expenditure up to 1981, the decline in research expenditure after this date resulted in spending per researcher falling 29 percent between 1981 and 1991 (16 percent excluding Nigeria). Only four countries (Botswana, South Africa, Swaziland, and Zimbabwe) were spending more per researcher in 1991 than in 1961. Of the decline in expenditures per researcher for all nineteen countries between 1981 and 1991, 12 percent can be attributed to the declining proportion of high-cost expatriate staff, and over 36 percent if South Africa and Nigeria (which employed few expatriates by 1981) are excluded. Using market exchange rates, 30 percent of all overall personnel costs in 1991 were used to pay the salaries and benefits of expatriate researchers (Pardey and Roseboom 1998).

Shortages of domestic funds have caused governments to turn increasingly to donor funds, as indicated by data from thirteen SSA countries where the share of agricultural research funds provided by donors rose from 34 percent in 1986 to 43 percent in 1991. Donor support declined in only four countries during this period. Greater reliance upon donor funds more than offsets the 14 percent decline in funds from governments during this period. However, donor dependency rates vary widely between countries, from 6 percent in Nigeria in the late 1980s to over 60 percent in Burkina Faso, Cape Verde, Mali, Senegal, Rwanda, Tanzania, and Zambia (Pardey, Roseboom, and Beintema 1997).

Agricultural Research Funding—Some Conclusions

This review of the data on research funding and expenditure has shown that:

- The deterioration in public funding of agricultural research may not be as severe or as universal as is widely perceived. Rates of growth have slowed (although even this had leveled off in developing countries by the late 1980s), but real declines are the exception rather than the rule, even in SSA.
- Agricultural research has been characterized by a rapid buildup of research personnel, declining levels of resources per researcher, and (especially in SSA) growing reliance on donor funds, none of which appear sustainable.
- The relative decline in research funding has been most pronounced in SSA, although it is not clear that SSA is particularly underfinanced in absolute terms. It was still spending more in 1991, per researcher or per dollar of AgGDP, than any other developing country region.

365

- There is therefore a danger that the lack of resources argument may be too freely used to explain poor performance (particularly in SSA), and may divert attention from the need to make more effective use of existing resources.

Agricultural Research Funding in Kenya

The most thorough assessment of aggregate expenditure data for Kenya is provided by the ISNAR data series 1961–91, which suggests that research financing by the public sector in Kenya has been relatively buoyant, growing by 4.3 percent annually in real terms over this period (table 15.2). Government institutes accounted for a fairly constant share (80–85%) of Kenya's total agricultural research expenditures by the nonprivate sector, with the semi-public institutions (the Coffee Research Foundation [CRF], Tea Research Foundation of Kenya [TRFK], and the National Irrigation Board) accounting for 13–18 percent, and academic institutions for 0–4 percent.

As a percentage of AgGDP, expenditures reached 1.7 percent in 1971, dipping to below 1.4 percent during the 1980s, and subsequently rising to almost 1.8 percent by 1991. The 1991 figure compares well with the SSA average of 0.7 percent and 0.5 percent for all developing countries (Alston, Pardey, and Roseboom 1998).

More recent data confirm that research expenditures by KARI alone peaked at 2 percent of AgGDP in 1991–92, but subsequently declined to 1 percent of AgGDP by 1997–98 (table 15.3). The rise in spending between 1987 and 1992 was driven by an increase in donor finance, much of it in capital infrastructure, equipment, and technical assistance provided under Phase I of the National Agricultural Research Project (NARP-I). During this period, donor finance accounted for over two-thirds of KARI total research budget.

Between 1992–93 and 1997–98 (NARP-Phase II), donor funding stabilized at K£30–35 million per year, but increased funding from the government of Kenya (GoK) and initiatives by KARI to generate funds internally reduced donor dependency levels to below 50 percent. In summary, although agricultural research in Kenya appears well funded, at least in comparison with other SSA countries, KARI is facing a declining financial capability in terms of both limited and unreliable provision of operating resources, and a degree of donor dependency that is perceived as being unsustainable.

Response to Financing Constraints

The KARI has responded to the financing constraints that are identified here in two ways. First, measures were introduced to reduce the extent of state financing in areas where the private sector might be willing to participate or beneficiaries might be willing to pay. Second, reforms were introduced to enhance the cost-effectiveness of remaining services through improved priority setting, by making services more user-oriented and responsive to demand, and by improving both the management of existing resources and the efficiency of service delivery. This section examines progress in the implementation of these reforms.

Table 15.2 Agricultural Researcher and Expenditure Series, Kenya, 1961–91

Agricultural Researcher and Expenditure[a]	Period							1961–91 Annual Growth Rate (%)
	1961–65	1966–70	1971–75	1976–80	1981–85	1986–90	1991	
Researchers (FTEs)	138.0	231.0	366.0	409.0	563.0	707.0	819.0	6.4
Expenditures								
(1985 Ksh million p.a.)	141.3	215.7	316.8	347.3	376.8	445.6	542.8	4.3
Expenditures (1985 PPP$):								
Government	12.9	n.a.	33.5	n.a.	54.9	61.1	76.6	—
Semi-public	3.7	n.a.	8.1	n.a.	8.5	13.1	13.2	—
Regional	7.6	n.a.	12.0	—	—	—	—	—
Academic	0.1	n.a.	1.0	n.a.	1.6	2.9	3.8	—
TOTAL	24.3	37.1	54.6	59.8	65.0	77.1	93.7	4.3
Exp./researcher (PPP$'000)	177.0	162.0	149.0	146.0	116.0	109.0	114.0	−1.9
Expenditures as % AgGDP	1.39	1.72	1.73	1.40	1.36	1.39	1.76	−0.4
SSA ave. exp. as % AgGDP	n.a.	n.a.	0.78	0.84	0.86	0.74	0.70	n.a.

Source: Roseboom and Pardey (1993, Tables 3 and 6); sub-Saharan Africa (SSA) averages from Alston, Pardey, and Roseboom (1998, Table 2).
a. FTE = full-time equivalent, PPP = purchasing power parity, AgGDP = agricultural gross domestic product, and SSA = sub-Saharan Africa.

Table 15.3 Kenya Agricultural Research Institute (KARI) Research Expenditures, K£ Million (current prices), 1983–84 to 1997–98

Period	AgGDP[a]	KARI Research Expenditure	Expenditure as % AgGDP[a]	Funding Sources			Funding as % Expenditure		
				GoK[b]	Donors	Internal Revenue	GoK[b]	Donors	Internal Revenue
1988–89	1,902.7	27.6	1.44	10.2	16.7	0.7	37	61	2
1989–90	2,088.4	36.5	1.74	10.7	25.0	0.8	29	69	2
1990–91	2,235.5	40.5	1.81	11.8	27.9	0.8	29	69	2
1991–92	2,337.7	47.0	2.01	14.5	31.8	0.7	31	68	1
1992–93	2,681.9	52.0	1.94	15.2	35.4	1.4	29	68	3
1993–94	3,583.1	56.0	1.56	21.9	32.9	1.2	39	59	2
1994–95	4,344.0	64.6	1.49	28.2	35.4	1.0	44	55	1
1995–96	5,428.8	70.3	1.29	32.2	35.2	2.9	46	50	4
1996–97	6,233.0	70.9	1.14	33.4	31.7	5.8	47	45	8
1997–98	7,006.0	73.6	1.05	38.5	32.1	3.0	52	44	4

Source: KARI records.
a. AgGDP = agricultural gross domestic product.
b. GoK = Government of Kenya.

In keeping with other NARS facing funding constraints, KARI has initiated moves to improve the effectiveness and accountability of the services it provides. It is attempting, through improved priority setting, focusing on adaptive research with a greater user-orientation, and the establishment of an Agricultural Research Fund (ARF), to support a competitive grants research program. In addition to encouraging greater efficiency of resource use, such measures have the added benefit of demonstrating to potential funding sources that the research system is directly responsive to the expressed needs of its clients.

Priority Setting

In 1990, KARI undertook a major priority-setting exercise in response to growing budgetary constraints and in order to make a better match between research activities and government agricultural development goals and objectives. Previously, research resource allocation had been largely based on experience and intuition, and it was recognized that a more systematic and quantitative approach was needed. Taking into account time and resources, available data, the details of analysis required, and analytical capacity within KARI, a scoring model approach was adopted for its ease of use, its limited data requirements, and the ability to consider multiple objectives (box 15.1). The results provided "a framework for decision making and research management within KARI's programs and projects" (KARI 1995c). However, although the exercise was influential in readjusting thinking and stated priorities, it appears as yet to have had only a modest impact on resource allocation decisions.

Attention is currently focused on defining priorities within commodity and factor program areas. This exercise involves a sophisticated economic surplus methodology that attempts to estimate increases in producer and consumer surplus arising from the successful development and adoption of new technology, and thus makes efficiency the key criterion for determining priorities (KARI 1995b). The extent to which other factors, notably equity, should be incorporated into the priority-setting exercise, is the subject of ongoing debate. However, the advocates of the economic surplus approach explicitly recognize that the process of priority setting and resource allocation cannot be made by reference to economic criteria alone.

As indicated previously, comparison of priority rankings for forty-two commodities with the proposed NARP-II budget allocations suggests that the two are only weakly correlated (the simple correlation coefficient for the two rankings is only 0.02). However, practical and political factors facing both government and donors inevitably limit the speed with which resources can be reallocated. In recognition of these factors, a full analysis would need to take into account the allocation of resources by commodity before the prioritization exercise, against which changes in resource allocation can be measured in addition to the fact that this is a function of time.

A key element of the exercise therefore is the submission of the technical results of each subcommittee for commodity priority setting to a stakeholder group of thirty to forty people, among which all interested parties (including producers and processors) are represented. This provides a forum within which the technical assumptions

Box 15.1 **Priority Setting: The Kenya Agricultural Research Institute (KARI) Scoring Model Approach**

In 1990, the KARI introduced a scoring approach to guide its research priority setting. Research activities were first classified into ten commodity research programs (comprising fifty-three individual commodities) and seven factor research programs (comprising twenty-eight separately identifiable components). Commodity research programs were ranked according to an "efficiency index" derived for each commodity by multiplying the value of production of each commodity by a series of "weights" reflecting:

- Foreign exchange earnings or savings potential,
- Potential adoption rate of new technology,
- Potential yield improvement,
- Probability of research success,
- Contribution to food security,
- Domestic and external trade potential, and
- Potential for expansion, equity, and employment.

Similarly, factor research programs were ranked by aggregating weighted scores (on a scale of 1 to 3) for the:

- Number and severity of the problem (given a weight of 65%),
- Complementarity with borrowed research (5%),
- Research cost (10%), and
- Effect of research on the variability of production (5%), sustainability of natural resource base (5%), labor use (5%), and capital (5%).

Results were published in what became known as the "Blue Book" (KARI 1991).

Comparison of KARI Commodity Priority Rankings and Proposed Narp-IIa Budget Allocations (Selected Crops)

Crops	KARI Priority Rating			Proposed NARP-II Budget		
	Original Rank[b]	Efficiency Share (%)[c]	Revised Rank	Rank	Percentage Share	Budget (US$'000)
Food crops:	—	58.4	—	—	59.0	11,264
Maize	4	33.9	1	1	22.9	4,370
Wheat	11	4.1	6	11	2.7	521
Rice	24	0.2	11	4	9.6	1,837
Sorghum and millet	19, 26	0.9	10	4	14.8	2,830
Potatoes and other tubers	(*)	7.5	4	3	5.0	948
Grain legumes	(*)	11.8	3	10	4.0	758
Horticulture and industrial crops:	—	41.6	—	—	41.0	7,809
Cotton	14	1.8	8	6	7.3	1,396
Oil crops	(*)	1.4	9	9	4.1	775
Pyrethrum	12	3.4	7	12	0.8	155
Sugarcane	8	5.3	5	2	16.8	3,211
Horticulture	(*)	29.7	2	8	5.4	1,022
Macadamia nuts	42	0.0	12	7	6.6	1,250
TOTAL	—	100.0	—	—	100.0	19,073

Source: KARI (1991, Table 2), KARI (1995a, part C).
a. NARP-II = National Agricultural Research Project, Phase II.
b. As specified in KARI (1991): (*) only individual component commodities were ranked.
c. Percentage share of aggregated efficiency index of commodities included in this analysis.

369

underlying the analysis (e.g., with respect to potential yield improvements or adoption rates) can be first discussed and modified, and the (amended) results can be further modified to take account of other factors, including equity considerations and regional issues. Gender is not explicitly referred to as a criterion in any of the written papers on priority setting, although it is the subject of ongoing debate through the Gender Task Force, which was established in March 1995 with representation of all departments. Its purpose is essentially to develop a strategy and action plan for getting gender issues mainstreamed into the research agenda. Among KARI professional staff, 24 percent are women, compared with 21 percent in the mid-1980s (Roseboom and Pardey 1993). This corresponds closely with the 23 percent of agricultural science graduates (1983–89) who are women.

Making Research More User-Oriented

The KARI operates a network of fifteen National Research Centers (NRCs), which undertake strategic and applied research in the various commodity and factor programs, and six Regional Research Centers (RRCs), which implement adaptive research programs in a geographically defined mandate area. Four of the NRCs also have regional mandates. At KARI headquarters, a Research Coordinating Committee (RCC) provides overall guidance to and coordination of the National and Adaptive Research Programs (NRPs and ARPs), and advises on the allocation of resources.

In an effort to make research more client-driven, KARI institutionalized a Farming Systems Approach to Research, Extension, and Training in 1991. This involves much greater use of participatory approaches to problem and constraint identification at the regional level that seek to ensure that research programs are targeted at developing relevant and needed technologies with a high chance of adoption. A Memorandum of Understanding signed between the Ministry of Agriculture, Livestock Development, and Marketing (MoALDM) and the Ministry of Research, Technical Training and Technology in 1993 that clearly specified the roles played by research, extension, and farmers in the process of technology development and transfer has further improved research-extension linkages.

On the basis of constraints identified by participatory rural appraisal (PRA) exercises, RRC staff prepare research proposals, which are then discussed by a Regional Research-Extension Advisory Committee (RREAC). How the proposed research addresses the particular needs of women is supposed to be a key criterion. Farmers are generally not directly represented, a practice defended by KARI staff on the grounds that discussion is relatively technical and that staff involved in the PRA exercise are well placed to represent them. Research proposals that are approved are passed on to the relevant Center Research Advisory Committees (CRACs), where they are considered before being recommended to KARI headquarters for incorporation into national research programs. Membership of these two committees overlaps considerably.

Some observations arising from discussion and interviews can be made. First, the effectiveness with which these committees operate varies considerably between centers. The frequency with which they meet ranges from quarterly to erratic, while at some centers the committees have to all intents and purposes been unified. In brief, the principle is generally thought to work well, but the practice often falls short of expectations. Part of this may be because of inadequate understanding on the part of some of the management officers within KARI, and lack of incentives to implement this very well thought out and structured approached.

Second, the view of those outside of KARI is that greater farmer representation is essential to maximize the prospects for a genuinely user-oriented research program that builds on farmers' own knowledge of possible solutions (as well as their identification of constraints). Greater farmer representation is also essential to persuade farmers of the merit of research and hence enhance the likelihood of direct financial contributions from the users of research, where appropriate. The representativeness of selected participants then becomes a key factor. The Kenyan National Farmers Union (KNFU) is the only national organization representing the small-scale farmer. Membership of the KNFU has increased from about two thousand to fifty thousand in the last seventeen years, but this still represents less than 2 percent of the estimated three million small-scale farmers. Ninety-five percent of members are "small" farmers (with fewer than twenty acres), and about 50 percent are reported to be women. Although growing rapidly from a small base, KNFU activities are constrained by reliance on membership subscriptions and limited external donations The KNFU was generally not represented on any of the CRACs or RREACs.

Third, even where the views of producers are adequately canvassed and incorporated into research planning at the center level, the process is obscure by which these concerns feed through the system into decisions regarding priority setting and resource allocation at the aggregate KARI level. This reflects the difficulties in reconciling priority-setting processes at project and program level referred to previously. A strong view was held at some RRCs that the effectiveness of PRA approaches to research priority setting would be significantly enhanced if accompanied by the decentralization of financial authority to individual RRCs.

Fourth, the severity of the financial constraint and donor dependency is tending to lead to designing research projects that are thought most likely to attract donor funding, and to adding new research ideas to ongoing donor-funded programs at individual centers in order to bypass the formal approval mechanisms. These processes tend to lead to some inertia and to continued donor influence over the research agenda.

Fifth, the possibility for nongovernmental organizations (NGOs) to serve as a bridge between farmers and scientists is being actively explored. Mbogoh, Shannon, and Mwangata (1995) evaluated a United Nations Development Programme (UNDP) dry land farming research, development, and extension project in Machakos District. They concluded that the practice of giving promising technology packages to NGO contact groups (women/farmer groups) for on-farm trials and feedback greatly enhanced the project's capacity to reach farmers throughout the semi-arid lands, and enhanced the sustainability of project activities.

Agricultural Research Fund

The ARF was established in February 1990 with a grant of US$521,000 from the U.S. Agency for International Development (USAID), and officially launched in July 1991. The ARF is aimed at promoting a more pluralistic research system through a system of competitive research grants that raises the quality, relevance, and cost-effectiveness of research within the framework of KARI priorities for supporting agricultural development (Echeverria and Elliott 2002).

The ARF is a discrete entity within KARI, managed by the Research Fund Management Committee (RFMC), whose members are appointed by the KARI Board of Management. Members of the RFMC include three from the universities and scientific community, two from government, and two from the private sector. In addition, KARI's director and deputy directors, ARF secretary (responsible for day-to-day management of the fund), and donor representatives sit as ex-officio members. Specific areas for research are defined each year based on information arising from the PRA surveys of farmer constraints described previously. The ARF is specifically designed to support applied research that will contribute directly to technology formulation and uptake by farmers and other end users, or lead to commercial applications (KARI 1996).

Invitations for research proposals are published in January and July of each year, with the appraisal process (involving an initial administrative and technical pre-screening followed by a more detailed peer review) completed within six months. The main criteria in reviewing proposals are:

- Involvement of stakeholders in formulation of the research proposal,
- Scientific merit and quality,
- Appropriateness of the research methodology,
- Likely achievement of objectives within the proposed time frame and budget,
- Expected economic benefits,
- Identification of performance indicators that can be monitored,
- Availability of necessary research facilities,
- Contribution in cash and kind from all sources,
- Proposed approach to hazardous procedures,
- Ethical considerations,
- Synergies to be obtained from teamwork and collaboration, and
- Links with academic institutions and postgraduate training.

Although awards can be authorized up to $100,000, the ARF guidelines indicate that grants for adaptive research will not normally exceed $37,000. To meet the costs of the substantial work associated with reviewing and administering large numbers of small grants, the ARF charges a 15 percent overhead on all research grants awarded. However, the overall management costs, including staff salaries that are presently donor-funded, are estimated as closer to 20 percent (Carney 1997). The ARF does not claim rights to any publications, inventions, or patents arising from a project.

Funding for the ARF under NARP-I comprised the initial contribution from USAID

($521,000), with additional amounts from the World Bank ($49,000 for adaptive research), and smaller sums from the Kenya Seed Company and Agricultural Research Foundation earmarked for specific research needs. Government funding was provided to cover operational costs.

Under NARP-II, USAID has contributed a further $250,000, the Department for International Development (DFID) $80,000, and the GoK $4 million in the form of an International Development Association (IDA) credit. Additional funding is expected to be forthcoming from other donors and private Kenyan organizations. Nevertheless, the total sums involved remain small: the figure $4.33 million for NARP-II represents just 2 percent of the total NARP-II budget.

Funds are maintained in a multidonor account, with funds from different donors and organizations held in separate subaccounts. Earmarking of funds for specific research areas by the different contributors is permitted, as are special conditions relating to proprietary rights and royalties. This implies that, far from being a consolidated funding mechanism, the ARF remains highly "projectized," with donors stipulating how funds are to be used and determining overall research objectives. This is likely to remain the case until a significant level of private-sector participation is achieved (Carney 1997).

Given the high level of donor dependency, the sustainability of the ARF is viewed with some skepticism by KARI management. In order to create further incentives for private-sector funding, a recent innovation has allowed the ARF to allocate matching funds in support of research grants financed by the private sector. Matching funds may come either from the untied ARF funds or from KARI where the proposed research is seen by KARI to be highly complementary to its work. In the long term, the objective is to attract sufficient funds from the private sector or GoK to establish an Endowment Fund by which the ARF's operations will be maintained. Attracting such a large sum of capital will, however, depend upon KARI or the ARF Secretariat being able to demonstrate a high level of financial management.

The extent to which the existence of an ARF results in higher-quality research offering better value for money depends significantly on the number of potentially competing institutes that might bid for resources, and the strength of the monitoring system. Kenya is perhaps better endowed than many African countries in this regard, although even here a shortcoming of the ARF has raised the problem of an insufficiently pluralistic and competitive research capability. However, an analysis of applications to and awards from the ARF since its inception implies that competition for awards has been stiff (table 15.4). Meanwhile, the fact that four of the twenty-nine USAID-funded projects under NARP-I were terminated for failure to adhere to their work plans is considered by the ARF Secretariat to confirm the rigor of the monitoring process.

Although ARF is administered with a high level of professionalism, less attention is being paid to assessing the cost-effectiveness of research and the client orientation of research outputs. It may still be too early for such an evaluation, but it would be critical in ensuring the future financial sustainability of the fund and in attracting a

Table 15.4 **Agricultural Research Fund (ARF) Applications and Awards to July 1998**

Source of application[a]	NARP-I[b] (1988 to 1995)			NARP-II[c] (1996 to July 1998)		
	Proposals Received	Proposals Accepted	Budget (KSh'000)	Proposals Received	Proposals Accepted	Budget (KSh'000)
University	114	23	31,104	87	11	13,520
KARI	28	6	2,873	41	9	11,863
Other public-sector institution	30	1	1,678	9	1	1,000
International research institution	2	2	2,518	4	3	2,950
Private sector/NGO	25	3	4,723	9	2	2,439
TOTAL	199	35	42,896	150	26	31,772

Source: ARF Secretariat, June 1998.
a. KARI = Kenya Agricultural Research Institute; and NGO = nongovernmental organization.
b. National Agricultural Research Program, Phase I.
c. National Agricultural Research Program, Phase II.

higher level of private-sector interest. The ARF must also clarify its research priorities and the apparent contradiction between a poverty-focused agenda to satisfy donors and the commercial orientation demanded by the private sector.

Staff Rationalization

In order to improve the effectiveness of existing resources, KARI is embarking on a staff rationalization program aimed at reducing overall numbers in employment and producing a more efficient ratio of scientific to support staff. The KARI total staff complement has fallen from 6,200 in 1989 to below 5,000 in 1998. The current ratio of scientific to support staff in KARI is 1:9. Following staff rationalization, KARI aims to reduce this ratio to 1:6, cutting the cost of personnel emoluments by Ksh 48 million per year, and improving the ratio of operation costs to personnel emoluments to 2:3. In doing this, KARI has developed comprehensive staffing norms that have entailed description of each and every job that it deems necessary and essential. This has shown that the KARI staff complement in the next millennium should not exceed 3,850, with about 500 research staff. The KARI has also resolved to concentrate in its core business of research, and to hire out services such as vehicle repairs, security, and maintenance of its now fully rehabilitated infrastructure of buildings, roads, and scientific equipment. When this is fully implemented KARI could do with a staff complement of about 2,900 staff and 500 scientists.

Managing Funding Sources

In accordance with the Science and Technology Act, KARI can receive funds in the form of grants, donations, gifts, fees, and subscriptions, and make disbursements therefrom. In practice, KARI has three main sources of funds: (1) GoK, (2) donors—

mainly bilateral and multilateral agencies with smaller contributions from foundations and the private sector, and (3) appropriation in aid (i.e., internally generated revenue). Although KARI negotiates with donors directly, it should be realized that donor funding is also public money and that KARI requires the political will of the government for approval of donor support.

Government of Kenya as Funding Source

Although KARI is a parastatal organization with its own board of management, it is answerable to the Ministry of Research and Technology. Its annual budgetary requirement is submitted to this ministry to be reflected in the government's budget every year. The KARI has very little control of this source of financing. While the personnel emolument is ensured every year, the operational budget has been slashed and reduced every year. This has made it most difficult for KARI to plan in the long term. Furthermore, the government quarterly financial controls make it impossible for KARI to use this source of funding for research, which requires a continuous flow of funds. In other words, it is practically impossible within the prevailing financial constraints for KARI to rely on government funding to conduct any meaningful research.

Multilateral Donors

The World Bank (IDA credit) has provided International Fund multilateral funding for KARI's NARP from the International Fund for Agricultural Development (IFAD), UNDP, the European Union (EU), and the African Development Bank (AfDB). Support from IFAD, UNDP, and the AfDB continued from ongoing activities before the reorganization of KARI and the formulation of NARP in 1987; World Bank and EU support began with the initiation of NARP.

Each multilateral funding agency has strict policies and conditions for the lending and provision of grant funds, often tied to policy or political conditionality, with additional measures designed to ensure the accountability of fund use. These conditions and procedures differ between agencies and over time, implying a heavy administrative burden upon the recipient implementing body (box 15.2).

A critical issue arises in planning a second phase without a gap that can cause damage or loss of what was achieved in the first phase. In the case of NARP, the first phase ended in October 1995 and the second started in June 1997—a gap of over two years. Fortunately, other donors who supported the project during this period were supporting most of the research activities. However, several civil works were not completed in three research centers. Although these were incorporated into the second phase, the delay meant that research activities could not continue optimally. An arrangement was made to provide a Project Preparation Facility (PPF) to prepare a second phase and support some operational costs, but this was not adequate to continue most priority research activities. This is an experience that KARI hopes will be avoided in the future.

Box 15.2   Preparations and Implementation of World Bank (International Development Association [IDA]) Funding for the National Agricultural Research Program Phase I (NARP-I) and Phase II (NARP-II)

Project Preparation (Identification). NARP-I was identified with assistance from the International Service for National Agricultural Research (ISNAR) and project preparation took place from 1985 to 1987. NARP-II was prepared by the Kenya Agricultural Research Institute (KARI), the Ministry of Agriculture, and the Ministry of Research and Technical Training, from November 1992 to April 1994.

Project Appraisal. This is the project formulation stage, when a team from the World Bank and the KARI reviewed all the elements described in the project preparation document. This culminated in the Staff Appraisal Report (SAR), which eventually became the main reference document of project implementation. The credit agreements were also derived from this process. The project appraisal stages for NARP-I and NARP-II each took more than one year.

Negotiations. At this stage, the implementation documents are agreed upon. The SAR and the various credit agreements are discussed in detail and every clause is agreed upon; this takes a few weeks.

Presentation to Board of Directors. After the negotiations, the borrower may need to meet a few conditions before the project is presented to the Board of Directors of the bank. The board may disagree and refer the project for further discussion with the borrower, but this rarely occurs. The bank and recipient government representative then sign the project. Only after this ceremony do the funds start to flow to the implementing agency.

Implementation. During implementation, the bank and the implementing agency, through supervision missions, closely monitor the project.

Mid-term Review. A major review of the project implementation is conducted halfway through the project period. During this review, all the implementation constraints are analyzed jointly by the bank and the borrower. If necessary, the staff appraisal and the project agreements may be revised to address the identified implementation constraints. In the case of NARP-I, significant changes were made during this review.

Implementation/Completion Review (ICR). Toward the end of the project, the bank and the borrower conduct an evaluation of the project where the outputs are compared with the objectives. NARP-I was judged as reasonably satisfactory and justifying the need for a second phase.

Project Audit Review. An independent consultant normally conducts this. In the case of NARP-I, it was concluded that the project was successful, and in some cases objectives had been achieved beyond expectation.

Summary and Conclusions

Although agricultural research in Kenya has been relatively well funded, KARI is increasingly faced with unreliable operating budgets and a high degree of donor dependency that is perceived as unsustainable. In order to make more effective use of existing resources, considerable effort is being devoted to improving priority setting, to making research more user-oriented, and to the awarding of competitive research grants through the ARF. The ARF has proved to be a popular innovation, although expensive to administer, and the extent to which it is generating more relevant and cost-effective research results is a question that remains largely unanswered.

Implications of Alternative Financing Options

In terms of future sustainability, the alternative and innovative approaches to agricultural research financing implemented by KARI are still in the early stages of development, and it is too early for a comprehensive assessment of their impact. However, some observations can be made regarding their fiscal, efficiency, and equity implications—all of which are key factors in determining sustainability.

Fiscal impact

State withdrawal, levy financing, and increased cost recovery all have the potential to generate substantial revenues or savings, but may simply prompt a corresponding reduction in GoK allocations to KARI. Commercial farming and other revenue-generating activities are unlikely to generate substantial resources, particularly when the full investment costs of any capital development are incorporated. With respect to revenue generation and cost recovery, the principle of revenue retention by KARI is essential, but likely to be agreed upon only if the overall KARI budget is not adversely affected. More fundamentally, KARI must be better able to demonstrate the positive benefits of services provided in order to justify and improve their budget allocations.

Measures to improve the cost-effectiveness of research do not generally have a direct impact on budgets, but may be expensive to implement (e.g., priority setting and more participatory approaches). However, such measures may have a positive indirect effect if they demonstrate that returns to research are improved, and if, by increasing user participation in the design and implementation of research programs, they generate more broad-based support and lobbying for KARI activities.

Efficiency impact

The KARI commercialization strategy can potentially lead to efficiency gains in service delivery and the investment of funds with higher social rates of return. Efficiency is also likely to be increased where user contributions are accompanied by a more direct say in how research budgets are allocated. However, the public pursuit of private financing, and the observed tendency for such contributions to have a disproportionate effect on the overall research agenda (e.g., in South Africa), may lead to some deviation from an efficient pattern of research activities and expenditures.

Levies are effectively a form of earmarked tax and have generally been regarded with disfavor in the public finance literature. This is partly because they restrict the ability of policy makers to allocate revenues to other investments that may yield higher social rates of return, and partly because they distort prices and are thus an inefficient form of taxation. However, increasing disillusionment with the ability or willingness of governments to spend tax revenues in accordance with efficiency criteria is resulting in a growing acceptance of the case in favor of earmarked taxes as a second-best solution.

Options to improve cost-effectiveness are designed to achieve a more efficient allocation of resources, in terms of securing more research outputs for less cost. For example, the KARI priority-setting model seeks to improve efficiency by maximizing producer and consumer surplus. However, the extent to which efficiency is actually improved depends substantially on:

- Accurate estimates concerning technical gains and the rate and extent of adoption of new technology;
- The weight given to efficiency as opposed to other criteria in determining priorities; and
- The extent to which government and donor budget allocations match the set of priorities so derived.

In the case of KARI, evidence suggests that the correlation between priorities and budget allocations may be relatively weak.

Although KARI believes that user participation in the design of research programs represents an efficient investment that will improve the effectiveness of research, no quantitative evaluation has yet been attempted. Given that more participatory approaches to research planning are often the first to be cut in times of budget reduction, such analysis would be highly desirable. Some loss in efficiency may also occur if resource allocation decisions are skewed in favor of particularly powerful interest groups that are able to dominate other users.

The operation of the ARF (and ultimately, consolidated funding mechanisms) has considerable potential to improve the efficiency of service delivery through coordinating effort and minimizing duplication. Competitive bidding for research grants and extension contracts may well produce gains in efficiency, particularly where there is a well-developed and competitive private sector and a public-sector capacity to manage and monitor.

Equity impact

Where the state withdraws from the provision of services there is always a concern that the poor will be neglected because the private sector will not find it profitable to serve them. However, concerns that privately funded research will ignore the particular needs of smallholders (e.g., seed varieties with appropriate storage, milling, and cooking characteristics) may be overstated where research benefits can be

378

appropriated (e.g., hybrid seeds). In a competitive environment where market share is critical, there seems little reason to believe that the private sector will be any less responsive to these needs than will the public sector. Indeed, greater private financing of research has the potential to improve equity where previous public funding represented a poorly targeted subsidy of largely private goods, provided that public-sector savings are redirected toward maintaining services to the poor or alternative, possibly more efficient, forms of poverty alleviation are implemented.

Although some of the reforms being introduced by KARI are indeed pushing the research agenda in favor of the commercial sector, 60 percent of the NARP-II budget is allocated toward food crops (box 15.1) and focused on crops and technologies relevant to resource-poor farmers. Where pro-poor research continues for welfare reasons, its cost-effectiveness as a means of poverty alleviation needs to be assessed alongside other possible means of achieving the same aim. Examples of such are public works programs, direct transfers, support for income-generating activities that are nonagricultural and over the longer term, and investment in rural infrastructure. Research may be effective at achieving efficiency objectives, but is often a blunt instrument for redistributive purposes (Alston, Norton, and Pardey 1995).

Despite measures to improve priority setting and ensure a competitive environment for allocating research grants, the degree to which the poor and marginalized are able to articulate their needs and make their interests heard is doubtful. There is a serious danger that initiatives seeking to increase user influence over the allocation of resources may be captured by the elite, the better off, and those who are more organized (Sims and Leonard 1989; Kaimowitz 1990). However, recent research on farmers' organizations suggests that the elite who typically fill leadership positions may in fact be doing a better job of identifying and addressing the needs of resource-poor farmers than does the conventional system (Carney 1996).

Recommendations

Faced with growing financial constraints, KARI has adopted an approach involving the commercialization of certain activities and measures to promote greater cost-effectiveness in remaining services. The extent to which these reforms are sustainable will depend upon their impact upon the KARI budget, the degree to which they lead to improved efficiency of resource use, and their distributional implications. Although it is too early to assess these implications in detail, some recommendations can be made for other NARS facing the same financing problems and where similar reforms are being considered.

- The introduction of commodity-specific levies to finance research should be encouraged where the marketing system is sufficiently concentrated to permit ready collection of levies (primarily relevant for industrially processed and export crops), or where producer groups are sufficiently homogeneous and organized to enable widespread voluntary collection that minimizes the problem of free-riding. Consideration should also be given to matching grants to encourage and

379

complement industry contributions, particularly where domestic consumers are key beneficiaries of research.

- User charges for analytical research functions should be increased toward full cost recovery. Where it can be demonstrated that free provision to the poor represents an effective form of support (compared with alternatives), a case can be made for some element of continued subsidy for selected beneficiaries. Where there are public health and safety or environmental implications, some degree of subsidy for such services may also be justified.

- The pursuit of other revenue-generating activities (particularly the commercial farming by public research institutes of surplus land to finance their activities) should generally be discouraged because of potential conflicts of interest and competition for inputs that frequently arise. Unless these can be overcome, sale or lease of such facilities represent better options.

- Priority setting for research expenditures has a crucial role to play, both in terms of marshalling donor resources around a domestically generated research agenda that meets national objectives and seeks to ensure a more efficient allocation of research financing, and in terms of raising the profile and appeal of agricultural research to domestic Ministries of Finance. Technical support to priority-setting processes in a form that maximizes staff and beneficiary participation should be encouraged.

- Measures to promote greater client orientation through farmer organizations are essential. However, the use of proxy representatives (drawn perhaps from the NGO community) for particular target groups that are insufficiently organized may be a more effective means of seeking to ensure that their research needs are adequately addressed. Training of research staff in participatory approaches to the analysis of needs and constraints of the poor and of women is also necessary.

- Agricultural research funds have their limitations, but are worth supporting to promote greater collaboration, cost sharing, and competition, and as a catalyst for broader reforms to public research institutions.

- Personnel numbers need to be controlled to ensure an efficient internal balance in research systems between personnel and nonpersonnel spending, perhaps as part of wider civil service reforms. Institutional and individual incentive systems need to be adjusted to reward activities that produce tangible benefits to research users.

- Support should be given to improved accounting and financial management procedures, enabling the more specific monitoring of expenditures and the allocation of resources to different research programs. Where management capacity is adequate, greater financial autonomy should be decentralized to the level of districts or individual research centers.

REFERENCES

Alston, Julian M., George W. Norton, and Philip G. Pardey. 1995. *Science under scarcity. Principles and practice for agricultural research evaluation and priority setting.* Ithaca, N.Y.: Cornell University Press.

Alston, Julian M., Philip G. Pardey, and Johannes Roseboom. 1998. Financing agricultural research: International investment patterns and policy perspectives. *World Development* 26:1057–72.

Brinkerhoff, D. W., J. D. Gage, and S. Gavian. 2002. *Sustainable agricultural research systems: Findings and lessons from reforms in Côte d'Ivoire, Ghana, Senegal, Tanzania, and Uganda.* Bethesda, Md.: Abt Assoc.

Carney, Diana. 1996. *Formal farmers' organizations in the agricultural technology system: Current roles and future challenges.* Natural Perspectives No. 14. London: Overseas Development Institute (ODI).

———. 1997. *Alternative systems for financing agricultural technology research and development in Uganda, Tanzania and Kenya.* Report to the Department for International Development (DFID), CNTR 97 3851A. London: Overseas Development Institute (ODI).

Echeverria, Ruben G., and Howard Elliott. 2002. Financing agricultural research by competitive funds. In *Agricultural research policy in an era of privatization,* ed. Derek Byerlee and Ruben G. Echeverria, 265–85. New York: CABI Publishing.

Evenson, Robert. 1987. International research centres: Their impact on spending for national agricultural research and extension. World Bank CGIAR Study Paper No. 22. Washington, D.C.: World Bank.

Evenson, Robert, and Yoav Kislev. 1975. *Agricultural research and productivity.* New Haven, Conn.: Yale University Press.

Kaimowitz, David. 1990. *Making the link: Agricultural research and technology transfer in developing countries.* Boulder, Colo.: Westview Press.

Kenya Agricultural Research Institute (KARI). 1991. *Kenya's agricultural research priorities to the year 2000.* Nairobi: KARI.

———. 1995a. *National Agricultural Research Program Phase II, Project Implementation Manual.* Final Version 25/09/95. Nairobi: KARI.

———. 1995b. *National Agricultural Research Program, Phase II project preparation report.* Nairobi: KARI.

———. 1995c. *Priority setting into the 21st century: A position paper by the priority setting working group.* Nairobi: KARI.

———. 1996. *Agricultural research fund: Competitive research grants program.* Nairobi: KARI.

Lipton, Michael. 1988. The place of agricultural research in the development of sub-Saharan Africa. *World Development* 16:1231–57.

Mbogoh, Stephen G., D. A. Shannon, and J. Mwangata. 1995. *Report of the technical evaluation mission, Dry Land Farming Research, Development and Extension Project (KEN/89/015), United Nations Development Program (UNDP).* Washington, D.C.: UNDP.

Oram, Peter A., and Vishva Bindlish. 1981. *Resource allocations to national agricultural research: Trends in the 1970s. A review of the third world systems.* The Hague: International Service for National Agricultural Research (ISNAR).

Pardey, Phillip G., and Johannes Roseboom. 1998. Trends in financing African agricultural research. In: *Financing agricultural research: A sourcebook,* ed. Steven R. Tabor, Willem Janssen, and Hilarion Bruneau, 307–20. The Hague: International Service for National Agricultural Research (ISNAR).

Pardey, Philip G., Johannes Roseboom, and Jock R. Anderson. 1991. *Agricultural research policy: International quantitative perspectives.* Cambridge, U.K.: Press Syndicate of the University of Cambridge.

Pardey, Philip G., Johannes Roseboom, and Nienke M. Beintema. 1997. Investments in African agricultural research. *World Development* 25:409–23.

Roseboom, Johannes, and Phillip G. Pardey. 1993. *Statistical brief on the national agricultural research system of Kenya.* Indicator series project (Phase II), Statistical Brief No. 5. The Hague: International Service for National Agricultural Research (ISNAR).

Sims, H., and David K. Leonard. 1989. The political economy of the development and transfer of agricultural technologies. Linkages Theme Paper No. 4. The Hague: International Service for National Agricultural Research (ISNAR).

Tabor, Steven R. 1998. Trends in agricultural research funding. In *Financing agricultural research: A sourcebook,* ed. Steven R. Tabor, Willem Janssen, and Hilarion Bruneau, 301–5. The Hague: International Service for National Agricultural Research (ISNAR).

Investing for Impact in Agricultural Research

MICHAEL WAITHAKA, MERCY KAMAU,
AND JULIUS MUNGAI

Management of Agricultural Research for a Desired Impact

What is the goal of agricultural research organizations? The ultimate goal of any agricultural research institute is to have a large and positive impact on the lives of its clientele at the local and national level. Impact is that change that may be attributed to use or adoption of a new technology by a targeted population. The impact may be at a household level, having caused changes in yields, income levels, or nutritional status, or at the macro level, including changes in employment, income, and foreign exchange earnings. However, the use of new agricultural technologies also may have negative impacts on the environment.

Types of Impact Assessment

Impact assessment involves evaluation of the economic, social, or environmental effects of agricultural research. Evaluation refers to judging, appraising, or determining the worth, value, or quality of research, whether it is proposed, ongoing, or completed. This is often done in terms of its relevance (appropriateness and importance of goals, objectives, problem, or target population), effectiveness (degree to which goals have been achieved), efficiency (cost-effectiveness of activities), or impact (the broad, long-term effects of research). A major purpose of impact assessment is to provide managers, scientists, or those who sponsor agricultural research with indications of its beneficial or negative effects. These can be examined after research is completed (ex post) to argue for continued investments, or during planning (ex ante) as an aid to priority setting. Lessons learned from impact assessments can be used to improve future research strategies, plans, and management (Ngigi 2003; Place et al. 2003).

Impact assessment may be ex ante, that is, carried out before research activities commence and serving as a vision of what a research organization has the potential to achieve. Or it may be ex post, that is, carried out after an organization has engaged in research activities for a period of time. Based on the importance that research organizations attach to causing an impact, impact assessment should be planned in advance. For a research organization to attain its desired goal, it must make choices about which activities it will engage in by clearly identifying its priority research areas (e.g., programs, themes, geographical areas, and even the clientele), and allocate its resources accordingly. The selection of priority research areas then becomes an important activity for the organization. Research organizations must also foster partnerships for effective technology transfer to enhance the magnitude and scope of change.

Developing Priority-Setting Capacity

Rationale for Setting Research Priorities

Priority setting for agricultural research is a popular topic because of the necessity of allocating limited funds to an increasing number of research goals. A few decades ago, research perspectives were rather clear. Development was defined as economic growth and research was expected to contribute to growth by increasing crop yields and livestock production. However, the evaluation of agricultural development has become more complex as new goals have emerged, such as equity, food security, social development and capacity building, gender issues, and sustainability. Also, participatory approaches are popular and an integrated approach to agricultural and rural development has become a common objective (Waithaka 1998; Janssen 1995). Budgetary constraints for agricultural research force research managers to focus on the most urgent problems in their mandate areas. This calls for strategic decisions with respect to allocation of the limited resources. Because of the magnitude and complexity of this problem, a structured process is required that rationally combines methods, experience, and intuition in priority setting (Mills 1998; Janssen and Waithaka 1998).

Because priority setting supports planning and resource allocation decisions, it should occur at the same level at which these decisions are made. Planning and resource allocation within a research system occur at four levels: national, institute, program, and project. At the national level, decisions are made on the level of investment to make in agricultural research vis-à-vis other agricultural sector activities, and on how funds are allocated to different components of the agricultural research system. At this level, decisions are based on broad national objectives, such as poverty alleviation, rural welfare, or growth in exports. Formal analysis is rare, but research organizations should be aware of how investment decisions are made, so as to effectively lobby for support. At the institute level, decisions are made on resource allocation across its major research programs and across major research zones within its mandate. The institute allocates resources on the basis of potential to contribute to its mandate. Here, formal analysis is important to bring in objectivity in identification.

Research organizations are compartmentalized into programs, whose activities have major impacts on their mandate areas. At this level, the priority-setting process should inform the potential benefits that can be gained from research themes and geographic areas, a "theme" being a set of closely related research activities that address a particular constraint. The methods used to arrive at priorities differ with the type of program. Commodity programs define their mandates in terms of agricultural output or input in different geographic areas that are relatively homogenous in environment or scope of technology user needs. Disciplinary programs, such as socioeconomics, have national mandates with outputs translating into interventions across a range of commodities and production factors. The results of such interventions cannot be formally defined; hence less formal methods are employed while comparing benefits from several research activities. Regional research programs, as with disciplinary programs, must evaluate benefits across multiple commodities and factors.

At lower levels, we have projects, a project being "a collection of specified activities and experiments with definite time frame, budgeted inputs, and definite outputs." Projects should be designed to address the priority research themes and geographic areas. This does not require formal priority-setting exercises, because it will be achieved through well-functioning priority-setting, planning, and resource allocation processes. Priority setting, being such an important and critical step in the management of any research institution, requires careful attention to the methodological choices and to the management of the process.

Methods Used in Priority Setting

Although priority setting as a subject has received much attention among agricultural researchers, most attention has been given to the methodological aspects. Basically, a priority-setting methodology requires the definition of a clear set of objectives, a well-defined set of possible activities, and an approach to compare the contribution of the activities toward the objectives (Contant and Bottomley 1988; Alston, Norton, and Pardey 1995).

Methods differ in their formal rigor, transparency, participation, time, and information requirements. Formal methods do not necessarily guarantee success, but they ensure a structured approach to making complex decisions. The method chosen must fit with the requirements of the organization, its goals, and its objectives. Because of the nature of the priority-setting process, no unique method is available that could cover all aspects of the problem or even solve them. Most common priority-setting methodologies fall under single-criterion or multiple-criteria approaches. In single-criterion approaches, one indicator is used that reflects the objective of the organization for which priorities are being set. The most common single-criterion methods are congruency analysis, cost-benefit and economic surplus, and linear programming models. Multiple-criteria approaches use several criteria, and the most common methods are production function, scoring models, the analytic hierarchy process, and mathematical programming models.

Single-criterion methods

In *congruency analysis*, the relative importance of a research subject depends on its relative importance according to a certain indicator (e.g., value of production, or area planted). Using this method, if commodity A has double the value of commodity B, the

385

amount of research resources allocated to A would be double the amount allocated to B, and minor subjects receive minor resources, thus delivering a budget allocation. Congruency analysis is a simple and straightforward method; it provides a good starting point for priority setting where the results are incorporated in more comprehensive multicriteria approaches.

Cost-benefit and economic surplus approaches estimate returns to investing in research by measuring the economic benefits of research over time to consumers and producers as a result of a shift in the supply function (Alston, Norton, and Pardey 1995). For each research activity, these approaches estimate the physical impact of research (e.g., a 10 percent increase in yields at the same cost per hectare) and translate this into a shift of the supply function. The effect of the supply shift on the market equilibrium (price and quantity) is estimated, as well as total benefits and efficiency losses. Activities with the highest research benefits are selected as priorities. When investment costs are incorporated, internal rates of return (ROR) can be calculated. Cost-benefit analysis assumes a constant price for calculating market value of research gains, while economic surplus takes into account price changes resulting from changes in supply. This approach has been used (Davis, Oram, and Ryan 1987; Mills and Karanja 1997). The strength of the cost-benefit and economic surplus approaches lies in their analytical rigor and the amount of information that goes into them (e.g., considering regions or social groups). They can also accommodate dynamics of growth in demand and supply, research and price spillover effects, and market distortions. They also distinguish benefits accruing to producers and consumers, or to different agents in the marketing channel, thereby being useful tools for policy analysis. The main disadvantage of these approaches is their heavy dependence on elaborate data (e.g., sizes of markets, size and nature of the supply shifts).

Optimization models are based on mathematical programming and compare a range of optimal technologies. The principle underlying this method is the determination of a set of research activities that maximize the aggregate value of a single- or multiple-objective function within the limits set by binding constraints on available resources. Most models address allocation of resources and selection of discrete research activities (Hazel and Norton 1986; Romero and Rehman 1989; Contant and Bottomley 1988). Linear programming, the simplest form of mathematical programming, has been explicitly used for planning under resource constraints. Estimated benefits from alternative research activities may be obtained from economic surplus methodologies, and incorporated in a planning context that recognizes more explicitly the constraints to research. Strengths of mathematical programming emanate from the high degree of manipulative power in response to decision-making conflicts (e.g., various levels of resources) between objectives and different types of decision rules. The main problem with linear programming is its dependency on exact data and the difficulty of defining relevant resource constraints in the long run, other than budget. When the budget is the only limitation, linear programming does not add anything to economic surplus methodology.

Multiple-criteria methods

The *production function* approach uses the concept of a production function, taking research expenditures as one argument in the function, and tries to quantify the impact of research on production. This relevant, but rough, approach has been used at an aggregate level (Fox 1987; Karanja 1990). Its usefulness depends on the possibility of separating a potential impact of research expenditures from the impact of other factors that determine the quantity of production.

Scoring models produce ordinal rankings of activities based on scores achieved on criteria scales relevant to stated objectives. They are frequently used for setting priorities where a number of criteria are identified, indicators are established for these criteria, and a score is given that indicates how a certain research activity contributes to it. After an activity has received a score on each criterion, a final score can be calculated once the weight (relative importance) of each is known, and once a method has been chosen for combining scores (e.g., by adding or multiplying). When scores can be defined in an objective manner (e.g., from statistical data), the contribution to the different criteria can be measured in specific units. Often these exact measurements are transformed into scores in order to combine scores on one criterion. Using scores rather than direct measurements is based on the need to combine assessments made in different measurement units.

Scoring models are widely used, as they have low data requirements and require few technical skills, thereby encouraging participation and transparency. The method combines both objective and subjective assessments where reliable information is hard to acquire. Also, advanced measurement methods, such as economic surplus approaches, can be integrated, as in Kelly, Ryan, and Patel (1995). The main disadvantage of scoring models is that when subjective information is used as a substitute for more rigorous data collection and objective definition, the outcomes become doubtful. Also, in the absence of formal rigor, it is tempting to include numerous objectives that are poorly defined or not very useful. There is also considerable arbitrariness and subjectivity in defining a set of weights attached to criteria and measurement components, and scores do not provide a clear translation into budgets.

The *analytic hierarchy process* (AHP) (Saaty 1980) has some characteristics of scoring models, in that criteria and the relative weights are defined. Its key components are the structuring of problems into hierarchy components of goals and subordinate features. It applies subjective judgment using pair-wise comparisons between a finite set of decision elements at each level of the hierarchy. The main advantage of AHP is that the alternative activities are not only being scored on the criteria but also are compared in a pair-wise fashion, and each time it is indicated how each activity contributes additionally to a certain criterion than another. Once all the pair-wise comparisons have been made, they are transformed into a type of score, which then leads to a final overall assessment. Because of the importance of pair-wise comparisons, AHP models are suited to problems with a limited number of alternatives and a high extent of subjectivity (Saaty 1980; Dyer and Forman 1992). Also, AHP models

387

are useful in situations where activities of a different nature are being compared, and where most of the data are subjective and the decision problem has multiple criteria dimensions. The main disadvantage of AHP is that pair-wise comparisons can be very tedious if each priority level has many activities.

Multiple-objective programming is an extension of linear programming in the sense that the objective function of the programming model combines not one, but several, criteria (in the sense that several criteria have to be satisfied) before the criterion can be maximized. In the same way that economic surplus approaches (one criterion) can be included in scoring models (multiple criteria), linear programming (one objective) can be included in multiple-objective programming (Romero and Rehman 1989). The disadvantages of multiple-objective programming resemble those of linear programming—considerable data requirements, and the difficulty of defining resource constraints in the long run.

The simple and the multiple-objective methods differ in their theoretical rigor, ease of use, participation, transparency, and simplicity (Janssen 1995). The most participative methods are those under multiple criteria. The easiest to use are congruency and multiple criteria. Economic surplus is strong in theoretical rigor, but poor in participation, transparency, and ease of use. Objective programming, like economic surplus, is strong in theoretical rigor, but poor in participation, transparency, and ease of use. Most of these methods stand to gain from increased user participation and transparency. Congruency can be improved with better targeting of clients and definition of objectives. Rapid appraisal methods such as preference and matrix scoring and ranking can improve scoring methods and AHP (Waithaka 1998).

Priority Setting in the Kenya Agricultural Research Institute (KARI)

Short- versus Long-Term Planning

As a way of enhancing its relevance, KARI is committed to well-thought-out strategic planning. A strategic plan embodies a long-term vision; considers stakeholders' needs; reflects government objectives as laid down in national sessional documents and development plans; and anticipates future trends, problems, and opportunities. The KARI mission is to develop and disseminate appropriate agricultural technologies in collaboration with stakeholders. The institute seeks to proactively contribute knowledge and creative solutions that are client-oriented, holistic, and systems oriented, gender-sensitive, sustainable, affordable, and participatory (Shapiro 1999).

In 1991, the first formal priority setting at institute level was carried out in recognition of a more systematic and quantitative approach. Taking into account time and resources, available data, the details of analysis required, analytical capacity within KARI, and the need to consider multiple objectives, a scoring model approach was adopted (KARI 1991). The process began with the reclassification of prevailing research programs into KARI commodity and factor programs. The criteria were agreed upon for assessing the contribution of these research programs to various national objectives. Four broad research programs were identified: food crops, livestock, horticultural and industrial crops, and factor programs (table 16.1). Commodity programs were ranked according to an "efficiency index" derived for each commodity by multiplying the value of production of each commodity by a series of weights. The weights reflect their foreign exchange earnings or savings potential, the potential adoption rate of new technology, potential yield improvement, probability of research success, contribution to food security, domestic and external trade potential, potential for expansion, equity, and employment potential. Similarly, factor research programs were ranked by aggregating weighted scores (on a scale of 1 to 3). This was for the number and severity of the problem (given a weight of 65 percent), complementarity with borrowed research (5%), research cost (10%), effect of research on the variability of production (5%), sustainability of natural resource base (5%), labor use (5%), and capital (5%) (KARI 1991).

Table 16.1 compares priority ranking and budget allocation in NARP-II. From the exercise, the highest-priority areas were adaptive research on dairy, sheep and goats, maize, pulses, sugarcane, and cotton (table 16.1, column 1). An interesting outcome was that the maize program, which has traditionally been perceived as the most important, and hence has received the most attention, came fourth, after livestock programs. Indeed, dairy was given a slightly higher allocation than maize. Beef, which was second, and goats, third, had a history of poor funding—a situation that was not revised in the budget allocation. Despite scanty funding, the beef program has done extremely well with KARI funds and collaboration with other programs, as illustrated by the forage sorghum work at the Beef Research Center in Lanet (Waithaka et al. 1999). In the factor programs, although crop protection was previously considered to be the most important program, soil and water management overtook it, and this was actually reflected in budgetary provisions. A comparison of priority rankings for fifty-three commodities with the proposed NARP-II budget allocations shows weak correlation (coefficient of 0.02), indicating that funding did not follow proclaimed priorities. It must be borne in mind that the priorities were set after budget allocation had been done. It is expected that in future rounds of funding, priority areas will be considered by linking past, present, and future allocations with effective completion of previous engagements and smooth transition toward new priority areas.

After the institute-wide exercise, the next step was to set priorities between research themes within programs. A priority-setting working group composed of senior management was set up to oversee the coordination of priority-setting efforts and the synthesis of that information for institute-wide exercises in the future. While determining methodologies and procedures, this group determined that more rigorous methods than scoring needed to be explored to capture the dynamics within programs. The criterion of choice was set to be efficiency, based on the argument that equity is largely captured when target groups or commodities are selected (KARI 1995a). Other criteria considered were sustainability, food self-sufficiency, food security, and foreign exchange earnings. Mills (1998) discusses the choice of different criteria. The socioeconomics division managed issues of analytical methods and assembly of relevant data.

Table 16.1 Comparison of Commodity Priority Rankings and the National Agricultural Research Program, Phase II (NARP-II) Budget Allocations

Commodity	Priority Ranking[a]	Budget Allocation (US$ 1,000)	Rank within Subgroup Budget	Rank by Overall Budget
Food crops:				
Maize	4	4,369	1	6
Wheat	11	521	6	21
Rice	24	1,837	3	9
Sorghum and millet	19, 26	2,829	2	8
Potatoes and tubers	7, 37, 49	948	4	16
Grain legumes	6, 29, 32	758	5	19
Livestock:				
Dairy	1	5,257	1	5
Beef	2	231	4	22
Sheep and goats	3	1,572	2	11
Poultry	10	980	3	16
Horticultural and industrial crops:				
Cotton	14	1,396	2	12
Oil crops	20–31	775	5	18
Pyrethrum	12	155	6	23
Sugarcane	8	3,211	1	7
Horticulture	5–48	1,022	4	15
Macadamias	42	1,250	3	13
Factor programs:				
Animal health	4–33	10,227	2	2
Socioeconomics	1, 4, 21, 27	6,774	3	3
Range management	2–30	6,421	4	4
Soil and water	4–33	14,064	1	1
Plant and genetics	3, 4, 13, 32	1,253	6	13
Crop protection	4, 18	1,649	5	10
Pasture and fodders	12, 22, 27	633	7	20

Source: KARI (1991, tables 2 and 3); and KARI (1995a, part C).
a. As specified in KARI (1991), tables 2 and 3. If more than four ranks, then the range of rank is shown.

A series of focused workshops, aimed at meeting the key objectives in the priority-setting process, were organized. This step-wise approach to priority setting in commodity research programs has provided a basis for the preparation of guidelines for priority setting for regional and factor-based programs. At this level, more rigorous economic surplus was used, with participation achieved through increased user involvement. Priorities have been set between research themes and activities. A key element of the exercise therefore is the submission of the technical results of each commodity priority-setting subcommittee to a stakeholder group. This provides a forum at which the assumptions underlying the analysis (e.g., with respect to potential yield improvements or adoption rates) are discussed and modified. The programs that have completed priority setting include:

- Maize,
- Wheat (Mills and Karanja 1997),
- Sorghum (Sorghum Program Priority Setting Working Group 1995),
- Millet (KARI 1995b; Audi and Priority Setting Working Group 1997),
- Cassava (Cassava Priority Setting Working Group 1995),
- Horticulture (Horticulture Priority Setting Working Group 1996),
- Dairy (KARI 1996),
- Animal health (Mulinge and McLeod 1998), and
- Soil fertility and plant nutrition (Soil Fertility and Plant Nutrition Priority Setting Working Group 1995).

Priority-setting exercises that are near completion are those of the rice, cotton, sugarcane, grain legumes, range research, and crop protection research programs, while those of regional research programs are yet to commence. However, guidelines for priority setting in regional programs have been developed. Most of the factor-based programs also have not gone very far in priority-setting activities, except for the pilot exercise with the Soil Fertility and Plant Nutrition Research Program. From this exercise, a set of guidelines and methods for factor-based priority setting has been developed with which the crop protection program has commenced its own process, with Kenya soil survey and irrigation and drainage management following suit. A major factor affecting the speed of completion of these exercises is the limited socioeconomic capacity within programs to provide the data and estimates of research potential, and at headquarters to facilitate the process, and the lack of readily available databases from which to draw information necessary for priority setting.

In several instances, the common priority-setting methods had to be adapted to suit varied situations and peculiarities. Studies giving experiences include commodity priority setting (Kamau, Kilambya, and Mills 1997), vegetables (Kamau and Mills 1998), and dairy (Janssen and Waithaka 1998). The next step is to conduct an institute-wide priority-setting exercise using the experience, information, and data gathered from the program exercises to guide the next NARP phase. Over the years, donors providing support for priority-setting activities have included the U.S. Agency for International Development (USAID) and the Rockefeller Foundation. Also providing support for specific activities are the Department for International Development (DFID) and the Netherlands Liaison Office (NLO). The major collaborating institution has been the International Service for National Agricultural Research (ISNAR), which has a long history of working with KARI to build capacity in research planning and program formulation. Since 1991, ISNAR has outposted three research fellows principally to provide technical support for priority setting in KARI.

391

Table 16.2 Restrictions on the Distribution of Benefits by Zones, the Dairy Research Program, Kenya Agricultural Research Institute (KARI)

Zone	NPV by Option[a] (Ksh million)		
	Option 1	Option 2	Option 3
Nairobi/Mombassa	3,480	3,143	1,683
1	6,667	6,628	3,887
2	32,080	29,671	12,366
3	12,621	11,532	6,448
4	27,023	20,787	9,667
5	2,189	1,841	1,118
6	6,133	7,813	8,386
All zones	90,195	81,418	43,559
Efficiency losses[b]	0	8,776	46,635

a. All options are run under maximizing efficiency objective (discounted net present value [NPV]).
b. Difference between NPV from Option 1 and NPV from option under consideration.
Option 1: Budget maximum Ksh 50 million, no other restrictions. Option 2: Budget maximum Ksh 50 million, agro-ecological zones (AEZs) 1, 5, and 6 receive together a minimum of 20 percent of research benefits. Option 3: Budget maximum Ksh 50 million, AEZs 1, 5, and 6 receive together a minimum of 30 percent of research benefits.

An Example of Program-Level Priority Setting: The Dairy Research Program

The Dairy Program priorities were set for six zones, depicted one to six in order of declining precipitation and increasing minimum temperatures spread across the country, and four research themes: animal breeding and genetic improvement, animal health, feed resources and utilization, and socioeconomics. Using multiple-objective programming, a first analysis took into account distributional concerns of economic benefits. The second analysis imposed upper and lower funding limits for themes, to restrict the number of activities from each theme that could appear in the solution. A third analysis was carried out respecting variations of the available program budget. The total benefits amounted to Ksh 90 billion over thirty years, and by region the highest benefits would accrue to zones 2, 4, 3, 1, 6, and 5 (table 16.2). By research themes, the highest benefits would accrue, in order, to feed resources and utilization, animal health, socioeconomics, and animal breeding and genetic improvement (Janssen and Waithaka 1998).

The effect of imposing a minimum benefit share to some of the less favored dairy regions (zones 1, 5, and 6) are shown in Option 2, table 16.2. Initially (at a minimum benefit share of 20 percent), the efficiency losses implied by this equity constraint are small. If the constraint is put at a higher level, the costs in foregone benefits amount to one half of the total possible benefits in the unconstrained scenario. Table 16.3 shows the effect of limitations in spending on the most promising theme (feed resources and utilization). Reducing the possible share of this theme in the final solution has major implications in terms of efficiency losses. Decision makers thus will need to assess with more care the importance they give to maintaining prominent roles for the other themes, at the cost of the feed resources and utilization theme.

Table 16.3 Restrictions on the Allocation of Research Budget by Theme, Kenya Agricultural Research Institute (KARI)

Option[a]	Net Present Value (NPV) (Ksh million) by Theme					
	Feed Resources and Utilization	Animal Health	Animal Breeding and Genetic Improvement	Socio-economics	All Themes	Efficiency Losses
Option 1	56,526	15,632	2,801	15,234	90,193	0
Option 2	39,217	23,869	2,801	15,234	81,121	9,072
Option 3	26,603	23,869	2,801	15,234	68,507	21,686

a. Difference between NPV from option 1 and NPV from option under consideration.
Option 1: Budget Ksh 50 million, no restriction on budget share by theme. Options 2 and 3: Budget Ksh 50 million, theme 1 (feed resources and utilization) maximum of 35 percent and 25 percent budget share, respectively

Other valuable insights can be gained from screening the range of funding levels from Ksh 30 million to Ksh 60 million to successfully implement the whole set of research activities. Box 16.1 shows the additional benefits from higher funding level. For example, if the dairy program invests Ksh 40 million instead of Ksh 30 million, additional net present value (NPV) amounts to around KSh 9,032 million with a B/C ratio of 1,324. The main conclusion that stands out from the results of tables 16.2 and 16.3 and box 16.1 is that all restrictions imposed on the decision space create very large efficiency losses. This information is of great practical value to decision makers because it clearly shows how economic potential is sacrificed in order to incorporate equity concerns or institutional factors.

Janssen and Waithaka (1998) further demonstrated the staff deployment that would arise between the eight dairy research centers if rationalization based on important regions and research themes were carried out (table 16.4).

Based on the expected benefits within mandate areas, Naivasha is the most important center, followed by both Kakamega and Kisii; then Embu, Kitale and Mtwapa; then Katumani and finally Muguga. Naivasha covers zones 1, 3, 4, and 6; while Kakamega covers only zone 2. Kisii covers zones 1, 2, and 4; and Embu covers zones 1, 2, 3, and 4. Kitale covers zones 1, 3, 4, and 6; Mtwapa covers zones 3, 4, 5, and 6;

Box 16.1 Variation of Available Research Budget, Kenya Agricultural Research Institute (KARI)

Research Budget Available (Ksh million, undiscounted)	Research Benefits in NPV (Ksh million)	Incremental Benefit/ Cost Ratio[a]
30	76,402.75	—
40	85,434.45	1,324
50	90,195.35	539
60	96,156.60	802

a. Incremental B/C ratio is defined as the ratio of increase of benefits and research costs (in net present value [NPV]) due to additional research funds between each step.

Table 16.4 Ranking of Kenya Agricultural Research Institute (KARI) Centers by Expected Benefits in the Mandate Area and Implications for Deployment of Researchers

Center	Ranking by Expected Benefits within Mandate Area	Most Important Zone within Mandate Area	Number of Researchers in Center	Number of Researchers Suggested after Redeployment
Naivasha	1	3	6	7
Kakamega	2	2	4	7
Kisii	2	1	2	7
Embu	4	4	5	4
Kitale	4	4	6	4
Mtwapa	4	7	3	4
Katumani	7	8	5	3
Muguga	8	4	7	2
TOTAL	—	—	38	38

Katumani covers zones 4 and 6; and Muguga covers zones 1, 2, 3, and 4. Kisii could take special responsibility for research for zone 1, Kakamega for zone 2, Naivasha for zone 3, Mtwapa for zone 5, and Katumani for zone 6. Although Kitale and Embu both cover zone 4, Embu, being more centrally placed, is favored over Kitale. Muguga has a wide coverage on most zones, but not to the extent covered by the other centers.

The dairy program had thirty-eight researchers within the eight centers in 1996. If these researchers were to be redeployed to reflect the share of economic benefits in the mandate region of the center, Kisii, Kakamega, Naivasha, and Mtwapa would receive additional staff. Muguga, Katumani, Kitale, and Embu would shed staff.

To obtain critical mass, dairy research could be restricted to the centers with the highest expected economic benefits to research. Muguga is ranked lowest among the eight centers and does not have high economic benefits for two of the zones it covers (3 and 4). Embu generates similar benefits to Kitale for zone 4. Mtwapa deals principally with zone 5, which is by far the least important zone in terms of economic benefits. Mtwapa can be left to concentrate on other research programs and Katumani

Table 16.5 Ranking of Five Kenya Agricultural Research Institute (KARI) Centers, Important Zones, and Researchers Present and Required

Center	Ranking on Zones	Most Important Zone	Researchers in Place	Researchers after Redeployment
Naivasha	1	3	6	9
Kisii	2	2	4	9
Kakamega	3	1	2	8
Kitale	4	4	6	6
Katumani	5	5	5	6
TOTAL	—	—	23	38

can then serve the eastern and coastal regions. Embu can forfeit its dairy mandate in favor of Kitale. Muguga can forfeit its dairy mandate, and Naivasha can take over to service Muguga's mandate areas in the Rift Valley and the central region. Table 16.5 shows the ranking of the remaining five centers and the number of their researchers before and after redeployment.

Ideally, because research priorities are meant to steer a long-run course for the institute, including the development of infrastructure and human capital, an institute-wide priority-setting exercise is supposed to be undertaken once every five to ten years. The results that, if the process is undertaken properly, are based on quantitative measures and consensus opinion should be adopted as the official guidelines for institute-wide resource allocation decisions.

Linking Priority Setting to Resource Allocation

The KARI has attached significant importance to priority setting as a means of guiding resource allocation decisions, demonstrating the value of agricultural research and claim over scarce public resources, and increasing its control over its research agenda by directing donor resources to its own priority areas. Despite the influence of priority setting in readjusting thinking and the stated priority research areas, however, it has had only a modest impact in influencing resource allocation decisions. As with institute-wide priorities, most program priorities have not been matched with resource allocation. Priority' research areas were not implemented because of rigidities in the system that resist change, the complexity of implementing recommendations such as moving or reducing staff within a hierarchical structure and complex organization, and lack of adequate funding.

On the one hand, this reflects the practical side of priority setting, in that it is not always easy to shift resources to reflect the new priorities in the short run. Issues of relocating staff and rationalization of centers are sensitive and at times political, calling for long-term implementation. On the other hand, a major assumption with priority setting is that programs will not take the newly set priorities and adopt them in one go. Rather, the assumption is that in future program planning, the recommendations will be considered and changes implemented gradually. This requires a monitoring and evaluation system that assesses ongoing activities and feeds the information gathered by this procedure into future planning processes. Although priorities have been set between themes in several programs, the link between the priority activities and budgeting has been weak. For priority setting to be effective, funds must be available in full and on time, irrespective of the source. To ensure that priorities are linked to allocation of funds, it is proposed that responsibility for priority setting and resource allocation be placed in the revamped office of the deputy director of research. This office will provide a common pool of resources for allocation to priority programs and projects, thereby reducing fragmented procedures, with their potential risk to donor and national agricultural research systems' (NARS') priorities (Shapiro 1999).

Another issue is that of putting too much emphasis on current problems (adaptive work), totally neglecting strategic work. A case in point is that of maize streak virus, which was not an issue in the 1980s, but gained importance in the 1990s and was controlled only because some strategic work (which was considered to be an academic area) was taking place.

Linking Research Investments to National Development Plans

The budget plays a crucial role in the cycle of research planning and management because it provides the essential link between planning and control. Its planning role is achieved by expressing in monetary terms the inputs needed to achieve the planned activities, where inputs are labor, materials, and equipment. Its control role is achieved by showing the inputs and other resources allocated to individual activities to enable scientists to undertake the tasks for which they are responsible. In other words, the responsibility for fulfilling a task such as breeding for a new variety of maize will be reflected by an amount allocated in the budget.

Public-sector organizations such as KARI are frequently faced with a lack of suitable output measurements, and therefore inputs consumed are often used as a measure of effectiveness. Thus the expenditure allocated in the budget for breeding a maize variety is crucially important because not only does it place a limit on the costs that can be incurred on this service, but it also reflects the planned level of service. Control can then be exercised by comparing budgeted results with actual results to ensure that expenditure levels are not exceeded and that planned activity levels are achieved.

The KARI's major sources of funds are the government of Kenya (GoK), multilateral and bilateral donors, internally generated revenue, and levy fees paid by the private sector. The government capacity to provide essential services has been increasingly strained by the large variance between revenues and expenditures, growing balance of payments difficulties, increasing demand for services, and a decline in efficiency within the public service. This has resulted in the curtailing of government expenditures, including those in agricultural research. The responsibility for setting ministerial and departmental budget ceilings, review of proposals, enforcement of priorities, and control of expenditures currently lies with the treasury. The treasury analyses national economic trends and spending patterns, and advises on the appropriate funding levels accordingly.

The KARI annual budgetary requirement is submitted to the parent ministry to be reflected in the government budget each year. The budget is an aggregation of individual scientists' budgets on research and development, submitted to the parent ministry for onward transmission to the treasury. In the treasury, the budget is captured in the national forward and annual budgets. The forward budget projects estimates for the next three years to link the annual budget more efficiently to the development plan. The development plan establishes the strategy and pattern of development to be pursued by the nation during a five-year period. It contains guidelines for government participation in the development process, including estimates of resource availability, appropriate public-sector activities, and priorities. The forward budget is based on ceilings approved by the government and reflects guidelines in the development plan.

It also provides the means for translating the pattern of development in the plan into prospective expenditures; for scheduling the implementation of programs, projects, and activities; and for ensuring effective coordination at the scheduling stage.

The annual printed estimates reflecting government priorities for the year emerge from a two-stage process. First, the annual budget specifies expenditures for one of the five years covered by the current forward budget. In the second stage, the annual budget is subjected to revision during the course of the fiscal year through supplementary appropriations. Subsequent publication of the appropriation accounts discloses actual budget out-turns and enables actual expenditures to be compared with the initial financial plan.

The KARI allocates government funds to its research centers through the authority to incur expenditures (AIE), which gives spending ceilings under various budget heads. Research centers access their budgets through standing imprest, which are surrendered as they are consumed until the funds are exhausted. The center directors are the accounting officers at the centers, and they spend the funds on behalf of the program heads and make returns to headquarters. In the recent past, underexpenditure of the authorized research budget has occurred, because of the government's failure to release allocated funds in full and on time, which has been a major concern. In the case of donor funds, the scientist is the cost center and is responsible for expending the project funds through the center director. Donors provide revolving funds through special center accounts. Replenishment of these accounts is made on the strength of expenditure statements submitted to donor liaison offices at KARI headquarters.

Centers generate revenue or appropriations in aid (AIA) from sale of research by-products (e.g., milk and seeds). The treasury has authorized KARI to keep 100 percent of its AIA, and in turn KARI management has authorized research centers to retain between 70 percent and 100 percent of the center-generated revenue. Centers are required to surrender the balance to headquarters accompanied by a plan for future activities using the retained revenue.

Financial/Accounting Systems and the Decentralization of Funds Management

Centralization Versus Decentralization

When KARI was created by the merger of the research department of the Ministry of Agriculture with research institutions of the defunct East African Community, it inherited a hierarchical administrative financial management structure that puts emphasis on control at the expense of responsiveness and efficiency. Although centralization has its strength in having one control center, its main weakness is that it easily loses touch with reality because of failure to keep in touch with all corners. It is also wasteful and inefficient when time and resources are spent seeking simple clearance from headquarters for day-to-day decision making.

Since the inception of KARI, many changes have occurred within the institute and also in its external environment. The treasury, donors, and farmers are now demanding more than just research products; they want actual impact, which was previously a less prominent concern. Funding agencies are also interested in transparency and accountability in the way research is conducted, and in measurable indicators of socioeconomic impact. The challenge to management is for a more entrepreneurial and outward-looking approach.

In response to these changes, KARI is transforming itself from a collection of traditionally organized research stations to an organization with an emphasis on the scientist, efficiency, and the consistency of its agenda with the national economic policy. This management style has led to the evolution of a decentralized general ledger account within the institution. This gradual shift toward decentralization ensures that local priorities can be adequately met and headquarters can facilitate the centers. Although this improves decision making at the center level, the situation could be improved and even more autonomy achieved if the centers were to take over major overheads such as staff remuneration and communications. If such drastic changes are made, efforts should be made to ensure that the decentralized units strive toward a common goal—fulfilling the mandate of the institute.

Project Financial Management System

To improve financial management and efficiency, KARI has put into place a state-of-the-art Project Financial Management System (PFMS). The PFMS is a computerized financial and accounting system, which was implemented in KARI in 1995 (Deloitte and Touche Consulting 1997). Because the computers at the centers and the central system at headquarters have no direct communication link, centers send their financial returns to the headquarters by diskette on a monthly basis. Plans are underway to link all centers through a computerized network.

The original PFMS was an online DOS-based integrated system, with several interlinked modules, which include budgeting, accounting, financial transactions, assets, and payroll. This has been upgraded to a Windows-based system, which is faster and more user-friendly. It has adequate capacity and configuration to process, record, and report financial transactions and related activities. It is based in the management and information department, and other users do not have online access to data or information within the PFMS system. The system produced timely accounts for the 1994–95 to the 1997–98 financial years and was useful in facilitating the closing of end-of-year accounts and the preparation of annual audit reports that were previously in arrears. Unlike in the past, returns from the centers are now current to the previous month.

The major strengths of PFMS are that the system produces timely reports because the entered information is processed online. The reports can be designed to meet different user requirements. The system can track budgets allocated to either projects or cost centers, and has facilities for preparing requests for reimbursement of costs. By capturing actual expenditure and the amounts budgeted for these expenditures, it enhances budget monitoring for different projects and the institute as a whole. The system satisfies general auditing and financial reporting needs in a decentralized, cost-effective, and efficient way. The decentralized general ledger system is capable of efficiently generating reports to various donors, resolving the cash flow bottleneck to researchers, and providing up-to-date information to management, particularly in the area of priority setting and budgeting. The system equally facilitates payroll, procurement, and fixed asset management, and cuts down on massive amounts of paperwork. The updated accounts are readily available to research managers at different levels in the institute.

The major problems with PFMS are the lack of adequately trained staff and the cumbersome coding required for input of information. Twenty out of the initial sixty personnel who were trained in the management of PFMS left the institute shortly afterward (World Bank 1998). Because some donors operate different systems, they need to be linked into the PFMS in order to reduce the chances of underreporting of their accounts. To cover staff shortfalls, other staff are being trained or recruited, and additional terminals are in place to enable managers to access financial information. The new system has reduced coding system problems and difficulties with incorrect coding of expenditures by centers. As a further refinement, plans are under way to link PFMS with planning, monitoring, and evaluation activities in order to improve on the quality of information being used for decision making.

Returns to Agricultural Research

Investments in research are usually costly, and in most cases the results are not immediate. Rationally, such resources should be allocated to those investments that ensure a high rate of return (ROR). Moreover, pressure on public and private investments in agricultural research has heightened the need to justify such investments vis-à-vis alternative public investments for development of the agricultural sector, such as extension and irrigation. Evaluation of the payoff from past investments in research systems is commonly referred to as ex-post impact assessment, while ex-ante approaches are used to estimate future returns to investments in research. Despite the availability of tools for assessing the impact of investments in research, only a few such assessments have been carried out, for several reasons, the main ones being:

- Lack of analytical capacity within programs;
- Inability of research institutes to retain trained economists who can carry out impact studies; and
- Lack of forward planning within programs so that data required for analysis may be generated.

Investments in agricultural research in both developed and developing countries have been shown to generate significant returns. Recent work on some African case studies reveal significant and positive ROR to investment in agricultural technology development and transfer in sub-Saharan Africa (Oehmke and Crawford 1993, 1996). Rates of return on investment for the projects studied were estimated to be 135 percent (Mali: maize), 31–92 percent (Senegal: cowpea), 40–60 percent (Kenya: maize), 40 percent (Nigeria: cocoa), 33 percent (Kenya: wheat), 21 percent (Zambia: maize), and 3 percent (Cameroon: cowpea). These studies imply that investments in research are justified. Rates of return are affected by the performance of other sectors concerned with development of the agricultural sector, such as extension and seed systems. For example, Karanja (1993) showed that reducing expenditures on extension by half reduced the ROR from over 60 to 46 percent. Reducing effectiveness on the seed system reduced ROR to 39 percent.

Using ex-ante assessment methodologies, yield projections and economic ROR were calculated for the NARP-II (Beynon et al. 1998). The calculation of an economic rate of return (ERR) for the project as a whole was constrained by data limitations. Yield improvements or cost reductions from use of technologies, the rate and extent of their adoption by farmers, and the productivity and output gains because of their application cannot be accurately predicted because they vary significantly across agro-ecological zones (AEZs). Benefits from improved technologies could also be influenced by external factors such as the availability of agricultural inputs and the efficiency of the marketing and distribution system. A limited economic analysis focusing on determining the expected benefits from research on food grains (maize, wheat, sorghum, and millet) was attempted. The analysis shows that research on food grains would yield an ERR of 24 percent, while the net present value of food grains research, based on a fifteen-year cash flow, discounted at the opportunity cost of capital of 12 percent, would amount to about US$70 million.

Weaknesses in Linkages between Priorities and Budgeting

Difficulty of Defining an Optimal Priority-Setting and Budgeting Process

Policymakers should be made aware that insufficient financing of recurrent operating costs results in important assets being underutilized, laying idle, or deteriorating at an unacceptable rate. It is therefore imperative that the government guarantees adequate funding for research operations and maintenance, commensurate with the level of scientific work and support services. As part of ensuring financial stability, budgetary revisions must be agreed upon by the parent ministry and the treasury in order to ensure that this condition is met at all times.

Research has both long- and short-term recurrent-cost budget requirements. The treasury operates on an annual budgetary basis and tries to stabilize cash flow requirements by spreading disbursements evenly over the year. This results in arbitrary budget cuts, which are done without consultation with the responsible scientists, resulting in research activities being only partially funded. It would be much better to do away with some projects or activities than to fund them partially. When funding shortfalls occur, scientists should be requested to readjust their priorities in line with the new budget ceilings. In many instances, it makes little difference if the recurrent-cost budget is inadequate for a month or two or is slightly lower one year than the next. However, for an agricultural research activity, the lack of sufficient operational resources during a crucial period of the cropping cycle may invalidate years of carefully planned experimentation.

Constraints on a Rationalized Budgeting Process

Rationalizing the size and scope of the research system makes it possible to mobilize more resources. This may bring about the need to downsize the research system to match the financial carrying capacity of the nation. Downsizing, of course, also has its costs. Research capacity may be lost during the process, researcher morale may suffer, and the expenses incurred for staff severance pay and disposing of outmoded buildings and equipment may be quite significant. Clear guidelines are needed to ensure that the downsizing exercise does not become overly politicized and that priority activities are protected during the process.

Multisourcing and Restricted Donor Funding

Generally, donors have been criticized for arguing that recurrent costs are not developmental and that grants and loans should be used for capital expenditures only. As a result, the impact of donor-assisted projects on recurrent costs has been twofold—there has been an increased demand on local budgetary resources to meet the recurrent cost component of projects, and a longer-term requirement to meet new levels of staffing and equipment provision created by capital spending. Although donors have made significant contributions to agricultural research, there is a price to be paid in relying too heavily on donor funds, including high transaction costs for the research institutes; loss of control of the research agenda; unbalanced incentive systems; loss of coherence in internal budgetary, accounting, and review systems; and major uncertainties in long-term planning. Efficiency criteria have seldom been used in allocating donor funds. The allocation decision is more in the control of the donor than of the NARS. The normal cycle of donor-assisted programs is too short to efficiently support agricultural research. There is evidence of donor fatigue, because donor support for agriculture and agricultural research in Africa has been on the decline. The remaining donors continue to offer expatriates who more often resemble students on learning missions.

Donor dependency also leads to fragmentation and lack of continuity in research efforts. Donors often ignore institutions' priorities and insist on their own priorities in commodities, problems, or regions. High-priority activities are neglected for "new mode" research subjects or approaches, for example, commodity research in the 1970s, farming systems research in the 1980s, and natural resource management in the 1990s (Byerlee and Alex 1998).

The KARI has equipped itself with the capability to manage fluctuations in the timing and levels of funds from the various sources. The effort to increase internally generated revenue would create buffer funds to ensure more flexibility in cash management. Other possible funding mechanisms that are being explored are matching grants, competitive grants, levies and check-offs, and endowments. The strengths and weaknesses of these mechanisms are discussed in Janssen (1998). Levies have been used successfully in export crops such as tea and coffee, but would be troublesome for food crops that are not formally marketed. Matching and competitive grants require much effort in fund-raising and can end up addressing the wrong agenda. Endowment funds would be a good choice, but they require an environment with well-developed capital markets.

Managing Cash Inflows and Disbursements

Characteristics of the Inflow of Financial Resources in KARI

Even though government spending on agricultural research has increased since the mid-1990s, the funding levels for these programs are generally below the levels that economic and social considerations would suggest as optimal. Currently, investment in research in all sectors is about 0.4 percent of the gross domestic product (GDP), of which about 0.3 percent is for agricultural research. For Kenya to meet food and raw material requirements by the year 2020, overall investments in agricultural research have to be increased to at least 1 percent of GDP (Ndiritu 1999).

The KARI is also facing a decline in financial capability in terms of limited and unreliable provision of operating resources, and a degree of donor dependency that is perceived as being unsustainable. In the past, the GoK has been unable to release all of the recurrent funds earmarked for KARI, but both the GoK and some donors have reportedly held back donor pledges to KARI. Increasing investment in agricultural research will require the support of stakeholders in both the public and the private sectors. The parent ministry has the responsibility of facilitating the participation of stakeholders and promoting dialogue between them.

The Gap between Managing Institutional Funds and Managing Scientific Research

Agricultural research systems, like complex machines, rust and decay when not regularly operated and properly maintained. In the extreme, inadequate recurrent-cost financing can bring research institute operations to a halt. If nothing of value is produced, funds dry up entirely, researchers become disenchanted for lack of opportunity to apply their talents, and morale plummets. Should the situation persist, the research system begins to decay. Insufficient operational budgets result in important assets being underutilized. Implications of inadequate funding are (Tabor 1998):

- A backlog of overdue repairs and maintenance;
- Researchers opting to absenteeism, having multiple jobs and moonlighting;
- A diversion of research property to nonresearch uses;
- Well-trained scientists becoming frustrated and leaving the system, in some cases abandoning research altogether; and
- Declines in the skills and operating capacity of staff because of reduced flow of research activities and dwindling contact among scientists working in similar disciplines.

If scientists become convinced that periodic funding shortages are likely to occur, they will adapt their behavior to deal with the constraint. Such adaptations may include a biasing of the research agenda away from long-gestating projects and operating-resource-intensive activities toward activities requiring fewer resources, and the allocation of large amounts of scientists' time to mobilizing sufficient operating resources. Such practices cause inefficiency and ineffectiveness in research activities and in the research system as a whole.

Insufficient recurrent-cost resources also make the research system highly vulnerable to programmatic biases introduced by donors, the private sector, and others willing to provide a small amount of "lifeline" resources. Institutes with recurrent-cost constraints are in a poor position to negotiate with external agencies supplying financing, because, without their support, activities might simply cease. As a result, high-priority research may be neglected in favor of low-priority work that happens to have a willing financier.

Future Options in Increasing the Efficiency of Resource Allocation and Fund Management

Improving Cost-Effectiveness

Several options are open for achieving a more efficient allocation of resources (in terms of securing more research outputs for less cost). For example, more quantitative forms of research priority setting are specifically aimed at improving efficiency (measured by producer and consumer surplus), even though the results of such analysis are often modified by other criteria (notably equity) during decision making on the allocation of priorities and resources. The extent to which efficiency is actually improved thus depends substantially on:

- The accuracy of the estimates concerning the technical gains due to and the rate and extent of adoption of new technology; and
- The weight given to efficiency as opposed to other criteria in setting priorities and the extent to which government and donor budget allocations match the set of derived priorities.

Analysis of data from Kenya suggests, for example, that the correlation between priorities and budget allocations is typically very weak (Beynon et al. 1998). Measures designed to increase the degree of user involvement in the design of research programs and the allocation of resources are intended to minimize waste from developing inappropriate technologies that stand little chance of being adopted, but may themselves be expensive to implement. Some loss in efficiency may also occur if resource allocation decisions are skewed in favor of particularly powerful interest groups that are able to dominate other users.

The operations of the agricultural research funds, and ultimately of the consolidated funding mechanisms, have considerable potential to improve the efficiency of service delivery through coordinating effort and minimizing duplication. Competitive bidding for research grants and extension contracts can be expected to produce gains in efficiency, but will work best where the private sector is well developed and competitive and the public sector has the capacity to manage and monitor. Lack of such capacity should not, however, preclude experimentation with such measures, because such capacity will develop partly through experience.

State withdrawal from direct control of research works best when there is already an active private sector and the macroeconomics and sectoral policy are conducive to further private investment in service provision. Levy financing will be most appropriate when the marketing structure is sufficiently concentrated to permit ready collection, while other commercialization, cost-recovery, and revenue-generation measures will work best where adequate financial management systems exist and collection costs are low. Many such measures will have a positive equity effect, but distributional concerns will be best protected when there is a political commitment to maintaining services to the poor or to implementing alternative and more efficient poverty-alleviation measures.

Priority setting will work best, and will be most likely to lead to desirable resource reallocation, when the need for efficiency-oriented priority setting is internally recognized and capacity exists for processes to be internally led. Measures to improve the user-orientation of service will work best when there is effective organization and representation of all interest groups, including those representing the resource poor, and when there is commitment to, and skills in, more participatory approaches to research. Reforms to the management of funding and the contracting out of service delivery will be most effective when transparent and efficient financial and contract management systems are in place.

Improving the Link between Priority Setting and Budgeting

Agricultural research priority setting is the process of making choices among a set of potential research activities. All functional agricultural research systems have followed either formal or informal priority-setting procedures to arrive at their research agendas. The formal procedures have been shown to improve both quality and transparency of complex resource allocation decisions by structuring information on client constraints and the potential of research to address these constraints. Clear and systematic presentation of priorities also assists national agricultural research organizations in taking a proactive role in soliciting support for the priority areas. Priority-setting processes can also be used to broaden participation in the formulation of the research agenda, and thereby to increase the organization's constituency base. Priority setting must be in step with strategic planning by sending sufficiently early signals of changing emphasis between programs and themes within programs. Such priorities should be derived through a consultative and participative consensus-building procedure. Only those projects that have been ranked highly should be funded, for priority-setting work to be successful.

To improve on the link between priority setting and budgeting requires bridging the gap of recurrent operating costs in financing that is a major drawback to timely availability of research funds. In the process of developing alternative funding sources, the following options to improve operational costs are adapted from Tabor (1998, 53–62) and should be considered. Decision makers need to:

Carefully screen new projects for recurrent-cost obligations

Projects aimed at institution-building rarely incorporate estimates of the full recurrent costs of maintaining capital works or of the ongoing training needed to keep the skills of project personnel up to date. Few project appraisals include the likely ongoing costs of replacing scientific assets that become economically or technically obsolete. The costs of replacing personnel who leave the institute because of promotions, transfers, or other forms of attrition are rarely estimated. If such costs are systematically underestimated, research systems are likely to end up running financially unsustainable projects.

Make appropriate use of recurrent-cost resources

Better management may be the solution to making more effective use of limited recurrent-cost resources. New management procedures may be necessary to correct problems of waste, corruption, and inefficient use of resources. The first step is to establish how recurrent-cost resources are being used. As management policies and procedures may be thrown into question in this process, it is important to obtain the views of both the managers and the scientists doing the research. Although expert committees can help to unearth deficiencies in recurrent-cost management and to identify strategies for improvement, measures must be taken at each level of the research system.

Individual researchers should be encouraged to share equipment, vehicles, and field site operations with colleagues. Careful coordination of research projects avoids duplication of effort and unnecessary outlays. Research program leaders should encourage the formation of research teams to optimize use of scarce recurrent resources. Options for the sharing of facilities and other resources between programs and projects should be identified. Research system leaders should document the extent of the recurrent-cost financing problem and forecast the shortfall. They should identify the causes of the problem and formulate strategies to address them. They should involve research managers at all levels in the search for solutions. They should formulate the needed changes in research policy and argue the merits of these recommendations before the relevant oversight bodies.

Downsize to the institution's recurrent-cost carrying capacity

When all other options have been exhausted, no choice may remain but to downsize the research system to match the financial carrying capacity of the nation. In some cases, rationalizing the size and scope of the research system makes it possible to mobilize more resources. Downsizing, of course, also has its costs (see *Constraints on a rationalized budgeting process,* above).

405

Restore confidence in the adequacy of recurrent resources

Perceptions tend to be self-fulfilling, particularly where financing is concerned. If sci-entists do not believe that the recurrent-funding problem has been satisfactorily resolved, they will continue to operate as if it is still a major problem. Sharing budg-etary information with scientific staff is the best way to restore their confidence. If sci-entists see that recurrent-cost commitments made at the time of budget approval have been honored, they will develop trust in the research system's capacity to meet essen-tial operating needs. This calls for transparency in the discussion and dissemination of financial information within the NARS.

Programming under Multiple Financial Sources

With their long experience in carrying out research supported by various donors, the IARCs have evolved some reasonably well functioning systems. Unlike public entities such as KARI, the IARCS can shift staff to priority research areas while not worrying much about the political ramifications of such moves. An example is drawn from the International Livestock Research Institute (ILRI) (George Kanza, personal communi-cation, 1998). The institute has developed complex, but functioning, network systems to track down expenses within both programs and regions. Senior accountants are familiar with the institute's financial management system and offer supervision and backstopping to the accounts' staff. To cater to institutional involvement, overheads are built into projects to reduce the burden on the institute. Administrative costs to cover communications, secretarial services, accounts administration, and control com-prise up to 20 percent of operational costs. Budgets are made over a long time hori-zon and are adjusted annually to keep track of changes in activities or priorities. Accountants are involved in budgeting formulation at the proposal stage to ensure that important aspects are not omitted in the final proposals. However, although the system puts more emphasis on research output and less on control, scientists continue to feel as if the accounting department is controlling their work too strongly.

Matching Budgeting to Organizational Structure

Organization refers to the way a system and its components interact with their envi-ronment and each other at all levels. Structure refers to the way work is divided into tasks and coordinated to achieve stable patterns of behavior and output (Elliot 1998). Most research institutions are structured with special attention to securing and retain-ing funding from governments, donors, own sources, and clients of research. However, structures that are highly suited to obtaining funds are not necessarily suited to exe-cuting research. Furthermore, funding mechanisms are country-sspecific and cannot easily be transplanted to other countries or regions; each country must cultivate its own.

In 1991 KARI had fifty-three commodity and thirty-three factor research pro-grams, and fifteen national research centers (four also with regional mandates), six regional centers, and ten subcenters spread over the country (KARI 1991). The KARI has taken steps to reconsider the distribution of emphasis between adaptive and strategic or basic research on commodities and factors. Organization and structure are driven by the need to match limited resources to highly complex problems. The KARI's current structure of regionally based adaptive research and national strategic research is based on the need for an expanded scope to address the needs of subsistence farming and rapidly increasing food needs, the increasing mandates from domestic and international research systems, and the evolution of agricultural and biological sciences. Adaptive research is characterized by significant heterogeneity in AEZs, underdeveloped market infrastructure, complex multiple enterprises, variable rainfall regimes, and low-input systems. This suggests a more decentralized and dispersed institutional structure that constrains movement toward economies of size or scale and development of capacity in strategic research (see chapter 7).

Achieving an optimum level of decentralization is made more difficult by the location specificity of both applied and adaptive research. Success of adaptive research depends critically on the consistent flow of new technologies and knowledge from applied research programs. With constraints on resources, there are trade-offs between the size of the commodity programs and the number of research programs included in the portfolio. Even so, the problem-solving capacity of adaptive research needs to be combined with the longer-term and more specialized applied research required to solve more intractable problems or produce real advances in yield potential. Thus, efficient allocation of funds between national commodity research programs and regional research centers lies beyond priority-setting and resource allocation procedures.

A crucial task for KARI is to implement the organizational structure proposed in the new strategic plan (Shapiro 1999). In this plan, the strategic objectives are to seek new and sustainable funding sources, improve internal and external communications, develop a participatory and consultative environment, decentralize management structures and systems, and implement an appropriate research paradigm embracing technology dissemination. These objectives call for the creation of an Office of Director of Research to oversee internal functions and to be assisted by the Office of Commercial Development, which will seek alternative funding avenues. A major task will be to develop an appropriate research paradigm that balances adaptive and strategic research. This strategy also recognizes the role of planning, monitoring, and evaluation in feeding the whole system that will be the responsibility of the director of research. The motive is to set in place an environment that guarantees maximum research output with minimum emphasis on control of the research process.

Lessons in Setting Research Priorities

1. Priority-setting exercises at the program level have been successful to the extent of refining methodologies to suit the peculiar needs of diverse programs.
2. A major weakness with priority setting has been that results have not always led to resource mobilization because of rigidity in the system, complexity of shifting resources, and lack of funds.

407

3. To enhance resource allocation, priority-setting activities should be in step with the strategic plan.

4. The question of decentralization versus centralization should focus on the future scope of the institute, following the guidelines of the strategic plan.

5. Once research funds are approved in the annual budgets, modifications should be avoided because there could be a risk of negating the whole investment process. The KARI needs to get firm commitment from the funding entities that approved funds will be available in full and on time.

6. Inasmuch as accounting and financial management procedures are necessary for fiscal discipline, the emphasis should be on facilitation of maximum research output and minimum control of the research process.

7. To take care of recurrent cost problems, efforts should be made to carefully screen new projects for recurrent cost obligations, to instill management practices aimed at appropriate use of recurrent-cost resources, and to downsize to the institution's recurrent cost carrying capacity.

8. Accountants should be involved in budget preparation to ensure that administrative and other overheads are included in project budgets.

9. The project financial management system that has been installed at KARI has improved financial management in the institute. However, this system needs to be used more widely by program leaders and senior management.

10. Alternative sources of funding must be aggressively sought to reduce overreliance on donor and state funding. Inasmuch as alternatives sources are sought, the government must be committed to the funding of agricultural research, particularly in areas where the private sector cannot and where collection of research revenue is problematic, for example, collection of cess from produce that is not marketed through formal channels.

REFERENCES

Alston, Julian M., George W. Norton, and Phillip G. Pardey. 1995. *Science under scarcity: Principles and practice for agricultural research evaluation and priority setting.* Ithaca, N.Y.: Cornell University Press.

Audi, Patrick O., and Priority Setting Working Group. 1997. *Priority setting for regional research programs: Assessing the impact of alternative interventions in Machakos, Makueni, Kitui and Mwingi Districts of Eastern Kenya.* Nairobi: Kenya Agricultural Research Institute (KARI).

Beynon, Jonathan, Stephen Akroyd, Alex Duncan, and Stephen Jones. 1998. *Financing the future: Options for agricultural research and extension in sub-Saharan Africa.* Oxford: Oxford Policy Management.

Byerlee, Derek, and Gary Alex. 1998. Towards more effective use of external assistance in building agricultural research systems. In *Financing agricultural research: A source,* ed. Steven R. Tabor, Willem Janssen, and Hilarion Bruneau, 97–113. The Hague: International Service for National Agricultural Research (ISNAR).

Cassava Priority Setting Working Group. 1995. *Cassava research priorities at KARI.* Nairobi: Kenya Agricultural Research Institute (KARI).

Contant, Rudolph B., and Anthony Bottomley. 1988. Priority setting in agricultural research. International Service for National Agricultural Research (ISNAR) Working Paper No. 10. The Hague: ISNAR.

Davis, Jeff S., Peter A. Oram, and James G. Ryan. 1987. Assessment of agricultural research priorities: An international perspective. Consultative Group on International Agricultural Research (CGIAR) Monograph No. 4. Canberra, Australia: Australian Centre for International Agricultural Research (ACIAR)

Deloitte and Touche Consulting. 1997. *KARI–revenue generation strategic review*. Overseas Development Administration contract reference: cntr 96 1193A. Final Report. Nairobi: KARI.

Dyer, Roger F., and Ernest H. Forman. 1992. *An analytical approach to marketing decisions*. Englewood Cliffs, N.J.: Prentice Hall International Editions.

Elliot, Howard. 1998. Financing agricultural research: Do organization and structure make a difference? In *Financing agricultural research: A source*, ed. Steven R. Tabor, Willem Janssen, and Hilarion Bruneau, 115–30. The Hague: International Service for National Agricultural Research, Netherlands (ISNAR).

Fox, Glen. 1987. Models of resource allocation in public agricultural research: A survey. *Journal of Agricultural Economics* 37:449–62.

Hazel, Peter B. R., and Roger D. Norton. 1986. *Mathematical programming for economic analysis in agriculture*. New York: Macmillan.

Horticulture Priority Setting Working Group. 1996. *Research priorities of KARI's horticulture program*. Nairobi: Kenya Agricultural Research Institute (KARI).

Janssen, Willem. 1995. Priority setting in agricultural and natural resource management research: Following Hamlet's dream or Macbeth's plan? In *Linking adoption studies and priority setting for livestock research. Workshop proceedings*, ed. Matthias Hitzel and Willem Janssen, 1–21. The Hague: International Service for National Agricultural Research (ISNAR).

———. 1998. Alternative funding mechanisms: How changes in the public sector affect agricultural research. In: *Financing agricultural research: A source book*, ed. Steven R. Tabor, Willem Janssen, and Hilarion Bruneau, 137–60. The Hague: International Service for National Agricultural Research (ISNAR).

Janssen, Willem, and Michael Waithaka, eds. 1998. *Priority setting in livestock research: The case of dairy program in KARI*. The Hague: International Service for National Agricultural Research (ISNAR).

Kamau, Mercy, Daniel Kilambya, and Bradford F. Mills. 1997. Commodity program priority setting: The experience of the Kenya Agricultural Research Institute. International Service for National Agricultural Research (ISNAR) Briefing Paper No. 34. The Hague: ISNAR.

Kamau, Mercy, and Bradford F. Mills. 1998. Technology, location and trade: Kenyan vegetables. *Agricultural Systems* 58:395–416.

Karanja, Daniel D. 1990. The rate of returns to maize research in Kenya (1955–88). Master's thesis, Michigan State University.

———.1993. An economic and institutional analysis of maize research in Kenya. Paper presented at the United States Agency for International Development (USAID)-Regional Economic Development Services Office for Eastern and Southern Africa (REDSO)-European Space Agency (ESA) conference of Agricultural Research Networks. Nairobi: International Laboratory for Research on Animal Diseases (ILRAD).

409

Kelly, T. G., James G. Ryan, and B. K. Patel. 1995. Applied participatory priority setting in agricultural research: Making trade-offs transparent and explicit. *Agricultural Systems* 49:177–216.

Kenya Agricultural Research Institute (KARI). 1991. *KARI's priorities to the year 2000.* Nairobi: KARI.

———. 1995a. *National Agricultural Research Programme Phase II, Project Implementation Manual, Final Version.* Nairobi: KARI.

———. 1995b. *Priority setting into the 21st century: A position paper by the priority-setting working group.* Nairobi: KARI.

———. 1996. *Priority setting for the KARI dairy program.* Nairobi: KARI.

Mills, Bradford, ed. 1998. *Agricultural research priority setting: Information investments for the improved use of research resources.* The Hague: International Service for National Agricultural Research (ISNAR).

Mills, Bradford, and Daniel D. Karanja. 1997. Process and methods for research program priority setting: The experience of the Kenya Agricultural Research Institute Wheat Program. *Food Policy* 22:63–79.

Mulinge, Wellington, and Anni McLeod. 1998. *Priorities for animal health research in KARI. Report for stakeholders.* Nairobi: Kenya Agricultural Research Institute (KARI).

Ndiritu, Cyrus. 1999. Agricultural research in the context of economic development. Paper presented to World Bank sponsored Rural Week, 21–23 March 1999, Washington, D.C.

Ngigi, Margaret. 2003. Success in African agriculture: The case of smallholder dairying in Eastern Africa. Paper presented at the In WEnt, IFPRI, NEPAD, CTA conference "Successes in African Agriculture," Pretoria, South Africa, 1–3 December.

Oehmke, James, and Eric W. Crawford. 1993. The impact of agricultural technology in sub-Saharan Africa: A synthesis of symposium findings. MSU International Development Paper No. 14. East Lansing: Michigan State University.

———. 1996. The impact of agricultural technology in sub-Saharan Africa. *Journal of African Economies* 5:271–92.

Place, Frank, Steve Franzel, Querish Noordin, and Bashir Jama. 2003. Improved fallows in Kenya, history, farmer practice and impacts. Paper presented at the In WEnt, IFPRI, NEPAD, CTA conference "Successes in African Agriculture," Pretoria, South Africa, 1–3 December.

Romero, Carlos E., and Tahir Rehman. 1989. *Multiple criteria analysis for agricultural decisions.* Developments in Agricultural Economics No. 5. Amsterdam: Elsevier Science Publishers.

Saaty, Thomas L. 1980. *The analytic hierarchy process.* New York: McGraw Hill.

Shapiro, Paul. 1999. *Strategic planning report KARI.* Vashon, Wash.: Paul Shapiro Associates.

Soil Fertility and Plant Nutrition Priority Setting Working Group. 1995. *Soil fertility and plant nutrition research priorities in Kenya.* Nairobi: Kenya Agricultural Research Institute (KARI).

Sorghum Program Priority Setting Working Group. 1995. *Sorghum research priorities at the KARI.* Nairobi: Kenya Agricultural Research Institute (KARI).

Tabor, Steven. 1998. Recurrent operating cost policies for agricultural research. In *Financing agricultural research: A source book,* ed. Steven R. Tabor, Willem Janssen, and Hilarion Bruneau, 47–63. The Hague: International Service for National Agricultural Research (ISNAR).

Waithaka, Michael. 1998. *Integration of a user perspective in research priority setting: The case of dairy technology adoption in Meru, Kenya.* Kommunikations und Beratung 22. Weikersheim, Germany: Margraf Verlag.

Waithaka, Michael, Tom Cusack, Ephraim Mukisira, Peterson Mwangi, Nancy Nganga, and Jane Wamuongo, eds. 1999. *An assessment of the impact of research programs undertaken by the Kenya Agricultural Research Institute.* First draft report. Nairobi: KARI.

World Bank. 1998. *National Agricultural Research Project II.* 10–26 February 1998, Nairobi, Kenya, Aide Memoir. Washington, D.C.: World Bank.

PART 5

Synthesis and Conclusions

Synthesis and Conclusions

SAM CHEMA, ADIEL N. MBABU, STEPHEN AKROYD, ROMANO M. KIOME, AND CYRUS G. NDIRITU

Lessons Learned in the Transformation of Kenya's National Agricultural Research

This study of the transformation of Kenya's national agricultural research has imparted several lessons that can be of use to other countries pursuing institutional reforms in Africa. These include:

- The transformation of institutions is an evolutionary process in response to identifiable stimuli.
- The nature of the transformation process greatly depends on the intensity of the stimuli, and, on the other hand, the institution's capacity to understand and respond to those stimuli.
- Thus, transformation processes are slow and often painful, requiring conscious and deliberate change strategies.

Transformation Process

Identifiable actors create institutions for a specific purpose in a particular historical moment. In the due course of time these objectives change, as do the historical actors themselves. These changes in the external and internal environments generate the necessary conditions for institutional transformations. External forces of institutional change are complex and dynamic. As chapters 2, 3, and 4 illustrate, these include interest groups in the politico-economy, diverse and ever-changing biophysical conditions, and the diverse and dynamic character of the client groups.

In Kenya, the agricultural sector is the pillar of economic and social development and it has served as an important arena for key actors in the political economy. As chapter 5 illustrates, agricultural research was first conceptualized to serve European commercial large-scale farmers in the early 1900s. However, in the 1950s the Swynnerton Plan opened the door to African smallholders and included them in the agricultural research system. The complex production systems of the smallholders have preoccupied Kenya's agricultural managers ever since.

Institutional Capacity to Respond to Stimuli for Change

Considering competing objectives among clients and stakeholders and the frequent changes in the relative ability to influence change, one can expect continuous pressures for institutional change to accommodate the ever-changing expectations. Signals for these expectations can be expressed in different forms at different operational levels—government policies, lobby groups, and stakeholder and client presentations. However, for an institution to effectively respond, it must have the capacity to register, process, and understand the expectations and to mobilize sufficient resources to meet those expectations. In other words, to respond effectively and efficiently, institutions must embrace a learning-by-doing culture.

In the case of the Kenya Agricultural Research Institute (KARI), as chapters 5 through 9 indicate, substantial efforts have been made to restructure the research organization, to improve decision-making processes, and to consolidate knowledge and skills for complex technology generation and dissemination. The point of departure for the transformation process was the decision to place smallholders at the heart of the institutional mission. The diversity and complexity of this task led to a paradigm shift—from science- to client-led research. Yet, the operationalization of this new paradigm was not easy. The first attempt to meet smallholder expectations in the 1950s led to a multiplication of science-led research that was ineffective. In the 1970s, the creation of farming systems units in headquarters also turned out to be ineffective. However, the consolidation of adaptive research programs in the National Agricultural Research Programme, Phase II (NARP-II) managed to bridge yield gaps between research stations and farmers. The current engagement in catalyzing extension agents and civil society in the delivery and utilization of agricultural technologies is expected to contribute significantly to the challenge of scaling up the adoption of the new technology.

A harmonized planning, monitoring, and evaluation (PM&E) system has been institutionalized to improving decision-making capacity. The system includes decentralization and stakeholder and client involvement in decision-making processes. Likewise, massive training programs have been undertaken to provide disciplinary depth and multidisciplinary breadth. This, in turn, provides the capacity to deal with the diverse scope required by the complex and dynamic smallholder production systems.

Strategies for the Management of Change

It is generally assumed that change automatically occurs once decisions to affect it have been reached. Such optimism neglects the fact that, more often than not, change generates both losers and winners. Needless to say, potential losers will do everything in their power to resist imminent change. In well-managed change processes, attempts are made to steer toward a win-win situation. The closer such a reality is to being reached, the less resistance is likely to be experienced. In the case of KARI, NARP-I initiated massive changes and, as chapter 6 indicates, the expectations were too optimistic. With that experience, KARI management developed proactive strategies to manage the change process in NARP-II. Task forces and thematic studies were initi-ated to promote brainstorming and consensus building.

Lessons from Objective-Based Linkages

Linkages and Partnership

The KARI's overall goal is poverty alleviation and food security for small-scale farmers and urban consumers within a sustainable environment of natural resources. Its main mission is to provide tested agricultural technologies as a contribution to the overall goal, but there are other research institutions, both national and international, contributing to this mission. KARI has learned that it must actively work with other key players engaged in both research and technology dissemination. These institutions include colleges and faculties of agriculture, as well as private organizations and nongovernmental organiza-tions (NGOs). In addition, ASARECA and the International Agricultural Research Cen-ters (IARCs) have all contributed to the national research agenda. Although partnerships with other research institutions have improved the quality of KARI's research, linkages with extension agencies are essential to diffuse new technologies to farmers. KARI's managers have developed partnerships with farmers through KARI's farming systems' approach to research, extension, and training (FSA-RET).

The Evolution of Goal-Oriented Linkages

National universities, private researchers, and other research institutions

The Agricultural Research Fund (ARF) has been the principal instrument that has been developed to foster partnerships with other national research organizations. This competitive fund was established in 1990 to solicit applications for research funding for projects, including those from other research institutes, such as the Kenya Try-panosomiasis Research Institute (KETRI). In order to encourage outsiders, the fund was not open to KARI scientists until later in the 1990s. Subsequently, scientists from KARI centers have been encouraged to compete nonpreferentially for grants from the fund. At the same time, projects of interdisciplinary and multi-institutional nature have been given preference.

Lessons learned with the ARF

To be sustainable, KARI feels that there is a need to develop a less donor-dependent mechanism for securing funds, because donor contributions have not always been consistent, leading to highly disruptive interruptions in research. Also, the small size of many funded projects has imposed high administrative costs and limited both the size of the partnership network and the depth of research that can be undertaken. The networking issue is being solved to some extent by giving preference to interdiscipli-nary and multi-institutional research proposals. The small size of each award is coun-tered by a plan to provide matching funds to scientists who can attract alternative financing. Excessive donor dependency can be reduced by encouraging alternative contributions and by persuading existing private-sector contributors to the KARI,

417

such as the Kenya Breweries Limited (KBL) and the Pyrethrum Board of Kenya (PBK), to channel some of their money through ARF.

Linkages with IARCs

In the past, the IARCs have used KARI, along with other national agricultural research systems (NARS), for germplasm and vaccine testing. In programs that have gained momentum during NARP-II, international scientists based in Kenya have been encouraged to submit joint bids with national scientists to the ARF to address KARI's priorities. The second mode of fostering collaboration has been through contracting IARC scientists to carry out research in areas where they have a comparative advantage. Wherever possible, a training element for national scientists has been incorporated in such contracts. A third avenue to partnerships has been through networking. Formerly, such networks were operated from the international centers. Since the establishment of the ASARECA, most of these networks are now coordinated through this association. The advantage is that the directors of NARS in east and central Africa manage ASARECA, bringing project formulation, monitoring, and impact assessment into close contact with the national programs.

Lessons learned

With the exception of projects funded through the ARF or contracted to IARCs, other collaborative projects in which KARI (and other NARS) has participated have tended to address alien goals. A new approach is needed to develop jointly conceived and funded projects consistent with the IARC's mandates, and those of NARS.

Linkage with Extension Agents

Crop agriculture

The evolution of Kenya's agricultural extension system and its linkages with research are discussed in chapter 11. In pre-KARI times, agricultural researchers considered their mission accomplished when the results of their research were written up, including appropriate recommendations, and a report was handed over to public extension agents. In the 1980s, with the advent of farming systems research (FSR), an attempt was made to involve extension agents in a farm-level evaluation of constraints facing farmers, followed by formulation and testing of problem-solving technologies. A major problem that has persisted to date is the lack of synchrony in funding these joint processes. A frequent result has been that researchers and extension personnel have not been able to consistently work on farm together, thus vitiating this important linkage. Incorporating researchers as an integral part of the extension process through the Training and Visit (T&V) Extension Project in the early 1980s was believed to be an important advance.

During NARP-I, an important step in the evolution of linkages was the establishment of a Research-Extension Liaison Division (RELD) to develop strong ties with KARI. Headed by a former senior research officer in the KARI, this decision appeared to be a significant step forward. A Memorandum of Understanding (MOU) was signed to formalize the linkages in 1993. The perennial problem of lack of synchrony in funding was handled through the creation of a joint research-extension bank account to facilitate activities mandated under the MOU. Regional Research Centers (RRCs) set up Center Research Advisory Committees (CRACs) chaired by provincial or district heads of Ministry of Agriculture operations. Until the T&V extension model was judged to have failed, this linkage appeared to be performing satisfactorily.

Animal agriculture

The term "animal agriculture" gained currency in the institutions that preceded the new KARI during the mid-1980s. This was in part prompted by the global debate on the depletion of the ozone layer and the role of livestock in this. It led to an internal debate on the need to legitimize and quantify the benefits livestock bring to the overall agricultural enterprise, especially to crop agriculture.

Animal health

Traditionally, veterinarians were left alone to pursue their own research program. It was generally perceived that they should focus on diseases of regional or Africa-wide importance, such as rinderpest, contagious bovine pleuropneumonia (CBPP), and East Coast fever. These three diseases were given a priority one ranking in NARP-I. Doubts about the ranking of animal health research in the mid-1970s were fuelled by a threatened cut in funding. The Food and Agriculture Organization (FAO) called a strategic meeting in 1978 to address this issue. The meeting was attended by institutions that were promoting postgraduate programs in veterinary epidemiology and economics from the University of Reading, the University of California at Davis, and the epidemiology unit in Canberra. In 1981 a Veterinary Epidemiology Unit was established at the veterinary research laboratory in Kenya to legitimize and quantify the role of animal health in national agricultural development. This unit was later merged with the KARI socioeconomic unit. A secondary purpose of the Veterinary Epidemiology Unit was to promote an appreciation among public veterinary officers of the importance of quantitative epidemiology in justifying animal health research. To that end, animal health research was involved in setting up a course in veterinary epidemiology at the University of Nairobi. Although this course was eventually established, interest in training of field officers emerged only in 2000. A formal request has been made to the University of Nairobi to look into the possibility of a postgraduate course for field veterinary officers. This is expected to facilitate linkages with KARI's research program, partly by reducing a long-standing intellectual gap between animal health researchers and the field services.

Identifying Linkages
Evolution of a mechanism to identify partners

We have acknowledged that linkages and partnerships are an important means of achieving KARI's goals. Partnerships, like priorities (see chapter 8 on PM&E and

419

chapter 15 on priority setting) are dynamic and are subject to change over time. In order to select optimum linkages for achievement of KARI goals, an iterative process needs to be developed. One way of doing this is to analyze the impediments that constrain the KARI and each of its partners in achieving their goals. This should be viewed as a management tool to be used at a variety of decision-making levels, including the project, program, and ultimately, institutional levels. Systems analytical methods, such as the Production to Consumption Systems Approach (PCSA) that evolved through Egerton University, have been used in the KARI smallholder dairy research and development project and in research on oilseeds for identifying key constraints on system performance.

Lessons on Financing Agricultural Research

World agricultural research expenditure has grown significantly in real (inflation-adjusted) terms over the last forty years. However, the funding for NARS in developing countries, especially in sub-Saharan Africa (SSA), has been baffling. In SSA the shortage of domestic funds for research has caused many governments to turn increasingly to donors. Although the reliance on donor funding often offsets the decline in support from African governments, one needs to question the relevance of research and the risk of neocolonialism through donor aid. There is also a danger that the lack of domestic support for research may be used to explain the poor performance and may divert attention from the need to make more effective use of national resources.

Agricultural research financing in Kenya was relatively buoyant in real terms up to about 1985. However, over the last fifteen years, funding of agricultural research in Kenya has been driven by an increase in donor finance, much of it in capital infrastructure, equipment, and technical assistance. Although the injection of such investment was vital to consolidate and fortify agricultural research, Kenya has experienced the effect of donor dependency in the form of brain drain and the declining morale of its scientists. To address these issues, KARI has embarked on various initiatives to increase the efficiency and the effectiveness of donor assistance. KARI is now trying to reduce government financing in areas where the private sector may be willing to participate or beneficiaries may be willing to pay. At the same time, reforms have to be introduced to enhance the cost-effectiveness of remaining services through down-sizing and improved priority setting, and by making services more user-oriented and responsive to demand. In addition, alternative sources of finance and commercialization of the outputs of agricultural research are options that are being aggressively explored.

Appendix

Robustness of Estimated Returns to Training and Visit Extension in Kenya

MADHUR GAUTAM AND JOCK R. ANDERSON

Introduction

This appendix re-examines the Bindlish and Evenson (1993, 1997) data and analysis touched upon in chapter 11. The effectiveness of the public agricultural extension service in Kenya is a controversial issue. Two successive International Development Association (IDA)-funded projects, the National Extension Projects I and II (NEP-I and II), have supported agricultural extension since 1982, at which time the World Bank assisted Kenya to introduce the Training and Visit (T&V) system of management. The objective of the projects was to make the Kenyan extension service more effective and efficient.

Toward the end of NEP-I in 1990, the Africa Technical Department of the World Bank undertook a study to evaluate the impact of the agricultural extension projects it had supported in Kenya and Burkina Faso. The Kenya study (Bindlish and Evenson 1993) estimated the returns to extension at 350 percent (marginal internal rate of return), with a "lower bound" estimate of 160 percent. The returns to extension in Burkina Faso (Bindlish, Evenson, and Gbetibouo 1997) were estimated in a similar fashion at 91 percent. Needless to say, supporters of this type of extension have welcomed these findings, notwithstanding the subtleties of the technical methods used to derive the results. Because the devil is in the detail, we must turn to these results again briefly in order to explore the robustness and thus the relevance of the findings.

This appendix is a version of a paper (Gautam and Anderson 1998) prepared as part of a wider Operations Evaluation Department (OED) effort to assess the value of extension investment in Kenya. The purpose is to test the robustness of the returns to agricultural extension in Kenya that Bindlish and Evenson (1993, revised in 1997) estimated. In doing so, the findings highlight the shortcomings of cross-sectional data in informing policy decisions. Specifically, three issues that could potentially have an important bearing on the results of Bindlish and Evenson (hereafter B&E in this appendix) are addressed. The first is the sensitivity of their results to possible omitted factors, particularly region-specific effects due to natural productivity potential or other factors. The matter is examined within the limits of the available cross-sectional data. The second is the sensitivity of the estimated returns to the functional form used for modeling agricultural production. The third concerns some data-related problems. All three are, in the final analysis, empirical issues, although the first two follow from well-established theoretical considerations in dealing with cross-sectional data and technology specification. As the following discussion explains, the results are sensitive to omitted regional effects and data considerations, but are seemingly robust with respect to the functional form for the production function.

A Brief Recap of the Bindlish and Evenson Study

The estimate by B&E of returns to the Kenyan T&V system was based on estimates from an empirical "meta"-production function. The study was designed to overcome a key limitation of most studies that have attempted to establish the impact of extension in a production-function framework, namely the specification of an appropriately exogenous variable for extension supply (Birkhaeuser, Evenson, and Feder 1991). Bindlish and Evenson use a variable based on frontline extension staff, specified as a ratio of extension workers to the number of farmers in each location (a subdistrict administrative unit—on the average, a district has six divisions, a division has six locations, and a location has six sublocations). They had tried other extension variables, including supervisors and subject matter specialists, but the results were not significantly different. Because the central government determines the allocation of staff to each location, the variable is exogenous to the household decision-making process and hence is a valid regressor for farm-level production function estimation. The actual data on staffing, however, were available only for 1990. For previous years, B&E had no choice but to construct staff-farm ratios rather arbitrarily, based on the number of years each staff member had been in the same location. The weighted staff-farm variable, constructed to capture the lagged impact of extension on productivity and the key variable in calculating the returns to extension is thus measured with error (Bindlish and Evenson 1993, 26, first and second paragraphs).

The original design of the B&E study was to obtain panel data by revisiting some 700 households that were interviewed in 1982 for the Kenya Rural Household Budget Survey (RHBS). The Central Bureau of Statistics (CBS) used "cluster" as a census enumeration unit for the 1982 RHBS sampling frame. In the sample, each cluster belongs to a distinct sublocation. Although the 1990 survey was able to collect the information needed to estimate a production function for about 670 households, comparable information for 1982 was lacking, preventing the estimation of a fixed or random effects model (Bindlish and Evenson 1993, 25). Given the circumstances, B&E were forced to estimate a cross-sectional production function using the 1990 data, supplemented by the information available from the 1982 survey, in an attempt to control for household- and area-specific factors affecting production. Household-specific effects were controlled by including total production and area cultivated by the household in 1982, and the 1990 age, education, and sex of the household head. To control for area-specific

424

characteristics, dummy variables for the "production potential" for the zones in which each cluster was located were included (for medium- and low-potential zones), as were the topography indicators (for hilly and undulating regions). To control for economic and infrastructure conditions characterizing the area, the regression included 1982 cluster-level means for variables representing access to roads, transport facilities, farm size, farm-level cropped area, farm-level livestock capital, value of cash crops produced, value of other crops produced, and household nonfarm income.

Bindlish and Evenson (1993) used a Cobb-Douglas functional form to model crop production, and they found the extension variable to be highly significant statistically and estimated the marginal rate of return on investment in extension to be about 350 percent (using the 415 observations that had all the necessary data). Subsequently, a data processing error was discovered, and after correcting for the error, B&E (1997) noted that the qualitative result did not change. Quantitatively, a re-estimation yields a statistically significant coefficient on extension of 0.25 instead of the 0.29 reported in the first report (Bindlish and Evenson 1993). The corresponding estimate of the returns to extension in Kenya is 278 percent (based on 418 "complete" observations). However, as discussed in the following, further measurement errors were discovered and the revised estimate is no longer valid.

Issues

The main concerns relate to model specification and data-related problems. The data issues are dealt with first in order to make the comparisons across different model specifications meaningful. On specification, the functional form issue is discussed first, followed by a discussion of the omitted region-specific factors.

Data issues

As part of the ongoing OED impact evaluation of agricultural extension projects in Kenya, an attempt was made to match up the 1990 farm-level output with the output from the 1982 RHBS data. For this purpose, both the 1990 B&E survey data and the 1982 RHBS data were obtained. A household- and cluster-level comparison across the years, however, revealed some differences and inconsistencies.

The most significant issue is the method of aggregation across crops to arrive at the farm-level output. A comparison of farm-level output across the years shows a significant drop in farm output (after accounting for farm area) from 1982 to 1990. The significance of the differences first came to light during an ongoing analysis of technical and efficiency changes from 1982 to 1990 and from 1990 to 1997. The initial results indicated significant technological regression from 1982 to 1990 and significant technological progress from 1990 to 1997. Neither could be satisfactorily explained by the events that have taken place in Kenya since 1982, and this prompted a closer look at the data. Further examination of the plot- and crop-level data from the 1990 survey, however, revealed that output quantities from different crops had been aggregated to estimate the farm-level output (and used as the dependent variable in B&E

425

production function estimation). Also, in the 1990 survey, output data were collected for only five major crops (maize, beans, sorghum, millet, and potatoes).

Needless to say, the production function estimates reported by B&E (1993 and 1997) are inappropriate. Nevertheless, it should be noted that the five crops, on the average, constitute about 70 percent of farm output value from the 1982 sample data and about 68 percent from the 1997 sample data. Thus, we can reasonably assume that a high percentage of farm output was captured during the 1990 survey. To proceed with the analysis, because the 1990 survey data do not have output prices, national prices have been used to estimate the farm-level output value for the 1990 sample. The prices were obtained from the Food and Agriculture Organization (FAO) database and cross-checked for consistency, where feasible, with the economic surveys for various years published by the CBS, Government of Kenya.

The benefit of access to the raw data from the 1982 RHBS survey also allowed a re-creation of the cluster- and household-level variables used by B&E (as contained in the processed set of 1990 data). A comparison of these variables revealed some differences (a) in the 1982 cluster- and farm-level control variables, and (b) in the agro-ecological control indicators.

As with the 1990 survey data, the 1982 cluster- and farm-level production variables used in the B&E analysis were inappropriately aggregated and had to be reconstructed. The quantities of crops produced, instead of their values, appear to have been summed and divided by an arbitrary factor of 12 to arrive at farm-level production used to control for household productivity differentials and for the cluster mean values of cash and other crop production. Other problematic variables are the cluster transportation and (road) infrastructure variables. What the coded values of these variables represent is unclear. For example, in some sublocations, all infrastructure variables (including those not used in the analysis) take the value 9, while most others take 1 or 2. In fact, alternative infrastructure variables are available in the 1982 data. These are the distances from the farm to the various types of road, and public transportation reported by households.

A comparison of the agro-ecological zone (AEZ) classification used for the B&E analysis with the AEZ classification variables available in the 1982 data also shows differences. In addition to the AEZ classification, B&E used indicators for the regional productivity potential (RPP) as a further control for differences in land quality. Because the 1982 data did not have comparable RPP indicators, these data were independently compiled. Given the differences observed in the AEZ indicators, a verification of the accuracy of the RPP indicators was sought as part of the ongoing OED impact study of extension projects in Kenya. The new indicators are based on information gathered from the respective district annual reports and farm management handbooks for Kenya. The RPP indicators are also substantially different from the indicators used by B&E. To determine which of the alternative sets of AEZ classification and RPP indicators to use, farm output was regressed on each set of indicators. The results show that the 1982 AEZ classification and the new RPP indicators have a higher explanatory power (R^2) for both the 1982 and 1990 farm-level production. Finally, to maintain the focus on methodological comparability, the aggregate data on district agricultural output and extension costs as well as the related assumptions used to calculate the rate of return to extension are the same as used by B&E (1993).

Functional Form

An overly restrictive functional form can provide misleading signals about the structure of the production process, and may yield estimates of coefficients that are not informative for policy formulation. Although the Cobb-Douglas form is convenient in its parsimony and ease of estimation, it imposes a priori restrictions on the coefficients that may not be valid. For example, it forces the elasticities of substitution to be unity between inputs, and the partial elasticities of production to be constant across varying input intensities. Of course, every functional form implies some restrictive features, so it is a matter of judgment as to what is feasible and reasonable to choose among many possible forms, while seeking not to impose restrictions that inhibit genuine insight.

The Kenya situation poses a particular difficulty. On the one hand, parsimony is highly desirable, given the cross-sectional nature of the data and the need to identify the effect of extension on productivity using a variable with modest degrees of freedom (the staff-farm ratio is available for seventy-one locations). Thus, a functional form that is fully flexible, such as the complete translog, is not feasible. Bindlish and Evenson specified the production function to include five "conventional" inputs (land, hired labor, proxy for family labor, "cash inputs," and fixed capital), one extension variable, five variables to control for household effects, four to control for weather effects, thirteen agro-ecological variables, and nine regional and infrastructure control variables. Nevertheless, it is desirable to test whether the functional form makes a significant difference to the coefficient of greatest interest, namely the extension supply variable. Because a complete characterization of the underlying production structure is not of immediate interest, the strategy is to allow some flexibility in the functional form with respect to variable inputs and the extension supply variable. The other, control, variables are still treated as intercept shifters. Although not fully satisfactory, this strategy allows a check on the stability of the elasticity of production with respect to the extension supply variable.

Among flexible functional forms, three alternative specifications were tried—the translog, the generalized Leontief, and the square-root quadratic. The models were applied to the original B&E specification, using the appropriately aggregated farm production as the dependent variable, but prior to introducing any of the other modifications. The translog performed the best in terms of goodness-of-fit (using adjusted R^2 statistic) of the estimated relationship, although the square-root quadratic performed better in terms of the coefficient of determination of the untransformed dependent variable. The results from the alternative specifications are not reported here. The estimate for the elasticity of production from the translog is 0.22, which is higher than the Cobb-Douglas estimate of 0.14 (detailed results for the Cobb-Douglas

427

analysis are presented in the following), but the elasticity from the square-root quadratic is lower, at 0.06. Both estimates are, however, just over one standard error apart from the Cobb-Douglas estimate.

These results thus suggest that, at least in this application, the Cobb-Douglas specification may not be too restrictive. To focus on the other issues, and to be brief, the rest of the discussion is based on results using the Cobb-Douglas functional form.

Specification

The main concerns in dealing with cross-sectional data include the handling of household- and region-specific effects. Bindlish and Evenson attempt to control for these effects by including locational characteristics and household human capital variables. These data are from the 1982 survey, as well as data collected for the 1990 study.

However, the specification issue remains because of the possibility that AEZs in different parts of the country (e.g., in different districts) are likely to have different production patterns and productivity. Further, it is also possible that deployment of extension staff, the key variable used to measure the supply of extension, is correlated with the productivity potential of each area. If the deployment is independent, the regression coefficient on the extension variable can be taken to represent the impact of extension on agricultural productivity, with the variation across locations providing the opportunity to measure an unbiased and efficient estimate of the impact of the marginal extension staff deployed. If, on the other hand, the regional productivity effects influence staff deployment (e.g., if higher-potential areas receive priority in staff assignments or receive relatively more staff, as planned for NEP-I), then the extension staff variable would implicitly also capture regional productivity differentials in addition to the impact of extension.

Even if the intended initial deployment by the center (Ministry headquarters in Nairobi) was neutral with respect to regional productivity potential, the problem might re-emerge if staff were able to transfer out of relatively undesirable locations into more desirable ones. This behavior would be understandable, with staff moving to locations with better amenities and access to infrastructure within each district, or moving to more progressive and dynamic districts. Subsequently, if that dynamism translates into higher value-added production, then the staff-farm ratio would again be "spuriously" positively correlated with the value of production.

From an empirical standpoint, the issue reduces to whether or not the cluster-level and other variables included in the B&E regression adequately control for region-specific effects. If not, then the regression will suffer from an "omitted variables" problem and will give biased and inconsistent estimates. In such an event, the extension staff variable would erroneously attribute to extension the effect of "natural" productivity differentials. Conversely, if staff deployment follows a standard rule of thumb (e.g., a predetermined staff-farm ratio as typically prescribed in T&V implementation plans) or if the turnover of staff is not region-specific, then the correlation between the regional productivity potential and the staff-farm ratio would probably be about zero. The estimated coefficient would remain an unbiased estimate.

Bindlish and Evenson (1997, 120) recognized this problem and attempted to control for the "staff deployment effect" by treating it as an "endogenous" variable. However, the specification bias in this case is one of omitted variables; the extension supply variable is correlated with the error term because it is correlated with omitted regional productivity effects. Bindlish and Evenson's (1997, 126) instrumenting equation validates this concern. For example, mean locational education level of household heads, the availability of extension under the previous system (reportedly biased toward more productive and progressive areas), and hilly terrain have a positive and significant effect in explaining the variation in the extension supply variable. Low- and medium-potential indicators have a negative sign. The number of farms and the mean household size in a location have an unexpected negative influence on staff allocation.

The appropriate solution would thus be to effectively control for productivity effects. If the problem is caused by omitted regional productivity effects, which creates the correlation between the staff-farm ratio and the error term, then including the regional fixed effects explicitly in the regression would eliminate the source of the problem. Factors other than regional productivity potential that influence the allocation of staff to different regions are unlikely to be correlated with errors associated with the farm-level production function. Hence, the staff-farm ratio will be independent of the production error term. If productivity effects cannot be effectively controlled for, then an instrumental variables approach could be used to overcome the problem. Unfortunately, valid instruments (i.e., determinants of staff allocation that are not correlated with the regional productivity differentials) are not available and in general would be rarely available. By instrumenting the extension supply variable on regional indicators, B&E exacerbated the problem, providing an explanation for the increase in magnitude of the estimated coefficient they reported. Given the positive correlation between the staff-farm ratio and productivity, as suggested by B&E's instrumenting equation, and assuming that natural productive potential will have a positive effect on output, we can show that the bias in the coefficient of staff-farm ratio should be upward using the standard "omitted variables" formula (Greene 1990). Based on their findings, however, B&E concluded that the estimate was biased downward.

Whether or not the estimated model suffers from specification errors can be tested. The procedure adopted is to include the district fixed effects to verify the robustness of the estimated coefficient on the staff-farm ratio. This is a rather weak test because within each district variation will occur across locations (and sublocations) in natural productivity potentials and hence, possibly, in staff-allocation. Nevertheless, given the limitations imposed by available data, a weak test is preferable to none.

The households sampled in the survey were from eighty-four clusters, each from a sublocation belonging to one of seventy-one distinct locations in seven districts. Among the observations available for estimation, the information on the extension variable is available for the seventy-one locations. Thus, on the one hand, variation appears to be sufficient in the key extension variable (the staff-farm ratio) to allow estimation of the impact of extension on productivity even after controlling for district fixed effects. On the other hand, the limited variation poses a dilemma, in that, given the already exten-sive use of dummy variables by B&E to control for the AEZ and regional productivity potential effects, including the district fixed effects might eliminate any meaningful variation in the extension-supply variable. With the data in hand, the analytical solu-tion to this problem is not obvious. However, its potential empirical significance is dealt with through a series of sequential tests to check the sensitivity of the staff-farm ratio coefficient. The details are discussed in the following results section.

Another potential problem with a district fixed effects estimation with a single cross-section is the possibility that the efficiency of the extension service varies by district. With the basic unit of organization of extension being the district, this could result in district fixed effects being indistinguishable from extension impact. This pos-sibility, however, goes against the basic premise of the T&V "system of management" introduced by NEP-I, and the intent of establishing a national system with a unified and consistent organizational structure in contrast to the previous extension system that was disparately organized and inefficient.

Whether or not this is the case is an empirical question and can be statistically tested by including cross terms for extension and district effects, in addition to pure district effects, to identify district-specific extension impact. If the districts are differ-entially efficient, the coefficients for each district will be significantly different from one another. Further, if homogeneity of extension effectiveness across districts can-not be rejected, then two further tests can be performed with a view to establishing the overall impact of extension, as measured by returns to extension expenditure. One test is the significance of a simple sum of the district-specific extension coefficients (implicitly assigning equal weight to each district in the sample). The second test is the significance of a weighted sum of district-specific extension effects, where the weights are the sample shares of each district in the total value of production.

Results

As a result of the aggregation error for farm production variables noted earlier, the results reported by B&E (1993, 1997) are not valid. Column 2 of table A-1 shows the correct estimates of the farm meta-production function (i.e., using the value of farm production). Note that, except for the correction made for the arithmetic errors in the creation of the extension variable, the other independent (or explanatory variables) and model specifications are exactly the same as were used in the original B&E (1993) analysis. (The original estimate for the coefficient on the extension variable was 0.29, and rate of return on extension investment was estimated to be 350 percent, with a lower bound of 160 percent. The lower bound corresponds to the rate of return asso-ciated with the lower limit of the 95 percent confidence interval for the estimated coefficient on the extension supply variable). The results in column 2 indicate a lower, but qualitatively similar, result. The extension coefficient is estimated at 0.14. However, it is barely significant at the 5 percent level. The marginal internal rate of return to T&V implied by this estimate is 161 percent; the lower bound estimate, however, is now negative. Thus, qualitatively it could be argued that the results, albeit not as robust, are still positive and along the lines reported by B&E (1997). This perhaps reflects the large share of maize in the farm-level output of sample farmers.

For the rest of the analysis, the results in column 2 of table A-1 are considered as the base case, or the B&E model, to which subsequent comparisons will be made. The remaining results are presented as follows. Using the same data as the B&E model (without any data modifications), extending the specification to allow for district fixed effects, column 3 of table A-1 gives the results of including district dummy variables. Column 4 replaces the extension variable with a series of cross-terms for district dummy variables and extension to test for differential efficiency of extension across districts. Incorporating the data modifications to the other explanatory variables, as discussed previously, table A-2 presents an alternative set of results. Columns 2, 3, and 4 of table A-2 present the results with the updated data corresponding to the respective models in table A-1.

The results in table A-1 demonstrate the sensitivity of the coefficient on the extension variable to district fixed effects, even without making any other changes. The coefficient on extension goes from 0.14 and significant at the 5 percent level, to -0.003 and not significant at the standard levels of significance. To verify whether any specification bias persists in the model with district fixed effects due to correlation between the staff-farm ratio and the error term, the instrumental variables (IV) technique was applied to the specification in column 3 of table A-1. As anticipated, the IV estimate of the staff-farm ratio coefficient, 0.04, was highly insignificant. The remaining models are estimated using OLS. An F test for the joint significance of the district fixed effects is highly significant, rejecting the hypothesis that the included location-specific and other variables adequately control for regional effects. In addition, the AEZ variables continue to be jointly significant in the presence of district dummy variables, suggesting that one set of variables is not a substitute for the other; that is, neither is dispensable. The two RPP indicators, however, become jointly insignificant in the presence of the district fixed effects.

As discussed previously, it is possible that by including too many fixed effects (for AEZs, RPPs, and districts) any meaningful or genuine variation in the extension supply variable may be reduced to the point of making it redundant. The large drop in the magnitude of the extension coefficient and its significance thus warrant some further investigation. To determine whether the base case result represents the genuine impact of extension or a spurious result because of omitted factors, a series of tests was performed. These included dropping the AEZ and RPP indicators to test the sensitivity of the coefficient on the extension supply variable. As noted previously, including the district fixed effects makes the RPP indicators jointly insignificant. Hence, unsurprisingly, when the RPP indicators are dropped, all coefficients and their standard errors remain virtually unchanged relative to the full fixed-effects model of column 2, table A-1. Next, the set of AEZ indicators was dropped (despite their joint significance noted previously). Again, there were no substantive (or significant) changes in the standard production parameters or in the extension coefficient.

431

Table A–1 Production Functions Using Bindlish and Evenson Data

Variable	Model I	Model II	Model III
Intercept	5.098** (0.557)	4.252** (0.600)	6.341** (0.768)
Log of area	0.458** (0.045)	0.440** (0.041)	0.426** (0.041)
Log of family size	0.276** (0.077)	0.198** (0.070)	0.174* (0.068)
Log of hired labor	0.032** (0.008)	0.021** (0.008)	0.020** (0.007)
Log of cash inputs	0.035* (0.018)	0.001 (0.017)	−0.009 (0.017)
Log of fixed farm capital	−0.028 (0.057)	0.030 (0.053)	0.021 (0.052)
Extension staff–farm ratio (Sfratio)	0.142* (0.071)	−0.003 (0.083)	
Sfratio x dummy variable for Machakos			0.717** (0.217)
Sfratio x dummy variable for Murang'a			1.009** (0.256)
Sfratio x dummy variable for Kisumu			−0.340* (0.138)
Sfratio x dummy variable for Kericho			−0.267 (0.241)
Sfratio x dummy variable for Taita Taveta			−0.242 (0.248)
Sfratio x dummy variable for Trans Nzoia			−0.629 (0.385)
Sfratio x dummy variable for Bungoma			−0.211 (0.197)
Farm output, 1982 (000 Ksh)	0.989** (0.230)	1.055** (0.218)	1.255** (0.217)
Farm area, 1982 (acres)	−0.029 (0.024)	−0.007 (0.022)	0.001 (0.022)
Age of head (years)	−0.003 (0.003)	−0.003 (0.003)	−0.003 (0.003)
Sex of head (female = 1)	0.001 (0.092)	0.091 (0.084)	0.043 (0.081)
Education of head (above primary = 1)	−0.029 (0.044)	−0.017 (0.041)	−0.008 (0.040)
Normal crop (normal = 1)	0.440** (0.145)	0.528** (0.140)	0.557** (0.143)
Failed crop (failed = 1)	0.184 (0.244)	0.667** (0.238)	0.538* (0.238)
1990 Cluster mean (Cm) for normal crop	0.298* (0.129)	0.356** (0.121)	0.340** (0.117)
1990 Cm for failed crop	−0.536 (0.292)	−0.726** (0.265)	−0.805** (0.258)
1982 Cm for access to roads	−0.009 (0.027)	−0.022 (0.030)	−0.032 (0.031)
1982 Cm for access to transport	0.011 (0.039)	0.029 (0.044)	0.015 (0.046)
1982 Cm for cropped area	−0.144** (0.040)	−0.146** (0.043)	−0.103* (0.045)
1982 Cm for farm size	0.091** (0.020)	0.026 (0.020)	0.016 (0.020)
1982 Cm for livestock value (000 Ksh)	0.023 (0.168)	0.336 (0.182)	0.144 (0.197)
1982 Cm for cash crop value (000 Ksh)	−0.029 (0.019)	0.015 (0.019)	0.014 (0.020)
1982 Cm for other crop value (000 Ksh)	−0.011 (0.015)	0.018 (0.015)	0.020 (0.015)
1982 Cm for nonfarm income (000 Ksh)	−0.127 (0.092)	−0.015 (0.088)	−0.017 (0.086)
Medium-potential zone dummy variable	−0.181 (0.117)	0.026 (0.109)	−0.108 (0.113)
Low-potential zone dummy variable	−0.372* (0.153)	0.248 (0.158)	−0.016 (0.170)
Hilly area dummy variable	−0.506** (0.160)	0.068 (0.174)	−0.027 (0.174)
Undulating area dummy variable	0.070 (0.120)	0.202 (0.139)	0.068 (0.153)
AEZ (range) Jt. Signif. (F value)	−0.94 to 0.55 (7.374)**	−0.65 to 0.25 (3.033)**	−0.99 to −0.15 (5.195)**
N	418.000	418.000	418.000
Adj. R2	0.646	0.713	0.735
Test for joint significance of district effects (F value)	15.843**	4.121**	
Test for the sum of Sfratio x district effects (F value)		0.003	
Test for the weighted sum of Sfratio x district effects (F value)			2.609

Source: Bindlish and Evenson 1993, 1997.
Note: Dependent variable is log of 1990 value of farm production. Standard errors are reported in parentheses. (*) indicates significance at 5% level, and (**) at 1% level. District effects, with Machakos as the base case, range from −0.23 to 1.48 for model II and from 1.63 to −0.19 for model III.

| Table A–2 | Production Functions Using Modified Data |

Variable	Model I	Model II	Model III
Intercept	3.207** (0.717)	2.953** (0.790)	3.947** (0.868)
Log of area	0.384** (0.041)	0.411** (0.040)	0.422** (0.040)
Log of family size	0.226** (0.068)	0.172** (0.064)	0.161* (0.064)
Log of hired labor	0.018* (0.007)	0.014* (0.007)	0.013 (0.007)
Log of cash inputs	0.024 (0.016)	0.001 (0.016)	0.008 (0.016)
Log of fixed farm capital	0.013 (0.048)	0.089 (0.047)	0.068 (0.047)
Extension staff–farm ratio (Sfratio)	−0.077 (0.069)	−0.110 (0.086)	
Sfratio x dummy variable for Machakos			0.432* (0.191)
Sfratio x dummy variable for Muranga			−0.201 (0.309)
Sfratio x dummy variable for Kisumu			−0.261 (0.184)
Sfratio x dummy variable for Kericho			−0.493** (0.188)
Sfratio x dummy variable for Taita Taveta			−0.106 (0.263)
Sfratio x dummy variable for Trans Nzoia			−0.235 (0.349)
Sfratio x dummy variable for Bungoma			−0.036 (0.181)
Farm output, 1982 (000 Ksh)	0.040** (0.009)	0.037** (0.008)	0.038** (0.008)
Farm area, 1982 (acres)	0.005 (0.013)	0.004 (0.013)	0.004 (0.012)
Age of head (years)	−0.001 (0.003)	−0.002 (0.002)	−0.003 (0.002)
Sex of head (female = 1)	0.097 (0.079)	0.134 (0.076)	0.107 (0.075)
Education of head (above primary = 1)	0.064 (0.141)	−0.041 (0.135)	−0.033 (0.135)
Normal crop (normal = 1)	0.631** (0.126)	0.562** (0.127)	0.516** (0.135)
Failed crop (failed = 1)	0.521** (0.201)	0.510** (0.194)	0.656** (0.202)
1990 Cluster mean (Cm) for normal crop	0.331** (0.111)	0.413** (0.108)	0.418** (0.108)
1990 Cm for failed crop	−0.611* (0.243)	−0.625** (0.230)	−0.617** (0.230)
1982 Cm for distance to AW roads	−0.064** (0.022)	−0.035 (0.023)	−0.020 (0.026)
1982 Cm for distance to dirt roads	0.035 (0.047)	0.045 (0.051)	0.021 (0.060)
1982 Cm for distance to transport	0.104** (0.024)	0.094** (0.025)	0.108** (0.029)
1982 Cm for cropped area	−0.076* (0.036)	−0.123** (0.038)	−0.075 (0.043)
1982 Cm for farm size	0.037** (0.014)	0.032* (0.014)	0.028 (0.015)
1982 Cm for livestock value (000 Ksh)	0.013 (0.018)	0.015 (0.018)	0.001 (0.024)
1982 Cm for cash crop value (000 Ksh)	−0.438** (0.060)	−0.227** (0.068)	−0.228** (0.082)
1982 Cm for other crop value (000 Ksh)	0.040* (0.018)	0.013 (0.020)	0.010 (0.021)
1982 Cm for nonfarm income (000 Ksh)	−0.018 (0.043)	−0.020 (0.043)	−0.009 (0.046)
Medium-potential zone dummy variable	−0.849** (0.177)	−0.398 (0.208)	−0.484* (0.224)
Low-potential zone dummy variable	−0.802** (0.250)	−0.396 (0.276)	−0.602 (0.314)
Hilly area dummy variable	0.054 (0.140)	0.211 (0.140)	0.234 (0.147)
Undulating area dummy variable	0.165 (0.097)	0.191 (0.117)	0.211 (0.138)
AEZ (range) Jt. Signif. (F value)	0.62 to 1.77 (3.319)**	0.216 to 1.572 (3.533)**	0.263 to 1.617 (3.263)**
N	455.00	455.00	455.00
Adj. R2	0.705	0.738	0.744
Test for joint significance of district effects (F value)	9.695**	5.023**	
Test for the sum of Sfratio x district effects (F value)		1.737	
Test for the weighted sum of Sfratio x district effects (F value)			1.150

Note: Dependent variable is log of 1990 value of farm production. Standard errors are reported in parentheses. (*) indicates significance at 5% level, and (**) at 1% level. District effects, with Machakos as the base case, range from −0.07 to 1.36 for model II and from −1.09 to 0.15 for model III. AW roads refer to all-weather roads.

Further, the overall model-fit is better with district fixed effects and without AEZs (adjusted R^2 of 0.70) compared to the base case model (adjusted R^2 of 0.65). Finally, dropping all the RPP and AEZ indicators, the model-fit continues to be superior (adjusted R^2 of 0.70), while the estimated coefficients are not substantively different from the full fixed-effects model.

These tests reveal the importance of the district-specific effects in explaining the productivity differences across households. They also provide confidence that, while it is theoretically possible that too many fixed effects can be more of a nuisance than an aid in statistical inference, in this empirical application this is not the case.

To test the hypothesis that extension may be differentially efficient across districts, and hence that the district effects are obscuring the extension impact, column 3 of table A-1 presents the results of the regression including cross-terms between district effects and extension. Two of the districts (Machakos and Muranga) have positive and statistically significant coefficients, while one (Kisumu) has a statistically significant negative coefficient. All the remaining districts have an insignificant coefficient, but the sign is negative. Although the signs on the individual district effects are interesting by themselves, from the evaluation viewpoint, the overall impact of extension is of greatest interest. Toward this end, the two tests mentioned previously are performed. One is the sum of the coefficients on the seven cross-terms, which turns out to be small (0.037) and insignificant. A more appropriate test is the significance of the weighted sum of district-specific extension effects, where the weights are the sample shares of each district in total output. The results of including cross-terms between district effects and extension indicate a negative overall extension impact (–0.246), which is statistically insignificant.

As sketched previously, some modifications need to be made to the variables used in the analyses reported in table A-1:

- The correct value of 1982 farm-level production needs to be used;
- New indicators (dummy variables) for medium- and low-potential zones need to be used;
- The AEZ classification available in the 1982 RHBS data set should be used;
- The household head's education status needs to be re-specified to dummy variables for primary and higher levels of education;
- Updated cluster-level means for nonfarm income, production, farm size, and livestock values need to be used; and
- The cluster-level infrastructure variables need to be replaced by the corresponding means for distance to all-weather roads (which includes tarmac and all-weather gravel roads), distance to dirt roads, and distance to nearest bus/*matatu* routes.

The results of including these modifications are presented in table A-2, columns 2–4, corresponding to those of table A-1. In column 2, table A-2, even the basic model without district effects shows that with updated variables, the extension variable is now no longer significant at any conventional level, and in fact has a negative coefficient

(–0.08). Given the significant impact of the new variables on the extension coefficient, a sensitivity analysis was undertaken to determine which variables had the biggest impact. Results (not reported) show that the new RPP indicators have the largest impact (reducing the extension coefficient to 0.04 and insignificant), followed by the 1982 cluster means for infrastructure variables, area, production, livestock assets, and nonfarm income (reducing the extension coefficient to 0.11 and insignificant).

The traditional input variables have coefficients similar to those for the base model in column 2 of table A-1. The test for district-specific effects, column 3, table A-2, shows that district effects continue to be jointly significant. The extension coefficient contin- ues to be statistically insignificant and negative. The sensitivity tests show that the extension coefficient fails to attain significance or substantively change in magnitude even when the AEZ and RPP indicators are excluded in the presence of district fixed effects. Finally, the district-specific extension efficiency is tested in column 4, where now only the coefficient for Machakos is positive and significant, while the coefficient for Kericho is negative and significant; the others are all negative but insignificant. The test results in column 4 also show that the simple sum of district-specific extension effects is negative (–0.9), although it is insignificant. The weighted sum of the impact of extension across districts is also negative (–0.15) and insignificant.

The marginal rate of return to extension implied by the estimated coefficients from all models in table A-2 is negative. For none of the models in table A-2 does the extension coefficient have a positive sign.

Conclusions

The results point to two intriguing implications. One concerns the pattern of the district-specific effects, and the other concerns the overall impact of the extension "system," and thus the returns to extension. On the first, only the two districts closest to Nairobi—Muranga and Machakos—have positive and significant coefficients in the first set of results (using the original B&E data), while in the second set only Machakos is significantly positive (using modified data). The factors underlying the differential effectiveness of extension across districts are not explored in this appendix. However, the results suggest that extension appears to be more effective in districts that are better connected to Nairobi, perhaps because of better infrastructure.

The second implication of this analysis is that, in the aggregate, the impact of T&V extension in Kenya is not discernible from the available data. The results also suggest a differential impact across districts. A value-weighted sum of district-specific impacts is used to determine the aggregate impact and to test if it is significantly different from zero. (Although it is counterintuitive that extension could reduce the productivity of farmers, as implied by the negative coefficients for some districts, it may be possible at the whole-farm level, say, by advising inappropriate crop mixes). The test shows that the hypothesis that T&V had no impact in Kenya between 1982 and 1990 cannot be rejected, implying that the sample data fail to show a positive rate of return on the investment in T&V.

The findings highlight two issues. First is the sensitivity of empirical results to potential data errors and model misspecification, errors that can yield misleading policy implications and investment signals. This is particularly important when dealing with cross-sectional and imperfect data, often all that are available in many countries. The B&E study provides a pertinent example where seemingly innocuous data errors and alternative specifications lead to strikingly different results. An important lesson is the need for greater vigilance in empirical analyses (especially data quality) used to inform or support policy development, including the need to validate potentially influential empirical findings.

The second issue concerns the effectiveness of the T&V system of extension management. For Kenya, the anticipated impact of T&V on agricultural productivity is not discernible from the available data using some refinements of the approach earlier taken by B&E. The differential impact across districts also questions the efficacy of imposing a single national system for extension services.

As is the case in such empirical studies, the results reported here are situation-specific and are subject to the limitations imposed by available data. To firmly establish the achievement of concrete results and to draw broad policy implications, the need to rigorously establish impact and to validate the empirical findings in other settings with the use of appropriate data cannot be overstated. Household panel data would have been particularly helpful in overcoming some of the problems that appear to have a significant bearing on B&E's results on the returns to extension in Kenya.

ACKNOWLEDGMENTS

The generous assistance of Robert Evenson and Vishva Bindlish in making available the 1990 data set and of Steven Block for the 1982 data is warmly acknowledged. The help of the Tegemeo Institute of Egerton University, Kenya, is gratefully acknowledged for the compilation of the RPP indicators for the study areas.

REFERENCES

Bindlish, Vishva, and Robert E. Evenson. 1993. Evaluation of the performance of T&V extension in Kenya. World Bank Technical Paper No. 208, Africa Technical Department Series. Washington, D.C.: World Bank.

———. 1997. The impact of T&V extension in Africa: The experience of Kenya and Burkina Faso. *World Bank Research Observer* 12:183–201.

Bindlish, Vishva, Robert E. Evenson, and Mathurin Gbetibouo. 1997. Evaluation of T&V based extension in Burkina Faso. World Bank Technical Paper No. 226, Africa Technical Department Series. Washington, D.C.: World Bank.

Birkhaeuser, Dean, Robert E. Evenson, and Gershon Feder. 1991. The economic impact of agricultural extension: A review. *Economic Development and Cultural Change* 39:507–21.

Gautam, Madhur, and Jock R. Anderson. 1998. *Reconsidering the evidence on the returns to T&V extension in Kenya.* Policy and Research Paper Series. Washington, D.C.: World Bank.

Greene, W. H. 1990. *Econometric analysis.* New York: Macmillan.

436

Contributors

Jock R. Anderson, *Operations Evaluation Department, World Bank, Washington, D.C*

Stephen Akroyd, *International Service for National Agricultural Research (ISNAR), The Hague*

Gem Arwings-Kodhek, *Egerton University, Tegemeo Institute, Kenya*

Derek Byerlee, *Agriculture and Rural Development Department, World Bank, Washington, D.C.*

Sam Chema, *Agricultural Research Foundation, Nairobi, Kenya*

Joel I. Cohen, *International Service for National Agricultural Research (ISNAR) at International Food Policy Research Institute (IFPRI), Washington, D.C.*

John Curry, *Food and Agriculture Organization (FAO), Rome, Italy*

Matt Dagg, *Consultant, formerly with International Service for National Agricultural Research (ISNAR)*

Carl K. Eicher, *University Distinguished Professor Emeritus, Department of Agricultural Economics, Michigan State University*

Howard Elliott, *Association for Strengthening Agricultural Research in East and Central Africa (ASARECA), Entebbe, Uganda*

Pablo Eyzaguirre, *Principal Scientist, International Plant Genetic Resources Institute (IPGRI), Rome*

Madhur Gautam, *World Bank, Washington, D.C.*

Douglas Horton, *Consultant, formerly with International Service for National Agricultural Research (ISNAR), The Hague*

Mercy Kamau, *Socio-economist, Kenya Agricultural Research Institute (KARI), currently attached to Tegemeo Institute of Policy and Development, Nairobi, Kenya*

Jacob Kampen, *Consultant in sustainable agricultural development, formerly lead specialist in agricultural research, sub-Saharan Africa Region, World Bank, Washington, D.C.*

Lilian Kimani, *Consultant, KK Consulting Associates, Nairobi, Kenya*

Romano M. Kiome, *Director, Kenya Agriculture Research Institute (KARI), Kenya*

Kithinji Kiragu, *Assistant Director, Human Resource Development, Kenya Agricultural Research Institute (KARI), Kenya*

John Lynam, *Associate Director, Food Security, Rockefeller Foundation, Nairobi, Kenya*

Adiel N. Mbabu, *Association for Strengthening Agricultural Research in East and Central Africa (ASARECA), Entebbe, Uganda*

Geoffrey C. Mrema, *The Food and Agriculture Organization (FAO) Rome, formerly Executive Secretary, Association for Strengthening Agricultural Research in East and Central Africa (ASARECA), Entebbe, Uganda*

Julius Mungai, *Consultant, Nairobi, Kenya*

Joseph Mureithi, *Assistant Director, Kenya Agricultural Research Institute (KARI), Kenya*

Stephen M. Nandwa, *Kenya Agricultural Research Institute (KARI), Kenya*

David Ndii, *Lecturer, Department of Economics, University of Nairobi, Kenya*

Cyrus G. Ndiritu, *Consultant in Agricultural Systems and Rural Development, formerly Director, Kenya Agricultural Research Institute (KARI), Kenya*

Mahamood Noor, *World Bank, Washington, D.C.*

Steven Were Omamo, *International Food Policy Research Institute (IFPRI), Kampala, Uganda*

Hillary N. K. Ondatto, *Senior Human Resource Development Officer, Kenya Agricultural Research Institute (KARI), Kenya*

Ruth Oniang'o, *Professor, Jomo Kenyatta University of Agriculture and Technology, Nairobi, Kenya*

Moctar Toure, *Global Environment Fund, Washington D.C., formerly World Bank, Washington, D.C.*

John S. Wafula, *African Biotechnology Stakeholders Forum (ABSF)*

Michael Waithaka, *Kenya Agricultural Research Institute (KARI) — International Livestock Research Institute (ILRI), Nairobi, Kenya*

Samuel Wakhusama Wanyangu, *International Service for the Acquisition of Agrio-biotech Application (ISAAA) AfriCenter*

Markus Walsh, *International Centre for Research in Agro forestry (ICRAF) Kenya*

Fred J. Wangati, *Consultant in Agricultural Research and Development, formerly Secretary to the National Science Research Council of Kenya*

Michigan State University Press is committed to preserving ancient forests and natural resources. We have elected to print this title on 50# Nature's Natural, which is 90% recycled (50% post-consumer waste). As a result of our paper choice, Michigan State University Press has saved the following natural resources*:

13.2	Trees (40 feet in height)
3,850	Gallons of Water
2,255	Kilowatt-hours of Electricity
33	Pounds of Air Pollution

We are a member of Green Press Initiative—a nonprofit program dedicated to supporting book publishers in maximizing their use of fiber that is not sourced from ancient or endangered forests. For more informa-

*Environmental benefits were calculated based on research provided by Conservatree and Cali-